PENGUIN TW

THE PENGUIN E

Eric Arthur Blair (George Orwell) was born in 1903 in India, where his father worked for the Civil Service. The family moved to England in 1907 and in 1917 Orwell entered Eton, where he contributed regularly to the various college magazines. From 1922 to 1927 he served with the Indian Imperial Police in Burma, an experience that inspired his first novel, *Burmese Days* (1934). Several years of poverty followed. He lived in Paris for two years before returning to England, where he worked successively as a private tutor, schoolteacher and bookshop assistant, and contributed reviews and articles to a number of periodicals. *Down and Out in Paris and London* was published in 1933. In 1936 he was commissioned by Victor Gollancz to visit areas of mass unemployment in Lancashire and Yorkshire and *The Road to Wigan Pier* (1937) is a powerful description of the poverty he saw there. At the end of 1936 Orwell went to Spain to fight for the Republicans and was wounded. *Homage to Catalonia* is his account of the civil war. He was admitted to a sanatorium in 1938 and from then on was never fully fit. He spent six months in Morocco and there wrote *Coming Up for Air*. During the Second World War he served in the Home Guard and worked for the BBC Eastern Service from 1941 to 1943. As literary editor of *Tribune* he contributed a regular page of political and literary commentary, and he also wrote for the *Observer* and later the *Manchester Evening News*. His unique political allegory, *Animal Farm*, was published in 1945, and it was this novel, together with *Nineteen Eighty-Four* (1949), that brought him world-wide fame.

George Orwell died in London in January 1950. A few days before, Desmond MacCarthy had sent him a message of greeting in which he wrote: 'You have made an indelible mark on English literature . . . you are among the few memorable writers of your generation.'

Bernard Crick is Emeritus Professor of Politics at Birkbeck College, London, and Honorary Fellow of Edinburgh University. He is best-known for his book *In Defence of Politics* which since its publication in 1964 has sold over a quarter of a million copies; a new Penguin edition appeared in 1993. His prize-winning *George Orwell: A Life* is published by Penguin. *Essays on Politics and Literature* and *Political Thoughts and Polemics* are, among his other books, two collections of essays.

The footnotes in this edition are taken from the four-volume *Collected Essays, Journalism and Letters of George Orwell* edited by Sonia Orwell and Ian Angus.

THE PENGUIN ESSAYS OF

GEORGE ORWELL

Dauna Reid
Oct 94
Edinburgh.

PENGUIN BOOKS
IN ASSOCIATION WITH
Martin Secker & Warburg

PENGUIN BOOKS

Published by the Penguin Group
Penguin Books Ltd, 27 Wrights Lane, London W8 5TZ, England
Penguin Books USA Inc., 375 Hudson Street, New York, New York 10014, USA
Penguin Books Australia Ltd, Ringwood, Victoria, Australia
Penguin Books Canada Ltd, 10 Alcorn Avenue, Toronto, Ontario, Canada M4V 3B2
Penguin Books (NZ) Ltd, 182–190 Wairau Road, Auckland 10, New Zealand

Penguin Books Ltd, Registered Offices: Harmondsworth, Middlesex, England

The Collected Essays, Journalism and Letters of George Orwell, Volume 1
first published by Martin Secker & Warburg 1968
Published in Penguin Books 1968

The Collected Essays, Journalism and Letters of George Orwell, Volume 2
first published by Martin Secker & Warburg 1968
Published in Penguin Books 1970

The Collected Essays, Journalism and Letters of George Orwell, Volume 3
first published by Martin Secker & Warburg 1968
Published in Penguin Books 1970

The Collected Essays, Journalism and Letters of George Orwell, Volume 4
first published by Martin Secker & Warburg 1968
Published in Penguin Books 1970

This volume published as *The Penguin Essays of George Orwell*, 1984
Reprinted with an Introduction 1994
1 3 5 7 9 10 8 6 4 2

The essays in this volume appeared in *The Collected Essays, Journalism and Letters of George Orwell, Volumes 1–4* edited by Sonia Orwell and Ian Angus

Printed in England by Clays Ltd, St Ives plc
Set in VIP Bembo

CONTENTS

Introduction: An Essay

The American critic Irving Howe has called Orwell 'the greatest English essayist since Hazlitt, maybe since Dr Johnson'. So an introduction was perhaps always needed to this fine collection of Orwell's longer, major essays and well-judged selection of the many shorter ones, if only to show that they are not merely pleasant appendages to his real books, but may well constitute his lasting claim to greatness as a writer. Orwell needs to be read as, at least, a considerable figure in this once-famous and specifically English tradition or *genre* of writing – even if behind all the English writers lurks the speculative curiosity of the benign father-figure of the essay, Michel de Montaigne, and his first great translator into English, John Florio. Even in Orwell's lifetime two books of his essays were published, though it was easier to publish essays then than now. To argue the primacy of his essays may release some guilt and puzzlement among many who believe that Orwell is a great figure but cannot honestly say that any one of his books measures up to his fame.[1]

Kipling asked 'What should they know of England who only England know?' Lecturing to teachers of English in Czechoslovakia and Poland shortly after the collapse of Soviet power, I was moved to ask 'What do they know of Orwell who only *Animal Farm* and *Nineteen Eighty-Four* know?' But Orwell's two last books, satires of very different kinds although fully consistent in meaning, almost alone gave him his international fame. Both books were promptly translated into many languages, and samizdat translations and smuggled copies were circulated in Poland, Czechoslovakia, Hungary and the Soviet Union. Orwell even wrote an introduction for a Ukrainian translation of *Animal Farm* in 1946 explaining his intention and who he was. Moreover, thanks to its reputation as a model of English plain style, *Animal Farm* soon became a set book for the advanced level examination of the Cambridge Proficiency in English Language, and so was openly used in language schools in South American dictatorships and throughout Africa. The censors read the text as though the pigs represented Russian Communism and nothing else, but students in Chile had no doubt that their General Pinochet was a big pig too, and in grim Paraguay resemblances between 'Napoleon' and General Stroessner were silently noted. An Arab dissident imprisoned in Zanzibar in the 1960s by President Julius Nyerere spent part of his time inside translating *Animal Farm* into Swahili; but when released he found that there was already a Swahili version, produced at Nyerere's own command. Satire can mean different things to different people.

Readers in Eastern Europe and Russia also thought that the satires were simply aimed at Communism. The books were, without any doubt, primarily aimed at Communism, but not at Communism alone; like in much great satire, the targets were wider and manifold. Consider, in *Nineteen Eighty-Four*, Julia's job in Minitrue: she worked a machine churning out pornographic novels to corrupt and debase the proles, to whom the Party also surreptitiously gave, for the same grand purpose, alcohol, drugs, 'films oozing with sex' and 'rubbishy newspapers containing almost nothing but sport, crime and astrology'. That was not the behaviour of the parties of either Stalin or Hitler: they propagandized, enlisted and mobilized the masses. The target for that barb is surely closer to home: Julia's job must be a savagely Swiftian satire on the British Press and reading public (whether the debauched or the debauchers). Orwell mocked the power-hungry wherever they were; the Communist Party was only the worst case. In any case, it is in the nature of imaginative satire for the targets to become wider over time. A good cap fits many heads, or can be made to do so with only a little stretching. Swift's *Gulliver's Travels* has outlived the politics of his age: we laugh at minor, Lilliputian rulers who think they are big and powerful, and we curse the clumsy giants of Brobdingnag who don't notice the small folk on whom they are treading.

If my friends in Eastern Europe had known Orwell as an essayist, known the speculative, humorous, mockingly provocative man, they might have read *Nineteen Eighty-Four* less literally and more as satire than as prophecy, seen it as part of – was it Brecht who said, or am I inventing? Perhaps it was Orwell himself – 'the laughter of free men', a potent weapon against tyranny and oppression, whether domestic or political. But to demote Orwell from prophet to essayist, or perhaps to promote him from minor novelist to great essayist, means facing certain difficulties in reading essays in general, his in particular. There is a price to be paid for Eric Blair's literary strategy of creating (or perhaps, more precisely, letting evolve) the adopted persona of George Orwell the plain, blunt, honest man – a friend not of 'the people', certainly not of 'the proletariat', but of 'the common man'. There are dangers in Orwell's much-praised plain style. One can tell lies or spin stories in monosyllables and simple sentences.

Orwell chose to write in the plain style for the very reason that he thought it the best way to reach the common reader and to convey truths. He saw the common reader as potentially the idealized 'common man' of Thomas Jefferson and Immanuel Kant (with perhaps a dash of Jean Jacques Rousseau too): a creature of common sense and decency, neither servile nor needing servants, who could do most things with his own hands and who wore any formal learning lightly. The common man was the best hope for civilization, rather than proletarian man or aristocracies or élites of any kind. Orwell tried to follow in the footsteps of Charles Dickens and H. G. Wells by writing, for both political and literary reasons, for those whose only university had been the public library. His chosen public was not the professional middle class or the intelligentsia but that lower-middle class who had only had secondary education, together with the self-educated working class. Although he was fully conversant with modernist, even futurist literature (as shown by his good understanding of and sympathy with Joyce's *Ulysses*, Henry Miller's *Tropic of Capricorn* and Zamyatin's *We*), he deliberately avoided, in all his pre-war novels but one, those devices of modernism which, to his way of thinking, had begun to make the modern novel inaccessible to the common man – books by intellectuals for intellectuals, needing a university degree in English Literature to be understood. The only exception was his early, unhappy experiment, *A Clergyman's Daughter*, in which each chapter attempted a different style and perspective. In fact, to judge by the sales of his pre-war novels (never more than three or four thousand), Orwell failed to reach the common man at all – until the fame and notoriety of *Animal Farm* and *Nineteen Eighty-Four*.

Critical opinion in Britain comes increasingly to value Orwell as an essayist, if one uses that term broadly to include criticism, long book reviews, column journalism and short polemics as well as conventional essays and the digressive, serio-comic passages in *The Road to Wigan Pier* and *The Lion and the Unicorn* (printed here as an essay, although strictly speaking a short polemical book or long pamphlet).[2] Consider this famous passage from the first essay in this volume, 'Why I Write' (1946):

What I have most wanted to do throughout the past ten years is to make political writing into an art. My starting point is always a feeling of partisanship, a sense of injustice. When I sit down to write a book, I do not say to myself, 'I am going to produce a work of art.' I write it because there is some lie I want to expose, some fact to which I want to draw attention, and my initial concern is to get a hearing. But I could not do the work of writing a book, or even a long magazine article, if it were not also an aesthetic experience. Anyone who cares to examine my work will see that even when it is downright propaganda it contains much that a full-time politician would consider irrelevant. I am not able, and I do not want, completely to abandon the world-view that I acquired in childhood. So long as I remain alive and well I shall continue to feel strongly about prose style, to love the surface of the earth and to take pleasure in solid objects and scraps of useless information. It is no use trying to suppress that side of myself. The job is to reconcile my ingrained likes and dislikes with the essentially public, non-individual activities that this age forces on all of us.

The essay form well suited Orwell, as he slowly came to realize. But it can be misleading to place 'Why I Write' out of temporal order (following the four volumes of the 1968 *Collected Essays, Journalism and Letters of George Orwell*) for it was, at the time it was written, an afterthought in mid-career, not a premeditated manifesto or solemn statement of intent. Moreover, it arose simply as a response to an invitation to take part in a symposium on 'Why I Write' in *Gangrel*, a short-lived journal with a tiny circulation. The author was still making his way and had to seize almost any chance to get into print, some fortunate, many highly opportunistic. Too much should not be read into the choice of subject matter, nor yet into omissions.[3]

The essay is a peculiar but reasonably specific form of writing. It can be moral, didactic and serious, even propagandistic, up to a point; but it is not a sermon, it has more informality and flexibility; above all it leaves the reader in some uncertainty about what is going to be said next, how the discursive argument will develop; and the argument will not be conclusive or structured logically – an essay may be quite content to raise an issue, force it on a reader's attention, but then to ruminate and speculate, neither to orate nor pontificate; above all it will seem personal not objective, will give a sense of listening to an extended conversation by an odd but interesting individual. An essay may refer to facts, evidence and authorities, but only in passing; it is not, like a legal advocacy, an ordered argument set out logically step by step. An essay speculates and enquires, as if the author is thinking aloud; it must not appear over-contrived, but rather appear to be a set of free associations made by a sensitive and well-stocked mind.

Orwell's wish 'to make political writing into an art' led to a bold but carefully phrased claim for the originality of his essays on the 'blurb' or dust-jacket copy of his *Critical Essays* of 1946 (which must have been approved by Orwell, ever suspicious of publishers for creating misleading appearances):

In these essays Mr Orwell applies to writers as diverse as Dickens, Kipling, Frank Richards and P. G. Wodehouse a new method of critical analysis. They are not political tracts, their main emphasis is literary, but they start out with the assumption that every writer is in some sense a propagandist and that subject-matter, imagery, even tricks of style are ultimately governed by the 'message' that the writer is trying to put across. This is the method which Orwell applies in the essays on Dickens, Wells, Kipling, Yeats, Dali and Koestler. But of special interest are the pieces dealing with the school stories in the *Gem* and *Magnet*, with seaside comic postcards, with the burlesques and comedies of P. G. Wodehouse and with the gangster stories of James Hadley Chase. In each of these Orwell demonstrates that what appears to be the very lightest of entertainment has a definable world-view and even a conscious purpose behind it, and that a book which has no literary value whatever may have the highest symptomatic importance. These essays are among the very few attempts that have been made in England to study popular art seriously.

The complete polemicist or propagandist knows exactly what he wants to say, but a natural essayist like Orwell, even when he sets out to write a polemic, will say, as he himself noted, much that is irrelevant. He stops to explore side issues, and enjoys the play of imagination and the actual act of writing too much ever to be either a reliable polemicist or a wholly objective sociologist.

Perhaps, however, by writing and thinking in a more independent and entertaining manner than the paid party hack writing to order, the essayist or the true writer can actually, on some occasions, be the more effective polemicist. But not reliably so. Orwell once said that 'a writer cannot be a *loyal* member of a political party'. I have italicized 'loyal', for at the time he wrote it he was a member of a political party, albeit a fairly small one – the Independent Labour Party (ILP)[4]. Indeed, he set himself up to be 'the conscience of the Left', someone who delighted in rubbing his own cat's fur backwards – much like the football supporters who bellow at their own side, 'What a load of rubbish! Sell 'em!' For instance, when writing a column in *Tribune* (a left-wing magazine, more or less pro-Labour) during the war, he set his readers a cunningly baited trap. One week he devoted almost the whole column to rabbiting on about what a good bargain was a sixpenny

Woolworth's rose. Angry letters rolled in and the usual high-minded threats to cancel non-existent subscriptions: 'As our glorious Russian allies fight for their lives at Stalingrad how dare he . . .'; 'Not what we want'; 'Footling trivialities'; 'Not serious'. Orwell replied that his idea of a just, egalitarian, classless society was not one in which great issues alone were discussed, but one in which there was time to sit and stare, to enjoy nature and leisure; such ideals must not be forgotten, especially in times of deadly crisis: they were part of his idea of the classless society. And he kept reverting to this theme, nagging or teasing his readers: 'I had better not continue too long on this subject, because the last time I mentioned flowers in this column an indignant lady wrote to say that flowers are bourgeois.' 'Some Thoughts on the Common Toad' makes the same serious point more fully, in plain style and comic tone:

> How many a time have I stood watching the toads mating, or a pair of hares having a boxing match in the young corn, and thought of all the important persons who would stop me enjoying this if they could. But luckily they can't. So long as you are not actually ill, hungry, frightened or immured in a prison or a holiday camp, spring is still spring . . . the earth is still going round the sun, and neither the dictators nor the bureaucrats, deeply as they disapprove of the process, are able to prevent it.

Here Orwell plays a fine old central European cultural role, the 'wise fool', or if not always quite that, at least the Chaplinesque little fellow subverting the pomposity of both statesmen and intellectuals. And he implies, more profoundly, that human life must strike a balance between material progress (which he values as the basis of any hope for the poor and the dispossessed) and preserving nature. Today we would see a bit of a green one in his red.

Orwell's two most famous books, though different in structure, are both written in the plain style, at times with almost monotonous monosyllabic intensity. But this does not prevent fundamentally different readings of them. Is *Animal Farm* a lament for the Revolution that failed, the betrayal by the pigs of the other animals, or a sad parable that all revolutions will fail because there is too much pig in us all? There is no doubt about the author's intention, but sensible people have also read it in the second sense. Fellow British democratic Socialists (Orwell always capitalized the two terms thus) would want to label such a reading as that of 'American Cold War warriors', which is true enough; but this gloomy interpretation must have seemed the only one possible to readers under Communist oppression in Eastern Europe and Russia. *Nineteen Eighty-Four* also has only a seeming simplicity: the text has been read in a bewildering number of different ways. Some, for instance, read it as Orwell's prophecy of what he thought was likely to happen in the Western world, but others see it as a satire exposing the pretensions, even the impossibility, of total power of any kind. Consider only the famous last passage:

He gazed up at the enormous face. Forty years it had taken him to learn what kind of smile was hidden beneath the dark moustache. O cruel, needless misunderstanding! O stubborn, self-willed exile from the loving breast! Two gin-scented tears trickled down the sides of his nose. But it was all right, everything was all right, the struggle was finished. He had won the victory over himself. He loved Big Brother.

THE END

Many heavy-weight critics have read this as terrible black pessimism: Everyman defeated by the totalitarian state, and not even killed but brainwashed into loving it. Orwell becomes an English Kafka or a sane Nietzsche with common sense. But I see better sense behind Anthony Burgess's provocative exaggeration that it is 'a comic novel'.[5] It is often missed that the darkness contains much of what the Germans well call from long experience *Galgenhumor*, 'gallows humour', or what we now call a whole literary mode, 'black humour'. *Nineteen Eighty-Four* is of a piece with the sardonic, mocking tone of several of Orwell's major essays – such as that on pornography and violence, 'Benefit of Clergy: Some Notes on Salvador Dali'.

Consider the language of this 'last' passage closely. It is either grotesquely and incompetently overwritten, or it is broad satire all the way. Why else the sudden lapse into parody of popular, romantic novels: 'O cruel . . . O stubborn . . .'? Why else the ludicrous 'gin-scented tears' trickling down not even the dignified face, but the comic 'nose', the 'sides' of it moreover? 'Victory over himself' has no totalitarian resonance but was a common catch-phrase of British soap-box, street-corner evangelists and temperance reformers (a point unhappily difficult for most translators to catch): it was that kind of 'struggle', not class or race *Kampf*. I read the passage as saying that the Party can break Winston Smith but that it cannot remake him in any heroic image, only as a miserable, beaten, frightened drunk, neither dedicated proletarian nor purified Aryan. And notice it is not 'the last passage', as is so often sepulchrally said. After 'THE END' comes the 'Appendix'. I suspect that the capitalized 'THE END' is another little bit of *Galgenhumor*, for it appears in no other book by the same publisher in this period, but usually only appeared in popular novelettes and at the end of Hollywood B-movies – presumably in case the reader or viewer ran one into the next by mistake. The Appendix, 'The Principles of Newspeak', is the real conclusion and states that because it is a 'slow and difficult business', the final translation into Newspeak of 'Shakespeare, Milton, Swift, Byron, Dickens and some others' (all Orwell's favourites) has had to be postponed until 'so late a date as 2050'. This year, next year, sometime, never.[6]

If we read the book as dark pessimism (for which there is warrant, especially in the torture scenes and the image of the future as 'a boot stamping on a human face – for ever'), then this Appendix either has to be ignored or made into a rather incompetent afterthought about the nature of language which somehow the author could not work into the text proper. But if we see the book as satire, specifically Swiftian satire, then the 'Appendix' becomes part of the text and tells us that the author believes language cannot be controlled by the State or the Academy (he was of the demotic or colloquial rather than the structuralist school of linguistics, whether he knew it or not). This is consistent with Orwell's views on language and literature expressed in several essays, his 'Propaganda and Demotic Speech' (1944) and more fully and famously in 'Politics and the English Language' (1946), although admittedly the view is darker in 'The Prevention of Literature' (1946), when he seems to admit the *possibility* (but perhaps only as a rhetorical warning) of total thought control and the destruction of imaginative literature. But I am now in deep water, especially as a sometime political philosopher trying to talk to, among others (I hope), teachers, students and critics of English. I know that a text is a text and that an author's intentions are not always met in the imaginative act of writing, and that all texts can be and are read differently in different contexts (especially political ones), and nowadays can be deconstructed according to fancy and at will. So I should not push my interpretations too far, or at all. The only point I need to make is that the plain style can be ambiguous, and is no guarantor of truth. The American critic Hugh Kenner, in a notable essay 'The Politics of the Plain Style', has shown that the choice of a plain style is as much a rhetorical device, whether for Lincoln or for Orwell, as the choice to write or speak in Ciceronian or Churchillian prose.[7] The high style connotes authority and tradition and the plain style connotes common sense and the common man, but both are relative terms, and both are artificial. Kenner makes a simple but important philosophical point and offers a sobering literary example. The philosophical point is quite simply that we cannot tell the truth of any sentence from the syntax, grammar or semantics. 'A camel sits on my shoulder telling me what to write' is a better sentence than 'Meaning is an epistemological arrest of experience or a contextually modulated interaction between authorial intentionality, contingently received text and subjectively deconstructed interpretation', but it cannot be true, whereas the bad sentence may well be true (if it is not simply a tautology, possibly even a truism, but even then can be reasonably construed as logically true – true by definition). In the famous and purgative 'Politics and the English Language' Orwell implies, by quoting so much bad and biased political prose, that good plain prose is contraceptive against propaganda. But his essay could be read by propagandists as sensible advice to keep the propaganda plain and simple: 'Love thy leader as thyself', 'Relax with a ciggy'. Besides, Orwell's plain style, while an admirable introduction to English prose, is not appropriate to all circumstances. Learning does need some special vocabularies, even if far less often than academics (talking mainly to each other) suppose. And have you ever tried (I use an Orwell-like 'button-holing' tactic) writing an obituary in an Orwell-like, conversational manner? I have. Not on.

Writing in the first person should be seen as a literary device before ever we look to it as a possible guarantee of authentic autobiography. Kenner cites the classic case of *The Life and Strange Surprising Adventures of Robinson Crusoe*. The original title page had on it 'Written by Himself', and not until several months later did the astonished reading public realize that the prince of Grub Street hacks, Daniel Defoe, had pulled a fast one on them again. An even more interesting case was Defoe's *Journal of the Plague Year*, written in the first person with his own name to it, full of facts, personal narratives and even mortality statistics drawn from Parish records and other sources. There is only one problem: Defoe's date of birth is not certain, but the real Defoe rather than the fictive 'I' of the eye-witness observer can only have been four or five years old at the time of the plague; yet the facts and figures, much used and checked by social and medical historians, appear to be true and accurate. He must have interviewed older survivors, searched the records diligently and then written the account as a fictive Defoe.

I was told by an old man while working on my biography of Orwell that it was not Eric Blair who was caned in front of the whole school for bed-wetting, as Orwell wrote in 'Such, Such Were the Joys', but someone else. Who knows? But if it was someone else, and if Orwell did not attend a hanging or shoot an elephant, does it matter? Do we then call him a liar and think him exposed, or admire him all the more as a skilful writer of short stories or 'colour sketches'? The distinction between an essay and a short story is not absolute. 'Such, Such Were the Joys', 'A Hanging' and 'Shooting an Elephant' could equally well be printed in an anthology of short stories, and the first two also in an anthology of polemical writing. Both the short story and the essay based on direct experience – or claiming to be based on experience – were a typical form of British writing in the 1930s. Orwell was only one of many who used this convention or literary strategy. 'Shooting an Elephant' (1936) was republished in 1940 in a Penguin New Writing collection edited by John Lehmann, in which ten out of the fourteen contributions were written in the first person and raise the same problem as Orwell's – short story or essay? Neither term is used by Lehmann in his Foreword, just 'writing'; true, he calls them all 'imaginative literature', but then also 'a return to the realistic tradition of Defoe and Fielding', with 'an interest in speed and vigour of narrative'.

No one supposes that in *Plain Tales From the Hills* Kipling was under the table when the Colonel proposed to Mrs Hackerby, nor that H. G. Wells saw the Martians land or had dinner with the time traveller back from the horrific future. These were plainly fictions. But Orwell's development of the literary persona of a plain, blunt, honest man was so successful that he brought problems of criticism upon himself. He had done some, perhaps most, of the things of which he wrote about in the first person. But if you build a reputation on first-hand narrative and honesty, the common reader may come to admire what he or she reads more for the truth than for the art of it, to admire the honesty of the man more than the writing; so may then feel, if any part of the narrative or story is shown to be untrue (it is unlikely that Orwell attended a hanging in Burma or was in hospital in Paris for as long as he implies), that both the essay, short story, colour sketch or article (whichever it is) and the man are demeaned or diminished. And literary critics could come to underestimate both his imaginative, creative powers and his critical ability.[8]

In a highly original essay, 'Politics vs Literature: An Examination of *Gulliver's Travels*', Orwell faced (as most scholars and critics had not) the moral enormity of Jonathan Swift, the depth of his hatred of and disgust at humanity, but could, nonetheless, acknowledge and characterize his genius.

Swift did not possess ordinary wisdom, but he did possess a terrible intensity of vision, capable of picking out a single hidden truth and then magnifying it and distorting it. The durability of *Gulliver's Travels* goes to show that if the force of belief is behind it, a world-view which only just passes the test of sanity is sufficient to produce a great work of art.

Orwell's seminal essay 'Charles Dickens' was written without any use of formal literary theory or academic discourse (he would have said 'jargon') and at a time when Dickens had been demoted by nearly all serious critics, except the irascible Leavises, to the patronizing pint-size of an over-productive Victorian popular novelist. It began Dickens's rehabilitation as one of the great English novelists. Orwell's feeling for Dickens is so intense that the physical and psychological portrait in the concluding paragraph is often taken as an unconscious self-portrait. Stocks in Kipling were also, more understandably, quoted low when Orwell wrote his essay 'Rudyard Kipling', but it began a sorting of the wheat from the chaff in Kipling's remarkably mixed achievement. In this essay Orwell coins the phrase 'good bad poetry', which gives us a way of appreciating popular writing as good or bad of its kind. This enabled Orwell to produce his wholly original essays 'Boys' Weeklies' and 'The Art of Donald McGill', which provided a way into the sociology of literature so much more tolerant and open-ended than the Marxist interpretation. Orwell never denied the second-rate nature of much of this matter, but equally he could condemn the political morality of Yeats, Pound and even Eliot, while acknowledging their genius. And in 'In Defence of P. G. Wodehouse' he sees that Wodehouse, so good of his kind, was a naïve idiot, not a Nazi sympathizer. But the defender of Dickens and Kipling against the scorn of intellectuals and modernists could himself, in 'Inside the Whale', present a brilliant appreciation of the surrealism of Henry Miller while being bitterly critical (in a somewhat over-diffuse essay of galloping digressions) of the social irresponsibility of Miller and others. He targets the very god of the common man in literature more precisely in 'Wells, Hitler and the World State'. Orwell accuses Wells of a scientific rationalism that could not take Hitler seriously, belittling both his threat and appeal.

The people who say that Hitler is Antichrist, or alternatively, the Holy Ghost, are nearer an understanding of the truth than the intellectuals who for ten dreadful years have kept it up that he is merely a figure out of comic opera, not worth taking seriously. All that this idea really reflects is the sheltered conditions of English life.

But before one can say 'biting the hand that fed him' one comes, in the penultimate paragraph, to the most beautiful and empathetic encomium on the early Wells, full of affectionate humour, modulating – as essays can – from the ironic, almost sarcastic, rage of his opening.

Many of Orwell's sophisticated friends of the days of his late fame came to treat him, however, as if he was a naïve and amateur writer, a *Douanier* Rousseau of letters, to be valued for his simple honesty and authenticity rather than for his art. Even his second wife, Sonia, a highly intelligent and literary person who guarded his reputation well, said to me that he was like the painter Stanley Spencer, which urged me to remark that the naïve visionary had been a prize-winning student at the Slade. And once she shouted at me over lunch, irritated by such remorseless pedantry, 'But of course he shot a fucking elephant, he said so didn't he?' The other Orwell biographer, Michael Sheldon, agrees with her. He has no doubt that 'Shooting an Elephant' is a memoir, just as 'Everything about the sketch "A Hanging" suggests that it is based on a real experience. It is a riveting piece of work whose emotional power comes from a slow but steady accumulation of details.' But there are many 'riveting' stories that we know to be made up the: pretence to be real is part of what makes them 'riveting'. Hugh Kenner is right: the truth of a proposition cannot be inferred from the syntax.

Orwell himself seemed to believe that it is more difficult to lie in monosyllables than in polysyllables, but like many people, he confused meaning with truth. So we must beware not merely of 'flowery tongued Odysseus' but of the plain-spoken man. I have met politicians who pretend to be tongue-tied and ordinary, and who take pains to 'speak bad'. Lincoln once remarked that '"Honest Abe" is very useful to Abraham Lincoln', and yet Lincoln was, like Orwell, an unusually honest man. Like Kenner, I do not wish to debunk Orwell; on the contrary I would like to shift the attention from his character to his writing and to present him as a great essayist, rather than the author of two considerable satires and a handful of minor novels that might no longer be read but for the fame of these two books and the joy of his essays. We can argue until the cows come home whether 'Shooting an Elephant' and 'A Hanging' are to be classified as essays or short stories, but what we cannot do is to use them uncritically as autobiography just because they sound authentic. For part of the skill of the essayist, as of the story writer who uses the fictive first person, is not just to create that famous 'momentary suspension of disbelief' but also a lasting uncertainty about whether we are reading fact or fiction. The good essay is speculative and open-ended: the reader is engaged in a lively conversation, and even when argued with, is not addressed didactically or polemically brow-beaten. The common man, while he hates being talked down to quite as much as feeling that all is semiotically above his head, is not always aware of or happy with these conventions: he can sometimes find frivolity in the essayist and yearn for serious instruction from someone trustworthy and less tricksy. I have encountered many non-university readers of Orwell (it is hard to think of any other serious author who is still so widely read by the common reader in English-speaking countries) who are just as discomforted as Sonia was to have the literal truth of anything he said doubted. I can almost hear his sardonic, rusty laughter.

Orwell could use broad humour for serious effect, rather than explicit moral argument, in a way both appealing and accessible to the common reader – unless such a reader feels himself lambasted:

> One sometimes gets the impression that the mere words 'Socialism' and 'Communism' draw towards them with magnetic force every fruit-juice drinker, nudist, sandal-wearer, sex maniac, Quaker, 'Nature Cure' quack, pacifist and feminist in England . . .

In the next equally digressive chapter of *The Road to Wigan Pier* he mocks those who think they can abolish class distinctions as easily as attending '"summer schools" where the proletarian and the repentant bourgeois are supposed to fall upon one another's necks and be brothers for ever'. Oh yes, there can be mixing on equal terms 'rather like the animals in one of those "Happy Family" cages [at a fair] where a dog, a cat, two ferrets, a rabbit, and three canaries preserve an armed truce while the showman's eye is on them'. But Orwell was a socialist, remember (of a peculiarly English kind), and he did believe strongly that one should try to break down class barriers.

It is this kind of *Sattweis*, sad and wise, humour that the readers of his wartime *Tribune* weekly column enjoyed, or at any rate grew to expect, as he leavened the polemics, varying the tone and pace with the skill of a good essayist. This image of Orwell is very different from the 'Orwellian' image of *Nineteen Eighty-Four*. The lighter tone of *Animal Farm* is more typical of his best writing and more 'Orwell-like': the lover of nature and of small, odd things; the humanist, not the misogynist – and the humanist who makes jokes at his own pessimism. Orwell told his *Tribune* readers that he was going to make the worst possible prophecy for the year 1946: it would be as bad as 1945. His essays often propound tongue-in-cheek paradoxes to provoke thought. But whereas G. K. Chesterton did this famously in a flamboyant, high literary style, Orwell's voice is conversational – for example, he remarks in 'The Sporting Spirit' *à propos* the visit of the Moscow Dynamo football team to Arsenal in 1945, 'that sport is an unfailing cause of ill-will, and that if such a visit as this had any effect at all on Anglo-Soviet relations, it could only be to make them slightly worse than before'.

Orwell could even reflect on the nature of humour without being pretentious, for he saw comedy and tragedy as always close in human life. In his essay 'The Art of Donald McGill', plumbing the moral depths of popular vulgar, comic picture postcards, he says that we all have in our minds inseparably both Don Quixote, hero and saint, and Sancho Panza, the 'unofficial self, the voice of the belly protesting against the soul'.

A dirty joke is not, of course, a serious attack upon morality, but it is a sort of mental rebellion, a momentary wish that things were otherwise. So also with all other jokes, which always centre round cowardice, laziness, dishonesty, or some other quality which society cannot afford to encourage. Society has always to demand a little more from human beings than it will get in practice. It has to demand faultless discipline and self-sacrifice, it must expect its subjects to work hard, pay their taxes, and be faithful to their wives, it must assume that men think it glorious to die on the battlefield and women want to wear themselves out with child-bearing. The whole of what one may call official literature is founded on such assumptions. I never read the proclamations of generals before battle, the speeches of Fuehrers and prime ministers, the solidarity songs of public schools and left-wing political parties, national anthems, Temperance tracts, Papal encyclicals and sermons against gambling and contraception, without seeming to hear in the background a chorus of raspberries from all the millions of common men to whom these high sentiments make no appeal. Nevertheless the high sentiments always win in the end, leaders who offer blood, toil, tears and sweat always get more out of their followers than those who offer safety and a good time . . . It is only that the other element in man, the lazy, cowardly, debt-bilking adulterer who is inside all of us, can never be suppressed altogether and needs a hearing occasionally.

To revert for a moment to the question of the fictive 'I': would it really matter if that same large chorus of common men were to cry, 'Come off it, Governor, you've never read proclamations and whatnot of generals before battle in your life.' For this passage is a good example of Orwell using the comic to be profound, and being profound about the nature of the comic. He makes an important theoretical point in plain language, just as in the previously quoted passage, when discussing the difficulties of crossing class barriers, he avoids theoretical discourse and just makes the seemingly casual but profound and morally disturbing observation that the classes actually meet as equals only in 'summer schools'. When I have read that passage to mixed audiences it goes down a treat, provoking the laughter of recognition; but academic audiences resist it, finding it patronizing, patriotic, romantic and 'untheorized'.

Orwell's use of the plain style also reveals something surprising about the commonsensical writer: an almost metaphysical intensity about the value of ordinary things, a kind of secular pietism. Agnostic though he was, his language is soaked in Protestant imagery, the sense of everything in the world being part of God's own deliberate creation and his 'wonder-working providence'. Consider George Bowling, the fat and sweaty commercial traveller of his immediate pre-war novel, *Coming Up for Air*. Bowling, a lower-middle-class common man if ever there was, is bored stiff with his boring wife, his boring job, his nasty children, and he is nostalgic, almost rotten with nostalgia; so he vanishes for a couple of days – not chasing another woman, as Hilda suspects, but to revisit scenes of childhood and wallow in memory. He ruminates:

I've always had that peculiar feeling for fishing. You'll think it damned silly, no doubt, but I've actually half a wish to go fishing even now, when I'm fat and forty-five and got two kids and a house in the suburbs. Why? Because in a manner of speaking I *am* sentimental about my childhood – not my own particular childhood, but the civilisation which I grew up in and which is now, I suppose, just about at its last kick. And fishing is somehow typical of that civilisation. As soon as you think of fishing you think of things that don't belong to the modern world. The very idea of sitting all day under a willow tree beside a quiet pool – and being able to find a quiet pool to sit beside – belongs to the time before the war, before the radio, before aeroplanes, before Hitler. There's a kind of peacefulness even in the names of English coarse fish. Roach, rudd, dace, bleak, barbel, bream, gudgeon, pike, chub, carp, tench. They're solid kind of names. The people who made them up hadn't heard of machine-guns, they didn't live in terror of the sack or spend their time eating aspirins, going to the pictures and wondering how to keep out of the concentration camp.

Does anyone go fishing nowadays, I wonder? Anywhere within a hundred miles of London there are no fish left to catch . . . who fishes in mill-streams or moats or cow ponds any longer? Where are the English coarse fish now? When I was a kid every pond and stream had fish in it. Now all the ponds are drained, and when the streams aren't poisoned with chemicals from factories they're full of rusty tins and motor-bike tyres.[9]

Notice how close this is to 'Some Thoughts on the Common Toad'. And, leaving aside the characteristic comic, sardonic exaggeration of the last paragraph, think of the invocation and litany of 'solid' names, and recall the passage from 'Why I Write' where he speaks of his love of 'the surface of the earth' and of 'pleasure in solid objects and scraps of useless information'. Secularist though he was, it is as if all things in nature and even unlikely artefacts have spiritual value and should be loved, respected; he implies a proper, almost sacred order between man and nature that the factories, aspirins and bombs threaten, and can destroy if not controlled Proto-ecologist?

A strikingly similar passage occurs in the work of another British secular writer H. G. Wells. It is not easy to escape from Protestantism, certainly not just by ceasing to believe in God. Wells turns pietistic not even over fish but over beer bottles. In *The History of Mr Polly*, poor old Polly has run away from his nagging wife and his boring shop, burned it down in fact (neither writer is a model for feminists or free-marketeers), and has gone tramping – a 'Quest', of course.

The nearer he came to the place the more he liked it. The windows on the ground floor were long and low, and they had pleasing red blinds. The green tables outside were agreeably ringed with memories of former drinks . . . Against the wall was a broken oar, two boat hooks and the stained and faded red cushions of a pleasure boat. One went up three steps to the glass steps to the glass-panelled door and peeped into a broad, low room with a bar and a beer-engine, behind which there were many bright and helpful-looking bottles against mirrors, and great and little pewter measures, and bottles fastened in brass wire upside down, with their corks replaced by taps, and a white china cask labelled 'Shrub', and cigar boxes and boxes of cigarettes, and a couple of Toby jugs and a beautifully coloured hunting scene framed and glazed, showing the most elegant people taking Piper's Cherry Brandy, and . . . satirical verses against swearing and asking for credit, and three very bright, red-cheeked apples and a round-shaped clock.

But these were the mere background to the really pleasant thing in the spectacle, which was quite the plumpest woman Mr Polly had ever seen . . .[10]

But these things are certainly not 'mere background'; for Wells they were as much part of 'the rich tapestry of life' as the plump woman. And remember that, for Orwell, 'the proles had stayed human. They had not become hardened inside.' To them what mattered, Winston Smith realized, were not the great questions raised by the Party, but 'individual relationships, and a completely helpless gesture, an embrace, a tear, a word spoken to a dying man, could have value in itself' – just like the piece of coral from a bygone era that Winston finds in the junk shop. Does one call all this a kind of commonsensical mysticism, or the mysticism of common sense? Life is all right, good even, if one looks at it with the simple wonder of a childexploring everything as new, or with the heightened delight in ordinary things of a stoical person who knows that he or she is soon to die.

Orwell's plain style and his great skill in using the essay as a mode of expression are part of his cult of the ordinary, his faith in common sense and the common man. I find this very attractive. Of course, one does rather have to pick and choose what one praises or accepts as ordinary. But an account of how that is done could only be a treatise on phenomenology in the German or French manner, not an English essay.

When considering what seems ordinary or important to Orwell, it should be remembered that the evidence for his priorities at any given time is necessarily incomplete. Only after the success of *Animal Farm* could he pick his shots, turn down some offers of work, and accept others or determine to write without having to consider too closely, like any relatively unknown writer, what journals there were and what their editors favoured, and without having to adapt the writing to the form, if not the colour, of a particular periodical. Like Aristotle's good rhetorician, the essayist must know not just a subject and have something to say about it, but must know an audience and how to reach it. Unlike a modern columnist-essayist such as Neal Ascherson, Sean French, Christopher Hitchens, Bernard Levin or Hugo Young (all obviously influenced by him), Orwell cannot be found pontificating or puzzling on every major issue of his day, despite his political commitment, despite the fact that his best writing was, in the broadest sense, on political topics. Partly he lacked opportunity (for about two years his only regular column was in *Tribune* – which had a slightly wider circulation then) and partly he wished to convey, in his books as well as his essays, a general set of humanistic and democratic attitudes and beliefs far more than to provide a commentary on events: the precise subject matter was almost immaterial. In any case, the essayist who is a writer still making his way has a great deal more freedom than opportunity. Perhaps this is why so many of the finest English essayists have come from obscurity, even poverty, which has made them, when reflecting on ordinary life, so much more attractive and interesting to most of us today than the elegant, Augustan mannerisms of Addison, Steele and the old *Spectator* essayists.

Bernard Crick

NOTES

1. Until the publication in 1964 of the four volumes of *The Collected Essays, Journalism and Letters of George Orwell* (Secker & Warburg, London), it was very difficult to get an overview of Orwell's essays, mostly buried in long-dead, small magazines. (Even the *C.E.* had significant omissions.) A small number appeared in *Critical Essays* (1946) and *Shooting an Elephant* (1950), prepared in his lifetime; more appeared posthumously in *England Your England* (1953) and, incorporating many of these, the misnamed selection, *Collected Essays* (1961). In the many obituaries and evaluations that followed his death in 1950, writers and critics committed themselves to influential interpretations; but with no chance of reading the main body of his work, they concentrated on the famous two last satires – as did most early scholarly works on Orwell, especially in the United States. Therefore most opinions were fixed before a full range of the essays could be read, so these were received as an appendage to his main achievement, rather than (as I suspect) as his best work. (See Robert Klitzke, 'Orwell and His Critics: an enquiry into the reception of and critical debate about George Orwell's political works', Ph.D. thesis, London University, 1977.)
2. See my Introduction to the Penguin edition of *The Lion and the Unicorn: Socialism and the English Genius*, (Penguin Harmondsworth, 1982).
3. I thank Dr Peter Marks of the University of Hull for this important and sobering point, among others. His Ph.D. thesis, 'Orwell's Essays' (Edinburgh University, 1982), is the only sustained critical work on the subject. It deserves a wide readership.
4. The ILP was a small formation of left-wing 'English socialists', a fusion or alliance (less common in Scotland or Wales) of non-Marxist secular moralists, Christian socialists and independent Marxists (with *some* sympathies with Trotsky on international relations), united by both fierce egalitarianism and libertarianism, also

by a common hatred of the Communist Party. See 'Orwell and English Socialism' in my *Essays on Politics and Literature* (Edinburgh University Press, Edinburgh, 1989).

5. Anthony Burgess, *1985*, Hutchinson, London, 1978, p. 20.
6. In my critical and annotated edition of George Orwell's *Nineteen Eighty-Four* (Clarendon Press, Oxford, 1984), I put the case for reading the book as specifically Swiftian satire. See also Frank Winter, 'Was Orwell a Secret Optimist? The Narrative Function of the 'Appendix' to *Nineteen Eighty-Four*', in Benoit J. Suykerbuyk (ed.), *Essays From Oceania and Eurasia: George Orwell and 1984* (Progressef, Antwerp, 1984), pp. 79–90.
7. Hugh Kenner, 'The Politics of the Plain Style', in Robert Mulvihill (ed.), *Reflection on America, 1984: an Orwell Symposium* (University of Georgia Press, Athens, Ga., 1966), pp. 58–65.
8. Not David Lodge who, in his *Modes of Modern Writing* (Edward Arnold, London, 1977, pp. 9–17) shows that 'Shooting an Elephant' and 'A Hanging' work well as 'symbolic structures', works of art, irrespective of whether they are fact, fiction or a bit of both. See also the Introduction to my *George Orwell: A Life* (Penguin, Harmondsworth, 1992, third edition, pp. 29–39); unhappily, if honestly, in that edition I had to relate new evidence that Orwell did shoot an elephant (pp. 586–9). But Lodge's point still stands.
9. George Orwell, *Coming Up for Air*, 1939, section 4. The sentence 'Where are the English coarse fish now?' contains a once-powerful historical echo and political parallel. Every English schoolboy used to know that the brave Protestant, Bishop Hugh Latimer, came out of prison and preached a sermon in front of Henry VIII against the new, economically efficient, privatized enclosures taken from the old common lands, favoured by the king's courtiers: 'the sheep are eating up the land . . . Where are the English yeomen now?'
10. H. G. Wells, *The History of Mr Polly*, chapter IX, section 3.

Bibliographical Note

The note at the end of each essay gives the original journal and year of publication. The initials that follow stand for the volumes of selected essays in which it was reprinted, whether in Britain or the USA. Sometimes the same collection has a different title in the two countries, but some of the collections were different. *C.E.* is *Collected Essays, Journalism and Letters* (4 vols.); *Cr.E.* is *Critical Essays*; *D.D.* is *Dickens, Dali and Others*; *E.Y.E.* is *England Your England*; *I.T.W.* is *Inside the Whale*; *O.R.* is the *Orwell Reader*; *S.E.* is *Shooting an Elephant*; and *S.J.* is *Such, Such Were the Joys*.

This volume of essays follows the 1968 text of *Collected Essays, Journalism and Letters* edited by Ian Angus and Sonia Orwell but will in time be changed to follow the completely re-edited text of Dr Peter Davison's *The Complete Works of George Orwell* (Secker & Warburg, 1986–). All recent reissues of Orwell's books in Penguin have followed Davison's text although his masterly notes and commentaries are in the Secker & Warburg edition.

Also Parts I and II wer reworked as a book, *The English People* (1947).

Horizon, September 1941; *Cr.E.*, *D.D.*; *O.R.*; *C.E.*

1. Why I Write

From a very early age, perhaps the age of five or six, I knew that when I grew up I should be a writer. Between the ages of about seventeen and twenty-four I tried to abandon this idea, but I did so with the consciousness that I was outraging my true nature and that sooner or later I should have to settle down and write books.

I was the middle child of three, but there was a gap of five years on either side, and I barely saw my father before I was eight. For this and other reasons I was somewhat lonely, and I soon developed disagreeable mannerisms which made me unpopular throughout my schooldays. I had the lonely child's habit of making up stories and holding conversations with imaginary persons, and I think from the very start my literary ambitions were mixed up with the feeling of being isolated and undervalued. I knew that I had a facility with words and a power of facing unpleasant facts, and I felt that this created a sort of private world in which I could get my own back for my failure in everyday life. Nevertheless the volume of serious – i.e. seriously intended – writing which I produced all through my childhood and boyhood would not amount to half a dozen pages. I wrote my first poem at the age of four or five, my mother taking it down to dictation. I cannot remember anything about it except that it was about a tiger and the tiger had 'chair-like teeth' – a good enough phrase, but I fancy the poem was a plagiarism of Blake's 'Tiger, Tiger'. At eleven, when the war of 1914–18 broke out, I wrote a patriotic poem which was printed in the local newspaper, as was another, two years later, on the death of Kitchener. From time to time, when I was a bit older, I wrote bad and usually unfinished 'nature poems' in the Georgian style. I also, about twice, attempted a short story which was a ghastly failure. That was the total of the would-be serious work that I actually set down on paper during all those years.

However, throughout this time I did in a sense engage in literary activities. To begin with there was the made-to-order stuff which I produced quickly, easily and without much pleasure to myself. Apart from school work, I wrote *vers d'occasion*, semi-comic poems which I could turn out at what now seems to me astonishing speed – at fourteen

I wrote a whole rhyming play, in imitation of Aristophanes, in about a week – and helped to edit school magazines, both printed and in manuscript. These magazines were the most pitiful burlesque stuff that you could imagine, and I took far less trouble with them than I now would with the cheapest journalism. But side by side with all this, for fifteen years or more, I was carrying out a literary exercise of a quite different kind: this was the making up of a continuous 'story' about myself, a sort of diary existing only in the mind. I believe this is a common habit of children and adolescents. As a very small child I used to imagine that I was, say, Robin Hood, and picture myself as the hero of thrilling adventures, but quite soon my 'story' ceased to be narcissistic in a crude way and became more and more a mere description of what I was doing and the things I saw. For minutes at a time this kind of thing would be running through my head: 'He pushed the door open and entered the room. A yellow beam of sunlight, filtering through the muslin curtains, slanted on to the table, where a matchbox, half open, lay beside the inkpot. With his right hand in his pocket he moved across to the window. Down in the street a tortoiseshell cat was chasing a dead leaf,' etc. etc. This habit continued till I was about twenty-five, right through my non-literary years. Although I had to search, and did search, for the right words, I seemed to be making this descriptive effort almost against my will, under a kind of compulsion from outside. The 'story' must, I suppose, have reflected the styles of the various writers I admired at different ages, but so far as I remember it always had the same meticulous descriptive quality.

When I was about sixteen I suddenly discovered the joy of mere words, i.e. the sounds and associations of words. The lines from *Paradise Lost*,

> So hee with difficulty and labour hard
> Moved on: with difficulty and labour hee,

which do not now seem to me so very wonderful, sent shivers down my backbone; and the spelling 'hee' for 'he' was an added pleasure. As for the need to describe things, I knew all about it already. So it is clear what kind of books I wanted to write, in so far as I could be said to want to write books at that time. I wanted to write enormous naturalistic novels with unhappy endings, full of detailed descriptions and arresting similes, and also full of purple passages in which words were used partly for the sake of their sound. And in fact my first complete novel, *Burmese Days*, which I wrote when I was thirty but projected much earlier, is rather that kind of book.

I give all this background information because I do not think one can assess a writer's motives without knowing something of his early development. His subject-matter will be determined by the age he lives in – at least this is true in tumultuous, revolutionary ages like our own – but before he ever begins to write he will have acquired an emotional attitude from which he will never completely escape. It is his job, no doubt, to discipline his temperament and avoid getting stuck at some immature stage, or in some perverse mood: but if he escapes from his early influences altogether, he will have killed his impulse to write. Putting aside the need to earn a living, I think there are four great motives for writing, at any rate for writing prose. They exist in different degrees in every writer, and in any one writer the proportions will vary from time to time, according to the atmosphere in which he is living. They are:

1. Sheer egoism. Desire to seem clever, to be talked about, to be remembered after death, to get your own back on grown-ups who snubbed you in childhood, etc. etc. It is humbug to pretend that this is not a motive, and a strong one. Writers share this characteristic with scientists, artists, politicians, lawyers, soldiers, successful businessmen – in short, with the whole top crust of humanity. The great mass of human beings are not acutely selfish. After the age of about thirty they abandon individual ambition – in many cases, indeed, they almost abandon the sense of being individuals at all – and live chiefly for others, or are simply smothered under drudgery. But there is also the minority of gifted, wilful people who are determined to live their own lives to the end, and writers belong in this class. Serious writers, I should say, are on the whole more vain and self-centred than journalists, though less interested in money.

2. Aesthetic enthusiasm. Perception of beauty in the external world, or, on the other hand, in words and their right arrangement. Pleasure in the impact or one sound on another, in the firmness of good prose or the rhythm of a good story. Desire to share an experience which one feels is valuable and ought not to be missed. The aesthetic motive is very feeble in a lot of writers, but even a pamphleteer or a writer of textbooks will have pet words and phrases which appeal to him for non-utilitarian reasons; or he may feel strongly about typography, width of margins, etc. Above the level of a railway guide, no book is quite free from aesthetic considerations.

3. Historical impulse. Desire to see things as they are, to find out true facts and store them up for the use of posterity.

4. Political purpose – using the word 'political' in the widest possible sense. Desire to push the world in a certain direction, to alter other people's idea of the kind of society that they should strive after. Once again, no book is genuinely free from political bias. The opinion that art should have nothing to do with politics is itself a political attitude.

It can be seen how these various impulses must war against one another, and how they must fluctuate from person to person and from time to time. By nature – taking your 'nature' to be the state you have attained when you are first adult – I am a person in whom the first three motives would outweigh the fourth. In a peaceful age I might have written ornate or merely descriptive books, and might have remained almost unaware of my political loyalties. As it is I have been forced into becoming a sort of pamphleteer. First I spent five years in a unsuitable profession (the Indian Imperial Police, in Burma), and then I underwent poverty and the sense of failure. This increased my natural hatred of authority and made me for the first time fully aware of the existence of the working classes, and the job in Burma had given me some understanding of the nature of imperialism: but these experiences were not enough to give me an accurate political orientation. Then came Hitler, the Spanish Civil War, etc. By the end of 1935 I had still failed to reach a firm decision. I remember a little poem that I wrote at that date, expressing my dilemma:

A happy vicar I might have been
Two hundred years ago,
To preach upon eternal doom
And watch my walnuts grow

But born, alas, in an evil time,
I missed that pleasant haven,
For the hair has grown on my upper lip
And the clergy are all clean-shaven.

And later still the times were good,
We were so easy to please,
We rocked our troubled thoughts to sleep
On the bosoms of the trees.

All ignorant we dared to own
The joys we now dissemble;
The greenfinch on the apple bough
Could make my enemies tremble.

But girls' bellies and apricots,
Roach in a shaded stream,

Horses, ducks in flight at dawn,
All these are a dream.

It is forbidden to dream again;
We maim our joys or hide them;
Horses are made of chromium steel
And little fat men shall ride them.

I am the worm who never turned,
The eunuch without a harem;
Between the priest and the commissar
I walk like Eugene Aram;

And the commissar is telling my fortune
While the radio plays,
But the priest has promised an Austin Seven,
For Duggie always pays.

I dreamed I dwelt in marble halls,
And woke to find it true;
I wasn't born for an age like this;
Was Smith? Was Jones? Were you?[1]

The Spanish war and other events in 1936–7 turned the scale and thereafter I knew where I stood. Every line of serious work that I have written since 1936 has been written, directly or indirectly, *against* totalitarianism and *for* democratic Socialism, as I understand it. It seems to me nonsense, in a period like our own, to think that one can avoid writing of such subjects. Everyone writes of them in one guise or another. It is simply a question of which side one takes and what approach one follows. And the more one is conscious of one's political bias, the more chance one has of acting politically without sacrificing one's aesthetic and intellectual integrity.

What I have most wanted to do throughout the past ten years is to make political writing into an art. My starting point is always a feeling of partisanship, a sense of injustice. When I sit down to write a book, I do not say to myself, 'I am going to produce a work of art.' I write it because there is some lie that I want to expose, some fact to which I want to draw attention, and my initial concern is to get a hearing. But I could not do the work of writing a book, or even a long magazine article, if it were not also an aesthetic experience. Anyone who cares to examine my work will see that even when it is downright propaganda it contains much that a full-time politician would consider irrelevant. I am not able,

1. This poem first appeared in the *Adelphi*, December 1936.

and I do not want, completely to abandon the world-view that I acquired in childhood. So long as I remain alive and well I shall continue to feel strongly about prose style, to love the surface of the earth, and to take pleasure in solid objects and scraps of useless information. It is no use trying to suppress that side of myself. The job is to reconcile my ingrained likes and dislikes with the essentially public, non-individual activities that this age forces on all of us.

It is not easy. It raises problems of construction and of language, and it raises in a new way the problem of truthfulness. Let me give just one example of the cruder kind of difficulty that arises. My book about the Spanish Civil War, *Homage to Catalonia*, is, of course, a frankly political book, but in the main it is written with a certain detachment and regard for form. I did try very hard in it to tell the whole truth without violating my literary instincts. But among other things it contains a long chapter, full of newspaper quotations and the like, defending Trotskyists who were accused of plotting with Franco. Clearly such a chapter, which after a year or two would lose its interest for any ordinary reader, must ruin the book. A critic whom I respect read me a lecture about it. 'Why did you put in all that stuff?' he said. 'You've turned what might have been a good book into journalism.' What he said was true, but I could not have done otherwise. I happened to know, what very few people in England had been allowed to know, that innocent men were being falsely accused. If I had not been angry about that I should never have written the book

In one form or another this problem comes up again. The problem of language is subtler and would take too long to discuss. I will only say that of later years I have tried to write less picturesquely and more exactly. In any case I find that by the time you have perfected any style of writing, you have always outgrown it. *Animal Farm* was the first book in which I tried, with full consciousness of what I was doing, to fuse political purpose and artistic purpose into one whole. I have not written a novel for seven years, but I hope to write another fairly soon. It is bound to be a failure, every book is a failure, but I know with some clarity what kind of book I want to write.

Looking back through the last page or two, I see that I have made it appear as though my motives in writing were wholly public-spirited. I don't want to leave that as the final impression. All writers are vain, selfish and lazy, and at the very bottom of their motives there lies a mystery. Writing a book is a horrible, exhausting struggle, like a long bout of some painful illness. One would never undertake such a thing if one were not driven on by some demon whom one can neither resist nor understand. For all one knows that demon is simply the same instinct that makes a baby squall for attention. And yet it is also true that one can write nothing readable unless one constantly struggles to efface one's own personality. Good prose is like a window pane. I cannot say with certainty which of my motives are the strongest, but I know which of them deserve to be followed. And looking back through my work, I see that it is invariably where I lacked a *political* purpose that I wrote lifeless books and was betrayed into purple passages, sentences without meaning, decorative adjectives and humbug generally.

Gangrel [No. 4, Summer], 1946; *S.J.*; *E.Y.E.*; *O.R.*; *C.E.*

2. The Spike

It was late afternoon. Forty-nine of us, forty-eight men and one woman, lay on the green waiting for the spike to open. We were too tired to talk much. We just sprawled about exhaustedly, with home-made cigarettes sticking out of our scrubby faces. Overhead the chestnut branches were covered with blossom, and beyond that great woolly clouds floated almost motionless in a clear sky. Littered on the grass, we seemed dingy, urban riff-raff. We defiled the scene, like sardine-tins and paper bags on the seashore.

What talk there was ran on the Tramp Major of this spike. He was a devil, everyone agreed, a tartar, a tyrant, a bawling, blasphemous, uncharitable dog. You couldn't call your soul your own when he was about, and many a tramp had he kicked out in the middle of the night for giving a back answer. When you came to be searched he fair held you upside down and shook you. If you were caught with tobacco there was hell to pay, and if you went in with money (which is against the law) God help you.

I had eightpence on me. 'For the love of Christ, mate,' the old hands advised me, 'don't you take it in. You'd get seven days for going into the spike with eightpence!'

So I buried my money in a hole under the hedge, marking the spot with a lump of flint. Then we set about smuggling our matches and tobacco, for it is forbidden to take these into nearly all spikes, and one is supposed to surrender them at the gate. We hid them in our socks, except for the twenty or so per cent who had no socks, and had to carry the tobacco in their boots, even under their very toes. We stuffed our ankles with contraband until anyone seeing us might have imagined an outbreak of elephantiasis. But it is an unwritten law that even the sternest Tramp Majors do not search below the knee, and in the end only one man was caught. This was Scotty, a little hairy tramp with a bastard accent sired by cockney out of Glasgow. His tin of cigarette ends fell out of his sock at the wrong moment, and was impounded.

At six the gates swung open and we shuffled in. An official at the gate entered our names and other particulars in the register and took our bundles away from us. The woman was sent off to the workhouse, and we others into the spike. It was a gloomy, chilly, limewashed place, consisting only of a bathroom and dining-room and about a hundred narrow stone cells. The terrible Tramp Major met us at the door and herded us into the bathroom to be stripped and searched. He was a gruff, soldierly man of forty, who gave the tramps no more ceremony than sheep at the dipping-pond, shoving them this way and that and shouting oaths in their faces. But when he came to myself, he looked hard at me, and said:

'You are a gentleman?'

'I suppose so,' I said.

He gave me another long look. 'Well, that's bloody bad luck, guv'nor,' he said, 'that's bloody bad luck, that is.' And thereafter he took it into his head to treat me with compassion, even with a kind of respect.

It was a disgusting sight, that bathroom. All the indecent secrets of our underwear were exposed; the grime, the rents and patches, the bits of string doing duty for buttons, the layers upon layers of fragmentary garments, some of them mere collections of holes, held together by dirt. The room became a press of steaming nudity, the sweaty odours of the tramps competing with the sickly, sub-faecal stench native to the spike. Some of the men refused the bath, and washed only their 'toe-rags', the horrid, greasy little clouts which tramps bind round their feet. Each of us had three minutes in which to bathe himself. Six greasy, slippery roller towels had to serve for the lot of us.

When we had bathed our own clothes were taken away from us, and we were dressed in the workhouse shirts, grey cotton things like nightshirts, reaching to the middle of the thigh. Then we were sent into the dining-room, where supper was set out on the deal tables. It was the invariable spike meal, always the same, whether breakfast, dinner or supper – half a pound of bread, a bit of margarine, and a pint of so-called tea. It took us five minutes to gulp down the cheap, noxious food. Then the Tramp Major served us with three cotton blankets each, and drove us off to our cells for the night. The doors were locked on the outside a little before seven in the evening, and would stay locked for the next twelve hours.

The cells measured eight feet by five, and had no lighting apparatus except a tiny, barred window high up in the wall, and a spyhole in the door. There were no bugs, and we had bedsteads and straw palliasses, rare luxuries both. In many spikes one sleeps on a wooden shelf, and in some on the bare floor, with a rolled-up coat for a pillow. With a cell to myself, and a bed, I was hoping for a sound night's rest. But I did not get it, for there is always something wrong in the spike, and the peculiar shortcoming here, as I discovered immediately, was the cold. May had begun, and in honour of the season – a little sacrifice to the gods of spring, perhaps – the authorities had cut off the steam from the hot pipes. The cotton blankets were almost useless. One spent the night in turning from side to side, falling asleep for ten minutes and waking half frozen, and watching for dawn.

As always happens in the spike, I had at last managed to fall comfortably asleep when it was time to get up. The Tramp Major came marching down the passage with his heavy tread, unlocking the doors and yelling to us to show a leg. Promptly the passage was full of squalid shirt-clad figures rushing for the bathroom, for there was only one tub full of water between us all in the morning, and it was first come first served. When I arrived twenty tramps had already washed their faces. I gave one glance at the black scum on top of the water, and decided to go dirty for the day.

We hurried into our clothes, and then went to the dining-room to bolt our breakfast. The bread was much worse than usual, because the military-minded idiot of a Tramp Major had cut it into slices overnight, so that it was as hard as ship's biscuit. But we were glad of our tea after the cold, restless night. I do not know what tramps would do without tea, or rather the stuff they miscall tea. It is their food, their medicine, their panacea for all evils. Without the half gallon or so of it that they suck down a day, I truly believe they could not face existence.

After breakfast we had to undress again for the medical inspection, which is a precaution against smallpox. It was three quarters of an hour before the doctor arrived, and one had time now to look about him and see what manner of men we were. It was an instructive sight. We stood shivering naked to the waist in two long ranks in the passage. The filtered light, bluish and cold, lighted us up with unmerciful clarity. No one can imagine, unless he has seen such a thing, what pot-bellied, degenerate curs we looked. Shock heads, hairy, crumpled faces, hollow chests, flat feet, sagging muscles – every kind of malformation and physical rottenness were there. All were flabby and discoloured, as all tramps are under their deceptive sunburn. Two or three figures seen there stay ineradicably in my mind. Old 'Daddy', aged seventy-four, with his truss, and his red, watering eyes: a herring-gutted starveling, with sparse beard and sunken cheeks, looking like the corpse of Lazarus in some primitive picture: an imbecile, wandering hither and thither with vague giggles, coyly pleased because his trousers constantly slipped down and left him nude. But few of us were greatly better than these; there were not ten decently built men among us, and half, I believe, should have been in hospital.

This being Sunday, we were to be kept in the spike over the week-end. As soon as the doctor had gone we were herded back to the dining-room, and its door shut upon us. It was a lime-washed, stone-floored room, unspeakably dreary with its furniture of deal boards and benches, and its prison smell. The windows were so high up that one could not look outside, and the sole ornament was a set of Rules threatening dire penalties to any casual who misconducted himself. We packed the room so tight that one could not move an elbow without jostling somebody. Already, at eight o'clock in the morning, we were bored with our captivity. There was nothing to talk about except the petty gossip of the road, the good and bad spikes, the charitable and uncharitable counties, the iniquities of the police and the Salvation Army. Tramps hardly ever get away from these subjects; they talk, as it were, nothing but shop. They have nothing worthy to be called conversation, because emptiness of belly leaves no speculation in their souls. The world is too much with them. Their next meal is never quite secure, and so they cannot think of anything except the next meal.

Two hours dragged by. Old Daddy, witless with age, sat silent, his back bent like a bow and his inflamed eyes dripping slowly on to the floor. George, a dirty old tramp notorious for the queer habit of sleeping in his hat, grumbled about a parcel of tommy that he had lost on the road. Bill the moocher, the best built man of us all, a Herculean sturdy beggar who smelt of beer even after twelve hours in the spike, told tales of mooching, of pints stood him in the boozers, and of a parson who had preached to the police and got him seven days. William and Fred, two young ex-fishermen from Norfolk, sang a sad song about Unhappy Bella, who was betrayed and died in the snow. The imbecile drivelled about an imaginary toff who had once given him two hundred and fifty-seven golden sovereigns. So the time passed, with dull talk and dull obscenities. Everyone was smoking, except Scotty, whose tobacco had been seized, and he was so miserable in his smokeless state that I stood him the making of a cigarette. We smoked furtively, hiding our cigarettes like schoolboys when we heard the Tramp Major's step, for smoking, though connived at, was officially forbidden.

Most of the tramps spent ten consecutive hours in this dreary room. It is hard to imagine how they put up with it. I have come to think that boredom is the worst of all a tramp's evils, worse than hunger and discomfort, worse even than the constant feeling of being socially disgraced. It is a silly piece of cruelty to confine an ignorant man all day with nothing to do; it is like chaining a dog in a barrel. Only an educated man, who has consolations within himself, can endure confinement. Tramps, unlettered types as nearly all of them are, face their poverty with blank, resourceless minds. Fixed for ten hours on a comfortless bench, they know no way of occupying themselves, and if they think at all it is to whimper about hard luck and pine for work. They have not the stuff in them to endure the horrors of idleness. And so, since so much of their lives is spent in doing nothing, they suffer agonies from boredom.

I was much luckier than the others, because at ten o'clock the Tramp Major picked me out for the most coveted of all jobs in the spike, the job of helping in the workhouse kitchen. There was not really any work to be done there, and I was able to make off and hide in a shed used for storing potatoes, together with some workhouse paupers who were skulking to avoid the Sunday-morning service. There was a stove burning there, and comfortable packing cases to sit on, and back numbers of the *Family Herald*, and even a copy of *Raffles* from the workhouse library. It was paradise after the spike.

Also, I had my dinner from the workhouse table, and it was one of the biggest meals I have ever eaten. A tramp does not see such a meal twice in the year, in the spike or out of it. The paupers told me that they always gorged to the bursting point on Sundays, and went hungry six days of the week. When the meal was over the cook set me to do the washing up, and told me to throw away the food that remained. The wastage was astonishing; great dishes of beef, and bucketfuls of bread and vegetables, were pitched away like rubbish, and then defiled with tea-leaves. I filled five dustbins to overflowing with good food. And while I did so my fellow tramps were sitting two hundred yards away in the spike, their bellies half filled with the spike dinner of the everlasting bread and tea, and perhaps two cold boiled potatoes each in honour of Sunday. It appeared that the food was thrown away from deliberate policy, rather than that it should be given to the tramps.

At three I left the workhouse kitchen and went back to the spike. The boredom in that crowded, comfortless room was now unbearable. Even smoking had ceased, for a tramp's only tobacco is picked-up cigarette ends, and, like a browsing beast, he starves if he is long away from the pavement-pasture. To occupy the time I talked with a rather superior tramp, a young carpenter who wore a collar and tie, and was on the road, he said, for lack of a set of tools. He kept a little aloof from the other tramps, and held himself more like a free man than a casual. He had literary tastes, too, and carried one of Scott's novels on all his wanderings. He told me he never entered a spike unless driven there by hunger, sleeping under hedges and behind ricks in preference. Along the south coast he had begged by day and slept in bathing-machines for weeks at a time.

We talked of life on the road. He criticized the system which makes a tramp spend fourteen hours a day in the spike, and the other ten in walking and dodging the police. He spoke of his own case – six months at the public charge for want of three pounds' worth of tools. It was idiotic, he said.

Then I told him about the wastage of food in the workhouse kitchen, and what I thought of it. And at that he changed his tune immediately. I saw that I had awakened the pew-renter who sleeps in every English workman. Though he had been famished along with the rest, he at once saw reasons why the food should have been thrown away rather than given to the tramps. He admonished me quite severely.

'They have to do it,' he said. 'If they made these places too pleasant you'd have all the scum of the country flocking into them. It's only the bad food as keeps all that scum away. These tramps are too lazy to work, that's all that's wrong with them. You don't want to go encouraging of them. They're scum.'

I produced arguments to prove him wrong, but he would not listen. He kept repeating:

'You don't want to have any pity on these tramps – scum, they are. You don't want to judge them by the same standards as men like you and me. They're scum, just scum.'

It was interesting to see how subtly he disassociated himself from his fellow tramps. He has been on the road six months, but in the sight of God, he seemed to imply, he was not a tramp. His body might be in the spike, but his spirit soared far away, in the pure aether of the middle classes.

The clock's hands crept round with excruciating slowness. We were too bored even to talk now, the only sound was of oaths and reverberating yawns. One would force his eyes away from the clock for what seemed an age, and then look back again to see that the hands had advanced three minutes. Ennui clogged our souls like cold mutton fat. Our bones ached because of it. The clock's hands stood at four, and supper was not till six, and there was nothing left remarkable beneath the visiting moon.

At last six o'clock did come, and the Tramp Major and his assistant arrived with supper. The yawning tramps brisked up like lions at feeding-time. But the meal was a dismal disappointment. The bread, bad enough in the morning, was now positively uneatable; it was so hard that even the strongest jaws could make little impression on it. The older men went almost supperless, and not a man could finish his portion, hungry though most of us were. When we had finished, the blankets were served out immediately, and we were hustled off once more to the bare, chilly cells.

Thirteen hours went by. At seven we were awakened, and rushed forth to squabble over the water in the bathroom, and bolt our ration of bread and tea. Our time in the spike was up, but we could not go until the doctor had examined us again, for the authorities have a terror of smallpox and its distribution by tramps. The doctor kept us waiting two hours this time, and it was ten o'clock before we finally escaped.

At last it was time to go, and we were let out into the yard. How bright everything looked, and how sweet the winds did blow, after the gloomy, reeking spike! The Tramp Major handed each man his bundle of confiscated possessions, and a hunk of bread and cheese for midday dinner, and then we took the road, hastening to get out of sight of the spike and its discipline. This was our interim of freedom. After a day and two nights of wasted time we had eight hours or so to take our recreation, to scour the roads for cigarette ends, to beg, and to look for work. Also, we had to make our ten, fifteen, or it might be twenty miles to the next spike, where the game would begin anew.

I disinterred my eightpence and took the road with Nobby, a respectable, downhearted tramp who carried a spare pair of boots and visited all the Labour Exchanges. Our late companions were scattering north, south, east and west, like bugs into a mattress. Only the imbecile loitered at the spike gates, until the Tramp Major had to chase him away.

Nobby and I set out for Croydon. It was a quiet road, there were no cars passing, the blossom covered the chestnut trees like great wax candles. Everything was so quiet and smelt so clean, it was hard to realize that only a few minutes ago we had been packed with that band of prisoners in a stench of drains and soft soap. The others had all disappeared; we two seemed to be the only tramps on the road.

Then I heard a hurried step behind me, and felt a tap on my arm. It was little Scotty, who had run panting after us. He pulled a rusty tin box from his pocket. He wore a friendly smile, like a man who is repaying an obligation.

'Here y'are, mate,' he said cordially. 'I owe you some fag ends. You stood me a smoke yesterday. The Tramp Major give me back my box of fag ends when we come out this morning. One good turn deserves another – here y'are.'

And he put four sodden, debauched, loathly cigarette ends into my hand.

Eric Blair

Adelphi, April 1931; later reduced and reshaped to form Chapters 27 and 35 of *Down and Out in Paris and London*.

3. A Hanging

It was in Burma, a sodden morning of the rains. A sickly light, like yellow tinfoil, was slanting over the high walls into the jail yard. We were waiting outside the condemned cells, a row of sheds fronted with double bars, like small animal cages. Each cell measured about ten feet by ten and was quite bare within except for a plank bed and a pot of drinking water. In some of them brown silent men were squatting at the inner bars, with their blankets draped round them. These were the condemned men, due to be hanged within the next week or two.

One prisoner had been brought out of his cell. He was a Hindu, a puny wisp of a man, with a shaven head and vague liquid eyes. He had a thick, sprouting moustache, absurdly too big for his body, rather like the moustache of a comic man on the films. Six tall Indian warders were guarding him and getting him ready for the gallows. Two of them stood by with rifles and fixed bayonets, while the others handcuffed him, passed a chain through his handcuffs and fixed it to their belts, and lashed his arms tight to his sides. They crowded very close about him, with their hands always on him in a careful, caressing grip, as though all the while feeling him to make sure he was there. It was like men handling a fish which is still alive and may jump back into the water. But he stood quite unresisting, yielding his arms limply to the ropes, as though he hardly noticed what was happening.

Eight o'clock struck and a bugle call, desolately thin in the wet air, floated from the distant barracks. The superintendent of the jail, who was standing apart from the rest of us, moodily prodding the gravel with his stick, raised his head at the sound. He was an army doctor, with a grey toothbrush moustache and a gruff voice. 'For God's sake hurry up, Francis,' he said irritably. 'The man ought to have been dead by this time. Aren't you ready yet?'

Francis, the head jailer, a fat Dravidian in a white drill suit and gold spectacles, waved his black hand. 'Yes sir, yes sir,' he bubbled. 'All iss satisfactorily prepared. The hangman iss waiting. We shall proceed.'

'Well, quick march, then. The prisoners can't get their breakfast till this job's over.'

We set out for the gallows. Two warders marched on either side of the prisoner, with their rifles at the slope; two others marched close against him, gripping him by arm and shoulder, as though at once pushing and supporting him. The rest of us, magistrates and the like, followed behind. Suddenly, when we had gone ten yards, the procession stopped short without any order or warning. A dreadful thing had happened – a dog, come goodness knows whence, had appeared in the yard. It came bounding among us with a loud volley of barks, and leapt round us wagging its whole body, wild with glee at finding so many human beings together. It was a large woolly dog, half Airedale, half pariah. For a moment it pranced round us, and then, before anyone could stop it, it had made a dash for the prisoner, and jumping up tried to lick his face. Everyone stood aghast, too taken aback even to grab at the dog.

'Who let that bloody brute in here?' said the superintendent angrily. 'Catch it, someone!'

A warder, detached from the escort, charged clumsily after the dog, but it danced and gambolled just out of his reach, taking everything as part of the game. A young Eurasian jailer picked up a handful of gravel and tried to stone the dog away, but it dodged the stones and came after us again. Its yaps echoed from the jail walls. The prisoner, in the grasp of the two warders, looked on incuriously, as though this was another formality of the hanging. It was several minutes before someone managed to catch the dog. Then we put my handkerchief through its collar and moved off once more, with the dog still straining and whimpering.

It was about forty yards to the gallows. I watched the bare brown back of the prisoner marching in front of me. He walked clumsily with his bound arms, but quite steadily, with that bobbing gait of the Indian who never straightens his knees. At each step his muscles slid neatly into place, the lock of hair on his scalp danced up and down, his feet printed themselves on the wet gravel. And once, in spite of the men who gripped him by each shoulder, he stepped slightly aside to avoid a puddle on the path.

It is curious, but till that moment I had never realized what it means to destroy a healthy, conscious man. When I saw the prisoner step aside to avoid the puddle, I saw the mystery, the unspeakable wrongness, of cutting a life short when it is in full tide. This man was not dying, he was alive just as we were alive. All the organs of his body were working – bowels digesting food, skin renewing itself, nails growing, tissues forming – all toiling away in solemn foolery. His nails would still be growing when he stood on the drop, when he was falling through the air with a tenth of a second to live. His eyes saw the yellow gravel and the grey walls, and his brain still remembered, foresaw, reasoned – reasoned even about puddles. He and we were a party of men walking together, seeing, hearing, feeling, understanding the same world; and in two minutes, with a sudden snap, one of us would be gone – one mind less, one world less.

The gallows stood in a small yard, separate from the main grounds of the prison, and overgrown with tall prickly weeds. It was a brick erection like three sides of a shed, with planking on top, and above that two beams and a crossbar with the rope dangling. The hangman, a grey-haired convict in the white uniform of the prison, was waiting beside his machine. He greeted us with a servile crouch as we entered. At a word from Francis the two warders, gripping the prisoner more closely than ever, half led, half pushed him to the gallows and helped him clumsily up the ladder. Then the hangman climbed up and fixed the rope round the prisoner's neck.

We stood waiting, five yards away. The warders had formed in a rough circle round the gallows. And then, when the noose was fixed, the prisoner began crying out on his god. It was a high, reiterated cry of 'Ram! Ram! Ram! Ram!', not urgent and fearful like a prayer or a cry for help, but steady, rhythmical, almost like the tolling of a bell. The dog answered the sound with a whine. The hangman, still standing on the gallows, produced a small cotton bag like a flour bag and drew it down over the prisoner's face. But the sound, muffled by the cloth, still persisted, over and over again: 'Ram! Ram! Ram! Ram! Ram!'

The hangman climbed down and stood ready, holding the lever. Minutes seemed to pass. The steady, muffled crying from the prisoner went on and on, 'Ram! Ram! Ram!' never faltering for an instant. The superintendent, his head on his chest, was slowly poking the ground with his stick; perhaps he was counting the cries, allowing the prisoner a fixed number – fifty, perhaps, or a hundred. Everyone had changed colour. The Indians had gone grey like bad coffee, and one or two of the bayonets were wavering. We looked at the lashed, hooded man on the drop, and listened to his cries – each cry another second of life; the same thought was in all our minds: oh, kill him quickly, get it over, stop that abominable noise!

Suddenly the superintendent made up his mind. Throwing up his head he made a swift motion with his stick. 'Chalo!' he shouted almost fiercely.

There was a clanking noise, and then dead silence. The prisoner had vanished, and the rope was twisting on itself. I let go of the dog, and it galloped immediately to the back of the gallows; but when it got there it stopped short, barked, and then retreated into a corner of the yard, where it stood among the weeds, looking timorously out at us. We went round the gallows to inspect the prisoner's body. He was dangling with his toes pointed straight downwards, very slowly revolving, as dead as a stone.

The superintendent reached out with his stick and poked the bare body; it oscillated, slightly, '*He's* all right,' said the superintendent. He backed out from under the gallows, and blew out a deep breath. The moody look had gone out of his face quite suddenly. He glanced at his wrist-watch. 'Eight minutes past eight. Well, that's all for this morning, thank God.'

The warders unfixed bayonets and marched away. The dog, sobered and conscious of having misbehaved itself, slipped after them. We walked out of the gallows yard, past the condemned cells with their waiting prisoners, into the big central yard of the prison. The convicts, under the command of warders armed with lathis, were already receiving their breakfast. They squatted in long rows, each man holding a tin pannikin, while two warders with buckets marched round ladling out rice; it seemed quite a homely, jolly scene, after the hanging. An enormous relief had come upon us now that the job was done. One felt an impulse to sing, to break into a run, to snigger. All at once everyone began chattering gaily.

The Eurasian boy walking beside me nodded towards the way we had come, with a knowing smile: 'Do you know, sir, our friend (he meant the dead man), when he heard his appeal had been dismissed, he pissed on the floor of his cell. From fright. – Kindly take one of my cigarettes, sir. Do you not admire my new silver case, sir? From the boxwallah, two rupees eight annas. Classy European style.'

Several people laughed – at what, nobody seemed certain.

Francis was walking by the superintendent, talking garrulously: 'Well, sir, all hass passed off with the utmost satisfactoriness. It wass all finished – flick! like that. It iss not always so – oah, no! I have known cases where the doctor wass obliged to go beneath the gallows and pull the prisoner's legs to ensure decease. Most disagreeable!'

'Wriggling about, eh? That's bad,' said the superintendent.

'Ach, sir, it iss worse when they become refractory! One man, I recall, clung to the bars of hiss cage when we went to take him out. You will scarcely credit, sir, that it took six warders to dislodge him, three pulling at each leg. We reasoned with him. "My dear fellow," we said, "think of all the pain and trouble you are causing to us!" But no, he would not listen! Ach, he wass very troublesome!'

I found that I was laughing quite loudly. Everyone was laughing. Even the superintendent grinned in a tolerant way. 'You'd better all come out and have a drink,' he said quite genially. 'I've got a bottle of whisky in the car. We could do with it.'

We went through the big double gates of the prison, into the road. 'Pulling at his legs!' exclaimed a Burmese magistrate suddenly, and burst into a loud chuckling. We all began laughing again. At that moment Francis's anecdote seemed extraordinarily funny. We all had a drink together, native and European alike, quite amicably. The dead man was a hundred yards away.

Eric A. Blair

Adelphi, August 1931; *New Savoy*, 1946; *S.E.*; *O.R.*; *C.E.*

4. Shooting an Elephant

In Moulmein, in Lower Burma, I was hated by large numbers of people – the only time in my life that I have been important enough for this to happen to me. I was sub-divisional police officer of the town, and in an aimless, petty kind of way anti-European feeling was very bitter. No one had the guts to raise a riot, but if a European woman went through the bazaars alone somebody would probably spit betel juice over her dress. As a police officer I was an obvious target and was baited whenever it seemed safe to do so. When a nimble Burman tripped me up on the football field and the referee (another Burman) looked the other way, the crowd yelled with hideous laughter. This happened more than once. In the end the sneering yellow faces of young men that met me everywhere, the insults hooted after me when I was at a safe distance, got badly on my nerves. The young Buddhist priests were the worst of all. There were several thousands of them in the town and none of them seemed to have anything to do except stand on street corners and jeer at Europeans.

All this was perplexing and upsetting. For at that time I had already made up my mind that imperialism was an evil thing and the sooner I chucked up my job and got out of it the better. Theoretically – and secretly, of course – I was all for the Burmese and all against their oppressors, the British. As for the job I was doing, I hated it more bitterly than I can perhaps make clear. In a job like that you see the dirty work of Empire at close quarters. The wretched prisoners huddling in the stinking cages of the lock-ups, the grey, cowed faces of the long-term convicts, the scarred buttocks of the men who had been flogged with bamboos – all these oppressed me with an intolerable sense of guilt. But I could get nothing into perspective. I was young and ill-educated and I had had to think out my problems in the utter silence that is imposed on every Englishman in the East. I did not even know that the British Empire is dying, still less did I know that it is a great deal better than the younger empires that are going to supplant it. All I knew was that I was stuck between my hatred of the empire I served and my rage against the evil-spirited little beasts who tried to make my job impossible. With one part of my mind I thought of the British Raj as an unbreakable tyranny, as something clamped down, *in saecula saeculorum*, upon the will of prostrate peoples; with another part I thought that the greatest joy in the world would be to drive a bayonet into a Buddhist priest's guts. Feelings like these are the normal by-products of imperialism; ask any Anglo-Indian official, if you can catch him off duty.

One day something happened which in a roundabout way was enlightening. It was a tiny incident in itself, but it gave me a better glimpse than I had had before of the real nature of imperialism – the real motives for which despotic governments act. Early one morning the sub-inspector at a police station the other end of town rang me up on the phone and said that an elephant was ravaging the bazaar. Would I please come and do something about it? I did not know what I could do, but I wanted to see what was happening and I got on to a pony and started out. I took my rifle, an old .44 Winchester and much too small to kill an elephant, but I thought the noise might be useful *in terrorem*. Various Burmans stopped me on the way and told me about the elephant's doings. It was not, of course, a wild elephant, but a tame one which had gone 'must'. It had been chained up as tame elephants always are when their attack of 'must' is due, but on the previous night it had broken its chain and escaped. Its mahout, the only person who could manage it when it was in that state, had set out in pursuit, but he had taken the wrong direction and was now twelve hours' journey away, and in the morning the elephant had suddenly reappeared in the town. The Burmese population had no weapons and were quite helpless against it. It had already destroyed somebody's bamboo hut, killed a cow and raided some fruit-stalls and devoured the stock; also it had met the municipal rubbish van, and, when the driver jumped out and took to his heels, had turned the van over and inflicted violence upon it.

The Burmese sub-inspector and some Indian constables were waiting for me in the quarter where the elephant had been seen. It was a very poor quarter, a labyrinth of squalid bamboo huts, thatched with palm-leaf, winding all over a steep hillside. I remember that it was a cloudy stuffy morning at the beginning of the rains. We began questioning the people as to where the elephant had gone, and, as usual, failed to get any definite information. That is invariably the case in the East; a story always sounds clear enough at a distance, but the nearer you get to the scene of events the vaguer it becomes. Some of the people said that the elephant had gone in one direction, some said that he had gone in another, some professed not even to have heard of any elephant. I had almost made up my mind that the whole story was a pack of lies, when we heard yells a little distance away. There was a loud, scandalized cry of 'Go away, child! Go away this instant!' and an old woman with a switch in her hand came round the corner of a hut, violently shooing away a crowd of naked children. Some more women followed, clicking their tongues and exclaiming; evidently there was something there that the children ought not to have seen. I rounded the hut and saw a man's dead body sprawling in the mud. He was an Indian, a black Dravidian coolie, almost naked, and he could not have been dead many minutes. The people said that the elephant had come suddenly upon him round the corner of the hut, caught him with its trunk, put its foot on his back and ground him into the earth. This was the rainy season and the ground was soft, and his face had scored a trench a foot deep and a couple of yards long. He was lying on his belly with arms crucified and head sharply twisted to one side. His face was coated with mud, the eyes wide open, the teeth bared and grinning with an expression of unendurable agony. (Never tell me, by the way, that the dead look peaceful. Most of the corpses I have seen looked devilish.) The friction of the great beast's foot had stripped the skin from his back as neatly as one skins a rabbit. As soon as I saw the dead man I sent an orderly to a friend's house near by to borrow an elephant rifle. I had already sent back the pony, not wanting it to go mad with fright and throw me if it smelled the elephant.

The orderly came back in a few minutes with a rifle and five cartridges, and meanwhile some Burmans had arrived and told us that the elephant was in the paddy fields below, only a few hundred yards away. As I started forward practically the whole population of the quarter flocked out of their houses and followed me. They had seen the rifle and were all shouting excitedly that I was going to shoot the elephant. They had not shown much interest in the elephant when he was merely ravaging their homes, but it was different now that he was going to be shot. It was a bit of fun to them, as it would be to an English crowd; besides, they wanted the meat. It made me vaguely uneasy. I had no intention of shooting the elephant – I had merely sent for the rifle to defend myself if necessary – and it is always unnerving to have a crowd following you. I marched down the hill, looking and feeling a fool, with the rifle over my shoulder and an ever-growing army of people jostling at my heels. At the bottom when you got away from the huts there was a metalled road and beyond that a miry waste of paddy fields a thousand yards across, not yet ploughed but soggy from the first rains and dotted with coarse grass. The elephant was standing eighty yards from the road, his left side towards us. He took not the slightest notice of the crowd's approach. He was tearing up bunches of grass, beating them against his knees to clean them and stuffing them into his mouth.

I had halted on the road. As soon as I saw the elephant I knew with perfect certainty that I ought not to shoot him. It is a serious matter to shoot a working elephant – it is comparable to destroying a huge and costly piece of machinery – and obviously one ought not to do it if it can possibly be avoided. And at that distance, peacefully eating, the elephant looked no more dangerous than a cow. I thought then and I think now that his attack of 'must' was already passing off; in which case he would merely wander harmlessly about until the mahout came back and caught him. Moreover, I did not in the least want to shoot him. I decided that I would watch him for a little while to make sure that he did not turn savage again, and then go home.

But at that moment I glanced round at the crowd that had followed me. It was an immense crowd, two thousand at the least and growing every minute. It blocked the road for a long distance on either side. I looked at the sea of yellow faces above the garish clothes – faces all happy and excited over this bit of fun, all certain that the elephant was going to be shot. They were watching me as they would watch a conjurer about to perform a trick. They did not like me, but with the magical rifle in my hands I was momentarily worth watching. And suddenly I realized that I should have to shoot the elephant after all. The people expected it of me and I had got to do it; I could feel their two thousand wills pressing me forward, irresistibly. And it was at this moment, as I stood there with the rifle in my hands, that I first grasped the hollowness, the futility of the white man's dominion in the East. Here was I, the white man with his gun, standing in front of the unarmed native crowd – seemingly the leading actor of the piece; but in reality I was only an absurd puppet pushed to and fro by the will of those yellow faces behind. I perceived in this moment that when the white man turns tyrant it is his own freedom that he destroys. He becomes a sort of hollow, posing dummy, the conventionalized figure of a sahib. For it is the condition of his rule that he shall spend his life in trying to impress the 'natives' and so in every crisis he has got to do what the 'natives' expect of him. He wears a mask, and his face grows to fit it. I had got to shoot the elephant. I had committed myself to doing it when I sent for the rifle. A sahib has got to act like a sahib; he has got to appear resolute, to know his own mind and do definite things. To come all that way, rifle in hand, with two thousand people marching at my heels, and then to trail feebly away, having done nothing – no, that was impossible. The crowd would laugh at me. And my whole life, every white man's life in the East, was one long struggle not be be laughed at.

But I did not want to shoot the elephant. I watched him beating his bunch of grass against his knees, with that pre-occupied grandmotherly air that elephants have. It seemed to me that it would be murder to shoot him. At that age I was not squeamish about killing animals, but I had never shot an elephant and never wanted to. (Somehow it always seems worse to kill a *large* animal.) Besides, there was the beast's owner to be considered. Alive, the elephant was worth at least a hundred pounds; dead, he would only be worth the value of his tusks – five pounds, possibly. But I had got to act quickly. I turned to some experienced-looking Burmans who had been there when we arrived, and asked them how the elephant had been behaving. They all said the same thing: he took no notice of you if you left him alone, but he might charge if you went too close to him.

It was perfectly clear to me what I ought to do. I ought to walk up to within, say, twenty-five yards of the elephant and test his behaviour. If he charged I could shoot, if he took no notice of me it would be safe to leave him until the mahout came back. But also I knew that I was going to do no such thing. I was a poor shot with a rifle and the ground was soft mud into which one would sink at every step. If the elephant charged and I missed him, I should have about as much chance as a toad under a steam-roller. But even then I was not thinking particularly of my own skin, only the watchful yellow faces behind. For at that moment, with the crowd watching me, I was not afraid in the ordinary sense, as I would have been if I had been alone. A white man mustn't be frightened in front of 'natives'; and so, in general, he isn't frightened. The sole thought in my mind was that if anything went wrong those two thousand Burmans would see me pursued, caught, trampled on and reduced to a grinning corpse like that Indian up the hill. And if that happened it was quite probable that some of them would laugh. That would never do. There was only one alternative. I shoved the cartridges into the magazine and lay down on the road to get a better aim.

The crowd grew very still, and a deep, low, happy sigh, as of people who see the theatre curtain so up at last, breathed from innumerable throats. They were going to have their bit of fun after all. The rifle was a beautiful German thing with cross-hair sights. I did not then know that in shooting an elephant one should shoot to cut an imaginary bar running from ear-hole to ear-hole. I ought therefore, as the elephant was sideways on, to have aimed straight at his ear-hole; actually I aimed several inches in front of this, thinking the brain would be further forward.

When I pulled the trigger I did not hear the bang or feel the kick – one never does when a shot goes home – but I heard the devilish roar of glee that went up from the crowd. In that instant, in too short a time, one would have thought, even for the bullet to get there, a mysterious, terrible change had come over the elephant. He neither stirred nor fell, but every line of his body had altered. He looked suddenly stricken, shrunken, immensely old, as though the frightful impact of the bullet had paralysed him without knocking him down. At last, after what seemed a long time – it might have been five seconds, I dare say – he sagged flabbily to his knees. His mouth slobbered. An enormous senility seemed to have settled upon him. One could have imagined him thousands of years old. I fired again into the same spot. At the second shot he did not collapse but climbed with desperate slowness to his feet and stood weakly upright, with legs sagging and head drooping. I fired a third time. That was the shot that did for him. You could see the agony of it jolt his whole body and knock the last remnant of strength from his legs. But in falling he seemed for a moment to rise, for as his hind legs collapsed beneath him he seemed to tower upwards like a huge rock toppling, his trunk reaching skyward like a tree. He trumpeted, for the first and only time. And then down he came, his belly towards me, with a crash that seemed to shake the ground even where I lay.

I got up. The Burmans were already racing past me across the mud. It was obvious that the elephant would never rise again, but he was not dead. He was breathing very rhythmically with long rattling gasps, his great mound of a side painfully rising and falling. His mouth was wide open – I could see far down into caverns of pale pink throat. I waited a long time for him to die, but his breathing did not weaken. Finally I fired two remaining shots into the spot where I thought his heart must be. The thick blood welled out of him like red velvet, but still he did not die. His body did not even jerk when the shots hit him, the tortured breathing continued without a pause. He was dying, very slowly and in great agony, but in some world remote from me where not even a bullet could damage him further. I felt that I had got to put an end to that dreadful noise. It seemed dreadful to see the great beast lying there, powerless to move and yet powerless to die, and not even to be able to finish him. I sent back for my small rifle and poured shot after shot into his heart and down his throat. They seemed to make no impression. The tortured gasps continued as steadily as the ticking of a clock.

In the end I could not stand it any longer and went away. I heard later that it took him half an hour to die. Burmans were arriving with dahs and baskets even before I left, and I was told they had stripped his body almost to the bones by the afternoon.

Afterwards, of course, there were endless discussions about the shooting of the elephant. The owner was furious, but he was only an Indian and could do nothing. Besides, legally I had done the right thing, for a mad elephant has to be killed, like a mad dog, if its owner fails to control it. Among the Europeans opinion was divided. The older men said I was right, the younger men said it was a damn shame to shoot an elephant for killing a coolie, because an elephant was worth more than any damn Coringhee coolie. And afterwards I was very glad that the coolie had been killed; it put me legally in the right and it gave me a sufficient pretext for shooting the elephant. I often wondered whether any of the others grasped that I had done it solely to avoid looking a fool.

New Writing, No. 2, Autumn 1936; *Penguin New Writing*, No. 1, [November] 1940; broadcast in the B.B.C. Home Service, 12 October 1948; *O.R.*; *C.E.*

5. Bookshop Memories

When I worked in a second-hand bookshop – so easily pictured, if you don't work in one, as a kind of paradise where charming old gentlemen browse eternally among calf-bound folios – the thing that chiefly struck me was the rarity of really bookish people. Our shop had an exceptionally interesting stock, yet I doubt whether ten per cent of our customers knew a good book from a bad one. First edition snobs were much commoner than lovers of literature, but oriental students haggling over cheap textbooks were commoner still, and vague-minded women looking for birthday presents for their nephews were commonest of all.

Many of the people who came to us were of the kind who would be a nuisance anywhere but have special opportunities in a bookshop. For example, the dear old lady who 'wants a book for an invalid' (a very common demand, that), and the other dear old lady who read such a nice book in 1897 and wonders whether you can find her a copy. Unfortunately she doesn't remember the title or the author's name or what the book was about, but she does remember that it had a red cover. But apart from these there are two well-known types of pest by whom every second-hand bookshop is haunted. One is the decayed person smelling of old breadcrusts who comes every day, sometimes several times a day, and tries to sell you worthless books. The other is the person who orders large quantities of books for which he has not the smallest intention of paying. In our shop we sold nothing on credit, but we would put books aside, or order them if necessary, for people who arranged to fetch them away later. Scarcely half the people who ordered books from us ever came back. It used to puzzle me at first. What made them do it? They would come in and demand some rare and expensive book, would make us promise over and over again to keep it for them, and then would vanish never to return. But many of them, of course, were unmistakable paranoiacs. They used to talk in a grandiose manner about themselves and tell the most ingenious stories to explain how they had happened to come out of doors without any money – stories which, in many cases, I am sure they themselves believed. In a town like London there are always plenty of not quite certifiable lunatics walking the streets, and they tend to gravitate towards bookshops, because a bookshop is one of the few places where you can hang about for a long time without spending any money. In the end one gets to know these people almost at a glance. For all their big talk there is something moth-eaten and aimless about them. Very often, when we were dealing with an obvious paranoiac, we would put aside the books he asked for and then put them back on the shelves the moment he had gone. None of them, I noticed, ever attempted to take books away without paying for them; merely to order them was enough – it gave them, I suppose, the illusion that they were spending real money.

Like most second-hand bookshops we had various sidelines. We sold second-hand typewriters, for instance, and also stamps – used stamps, I mean. Stamp-collectors are a strange, silent, fish-like breed, of all ages, but only of the male sex; women, apparently, fail to see the peculiar charm of gumming bits of coloured paper into albums. We also sold sixpenny horoscopes compiled by somebody who claimed to have foretold the Japanese earthquake. They were in sealed envelopes and I never opened one of them myself, but the people who bought them often came back and told us how 'true' their horoscopes had been. (Doubtless any horoscope seems 'true' if it tells you that you are highly attractive to the opposite sex and your worst fault is generosity.) We did a good deal of business in children's books, chiefly 'remainders'. Modern books for children are rather horrible things, especially when you see them in the mass. Personally I would sooner give a child a copy of Petronius Arbiter than *Peter Pan*, but even Barrie seems manly and wholesome compared with some of his later imitators. At Christmas time we spent a feverish ten days struggling with Christmas cards and calendars, which are tiresome things to sell but good business while the season lasts. It used to interest me to see the brutal cynicism with which Christian sentiment is exploited. The touts from the Christmas card firms used to come round with their catalogues as early as June. A phrase from one of their invoices sticks in my memory. It was: '2 doz. Infant Jesus with rabbits'.

But our principle sideline was a lending library – the usual 'twopenny no-deposit' library of five or six hundred volumes, all fiction. How the book thieves must love those libraries! It is the easiest crime in the world to borrow a book at one shop for twopence, remove the label and sell it at another shop for a shilling. Nevertheless booksellers generally find that it pays them better to have a certain number of books stolen (we used to lose about a dozen a month) than to frighten customers away by demanding a deposit.

Our shop stood exactly on the frontier between Hampstead and Camden Town, and we were frequented by all types from baronets to bus-conductors. Probably our library subscribers were a fair cross-section of London's reading public. It is therefore worth noting that of all the authors in our library the one who 'went out' the best was – Priestley? Hemingway? Walpole? Wodehouse? No, Ethel M. Dell, with Warwick Deeping a good second and Jeffrey Farnol, I should say, third. Dell's novels, of course, are read solely by women, but by women of all kinds and ages and not, as one might expect, merely by wistful spinsters and the fat wives of tobacconists. It is not true that men don't read novels, but it is true that there are whole branches of fiction that they avoid. Roughly speaking, what one might call the average novel – the ordinary, good-bad, Galsworthy-and-water stuff which is the norm of the English novel – seems to exist only for women. Men read either the novels it is possible to respect, or detective stories. But their consumption of detective stories is terrific. One of our subscribers to my knowledge read four or five detective stories every week for over a year, besides others which he got from another library. What chiefly surprised me was that he never read the same book twice. Apparently the whole of that frightful torrent of trash (the pages read every year would, I calculated, cover nearly three quarters of an acre) was stored for ever in his memory. He took no notice of titles or author's names, but he could tell by merely glancing into a book whether he had 'had it already'.

In a lending library you see people's real tastes, not their pretended ones, and one thing that strikes you is how completely the 'classical' English novelists have dropped out of favour. It is simply useless to put Dickens, Thackeray, Jane Austen, Trollope, etc. into the ordinary lending library; nobody takes them out. At the mere sight of a nineteenth-century novel people say, 'Oh, but that's *old*!' and shy away immediately. Yet it is always fairly easy to *sell* Dickens, just as it is always easy to sell Shakespeare. Dickens is one of those authors whom people are 'always meaning to' read, and, like the Bible, he is widely known at second hand. People know by hearsay that Bill Sikes was a burglar and that Mr

Micawber had a bald head, just as they know by hearsay that Moses was found in a basket of bulrushes and saw the 'back parts' of the Lord. Another thing that is very noticeable is the growing unpopularity of American books. And another – the publishers get into a stew about this every two or three years – is the unpopularity of short stories. The kind of person who asks the librarian to choose a book for him nearly always starts by saying 'I don't want short stories', or 'I do not desire little stories', as a German customer of ours used to put it. If you ask them why, they sometimes explain that it is too much fag to get used to a new set of characters with every story; they like to 'get into' a novel which demands no further thought after the first chapter. I believe, though, that the writers are more to blame here than the readers. Most modern short stories, English and American, are utterly lifeless and worthless, far more so than most novels. The short stories which *are* stories are popular enough, *vide* D. H. Lawrence, whose short stories are as popular as his novels.

Would I like to be a bookseller *de métier*? On the whole – in spite of my employer's kindness to me, and some happy days I spent in the shop – no.

Given a good pitch and the right amount of capital, any educated person ought to be able to make a small secure living out of a bookshop. Unless one goes in for 'rare' books it is not a difficult trade to learn, and you start at a great advantage if you know anything about the insides of books. (Most booksellers don't. You can get their measure by having a look at the trade papers where they advertise their wants. If you don't see an ad. for Boswell's *Decline and Fall* you are pretty sure to see one for *The Mill on the Floss* by T. S. Eliot.) Also it is a humane trade which is not capable of being vulgarized beyond a certain point. The combines can never squeeze the small independent bookseller out of existence as they have squeezed the grocer and the milkman. But the hours of work are very long – I was only a part-time employee, but my employer put in a seventy-hour week, apart from constant expeditions out of hours to buy books – and it is an unhealthy life. As a rule a bookshop is horribly cold in winter, because if it is too warm the windows get misted over, and a bookseller lives on his windows. And books give off more and nastier dust than any other class of objects yet invented, and the top of a book is the place where every bluebottle prefers to die.

But the real reason why I should not like to be in the book trade for life is that while I was in it I lost my love of books. A bookseller has to tell lies about books, and that gives him a distaste for them; still worse is the fact that he is constantly dusting them and hauling them to and fro.

There was a time when I really did love books – loved the sight and smell and feel of them, I mean, at least if they were fifty or more years old. Nothing pleased me quite so much as to buy a job lot of them for a shilling at a country auction. There is a peculiar flavour about the battered unexpected books you pick up in that kind of collection: minor eighteenth-century poets, out-of-date gazeteers, odd volumes of forgotten novels, bound numbers of ladies' magazines of the sixties. For casual reading – in your bath, for instance, or late at night when you are too tired to go to bed, or in the odd quarter of an hour before lunch – there is nothing to touch a back number of the *Girl's Own Paper*. But as soon as I went to work in the bookshop I stopped buying books. Seen in the mass, five or ten thousand at a time, books were boring and even slightly sickening. Nowadays I do buy one occasionally, but only if it is a book that I want to read and can't borrow, and I never buy junk. The sweet smell of decaying paper appeals to me no longer. It is too closely associated in my mind with paranoiac customers and dead bluebottles.

Fortnightly, November 1936

6. Marrakech

As the corpse went past the flies left the restaurant table in a cloud and rushed after it, but they came back a few minutes later.

The little crowd of mourners – all men and boys, no women – threaded their way across the market-place between the piles of pomegranates and the taxis and the camels, wailing a short chant over and over again. What really appeals to the flies is that the corpses here are never put into coffins, they are merely wrapped in a piece of rag and carried on a rough wooden bier on the shoulders of four friends. When the friends get to the burying-ground they hack an oblong hole a foot or two deep, dump the body in it and fling over a little of the dried-up lumpy earth, which is like broken brick. No gravestone, no name, no identifying mark of any kind. The burying-ground is merely a huge waste of hummocky earth, like a derelict building-lot. After a month or two no one can even be certain where his own relatives are buried.

When you walk through a town like this – two hundred thousand inhabitants, of whom at least twenty thousand own literally nothing except the rags they stand up in – when you see how the people live, and still more how easily they die, it is always difficult to believe that you are walking among human beings. All colonial empires are in reality founded upon that fact. The people have brown faces – besides, there are so many of them! Are they really the same flesh as yourself? Do they even have names? Or are they merely a kind of undifferentiated brown stuff, about as individual as bees or coral insects? They rise out of the earth, they sweat and starve for a few years, and then they sink back into the nameless mounds of the graveyard and nobody notices that they are gone. And even the graves themselves soon fade back into the soil. Sometimes, out for a walk, as you break your way through the prickly pear, you notice that it is rather bumpy underfoot, and only a certain regularity in the bumps tells you that you are walking over skeletons.

I was feeding one of the gazelles in the public gardens.

Gazelles are almost the only animals that look good to eat when they are still alive, in fact, one can hardly look at their hindquarters without thinking of mint sauce. The gazelle I was feeding seemed to know that this thought was in my mind, for though it took the piece of bread I was holding out it obviously did not like me. It nibbled rapidly at the bread, then lowered its head and tried to butt me, then took another nibble and then butted again. Probably its idea was that if if could drive me away the bread would somehow remain hanging in mid-air.

An Arab navvy working on the path nearby lowered his heavy hoe and sidled towards us. He looked from the gazelle to the bread and from the bread to the gazelle, with a sort of quiet amazement, as though he had never seen anything quite like this before. Finally he said shyly in French: '*I* could eat some of that bread.'

I tore off a piece and he stowed it gratefully in some secret place under his rags. This man is an employee of the Municipality.

When you go through the Jewish quarters you gather some idea of what the medieval ghettoes were probably like. Under their Moorish rulers the Jews were only allowed to own land in certain restricted areas, and after centuries of this kind of treatment they have ceased to bother about overcrowding. Many of the streets are a good deal less than six feet wide, the houses are completely windowless, and sore-eyed children cluster everywhere in unbelievable numbers, like clouds of flies. Down the centre of the street there is generally running a little river of urine.

In the bazaar huge families of Jews, all dressed in the long black robe and little black skull-cap, are working in dark fly-infested booths that look like caves. A carpenter sits cross-legged at a prehistoric lathe, turning chair-legs at lightning speed. He works the lathe with a bow in his right hand and guides the chisel with his left foot, and thanks to a lifetime of sitting in this position his left leg is warped out of shape. At his side his grandson, aged six, is already starting on the simpler parts of the job.

I was just passing the coppersmiths' booths when somebody noticed that I was lighting a cigarette. Instantly, from the dark holes all round, there was a frenzied rush of Jews, many of them old grandfathers with flowing grey beards, all clamouring for a cigarette. Even a blind man somewhere at the back of one of the booths heard a rumour of cigarettes and came crawling out, groping in the air with his hand. In about a minute I had used up the whole packet. None of these people, I suppose, works less than twelve hours a day, and every one of them looks on a cigarette as a more or less impossible luxury.

As the Jews live in self-contained communities they follow the same trades as the Arabs, except for agriculture. Fruitsellers, potters, silversmiths, blacksmiths, butchers, leatherworkers, tailors, water-carriers, beggars, porters – whichever way you look you see nothing but Jews. As a matter of fact there are thirteen thousand of them, all living in the space of a few acres. A good job Hitler isn't here. Perhaps he is on his way, however. You hear the usual dark rumours about the Jews, not only from the Arabs but from the poorer Europeans.

'Yes, *mon vieux*, they took my job away from me and gave it to a Jew. The Jews! They're the real rulers of this country, you know. They've got all the money. They control the banks, finance – everything.'

'But,' I said, 'isn't it a fact that the average Jew is a labourer working for about a penny an hour?'

'Ah, that's only for show! They're all moneylenders really. They're cunning, the Jews.'

In just the same way, a couple of hundred years ago, poor old women used to be burned for witchcraft when they could not even work enough magic to get themselves a square meal.

All people who work with their hands are partly invisible, and the more important the work they do, the less visible they are. Still, a white skin is always fairly conspicuous. In northern Europe, when you see a labourer ploughing a field, you probably give him a second glance. In a hot country, anywhere south of Gibraltar or east of Suez, the chances are that you don't even see him. I have noticed this again and again. In a tropical landscape one's eye takes in everything except the human beings. It takes in the dried-up soil, the prickly pear, the palm-tree and the distant mountain, but it always misses the peasant hoeing at his patch. He is the same colour as the earth, and a great deal less interesting to look at.

It is only because of this that the starved countries of Asia and Africa are accepted as tourist resorts. No one would think of running cheap trips to the Distressed Areas. But where the human beings have brown skins their poverty is simply not noticed. What does Morocco mean to a Frenchman? An orange-grove or a job in government service. Or to an Englishman? Camels, castles, palm-trees, Foreign Legionnaires, brass trays and bandits. One could probably live here for years without noticing that for nine tenths of the people the reality of life is an endless, back-breaking struggle to wring a little food out of an eroded soil.

Most of Morocco is so desolate that no wild animal bigger than a hare can live on it. Huge areas which were once covered with forest have turned into a treeless waste where the soil is exactly like broken-up brick. Nevertheless a good deal of it is cultivated, with frightful labour. Everything is done by hand. Long lines of women, bent double like inverted capital Ls, work their way slowly across the fields, tearing up the prickly weeds with their hands, and the peasant gathering lucerne for fodder pulls it up stalk by stalk instead of reaping it, thus saving an inch or two on each stalk. The plough is a wretched wooden thing, so frail that one can easily carry it on one's shoulder, and fitted underneath with a rough iron spike which stirs the soil to a depth of about four inches. This is as much as the strength of the animals is equal to. It is usual to plough with a cow and a donkey yoked together. Two donkeys would not be quite strong enough, but on the other hand two cows would cost a little more to feed. The peasants possess no harrows, they merely plough the soil several times over in different directions, finally leaving it in rough furrows, after which the whole field has to be shaped with hoes into small oblong patches, to conserve water. Except for a day or two after the rare rainstorms there is never enough water. Along the edges of the fields channels are hacked out to a depth of thirty or forty feet to get at the tiny trickles which run through the subsoil.

Every afternoon a file of very old women passes down the road outside my house, each carrying a load of firewood. All of them are mummified with age and the sun, and all of them are tiny. It seems to be generally the case in primitive communities that the women, when they get beyond a certain age, shrink to the size of children. One day a poor old creature who could not have been more than four feet tall crept past me under a vast load of wood. I stopped her and put a five-sou piece (a little more than a farthing) into her hand. She answered with a shrill wail, almost a scream, which was partly gratitude but mainly surprise. I suppose that from her point of view, by taking any notice of her, I seemed almost to be violating a law of nature. She accepted her status as an old woman, that is to say as a beast of burden. When a family is travelling it is quite usual to see a father and a grown-up son riding on donkeys, and an old woman following on foot, carrying the baggage.

But what is strange about these people is their invisibility. For several weeks, always at about the same time of day, the file of old women had hobbled past the house with their firewood, and though they had registered themselves on my eyeballs I cannot truly say that I had seen them. Firewood was passing – that was how I saw it. It was only that one day I happened to be walking behind them, and the curious up-and-down motion of a load of wood drew my attention to the human being underneath it. Then for the first time I noticed the poor old earth-coloured bodies, bodies reduced to bones and leathery skin, bent double under the crushing weight. Yet I suppose I had not been five minutes on Moroccan soil before I noticed the overloading of the donkeys and was infuriated by it. There is no question that the donkeys are damnably treated. The Moroccon donkey is hardly bigger than a St Bernard dog, it carries a load which in the British army would be considered too much for a fifteen-hands mule, and very often its pack-saddle is not taken off its back for weeks together. But what is peculiarly pitiful is that it is the most willing creature on earth, it follows its master like a dog and does not need either bridle or halter. After a dozen years of devoted work it suddenly drops dead, whereupon its master tips it into the ditch and the village dogs have torn its guts out before it is cold.

This kind of thing makes one's blood boil, whereas – on the whole – the plight of the human beings does not. I am not commenting, merely pointing to a fact. People with brown skins are next door to invisible. Anyone can be sorry for the donkey with its galled back, but it is generally owing to some kind of accident if one even notices the old woman under her load of sticks.

As the storks flew northward the Negroes were marching southward – a long, dusty column, infantry, screw-gun batteries and then more infantry, four or five thousand men in all, winding up the road with a clumping of boots and a clatter of iron wheels.

They were Senegalese, the blackest Negroes in Africa, so black that sometimes it is difficult to see whereabouts on their necks the hair begins. Their splendid bodies were hidden in reach-me-down khaki uniforms, their feet squashed into boots that looked like blocks of wood, and every tin hat seemed to be a couple of sizes too small. It was very hot and the men had marched a long way. They slumped under the weight of their packs and the curiously sensitive black faces were glistening with sweat.

As they went past a tall, very young Negro turned and caught my eye. But the look he gave me was not in the least the kind of look you might expect. Not hostile, not contemptuous, not sullen, not even inquisitive. It was the shy, wide-eyed Negro look, which actually is a look of profound respect. I saw how it was. This wretched boy, who is a French citizen and has therefore been dragged from the forest to scrub floors and catch syphilis in garrison towns, actually has feelings of reverence before a white skin. He has been taught that the white race are his masters, and he still believes it.

But there is one thought which every white man (and in this connexion it doesn't matter twopence if he calls himself a Socialist) thinks when he sees a black army marching past. 'How much longer can we go on kidding these people? How long before they turn their guns in the other direction?'

It was curious, really. Every white man there has this thought stowed somewhere or other in his mind. I had it, so had the other onlookers, so had the officers on their sweating chargers and the white N.C.O.s marching in the ranks. It was a kind of secret which we all knew and were too clever to tell; only the Negroes didn't know it. And really it was almost like watching a flock of cattle to see the long column, a mile or two miles of armed men, flowing peacefully up the road, while the great white birds drifted over them in the opposite direction, glittering like scraps of paper.

Written [Spring] 1939

New Writing, Christmas 1939: *S.J.*; *E.Y.E.*; C.E.

7. Charles Dickens

I

Dickens is one of those writers who are well worthing stealing. Even the burial of his body in Westminster Abbey was a species of theft, if you come to think of it.

When Chesterton wrote his Introductions to the Everyman Edition of Dickens's works, it seemed quite natural to him to credit Dickens with his own highly individual brand of medievalism, and more recently a Marxist writer, Mr T. A. Jackson,[1] has made spirited efforts to turn Dickens into a bloodthirsty revolutionary. The Marxist claims him as 'almost' a Marxist, the Catholic claims him as 'almost' a Catholic, and both claim him as a champion of the proletariat (or 'the poor', as Chesterton would have put it). On the other hand, Nadezhda Krupskaya, in her little book on Lenin, relates that towards the end of his life Lenin went to see a dramatized version of *The Cricket on the Hearth*, and found Dickens's 'middle-class sentimentality' so intolerable that he walked out in the middle of a scene.

Taking 'middle-class' to mean what Krupskaya might be expected to mean by it, this was probably a truer judgement than those of Chesterton and Jackson. But it is worth noticing that the dislike of Dickens implied in this remark is something unusual. Plenty of people have found him unreadable, but very few seem to have felt any hostility towards the general spirit of his work. Some years ago Mr Bechhofer Roberts published a full-length attack on Dickens in the form of a novel (*This Side Idolatry*), but it was a merely personal attack, concerned for the most part with Dickens's treatment of his wife. It dealt with incidents which not one in a thousand of Dickens's readers would ever hear about, and which no more invalidate his work than the second-best bed invalidates *Hamlet*. All that the book really demonstrated was that a writer's literary personality has little or nothing to do with his private character. It is quite possible that in private life Dickens was just the kind of insensitive egoist that Mr Bechhofer Roberts makes him appear. But in his published work there is implied a personality quite different from this, a personality which has won him far more friends than enemies. It might well have been otherwise, for even if Dickens was a bourgeois, he was certainly a

1. *Charles Dickens: The Progress of a Radical* by T. A. Jackson, 1937.

subversive writer, a radical, one might truthfully say a rebel. Everyone who has read widely in his work has felt this. Gissing, for instance, the best of the writers on Dickens, was anything but a radical himself, and he disapproved of this strain in Dickens and wished it were not there, but it never occurred to him to deny it. In *Oliver Twist*, *Hard Times*, *Bleak House*, *Little Dorrit*, Dickens attacked English institutions with a ferocity that has never since been approached. Yet he managed to do it without making himself hated, and, more than this, the very people he attacked have swallowed him so completely that he has become a national institution himself. In its attitude towards Dickens the English public has always been a little like the elephant which feels a blow with a walking stick as a delightful tickling. Before I was ten years old I was having Dickens ladled down my throat by schoolmasters in whom even at that age I could see a strong resemblance to Mr Creakle, and one knows without needing to be told that lawyers delight in Serjeant Buzfuz and that *Little Dorrit* is a favourite in the Home Office. Dickens seems to have succeeded in attacking everybody and antagonizing nobody. Naturally this makes one wonder whether after all there was something unreal in his attack upon society. Where exactly does he stand, socially, morally and politically? As usual, one can define his position more easily if one starts by deciding what he was *not*.

In the first place he was *not*, as Messrs Chesterton and Jackson seem to imply, a 'proletarian' writer. To begin with, he does not write about the proletariat, in which he merely resembles the overwhelming majority of novelists, past and present. If you look for the working classes in fiction, and especially English fiction, all you find is a hole. This statement needs qualifying perhaps. For reasons that are easy enough to see, the agricultural labourer (in England a proletarian) gets a fairly good showing in fiction, and a great deal has been written about criminals, derelicts and, more recently, the working-class intelligentsia. But the ordinary town proletariat, the people who make the wheels go round, have always been ignored by novelists. When they do find their way between the covers of a book, it is nearly always as objects of pity or as comic relief. The central action of Dickens's stories almost invariably takes place in middle-class surroundings. If one examines his novels in detail one finds that his real subject-matter is the London commercial bourgeoisie and their hangers-on – lawyers, clerks, tradesmen, innkeepers, small craftsmen and servants. He has no portrait of an agricultural worker, and only one (Stephen Blackpool in *Hard Times*) of an industrial worker. The Plornishes in *Little Dorrit* are probably his best picture of a working-class family – the

Peggottys, for instance, hardly belong to the working class – but on the whole he is not successful with this type of character. If you ask any ordinary reader which of Dickens's proletarian characters he can remember, the three he is almost certain to mention are Bill Sikes, Sam Weller and Mrs Gamp. A burglar, a valet and a drunken midwife – not exactly a representative cross-section of the English working class.

Secondly, in the ordinarily accepted sense of the word, Dickens is not a 'revolutionary' writer. But his position here needs some defining.

Whatever else Dickens may have been, he was not a hole-and-corner soul-saver, the kind of well-meaning idiot who thinks that the world will be perfect if you amend a few by-laws and abolish a few anomalies. It is worth comparing him with Charles Reade, for instance. Reade was a much better informed man than Dickens, and in some ways more public-spirited. He really hated the abuses he could understand, he showed them up in a series of novels which for all their absurdity are extremely readable, and he probably helped to alter public opinion on a few minor but important points. But it was quite beyond him to grasp that, given the existing form of society, certain evils *cannot* be remedied. Fasten upon this or that minor abuse, expose it, drag it into the open, bring it before a British jury, and all will be well – that is how he sees it. Dickens at any rate never imagined that you can cure pimples by cutting them off. In every page of his work one can see a consciousness that society is wrong somewhere at the root. It is when one asks 'Which root?' that one begins to grasp his position.

The truth is that Dickens's criticism of society is almost exclusively moral. Hence the utter lack of any constructive suggestion anywhere in his work. He attacks the law, parliamentary government, the educational system and so forth, without ever clearly suggesting what he would put in their places. Of course it is not necessarily the business of a novelist, or a satirist, to make constructive suggestions, but the point is that Dickens's attitude is at bottom not even *de*structive. There is no clear sign that he wants the existing order to be overthrown, or that he believes it would make very much difference if it *were* overthrown. For in reality his target is not so much society as 'human nature'. It would be difficult to point anywhere in his books to a passage suggesting that the economic system is wrong *as a system*. Nowhere, for instance, does he make any attack on private enterprise or private property. Even in a book like *Our Mutual Friend*, which turns on the power of corpses to interfere with living people by means of idiotic wills, it does not occur to him to suggest that individuals ought not to have this irresponsible power. Of course one can draw this inference for oneself, and one can draw it again from the remarks about Bounderby's will at the end of *Hard Times*, and indeed from the whole of Dickens's work one can infer the evil of *laissez-faire* capitalism; but Dickens makes no such inference himself. It is said that Macaulay refused to review *Hard Times* because he disapproved of its 'sullen Socialism'. Obviously Macaulay is here using the word 'Socialism' in the same sense in which, twenty years ago, a vegetarian meal or a Cubist picture used to be referred to as 'Bolshevism'. There is not a line in the book that can properly be called Socialistic; indeed, its tendency if anything is pro-capitalist, because its whole moral is that capitalists ought to be kind, not that workers ought to be rebellious. Bounderby is a bullying windbag and Gradgrind has been morally blinded, but if they were better men, the system would work well enough – that, all through, is the implication. And so far as social criticism goes, one can never extract much more from Dickens than this, unless one deliberately reads meanings into him. His whole 'message' is one that at first glance looks like an enormous platitude: If men would behave decently the world would be decent.

Naturally this calls for a few characters who are in positions of authority and who *do* behave decently. Hence that recurrent Dickens figure, the Good Rich Man. This character belongs especially to Dickens's early optimistic period. He is usually a 'merchant' (we are not necessarily told what merchandise he deals in), and he is always a superhumanly kind-hearted old gentleman who 'trots' to and fro, raising his employees' wages, patting children on the head, getting debtors out of jail and, in general, acting the fairy godmother. Of course he is a pure dream figure, much further from real life than, say, Squeers or Micawber. Even Dickens must have reflected occasionally that anyone who was so anxious to give his money away would never have acquired it in the first place. Mr Pickwick, for instance, had 'been in the city', but it is difficult to imagine him making a fortune there. Nevertheless this character runs like a connecting thread through most of the earlier books. Pickwick, the Cheerybles, old Chuzzlewit, Scrooge – it is the same figure over and over again, the good rich man, handing out guineas. Dickens does however show signs of development here. In the books of the middle period the good rich man fades out to some extent. There is no one who plays this part in *A Tale of Two Cities*, nor in *Great Expectations* – *Great Expectations* is, in fact definitely an attack on patronage – and in *Hard Times* it is only very doubtfully played by Gradgrind after his reformation. The character reappears in a rather different form as Meagles in *Little Dorrit* and John

Jarndyce in *Bleak House* – one might perhaps add Betsy Trotwood in *David Copperfield*. But in these books the good rich man has dwindled from a 'merchant' to a *rentier*. This is significant. A *rentier* is part of the possessing class, he can and, almost without knowing it, does make other people work for him, but he has very little direct power. Unlike Scrooge or the Cheerybles, he cannot put everything right by raising everybody's wages. The seeming inference from the rather despondent books that Dickens wrote in the fifties is that by that time he had grasped the helplessness of well-meaning individuals in a corrupt society. Nevertheless in the last completed novel, *Our Mutual Friend* (published 1864–5), the good rich man comes back in full glory in the person of Boffin. Boffin is a proletarian by origin and only rich by inheritance, but he is the usual *deus ex machina*, solving everybody's problems by showering money in all directions. He even 'trots' like the Cheerybles. In several ways *Our Mutual Friend* is a return to the earlier manner, and not an unsuccessful return either. Dickens's thoughts seem to have come full circle. Once again, individual kindliness is the remedy for everything.

One crying evil of his time that Dickens says very little about is child labour. There are plenty of pictures of suffering children in his books, but usually they are suffering in schools rather than in factories. The one detailed account of child labour that he gives is the description in *David Copperfield* of little David washing bottles in Murdstone & Grinby's warehouse. This, of course, is autobiography. Dickens himself, at the age of ten, had worked in Warren's blacking factory in the Strand, very much as he describes it here. It was a terribly bitter memory to him, partly because he felt the whole incident to be discreditable to his parents, and he even concealed it from his wife till long after they were married. Looking back on this period, he says in *David Copperfield*:

> It is a matter of some surprise to me, even now, that I can have been so easily thrown away at such an age. A child of excellent abilities and with strong powers of observation, quick, eager, delicate, and soon hurt bodily or mentally, it seems wonderful to me that nobody should have made any sign in my behalf. But none was made; and I became, at ten years old, a little labouring hind in the service of Murdstone & Grinby.

And again, having described the rough boys among whom he worked:

> No words can express the secret agony of my soul as I sunk into this companionship . . . and felt my hopes of growing up to be a learned and distinguished man crushed in my bosom.

Obviously it is not David Copperfield who is speaking, it is Dickens himself. He uses almost the same words in the autobiography that he began and abandoned a few months earlier. Of course Dickens is right in saying that a gifted child ought not to work ten hours a day pasting labels on bottles, but what he does not say is that *no* child ought to be condemned to such a fate, and there is no reason for inferring that he thinks it. David escapes from the warehouse, but Mick Walker and Mealy Potatoes and the others are still there, and there is no sign that this troubles Dickens particularly. As usual, he displays no consciousness that the *structure* of society can be changed. He despises politics, does not believe that any good can come out of Parliament – he had been a parliamentary shorthand writer, which was no doubt a disillusioning experience – and he is slightly hostile to the most hopeful movement of his day, trade unionism. In *Hard Times* trade unionism is represented as something not much better than a racket, something that happens because employers are not sufficiently paternal. Stephen Blackpool's refusal to join the union is rather a virtue in Dickens's eyes. Also, as Mr Jackson has pointed out, the apprentices' association in *Barnaby Rudge*, to which Sim Tappertit belongs, is probably a hit at the illegal or barely legal unions of Dickens's own day, with their secret assemblies, passwords and so forth. Obviously he wants the workers to be decently treated, but there is no sign that he wants them to take their destiny into their own hands, least of all by open violence.

As it happens, Dickens deals with revolution in the narrower sense in two novels, *Barnaby Rudge* and *A Tale of Two Cities*. In *Barnaby Rudge* it is a case of rioting rather than revolution. The Gordon Riots of 1780, though they had religious bigotry as a pretext, seem to have been little more than a pointless outburst of looting. Dickens's attitude to this kind of thing is sufficiently indicated by the fact that his first idea was to make the ringleaders of the riots three lunatics escaped from an asylum. He was dissuaded from this, but the principal figure of the book is in fact a village idiot. In the chapters dealing with the riots Dickens shows a most profound horror of mob violence. He delights in describing scenes in which the 'dregs' of the population behave with atrocious bestiality. These chapters are of great psychological interest, because they show how deeply he had brooded on this subject. The things he describes can only have come out of his imagination, for no riots on anything like the same scale had happened in his lifetime. Here is one of his descriptions, for instance:

If Bedlam gates had been flung open wide, there would not have issued forth such maniacs as the frenzy of that night had made. There were men there who danced and trampled on the beds of flowers as though they trod down human enemies, and wrenched them from their stalks, like savages who twisted human necks. There were men who cast their lighted torches in the air, and suffered them to fall upon their heads and faces, blistering the skin with deep unseemly burns. There were men who rushed up to the fire, and paddled in it with their hands as if in water; and others who were restrained by force from plunging in, to gratify their deadly longing. On the skull of one drunken lad – not twenty, by his looks – who lay upon the ground with a bottle to his mouth, the lead from the roof came streaming down in a shower of liquid fire, white hot, melting his head like wax . . . But of all the howling throng not one learnt mercy from, or sickened at these sights; nor was the fierce, besotted, senseless rage of one man glutted.

You might almost think you were reading a description of 'red' Spain by a partisan of General Franco. One ought, of course, to remember that when Dickens was writing, the London 'mob' still existed. (Nowadays there is no mob, only a flock.) Low wages and the growth and shift of population had brought into existence a huge, dangerous slum-proletariat, and until the early middle of the nineteenth century there was hardly such a thing as a police force. When the brickbats began to fly there was nothing between shuttering your windows and ordering the troops to open fire. In *A Tale of Two Cities* he is dealing with a revolution which was really *about* something, and Dickens's attitude is different, but not entirely different. As a matter of fact, *A Tale of Two Cities* is a book which tends to leave a false impression behind, especially after a lapse of time.

The one thing that everyone who has read *A Tale of Two Cities* remembers is the Reign of Terror. The whole book is dominated by the guillotine – tumbrils thundering to and fro, bloody knives, heads bouncing into the basket, and sinister old women knitting as they watch. Actually these scenes only occupy a few chapters, but they are written with terrible intensity, and the rest of the book is rather slow going. But *A Tale of Two Cities* is not a companion volume to *The Scarlet Pimpernel*. Dickens sees clearly enough that the French Revolution was bound to happen and that many of the people who were executed deserved what they got. If, he says, you behave as the French aristocracy had behaved, vengeance will follow. He repeats this over and over again. We are constantly being reminded that while 'my lord' is lolling in bed, with four liveried footmen serving his chocolate and the peasants starving outside, somewhere in the forest a tree is growing which will presently be sawn into planks for the platform of the guillotine, etc. etc. etc. The inevitability of the Terror, given its causes, is insisted upon in the clearest terms:

> It was too much the way . . . to talk of this terrible Revolution as if it were the only harvest ever known under the skies that had not been sown – as if nothing had ever been done, or omitted to be done, that had led to it – as if observers of the wretched millions in France, and of the misused and perverted resources that should have made them prosperous, had not seen it inevitably coming, years before, and had not in plain terms recorded what they saw.

And again:

> All the devouring and insatiate monsters imagined since imagination could record itself, are fused in the one realization, Guillotine. And yet there is not in France, with its rich variety of soil and climate, a blade, a leaf, a root, a sprig, a peppercorn, which will grow to maturity under conditions more certain than those that have produced this horror. Crush humanity out of shape once more, under similar hammers, and it will twist itself into the same tortured forms.

In other words, the French aristocracy had dug their own graves. But there is no perception here of what is now called historic necessity. Dickens sees that the results are inevitable, given the causes, but he thinks that the causes might have been avoided. The Revolution is something that happens because centuries of oppression have made the French peasantry sub-human. If the wicked nobleman could somehow have turned over a new leaf, like Scrooge, there would have been no Revolution, no *jacquerie*, no guillotine – and so much the better. This is the opposite of the 'revolutionary' attitude. From the 'revolutionary' point of view the class-struggle is the main source of progress, and therefore the nobleman who robs the peasant and goads him to revolt is playing a necessary part, just as much as the Jacobin who guillotines the nobleman. Dickens never writes anywhere a line that can be interpreted as meaning this. Revolution as he sees it is merely a monster that is begotten by tyranny and always ends by devouring its own instruments. In Sydney Carton's vision at the foot of the guillotine, he foresees Defarge and the other leading spirits of the Terror all perishing under the same knife – which, in fact, was approximately what happened.

And Dickens is very sure that revolution *is* a monster. That is why everyone remembers the revolutionary scenes in *A Tale of Two Cities*; they have the quality of nightmare, and it is Dickens's own nightmare. Again and again he insists upon the meaningless horrors of revolution – the mass-butcheries, the injustice, the ever-present terror of spies, the frightful blood-lust of the mob. The descriptions of the Paris mob – the description, for instance, of the crowd of murderers struggling round the grindstone to sharpen their weapons before butchering the prisoners in the September massacres – outdo anything in *Barnaby Rudge*. The revolutionaries appear to him simply as degraded savages – in fact, as lunatics. He broods over their frenzies with a curious imaginative intensity. He describes them dancing the 'Carmagnole', for instance:

> There could not be fewer than five hundred people, and they were dancing like five thousand demons. . . . They danced to the popular Revolution song, keeping a ferocious time that was like a gnashing of teeth in unison. . . . They advanced, retreated, struck at one another's hands, clutched at one another's heads, spun round alone, caught one another, and spun round in pairs, until many of them dropped. . . . Suddenly they stopped again, paused, struck out the time afresh, forming into lines the width of the public way, and, with their heads low down and their hands high up, swooped screaming off. No fight could have been half so terrible as this dance. It was so emphatically a fallen sport – a something, once innocent, delivered over to all devilry.

He even credits some of these wretches with a taste for guillotining children. The passage I have abridged above ought to be read in full. It and others like it show how deep was Dickens's horror of revolutionary hysteria. Notice, for instance, that touch, 'with their heads low down and their hands high up' etc., and the evil vision it conveys. Madame Defarge is a truly dreadful figure, certainly Dickens's most successful attempt at a *malignant* character. Defarge and others are simply 'the new oppressors who have risen on the destruction of the old', the revolutionary courts are presided over by 'the lowest, cruellest and worst populace', and so on and so forth. All the way through Dickens insists upon the nightmare insecurity of a revolutionary period, and in this he shows a great deal of prescience. 'A law of the suspected, which struck away all security for liberty or life, and delivered over any good and innocent person to any bad and guilty one; prisons gorged with people who had committed no offence, and could obtain no hearing' – it would apply pretty accurately to several countries today.

The apologists of any revolution generally try to minimize its horrors; Dickens's impulse is to exaggerate them – and from a historical point of view he has certainly exaggerated. Even the Reign of Terror was a much smaller thing than he makes it appear. Though he quotes no figures, he gives the impression of a frenzied massacre lasting for years, whereas in reality the whole of the Terror, so far as the number of deaths goes, was a joke compared with one of Napoleon's battles. But the bloody knives and the tumbrils rolling to and fro create in his mind a special, sinister vision which he has succeeded in passing on to generations of readers. Thanks to Dickens, the very word 'tumbril' has a murderous sound; one forgets that a tumbril is only a sort of farm-cart. To this day, to the average Englishman, the French Revolution means no more than a pyramid of several heads. It is a strange thing that Dickens, much more in sympathy with the ideas of the Revolution than most Englishmen of his time, should have played a part in creating this impression.

If you hate violence and don't believe in politics, the only major remedy remaining is education. Perhaps society is past praying for, but there is always hope for the individual human being, if you can catch him young enough. This belief partly accounts for Dickens's preoccupation with childhood.

No one, at any rate no English writer, has written better about childhood than Dickens. In spite of all the knowledge that has accumulated since, in spite of the fact that children are now comparatively sanely treated, no novelist has shown the same power of entering into the child's point of view. I must have been about nine years old when I first read *David Copperfield*. The mental atmosphere of the opening chapters was so immediately intelligible to me that I vaguely imagined they had been written *by a child*. And yet when one re-reads the book as an adult and sees the Murdstones, for instance, dwindle from gigantic figures of doom into semi-comic monsters, these passages lose nothing. Dickens has been able to stand both inside and outside the child's mind, in such a way that the same scene can be wild burlesque or sinister reality, according to the age at which one reads it. Look, for instance, at the scene in which David Copperfield is unjustly suspected of eating the mutton chops; or the scene in which Pip, in *Great Expectations*, coming back from Miss Havisham's house and finding himself completely unable to describe what he has seen, takes refuge in a series of outrageous lies – which, of course, are eagerly believed. All the isolation of childhood is there. And how accurately he has recorded the mechanisms of the child's mind, its visualizing tendency, its sensitiveness to certain kinds of impression. Pip relates how in his childhood his ideas about his dead parents were derived from their tombstones:

The shape of the letters on my father's, gave me an odd idea that he was a square, stout, dark man, with curly black hair. From the character and turn of the inscription, 'ALSO GEORGIANA, WIFE OF THE ABOVE', I drew a childish conclusion that my mother was freckled and sickly. To five little stone lozenges, each about a foot and a half long, which were arranged in a neat row beside their grave, and were sacred to the memory of five little brothers of mine . . . I am indebted for a belief I religiously entertained that they had all been born on their backs with their hands in their trouser-pockets, and had never taken them out in this state of existence.

There is a similar passage in *David Copperfield*. After biting Mr Murdstone's hand, David is sent away to a school and obliged to wear on his back a placard saying, 'Take care of him. He bites.' He looks at the door in the playground where the boys have carved their names, and from the appearance of each name he seems to know in just what tone of voice the boy will read out the placard:

> There was one boy – a certain J. Steerforth – who cut his name very deep and very often, who, I conceived, would read it in a rather strong voice, and afterwards pull my hair. There was another boy, one Tommy Traddles, who I dreaded would make game of it, and pretend to be dreadfully frightened of me. There was a third, George Demple, who I fancied would sing it.

When I read this passage as a child, it seemed to me that those were exactly the pictures that those particular names would call up. The reason, of course, is the sound-associations of the words (Demple – 'temple'; Traddles – probably 'skedaddle'). But how many people, before Dickens, had ever noticed such things? A sympathetic attitude towards children was a much rarer thing in Dickens's day than it is now. The early nineteenth century was not a good time to be a child. In Dickens's youth children were still being 'solemnly tried at a criminal bar, where they were held up to be seen', and it was not so long since boys of thirteen had been hanged for petty theft. The doctrine of 'breaking the child's spirit' was in full vigour, and *The Fairchild Family*[2] was a standard book for children till late into the century. This evil book is now issued in pretty-pretty expurgated editions, but it is well worth reading in the original version. It gives one some idea of the lengths to which child-discipline was sometimes carried. Mr Fairchild, for instance, when he catches his children quarrelling, first thrashes them, reciting Doctor Watts's 'Let dogs delight to bark and bite' between blows of the cane, and then takes them to spend the afternoon beneath a gibbet where the rotting corpse of a murderer is hanging. In the earlier part of the century scores of thousands of children, aged sometimes as young as six, were literally worked to death in the mines or cotton mills, and even at the fashionable public

2. *The History of the Fairchild Family* by May M. Sherwood, 3 parts, 1818–47.

schools boys were flogged till they ran with blood for a mistake in their Latin verses. One thing which Dickens seems to have recognized, and which most of his contemporaries did not, is the sadistic sexual element in flogging. I think this can be inferred from *David Copperfield* and *Nicholas Nickleby*. But mental cruelty to a child infuriates him as much as physical, and though there is a fair number of exceptions, his schoolmasters are generally scoundrels.

Except for the universities and the big public schools, every kind of education then existing in England gets a mauling at Dickens's hands. There is Doctor Blimber's Academy, where little boys are blown up with Greek until they burst, and the revolting charity schools of the period, which produced specimens like Noah Claypole and Uriah Heep, and Salem House, and Dotheboys Hall, and the disgraceful little dame-school kept by Mr Wopsle's great-aunt. Some of what Dickens says remains true even today. Salem House is the ancestor of the modern 'prep school', which still has a good deal of resemblance to it; and as for Mr Wopsle's great-aunt, some old fraud of much the same stamp is carrying on at this moment in nearly every small town in England. But, as usual, Dickens's criticism is neither creative nor destructive. He sees the idiocy of an educational system founded on the Greek lexicon and the wax-ended cane; on the other hand, he has no use for the new kind of school that is coming up in the fifties and sixties, the 'modern' school, with its gritty insistence on 'facts'. What, then, *does* he want? As always, what he appears to want is a moralized version of the existing thing – the old type of school, but with no caning, no bullying or underfeeding, and not quite so much Greek. Doctor Strong's school, to which David Copperfield goes after he escapes from Murdstone & Grinby's, is simply Salem House with the vices left out and a good deal of 'old grey stones' atmosphere thrown in:

> Doctor Strong's was an excellent school, as different from Mr Creakle's as good is from evil. It was very gravely and decorously ordered, and on a sound system; with an appeal, in everything, to the honour and good faith of the boys . . . which worked wonders. We all felt that we had a part in the management of the place, and in sustaining its character and dignity. Hence, we soon became warmly attached to it – I am sure I did for one, and I never knew, in all my time, of any boy being otherwise – and learnt with a good will, desiring to do it credit. We had noble games out of hours, and plenty of liberty; but even then, as I remember, we were well spoken of in the town, and rarely did any disgrace, by our appearance or manner, to the reputation of Doctor Strong and Doctor Strong's boys.

In the woolly vagueness of this passage one can see Dickens's utter lack of any educational theory. He can imagine the *moral* atmosphere of a good school, but nothing further. The boys 'learnt with a good will', but what did they learn? No doubt it was Doctor Blimber's curriculum, a little watered down. Considering the attitude to society that is everywhere implied in Dickens's novels, it comes as rather a shock to learn that he sent his eldest son to Eton and sent all his children through the ordinary educational mill. Gissing seems to think that he may have done this because he was painfully conscious of being under-educated himself. Here perhaps Gissing is influenced by his own love of classical learning. Dickens had had little or no formal education, but he lost nothing by missing it, and on the whole he seems to have been aware of this. If he was unable to imagine a better school than Doctor Strong's, or, in real life, than Eton, it was probably due to an intellectual deficiency rather different from the one Gissing suggests.

It seems that in every attack Dickens makes upon society he is always pointing to a change of spirit rather than a change of structure. It is hopeless to try and pin him down to any definite remedy, still more to any political doctrine. His approach is always along the moral plane, and his attitude is sufficiently summed up in that remark about Strong's school being as different from Creakle's 'as good is from evil'. Two things can be very much alike and yet abysmally different. Heaven and Hell are in the same place. Useless to change institutions without a 'change of heart' – that, essentially, is what he is always saying.

If that were all, he might be no more than a cheer-up writer, a reactionary humbug. A 'change of heart' is in fact *the* alibi of people who do not wish to endanger the *status quo*. But Dickens is not a humbug, except in minor matters, and the strongest single impression one carries away from his books is that of a hatred of tyranny. I said earlier that Dickens is not *in the accepted sense* a revolutionary writer. But it is not at all certain that a merely moral criticism of society may not be just as 'revolutionary' – and revolution, after all, means turning things upside down – as the politico-economic criticism which is fashionable at this moment. Blake was not a politician, but there is more understanding of the nature of capitalist society in a poem like 'I wander through each charter'd street' than in three quarters of Socialist literature. Progress is not an illusion, it happens, but it is slow and invariably disappointing. There is always a new tyrant waiting to take over from the old – generally not quite so bad, but still a tyrant. Consequently two view-points are always tenable. The one, how can you improve human nature until you have changed the system? The other, what is the use of changing the system before you have improved human nature? They appeal to different individuals, and they probably show a tendency to alternate in point of time. The moralist and the revolutionary are constantly undermining one another. Marx exploded a hundred tons of dynamite beneath the moralist position, and we are still living in the echo of that tremendous crash. But already, somewhere or other, the sappers are at work and fresh dynamite is being stamped in place to blow Marx at the moon. Then Marx, or somebody like him, will come back with yet more dynamite, and so the process continues, to an end we cannot yet foresee. The central problem – how to prevent power from being abused – remains unsolved. Dickens, who had not the vision to see that private property is an obstructive nuisance, had the vision to see that. 'If men would behave decently the world would be decent' is not such a platitude as it sounds.

II

More completely than most writers, perhaps, Dickens can be explained in terms of his social origin, though actually his family history was not quite what one would infer from his novels. His father was a clerk in government service, and through his mother's family he had connexions with both the army and the navy. But from the age of nine onwards he was brought up in London in commercial surroundings, and generally in an atmosphere of struggling poverty. Mentally he belongs to the small urban bourgeoisie, and he happens to be an exceptionally fine specimen of this class, with all the 'points', as it were, very highly developed. That is partly what makes him so interesting. If one wants a modern equivalent, the nearest would be H. G. Wells, who has had a rather similar history and who obviously owes something to Dickens as a novelist. Arnold Bennett was essentially of the same type, but, unlike the other two, he was a midlander, with an industrial and Nonconformist rather than commercial and Anglican background.

The great disadvantage, and advantage, of the small urban bourgeois is his limited outlook. He sees the world as a middle-class world, and everything outside those limits is either laughable or slightly wicked. On the one hand, he has no contact with industry or the soil; on the other, no contact with the governing classes. Anyone who has studied Wells's novels in detail will have noticed that though he hates the aristocrat like poison, he has no particular objection to the plutocrat, and no enthusiasm for the proletarian. His most hated types, the people he believes to be responsible for all human ills, are kings, landowners, priests, nationalists, soldiers, scholars and peasants. At first sight a list beginning with kings and ending with peasants looks like a mere omnium gatherum, but in reality all these people have a common factor. All of them are archaic types, people who are governed by tradition and whose eyes are turned towards the past – the opposite, therefore, of the rising bourgeois who has put his money on the future and sees the past simply as a dead hand.

Actually, although Dickens lived in a period when the bourgeoisie was really a rising class, he displays this characteristic less strongly than Wells. He is almost unconscious of the future and has a rather sloppy love of the picturesque (the 'quaint old church' etc.). Nevertheless his list of most hated types is like enough to Wells's for the similarity to be striking. He is vaguely on the side of the working class – has a sort of generalized sympathy with them because they are oppressed – but he does not in reality know much about them; they come into his books chiefly as servants, and comic servants at that. At the other end of the scale he loathes the aristocrat and – going one better than Wells in this – loathes the big bourgeois as well. His real sympathies are bounded by Mr Pickwick on the upper side and Mr Barkis on the lower. But the term 'aristocrat', for the type Dickens hates, is vague and needs defining.

Actually Dickens's target is not so much the great aristocracy, who hardly enter into his books, as their petty offshoots, the cadging dowagers who live up mews in Mayfair, and the bureaucrats and professional soldiers. All through his books there are countless hostile sketches of these people, and hardly any that are friendly. There are practically no friendly pictures of the land-owning class, for instance. One might make a doubtful exception of Sir Leicester Dedlock; otherwise there is only Mr Wardle (who is a stock figure – the 'good old squire') and Haredale in *Barnaby Rudge*, who has Dickens's sympathy because he is a persecuted Catholic. There are no friendly pictures of soldiers (i.e. officers), and none at all of naval men. As for his bureaucrats, judges and magistrates, most of them would feel quite at home in the Circumlocution Office. The only official whom Dickens handles with any kind of friendliness are, significantly enough, policemen.

Dickens's attitude is easily intelligible to an Englishman, because it is part of the English puritan tradition, which is not dead even at this day. The class Dickens belonged to, at least by adoption, was growing suddenly rich after a couple of centuries of obscurity. It had grown up mainly in the big towns, out of contact with agriculture, and politically impotent; government, in its experience, was something which either interfered or persecuted. Consequently it was a class with no tradition of public service and not much tradition of usefulness. What now strikes us as remarkable about the new moneyed class of the nineteenth century is their complete irresponsibility; they see everything in terms of individual success, with hardly any consciousness that the community exists. On the other hand, a Tite Barnacle, even when he was neglecting his duties, would have some vague notion of what duties he was neglecting. Dickens's attitude is never irresponsible, still less does he take the money-grubbing Smilesian line; but at the back of his mind there is usually a half-belief that the whole apparatus of government is unnecessary. Parliament is simply Lord Coodle and Sir Thomas Doodle, the Empire is simply Major Bagstock and his Indian servant, the army is simply Colonel Chowser and Doctor Slammer, the public services are simply Bumble and the Circumlocution Office – and so on and so forth. What he does not see, or only intermittently sees, is that Coodle and Doodle and all the other corpses left over from the eighteenth century *are* performing a function which neither Pickwick nor Boffin would ever bother about.

And of course this narrowness of vision is in one way a great advantage to him, because it is fatal for a caricaturist to see too much. From Dickens's point of view 'good' society is simply a collection of village idiots. What a crew! Lady Tippins! Mrs Gowan! Lord Verisopht! The Honourable Bob Stables! Mrs Sparsit (whose husband was a Powler)! The Tite Barnacles! Nupkins! It is practically a case-book in lunacy. But at the same time his remoteness from the landowning-military-bureaucratic class incapacitates him for full-length satire. He only succeeds with this class when he depicts them as mental defectives. The accusation which used to be made against Dickens in his life-time, that he 'could not paint a gentleman', was an absurdity, but it is true in this sense, that what he says against the 'gentleman' class is seldom very damaging. Sir Mulberry Hawk, for instance, is a wretched attempt at the wicked-baronet type. Harthouse in *Hard Times* is better, but he would be only an ordinary achievement for Trollope or Thackeray. Trollope's thoughts hardly move outside the 'gentleman' class, but Thackeray has the great advantage of having a foot in two moral camps. In some ways his outlook is very similar to Dickens's. Like Dickens, he identifies with the puritanical moneyed class against the card-playing, debt-bilking aristocracy. The eighteenth century, as he sees it, is sticking out into the nineteenth in the person of the wicked Lord Steyne. *Vanity Fair* is a full-length version of what Dickens did for a few chapters in *Little Dorrit*. But by origins and upbringing Thackeray happens to be somewhat nearer to the class he is satirizing. Consequently he can produce such comparatively subtle types as, for instance, Major Pendennis and Rawdon Crawley. Major Pendennis is a shallow old snob, and Rawdon Crawley is a thick-headed ruffian who sees nothing wrong in living for years by swindling tradesmen; but what Thackeray realizes is that according to their tortuous code they are neither of them bad men. Major Pendennis would not sign a dud cheque, for instance. Rawdon certainly would, but on the other hand he would not desert a friend in a tight corner. Both of them would behave well on the field of battle – a thing that would not particularly appeal to Dickens. The result is that at the end one is left with a kind of amused tolerance for Major Pendennis and with something approaching respect for Rawdon; and yet one sees, better than any diatribe could make one, the utter rottenness of that kind of cadging, toadying life on the fringes of smart society. Dickens would be quite incapable of this. In his hands both Rawdon and the Major would dwindle to traditional caricatures. And, on the whole, his attacks on 'good' society are rather perfunctory. The aristocracy and the big bourgeoisie exist in his books chiefly as a kind of 'noises off', a haw-hawing chorus somewhere in the wings, like Podsnap's dinner-parties. When he produces a really subtle and damaging portrait, like John Dorrit or Harold Skimpole, it is generally of some rather middling, unimportant person.

One very striking thing about Dickens, especially considering the time he lived in, is his lack of vulgar nationalism. All peoples who have reached the point of becoming nations tend to despise foreigners, but there is not much doubt that the English-speaking races are the worst offenders. Once can see this from the fact that as soon as they become fully aware of any foreign race, they invent an insulting nickname for it. Wop, Dago, Froggy, Squarehead, Kike, Sheeny, Nigger, Wog, Chink, Greaser, Yellowbelly – these are merely a selection. Any time before 1870 the list would have been shorter because the map of the world was different from what it is now, and there were only three or four foreign races that had fully entered into the English consciousness. But towards these, and especially towards France, the nearest and best-hated nation, the English attitude of patronage was so intolerable that English 'arrogance' and 'xenophobia' are still a legend. And of course they are not a completely untrue legend even now. Till very recently nearly all English children were brought up to despise the southern European races, and history as taught in schools was mainly a list of battles won by England. But one has got to read, say, the *Quarterly Review* of the thirties to know what boasting really is. Those were the days when the English built up their legend of themselves as 'sturdy islanders' and 'stubborn hearts of oak' and when it was accepted as a kind of scientific fact that one Englishman was the equal of three foreigners. All through nineteenth-century novels and comic papers there runs the traditional figure of the 'Froggy' – a small ridiculous man with a tiny beard and a pointed top-hat, always jabbering and gesticulating, vain, frivolous and fond of boasting of his martial exploits, but generally taking to flight when real danger appears. Over against him was John Bull, the 'sturdy English yeoman', or (a more public-school version) the 'strong, silent Englishman' of Charles Kingsley, Tom Hughes and others.

Thackeray, for instance, has this outlook very strongly, though there are moments when he sees through it and laughs at it. The one historical fact that is firmly fixed in his mind is that the English won the battle of Waterloo. One never reads far in his books without coming upon some reference to it. The English, as he sees it, are invincible because of their tremendous physical strength, due mainly to living on beef. Like most Englishmen of his time, he has the curious illusion that the English are larger than other people (Thackeray, as it happened, *was* larger than most people), and therefore he is capable of writing passages like this:

> I say to you that you are better than a Frenchman. I would lay even money that you who are reading this are more than five feet seven in height, and weigh eleven stone; while a Frenchman is five feet four and does not weigh nine. The Frenchman has after his soup a dish of vegetables, where you have one of meat. You are a different and superior animal – a French-beating animal (the history of hundreds of years has shown you to be so), etc. etc.

There are similar passages scattered all through Thackeray's works. Dickens would never be guilty of anything of the kind. It would be an exaggeration to say that he nowhere pokes fun at foreigners, and of course, like nearly all nineteenth-century Englishmen, he is untouched by European culture. But never anywhere does he indulge in the typical English boasting, the 'island race', 'bulldog breed', 'right little, tight little island' style of talk. In the whole of *A Tale of Two Cities* there is not a line that could be taken as meaning, 'Look how those wicked Frenchmen behave!' The one place where he seems to display a normal hatred of foreigners is in the American chapters of *Martin Chuzzlewit*. This, however, is simply the reaction of a generous mind against cant. If Dickens were alive today he would make a trip to Soviet Russia and come back with a book rather like Gide's *Retour de l'U.R.S.S.* But he is remarkably free from the idiocy of regarding nations as individuals. He seldom even makes jokes turning on nationality. He does not exploit the comic Irishman and the comic Welshman, for instance, and not because he objects to stock characters and ready-made jokes, which obviously he does not. It is perhaps more significant that he shows no prejudice against Jews. It is true that he takes it for granted (*Oliver Twist* and *Great Expectations*) that a receiver of stolen goods will be a Jew, which at the time was probably justified. But the 'Jew joke', endemic in English literature until the rise of Hitler, does not appear in his books, and in *Our Mutual Friend* he makes a pious though not very convincing attempt to stand up for the Jews.

Dickens's lack of vulgar nationalism is in part the mark of a real largeness of mind, and in part results from his negative, rather unhelpful political attitude. He is very much an Englishman, but he is hardly aware of it – certainly the thought of being an Englishman does not thrill him. He has no imperialist feeling, no discernible views on foreign politics, and is untouched by the military tradition. Temperamentally he is much nearer to the small Nonconformist tradesman who looks down on the 'red-coats' and thinks that war is wicked – a one-eyed view, but, after all, war *is* wicked. It is noticeable that Dickens hardly writes of war, even to denounce it. With all his marvellous powers of description, and of describing things he had never seen, he never describes a battle, unless one counts the attack on the Bastille in *A Tale of Two Cities*. Probably the subject would not strike him as interesting, and in any case he would not regard a battlefield as a place where anything worth settling could be settled. It is one up to the lower-middle-class, puritan mentality.

III

Dickens had grown up near enough to poverty to be terrified of it, and in spite of his generosity of mind, he is not free from the special prejudices of the shabby-genteel. It is usual to claim him as a 'popular' writer, a champion of the 'oppressed masses'. So he is, so long as he thinks of them as oppressed; but there are two things that condition his attitude. In the first place, he is a south of England man, and a cockney at that, and therefore out of touch with the bulk of the real oppressed masses, the industrial and agricultural labourers. It is interesting to see how Chesterton, another cockney, always presents Dickens as the spokesman of 'the poor', without showing much awareness of who 'the poor' really are. To Chesterton 'the poor' means small shopkeepers and servants. Sam Weller, he says, 'is the great symbol in English literature of the populace peculiar to England'; and Sam Weller is a valet! The other point is that Dickens's early experiences have given him a horror of proletarian roughness. He shows this unmistakably whenever he writes of the poorest of the poor, the slum-dwellers. His descriptions of the London slums are always full of undisguised repulsion:

> The ways were foul and narrow; the shops and houses wretched; and people half naked, drunken, slipshod and ugly. Alleys and archways, like so many cesspools, disgorged their offences of smell, and dirt, and life, upon the straggling streets; and the whole quarter reeked with crime, and filth, and misery, etc. etc.

There are many similar passages in Dickens. From them one gets the impression of whole submerged populations whom he regards as being beyond the pale. In rather the same way the modern doctrinaire Socialist contemptuously writes off a large block of the population as 'lumpenproletariat'. Dickens also shows less understanding of criminals than one would expect of him. Although he is well aware of the social and economic causes of crime, he often seems to feel that when a man has once broken the law he has put himself outside human society. There is a chapter at the end of *David Copperfield* in which David visits the prison where Littimer and Uriah Heep are serving their sentences. Dickens actually seems to regard the horrible 'model' prisons, against which Charles Reade delivered his memorable attack in *It is Never Too Late to Mend*, as too humane. He complains that the food is too good! As soon as he comes up against crime or the worst depths of poverty, he shows traces of the 'I've always kept myself respectable' habit of mind. The attitude of Pip (obviously the attitude of Dickens himself) towards Magwitch in *Great Expectations* is extremely interesting. Pip is conscious all along of his ingratitude towards Joe, but far less so of his ingratitude towards Magwitch. When he discovers that the person who has loaded him with benefits for years is actually a transported convict, he falls into frenzies of disgust. 'The abhorrence in which I held the man, the dread I had of him, the repugnance with which I shrank from him, could not have been exceeded if he had been some terrible beast', etc. etc. So far as one can discover from the text, this is not because when Pip was a child he had been terrorized by Magwitch in the churchyard; it is because Magwitch is a criminal and a convict. There is an even more 'kept-myself-respectable' touch in the fact that Pip feels as a matter of course that he cannot take Magwitch's money. The money is not the product of a crime, it has been honestly acquired; but it is an ex-convict's money and therefore 'tainted'. There is nothing psychologically false in this, either.

Psychologically the latter part of *Great Expectations* is about the best thing Dickens ever did; throughout this part of the book one feels 'Yes, that is just how Pip would have behaved.' But the point is that in the matter of Magwitch, Dickens identifies with Pip, and his attitude is at bottom snobbish. The result is that Magwitch belongs to the same queer class of characters as Falstaff and, probably, Don Quixote – characters who are more pathetic than the author intended.

When it is a question of the non-criminal poor, the ordinary, decent, labouring poor, there is of course nothing contemptuous in Dickens's attitude. He has the sincerest admiration for people like the Peggottys and the Plornishes. But it is questionable whether he really regards them as equals. It is of the greatest interest to read Chapter XI of *David Copperfield* and side by side with it the autobiographical fragment (parts of this are given in Forster's *Life*, in which Dickens expresses his feelings about the blacking-factory episode a great deal more strongly than in the novel. For more than twenty years afterwards the memory was so painful to him that he would go out of his way to avoid that part of the Strand. He says that to pass that way 'made me cry, after my eldest child could speak'. The text makes it quite clear that what hurt him most of all, then and in retrospect, was the enforced contact with 'low' associates:

> No words can express the secret agony of my soul as I sunk into this companionship; compared these everyday associates with those of happier childhood. . . . But I held some station at the blacking warehouse too. . . . I soon became at least as expeditious and as skilful with my hands as either of the other boys. Though perfectly familiar with them, my conduct and manners were different enough from theirs to place a space between us. They, and the men, always spoke of me as 'the young gentleman'. A certain man . . . used to call me 'Charles' sometimes in speaking to me; but I think it was mostly when we were very confidential. . . . Poll Green uprose once, and rebelled against the 'young gentleman' usage; but Bob Fagin settled him speedily.

It was as well that there should be 'a space between us', you see. However much Dickens may admire the working classes, he does not wish to resemble them. Given his origins, and the time he lived in, it could hardly be otherwise. In the early nineteenth century class-animosities may have been no sharper than they are now, but the surface differences between class and class were enormously greater. The 'gentleman' and the 'common man' must have seemed like different species of animal. Dickens is quite genuinely on the side of the poor against the rich, but it would be next door to impossible for him not to think of a working-class exterior as a stigma. In one of Tolstoy's fables the peasants of a certain village judge every stranger who arrives from the state of his hands. If his palms are hard from work, they let him in; if his palms are soft, out he goes. This would be hardly intelligible to Dickens; all his heroes have soft hands. His younger heroes – Nicholas Nickleby, Martin Chuzzlewit, Edward Chester, David Copperfield, John Harmon – are usually of the type known as 'walking gentlemen'. He likes a bourgeois exterior and a bourgeois (not aristocratic) accent. One curious symptom of this is that he will not allow anyone who is to play a heroic part to speak like a working man. A comic hero like Sam Weller, or a merely pathetic figure like Stephen Blackpool, can speak with a broad accent, but the *jeune premier* always speaks the then equivalent of B.B.C. This is so, even when it involves absurdities. Little Pip, for instance, is brought up by people speaking broad Essex, but talks upper-class English from his earliest childhood; actually he would have talked the same dialect as Joe, or at least as Mrs Gargery. So also with Biddy Wopsle, Lizzie Hexam, Sissie Jupe, Oliver Twist – one ought perhaps to add Little Dorrit. Even Rachel in *Hard Times* has barely a trace of Lancashire accent, an impossibility in her case.

One thing that often gives the clue to a novelist's real feelings on the class question is the attitude he takes up when class collides with sex. This is a thing too painful to be lied about, and consequently it is one of the points at which the 'I'm-not-a-snob' pose tends to break down.

One sees that at its most obvious where a class-distinction is also a colour-distinction. And something resembling the colonial atitude ('native' women are fair game, white women are sacrosanct) exists in a veiled form in all-white communities, causing bitter resentment on both sides. When this issue arises, novelists often revert to crude class-feelings which they might disclaim at other times. A good example of 'class-conscious' reaction is a rather forgotten novel, *The People of Clopton*, by Andrew Barton. The author's moral code is quite clearly mixed up with class-hatred. He feels the seduction of a poor girl by a rich man to be something atrocious, a kind of defilement, something quite different from her seduction by a man in her own walk of life. Trollope deals with this theme twice (*The Three Clerks* and *The Small House at Allington*) and, as one might expect, entirely from the upper-class angle. As he sees it, an affair with a barmaid or a landlady's daughter is simply an 'entanglement' to be escaped from. Trollope's moral standards are strict, and he does not allow the seduction actually to happen, but the implication is always that a working-class girl's feelings do not greatly matter. In *The Three Clerks* he even gives the typical class-reaction by noting that the girl 'smells'. Meredith (*Rhoda Fleming*) takes more the 'class-conscious' viewpoint. Thackeray, as often, seems to hesitate. In *Pendennis* (Fanny Bolton) his attitude is much the same as Trollope's; in *A Shabby Genteel Story* it is nearer to Meredith's.

One could divine a good deal about Trollope's social origin, or Meredith's, or Barton's, merely from their handling of the class-sex theme. So one can with Dickens, but what emerges, as usual, is that he is more inclined to identify himself with the middle class than with the proletariat. The one incident that seems to contradict this is the tale of the young peasant-girl in Doctor Manette's manuscript in *A Tale of Two Cities*. This, however, is merely a costume-piece put in to explain the implacable hatred of Madame Defarge, which Dickens does not pretend to approve of. In *David Copperfield*, where he is dealing with a typical nineteenth-century seduction, the class-issue does not seem to strike him as paramount. It is a law of Victorian novels that sexual misdeeds must not go unpunished, and so Steerforth is drowned on Yarmouth sands, but neither Dickens, nor old Peggotty, nor even Ham, seems to feel that Steerforth has added to his offence by being the son of rich parents. The Steerforths are moved by class-motives, but the Peggottys are not – not even in the scene between Mrs Steerforth and old Peggotty; if they were, of course, they would probably turn against David as well as against Steerforth.

In *Our Mutual Friend* Dickens treats the episode of Eugene Wrayburn and Lizzie Hexam very realistically and with no appearance of class bias. According to the 'unhand me, monster' tradition, Lizzie ought either to 'spurn' Eugene or to be ruined by him and throw herself off Waterloo Bridge; Eugene ought to be either a heartless betrayer or a hero resolved upon defying society. Neither behaves in the least like this. Lizzie is frightened by Eugene's advances and actually runs away from them, but hardly pretends to dislike them; Eugene is attracted by her, has too much decency to attempt seducing her and dare not marry her because of his family. Finally they are married and no one is any the worse, except perhaps Mr Twemlow, who will lose a few dinner engagements. It is all very much as it might have happened in real life. But a 'class-conscious' novelist would have given her to Bradley Headstone.

But when it is the other way about – when it is a case of a poor man aspiring to some woman who is 'above' him – Dickens instantly retreats into the middle-class attitude. He is rather fond of the Victorian notion of a woman (woman with a capital W) being 'above' a man. Pip feels that

Estella is 'above' him, Esther Summerson is 'above' Guppy, Little Dorrit is 'above' John Chivery, Lucy Manette is 'above' Sydney Carton. In some of these the 'above'-ness is merely moral, but in others it is social. There is a scarcely mistakable class-reaction when David Copperfield discovers that Uriah Heep is plotting to marry Agnes Wickfield. The disgusting Uriah suddenly announces that he is in love with her:

> 'Oh, Master Copperfield, with what a pure affection do I love the ground my Agnes walks on.'
>
> I believe I had the delirious idea of seizing the red-hot poker out of the fire, and running him through with it. It went from me with a shock, like a ball fired from a rifle: but the image of Agnes, outraged by so much as a thought of this red-headed animal's, remained in my mind (when I looked at him, sitting all awry as if his mean soul griped his body) and made me giddy. . . . 'I believe Agnes Wickfield to be as far above *you* (David says later on), and as far removed from all *your* aspirations, as that moon herself.'

Considering how Heep's general lowness – his servile manners, dropped aitches and so forth – has been rubbed in throughout the book, there is not much doubt about the nature of Dickens's feelings. Heep, of course, is playing a villainous part, but even villains have sexual lives; it is the thought of the 'pure' Agnes in bed with a man who drops his aitches that really revolts Dickens. But his usual tendency is to treat a man in love with a woman who is 'above' him as a joke. It is one of the stock jokes of English literature, from Malvolio onwards. Guppy in *Bleak House* is an example, John Chivery is another, and there is a rather ill-natured treatment of this theme in the 'swarry' in *Pickwick Papers*. Here Dickens describes the Bath footmen as living a kind of fantasy-life, holding dinner-parties in imitation of their 'betters' and deluding themselves that their young mistresses are in love with them. This evidently strikes him as very comic. So it is, in a way, though one might question whether it is not better for a footman even to have delusions of this kind than simply to accept his status in the spirit of the catechism.

In his attitude towards servants. Dickens is not ahead of his age. In the nineteenth century the revolt against domestic service was just beginning, to the great annoyance of everyone with over £500 a year. An enormous number of the jokes in nineteenth-century comic papers deal with the uppishness of servants. For years *Punch* ran a series of jokes called 'Servant Gal-isms', all turning on the then astonishing fact that a servant is a human being. Dickens is sometimes guilty of this kind of thing himself. His books abound with the ordinary comic servants; they are dishonest

(*Great Expectations*), incompetent (*David Copperfield*), turn up their noses at good food (*Pickwick Papers*) etc. etc. – all rather in the spirit of the suburban housewife with one down-trodden cook-general. But what is curious, in a nineteenth-century radical, is that when he wants to draw a sympathetic picture of a servant, he creates what is recognizably a feudal type. Sam Weller, Mark Tapley, Clara Peggotty are all of them feudal figures. They belong to the genre of the 'old family retainer'; they identify themselves with their master's family and are at once doggishly faithful and completely familiar. No doubt Mark Tapley and Sam Weller are derived to some extent from Smollett, and hence from Cervantes; but it is interesting that Dickens should have been attracted by such a type. Sam Weller's attitude is definitely medieval. He gets himself arrested in order to follow Mr Pickwick into the Fleet, and afterwards refuses to get married because he feels that Mr Pickwick still needs his services. There is a characteristic scene between them:

> 'Vages or no vages, board or no board, lodgin' or no lodgin', Sam Veller, as you took from the old inn in the Borough, sticks by you, come what may . . . '
>
> 'My good fellow,' said Mr Pickwick, when Mr Weller had sat down again, rather abashed at his own enthusiasm, 'you are bound to consider the young woman also.'
>
> 'I do consider the young 'ooman, sir,' said Sam. 'I have considered the young 'ooman. I've spoke to her. I've told her how I'm sitivated; she's ready to vait till I'm ready, and I believe she vill. If she don't, she's not the young 'ooman I take her for, and I give her up with readiness.'

It is easy to imagine what the young woman would have said to this in real life. But notice the feudal atmosphere. Sam Weller is ready as a matter of course to sacrifice years of life to his master, and he can also sit down in his master's presence. A modern manservant would never think of doing either. Dickens's views on the servant question do not get much beyond wishing that master and servant would love one another. Sloppy in *Our Mutual Friend*, though a wretched failure as a character, represents the same kind of loyalty as Sam Weller. Such loyalty, of course, is natural, human and likeable; but so was feudalism.

What Dickens seems to be doing, as usual, is to reach out for an idealized version of the existing thing. He was writing at a time when domestic service must have seemed a completely inevitable evil. There were no labour-saving devices, and there was huge inequality of wealth. It was an age of enormous families, pretentious meals and inconvenient houses, when the slavery drudging fourteen hours a day in the basement kitchen was something too normal to be noticed. And given the *fact* of servitude, the feudal relationship is the only tolerable one. Sam Weller and Mark Tapley are dream figures, no less than the Cheerybles. If there have got to be masters and servants, how much better that the master should be Mr Pickwick and the servant should be Sam Weller. Better still, of course, if servants did not exist at all – but this Dickens is probably unable to imagine. Without a high level of mechanical development, human equality is not practically possible; Dickens goes to show that it is not imaginable either.

IV

It is not merely a coincidence that Dickens never writes about agriculture and writes endlessly about food. He was a cockney, and London is the centre of the earth in rather the same sense that the belly is the centre of the body. It is a city of consumers, of people who are deeply civilized but not primarily useful. A thing that strikes one when one looks below the surface of Dickens's books is that, as nineteenth-century novelists go, he is rather ignorant. He knows very little about the way things really happen. At first sight this statement looks flatly untrue, and it needs some qualification.

Dickens had had vivid glimpses of 'low life' – life in a debtor's prison, for example – and he was also a popular novelist and able to write about ordinary people. So were all the characteristic English novelists of the nineteenth century. They felt at home in the world they lived in, whereas a writer nowadays is so hopelessly isolated that the typical modern novel is a novel about a novelist. Even when Joyce, for instance, spends a decade or so in patient efforts to make contact with the 'common man', his 'common man' finally turns out to be a Jew, and a bit of a highbrow at that. Dickens at least does not suffer from this kind of thing. He has no difficulty in introducing the common motives, love, ambition, avarice, vengeance and so forth. What he does not noticeably write about, however, is *work*.

In Dickens's novels anything in the nature of work happens off-stage. The only one of his heroes who has a plausible profession is David Copperfield, who is first a shorthand writer and then a novelist, like Dickens himself. With most of the others, the way they earn their living is very much in the background. Pip, for instance, 'goes into business' in Egypt; we are not told what business, and Pip's working life occupies about half a page of the book. Clennam has been in some unspecified business in China, and later goes into another barely specified business with Doyce. Martin Chuzzlewit is an architect, but does not seem to get much time for practising. In no case do their adventures spring directly out of their work. Here the contrast between Dickens and, say, Trollope is startling. And one reason for this is undoubtedly that Dickens knows very little about the professions his characters are supposed to follow. What exactly went on in Gradgrind's factories? How did Podsnap make his money? How did Merdle work his swindles? One knows that Dickens could never follow up the details of parliamentary elections and Stock Exchange rackets as Trollope could. As soon as he has to deal with trade, finance, industry or politics he takes refuge in vagueness, or in satire. This is the case even with legal processes, about which actually he must have known a good deal. Compare any lawsuit in Dickens with the lawsuit in *Orley Farm*, for instance.

And this partly accounts for the needless ramifications of Dickens's novels, the awful Victorian 'plot'. It is true that not all his novels are alike in this. *A Tale of Two Cities* is a very good and fairly simple story, and so in its different way is *Hard Times*; but these are just the two which are always rejected as 'not like Dickens' – and incidentally they were not published in monthly numbers.[3] The two first-person novels are also good stories, apart from their sub-plots. But the typical Dickens novel, *Nicholas Nickleby*, *Oliver Twist*, *Martin Chuzzlewit*, *Our Mutual Friend*, always exists round a framework of melodrama. The last thing anyone remembers about these books is their central story. On the other hand, I suppose no one has ever read them without carrying the memory of individual pages to the day of his death. Dickens sees human beings with the most intense vividness, but he sees them always in private life, as 'characters', not as functional members of society; that is to say, he sees them statically. Consequently his greatest success is *The Pickwick Papers*, which is not a story at all, merely a series of sketches; there is little attempt at development – the characters simply go on and on, behaving like idiots, in a kind of eternity. As soon as he tries to bring his characters into action, the melodrama begins. He cannot make the action revolve round their ordinary occupations; hence the crossword puzzle of coincidences, intrigues, murders, disguises, buried wills, long-lost brothers, etc. etc.

3. *Hard Times* was published as a serial in *Household Words* and *Great Expectations* and *A Tale of Two Cities* in *All the Year Round*. Forster says that the shortness of the weekly instalments made it 'much more difficult to get sufficient interest into each'. Dickens himself complained of the lack of 'elbow-room'. In other words, he had to stick more closely to the story. [Author's footnote.]

In the end even people like Squeers and Micawber get sucked into the machinery.

Of course it would be absurd to say that Dickens is a vague or merely melodramatic writer. Much that he wrote is extremely factual, and in the power of evoking visual images he has probably never been equalled. When Dickens has once described something you see it for the rest of your life. But in a way the concreteness of his vision is a sign of what he is missing. For, after all, that is what the merely casual onlooker always sees – the outward appearance, the non-functional, the surfaces of things. No one who is really involved in the landscape ever sees the landscape. Wonderfully as he can describe an *appearance*, Dickens does not often describe a *process*. The vivid pictures that he succeeds in leaving in one's memory are nearly always the pictures of things seen in leisure moments, in the coffee-rooms of country inns or through the windows of a stage-coach; the kind of things he notices are inn-signs, brass door-knockers, painted jugs, the interiors of shops and private houses, clothes, faces and, above all, food. Everything is seen from the consumer-angle. When he writes about Coketown he manages to evoke, in just a few paragraphs, the atmosphere of a Lancashire town as a slightly disgusted southern visitor would see it. 'It had a black canal in it, and a river that ran purple with evil-smelling dye, and vast piles of buildings full of windows where there was a rattling and a trembling all day long, and where the piston of the steam-engine worked monotonously up and down, like the head of an elephant in a state of melancholy madness.' That is as near as Dickens ever gets to the machinery of the mills. An engineer or a cotton-broker would see it differently; but then neither of them would be capable of that impressionistic touch about the heads of the elephants.

In a rather different sense his attitude to life is extremely unphysical. He is a man who lives through his eyes and ears rather than through his hands and muscles. Actually his habits were not so sedentary as this seems to imply. In spite of rather poor health and physique, he was active to the point of restlessness; throughout his life he was a remarkable walker, and he could at any rate carpenter well enough to put up stage scenery. But he was not one of those people who feel a need to use their hands. It is difficult to imagine him digging at a cabbage-patch, for instance. He gives no evidence of knowing anything about agriculture, and obviously knows nothing about any kind of game or sport. He has no interest in pugilism, for instance. Considering the age in which he was writing, it is astonishing how little physical brutality there is in Dickens's novels. Martin Chuzzlewit and Mark Tapley, for instance, behave with the most remarkable mildness towards the Americans who are constantly menacing them with revolvers and bowie-knives. The average English or American novelist would have had them handing out socks on the jaw and exchanging pistol-shots in all directions. Dickens is too decent for that; he sees the stupidity of violence, and also he belongs to a cautious urban class which does not deal in socks on the jaw, even in theory. And this attitude towards sport is mixed up with social feelings. In England, for mainly geographical reasons, sport, especially field-sports, and snobbery are inextricably mingled. English Socialists are often flatly incredulous when told that Lenin, for instance, was devoted to shooting. In their eyes shooting, hunting, etc. are simply snobbish observances of the landed gentry; they forget that these things might appear differently in a huge virgin country like Russia. From Dickens's point of view almost any kind of sport is at best a subject of satire. Consequently one side of nineteenth-century life – the boxing, racing, cock-fighting, badger-digging, poaching, rat-catching side of life, so wonderfully embalmed in Leech's illustrations to Surtees – is outside his scope.

What is more striking, in a seemingly 'progressive' radical, is that he is not mechanically minded. He shows no interest either in the details of machinery or in the things machinery can do. As Gissing remarks, Dickens nowhere describes a railway journey with anything like the enthusiasm he shows in describing journeys by stage-coach. In nearly all of his books one has a curious feeling that one is living in the first quarter of the nineteenth century, and in fact, he does tend to return to this period. *Little Dorrit*, written in the middle fifties, deals with the late twenties; *Great Expectations* (1861) is not dated, but evidently deals with the twenties and thirties. Several of the inventions and discoveries which have made the modern world possible (the electric telegraph, the breech-loading gun, india-rubber, coal gas, wood-pulp paper) first appeared in Dickens's lifetime, but he scarcely notes them in his books. Nothing is queerer than the vagueness with which he speaks of Doyce's 'invention' in *Little Dorrit*. It is represented as something extremely ingenious and revolutionary, 'of great importance to his country and his fellow creatures', and it is also an important minor link in the book; yet we are never told what the 'invention' is! On the other hand, Doyce's physical appearance is hit off with the typical Dickens touch; he has a peculiar way of moving his thumb, a way characteristic of engineers. After that, Doyce is firmly anchored in one's memory; but, as usual, Dickens has done it by fastening on something external.

There are people (Tennyson is an example) who lack the mechanical faculty but can see the social possibilities of machinery. Dickens has not this stamp of mind. He shows very little consciousness of the future. When he speaks of human progress it is usually in terms of *moral* progress – men growing better; probably he would never admit that men are only as good as their technical development allows them to be. At this point the gap between Dickens and his modern analogue, H. G. Wells, is at its widest. Wells wears the future round his neck like a millstone, but Dickens's unscientific cast of mind is just as damaging in a different way. What it does is to make any *positive* attitude more difficult for him. He is hostile to the feudal, agricultural past and not in real touch with the industrial present. Well, then, all that remains is the future (meaning science, 'progress' and so forth), which hardly enters into his thoughts. Therefore, while attacking everything in sight, he has no definable standard of comparison. As I have pointed out already, he attacks the current educational system with perfect justice. and yet, after all, he has no remedy to offer except kindlier schoolmasters. Why did he not indicate what a school *might* have been? Why did he not have his own sons educated according to some plan of his own, instead of sending them to public schools to be stuffed with Greek? Because he lacked that kind of imagination. He has an infallible moral sense, but very little intellectual curiosity. And here one comes upon something which really is an enormous deficiency in Dickens, something that really does make the nineteenth century seem remote from us – that he has no ideal of *work*.

With the doubtful exception of David Copperfield (merely Dickens himself), one cannot point to a single one of his central characters who is primarily interested in his job. His heroes work in order to make a living and to marry the heroine, not because they feel a passionate interest in one particular subject. Martin Chuzzlewit, for instance, is not burning with zeal to be an architect; he might just as well be a doctor or a barrister. In any case, in the typical Dickens novel, the *deus ex machina* enters with a bag of gold in the last chapter and the hero is absolved from further struggle. The feeling, 'This is what I came into the world to do. Everything else is uninteresting. I will do this even if it means starvation', which turns men of differing temperaments into scientists, inventors, artists, priests, explorers and revolutionaries – this motif is almost entirely absent from Dickens's books. He himself, as is well known, worked like a slave and believed in his work as few novelists have ever done. But there seems to be no calling except novel-writing (and perhaps acting) towards which he can imagine this kind of devotion. And, after all, it is natural enough, considering his rather negative attitude towards society. In the last resort there is nothing he admires except common decency. Science is uninteresting and machinery is cruel and ugly (the heads of the elephants). Business is only for ruffians like Bounderby. As for politics – leave that to the Tite Barnacles. Really there is no objective except to marry the heroine, settle down, live solvently and be kind. And you can do that much better in private life.

Here, perhaps, one gets a glimpse of Dickens's secret imaginative background. What did he think of as the most desirable way to live? When Martin Chuzzlewit had made it up with his uncle, when Nicholas Nickleby had married money, when John Harmon had been enriched by Boffin – what did they *do?*

The answer evidently is that they did nothing. Nicholas Nickleby invested his wife's money with the Cheerybles and 'became a rich and prosperous merchant', but as he immediately retired into Devonshire, we can assume that he did not work very hard. Mr and Mrs Snodgrass 'purchased and cultivated a small farm, more for occupation than profit'. That is the spirit in which most of Dickens's books end – a sort of radiant idleness. Where he appears to disapprove of young men who do not work (Harthouse, Harry Gowan, Richard Carstone, Wrayburn before his reformation), it is because they are cynical and immoral or because they are a burden on somebody else; if you are 'good', and also self-supporting, there is no reason why you should not spend fifty years in simply drawing your dividends. Home life is always enough. And, after all, it was the general assumption of his age. The 'genteel sufficiency', the 'competence', the 'gentleman of independent means' (or 'in easy circumstances') – the very phrases tell one all about the strange, empty dream of the eighteenth- and nineteenth-century middle bourgeoisie. It was a dream of *complete idleness*. Charles Reade conveys its spirit perfectly in the ending of *Hard Cash*. Alfred Hardie, hero of *Hard Cash*, is the typical nineteenth-century novel hero (public-school style), with gifts which Reade describes as amounting to 'genius'. He is an old Etonian and a scholar of Oxford, he knows most of the Greek and Latin classics by heart, he can box with prize-fighters and win the Diamond Sculls at Henley. He goes through incredible adventures in which, of course, he behaves with faultless heroism, and then, at the age of twenty-five, he inherits a fortune, marries his Julia Dodd and settles down in the suburbs of Liverpool, in the same house as his parents-in-law:

> They lived together at Albion Villa, thanks to Alfred. . . . Oh, you happy little villa! You were as like Paradise as any mortal dwelling can be. A day came,

however, when your walls could no longer hold all the happy inmates. Julia presented Alfred with a lovely boy; enter two nurses and the villa showed symptoms of bursting. Two months more, and Alfred and his wife overflowed into the next villa. It was but twenty yards off; and there was a double reason for the migration. As often happens after a long separation, Heaven bestowed on Captain and Mrs Dodd another infant to play about their knees, etc. etc. etc.

This is the type of the Victorian happy ending – a vision of a huge, loving family of three or four generations, all crammed together in the same house and constantly multiplying, like a bed of oysters. What is striking about it is the utterly soft, sheltered, effortless life that it implies. It is not even a violent idleness, like Squire Western's. That is the significance of Dickens's urban background and his non-interest in the blackguardly-sporting-military side of life. His heroes, once they had come into money and 'settled down', would not only do no work; they would not even ride, hunt, shoot, fight duels, elope with actresses or lose money at the races. They would simply live at home in feather-bed respectability, and preferably next door to a blood-relation living exactly the same life:

The first act of Nicholas, when he became a rich and prosperous merchant, was to buy his father's old house. As time crept on, and there came gradually about him a group of lovely children, it was altered and enlarged; but none of the old rooms were ever pulled down, no old tree was ever rooted up, nothing with which there was any association of bygone times was ever removed or changed.

Within a stone's-throw was another retreat enlivened by children's pleasant voices too; and here was Kate . . . the same true, gentle creature, the same fond sister, the same in the love of all about her, as in her girlish days.

It is the same incestuous atmosphere as in the passage quoted from Reade. And evidently this is Dickens's ideal ending. It is perfectly attained in *Nicholas Nickleby*, *Martin Chuzzlewit* and *Pickwick*, and it is approximated to in varying degrees in almost all the others. The exceptions are *Hard Times* and *Great Expectations* – the latter actually has a 'happy ending', but it contradicts the general tendency of the book, and it was put in at the request of Bulwer Lytton.

The ideal to be striven after, then, appears to be something like this: a hundred thousand pounds, a quaint old house with plenty of ivy on it, a sweetly womanly wife, a horde of children, and no work. Everything is safe, soft, peaceful and, above all, domestic. In the moss-grown churchyard down the road are the graves of the loved ones who passed away before the happy ending happened. The servants are comic and feudal, the children prattle round your feet, the old friends sit at your fireside, talking of past days, there is the endless succession of enormous meals, the cold punch and sherry negus, the feather beds and warming-pans, the Christmas parties with charades and blind man's bluff; but nothing ever happens, except the yearly child-birth. The curious thing is that it is a genuinely happy picture, or so Dickens is able to make it appear. The thought of that kind of existence is satisfying to him. This alone would be enough to tell one that more than a hundred years have passed since Dicken's first book was written. No modern man could combine such purposelessness with so much vitality.

V

By this time anyone who is a lover of Dickens, and who has read as far as this, will probably be angry with me.

I have been discussing Dickens simply in terms of his 'message', and almost ignoring his literary qualities. But every writer, especially every novelist, *has* a 'message', whether he admits it or not, and the minutest details of his work are influenced by it. All art is propaganda. Neither Dickens himself nor the majority of Victorian novelists would have thought of denying this. On the other hand, not all propaganda is art. As I said earlier, Dickens is one of those writers who are felt to be worth stealing. He has been stolen by Marxists, by Catholics and, above all, by Conservatives. The question is, What is there to steal? Why does anyone care about Dickens? Why do *I* care about Dickens?

That kind of question is never easy to answer. As a rule, an aesthetic preference is either something inexplicable or it is so corrupted by non-aesthetic motives as to make one wonder whether the whole of literary criticism is not a huge network of humbug. In Dickens's case the complicating factor is his familiarity. He happens to be one of those 'great authors' who are ladled down everyone's throat in childhood. At the time this causes rebellion and vomiting, but it may have different after-effects in later life. For instance, nearly everyone feels a sneaking affection for the patriotic poems that he learned by heart as a child, 'Ye Mariners of England', 'The Charge of the Light Brigade' and so forth. What one enjoys is not so much the poems themselves as the memories they call up. And with Dickens the same forces of association are at work. Probably there are copies of one or two of his books lying about in an actual majority of English homes. Many children begin to know his characters by sight before they can even read, for on the whole Dickens was lucky in his illustrators. A thing that is absorbed as early as that does not come up against any critical judgement. And when one thinks of this, one thinks of all that is bad and silly in Dickens – the cast-iron 'plots', the characters who don't come off, the *longueurs*, the paragraphs in blank verse, the awful pages of 'pathos'. And then the thought arises, when I say I like Dickens, do I simply mean that I like thinking about my childhood? Is Dickens merely an institution?

If so, he is an institution that there is no getting away from. How often one really thinks about any writer, even a writer one cares for, is a difficult thing to decide; but I should doubt whether anyone who has actually read Dickens can go a week without remembering him in one context or another. Whether you approve of him or not, he is *there* like the Nelson Column. At any moment some scene or character, which may come from some book you cannot even remember the name of, is liable to drop into your mind. Micawber's letters! Winkle in the witness box! Mrs Gamp! Mrs Wititterly and Sir Tumley Snuffim! Todger's! (George Gissing said that when he passed the Monument it was never of the Fire of London that he thought, always of Todgers's.) Mrs Leo Hunter! Squeers! Silas Wegg and the Decline and Fall-off of the Russian Empire! Miss Mills and the Desert of Sahara! Wopsle acting Hamlet! Mrs Jellyby! Mantalini! Jerry Cruncher! Barkis! Pumblechook! Tracy Tupman! Skimpole! Joe Gargery! Pecksniff! – and so it goes on and on. It is not so much a series of books, it is more like a world. And not a purely comic world either, for part of what one remembers in Dickens is his Victorian morbidness and necrophilia and the blood-and-thunder scenes – the death of Sikes, Krook's spontaneous combustion, Fagin in the condemned cell, the women knitting round the guillotine. To a surprising extent all this has entered even into the minds of people who do not care about it. A music-hall comedian can (or at any rate could quite recently) go on the stage and impersonate Micawber or Mrs Gamp with a fair certainty of being understood, although not one in twenty of the audience had ever read a book of Dickens's right through. Even people who affect to despise him quote him unconsciously.

Dickens is a writer who can be imitated, up to a certain point. In genuinely popular literature – for instance, the Elephant and Castle version of *Sweeny Todd* – he has been plagiarized quite shamelessly. What has been imitated, however, is simply a tradition that Dickens himself took from earlier novelists and developed, the cult of 'character', i.e. eccentricity. The thing that cannot be imitated is his fertility of invention, which is invention not so much of characters, still less of 'situations', as of turns of phrase and concrete details. The outstanding, unmistakable mark of Dickens's writing is the *unnecessary detail.* Here is an example of what I mean. The story given below is not particularly funny, but there is one phrase in it that is as individual as a fingerprint. Mr Jack Hopkins, at Bob Sawyer's party, is telling the story of the child who swallowed its sister's necklace:

> Next day, child swallowed two beads; the day after that, he treated himself to three, and so on, till in a week's time he had got through the necklace – five-and-twenty beads in all. The sister, who was an industrious girl and seldom treated herself to a bit of finery, cried her eyes out at the loss of the necklace; looked high and low for it; but I needn't say, didn't find it. A few days afterwards, the family were at dinner – baked shoulder of mutton and potatoes under it – the child, who wasn't hungry, was playing about the room, when suddenly there was heard the devil of a noise, like a small hailstorm. 'Don't do that, my boy,' says the father. 'I ain't a-doin' nothing,' said the child. 'Well, don't do it again,' said the father. There was a short silence, and then the noise began again, worse than ever. 'If you don't mind what I say, my boy,' said the father, 'you'll find yourself in bed, in something less than a pig's whisper.' He gave the child a shake to make him obedient, and such a rattling ensued as nobody ever heard before. 'Why, dam' me, it's *in* the child,' said the father; 'he's got the croup in the wrong place!' 'No, I haven't, father,' said the child, beginning to cry, 'it's the necklace; I swallowed it, father.' The father caught the child up, and ran with him to the hospital, the beads in the boy's stomach rattling all the way with the jolting; and the people looking up in the air, and down in the cellars, to see where the unusual sound came from. 'He's in the hospital now,' said Jack Hopkins, 'and he makes such a devil of a noise when he walks about, that they're obliged to muffle him in a watchman's coat, for fear he should wake the patients.'

As a whole, this story might come out of any nineteenth-century comic paper. But the unmistakable Dickens touch, the thing nobody else would have thought of, is the baked shoulder of mutton and potatoes under it. How does this advance the story? The answer is that it doesn't. It is something totally unnecessary, a florid little squiggle on the edge of the page; only, it is by just these squiggles that the special Dickens atmosphere is created. The other thing one would notice here is that Dickens's way of telling a story takes a long time. An interesting example, too long to quote, is Sam Weller's story of the obstinate patient in Chapter XLIV of *The Pickwick Papers.* As it happens, we have a standard of comparison here, because Dickens is plagiarizing, consciously or unconsciously. The story is also told by some ancient Greek writer. I cannot now find the passage, but I read it years ago as a boy at school, and it runs more or less like this:

A certain Thracian, renowned for his obstinacy, was warned by his physician that if he drank a flagon of wine it would kill him. The Thracian thereupon drank the flagon of wine and immediately jumped off the house-top and perished. 'For,' said he, 'in this way I shall prove that the wine did not kill me.'

As the Greek tells it, that is the whole story – about six lines. As Sam Weller tells it, it takes round about a thousand words. Long before getting to the point we have been told all about the patient's clothes, his meals, his manners, even the newspapers he reads, and about the peculiar construction of the doctor's carriage, which conceals the fact that the coachman's trousers do not match his coat. Then there is the dialogue between the doctor and the patient. " 'Crumpets is wholesome, sir," said the patient. "Crumpets is *not* wholesome sir," says the doctor, wery fierce,' etc. etc. In the end the original story has been buried under the details. And in all of Dickens's most characteristic passages it is the same. His imagination overwhelms everything, like a kind of weed. Squeers stands up to address his boys, and immediately we are hearing about Bolder's father who was two pounds ten short, and Mobb's stepmother who took to her bed on hearing that Mobbs wouldn't eat fat and hoped Mr Squeers would flog him into a happier state of mind. Mrs Leo Hunter writes a poem, 'Expiring Frog'; two full stanzas are given. Boffin takes a fancy to pose as a miser, and instantly we are down among the squalid biographies of eighteenth-century misers, with names like Vulture Hopkins and the Rev. Blewberry Jones, and chapter headings like 'The Story of the Mutton Pies' and 'The Treasures of a Dunghill'. Mrs Harris, who does not even exist, has more detail piled on to her than any three characters in an ordinary novel. Merely in the middle of a sentence we learn, for instance, that her infant nephew has been seen in a bottle at Greenwich Fair, along with the pink-eyed lady, the Prussian dwarf and the living skeleton. Joe Gargery describes how the robbers broke into the house of Pumblechook, the corn and seed merchant – 'and they took his till, and they took his cashbox, and they drinked his wine, and they partook of his wittles, and they slapped his face, and they pulled his nose, and they tied him up to his bedpust, and they give him a dozen, and they stuffed his mouth full of flowering annuals to perwent his crying out'. Once again the unmistakable Dickens touch, the flowering annuals; but any other novelist would only have mentioned about half of these outrages. Everything is piled up and up, detail on detail, embroidery on embroidery. It is futile to object that this kind of thing is rococo – one might as well make the same objection to a wedding-cake. Either you like it or you do not like it. Other nineteenth-century writers Surtees, Barham, Thackeray, even Marryat, have something of Dickens's profuse, overflowing quality, but none of them on anything like the same scale. The appeal of all these writers now depends partly on period-flavour, and though Marryat is still officially a 'boys' writer' and Surtees has a sort of legendary fame among hunting men, it is probable that they are read mostly by bookish people.

Significantly, Dickens's most successful books (not his *best* books) are *The Pickwick Papers*, which is not a novel, and *Hard Times* and *A Tale of Two Cities*, which are not funny. As a novelist his natural fertility greatly hampers him, because the burlesque which he is never able to resist is constantly breaking into what ought to be serious situations. There is a good example of this in the opening chapter of *Great Expectations*. The escaped convict, Magwitch, has just captured the six-year-old Pip in the churchyard. The scene starts terrifyingly enough, from Pip's point of view. The convict, smothered in mud and with his chain trailing from his leg, suddenly starts up among the tombs, grabs the child, turns him upside down and robs his pockets. Then he begins terrorizing him into bringing food and a file:

> He held me by the arms in an upright position on the top of the stone, and went on in these fearful terms:
>
> 'You bring me, tomorrow morning early, that file and them wittles. You bring the lot to me, at that old Battery over yonder. You do it, and you never dare to say a word or dare to make a sign concerning your having seen such a person as me, or any person sumever, and you shall be let to live. You fail, or you go from my words in any partickler, no matter how small it is, and your heart and liver shall be tore out, roasted and ate. Now, I ain't alone, as you may think I am. There's a young man hid with me, in comparison with which young man I am a Angel. That young man hears the words I speak. That young man has a secret way pecooliar to himself, of getting at a boy, and at his heart, and at his liver. It is in wain for a boy to attempt to hide himself from that young man. A boy may lock his door, may be warm in bed, may tuck himself up, may draw the clothes over his head, may think himself comfortable and safe, but that young man will softly creep and creep his way to him and tear him open. I am keeping that young man from harming you at the present moment, but with great difficulty. I find it wery hard to hold that young man off of your inside. Now, what do you say?'

Here Dickens has simply yielded to temptation. To begin with, no starving and hunted man would speak in the least like that. Moreover, although the speech shows a remarkable knowledge of the way in which a child's mind works, its actual words are quite out of tune with what is to follow. It turns Magwitch into a sort of pantomime wicked uncle, or, if one sees him through the child's eyes, into an appalling monster. Later in the book he is to be represented as neither, and his exaggerated gratitude, on which the plot turns, is to be incredible because of just this speech. As usual, Dickens's imagination has overwhelmed him. The picturesque details were too good to be left out. Even with characters who are more of a piece than Magwitch he is liable to be tripped up by some seductive phrase. Mr Murdstone, for instance, is in the habit of ending David Copperfield's lessons every morning with a dreadful sum in arithmetic. 'If I go into a cheesemonger's shop, and buy five thousand double-Gloucester cheeses at fourpence halfpenny each, present payment,' it always begins. Once again the typical Dickens detail, the double-Gloucester cheeses. But it is far too human a touch for Murdstone; he would have made it five thousand cashboxes. Every time this note is struck, the unity of the novel suffers. Not that it matters very much, because Dickens is obviously a writer whose parts are greater than his wholes. He is all fragments, all details – rotten architecture, but wonderful gargoyles – and never better than when he is building up some character who will later on be forced to act inconsistently.

Of course it is not usual to urge against Dickens that he makes his characters behave inconsistently. Generally he is accused of doing just the opposite. His characters are supposed to be mere 'types', each crudely representing some single trait and fitted with a kind of label by which you recognize him. Dickens is 'only a caricaturist' – that is the usual accusation, and it does him both more and less than justice. To begin with, he did not think of himself as a caricaturist, and was constantly setting into action characters who ought to have been purely static. Squeers, Micawber, Miss Mowcher,[4] Wegg, Skimpole, Pecksniff and many others are finally involved in 'plots' where they are out of place and where they behave quite incredibly. They start off as magic-lantern slides and they end by getting mixed up in a third-rate movie. Sometimes one can put one's finger on a single sentence in which the original illusion is destroyed. There is such a sentence in *David Copperfield*. After the famous dinner-party (the one where the leg of mutton was underdone), David is showing his guests out. He stops Traddles at the top of the stairs:

4. Dickens turned Miss Mowcher into a sort of heroine because the real woman whom he had caricatured had read the earlier chapters and was bitterly hurt. He had previously meant her to play a villainous part. But *any* action by such a character would seem incongruous. [Author's footnote.]

'Traddles,' said I, 'Mr Micawber don't mean any harm, poor fellow: but if I were you I wouldn't lend him anything.'

'My dear Mr Copperfield,' returned Traddles smiling, 'I haven't got anything to lend.'

'You have got a name, you know,' I said.

At the place where one reads it this remark jars a little, though something of the kind was inevitable sooner or later. The story is a fairly realistic one, and David is growing up; ultimately he is bound to see Mr Micawber for what he is, a cadging scoundrel. Afterwards. of course, Dickens's sentimentality overcomes him and Micawber is made to turn over a new leaf. But from then on the original Micawber is never quite recaptured, in spite of desperate efforts. As a rule, the 'plot' in which Dickens's characters get entangled is not particularly credible, but at least it makes some pretence at reality, whereas the world to which they belong is a never-never land, a kind of eternity. But just here one sees that 'only a caricaturist' is not really a condemnation. The fact that Dickens is always thought of as a caricaturist, although he was constantly trying to be something else, is perhaps the surest mark of his genius. The monstrosities that he created are still remembered as monstrosities, in spite of getting mixed up in would-be probable melodramas. Their first impact is so vivid that nothing that comes afterwards effaces it. As with the people one knew in childhood, one seems always to remember them in one particular attitude, doing one particular thing. Mrs Squeers is always ladling out brimstone and treacle, Mrs Gummidge is always weeping, Mrs Gargery is always banging her husband's head against the wall, Mrs Jellyby is always scribbling tracts while her children fall into the area – and there they all are, fixed for ever like little twinkling miniatures painted on snuff-box lids, completely fantastic and incredible, and yet somehow more solid and infinitely more memorable than the efforts of serious novelists. Even by the standards of his time Dickens was an exceptionally artificial writer. As Ruskin said, he 'chose to work in a circle of stage fire'. His characters are even more distorted and simplified than Smollett's. But there are no rules in novel writing, and for any work of art there is only one test worth bothering about – survival. By this test Dickens's characters have succeeded, even if the people who remember them hardly think of them as human beings. They are monsters but at any rate they *exist*.

But all the same there is a disadvantage in writing about monsters. It amounts to this, that it is only certain moods that Dickens can speak to. There are large areas of the human mind that he never touches. There is no poetic feeling anywhere in his books, and no genuine tragedy, and even sexual love is almost outside his scope. Actually his books are not so sexless as they are sometimes declared to be, and considering the time in which he was writing, he is reasonably frank. But there is not a trace in him of the feeling that one finds in *Manon Lescaut*, *Salammbô*, *Carmen*, *Wuthering Heights*. According to Aldous Huxley, D. H. Lawrence once said that Balzac was 'a gigantic dwarf', and in a sense the same is true of Dickens. There are whole worlds which he either knows nothing about or does not wish to mention. Except in a rather roundabout way, one cannot *learn* very much from Dickens. And to say this is to think almost immediately of the great Russian novelists of the nineteenth century. Why is it that Tolstoy's grasp seems to be so much larger then Dickens's – why is it that he seems able to tell you so much more *about yourself*? It is not that he is more gifted, or even, in the last analysis, more intelligent. It is because he is writing about people who are growing. His characters are struggling to make their souls, whereas Dickens's are already finished and perfect. In my own mind Dickens's people are present far more often and far more vividly than Tolstoy's, but always in a single unchangeable attitude, like pictures or pieces of furniture. You cannot hold an imaginary conversation with a Dickens character as you can with, say, Pierre Bezukhov. And this is not merely because of Tolstoy's greater seriousness, for there are also comic characters that you can imagine yourself talking to – Bloom, for instance, or Pécuchet, or even Wells's Mr Polly. It is because Dickens's characters have no mental life. They say perfectly the thing that they have to say, but they cannot be conceived as talking about anything else. They never learn, never speculate. Perhaps the most meditative of his characters is Paul Dombey, and his thoughts are mush. Does this mean that Tolstoy's novels are 'better' than Dickens's? The truth is that it is absurd to make such comparisons in terms of 'better' and 'worse'. If I were forced to compare Tolstoy with Dickens, I should say that Tolstoy's appeal will probably be wider in the long run, because Dickens is scarcely intelligible outside the English-speaking culture; on the other hand, Dickens is able to reach simple people, which Tolstoy is not. Tolstoy's characters can cross a frontier, Dickens's can be portrayed on a cigarette card.[5] But one is no more obliged to choose between them than between a sausage and a rose. Their purposes barely intersect.

5. Messrs John Player & Sons issued two series of cigarette cards entitled 'Characters from Dickens' in 1913; they reissued them as a single series in 1923.

VI

If Dickens had been *merely* a comic writer, the chances are that no one would now remember his name. Or at best a few of his books would survive in rather the same way as books like *Frank Fairleigh*, *Mr Verdant Green* and *Mrs Caudle's Curtain Lectures*,[6] as a sort of hangover of the Victorian atmosphere, a pleasant little whiff of oysters and brown stout. Who has not felt sometimes that it was 'a pity' that Dickens ever deserted the vein of *Pickwick* for things like *Little Dorrit* and *Hard Times*? What people always demand of a popular novelist is that he shall write the same book over and over again, forgetting that a man who would write the same book twice could not even write it once. Any writer who is not utterly lifeless moves upon a kind of parabola, and the downward curve is implied in the upward one. Joyce has to start with the frigid competence of *Dubliners* and end with the dream-language of *Finnegans Wake*, but *Ulysses* and *Portrait of the Artist* are part of the trajectory. The thing that drove Dickens forward into a form of art for which he was not really suited, and at the same time caused us to remember him, was simply the fact that he was a moralist, the consciousness of 'having something to say'. He is always preaching a sermon, and that is the final secret of his inventiveness. For you can only create if you can *care*. Types like Squeers and Micawber could not have been produced by a hack writer looking for something to be funny about. A joke worth laughing at always has an idea behind it, and usually a subversive idea. Dickens is able to go on being funny because he is in revolt against authority, and authority is always there to be laughed at. There is always room for one more custard pie.

His radicalism is of the vaguest kind, and yet one always knows that it is there. That is the difference between being a moralist and a politician. He has no constructive suggestions, not even a clear grasp of the nature of the society he is attacking, only an emotional perception that something is wrong. All he can finally say is, 'Behave decently', which, as I suggested earlier, is not necessarily so shallow as it sounds. Most revolutionaries are potential Tories, because they imagine that everything can be put right by altering the *shape* of society; once that change is effected, as it sometimes is, they see no need for any other. Dickens has not this kind of mental coarseness. The vagueness of his discontent is the mark of its permanence. What he is out against is not this or that institution, but, as

6. *Frank Fairleigh* by F. E. Smedley, 1850; *The Adventurers of Mr Verdant Green* by Cuthbert Bede (pseud. of Edward Bradley), 1853; *Mrs Caudle's Curtain Lectures* by Douglas Jerrold (reprinted from *Punch*, 1846).

Chesterton put it, 'an expression on the human face'. Roughly speaking, his morality is the Christian morality, but in spite of his Anglican upbringing he was essentially a Bible-Christian, as he took care to make plain when writing his will. In any case he cannot properly be described as a religious man. He 'believed', undoubtedly, but religion in the devotional sense does not seem to have entered much into his thoughts.[7] Where he is Christian is in his quasi-instinctive siding with the oppressed against the oppressors. As a matter of course he is on the side of the underdog, always and everywhere. To carry this to its logical conclusion one has got to change sides when the underdog becomes an upperdog, and in fact Dickens does tend to do so. He loathes the Catholic Church, for instance, but as soon as the Catholics are persecuted (*Barnaby Rudge*) he is on their side. He loathes the aristocratic class even more, but as soon as they are really overthrown (the revolutionary chapters in *A Tale of Two Cities*) his sympathies swing round. Whenever he departs from this emotional attitude he goes astray. A well-known example is at the ending of *David Copperfield*, in which everyone who reads it feels that something has gone wrong. What is wrong is that the closing chapters are pervaded, faintly but noticeably, by the cult of success. It is the gospel according to Smiles, instead of the gospel according to Dickens. The attractive, out-at-elbow characters are got rid of, Micawber makes a fortune, Heep gets into prison – both of these events are flagrantly impossible – and even Dora is killed off to make way for Agnes. If you like, you can read Dora as Dickens's wife and Agnes as his sister-in-law, but the essential point is that Dickens has 'turned respectable' and done violence to his own nature. Perhaps that is why Agnes is the most disagreeable of his heroines, the real legless angel of Victorian romance, almost as bad as Thackeray's Laura.

No grown-up person can read Dickens without feeling his limitations, and yet there does remain his native generosity of mind, which acts as a kind of anchor and nearly always keeps him where he belongs. It is probably the central secret of his popularity. A good-tempered antinom-

7. From a letter to his youngest son (in 1868): 'You will remember that you have never at home been harassed about religious observances, or mere formalities. I have always been anxious not to weary my children with such things, before they are old enough to form opinions respecting them. You will therefore understand the better that I now most solemnly impress upon you the truth and beauty of the Christian Religion, as it came from Christ Himself, and the impossibility of your going far wrong if you humbly but heartily respect it . . . Never abandon the wholesome practice of saying your own private prayers, night and morning. I have never abandoned it myself, and I know the comfort of it.' [Author's footnote.]

ianism rather of Dickens's type is one of the marks of western popular culture. One sees it in folk-stories and comic songs, in dream-figures like Mickey Mouse and Popeye the Sailor (both of them variants of Jack the Giant-Killer), in the history of working-class Socialism, in the popular protests (always ineffective but not always a sham) against imperialism, in the impulse that makes a jury award excessive damages when a rich man's car runs over a poor man; it is the feeling that one is always on the side of the underdog, on the side of the weak against the strong. In one sense it is a feeling that is fifty years out of date. The common man is still living in the mental world of Dickens, but nearly every modern intellectual has gone over to some or other form of totalitarianism. From the Marxist or Fascist point of view, nearly all that Dickens stands for can be written off as 'bourgeois morality'. But in moral outlook no one could be more 'bourgeois' than the English working classes. The ordinary people in the western countries have never entered, mentally, into the world of 'realism' and power politics. They may do so before long, in which case Dickens will be as out of date as the cab-horse. But in his own age and ours he has been popular chiefly because he was able to express in a comic, simplified and therefore memorable form the native decency of the common man. And it is important that from this point of view people of very different types can be described as 'common'. In a country like England, in spite of its class-structure there does exist a certain cultural unity. All through the Christian ages, and especially since the French Revolution, the western world has been haunted by the idea of freedom and equality; it is only an *idea*, but it has penetrated to all ranks of society. The most atrocious injustices, cruelties, lies, snobberies exist everywhere, but there are not many people who can regard these things with the same indifference as, say, a Roman slave-owner. Even the millionaire suffers from a vague sense of guilt, like a dog eating a stolen leg of mutton. Nearly everyone, whatever his actual conduct may be, responds emotionally to the idea of human brotherhood. Dickens voiced a code which was and on the whole still is believed in, even by people who violate it. It is difficult otherwise to explain why he could be both read by working people (a thing that has happened to no other novelist of his stature) and buried in Westminster Abbey.

When one reads any strongly individual piece of writing, one has the impression of seeing a face somewhere behind the page. It is not necessarily the actual face of the writer. I feel this very strongly with Swift, with Defoe, with Fielding, Stendhal, Thackeray, Flaubert, though in several cases I do not know what these people looked like and do not want to know. What one sees is the face that the writer *ought* to have. Well, in the case of Dickens I see a face that is not quite the face of Dickens's photographs, though it resembles it. It is the face of a man of about forty, with a small beard and a high colour. He is laughing, with a touch of anger in his laughter, but no triumph, no malignity. It is the face of a man who is always fighting against something, but who fights in the open and is not frightened, the face of a man who is *generously angry* – in other words, of a nineteenth-century liberal, a free intelligence, a type hated with equal hatred by all the smelly little orthodoxies which are now contending for our souls.

Written 1939

I.T.W. (slightly revised) *Cr. E.*; *D.D.*; C.E.

8. Boys' Weeklies

You never walk through any poor quarter in any big town without coming upon a small newsagent's shop. The general appearance of these shops is always very much the same: a few posters for the *Daily Mail* and the *News of the World* outside, a poky little window with sweet-bottles and packets of Players, and a dark interior smelling of liquorice allsorts and festooned from floor to ceiling with vilely printed twopenny papers, most of them with lurid cover illustrations in three colours.

Except for the daily and evening papers, the stock of these shops hardly overlaps at all with that of the big newsagents. Their main selling line is the twopenny weekly, and the number and variety of these are almost unbelievable. Every hobby and pastime – cage-birds, fretwork, carpentering, bees, carrier-pigeons, home conjuring, philately, chess – has at least one paper devoted to it, and generally several. Gardening and livestock-keeping must have at least a score between them. Then there are the sporting papers, the radio papers, the children's comics, the various snippet papers such as *Tit-Bits*, the large range of papers devoted to the movies and all more or less exploiting women's legs, the various trade papers, the women's story-papers (the *Oracle*, *Secrets*, *Peg's Paper*, etc. etc.), the needlework papers – these so numerous that a display of them alone will often fill an entire window – and in addition the long series of

'Yanks Mags' (*Fight Stories*, *Action Stories*, *Western Short Stories*, etc.), which are imported shop-soiled from America and sold at twopence-halfpenny or threepence. And the periodical proper shades off into the fourpenny novelette, the *Aldine Boxing Novels*, the *Boys' Friend Library*, the *School-girls' Own Library* and many others.

Probably the contents of these shops is the best available indication of what the mass of the English people really feels and thinks. Certainly nothing half so revealing exists in documentary form. Best-seller novels, for instance, tell one a great deal, but the novel is aimed almost exclusively at people above the £4-a-week level. The movies are probably a very unsafe guide to popular taste, because the film industry is virtually a monopoly, which means that it is not obliged to study its public at all closely. The same applies to some extent to the daily papers, and most of all to the radio. But it does not apply to the weekly paper with a smallish circulation and specialized subject-matter. Papers like the *Exchange and Mart*, for instance, or *Cage-Birds*, or the *Oracle*, or *Prediction*, or the *Matrimonial Times*, only exist because there is a definite demand for them, and they reflect the minds of their readers as a great national daily with a circulation of millions cannot possibly do.

Here I am only dealing with a single series of papers, the boys' twopenny weeklies, often inaccurately described as 'penny dreadfuls'. Falling strictly within this class there are at present ten papers, the *Gem*, *Magnet*, *Modern Boy*, *Triumph* and *Champion*, all owned by the Amalgamated Press, and the *Wizard*, *Rover*, *Skipper*, *Hotspur* and *Adventure*, all owned by D. C. Thomson & Co. What the circulations of these papers are, I do not know. The editors and proprietors refuse to name any figures, and in any case the circulation of a paper carrying serial stories is bound to fluctuate widely. But there is no question that the combined public of the ten papers is a very large one. They are on sale in every town in England, and nearly every boy who reads at all goes through a phase of reading one or more of them. The *Gem* and *Magnet*, which are much the oldest of these papers, are of rather different type from the rest, and they have evidently lost some of their popularity during the past few years. A good many boys now regard them as old-fashioned and 'slow'. Nevertheless I want to discuss them first, because they are more interesting psychologically than the others, and also because the mere survival of such papers into the nineteen-thirties is a rather startling phenomenon.

The *Gem* and *Magnet* are sister-papers (characters out of one paper frequently appear in the other), and were both started more than thirty years ago. At that time, together with *Chums* and the old *B[oy's] O[wn]*

P[aper], they were the leading players for boys, and they remained dominant till quite recently. Each of them carries every week a fifteen- or twenty-thousand word school story, complete in itself, but usually more or less connected with the story of the week before. The *Gem* in addition to its school story carries one or more adventure serials. Otherwise the two papers are so much alike that they can be treated as one, though the *Magnet* has always been the better known of the two, probably because it possesses a really first-rate character in the fat boy, Billy Bunter.

The stories are stories of what purports to be public-school life, and the schools (Greyfriars in the *Magnet* and St Jim's in the *Gem*) are represented as ancient and fashionable foundations of the type of Eton or Winchester. All the leading characters are fourth-form boys aged fourteen or fifteen, older or younger boys only appearing in very minor parts. Like Sexton Blake and Nelson Lee, these boys continue week after week and year after year, never growing any older. Very occasionally a new boy arrives or a minor character drops out, but in at any rate the last twenty-five years the personnel has barely altered. All the principal characters in both papers – Bob Cherry, Tom Merry, Harry Wharton, Johnny Bull, Billy Bunter and the rest of them – were at Greyfriars or St Jim's long before the Great War, exactly the same age as at present, having much the same kind of adventures and talking almost exactly the same dialect. And not only the characters but the whole atmosphere of both the *Gem* and *Magnet* has been preserved unchanged, partly by means of very elaborate stylization. The stories in the *Magnet* are signed 'Frank Richards' and those in the *Gem* 'Martin Clifford', but a series lasting thirty years could hardly be the work of the same person every week.[1] Consequently they have to be written in a style that is easily imitated – an extraordinary, artificial, repetitive style, quite different from anything else now existing in English literature. A couple of extracts will do as illustrations. Here is one from the *Magnet*:

> Groan!
> 'Shut up, Bunter!'
> Groan!
> Shutting up was not really in Billy Bunter's line. He seldom shut up, though often requested to do so. On the present awful occasion the fat Owl of Greyfriars was less inclined than ever to shut up. And he did not shut up! He groaned, and groaned, and went on groaning.

1. This is quite incorrect. These stories have been written throughout the whole period by 'Frank Richards' and 'Martin Clifford', who are one and the same person! See articles in *Horizon*, May 1940, and *Summer Pie*, summer 1944. [Author's footnote 1945.]

Even groaning did not fully express Bunter's feeling. His feelings, in fact, were inexpressible.

There were six of them in the soup! Only one of the six uttered sounds of woe and lamentation. But that one, William George Bunter, uttered enough for the whole party and a little over.

Harry Wharton & Co. stood in a wrathy and worried group. They were landed and stranded, diddled, dished and done! etc. etc. etc.

Here is one from the *Gem*:

'Oh cwumbs!'
'Oh gum!'
'Oooogh!'
'Urrggh!'

Arthur Augustus sat up dizzily. He grabbed his handkerchief and pressed it to his damaged nose. Tom Merry sat up, gasping for breath. They looked at one another.

'Bai Jove! This is a go, deah boy!' gurgled Arthur Augustus. 'I have been thwown into a quite a fluttah! Oogh! The wottahs! The wuffians! The fearful outsidahs! Wow!' etc. etc. etc.

Both of these extracts are entirely typical; you would find something like them in almost every chapter of every number, today or twenty-five years ago. The first thing that anyone would notice is the extraordinary amount of tautology (the first of these two passages contains a hundred and twenty-five words and could be compressed into about thirty), seemingly designed to spin out the story, but actually playing its part in creating the atmosphere. For the same reason various facetious expressions are repeated over and over again; 'wrathy', for instance, is a great favourite, and so is 'diddled, dished and done'. 'Oooogh!' 'Grooo!' and 'Yaroo!' (stylized cries of pain) recur constantly, and so does 'Ha! ha! ha!', always given a line to itself, so that sometimes a quarter of a column or thereabouts consists of 'Ha! ha! ha!' The slang ('Go and eat coke!', 'What the thump!', 'You frabjous ass!', etc. etc.) has never been altered, so that the boys are now using slang which is at least thirty years out of date. In addition, the various nicknames are rubbed in on every possible occasion. Every few lines we are reminded that Harry Wharton & Co. are 'the Famous Five', Bunter is always 'the fat Owl' or 'the Owl of the Remove', Vernon-Smith is always 'the Bounder of Greyfriars', Gussy (the Honourable Arthur Augustus D'Arcy) is always 'the swell of St Jim's', and so on and so forth. There is a constant, untiring effort to keep the atmosphere intact and to make sure that every new reader learns immediately who is who. The result has been to make Greyfriars and St Jim's into an extraordinary little world of their own, a world which cannot be taken seriously by anyone over fifteen, but which at any rate is not easily forgotten. By a debasement of the Dickens technique a series of stereotyped 'characters' has been built up, in several cases very successfully. Billy Bunter, for instance, must be one of the best-known figures in English fiction; for the mere number of people who know him he ranks with Sexton Blake, Tarzan, Sherlock Holmes and a handful of characters in Dickens.

Needless to say, these stories are fantastically unlike life at a real public school. They run in cycles of rather differing types, but in general they are the clean-fun, knockabout type of story, with interest centring round horseplay, practical jokes, ragging masters, fights, canings, football, cricket and food. A constantly recurring story is one in which a boy is accused of some misdeed committed by another and is too much of a sportsman to reveal the truth. The 'good' boys are 'good' in the clean-living Englishman tradition – they keep in hard training, wash behind their ears, never hit below the belt, etc. etc. – and by way of contrast there is a series of 'bad' boys, Racke, Crooke, Loder and others, whose badness consists in betting, smoking cigarettes and frequenting public houses. All these boys are constantly on the verge of expulsion, but as it would mean a change of personnel if any boy were actually expelled, no one is ever caught out in any really serious offence. Stealing, for instance, barely enters as a motif. Sex is completely taboo, especially in the form in which it actually arises at public schools. Occasionally girls enter into the stories, and very rarely there is something approaching a mild flirtation, but it is always entirely in the spirit of clean fun. A boy and a girl enjoy going for bicycle rides together – that is all it ever amounts to. Kissing, for instance, would be regarded as 'soppy'. Even the bad boys are presumed to be completely sexless. When the *Gem* and *Magnet* were started, it is probable that there was a deliberate intention to get away from the guilty sex-ridden atmosphere that pervaded so much of the earlier literature for boys. In the nineties the *Boy's Own Paper*, for instance, used to have its correspondence columns full of terrifying warnings against masturbation, and books like *St Winifred's* and *Tom Brown's Schooldays* were heavy with homosexual feeling, though no doubt the authors were not fully aware of it. In the *Gem* and *Magnet* sex simply does not exist as a problem. Religion is also taboo; in the whole thirty years' issue of the two papers the word 'God' probably does not occur, except in 'God save the King'. On the other hand, there has always been a very strong 'temperance' strain.

Drinking and, by association, smoking are regarded as rather disgraceful even in an adult ('shady' is the usual word), but at the same time as something irresistibly fascinating, a sort of substitute for sex. In their moral atmosphere the *Gem* and *Magnet* have a great deal in common with the Boy Scout movement, which started at about the same time.

All literature of this kind is partly plagiarism. Sexton Blake, for instance, started off quite frankly as an imitation of Sherlock Holmes, and still resembles him fairly strongly; he has hawk-like features, lives in Baker Street, smokes enormously and puts on a dressing-gown when he wants to think. The *Gem* and *Magnet* probably owe something to the school story writers who were flourishing when they began, Gunby Hadath, Desmond Coke and the rest, but they owe more to nineteenth-century models. In so far as Greyfriars and St Jim's are like real schools at all, they are much more like Tom Brown's Rugby than a modern public school. Neither school has an O.T.C. for instance, games are not compulsory, and the boys are even allowed to wear what clothes they like. But without doubt the main origin of these papers is *Stalky & Co.* This book has had an immense influence on boys' literature, and it is one of those books which have a sort of traditional reputation among people who have never even seen a copy of it. More than once in boys' weekly papers I have come across a reference to *Stalky & Co.* in which the word was spelt 'Storky'. Even the name of the chief comic among the Greyfriars masters, Mr Prout, is taken from *Stalky & Co.* and so is much of the slang: 'jape', 'merry', 'giddy', 'bizney' (business), 'frajbous', 'don't' for 'doesn't' – all of them out of date even when *Gem* and *Magnet* started. There are also traces of earlier origins. The name 'Greyfriars' is probably taken from Thackeray, and Gosling, the school porter in the *Magnet*, talks in an imitation of Dickens's dialect.

With all this, the supposed 'glamour' of public-school life is played for all it is worth. There is all the usual paraphernalia – lock-up, roll-call, house matches, fagging, prefects, cosy teas round the study fire, etc. etc. – and constant reference to the 'old school', the 'old grey stones' (both schools were founded in the early sixteenth century), the 'team spirit' of the 'Greyfriars men'. As for the snob-appeal, it is completely shameless. Each school has a titled boy or two whose titles are constantly thrust in the reader's face; other boys have the names of well-known aristocratic families, Talbot, Manners, Lowther. We are for ever being reminded that Gussy is the Honourable Arthur A. D'Arcy, son of Lord Eastwood, that Jack Blake is heir to 'broad acres', that Hurree Jamset Ram Singh (nicknamed Inky) is the Nabob of Bhanipur, that Vernon-Smith's father is a millionaire. Till recently the illustrations in both papers always depicted the boys in clothes imitated from those of Eton; in the last few years Greyfriars has changed over to blazers and flannel trousers, but St Jim's still sticks to the Eton jacket, and Gussy sticks to his top-hat. In the school magazine which appears every week as part of the *Magnet*, Harry Wharton writes an article discussing the pocket-money received by the 'fellows in the Remove', and reveals that some of them get as much as five pounds a week! This kind of thing is a perfectly deliberate incitement to wealth-fantasy. And here it is worth noticing a rather curious fact, and that is that the school story is a thing peculiar to England. So far as I know, there are extremely few school stories in foreign languages. The reason, obviously, is that in England education is mainly a matter of status. The most definite dividing line between the petite bourgeoisie and the working class is that the former pay for their education, and within the bourgeoisie there is another unbridgeable gulf between the 'public' school and the 'private' school. It is quite clear that there are tens and scores of thousands of people to whom every detail of life at a 'posh' public school is wildly thrilling and romantic. They happen to be outside that mystic world of quadrangles and house-colours, but they yearn after it, day-dream about it, live mentally in it for hours at a stretch. The question is, Who are these people? Who reads the *Gem* and *Magnet*?

Obviously one can never be quite certain about this kind of thing. All I can say from my own observation is this. Boys who are likely to go to public schools themselves generally read the *Gem* and *Magnet*, but they nearly always stop reading them when they are about twelve; they may continue for another year from force of habit, but by that time they have ceased to take them seriously. On the other hand, the boys at very cheap private schools, the schools that are designed for people who can't afford a public school but consider the council schools 'common', continue reading the *Gem* and *Magnet* for several years longer. A few years ago I was a teacher at two of these schools myself. I found that not only did virtually all the boys read the *Gem* and *Magnet*, but that they were still taking them fairly seriously when they were fifteen or even sixteen. These boys were the sons of shopkeepers, office employees and small business and professional men, and obviously it is this class that the *Gem* and *Magnet* are aimed at. But they are certainly read by working-class boys as well. They are generally on sale in the poorest quarters of big towns, and I have known them to be read by boys whom one might expect to be completely immune from public-school 'glamour'. I have seen a young coal miner, for instance, a lad who had already worked a year or two underground, eagerly reading the *Gem*. Recently I offered a batch of English papers to some British legionaries of the French Foreign Legion in North Africa; they picked out the *Gem* and *Magnet* first. Both papers are much read by girls,[2] and the Pen Pals' department of the *Gem* shows that it is read in every corner of the British Empire, by Australians, Canadians, Palestine Jews, Malays, Arabs, Straits Chinese, etc. etc. The editors evidently expect their readers to be aged round about fourteen, and the advertisements (milk chocolate, postage stamps, water pistols, blushing cured, home conjuring tricks, itching-powder, the Phine Phun Ring which runs a needle into your friend's hand, etc. etc.) indicate roughly the same age; there are also the Admiralty advertisements, however, which call for youths between seventeen and twenty-two. And there is no question that these papers are also read by adults. It is quite common for people to write to the editor and say that they have read every number of the *Gem* or *Magnet* for the past thirty years. Here, for instance, is a letter from a lady in Salisbury:

> I can say of your splendid yarns of Harry Wharton & Co. of Greyfriars, that they never fail to reach a high standard. Without doubt they are the finest stories of their type on the market today, which is saying a good deal. They seem to bring you face to face with Nature. I have taken the *Magnet* from the start, and have followed the adventures of Harry Wharton & Co. with rapt interest. I have no sons, but two daughters, and there's always a rush to be the first to read the grand old paper. My husband, too, was a staunch reader of the *Magnet* until he was suddenly taken away from us.

It is well worth getting hold of some copies of the *Gem* and *Magnet*, especially the *Gem*, simply to have a look at the correspondence columns. What is truly startling is the intense interest with which the pettiest details of life at Greyfriars and St Jim's are followed up. Here, for instance, are a few of the questions sent in by readers:

> 'What age is Dick Roylance?' 'How old is St Jim's?' 'Can you give me a list of the Shell and their studies?' 'How much did D'Arcy's monocle cost?' 'How is it fellows like Crooke are in the Shell and decent fellows like yourself are only in the Fourth?' 'What are the Form captain's three chief duties?' 'Who is the chemistry master at St Jim's?' (From a girl) 'Where is St Jim's situated? *Could* you tell me how to get there, as I would love to see the building? Are you boys just 'phoneys', as I think you are?'

2. There are several corresponding girls' papers. The *Schoolgirl* is companion-paper to the *Magnet* and has stories by 'Hilda Richards'. The characters are interchangeable to some extent. Bessie Bunter, Billy Bunter's sister, figures in the *Schoolgirl*. [Author's footnote.]

It is clear that many of the boys and girls who write these letters are living a complete fantasy-life. Sometimes a boy will write, for instance, give his age, height, weight, chest and biceps measurements and asking which member of the Shell or Fourth Form he most exactly resembles. The demand for a list of the studies on the Shell passage, with an exact account of who lives in each, is a very common one. The editors, of course, do everything in their power to keep up the illusion. In the *Gem* Jack Blake is supposed to write the answers to correspondents, and in the *Magnet* a couple of pages is always given up to the school magazine (the *Greyfriars Herald*, edited by Harry Wharton), and there is another page in which one or other character is written up each week. The stories run in cycles, two or three characters being kept in the foreground for several weeks at a time. First there will be a series of rollicking adventure stories, featuring the Famous Five and Billy Bunter; then a run of stories turning on mistaken identity, with Wibley (the make-up wizard) in the star part; then a run of more serious stories in which Vernon-Smith is trembling on the verge of expulsion. And here one comes upon the real secret of the *Gem* and *Magnet* and the probable reason why they continue to be read in spite of their obvious out-of-dateness.

It is that the characters are so carefully graded as to give almost every type of reader a character he can identify himself with. Most boys' papers aim at doing this, hence the boy-assistant (Sexton Blake's Tinker, Nelson Lee's Nipper, etc.) who usually accompanies the explorer, detective or what-not on his adventures. But in these cases there is only one boy, and usually it is much the same type of boy. In the *Gem* and *Magnet* there is a model for nearly everybody. There is the normal, athletic, high-spirited boy (Tom Merry, Jack Blake, Frank Nugent), a slightly rowdier version of this type (Bob Cherry), a more aristocratic version (Talbot, Manners), a quieter, more serious version (Harry Wharton), and a stolid, 'bulldog' version (Johnny Bull). Then there is the reckless, dare-devil type of boy (Vernon-Smith), the definitely 'clever', studious boy (Mark Linley, Dick Penfold), and the eccentric boy who is not good at games but possesses some special talent (Skinner, Wibley). And there is the scholarship-boy (Tom Redwing), an important figure in this class of story because he makes it possible for boys from very poor homes to project themselves into the public-school atmosphere. In addition there are Australian, Irish, Welsh, Manx, Yorkshire and Lancashire boys to play upon local patriotism. But the subtlety of characterization goes deeper than this. If one studies the correspondence columns one sees that there is probably *no* character in the *Gem* and *Magnet* whom some or other reader does not identify with, except the out-and-out comics, Coker, Billy Bunter, Fisher T. Fish (the money-grubbing American boy) and, of course, the masters. Bunter, though in his origin he probably owed something to the fat boy in *Pickwick*, is a real creation. His tight trousers against which boots and canes are constantly thudding, his astuteness in search of food, his postal order which never turns up, have made him famous wherever the Union Jack waves. But he is not a subject for day-dreams. On the other hand, another seeming figure of fun, Gussy (the Honourable Arthur A. D'Arcy, 'the swell of St Jim's'), is evidently much admired. Like everything else in the *Gem* and *Magnet*, Gussy is at least thirty years out of date. He is the 'knut' of the early twentieth century or even the 'masher' of the nineties ('Bai Jove, deah boy!' and 'Weally, I shall be obliged to give you a feahful thwashin!'), the monocled idiot who made good on the fields of Mons and Le Cateau. And his evident popularity goes to show how deep the snob-appeal of this type is. English people are extremely fond of the titled ass (cf. Lord Peter Wimsey) who always turns up trumps in the moment of emergency. Here is a letter from one of Gussy's girl admirers:

I think you're too hard on Gussy. I wonder he's still in existence, the way you treat him. He's my hero. Did you know I write lyrics? How's this – to the tune of 'Goody Goody'?

Gonna get my gas-mask, join the A.R.P.
'Cos I'm wise to all those bombs you drop on me.
Gonna dig myself a trench
Inside the garden fence;
Gonna seal my windows up with tin
So that the tear gas can't get in;
Gonna park my cannon right outside the kerb
With a note to Adolf Hitler: 'Don't disturb!'
And if I never fall in Nazi hands
That's soon enough for me
Gonna get my gas-mask, join the A.R.P.

P.S. – Do you get on well with girls?

I quote this in full because (dated April 1939) it is interesting as being probably the earliest mention of Hitler in the *Gem*. In the *Gem* there is also a heroic fat boy, Fatty Wynn, as a set-off against Bunter. Vernon-Smith, 'the Bounder of the Remove', a Byronic character, always on the verge of the sack, is another great favourite. And even some of the cads probably have their following. Loder, for instance, 'the rotter of the Sixth', is a cad, but he is also a highbrow and given to saying sarcastic things about football and the team spirit. The boys of the Remove only think him all the more of a cad for this, but a certain type of boy would probably identify with him. Even Racke, Crooke and Co. are probably admired by small boys who think it diabolically wicked to smoke cigarettes. (A frequent question in the correspondence column: 'What brand of cigarettes does Racke smoke?')

Naturally the politics of the *Gem* and *Magnet* are Conservative, but in a completely pre-1914 style, with no Fascist tinge. In reality their basic political assumptions are two: nothing ever changes, and foreigners are funny. In the *Gem* of 1939 Frenchmen are still Froggies and Italians are still Dagoes. Mossoo, the French master at Greyfriars, is the usual comic-paper Frog, with pointed beard, pegtop trousers, etc. Inky, the Indian boy, though a rajah, and therefore possessing snob-appeal, is also the comic babu of the *Punch* tradition. ("The rowfulness is not the proper caper, my esteemed Bob," said Inky. "Let dogs delight in the barkfulness and bitefulness, but the soft answer is the cracked pitcher that goes longest to a bird in the bush, as the English proverb remarks.") Fisher T. Fish is the old-style stage Yankee ("Waal, I guess," etc.) dating from a period of Anglo-American jealousy. Wun Lung, the Chinese boy (he has rather faded out of late, no doubt because some of the *Magnet's* readers are Straits Chinese), is the nineteenth-century pantomime Chinaman, with saucer-shaped hat, pigtail and pidgin-English. The assumption all along is not only that foreigners are comics who are put there for us to laugh at, but that they can be classified in much the same way as insects. That is why in all boys' papers, not only the *Gem* and *Magnet*, a Chinese is invariably portrayed with a pigtail. It is the thing you recognize him by, like the Frenchman's beard or the Italian's barrel-organ. In papers of this kind it occasionally happens that when the setting of a story is in a foreign country some attempt is made to describe the natives as individual human beings, but as a rule it is assumed that foreigners of any one race are all alike and will conform more or less exactly to the following patterns:

FRENCHMAN: Excitable. Wears beard, gesticulates wildly.
SPANIARD, MEXICAN etc.: Sinister, treacherous.
ARAB, AFGHAN etc.: Sinister, treacherous.
CHINESE: Sinister, treacherous. wears pigtails.
ITALIAN: Excitable. Grinds barrel-organ or carries stiletto.
SWEDE, DANE etc.: Kind-hearted, stupid.
NEGRO: Comic, very faithful.

The working classes only enter into the *Gem* and *Magnet* as comics or semi-villains (race-course touts etc.). As for class-friction, trade unionism, strikes, slumps, unemployment, Fascism and civil war – not a mention. Somewhere or other in the thirty years' issue of the two papers you might perhaps find the word 'Socialism', but you would have to look a long time for it. If the Russian Revolution is anywhere referred to, it will be indirectly, in the word 'Bolshy' (meaning a person of violent disagreeable habits). Hitler and the Nazis are just beginning to make their appearance, in the sort of reference I quoted above. The war crisis of September 1938 made just enough impression to produce a story in which Mr Vernon-Smith, the Bounder's millionaire father, cashed in on the general panic by buying up country houses in order to sell them to 'crisis scuttlers'. But that is probably as near to noticing the European situation as the *Gem* and *Magnet* will come, until the war actually starts.[3] That does not mean these papers are unpatriotic – quite the contrary! Throughout the Great War the *Gem* and *Magnet* were perhaps the most consistently and cheerfully patriotic papers in England. Almost every week the boys caught a spy or pushed a conchy into the army, and during the rationing period 'EAT LESS BREAD' was printed in large type on every page. But their patriotism has nothing whatever to do with power politics or 'ideological' warfare. It is more akin to family loyalty, and actually it gives one a valuable clue to the attitude of ordinary people, especially the huge untouchable block of the middle class and the better-off working class. These people are patriotic to the middle of their bones, but they do not feel that what happens in foreign countries is any of their business. When England is in danger they rally to its defence as a matter of course, but in between times they are not interested. After all, England is always in the right and England always wins, so why worry? It is an attitude that has been shaken during the past twenty years, but not so deeply as is sometimes supposed. Failure to understand it is one of the reasons why left-wing political parties are seldom able to produce an acceptable foreign policy.

The mental world of the *Gem* and *Magnet*, therefore, is something like this:

The year is 1910 – or 1940, but it is all the same. You are at Greyfriars, a rosy-cheeked boy of fourteen in posh, tailor-made clothes, sitting down to tea in your study on the Remove passage after an exciting game of football which was won by an odd goal in the last half-minute. There is a cosy fire in the study, and outside the wind is whistling. The ivy clusters thickly round the old grey stones. The King is on his throne and the

3. This was written some months before the outbreak of war. Up to the end of September 1939 no mention of the war has appeared in either paper. [Author's footnote.]

pound is worth a pound. Over in Europe the comic foreigners are jabbering and gesticulating, but the grim grey battleships of the British Fleet are steaming up the Channel and at the outposts of Empire the monocled Englishmen are holding the niggers at bay. Lord Mauleverer has just got another fiver and we are all settling down to a tremendous tea of sausages, sardines, crumpets, potted meat, jam and doughnuts. After tea we shall sit round the study fire having a good laugh at Billy Bunter and discussing the team for next week's match against Rookwood. Everything is safe, solid and unquestionable. Everything will be the same for ever and ever. That approximately is the atmosphere.

But now turn from the *Gem* and *Magnet* to the more up-to-date papers which have appeared since the Great War. The truly significant thing is that they have more points of resemblance to the *Gem* and *Magnet* than points of difference. But it is better to consider the differences first.

There are eight of these newer papers, the *Modern Boy*, *Triumph*, *Champion*, *Wizard*, *Rover*, *Skipper*, *Hotspur* and *Adventure*. All of these have appeared since the Great War, but except for the *Modern Boy* none of them is less than five years old. Two papers which ought also to be mentioned briefly here, though they are not strictly in the same class as the rest, are the *Detective Weekly* and the *Thriller*, both owned by the Amalgamated Press. The *Detective Weekly* has taken over Sexton Blake. Both of these papers admit a certain amount of sex-interest into their stories, and though certainly read by boys, they are not aimed at them exclusively. All the others are boys' papers pure and simple, and they are sufficiently alike to be considered together. There does not seem to be any notable difference between Thomson's publications and those of the Amalgamated Press.

As soon as one looks at these papers one sees their technical superiority to the *Gem* and *Magnet*. To begin with, they have the great advantage of not being written entirely by one person. Instead of one long complete story, a number of the *Wizard* or *Hotspur* consists of half a dozen or more serials, none of which goes on for ever. Consequently there is far more variety and far less padding, and none of the tiresome stylization and facetiousness of the *Gem* and *Magnet*. Look at these two extracts, for example:

Billy Bunter groaned.

A quarter of an hour had elapsed out of the two hours that Bunter was booked for extra French.

In a quarter of an hour there were only fifteen minutes! But every one of those minutes seemed inordinately long to Bunter. They seemed to crawl by like tired snails.

Looking at the clock in Class-room No. 10 the fat Owl could hardly believe that only fifteen minutes had passed. It seemed more like fifteen hours, if not fifteen days!

Other fellows were in extra French as well as Bunter. They did not matter. Bunter did! (*Magnet*.)

After a terrible climb, hacking out handholds in the smooth ice every step of the way up, Sergeant Lionheart Logan of the Mounties was now clinging like a human fly to the face of an icy cliff, as smooth and treacherous as a giant pane of glass.

An Arctic blizzard, in all its fury was buffeting his body, driving the blinding snow into his face, seeking to tear his fingers loose from their handholds and dash him to death on the jagged boulders which lay at the foot of the cliff a hundred feet below.

Crouching among those boulders were eleven villainous trappers who had done their best to shoot down Lionheart and his companion, Constable Jim Rogers – until the blizzard had blotted the two Mounties out of sight from below. (*Wizard*.)

The second extract gets you some distance with the story, the first takes a hundred words to tell you that Bunter is in the detention class. Moreover, by not concentrating on school stories (in point of numbers the school story slightly predominates in all these papers, except the *Thriller* and *Detective Weekly*), the *Wizard*, *Hotspur*, etc. have far greater opportunities for sensationalism. Merely looking at the cover illustrations of the papers which I have on the table in front of me, here are some of the things I see. On one a cowboy is clinging by his toes to the wing of an aeroplane in mid-air and shooting down another aeroplane with his revolver. On another a Chinese is swimming for his life down a sewer with a swarm of ravenous-looking rats swimming after him. On another an engineer is lighting a stick of dynamite while a steel robot feels for him with its claws. On another a man in airman's costume is fighting bare-handed against a rat somewhat larger than a donkey. On another a nearly naked man of terrific muscular development has just seized a lion by the tail and flung it thirty yards over the wall of an arena, with the words, 'Take back your blooming lion!' Clearly no school story can compete with this kind of thing. From time to time the school buildings may catch fire or the French master may turn out to be the head of an international anarchist gang, but in a general way the interest must centre round cricket, school rivalries, practical jokes, etc. There is not much room for bombs, death-rays, sub-machine-guns, aeroplanes, mustangs, octopuses, grizzly bears or gangsters.

Examination of a large number of these papers shows that, putting aside school stories, the favourite subjects are Wild West, Frozen North, Foreign Legion, crime (always from the detective's angle), the Great War (Air Force or Secret Service, not the infantry), the Tarzan motif in varying forms, professional football, tropical exploration, historical romance (Robin Hood, Cavaliers and Roundheads, etc.) and scientific invention. The Wild West still leads, at any rate as a setting, though the Red Indian seems to be fading out. The one theme that is really new is the scientific one. Death-rays, Martians, invisible men, robots, helicopters and interplanetary rockets figure largely; here and there there are even far-off rumours of psychotherapy and ductless glands. Whereas the *Gem* and *Magnet* derive from Dickens and Kipling, the *Wizard*, *Champion*, *Modern Boy*, etc. owe a great deal to H. G. Wells, who, rather than Jules Verne, is the father of 'Scientifiction'. Naturally, it is the magical, Martian aspect of science that is most exploited, but one or two papers include serious articles on scientific subjects, besides quantities of informative snippets. (Examples: 'A Kauri tree in Queensland, Australia, is over 12,000 years old'; 'Nearly 50,000 thunderstorms occur every day'; 'Helium gas costs £1 per 1,000 cubic feet'; 'There are over 500 varieties of spiders in Great Britain'; 'London firemen use 14,000,000 gallons of water annually', etc. etc.) There is a marked advance in intellectual curiosity and, on the whole, in the demand made on the reader's attention. In practice the *Gem* and *Magnet* and the post-war papers are read by much the same public, but the mental age aimed at seems to have risen by a year or two years – an improvement probably corresponding to the improvement in elementary education since 1909.

The other thing that has emerged in the post-war boys' papers, though not to anything like the extent one would expect, is bully-worship and the cult of violence.

If one compares the *Gem* and *Magnet* with a genuinely modern paper, the thing that immediately strikes one is the absence of the leader-principle. There is no central dominating character; instead there are fifteen or twenty characters, all more or less on an equality, with whom readers of different types can identify. In the more modern papers this is not usually the case. Instead of identifying with a schoolboy of more or less his own age, the reader of the *Skipper*, *Hotspur*, etc. is led to identify with a G-man, with a Foreign Legionary, with some variant of Tarzan, with an air ace, a master spy, an explorer, a pugilist – at any rate with some single all-powerful character who dominates everyone about him and whose usual method of solving any problem is a sock on the jaw.

This character is intended as a superman, and as physical strength is the form of power that boys can best understand, he is usually a sort of human gorilla; in the Tarzan type of story he is sometimes actually a giant, eight or ten feet high. At the same time the scenes of violence in nearly all these stories are remarkably harmless and unconvincing. There is a great difference in tone between even the most bloodthirsty English paper and the threepenny Yank Mags, *Fight Stories*, *Action Stories*, etc. (not strictly boys' papers, but largely read by boys). In the Yank Mags you get real blood-lust, really gory descriptions of the all-in, jump-on-his-testicles style of fighting, written in a jargon that has been perfected by people who brood endlessly on violence. A paper like *Fight Stories*, for instance, would have very little appeal except to sadists and masochists. You can see the comparative gentleness of English civilization by the amateurish way in which prize-fighting is always described in the boys' weeklies. There is no specialized vocabulary. Look at these four extracts, two English, two American:

> When the gong sounded, both men were breathing heavily, and each had great red marks on his chest, Bill's chin was bleeding, and Ben had a cut over his right eye.
>
> Into their corners they sank, but when the gong clanged again they were up swiftly, and they went like tigers at each other. (*Rover*.)

> He walked in stolidly and smashed a clublike right to my face. Blood spattered and I went back on my heels, but surged in and ripped my right under his heart. Another right smashed full on Sven's already battered mouth, and, spitting out the fragments of a tooth, he crashed a flailing left to my body. (*Fight Stories*.)

> It was amazing to watch the black Panther at work. His muscles rippled and slid under his dark skin. There was all the power and grace of a giant cat in his swift and terrible onslaught.
>
> He volleyed blows with a bewildering speed for so huge a fellow. In a moment Ben was simply blocking with his gloves as well as he could. Ben was really a past-master of defence. He had many fine victories behind him. But the Negro's rights and lefts crashed through openings that hardly any other fighter could have found. (*Wizard*.)

> Haymakers which packed the bludgeoning weight of forest monarchs crashing down under the ax hurled into the bodies of the two heavies as they swapped punches. (*Fight Stories*.)

Notice how much more knowledgeable the American extracts sound. They are written for devotees of the prize-ring, the others are not. Also, it ought to be emphasized that on its level the moral code of the English boys' papers is a decent one. Crime and dishonesty are never held up to admiration, there is none of the cynicism and corruption of the American gangster story. The huge sale of the Yank Mags in England shows that there is a demand for that kind of thing, but very few English writers seem able to produce it. When hatred of Hitler became a major emotion in America, it was interesting to see how promptly 'anti-Fascism' was adapted to pornographic purposes by the editors of the Yank Mags. One magazine which I have in front of me is given up to a long, complete story, 'When Hell Came to America', in which the agents of a 'blood-maddened European dictator' are trying to conquer the U.S.A. with death-rays and invisible aeroplanes. There is the frankest appeal to sadism, scenes in which the Nazis tie bombs to women's backs and fling them off heights to watch them blown to pieces in mid-air, others in which they tie naked girls together by their hair and prod them with knives to make them dance, etc. etc. The editor comments solemnly on all this, and uses it as a plea for tightening up restrictions against immigrants. On another page of the same paper: 'LIVES OF THE HOTCHA CHORUS GIRLS. Reveals all the intimate secrets and fascinating pastimes of the famous Broadway Hotcha girls. NOTHING IS OMITTED. Price 10c.' 'HOW TO LOVE. 10c.' 'FRENCH PHOTO RING, 25c.' 'NAUGHTY NUDIES TRANSFERS. From the outside of the glass you see a beautiful girl, innocently dressed. Turn it around and look through the glass and oh! what a difference! Set of 3 transfers 25c.' etc. etc. etc. There is nothing at all like this in any English paper likely to be read by boys. But the process of Americanization is going on all the same. The American ideal, the 'he-man', the 'tough guy', the gorilla who puts everything right by socking everybody else on the jaw, now figures in probably a majority of boys' papers. In one serial now running in the *Skipper* he is always portrayed, ominously enough, swinging a rubber truncheon.

The development of the *Wizard*, *Hotspur*, etc., as against the earlier boys' papers, boils down to this: better technique, more scientific interest, more bloodshed, more leader-worship. But, after all, it is the *lack* of development that is the really striking thing.

To begin with, there is no political development whatever. The world of the *Skipper* and the *Champion* is still the pre-1914 world of the *Magnet* and the *Gem*. The Wild West story, for instance, with its cattle-rustlers, lynch-law and other paraphernalia belonging to the eighties, is a curiously archaic thing. It is worth noticing that in papers of this type it is always taken for granted that adventures only happen at the ends of the earth, in tropical forests, in Arctic wastes, in African deserts, on Western prairies, in Chinese opium dens – everywhere, in fact, except the place where things really *do* happen. That is a belief dating from thirty or forty years ago, when the new continents were in process of being opened up. Nowadays, of course, if you really want adventure, the place to look for it is in Europe. But apart from the picturesque side of the Great War, contemporary history is carefully excluded. And except that Americans are now admired instead of being laughed at, foreigners are exactly the same figures of fun that they always were. If a Chinese character appears, he is still the sinister pigtailed opium-smuggler of Sax Rohmer; no indication that things have been happening in China since 1912 – no indication that a war is going on there, for instance. If a Spaniard appears, he is still a 'dago' or a 'greaser' who rolls cigarettes and stabs people in the back; no indication that things have been happening in Spain. Hitler and the Nazis have not yet appeared, or are barely making their appearance. There will be plenty about them in a little while, but it will be from a strictly patriotic angle (Britain versus Germany), with the real meaning of the struggle kept out of sight as much as possible. As for the Russian Revolution, it is extremely difficult to find any reference to it in any of these papers. When Russia is mentioned at all it is usually in an information snippet (example: 'There are 29,000 centenarians in the U.S.S.R.'), and any reference to the Revolution is indirect and twenty years out of date. In one story in the *Rover*, for instance, somebody has a tame bear, and as it is a Russian bear, it is nicknamed Trotsky – obviously an echo of the 1917–23 period and not of recent controversies. The clock has stopped at 1910. Britannia rules the waves, and no one has heard of slumps, booms, unemployment, dictatorships, purges or concentration camps.

And in social outlook there is hardly any advance. The snobbishness is somewhat less open than in the *Gem* and *Magnet* – that is the most one can possibly say. To begin with, the school story, always partly dependent on snob-appeal, is by no means eliminated. Every number of a boys' paper includes at least one school story, these stories slightly outnumbering the Wild Westerns. The very elaborate fantasy-life of the *Gem* and *Magnet* is not imitated and there is more emphasis on extraneous adventure, but the social atmosphere (old grey stones) is much the same. When a new school is introduced at the beginning of a story we are often told in just about those words that 'it was a very posh school'. From time to time a story appears which is ostensibly directed *against* snobbery. The scholarship-boy (cf. Tom Redwing in the *Magnet*) makes fairly frequent appearances, and what is essentially the same theme is sometimes presented in this form; there is great rivalry between two schools, one of which considers itself more 'posh' than the other, and there are fights, practical jokes, football matches, etc. always ending in the discomfiture of the snobs. If one glances very superficially at some of these stories it is possible to imagine that a democratic spirit has crept into the boys' weeklies, but when one looks more closely one sees that they merely reflected the bitter jealousies that exist within the white-collar class. Their real function is to allow the boy who goes to a cheap private school (*not* a Council school) to feel that his school is just as 'posh' in the sight of God as Winchester or Eton. The sentiment of school loyalty ('We're better than the fellows down the road'), a thing almost unknown to the real working class, is still kept up. As these stories are written by many different hands, they do, of course, vary a good deal in tone. Some are reasonably free from snobbishness, in others money and pedigree are exploited even more shamelessly than in the *Gem* and *Magnet*. In one that I came across an actual *majority* of the boys mentioned were titled.

Where working-class characters appear, it is usually either as comics (jokes about tramps, convicts, etc.) or as prize-fighters, acrobats, cowboys, professional footballers and Foreign Legionaries – in other words, as adventurers. There is no facing of the facts about working-class life, or, indeed, about *working* life of any description. Very occasionally one may come across a realistic description of, say, work in a coal mine, but in all probability it will only be there as the background of some lurid adventure. In any case the central character is not likely to be a coal-miner. Nearly all the time the boy who reads these papers – in nine cases out of ten a boy who is going to spend his life working in a shop, in a factory or in some subordinate job in an office – is led to identify with people in positions of command, above all with people who are never troubled by shortage of money. The Lord Peter Wimsey figure, the seeming idiot who drawls and wears a monocle but is always to the fore in moments of danger, turns up over and over again. (This character is a great favourite in Secret Service stories.) And, as usual, the heroic characters all have to talk B.B.C.; they may talk Scottish or Irish or American, but no one in a star part is ever permitted to drop an aitch. Here it is worth comparing the social atmosphere of the boys' weeklies with that of the women's weeklies, the *Oracle*, the *Family Star*, *Peg's Paper*, etc.

The women's papers are aimed at an older public and are read for the most part by girls who are working for a living. Consequently they are on the surface much more realistic. It is taken for granted, for example, that nearly everyone has to live in a big town and work at a more or less dull job. Sex, so far from being taboo, is *the* subject. The short, complete stories, the special feature of these papers, are generally of the 'came the dawn' type: the heroine narrowly escapes losing her 'boy' to a designing rival, or the 'boy' loses his job and has to postpone marriage, but presently gets a better job. The changeling-fantasy (a girl brought up in a poor home is 'really' the child of rich parents) is another favourite. Where sensationalism comes in, usually in the serials, it arises out of the more domestic type of crime, such as bigamy, forgery or sometimes murder; no Martians, death-rays or international anarchist gangs. These papers are at any rate aiming at credibility, and they have a link with real life in their correspondence columns, where genuine problems are being discussed. Ruby M. Ayres's column of advice in the *Oracle*, for instance, is extremely sensible and well written. And yet the world of the *Oracle* and *Peg's Paper* is a pure fantasy-world. It is the same fantasy all the time, pretending to be richer than you are. The chief impression that one carries away from almost every story in these papers is of frightful, overwhelming 'refinement'. Ostensibly the characters are working-class people, but their habits, the interiors of their houses, their clothes, their outlook and, above all, their speech are entirely middle class. They are all living at several pounds a week above their income. And needless to say, that is just the impression that is intended. The idea is to give the bored factory-girl or worn-out mother of five a dream-life in which she pictures herself – not actually as a duchess (that convention has gone out) but as, say, the wife of a bank-manager. Not only is a five-to-six-pound-a-week standard of life set up as the ideal, it is tacitly assumed that that is how working-class people really *do* live. The major facts are simply not faced. It is admitted, for instance, that people sometimes lose their jobs; but then the dark clouds roll away and they get better jobs instead. No mention of unemployment as sometimes permanent and inevitable, no mention of the dole, no mention of trade unionism. No suggestion anywhere that there can be anything wrong with the system *as a system*; there are only individual misfortunes, which are generally due to somebody's wickedness and can in any case be put right in the last chapter. Always the dark clouds roll away, the kind employer raises Alfred's wages, and there are jobs for everybody except the drunks. It is still the world of the *Wizard* and the *Gem*, except that there are orange-blossoms instead of machine-guns.

The outlook inculcated by all these papers is that of a rather exceptionally stupid member of the Navy League in the year 1910. Yes, it may be said, but what does it matter? And in any case, what else do you expect?

Of course no one in his senses would want to turn the so-called penny dreadful into a realistic novel or a Socialist tract. An adventure story must of its nature be more or less remote from real life. But, as I have tried to make clear, the unreality of the *Wizard* and the *Gem* is not so artless as it looks. These papers exist because of a specialized demand, because boys at certain ages find it necessary to read about Martians, death-rays, grizzly bears and gangsters. They get what they are looking for, but they get it wrapped up in the illusions which their future employers think suitable for them. To what extent people draw their ideas from fiction is disputable. Personally I believe that most people are influenced far more than they would care to admit by novels, serial stories, films and so forth, and that from this point of view the worst books are often the most important, because they are usually the ones that are read earliest in life. It is probable that many people who could consider themselves extemely sophisticated and 'advanced' are actually carrying through life an imaginative background which they acquired in childhood from (for instance) Sapper and Ian Hay. If that is so, the boys' twopenny weeklies are of the deepest importance. Here is the stuff that is read somewhere between the ages of twelve and eighteen by a very large proportion, perhaps an actual majority, of English boys, including many who will never read anything else except newspapers; and along with it they are absorbing a set of beliefs which would be regarded as hopelessly out of date in the Central Office of the Conservative Party. All the better because it is done indirectly, there is being pumped into them the conviction that the major problems of our time do not exist, that there is nothing wrong with *laissez-faire* capitalism, that foreigners are unimportant comics and that the British Empire is a sort of charity-concern which will last for ever. Considering who owns these papers, it is difficult to believe that this is unintentional. Of the twelve papers I have been discussing (i.e. twelve including the *Thriller* and *Detective Weekly*) seven are the property of the Amalgamated Press, which is one of the biggest press-combines in the world and controls more than a hundred different papers. The *Gem* and *Magnet*, therefore, are closely linked up with the *Daily Telegraph* and the *Financial Times*. This in itself would be enough to rouse certain suspicions, even if it were not obvious that the stories in the boys' weeklies are politically vetted. So it appears that if you feel the need of a fantasy-life in which you travel to Mars and fight lions bare-handed (and what boy doesn't?) you can only have it by delivering yourself over, mentally, to people like Lord Camrose. For there is no competition. Throughout the whole of this run of papers the differences are negligible, and on this level no others exist. This raises the question, why is there no such thing as a left-wing boys' paper?

At first glance such an idea merely makes one slightly sick. It is so horribly easy to imagine what a left-wing boys' paper would be like, if it existed. I remember in 1920 or 1921 some optimistic person handing round Communist tracts among a crowd of public-school boys. The tract I received was of the question-and-answer kind:

Q. 'Can a Boy Communist be a Boy Scout, Comrade?'
A. 'No, Comrade.'
Q. 'Why, Comrade?'
A. 'Because, Comrade, a Boy Scout must salute the Union Jack, which is the symbol of tyranny and oppression,' etc. etc.

Now, suppose that at this moment somebody started a left-wing paper deliberately aimed at boys of twelve or fourteen. I do not suggest that the whole of its contents would be exactly like the tract I have quoted above, but does anyone doubt that they would be *something* like it? Inevitably such a paper would either consist of dreary uplift or it would be under Communist influence and given over to adulation of Soviet Russia; in either case no normal boy would ever look at it. Highbrow literature apart, the whole of the existing left-wing press, in so far as it is at all vigorously 'left', is one long tract. The one Socialist paper in England which could live a week on its merits *as a paper* is the *Daily Herald*, and how much Socialism is there in the *Daily Herald*? At this moment, therefore, a paper with a 'left' slant and at the same time likely to have an appeal to ordinary boys in their teens is something almost beyond hoping for.

But it does not follow that it is impossible. There is no clear reason why every adventure story should necessarily be mixed up with snobbishness and gutter patriotism. For, after all, the stories in the *Hotspur* and the *Modern Boy* are not Conservative tracts; they are merely adventure stories with a Conservative bias. It is fairly easy to imagine the process being reversed. It is possible, for instance, to imagine a paper as thrilling and lively as the *Hotspur*, but with subject-matter and 'ideology' a little more up to date. It is even possible (though this raises other difficulties) to imagine a women's paper at the same literary level as the *Oracle*, dealing in approximately the same kind of story, but taking rather more account of the realities of working-class life. Such things have been done before, though not in England. In the last years of the Spanish monarchy there was a large output in Spain of left-wing novelettes, some of them evidently of Anarchist origin. Unfortunately at the time when they were appearing I did not see their social significance, and I lost the collection of them that I had, but no doubt copies would still be procurable. In get-up and style of story they were very similar to the English fourpenny novelette, except that their inspiration was 'left'. If, for instance, a story described police pursuing Anarchists through the mountains, it would be from the point of view of the Anarchists and not of the police. An example nearer to hand is the Soviet film *Chapayev*, which has been shown a number of times in London. Technically, by the standards of the time when it was made, *Chapayev* is a first-rate film, but mentally, in spite of the unfamiliar Russian background, it is not so very remote from Hollywood. The one thing that lifts it out of the ordinary is the remarkable performance by the actor who takes the part of the White officer (the fat one) – a performance which looks very like an inspired piece of gagging. Otherwise the atmosphere is familiar. All the usual paraphernalia is there – heroic fight against odds, escape at the last moment, shots of galloping horses, love interest, comic relief. The film is in fact a fairly ordinary one, except that its tendency is 'left'. In a Hollywood film of the Russian Civil War the Whites would probably be angels and the Reds demons. In the Russian version the Reds are angels and the Whites demons. That also is a lie, but, taking the long view, it is a less pernicious lie than the other.

Here several difficult problems present themselves. Their general nature is obvious enough, and I do not want to discuss them. I am merely pointing to the fact that, in England, popular imaginative literature is a field that left-wing thought has never begun to enter. *All* fiction from the novels in the mushroom libraries downwards is censored in the interests of the ruling class. And boys' fiction above all, the blood-and-thunder stuff which nearly every boy devours at some time or other, is sodden in the worst illusions of 1910. The fact is only unimportant if one believes that what is read in childhood leaves no impression behind. Lord Camrose and his colleagues evidently believe nothing of the kind, and, after all, Lord Camrose ought to know.

Written 1939

Horizon, March 1940 (abridged); *I.T.W.*; (slightly revised) *Cr.E.*; *D.D.*; *C.E.*

9. Inside the Whale

I

When Henry Miller's novel, *Tropic of Cancer*, appeared in 1935, it was greeted with rather cautious praise, obviously conditioned in some cases by a fear of seeming to enjoy pornography. Among the people who praised it were T. S. Eliot, Herbert Read, Aldous Huxley, John dos Passos, Ezra Pound – on the whole, not the writers that are in fashion at this moment. And in fact the subject-matter of the book, and to a certain extent its mental atmosphere, belong to the twenties rather than to the thirties.

Tropic of Cancer is a novel in the first person, or autobiography in the form of a novel, whichever way you like to look at it. Miller himself insists that it is straight autobiography, but the tempo and method of telling the story are those of a novel. It is a story of the American Paris, but not along the usual lines, because the Americans who figure in it happen to be people without money. During the boom years, when dollars were plentiful and the exchange-value of the franc was low, Paris was invaded by such a swarm of artists, writers, students, dilettanti, sight-seers, debauchees and plain idlers as the world has probably never seen. In some quarters of the town the so-called artists must actually have outnumbered the working population – indeed, it has been reckoned that in the late twenties there were as many as 30,000 painters in Paris, most of them impostors. The populace had grown so hardened to artists that gruff-voiced lesbians in corduroy breeches and young men in Grecian or medieval costume could walk the streets without attracting a glance, and along the Seine banks by Notre Dame it was almost impossible to pick one's way between the sketching-stools. It was the age of dark horses and neglected genii; the phrase on everybody's lips was '*Quand je serai lancé*'. As it turned out, nobody was *lancé*, the slump descended like another Ice Age, the cosmopolitan mob of artists vanished, and the huge Montparnasse cafés which only ten years ago were filled till the small hours by hordes of shrieking poseurs have turned into darkened tombs in which there are not even any ghosts. It is this world – described in, among other novels, Wyndham Lewis's *Tarr* – that Miller is writing about, but he is dealing only with the under side of it, the lumpenproletarian fringe which has been able to survive the slump because it is composed partly of genuine artists and partly of genuine scoundrels. The neglected genii, the paranoiacs who are always 'going to' write the novel that will knock Proust into a cocked hat, are there, but they are only genii in the rather rare moments when they are not scouting about for the next meal. For the most part it is a story of bug-ridden rooms in working-men's hotels, of fights, drinking bouts, cheap brothels, Russian refugees, cadging, swindling and temporary jobs. And the whole atmosphere of the poor quarters of Paris as a foreigner sees them – the cobbled alleys, the sour reek of refuse, the bistros with their greasy zinc counters and worn brick floors, the green waters of the Seine, the blue cloaks of the Republican Guard, the crumbling iron urinals, the peculiar sweetish smell of the Métro stations, the cigarettes that come to pieces, the pigeons in the Luxembourg Gardens – it is all there, or at any rate the feeling of it is there.

On the face of it no material could be less promising. When *Tropic of Cancer* was published the Italians were marching into Abyssinia and Hitler's concentration camps were already bulging. The intellectual foci of the world were Rome, Moscow and Berlin. It did not seem to be a moment at which a novel of outstanding value was likely to be written about American dead-beats cadging drinks in the Latin Quarter. Of course a novelist is not obliged to write directly about contemporary history, but a novelist who simply disregards the major public events of the moment is generally either a footler or a plain idiot. From a mere account of the subject-matter of *Tropic of Cancer* most people would probably assume it to be no more than a bit of naughty-naughty left over from the twenties. Actually, nearly everyone who read it saw at once that it was nothing of the kind, but a very remarkable book. How or why remarkable? That question is never easy to answer. It is better to begin by describing the impression that *Tropic of Cancer* has left on my own mind.

When I first opened *Tropic of Cancer* and saw that it was full of unprintable words, my immediate reaction was a refusal to be impressed. Most people's would be the same, I believe. Nevertheless, after a lapse of time the atmosphere of the book, besides innumerable details, seemed to linger in my memory in a peculiar way. A year later Miller's second book, *Black Spring*, was published. By this time *Tropic of Cancer* was much more vividly present in my mind than it had been when I first read it. My first feeling about *Black Spring* was that it showed a falling-off, and it is a fact that it has not the same unity as the other book. Yet after another year there were many passages in *Black Spring* that had also rooted themselves in my memory. Evidently these books are of the sort to leave a flavour behind them – books that 'create a world of their own', as the saying goes. The books that do this are not necessarily good books, they may be good bad books like *Raffles* or the *Sherlock Holmes* stories, or perverse and morbid books like *Wuthering Heights* or *The House with the Green Shutters*. But now and again there appears a novel which opens up a new world not by revealing what is strange, but by revealing what is familiar. The truly remarkable thing about *Ulysses*, for instance, is the commonplaceness of its material. Of course there is much more in *Ulysses* than this, because Joyce is a kind of poet and also an elephantine pedant, but his real achievement has been to get the familiar on to paper. He dared – for it is a matter of *daring* just as much as of technique – to expose the imbecilities of the inner mind, and in doing so he discovered an America which was under everybody's nose. Here is a whole world of stuff which you have lived with since childhood, stuff which you supposed to be of its nature incommunicable, and somebody has managed to communicate it. The effect is to break down, at any rate momentarily, the solitude in which the human being lives. When you read certain passages in *Ulysses* you feel that Joyce's mind and your mind are one, that he knows all about you though he has never heard your name, that there exists some world outside time and space in which you and he are together. And though he does not resemble Joyce in other ways, there is a touch of this quality in Henry Miller. Not everywhere, because his work is very uneven, and sometimes, especially in *Black Spring*, tends to slide away into mere verbiage or into the squashy universe of the Surrealists. But read him for five pages, ten pages, and you feel the peculiar relief that comes not so much from understanding as from *being understood*. 'He knows all about me,' you feel; 'he wrote this specially for me.' It is as though you could hear a voice speaking to you, a friendly American voice, with no humbug in it, no moral purpose, merely an implicit assumption that we are all alike. For the moment you have got away from the lies and simplifications, the stylized, marionette-like quality of ordinary fiction, even quite good fiction, and are dealing with recognizable experiences of human beings.

But what kind of experience? What kind of human beings? Miller is writing about the man in the street, and it is incidentally rather a pity that it should be a street full of brothels. That is the penalty of leaving your native land. It means transferring your roots into shallower soil. Exile is probably more damaging to a novelist than to a painter or even a poet, because its effect is to take him out of contact with working life and narrow down his range to the street, the café, the church, the brothel and the studio. On the whole, in Miller's books you are reading about people living the expatriate life, people drinking, talking, meditating and fornicating, not about people working, marrying and bringing up children; a pity, because he would have described the one set of activities as well as the other. In *Black Spring* there is a wonderful flashback of New York, the swarming Irish-infested New York of the O. Henry period, but the Paris scenes are the best, and, granted their utter worthlessness as social types, the drunks and dead-beats of the cafés are handled with a feeling for character and a mastery of technique that are unapproached in any at all recent novel. All of them are not only credible but completely familiar; you have the feeling that all their adventures have happened to yourself. Not that they are anything very startling in the way of adventures. Henry gets a job with a melancholy Indian student, gets another job at a dreadful French school during a cold snap when the lavatories are frozen solid, goes on drinking bouts in Le Havre with his friend Collins, the sea captain, goes to brothels where there are wonderful Negresses, talks with his friend Van Norden, the novelist, who has got the great novel of the world in his head but can never bring himself to begin writing it. His friend Karl, on the verge of starvation, is picked up by a wealthy widow who wishes to marry him. There are interminable, Hamlet-like conversations in which Karl tries to decide which is worse, being hungry or sleeping with an old woman. In great detail he describes his visits to the widow, how he went to the hotel dressed in his best, how before going in he neglected to urinate, so that the whole evening was one long crescendo of torment, etc. etc. And after all, none of it is true, the widow doesn't even exist – Karl has simply invented her in order to make himself seem important. The whole book is in this vein, more or less. Why is it that these monstrous trivialities are so engrossing? Simply because the whole atmosphere is deeply familiar, because you have all the while the feeling that these things are happening to *you*. And you have this feeling because somebody has chosen to drop the Geneva language of the ordinary novel and drag the *real-politik* of the inner mind into the open. In Miller's case it is not so much a question of exploring the mechanisms of the mind as of owning up to everyday facts and everyday emotions. For the truth is that many ordinary people, perhaps an actual majority, do speak and behave in just the way that is recorded here. The callous coarseness with which the characters in *Tropic of Cancer* talk is very rare in fiction, but it is extremely common in real life; again and again I have heard just such conversations from people who were not even aware that they were talking coarsely. It is worth noticing that *Tropic of*

Cancer is not a young man's book. Miller was in his forties when it was published, and though since then he has produced three or four others, it is obvious that this first book had been lived with for years. It is one of those books that are slowly matured in poverty and obscurity, by people who know what they have got to do and therefore are able to wait. The prose is astonishing, and in parts of *Black Spring* it is even better. Unfortunately I cannot quote; unprintable words occur almost everywhere. But get hold of *Tropic of Cancer*, get hold of *Black Spring* and read especially the first hundred pages. They give you an idea of what can still be done, even at this late date, with English prose. In them, English is treated as a spoken language, but spoken *without fear*, i.e. without fear of rhetoric or of the unusual or poetical word. The adjective has come back, after ten years' exile. It is a flowing, swelling prose, a prose with rhythms in it, something quite different from the flat, cautious statements and snack-bar dialects that are now in fashion.

When a book like *Tropic of Cancer* appears, it is only natural that the first thing people notice should be its obscenity. Given our current notions of literary decency, it is not at all easy to approach an unprintable book with detachment. Either one is shocked and disgusted, or one is morbidly thrilled, or one is determined above all else not to be impressed. The last is probably the commonest reaction, with the result that unprintable books often get less attention than they deserve. It is rather the fashion to say that nothing is easier than to write an obscene book, that people only do it in order to get themselves talked about and make money, etc. etc. What makes it obvious that this is *not* the case is that books which are obscene in the police-court sense are distinctly uncommon. If there were easy money to be made out of dirty words, a lot more people would be making it. But, because 'obscene' books do not appear very frequently, there is a tendency to lump them together, as a rule quite unjustifiably. *Tropic of Cancer* has been vaguely associated with two other books, *Ulysses* and *Voyage au Bout de la Nuit*, but in neither case is there much resemblance. What Miller has in common with Joyce is a willingness to mention the inane squalid facts of everyday life. Putting aside differences of technique, the funeral scene in *Ulysses*, for instance, would fit into *Tropic of Cancer*; the whole chapter is a sort of confession, an *exposé* of the frightful inner callousness of the human being. But there the resemblance ends. As a novel, *Tropic of Cancer* is far inferior to *Ulysses*. Joyce is an artist, in a sense in which Miller is not and probably would not wish to be, and in any case he is attempting much more. He is exploring different states of consciousness, dream, reverie (the 'bronze-by-gold' chapter), drunkenness, etc., and dovetailing them all into a huge complex pattern, almost like a Victorian 'plot'. Miller is simply a hard-boiled person talking about life, an ordinary American businessman with intellectual courage and a gift for words. It is perhaps significant that he *looks* exactly like everyone's idea of an American businessman. As for the comparison with *Voyage au Bout de la Nuit*, it is even further from the point. Both books use unprintable words, both are in some sense autobiographical, but that is all. *Voyage au Bout de la Nuit* is a book-with-a-purpose, and its purpose is to protest against the horror and meaninglessness of modern life – actually, indeed, of *life*. It is a cry of unbearable disgust, a voice from the cesspool. *Tropic of Cancer* is almost exactly the opposite. The thing has become so unusual as to seem almost anomalous, but it is the book of a man who is happy. So is *Black Spring*, though slightly less so, because tinged in places with nostalgia. With years of lumpenproletarian life behind him, hunger, vagabondage, dirt, failure, nights in the open, battles with immigration officers, endless struggles for a bit of cash, Miller finds that he is enjoying himself. Exactly the aspects of life that fill Céline with horror are the ones that appeal to him. So far from protesting, he is *accepting*. And the very word 'acceptance' calls up his real affinity, another American, Walt Whitman.

But there is something rather curious in being Whitman in the nineteen-thirties. It is not certain that if Whitman himself were alive at this moment he would write anything in the least degree resembling *Leaves of Grass*. For what he is saying, after all, is 'I accept', and there is a radical difference between acceptance now and acceptance then. Whitman was writing in a time of unexampled prosperity, but more than that, he was writing in a country where freedom was something more than a word. The democracy, equality and comradeship that he is always talking about are not remote ideals, but something that existed in front of his eyes. In mid-nineteenth-century America men felt themselves free and equal, *were* free and equal, so far as that is possible outside a society of pure Communism. There was poverty and there were even class-distinctions, but except for the Negroes there was no permanently submerged class. Everyone had inside him, like a kind of core, the knowledge that he could earn a decent living, and earn it without boot-licking. When you read about Mark Twain's Mississippi raftsmen and pilots, of Bret Harte's Western gold miners, they seem more remote than the cannibals of the Stone Age. The reason is simply that they are free human beings. But it is the same even with the peaceful domesticated America of the Eastern states, the America of *Little Women*, *Helen's Babies* and *Riding Down from Bangor*. Life has a buoyant, carefree quality that you can feel as you read, like a physical sensation in your belly. It is this that Whitman is celebrating, though actually he does it very badly, because he is one of those writers who tell you what you ought to feel instead of making you feel it. Luckily for his beliefs, perhaps, he died too early to see the deterioration in American life that came with the rise of large-scale industry and the exploiting of cheap immigrant labour.

Miller's outlook is deeply akin to that of Whitman, and nearly everyone who has read him has remarked on this. *Tropic of Cancer* ends with an especially Whitmanesque passage, in which, after the lecheries, the swindles, the fights, the drinking bouts and the imbecilities, he simply sits down and watches the Seine flowing past, in a sort of mystical acceptance of the thing-as-it-is. Only, what is he accepting? In the first place, not America, but the ancient bone-heap of Europe, where every grain of soil has passed through innumerable human bodies. Secondly, not an epoch of expansion and liberty, but an epoch of fear, tyranny and regimentation. To say 'I accept' in an age like our own is to say that you accept concentration camps, rubber truncheons, Hitler, Stalin, bombs, aeroplanes, tinned food, machine-guns, putsches, purges, slogans, Bedaux belts, gas-masks, submarines, spies, *provocateurs*, press censorship, secret prisons, aspirins, Hollywood films and political murders. Not *only* those things, of course, but those things among others. And on the whole this is Henry Miller's attitude. Not quite always, because at moments he shows signs of a fairly ordinary kind of literary nostalgia. There is a long passage in the earlier part of *Black Spring*, in praise of the Middle Ages, which as prose must be one of the most remarkable pieces of writing in recent years, but which displays an attitude not very different from that of Chesterton. In *Max and the White Phagocytes* there is an attack on modern American civilization (breakfast cereals, cellophane, etc.) from the usual angle of the literary man who hates industrialism. But in general the attitude is 'Let's swallow it whole'. And hence the seeming preoccupation with indecency and with the dirty-handkerchief side of life. It is only seeming, for the truth is that life, ordinary everyday life, consists far more largely of horrors than writers of fiction usually care to admit. Whitman himself 'accepted' a great deal that his contemporaries found unmentionable. For he is not only writing of the prairie, he also wanders through the city and notes the shattered skull of the suicide, the 'grey sick faces of onanists', etc. etc. But unquestionably our own age, at any rate in western Europe, is less healthy and less hopeful than the age in which Whitman was writing. Unlike Whitman, we live in a *shrinking* world. The 'democratic vistas' have ended in barbed wire. There is less feeling of creation and growth, less and less emphasis on the cradle, endlessly rocking, more and more emphasis on the teapot, endlessly stewing. To accept civilization *as it is* practically means accepting decay. It has ceased to be a strenuous attitude and become a passive attitude – even 'decadent', if that word means anything.

But precisely because, in one sense, he is passive to experience, Miller is able to get nearer to the ordinary man than is possible to more purposive writers. For the ordinary man is also passive. Within a narrow circle (home life, and perhaps the trade union or local politics) he feels himself master of his fate, but against major events he is as helpless as against the elements. So far from endeavouring to influence the future, he simply lies down and lets things happen to him. During the past ten years literature has involved itself more and more deeply in politics, with the result that there is now less room in it for the ordinary man than at any time during the past two centuries. One can see the change in the prevailing literary attitude by comparing the books written about the Spanish Civil War with those written about the war of 1914–18. The immediately striking thing about the Spanish war books, at any rate those written in English, is their shocking dullness and badness. But what is more significant is that almost all of them, right-wing or left-wing, are written from a political angle, by cocksure partisans telling you what to think; whereas the books about the Great War were by common soldiers or junior officers who did not even pretend to understand what the whole thing was about. Books like *All Quiet on the Western Front*, *Le Feu*, *A Farewell to Arms*, *Death of a Hero*, *Good-Bye to All That*, *Memoirs of an Infantry Officer* and *A Subaltern on the Somme* were written not by propagandists but by *victims*. They are saying in effect, 'What the hell is all this about? God knows. All we can do is to endure.' And though he is not writing about war, nor, on the whole, about unhappiness, this is nearer to Miller's attitude than the omniscience which is now fashionable. The *Booster*, a short-lived periodical of which he was part-editor, used to describe itself in its advertisements as 'non-political, non-educational, non-progressive, non-co-operative, non-ethical, non-literary, non-consistent, non-contemporary', and Miller's own work could be described in nearly the same terms. It is a voice from the crowd, from the underling, from the third-class carriage, from the ordinary, non-political, non-moral, passive man.

I have been using the phrase 'ordinary man' rather loosely, and I have taken it for granted that the 'ordinary man' exists, a thing now denied by some people. I do not mean that the people Miller is writing about constitute a majority, still less that he is writing about proletarians. No

English or American novelist has as yet seriously attempted that. And again, the people in *Tropic of Cancer* fall short of being ordinary to the extent that they are idle, disreputable and more or less 'artistic'. As I have said already, this is a pity, but it is the necessary result of expatriation. Miller's 'ordinary man' is neither the manual worker nor the suburban householder, but the derelict, the *déclassé*, the adventurer, the American intellectual without roots and without money. Still, the experiences even of this type overlap fairly widely with those of more normal people. Miller has been able to get the most out of his rather limited material because he has had the courage to identify with it. The ordinary man, the 'average sensual man', has been given the power of speech, like Balaam's ass.

It will be seen that this is something out of date, or at any rate out of fashion. The average sensual man is out of fashion. The passive, non-political attitude is out of fashion. Preoccupation with sex and truthfulness about the inner life are out of fashion. American Paris is out of fashion. A book like *Tropic of Cancer*, published at such a time, must be either a tedious preciosity or something unusual, and I think a majority of the people who have read it would agree that it is not the first. It is worth trying to discover just what this escape from the current literary fashion means. But to do that one has got to see it against its background – that is, against the general development of English literature in the twenty years since the Great War.

II

When one says that a writer is fashionable one practically always means that he is admired by people under thirty. At the beginning of the period I am speaking of, the years during and immediately after the war, the writer who had the deepest hold upon the thinking young was almost certainly Housman. Among people who were adolescent in the years 1910–25, Housman had an influence which was enormous and is now not at all easy to understand. In 1920, when I was about seventeen, I probably knew the whole of *A Shropshire Lad* by heart. I wonder how much impression *A Shropshire Lad* makes at this moment on a boy of the same age and more or less the same cast of mind? No doubt he has heard of it and even glanced into it; it might strike him as rather cheaply clever – probably that would be about all. Yet these are the poems that I and my contemporaries used to recite to ourselves, over and over, in a kind of ecstasy, just as earlier generations had recited Meredith's 'Love in a Valley', Swinburne's 'Garden of Proserpine', etc. etc.

With rue my heart is laden
For golden friends I had,
For many a rose-lipt maiden
And many a lightfoot lad.

By brooks too broad for leaping
The lightfoot boys are laid;
The rose-lipt girls are sleeping
In fields where roses fade.

It just tinkles. But it did not seem to tinkle in 1920. Why does the bubble always burst? To answer that question one has to take account of the *external* conditions that make certain writers popular at certain times. Housman's poems had not attracted much notice when they were first published. What was there in them that appealed so deeply to a single generation, the generation born round about 1900?

In the first place, Housman is a 'country' poet. His poems are full of the charm of buried villages, the nostalgia of place names, Clunton and Clunbury, Knighton, Ludlow, 'on Wenlock Edge', 'in summer time on Bredon', thatched roofs and the jingle of smithies, the wild jonquils in the pastures, the 'blue, remembered hills'. War poems apart, English verse of the 1910–25 period is mostly 'country'. The reason no doubt was that the *rentier*-professional class was ceasing once and for all to have any real relationship with the soil; but at any rate there prevailed then, far more than now, a kind of snobbism of belonging to the country and despising the town. England at that time was hardly more an agricultural country than it is now, but before the light industries began to spread themselves it was easier to think of it as one. Most middle-class boys grew up within sight of a farm, and naturally it was the picturesque side of farm life that appealed to them – the ploughing, harvesting, stack-thrashing and so forth. Unless he has to do it himself a boy is not likely to notice the horrible drudgery of hoeing turnips, milking cows with chapped teats at four o'clock in the morning, etc. etc. Just before, just after and, for that matter, during the war was the great age of the 'nature poet', the heyday of Richard Jefferies and W. H. Hudson. Rupert Brooke's 'Grantchester', the star poem of 1913, is nothing but an enormous gush of 'country' sentiment, a sort of accumulated vomit from a stomach stuffed with place-names. Considered as a poem 'Grantchester' is something worse than worthless but as an illustration of what the thinking middle-class young of that period *felt* it is a valuable document.

Housman, however, did not enthuse over the rambler roses in the week-ending spirit of Brooke and the others. The 'country' motif is there all the time, but mainly as a background. Most of the poems have a quasi-human subject, a kind of idealized rustic, in reality Strephon or Corydon brought up to date. This in itself had a deep appeal. Experience shows that over-civilized people enjoy reading about rustics (key-phrase, 'close to the soil') because they imagine them to be more primitive and passionate than themselves. Hence the 'dark earth' novels of Sheila Kaye-Smith etc. And at that time a middle-class boy, with his 'country' bias, would identify with an agricultural worker as he would never have thought of doing with a town worker. Most boys had in their minds a vision of an idealized ploughman, gypsy, poacher, or gamekeeper, always pictured as a wild, free, roving blade, living a life of rabbit-snaring, cock-fighting, horses, beer and women. Masefield's 'Everlasting Mercy', another valuable period piece, immensely popular with boys round about the war years, gives you this vision in a very crude form. But Housman's Maurices and Terences could be taken seriously where Masefield's Saul Kane could not; on this side of him, Housman was Masefield with a dash of Theocritus. Moreover all his themes are adolescent – murder, suicide, unhappy love, early death. They deal with the simple, intelligible disasters that give you the feeling of being up against the 'bed-rock facts' of life:

The sun burns on the half-mown hill,
  By now the blood is dried;
And Maurice amongst the hay lies still
  And my knife is in his side.

And again:

They hang us now in Shrewsbury jail:
  The whistles blow forlorn,
And trains all night groan on the rail
  To men that die at morn.

It is all more or less in the same tune. Everything comes unstuck. 'Dick lies long in the churchyard, and Ned lies long in jail.' And notice also the exquisite self pity – the 'nobody loves me' feeling:

The diamond drops adorning
  Thy low mound on the lea,
These are the tears of morning,
  That weeps, but not for thee.

Hard cheese, old chap! Such poems might have been written expressly for adolescents. And the unvarying sexual pessimism (the girl always dies or marries somebody else) seemed like wisdom to boys who were herded together in public schools and were half-inclined to think of women as something unattainable. Whether Housman ever had the same appeal for girls I doubt. In his poems the women's point of view is not considered, she is merely the nymph, the siren, the treacherous half-human creature who leads you a little distance and then gives you the slip.

But Housman would not have appealed so deeply to the people who were young in 1920 if it had not been for another strain in him, and that was his blasphemous, antinomian, 'cynical' strain. The fight that always occurs between the generations was exceptionally bitter at the end of the Great War; this was partly due to the war itself, and partly it was an indirect result of the Russian Revolution, but an intellectual struggle was in any case due at about that date. Owing probably to the ease and security of life in England, which even the war hardly disturbed, many people whose ideas were formed in the eighties or earlier had carried them quite unmodified into the nineteen-twenties. Meanwhile, so far as the younger generation was concerned, the official beliefs were dissolving like sand-castles. The slump in religious belief, for instance, was spectacular. For several years the old-young antagonism took on a quality of real hatred. What was left of the war generation had crept out of the massacre to find their elders still bellowing the slogans of 1914, and a slightly younger generation of boys were writhing under dirty-minded celibate schoolmasters. It was to these that Housman appealed, with his implied sexual revolt and his personal grievance against God. He was patriotic, it was true, but in a harmless old-fashioned way, to the tune of red coats and 'God save the Queen' rather than steel helmets and 'Hang the Kaiser'. And he was satisfyingly anti-Christian – he stood for a kind of bitter, defiant paganism, a conviction that life is short and the gods are against you, which exactly fitted the prevailing mood of the young; and all in charming fragile verse that was composed almost entirely of words of one syllable.

It will be seen that I have discussed Housman as though he were merely a propagandist, an utterer of maxims and quotable 'bits'. Obviously he was more than that. There is no need to under-rate him now because he was over-rated a few years ago. Although one gets into trouble nowadays for saying so, there is a number of his poems ('Into my heart an air that kills', for instance, and 'Is my team ploughing?') that are not likely to remain long out of favour. But at bottom it is always a writer's tendency, his 'purpose', his 'message', that makes him liked or disliked. The proof of this is the extreme difficulty of seeing any literary merit in a book that seriously damages your deepest beliefs. And no book is ever truly neutral Some tendency or other is always discernible, in verse as much as in prose, even if it does no more than determine the form and the choice of imagery. But poets who attain wide popularity, like Housman, are as a rule definitely gnomic writers.

After the war, after Housman and the Nature poets, there appears a group of writers of completely different tendency – Joyce, Eliot, Pound, Lawrence, Wyndham Lewis, Aldous Huxley, Lytton Strachey. So far as the middle and late twenties go, these are 'the movement', as surely as the Auden–Spender group have been 'the movement' during the past few years. It is true that not all of the gifted writers of the period can be fitted into the pattern. E. M. Forster, for instance, though he wrote his best book in 1923 or thereabouts, was essentially pre-war, and Yeats does not seem in either of his phases to belong to the twenties. Others who were still living, Moore, Conrad, Bennett, Wells, Norman Douglas, had shot their bolt before the war ever happened. On the other hand, a writer who should be added to the group, though in the narrowly literary sense he hardly 'belongs', is Somerset Maugham. Of course the dates do not fit exactly; most of these writers had already published books before the war, but they can be classified as post-war in the same sense that the younger men now writing are post-slump. Equally, of course, you could read through most of the literary papers of the time without grasping that these people *are* 'the movement'. Even more then than at most times the big shots of literary journalism were busy pretending that the age-before-last had not come to an end. Squire ruled the *London Mercury*, Gibbs and Walpole were the gods of the lending libraries, there was a cult of cheeriness and manliness, beer and cricket, briar pipes and monogamy, and it was at all times possible to earn a few guineas by writing an article denouncing 'highbrows'. But all the same it was the despised highbrows who had captured the young. The wind was blowing from Europe, and long before 1930 it had blown the beer-and-cricket school naked, except for their knighthoods.

But the first thing one would notice about the group of writers I have named above is that they do not look like a group. Moreover several of them would strongly object to being coupled with several of the others. Lawrence and Eliot were in reality antipathetic, Huxley worshipped

Lawrence but was repelled by Joyce, most of the others would have looked down on Huxley, Strachey and Maugham, and Lewis attacked everyone in turn; indeed, his reputation as a writer rests largely on these attacks. And yet there is a certain temperamental similarity, evident enough now, though it would not have been so a dozen years ago. What it amounts to is *pessimism of outlook*. But it is necessary to make clear what is meant by pessimism.

If the keynote of the Georgian poets was 'beauty of Nature', the keynote of the post-war writers would be 'tragic sense of life'. The spirit behind Housman's poems, for instance, is not tragic, merely querulous; it is hedonism disappointed. The same is true of Hardy, though one ought to make an exception of *The Dynasts*. But the Joyce–Eliot group came later in time, puritanism is not their main adversary, they are able from the start to 'see through' most of the things that their predecessors had fought for. All of them are temperamentally hostile to the notion of 'progress'; it is felt that progress not only doesn't happen, but *ought not* to happen. Given this general similarity, there are, of course, differences of approach between the writers I have named as well as very different degrees of talent. Eliot's pessimism is partly the Christian pessimism, which implies a certain indifference to human misery, partly a lament over the decadence of western civilization ('We are the hollow men, we are the stuffed men' etc. etc.), a sort of twilight-of-the-gods feeling which finally leads him, in 'Sweeney Agonistes' for instance, to achieve the difficult feat of making modern life out to be worse than it is. With Strachey it is merely a polite eighteenth-century scepticism mixed up with a taste for debunking. With Maugham it is a kind of stoical resignation, the stiff upper lip of the pukka sahib somewhere East of Suez, carrying on with his job without believing in it, like an Antonine Emperor. Lawrence at first sight does not seem to be a pessimistic writer, because, like Dickens, he is a 'change-of-heart' man and constantly insisting that life here and now would be all right if only you looked at it a little differently. But what he is demanding is a movement away from our mechanized civilization, which is not going to happen, and which he knows is not going to happen. Therefore his exasperation with the present turns once more into idealization of the past, this time a safely mythical past, the Bronze Age. When Lawrence prefers the Etruscans (*his* Etruscans) to ourselves it is difficult not to agree with him, and yet, after all, it is a species of defeatism, because that is not the direction in which the world is moving. The kind of life that he is always pointing to, a life centring round the simple mysteries – sex, earth, fire, water, blood – is merely a lost cause. All he has been able to produce, therefore, is a wish that things would happen in a way in which they are manifestly not going to happen. 'A wave of generosity or a wave of death', he says, but it is obvious that there are no waves of generosity this side of the horizon. So he flees to Mexico, and then dies at forty-five, a few years before the wave of death gets going. It will be seen that once again I am speaking of these people as though they were not artists, as though they were merely propagandists putting a 'message' across. And once again it is obvious that all of them are more than that. It would be absurd, for instance, to look on *Ulysses* as *merely* a show-up of the horror of modern life, the 'dirty *Daily Mail* era', as Pound put it. Joyce actually is more of a 'pure artist' than most writers. But *Ulysses* could not have been written by someone who was merely dabbling with word-patterns; it is the product of a special vision of life, the vision of a Catholic who has lost his faith. What Joyce is saying is 'Here is life without God. Just look at it!' and his technical innovations, important though they are, are there primarily to serve this purpose.

But what is noticeable about all these writers is that what 'purpose' they have is very much up in the air. There is no attention to the urgent problems of the moment, above all no politics in the narrower sense. Our eyes are directed to Rome, to Byzantium, to Montparnasse, to Mexico, to the Etruscans, to the subconscious, to the solar plexus – to everything except the places where things are actually happening. When one looks back at the twenties, nothing is queerer than the way in which every important event in Europe escaped the notice of the English intelligentsia. The Russian Revolution, for instance, all but vanishes from the English consciousness between the death of Lenin and the Ukraine famine – about ten years. Throughout those years Russia means Tolstoy, Dostoyevsky and exiled counts driving taxi-cabs. Italy means picture-galleries, ruins, churches and museums – but not Blackshirts. Germany means films, nudism and psychoanalysis – but not Hitler, of whom hardly anyone had heard till 1931. In 'cultured' circles art-for-art's-saking extended practically to a worship of the meaningless. Literature was supposed to consist solely in the manipulation of words. To judge a book by its subject-matter was the unforgivable sin, and even to be aware of its subject-matter was looked on as a lapse of taste. About 1928, in one of the three genuinely funny jokes that *Punch* has produced since the Great War, an intolerable youth is pictured informing his aunt that he intends to 'write'. 'And what are you going to write about, dear?' asks the aunt. 'My dear aunt,' says the youth crushingly, 'one doesn't write *about* anything, one just *writes*.'

The best writers of the twenties did not subscribe to this doctrine, their 'purpose' is in most cases fairly overt, but it is usually a 'purpose' along moral-religious-cultural lines. Also, when translatable into political terms, it is in no case 'left'. In one way or another the tendency of all the writers in this group is conservative. Lewis, for instance, spent years in frenzied witch-smellings after 'Bolshevism', which he was able to detect in very unlikely places. Recently he has changed some of his views, perhaps influenced by Hitler's treatment of artists, but it is safe to bet that he will not go very far leftward. Pound seems to have plumped definitely for Fascism, at any rate the Italian variety. Eliot has remained aloof, but if forced at the pistol's point to choose between Fascism and some more democratic form of Socialism, would probably choose Fascism. Huxley starts off with the usual despair-of-life, then, under the influence of Lawrence's 'dark abdomen', tries something called Life-Worship, and finally arrives at pacifism – a tenable position, and at this moment an honourable one, but probably in the long run involving rejection of Socialism. It is also noticeable that most of the writers in this group have a certain tenderness for the Catholic Church, though not usually of a kind that an orthodox Catholic would accept.

The mental connexion between pessimism and a reactionary outlook is no doubt obvious enough. What is perhaps less obvious is just *why* the leading writers of the twenties were predominantly pessimistic. Why always the sense of decadence, the skulls and cactuses, the yearning after lost faith and impossible civilizations? Was it not, after all, *because* these people were writing in an exceptionally comfortable epoch? It is just in such times that 'cosmic despair' can flourish. People with empty bellies never despair of the universe, nor even think about the universe, for that matter. The whole period 1910–30 was a prosperous one, and even the war years were physically tolerable if one happened to be a non-combatant in one of the Allied countries. As for the twenties, they were the golden age of the *rentier*-intellectual, a period of irresponsibility such as the world had never before seen. The war was over, the new totalitarian states had not arisen, moral and religious taboos of all descriptions had vanished, and the cash was rolling in. 'Disillusionment' was all the fashion. Everyone with a safe £500 a year turned highbrow and began training himself in *taedium vitae*. It was an age of eagles and of crumpets, facile despairs, backyard Hamlets, cheap return tickets to the end of the night. In some of the minor characteristic novels of the period, books like *Told by an Idiot*, the despair-of-life reaches a Turkish-bath atmosphere of self-pity. And even the best writers of the time can be convicted of a too

Olympian attitude, a too great readiness to wash their hands of the immediate practical problem. They see life very comprehensively, much more so than those who come immediately before or after them, but they see it through the wrong end of the telescope. Not that that invalidates their books, as books. The first test of any work of art is survival, and it is a fact that a great deal that was written in the period 1910–30 has survived and looks like continuing to survive. One has only to think of *Ulysses*, *Of Human Bondage*, most of Lawrence's early work, especially his short stories, and virtually the whole of Eliot's poems up to about 1930, to wonder what is now being written that will wear so well.

But quite suddenly, in the years 1930–35, something happens. The literary climate changes. A new group of writers, Auden and Spender and the rest of them, has made its appearance, and although technically these writers owe something to their predecessors, their 'tendency' is entirely different. Suddenly we have got out of the twilight of the gods into a sort of Boy Scout atmosphere of bare knees and community singing. The typical literary man ceases to be a cultured expatriate with a leaning towards the Church, and becomes an eager-minded schoolboy with a leaning towards Communism. If the keynote of the writers of the twenties is 'tragic sense of life', the keynote of the new writers is 'serious purpose'.

The differences between the two schools are discussed at some length in Mr Louis MacNeice's book *Modern Poetry*. This book is, of course, written entirely from the angle of the younger group and takes the superiority of their standards for granted. According to Mr MacNeice:

> The poets of *New Signatures*,[1] unlike Yeats and Eliot, are emotionally partisan. Yeats proposed to turn his back on desire and hatred; Eliot sat back and watched other people's emotions with ennui and an ironical self-pity . . . The whole poetry, on the other hand, of Auden, Spender and Day Lewis implies that they have desires and hatreds of their own and, further, that they think some things *ought* to be desired and others hated.

And again:

> The poets of *New Signatures* have swung back . . . to the Greek preference for information or statement. The first requirement is to have something to say, and after that you must say it as well as you can.

In other words, 'purpose' has come back, the younger writers have

1. Published in 1932. [Authors footnote.]

'gone into politics'. As I have pointed out already, Eliot & Co. are not really so non-partisan as Mr MacNeice seems to suggest. Still, it is broadly true that in the twenties the literary emphasis was more on technique and less on subject-matter than it is now.

The leading figures in this group are Auden, Spender, Day Lewis, MacNeice, and there is a long string of writers of more or less the same tendency, Isherwood, John Lehmann, Arthur Calder-Marshall, Edward Upward, Alec Brown, Philip Henderson, and many others. As before, I am lumping them together simply according to tendency. Obviously there are very great variations in talent. But when one compares these writers with the Joyce–Eliot generation, the immediately striking thing is how much easier it is to form them into a group. Technically they are closer together, politically they are almost indistinguishable, and their criticisms of one another's work have always been (to put it mildly) good-natured. The outstanding writers of the twenties were of very varied origins, few of them had passed through the ordinary English educational mill (incidentally, the best of them, barring Lawrence, were not Englishmen), and most of them had had at some time to struggle against poverty, neglect, and even downright persecution. On the other hand, nearly all the younger writers fit easily into the public-school–university–Bloomsbury pattern. The few who are of proletarian origin are of the kind that is declassed early in life, first by means of scholarships and then by the bleaching-tub of London 'culture'. It is significant that several of the writers in this group have been not only boys but, subsequently, masters at public schools. Some years ago I described Auden as 'a sort of gutless Kipling'. As criticism this was quite unworthy, indeed it was merely a spiteful remark, but it is a fact that in Auden's work, especially his earlier work, an atmosphere of uplift – something rather like Kipling's 'If' or Newbolt's 'Play Up, Play Up, and Play the Game!' – never seems to be very far away. Take, for instance, a poem like 'You're leaving now, and it's up to you boys'.[2] It is pure scout-master, the exact note of the ten-minutes' straight talk on the dangers of self-abuse. No doubt there is an element of parody that he intends. And of course the rather priggish note that is common to most of these writers is a symptom of release. By throwing 'pure art' overboard they have freed themselves from the fear of being laughed at and vastly enlarged their scope. The prophetic side of Marxism, for example, is new material for poetry and has great possibilities:

2. This is in fact the first line of Poem No. 10 in Cecil Day Lewis's early volume of poetry *The Magnetic Mountain*.

We are nothing.
We have fallen
Into the dark and shall be destroyed.
Think though, that in this darkness
We hold the secret hub of an idea
Whose living sunlit wheel revolves in future years outside.
(Spender, *Trial of a Judge*.)

But at the same time, by being Marxized literature has moved no nearer to the masses. Even allowing for the time-lag, Auden and Spender are somewhat farther from being popular writers than Joyce and Eliot, let alone Lawrence. As before, there are many contemporary writers who are outside the current, but there is not much doubt about what *is* the current. For the middle and late thirties, Auden, Spender & Co. *are* 'the movement', just as Joyce, Eliot & Co. were for the twenties. And the movement is in the direction of some rather ill-defined thing called Communism. As early as 1934 or 1935 it was considered eccentric in literary circles not to be more or less 'left', and in another year or two there had grown up a left-wing orthodoxy that made a certain set of opinions absolutely *de rigueur* on certain subjects. The idea had begun to gain ground (*vide* Edward Upward and others) that a writer must either be actively 'left' or write badly. Between 1935 and 1939 the Communist Party had an almost irresistible fascination for any writer under forty. It became as normal to hear that so-and-so had 'joined' as it had been a few years earlier, when Roman Catholicism was fashionable, to hear that so-and-so had 'been received'. For about three years, in fact, the central stream of English literature was more or less directly under Communist control. How was it possible for such a thing to happen? And at the same time, what is meant by 'Communism'? It is better to answer the second question first.

The Communist movement in western Europe began as a movement for the violent overthrow of capitalism, and degenerated within a few years into an instrument of Russian foreign policy. This was probably inevitable when the revolutionary ferment that followed the Great War had died down. So far as I know, the only comprehensive history of this subject in English is Franz Borkenau's book, *The Communist International*. What Borkenau's facts even more than his deductions make clear is that Communism could never have developed along its present lines if any real revolutionary feeling had existed in the industrialized countries. In England, for instance, it is obvious that no such feeling has existed for years past. The pathetic membership figures of all extremist parties show this clearly. It is only natural, therefore, that the English Communist movement should be controlled by people who are mentally subservient to Russia and have no real aim except to manipulate British foreign policy in the Russian interest. Of course such an aim cannot be openly admitted, and it is this fact that gives the Communist party its very peculiar character. The more vocal kind of Communist is in effect a Russian publicity agent posing as an international Socialist. It is a pose that is easily kept up at normal times, but becomes difficult in moments of crisis, because of the fact that the U.S.S.R. is no more scrupulous in its foreign policy than the rest of the Great Powers. Alliances, changes of front, etc. which only make sense as part of the game of power politics have to be explained and justified in terms of international Socialism. Every time Stalin swaps partners, 'Marxism' has to be hammered into a new shape. This entails sudden and violent changes of 'line', purges, denunciations, systematic destruction of party literature, etc. etc. Every Communist is in fact liable at any moment to have to alter his most fundamental convictions, or leave the party. The unquestionable dogma of Monday may become the damnable heresy of Tuesday, and so on. This has happened at least three times during the past ten years. It follows that in any western country a Communist Party is always unstable and usually very small. Its long-term membership really consists of an inner ring of intellectuals who have identified with the Russian bureaucracy, and a slightly larger body of working-class people who feel a loyalty towards Soviet Russia without necessarily understanding its policies. Otherwise there is only a shifting membership, one lot coming and another going with each change of 'line'.

In 1930 the English Communist Party was a tiny, barely legal organization whose main activity was libelling the Labour Party. But by 1935 the face of Europe had changed, and left-wing politics changed with it. Hitler had risen to power and begun to re-arm, the Russian Five-Year Plans had succeeded, Russia had reappeared as a great military power. As Hitler's three targets of attack were, to all appearances, Great Britain, France and the U.S.S.R., the three countries were forced into a sort of uneasy *rapprochement*. This meant that the English or French Communist was obliged to become a good patriot and imperialist – that is, to defend the very things he had been attacking for the past fifteen years. The Comintern slogans suddenly faded from red to pink. 'World revolution' and 'Social Fascism' gave way to 'Defence of democracy' and 'Stop Hitler!' The years 1935–9 were the period of anti-Fascism and the Popular Front, the heyday of the Left Book Club, when red duchesses and 'broadminded' deans toured the battlefields of the Spanish war and Winston Churchill was the blue-eyed boy of the *Daily Worker*. Since then, of course, there has been yet another change of 'line'. But what is important for my purpose is that it was during the 'anti-Fascist' phase that the younger English writers gravitated towards Communism.

The Fascism-democracy dogfight was no doubt an attraction in itself, but in any case their conversion was due at about that date. It was obvious that *laissez-faire* capitalism was finished and that there had got to be some kind of reconstruction; in the world of 1935 it was hardly possible to remain politically indifferent. But why did these young men turn towards anything so alien as Russian Communism? Why should *writers* be attracted by a form of Socialism that makes mental honesty impossible? The explanation really lies in something that had already made itself felt before the slump and before Hitler: middle-class unemployment.

Unemployment is not merely a matter of not having a job. Most people can *get* a job of sorts, even at the worst of times. The trouble was that by 1930 there was no activity, except perhaps scientific research, the arts and left-wing politics, that a thinking person could believe in. The debunking of western civilization had reached its climax and 'disillusionment' was immensely widespread. Who now could take it for granted to go through life in the ordinary middle-class way, as a soldier, a clergyman, a stockbroker, an Indian Civil Servant or what not? And how many of the values by which our grandfathers lived could now be taken seriously? Patriotism, religion, the Empire, the family, the sanctity of marriage, the Old School Tie, birth, breeding, honour, discipline – anyone of ordinary education could turn the whole lot of them inside out in three minutes. But what do you achieve, after all, by getting rid of such primal things as patriotism and religion? You have not necessarily got rid of the need for *something to believe in*. There had been a sort of false dawn a few years earlier when numbers of young intellectuals, including several quite gifted writers (Evelyn Waugh, Christopher Hollis and others), had fled into the Catholic Church. It is significant that these people went almost invariably to the Roman Church and not, for instance, to the C. of E., the Greek Church or the Protestant sects. They went, that is, to the Church with a world-wide organization, the one with a rigid discipline, the one with power and prestige behind it. Perhaps it is even worth noticing that the only latter-day convert of really first-rate gifts, Eliot, has embraced not Romanism but Anglo-Catholicism, the ecclesiastical equivalent of Trotskyism. But I do not think one need look farther than this for the reason why the young writers of the thirties flocked into or towards the Communist Party. It was simply something to believe in. Here was a church, an army, an orthodoxy, a discipline. Here was a Fatherland and – at any rate since 1935 or thereabouts – a Fuehrer. All the loyalties and superstitions that the intellect had seemingly banished could come rushing back under the thinnest of disguises. Patriotism, religion, empire, military glory – all in one word, Russia. Father, king, leader, hero, saviour – all in one word, Stalin. God – Stalin. The devil – Hitler. Heaven – Moscow. Hell – Berlin. All the gaps were filled up. So, after all, the 'Communism' of the English intellectual is something explicable enough. It is the patriotism of the deracinated.

But there is one thing that undoubtedly contributed to the cult of Russia among the English intelligentsia during these years, and that is the softness and security of life in England itself. With all its injustices, England is still the land of habeas corpus, and the overwhelming majority of English people have no experience of violence or illegality. If you have grown up in that sort of atmosphere it is not at all easy to imagine what a despotic régime is like. Nearly all the dominant writers of the thirties belonged to the soft-boiled emancipated middle class and were too young to have effective memories of the Great War. To people of that kind such things as purges, secret police, summary executions, imprisonment without trial, etc. etc. are too remote to be terrifying. They can swallow totalitarianism *because* they have no experience of anything except liberalism. Look, for instance, at this extract from Mr Auden's poem 'Spain' (incidentally this poem is one of the few decent things that have been written about the Spanish war):

> Tomorrow for the young, the poets exploding like bombs,
> The walks by the lake, the weeks of perfect communion;
> Tomorrow the bicycle races
> Through the suburbs on summer evenings. But today the struggle.
>
> Today the deliberate increase in the chances of death,
> The conscious acceptance of guilt in the necessary murder;
> Today the expending of powers
> On the flat ephemeral pamphlet and the boring meeting.

The second stanza is intended as a sort of thumbnail sketch of a day in the life of a 'good party man'. In the morning a couple of political murders, a ten-minutes' interlude to stifle 'bourgeois' remorse, and then a hurried luncheon and a busy afternoon and evening chalking walls and distributing leaflets. All very edifying. But notice the phrase 'necessary murder'. It could only be written by a person to whom murder is at most a *word*. Personally I would not speak so lightly of murder. It so happens that I have seen the bodies of numbers of murdered men – I don't mean killed in battle, I mean murdered. Therefore I have some conception of what murder means – the terror, the hatred, the howling relatives, the post-mortems, the blood, the smells. To me, murder is something to be avoided. So it is to any ordinary person. The Hitlers and Stalins find murder necessary, but they don't advertise their callousness, and they don't speak of it as murder; it is 'liquidation', 'elimination' or some other soothing phrase. Mr Auden's brand of amoralism is only possible if you are the kind of person who is always somewhere else when the trigger is pulled. So much of left-wing thought is a kind of playing with fire by people who don't even know that fire is hot. The warmongering to which the English intelligentsia gave themselves up in the period 1935–9 was largely based on a sense of personal immunity. The attitude was very different in France, where the military service is hard to dodge and even literary men know the weight of a pack.

Towards the end of Mr Cyril Connolly's recent book, *Enemies of Promise*, there occurs an interesting and revealing passage. The first part of the book is, more or less, an evaluation of present-day literature. Mr Connolly belongs exactly to the generation of the writers of 'the movement', and with not many reservations their values are his values. It is interesting to notice that among prose writers he admires chiefly those specializing in violence – the would-be tough American school, Hemingway, etc. The latter part of the book, however, is autobiographical and consists of an account, fascinatingly accurate, of life at a preparatory school and Eton in the years 1910–20. Mr Connolly ends by remarking:

> Were I to deduce anything from my feelings on leaving Eton, it might be called *The Theory of Permanent Adolescence.* It is the theory that the experience undergone by boys at the great public schools are so intense as to dominate their lives and to arrest their development.

When you read the second sentence in this passage, your natural impulse is to look for the misprint. Presumably there is a 'not' left out, or something. But no, not a bit of it! He means it! And what is more, he is merely speaking the truth, in an inverted fashion. 'Cultured' middle-class life has reached a depth of softness at which a public-school education – five years in a lukewarm bath of snobbery – can actually be looked back upon as an eventful period. To nearly all the writers who have counted during the thirties, what more has ever happened than Mr Connolly records in *Enemies of Promise*? It is the same pattern all the time;

public school, university, a few trips abroad, then London. Hunger, hardship, solitude, exile, war, prison, persecution, manual labour – hardly even words. No wonder that the huge tribe known as 'the right left people' found it so easy to condone the purge-and-Ogpu side of the Russian régime and the horrors of the first Five-Year Plan. They were so gloriously incapable of understanding what it all meant.

By 1937 the whole of the intelligentsia was mentally at war. Left-wing thought had narrowed down to 'anti-Fascism', i.e. to a negative, and a torrent of hate-literature directed against Germany and the politicians supposedly friendly to Germany was pouring from the press. The thing that, to me, was truly frightening about the war in Spain was not such violence as I witnessed, nor even the party feuds behind the lines, but the immediate reappearance in left-wing circles of the mental atmosphere of the Great War. The very people who for twenty years had sniggered over their own superiority to war hysteria were the ones who rushed straight back into the mental slum of 1915. All the familiar war-time idiocies, spy-hunting, orthodoxy-sniffing (Sniff, sniff. Are you a good anti-Fascist?), the retailing of incredible atrocity stories, came back into vogue as though the intervening years had never happened. Before the end of the Spanish war, and even before Munich, some of the better of the left-wing writers were beginning to squirm. Neither Auden nor, on the whole, Spender wrote about the Spanish war in quite the vein that was expected of them. Since then there has been a change of feeling and much dismay and confusion, because the actual course of events has made nonsense of the left-wing orthodoxy of the last few years. But then it did not need very great acuteness to see that much of it was nonsense from the start. There is no certainty, therefore, that the next orthodoxy to emerge will be any better than the last.

On the whole the literary history of the thirties seems to justify the opinion that a writer does well to keep out of politics. For any writer who accepts or partially accepts the discipline of a political party is sooner or later faced with the alternative: toe the line, or shut up. It is, of course, possible to toe the line and go on writing – after a fashion. Any Marxist can demonstrate with the greatest of ease that 'bourgeois' liberty of thought is an illusion. But when he has finished his demonstration there remains the psychological *fact* that without this 'bourgeois' liberty the creative powers wither away. In the future a totalitarian literature may arise, but it will be quite different from anything we can now imagine. Literature as we know it is an individual thing, demanding mental honesty and a minimum of censorship. And this is even truer of prose than of verse. It is probably not a coincidence that the best writers of the thirties have been poets. The atmosphere of orthodoxy is always damaging to prose, and above all it is completely ruinous to the novel, the most anarchical of all forms of literature. How many Roman Catholics have been good novelists? Even the handful one could name have usually been bad Catholics. The novel is practically a Protestant form of art; it is a product of the free mind, of the autonomous individual. No decade in the past hundred and fifty years has been so barren of imaginative prose as the nineteen-thirties. There have been good poems, good sociological works, brilliant pamphlets, but practically no fiction of any value at all. From 1933 onwards the mental climate was increasingly against it. Anyone sensitive enough to be touched by the *zeitgeist* was also involved in politics. Not everyone, of course, was definitely *in* the political racket, but practically everyone was on its periphery and more or less mixed up in propaganda campaigns and squalid controversies. Communists and near-Communists had a disproportionately large influence in the literary reviews. It was a time of labels, slogans and evasions. At the worst moments you were expected to lock yourself up in a constipating little cage of lies; at the best a sort of voluntary censorship ('Ought I to say this? Is it pro-Fascist?') was at work in nearly everyone's mind. It is almost inconceivable that good novels should be written in such an atmosphere. Good novels are not written by orthodoxy-sniffers, nor by people who are conscience-stricken about their own unorthodoxy. Good novels are written by people who are *not frightened.* This brings me back to Henry Miller.

III

If this were a likely moment for the launching of 'schools' of literature, Henry Miller might be the starting-point of a new 'school'. He does at any rate mark an unexpected swing of the pendulum. In his books one gets right away from the 'political animal' and back to a viewpoint not only individualistic but completely passive – the viewpoint of a man who believes the world-process to be outside his control and who in any case hardly wishes to control it.

I first met Miller at the end of 1936, when I was passing through Paris on my way to Spain. What most intrigued me about him was to find that he felt no interest in the Spanish war whatever. He merely told me in forcible terms that to go to Spain at that moment was the act of an idiot. He could understand anyone going there from purely selfish motives, out of curiosity, for instance, but to mix oneself up in such things *from a sense of obligation* was sheer stupidity. In any case my ideas about combating Fascism, defending democracy, etc. etc. were all boloney. Our civilization was destined to be swept away and replaced by something so different that we should scarcely regard it as human – a prospect that did not bother him, he said. And some such outlook is implicit throughout his work. Everywhere there is the sense of the approaching cataclysm, and almost everywhere the implied belief that it doesn't matter. The only political declaration which, so far as I know, he has ever made in print is a purely negative one. A year or so ago an American magazine, the *Marxist Quarterly*, sent out a questionnaire to various American writers asking them to define their attitude on the subject of war. Miller replied in terms of extreme pacifism, but a merely personal pacifism, an individual refusal to fight, with no apparent wish to convert others to the same opinion – practically, in fact, a declaration of irresponsiblity.

However, there is more than one kind of irresponsibility. As a rule, writers who do not wish to identify themselves with the historical process of the moment either ignore it or fight against it. If they can ignore it, they are probably fools. If they can understand it well enough to want to fight against it, they probably have enough vision to realize that they cannot win. Look, for instance, at a poem like 'The Scholar Gypsy', with its railing against the 'strange disease of modern life' and its magnificent defeatist simile in the final stanza. It expresses one of the normal literary attitudes, perhaps actually the prevailing attitude during the last hundred years. And on the other hand there are the 'progressives', the yea-sayers, the Shaw-Wells type, always leaping forward to embrace the ego-projections which they mistake for the future. On the whole the writers of the twenties took the first line and the writers of the thirties the second. And at any given moment, of course, there is a huge tribe of Barries and Deepings and Dells who simply don't notice what is happening. Where Miller's work is symptomatically important is in its avoidance of any of these attitudes. He is neither pushing the world-process forward nor trying to drag it back, but on the other hand he is by no means ignoring it. I should say that he believes in the impending ruin of western civilization much more firmly than the majority of 'revolutionary' writers; only he does not feel called upon to do anything about it. He is fiddling while Rome is burning, and, unlike the enormous majority of people who do this, fiddling with his face towards the flames.

In *Max and the White Phagocytes* there is one of those revealing passages in which a writer tells you a great deal about himself while talking about somebody else. The book includes a long essay on the diaries of Anais Nin, which I have never read, except for a few fragments, and which I believe have not been published. Miller claims that they are the only truly feminine writing that has ever appeared, whatever that may mean. But the interesting passage is one in which he compares Anais Nin – evidently a completely subjective, introverted writer – to Jonah in the whale's belly. In passing he refers to an essay that Aldous Huxley wrote some years ago about El Greco's picture 'The Dream of Philip the Second'. Huxley remarks that the people in El Greco's pictures always look as though they were in the bellies of whales, and professes to find something peculiarly horrible in the idea of being in a 'visceral prison'. Miller retorts that, on the contrary, there are many worse things than being swallowed by whales, and the passage makes it clear that he himself finds the idea rather attractive. Here he is touching upon what is probably a very widespread fantasy. It is perhaps worth noticing that everyone, at least every English-speaking person, invariably speaks of Jonah and the *whale*. Of course the creature that swallowed Jonah was a fish, and is so described in the Bible (Jonah i, 17), but children naturally confuse it with a whale, and this fragment of baby-talk is habitually carried into later life – a sign, perhaps, of the hold that the Jonah myth has upon our imaginations. For the fact is that being inside a whale is a very comfortable, cosy, homelike thought. The historical Jonah, if he can be so called, was glad enough to escape, but in imagination, in day-dream, countless people have envied him. It is, of course, quite obvious why. The whale's belly is simply a womb big enough for an adult. There you are, in the dark, cushioned space that exactly fits you, with yards of blubber between yourself and reality, able to keep up an attitude of the completest indifference, no matter *what* happens. A storm that would sink all the battleships in the world would hardly reach you as an echo. Even the whale's own movements would probably be imperceptible to you. He might be wallowing among the surface waves or shooting down into the blackness of the middle seas (a mile deep, according to Herman Melville), but you would never notice the difference. Short of being dead, it is the final, unsurpassable stage of irresponsibility. And however it may be with Anais Nin, there is no question that Miller himself is inside the whale. All his best and most characteristic passages are written from the angle of Jonah, a willing Jonah. Not that he is especially introverted – quite the contrary. In his case the whale happens to be transparent. Only he feels no impulse to alter or control the process that he is undergoing. He has performed the essential Jonah act of allowing himself to be swallowed, remaining passive, *accepting*.

It will be seen what this amounts to. It is a species of quietism, implying either complete unbelief or else a degree of belief amounting to mysticism. The attitude is '*Je m'en fous*' or 'Though He slay me, yet will I trust in Him', whichever way you like to look at it; for practical purposes both are identical, the moral in either case being 'Sit on your bum'. But in a time like ours, is this a defensible attitude? Notice that it is almost impossible to refrain from asking this question. At the moment of writing we are still in a period in which it is taken for granted that books ought always to be positive, serious and 'constructive'. A dozen years ago this idea would have been greeted with titters. ('My dear aunt, one doesn't write *about* anything, one just *writes*'.) Then the pendulum swung away from the frivolous notion that art is merely technique, but it swung a very long distance, to the point of asserting that a book can only be 'good' if it is founded on a 'true' version of life. Naturally the people who believe this also believe that they are in possession of the truth themselves. Catholic critics, for instance, tend to claim that books are only 'good' when they are of Catholic tendency. Marxist critics make the same claim more boldly for Marxist books. For instance, Mr Edward Upward ('A Marxist Interpretation of Literature', in *The Mind in Chains*):

> Literary criticism which aims at being Marxist must . . . proclaim that no book written *at the present time* can be 'good' unless it is written from a Marxist or near-Marxist viewpoint.

Various other writers have made similar or comparable statements. Mr Upward italicizes 'at the present time' because he realizes that you cannot, for instance, dismiss *Hamlet* on the ground that Shakespeare was not a Marxist. Nevertheless his interesting essay only glances very shortly at this difficulty. Much of the literature that comes to us out of the past is permeated by and in fact founded on beliefs (the belief in the immortality of the soul, for example) which now seem to us false and in some cases contemptibly silly. Yet it is 'good' literature, if survival is any test. Mr Upward would no doubt answer that a belief which was appropriate several centuries ago might be inappropriate and therefore stultifying now. But this does not get one much farther, because it assumes that in any age there will be *one* body of belief which is the current approximation to truth, and that the best literature of the time will be more or less in harmony with it. Actually no such uniformity has ever existed. In seventeenth-century England, for instance, there was a religious and political cleavage which distinctly resembled the left-right antagonism of today. Looking back, most modern people would feel that the bourgeois-Puritan viewpoint was a better approximation to truth than the Catholic-feudal one. But it is certainly not the case that all or even a majority of the best writers of the time were Puritans. And more than this, there exist 'good' writers whose world-view would in *any* age be recognized as false and silly. Edgar Allan Poe is an example. Poe's outlook is at best a wild romanticism and at worst is not far from being insane in the literal clinical sense. Why is it, then, that stories like 'The Black Cat', 'The Tell-tale Heart', 'The Fall of the House of Usher' and so forth, which might very nearly have been written by a lunatic, do not convey a feeling of falsity? Because they are true within a certain framework, they keep the rules of their own peculiar world, like a Japanese picture. But it appears that to write successfully about such a world you have got to believe in it. One sees the difference immediately if one compares Poe's *Tales* with what is, in my opinion, an insincere attempt to work up a similar atmosphere, Julian Green's *Minuit*. The thing that immediately strikes one about *Minuit* is that there is no reason why any of the events in it should happen. Everything is completely arbitrary; there is no emotional sequence. But this is exactly what one does *not* feel with Poe's stories. Their maniacal logic, in its own setting, is quite convincing. When, for instance, the drunkard seizes the black cat and cuts its eyes out with his penknife, one knows exactly *why* he did it, even to the point of feeling that one would have done the same oneself. It seems therefore that for a creative writer possession of the 'truth' is less important than emotional sincerity. Even Mr Upward would not claim that a writer needs nothing beyond a Marxist training. He also needs talent. But talent, apparently, is a matter of being able to *care*, of really *believing* in your beliefs, whether they are true or false. The difference between, for instance, Céline and Evelyn Waugh is a difference of emotional intensity. It is the difference between genuine despair and a despair that is at least partly a pretence. And with this there goes another consideration which is perhaps less obvious: that there are occasions when an 'untrue' belief is more likely to be sincerely held than a 'true' one.

If one looks at the books of personal reminiscence written about the war of 1914–18, one notices that nearly all that have remained readable after a lapse of time are written from a passive, negative angle. They are the records of something completely meaningless, a nightmare happening in a void. That was not exactly the truth about the war, but it was the truth about the individual reaction. The soldier advancing into a machine-gun barrage or standing waist-deep in a flooded trench knew only that here was an appalling experience in which he was all but helpless. He was likelier to make a good book out of his helplessness and his ignorance than out of a pretended power to see the whole thing in perspective. As for the books that were written during the war itself, the best of them were nearly all the work of people who simply turned their backs and tried not to notice that the war was happening. Mr E. M. Forster has described how in 1917 he read 'Prufrock' and others of Eliot's early poems, and how it heartened him at such a time to get hold of poems that were 'innocent of public-spiritedness':

> They sang of private disgust and diffidence, and of people who seemed genuine because they were unattractive or weak . . . Here was a protest, and a feeble one, and the more congenial for being feeble . . . He who could turn aside to complain of ladies and drawing-rooms preserved a tiny drop of our self-respect, he carried on the human heritage.

That is very well said. Mr MacNeice, in the book I have referred to already, quotes this passage and somewhat smugly adds:

> Ten years later less feeble protests were to be made by poets and the human heritage carried on rather differently . . . The contemplation of a world of fragments becomes boring and Eliot's successors are more interested in tidying it up.

Similar remarks are scattered throughout Mr MacNeice's book. What he wishes us to believe is that Eliot's 'successors' (meaning Mr MacNeice and his friends) have in some way 'protested' more effectively than Eliot did by publishing 'Prufrock' at the moment when the Allied armies were assaulting the Hindenburg Line. Just where these 'protests' are to be found I do not know. But in the contrast between Mr Forster's comment and Mr MacNeice's lies all the difference between a man who knows what the 1914–18 war was like and a man who barely remembers it. The truth is that in 1917 there was nothing that a thinking and sensitive person could do, except to remain human, if possible. And a gesture of helplessness, even of frivolity, might be the best way of doing that. If I had been a soldier fighting in the Great War, I would sooner have got hold of 'Prufrock' than *The First Hundred Thousand* or Horatio Bottomley's *Letters to the Boys in the Trenches*. I should have felt, like Mr Forster, that by simply standing aloof and keeping in touch with pre-war emotions, Eliot was carrying on the human heritage. What a relief it would have been at such a time, to read about the hesitations of a middle-aged highbrow with a bald spot! So different from bayonet drill! After the bombs and the food queues and the recruiting posters, a human voice! What a relief!

But, after all, the war of 1914–18 was only a heightened moment in an almost continuous crisis. At this date it hardly even needs a war to bring home to us the disintegration of our society and the increasing helplessness of all decent people. It is for this reason that I think that the passive, non-co-operative attitude implied in Henry Miller's work is justified. Whether or not it is an expression of what people *ought* to feel, it probably comes somewhere near to expressing what they do feel. Once again it is the human voice among the bomb-explosions, a friendly American voice, 'innocent of public-spiritedness'. No sermons, merely the subjective truth. And along those lines, apparently, it is still possible for a good novel to be written. Not necessarily an edifying novel, but a novel worth reading and likely to be remembered after it is read.

While I have been writing this book[3] another European war has broken out. It will either last several years and tear western civilization to pieces, or it will end inconclusively and prepare the way for yet another war which will do the job once and for all. But war is only 'peace intensified'. What is quite obviously happening, war or no war, is the break-up of *laissez-faire* capitalism and of the liberal-Christian culture. Until recently the full implications of this were not foreseen, because it was generally imagined that Socialism could preserve and even enlarge the atmosphere of liberalism. It is now beginning to be realized how false this idea was. Almost certainly we are moving into an age of totalitarian dictatorships – an age in which freedom of thought will be at first a deadly sin and later on a meaningless abstraction. The autonomous individual is going to be stamped out of existence. But this means that literature, in the form in which we know it, must suffer at least a temporary death. The literature of liberalism is coming to an end and the literature of totalitarianism has not yet appeared and is barely imaginable. As for the writer, he is sitting on a melting iceberg; he is merely an anachronism, a hangover from the bourgeois age, as surely doomed as the hippopotamus. Miller seems to me a man out of the common because he saw and proclaimed this fact a long while before most of his contemporaries – at a time, indeed, when many of them were actually burbling about a renaissance of literature. Wyndham Lewis had said years earlier that the major history of the English language was finished, but he was basing this on different and rather trivial reasons. But from now onwards the all-important fact for the creative writer is going to be that this is not a writer's world. That

3. *Inside the Whale.*

does not mean that he cannot help to bring the new society into being, but he can take no part in the process *as a writer*. For *as a writer* he is a liberal, and what is happening is the destruction of liberalism. It seems likely, therefore, that in the remaining years of free speech any novel worth reading will follow more or less along the lines that Miller has followed – I do not mean in technique or subject-matter, but in implied outlook. The passive attitude will come back, and it will be more consciously passive than before. Progress and reaction have both turned out to be swindles. Seemingly there is nothing left but quietism – robbing reality of its terrors by simply submitting to it. Get inside the whale – or rather, admit that you are inside the whale (for you *are*, of course). Give yourself over to the world-process, stop fighting against it or pretending that you control it; simply accept it, endure it, record it. That seems to be the formula that any sensitive novelist is now likely to adopt. A novel on more positive, 'constructive' lines, and not emotionally spurious, is at present very difficult to imagine.

But do I mean by this that Miller is a 'great author', a new hope for English prose? Nothing of the kind. Miller himself would be the last to claim or want any such thing. No doubt he will go on writing – anybody who has once started always goes on writing – and associated with him there is a number of writers of approximately the same tendency, Lawrence Durrell, Michael Fraenkel and others, almost amounting to a 'school'. But he himself seems to me essentially a man of one book. Sooner or later I should expect him to descend into unintelligibility, or into charlatanism; there are signs of both in his later work. His last book, *Tropic of Capricorn*, I have not even read. This was not because I did not want to read it, but because the police and customs authorities have so far managed to prevent me from getting hold of it. But it would surprise me if it came anywhere near *Tropic of Cancer* or the opening chapters of *Black Spring*. Like certain other autobiographical novelists, he had it in him to do just one thing perfectly, and he did it. Considering what the fiction of the nineteen-thirties has been like, that is something.

Miller's books are published by the Obelisk Press in Paris. What will happen to the Obelisk Press, now that war has broken out and Jack Kahane, the publisher, is dead, I do not know, but at any rate the books are still procurable. I earnestly counsel anyone who has not done so to read at least *Tropic of Cancer*. With a little ingenuity, or by paying a little over the published price, you can get hold of it, and even if parts of it disgust you, it will stick in your memory. It is also an 'important' book, in a sense different from the sense in which that word is generally used.

As a rule novels are spoken of as 'important' when they are either a 'terrible indictment' of something or other or when they introduce some technical innovation. Neither of these applies to *Tropic of Cancer.* Its importance is merely symptomatic. Here in my opinion is the only imaginative prose writer of the slightest value who has appeared among the English-speaking races for some years past. Even if that is objected to as an overstatement, it will probably be admitted that Miller is a writer out of the ordinary, worth more than a single glance; and, after all, he is a completely negative, unconstructive, amoral writer, a mere Jonah, a passive accepter of evil, a sort of Whitman among the corpses. Symptomatically, that is more significant than the mere fact that five thousand novels are published in England every year and four thousand nine hundred of them are tripe. It is a demonstration of the *impossibility* of any major literature until the world has shaken itself into its new shape.

I.T.W.; *New Directions in Prose and Poetry*, 1940; *S.J.*; *E.Y.E.*; *C.E.*

10. My Country Right or Left

Contrary to popular belief, the past was not more eventful than the present. If it seems so it is because when you look backward things that happened years apart are telescoped together, and because very few of your memories come to you genuinely virgin. It is largely because of the books, films and reminiscences that have come between that the war of 1914–18 is now supposed to have had some tremendous, epic quality that the present one lacks.

But if you were alive during that war, and if you disentangle your real memories from their later accretions, you find that it was not usually the big events that stirred you at the time. I don't believe that the Battle of the Marne, for instance, had for the general public the melodramatic quality that it was afterwards given. I do not even remember hearing the phrase 'Battle of the Marne' till years later. It was merely that the Germans were twenty-two miles from Paris – and certainly that was terrifying enough, after the Belgian atrocity stories – and then for some reason they had turned back. I was eleven when the war started. If I honestly sort out my memories and disregard what I have learned since, I must admit that nothing in the whole war moved me so deeply as the loss of the *Titanic* had done a few years earlier. This comparatively petty disaster shocked the whole world, and the shock has not quite died away even yet. I remember the terrible, detailed accounts read out at the breakfast table (in those days it was a common habit to read the newspaper aloud), and I remember that in all the long list of horrors the one that most impressed me was that at the last the *Titanic* suddenly up-ended and sank bow foremost, so that the people clinging to the stern were lifted no less than three hundred feet into the air before they plunged into the abyss. It gave me a sinking sensation in the belly which I can still all but feel. Nothing in the war ever gave me quite that sensation.

Of the outbreak of war I have three vivid memories which, being petty and irrelevant, are uninfluenced by anything that has come later. One is of the cartoon of the 'German Emperor' (I believe the hated name 'Kaiser' was not popularized till a little later) that appeared in the last days of July. People were mildly shocked by this guying of royalty ('But he's such a handsome man, really!') although we were on the edge of war. Another is of the time when the army commandeered all the horses in our little country town, and a cabman burst into tears in the market-place when his horse, which had worked for him for years, was taken away from him. And another is of a mob of young men at the railway station, scrambling for the evening papers that had just arrived on the London train. And I remember the pile of peagreen papers (some of them were still green in those days), the high collars, the tightish trousers and the bowler hats, far better than I can remember the names of the terrific battles that were already raging on the French frontier.

Of the middle years of the war, I remember chiefly the square shoulders, bulging calves and jingling spurs of the artillerymen, whose uniform I much preferred to that of the infantry. As for the final period, if you ask me to say truthfully what is my chief memory, I must answer simply – margarine. It is an instance of the horrible selfishness of children that by 1917 the war had almost ceased to affect us, except through our stomachs. In the school library a huge map of the Western Front was pinned on an easel, with a red silk thread running across on a zig-zag of drawing-pins. Occasionally the thread moved half an inch this way or that, each movement meaning a pyramid of corpses. I paid no attention. I was at school among boys who were above the average level of intelligence, and yet I do not remember that a single major event of the time appeared to us in its true significance. The Russian Revolution, for instance, made no impression, except on the few whose parents happened to have money invested in Russia. Among the very young the pacifist reaction had set in long before the war ended. To be as slack as you dared on O.T.C. parades, and to take no interest in the war, was considered a mark of enlightenment. The young officers who had come back, hardened by their terrible experience and disgusted by the attitude of the younger generation to whom this experience meant just nothing, used to lecture us for our softness. Of course they could produce no argument that we were capable of understanding. They could only bark at you that war was 'a good thing', it 'made you tough', 'kept you fit', etc. etc. We merely sniggered at them. Ours was the one-eyed pacifism that is peculiar to sheltered countries with strong navies. For years after the war, to have any knowledge of or interest in military matters, even to know which end of a gun the bullet comes out of, was suspect in 'enlightened' circles. 1914–18 was written off as a meaningless slaughter, and even the men who had been slaughtered were held to be in some way to blame. I have often laughed to think of the recruiting poster, 'What did you do in the Great War, daddy?' (a child is asking this question of its shame-stricken father), and of all the men who must have been lured into the army by just that poster and afterwards despised by their children for not being Conscientious Objectors.

But the dead men had their revenge after all. As the war fell back into the past, my particular generation, those who had been 'just too young', became conscious of the vastness of the experience they had missed. You felt yourself a little less than a man, because you had missed it. I spent the years 1922–7 mostly among men a little older than myself who had been through the war. They talked about it unceasingly, with horror, of course, but also with a steadily growing nostalgia. You can see this nostalgia perfectly clearly in the English war-books. Besides, the pacifist reaction was only a phase, and even the 'just too young' had all been trained for war. Most of the English middle class are trained for war from the cradle onwards, not technically but morally. The earliest political slogan I can remember is 'We want eight (eight dreadnoughts) and we won't wait'. At seven years old I was a member of the Navy League and wore a sailor suit with 'H.M.S. *Invincible*' on my cap. Even before my public-school O.T.C. I had been in a private-school cadet corps. On and off, I have been toting a rifle ever since I was ten, in preparation not only for war but for a particular kind of war, a war in which the guns rise to a frantic orgasm of sound, and at the appointed moment you clamber out of the trench, breaking your nails on the sandbags, and stumble across mud and wire into the machine-gun barrage. I am convinced that part of the reason for the fascination that the Spanish Civil War had for people of about my age was that it was so like the Great War. At certain moments Franco was able to scrape together enough aeroplanes to raise the war to a modern level, and these were the turning-points. But for the rest it was a bad copy of 1914–18, a positional war of trenches, artillery, raids, snipers, mud, barbed wire, lice and stagnation. In early 1937 the bit of the Aragon front that I was on must have been very like a quiet sector in France in 1915. It was only the artillery that was lacking. Even on the rare occasions when all the guns in Huesca and outside it were firing simultaneously, there were only enough of them to make a fitful unimpressive noise like the ending of a thunderstorm. The shells from Franco's six-inch guns crashed loudly enough, but there were never more than a dozen of them at a time. I know that what I felt when I first heard artillery fired 'in anger', as they say, was at least partly disappointment. It was so different from the tremendous, unbroken roar that my senses had been waiting for for twenty years.

I don't quite know in what year I first knew for certain that the present war was coming. After 1936, of course, the thing was obvious to anyone except an idiot. For several years the coming war was a nightmare to me, and at times I even made speeches and wrote pamphlets against it. But the night before the Russo-German pact was announced I dreamed that the war had started. It was one of those dreams which, whatever Freudian inner meaning they may have, do sometimes reveal to you the real state of your feelings. It taught me two things, first, that I should be simply relieved when the long-dreaded war started, secondly, that I was patriotic at heart, would not sabotage or act against my own side, would support the war, would fight in it if possible. I came downstairs to find the newspaper announcing Ribbentrop's flight to Moscow.[1] So war was coming, and the Government, even the Chamberlain Government, was assured of my loyalty. Needless to say this loyalty was and remains merely a gesture. As with almost everyone I know, the Government has flatly refused to employ me in any capacity whatever, even as a clerk or a private soldier. But that does not alter one's feelings. Besides, they will be forced to make use of us sooner or later.

If I had to defend my reasons for supporting the war, I believe I could do so. There is no real alternative between resisting Hitler and surrender-

1. On 21 August 1939 Ribbentrop was invited to Moscow and on 23 August he and Molotov signed the Russo-German Pact.

ing to him, and from a Socialist point of view I should say that it is better to resist; in any case I can see no argument for surrender that does not make nonsense of the Republican resistance in Spain, the Chinese resistance to Japan, etc. etc. But I don't pretend that that is the emotional basis of my actions. What I knew in my dream that night was that the long drilling in patriotism which the middle classes go through had done its work, and that once England was in a serious jam it would be impossible for me to sabotage. But let no one mistake the meaning of this. Patriotism has nothing to do with conservatism. It is devotion to something that is changing but is felt to be mystically the same, like the devotion of the ex-White Bolshevik to Russia. To be loyal both to Chamberlain's England and to the England of tomorrow might seem an impossibility, if one did not know it to be an everyday phenomenon. Only revolution can save England, that has been obvious for years, but now the revolution has started, and it may proceed quite quickly if only we can keep Hitler out. Within two years, maybe a year, if only we can hang on, we shall see changes that will surprise the idiots who have no foresight. I dare say the London gutters will have to run with blood. All right, let them, if it is necessary. But when the red militias are billeted in the Ritz I shall still feel that the England I was taught to love so long ago and for such different reasons is somehow persisting.

I grew up in an atmosphere tinged with militarism, and afterwards I spent five boring years within the sound of bugles. To this day it gives me a faint feeling of sacrilege not to stand to attention during 'God save the King'. That is childish, of course, but I would sooner have had that kind of upbringing than be like the left-wing intellectuals who are so 'enlightened' that they cannot understand the most ordinary emotions. It is exactly the people whose hearts have *never* leapt at the sight of a Union Jack who will flinch from revolution when the moment comes. Let anyone compare the poem John Cornford wrote not long before he was killed ('Before the Storming of Huesca') with Sir Henry Newbolt's 'There's a breathless hush in the Close tonight'. Put aside the technical differences, which are merely a matter of period, and it will be seen that the emotional content of the two poems is almost exactly the same. The young Communist who died heroically in the International Brigade was public school to the core. He had changed his allegiance but not his emotions. What does that prove? Merely the possibility of building a Socialist on the bones of a Blimp, the power of one kind of loyalty to transmute itself into another, the spiritual need for patriotism and the military virtues, for which, however little the boiled rabbits of the Left may like them, no substitute has yet been found.

Folios of New Writing, Autumn 1940

11. The Lion and the Unicorn: Socialism and the English Genius

PART I: ENGLAND YOUR ENGLAND

I

As I write, highly civilized human beings are flying overhead, trying to kill me.

They do not feel any enmity against me as an individual, nor I against them. They are 'only doing their duty', as the saying goes. Most of them, I have no doubt, are kind-hearted law-abiding men who would never dream of committing murder in private life. On the other hand, if one of them succeeds in blowing me to pieces with a well-placed bomb, he will never sleep any the worse for it. He is serving his country, which has the power to absolve him from evil.

One cannot see the modern world as it is unless one recognizes the overwhelming strength of patriotism, national loyalty. In certain circumstances it can break down, at certain levels of civilization it does not exist, but as a *positive* force there is nothing to set beside it. Christianity and international Socialism are as weak as straw in comparison with it. Hitler and Mussolini rose to power in their own countries very largely because they could grasp this fact and their opponents could not.

Also, one must admit that the divisions between nation and nation are founded on real differences of outlook. Till recently it was thought proper to pretend that all human beings are very much alike, but in fact anyone able to use his eyes knows that the average of human behaviour differs enormously from country to country. Things that could happen in one country could not happen in another. Hitler's June purge, for instance, could not have happened in England. And, as western peoples go, the English are very highly differentiated. There is a sort of back-handed admission of this in the dislike which nearly all foreigners feel for our national way of life. Few Europeans can endure living in England, and even Americans often feel more at home in Europe.

When you come back to England from any foreign country, you have immediately the sensation of breathing a different air. Even in the first few minutes dozens of small things conspire to give you this feeling. The beer is bitterer, the coins are heavier, the grass is greener, the advertisements are more blatant. The crowds in the big towns, with their mild knobby faces, their bad teeth and gentle manners, are different from a European crowd. Then the vastness of England swallows you up, and you lose for a while your feeling that the whole nation has a single identifiable character. Are there really such things as nations? Are we not forty-six million individuals, all different? And the diversity of it, the chaos! The clatter of clogs in the Lancashire mill towns, the to-and-fro of the lorries on the Great North Road, the queues outside the Labour Exchanges, the rattle of pintables in the Soho pubs, the old maids biking to Holy Communion through the mists of the autumn morning – all these are not only fragments, but *characteristic* fragments, of the English scene. How can one make a pattern out of this muddle?

But talk to foreigners, read foreign books or newspapers, and you are brought back to the same thought. Yes, there *is* something distinctive and recognizable in English civilization. It is a culture as individual as that of Spain. It is somehow bound up with solid breakfasts and gloomy Sundays, smoky towns and winding roads, green fields and red pillar-boxes. It has a flavour of its own. Moreover it is continuous, it stretches into the future and the past, there is something in it that persists, as in a living creature. What can the England of 1940 have in common with the England of 1840? But then, what have you in common with the child of five whose photograph your mother keeps on the mantelpiece? Nothing, except that you happen to be the same person.

And above all, it is *your* civilization, it is *you*. However much you hate it or laugh at it, you will never be happy away from it for any length of time. The suet puddings and the red pillarboxes have entered into your soul. Good or evil, it is yours, you belong to it, and this side the grave you will never get away from the marks that it has given you.

Meanwhile England, together with the rest of the world, is changing. And like everything else it can change only in certain directions, which up to a point can be foreseen. That is not to say that the future is fixed, merely that certain alternatives are possible and others not. A seed may grow or not grow, but at any rate a turnip seed never grows into a parsnip. It is therefore of the deepest importance to try and determine what England *is*, before guessing what part England *can play* in the huge events that are happening.

II

National characteristics are not easy to pin down, and when pinned down they often turn out to be trivialities or seem to have no connexion with one another. Spaniards are cruel to animals, Italians can do nothing without making a deafening noise, the Chinese are addicted to gambling. Obviously such things don't matter in themselves. Nevertheless, nothing is causeless, and even the fact that Englishmen have bad teeth can tell something about the realities of English life.

Here are a couple of generalizations about England that would be accepted by almost all observers. One is that the English are not gifted artistically. They are not as musical as the Germans or Italians, painting and sculpture have never flourished in England as they have in France. Another is that, as Europeans go, the English are not intellectual. They have a horror of abstract thought, they feel no need for any philosophy or systematic 'world-view'. Nor is this because they are 'practical', as they are so fond of claiming for themselves. One has only to look at their methods of town planning and water supply, their obstinate clinging to everything that is out of date and a nuisance, a spelling system that defies analysis, and a system of weights and measures that is intelligible only to the compilers of arithmetic books, to see how little they care about mere efficiency. But they have a certain power of acting without taking thought. Their world-famed hypocrisy – their double-faced attitude towards the Empire, for instance – is bound up with this. Also, in moments of supreme crisis the whole nation can suddenly draw together and act upon a species of instinct, really a code of conduct which is understood by almost everyone, though never formulated. The phrase that Hitler coined for the Germans, 'a sleep-walking people', would have been better applied to the English. Not that there is anything to be proud of in being called a sleep-walker.

But here it is worth noting a minor English trait which is extremely well marked though not often commented on, and that is a love of flowers. This is one of the first things that one notices when one reaches England from abroad, especially if one is coming from southern Europe. Does it not contradict the English indifference to the arts? Not really, because it is found in people who have no aesthetic feeling whatever. What it does link up with, however, is another English characteristic which is so much a part of us that we barely notice it, and that is the addiction to hobbies and spare-time occupations, the *privateness* of English life. We are a nation of flower-lovers, but also a nation of stamp-collectors, pigeon-fanciers, amateur carpenters, coupon-snippers, darts-players, crossword-puzzle fans. All the culture that is most truly native centres round things which even when they are communal are not official – the pub, the football match, the back garden, the fireside and the 'nice cup of tea'. The liberty of the individual is still believed in, almost as in the nineteenth century. But this has nothing to do with economic liberty, the right to exploit others for profit. It is the liberty to have a home of your own, to do what you like in your spare time, to choose your own amusements instead of having them chosen for you from above. The most hateful of all names in an English ear is Nosey Parker. It is obvious, of course, that even this purely private liberty is a lost cause. Like all other modern people, the English are in process of being numbered, labelled, conscripted, 'co-ordinated'. But the pull of their impulses is in the other direction, and the kind of regimentation that can be imposed on them will be modified in consequence. No party rallies, no Youth Movements, no coloured shirts, no Jew-baiting or 'spontaneous' demonstrations. No Gestapo either, in all probability.

But in all societies the common people must live to some extent *against* the existing order. The genuinely popular culture of England is something that goes on beneath the surface, unofficially and more or less frowned on by the authorities. One thing one notices if one looks directly at the common people, especially in the big towns, is that they are not puritanical. They are inveterate gamblers, drink as much beer as their wages will permit, are devoted to bawdy jokes, and use probably the foulest language in the world. They have to satisfy these tastes in the face of astonishing, hypocritical laws (licensing laws, lottery acts, etc. etc.) which are designed to interfere with everybody but in practice allow everything to happen. Also, the common people are without definite religious belief, and have been so for centuries. The Anglican Church never had a real hold on them, it was simply a preserve of the landed gentry, and the Nonconformist sects only influenced minorities. And yet they have retained a deep tinge of Christian feeling, while almost forgetting the name of Christ. The power-worship which is the new religion of Europe, and which has infected the English intelligentsia, has never touched the common people. They have never caught up with power politics. The 'realism' which is preached in Japanese and Italian newspapers would horrify them. One can learn a good deal about the spirit of England from the comic coloured postcards that you see in the windows of cheap stationers' shops. These things are a sort of diary upon which the English people have unconsciously recorded themselves. Their old-fashioned outlook, their graded snobberies, their mixture of bawdiness and hypocrisy, their extreme gentleness, their deeply moral attitude to life, are all mirrored there.

The gentleness of the English civilization is perhaps its most marked characteristic. You notice it the instant you set foot on English soil. It is a land where the bus conductors are good-tempered and the policemen carry no revolvers. In no country inhabited by white men is it easier to shove people off the pavement. And with this goes something that is always written off by European observers as 'decadence' or hypocrisy, the English hatred of war and militarism. It is rooted deep in history, and it is strong in the lower-middle class as well as the working class. Successive wars have shaken it but not destroyed it. Well within living memory it was common for 'the redcoats' to be booed at in the streets and for the landlords of respectable public houses to refuse to allow soldiers on the premises. In peace time, even when there are two million unemployed, it is difficult to fill the ranks of the tiny standing army, which is officered by the county gentry and a specialized stratum of the middle class, and manned by farm labourers and slum proletarians. The mass of the people are without military knowledge or tradition, and their attitude towards war is invariably defensive. No politician could rise to power by promising them conquests or military 'glory', no Hymn of Hate has ever made any appeal to them. In the last war the songs which the soldiers made up and sang of their own accord were not vengeful but humorous and mock-defeatist.[1] The only enemy they ever named was the sergeant-major.

In England all the boasting and flag-wagging, the 'Rule Britannia' stuff, is done by small minorities. The patriotism of the common people is not vocal or even conscious. They do not retain among their historical memories the name of a single military victory. English literature, like other literatures, is full of battle-poems, but it is worth noticing that the ones that have won for themselves a kind of popularity are always a tale

1. For example:

> 'I don't want to join the bloody Army,
> I don't want to go unto the war;
> I want no more to roam,
> I'd rather stay at home,
> Living on the earnings of a whore.'

But it was not in that spirit that they fought. [Author's footnote.]

of disasters and retreats. There is no popular poem about Trafalgar or Waterloo, for instance. Sir John Moore's army at Corunna, fighting a desperate rearguard action before escaping overseas (just like Dunkirk!) has more appeal than a brilliant victory. The most stirring battle-poem in English is about a brigade of cavalry which charged in the wrong direction. And of the last war, the four names which have really engraved themselves on the popular memory are Mons, Ypres, Gallipoli and Passchendaele, every time a disaster. The names of the great battles that finally broke the German armies are simply unknown to the general public.

The reason why the English anti-militarism disgusts foreign observers is that it ignores the existence of the British Empire. It looks like sheer hypocrisy. After all, the English have absorbed a quarter of the earth and held on to it by means of a huge navy. How dare they then turn round and say that war is wicked?

It is quite true that the English are hypocritical about their Empire. In the working class this hypocrisy takes the form of not knowing that the Empire exists. But their dislike of standing armies is a perfectly sound instinct. A navy employs comparatively few people, and it is an external weapon which cannot affect home politics directly. Military dictatorships exist everywhere, but there is no such thing as a naval dictatorship. What English people of nearly all classes loathe from the bottom of their hearts is the swaggering officer type, the jingle of spurs and the crash of boots. Decades before Hitler was ever heard of, the word 'Prussian' had much the same significance in England as 'Nazi' has today. So deep does this feeling go that for a hundred years past the officers of the British army, in peace time, have always worn civilian clothes when off duty.

One rapid but fairly sure guide to the social atmosphere of a country is the parade-step of its army. A military parade is really a kind of ritual dance, something like a ballet, expressing a certain philosophy of life. The goose-step, for instance, is one of the most horrible sights in the world, far more terrifying than a dive-bomber. It is simply an affirmation of naked power; contained in it, quite consciously and intentionally, is the vision of a boot crashing down on a face. Its ugliness is part of its essence, for what it is saying is 'Yes, I *am* ugly, and you daren't laugh at me', like the bully who makes faces at his victim. Why is the goose-step not used in England? There are, heaven knows, plenty of army officers who would be only too glad to introduce some such thing. It is not used because the people in the street would laugh. Beyond a certain point, military display is only possible in countries where the common people dare not laugh at the army. The Italians adopted the goose-step at about the time when Italy passed definitely under German control, and, as one would expect, they do it less well than the Germans. The Vichy government, if it survives, is bound to introduce a stiffer parade-ground discipline into what is left of the French army. In the British army the drill is rigid and complicated, full of memories of the eighteenth century, but without definite swagger; the march is merely a formalized walk. It belongs to a society which is ruled by the sword, no doubt, but a sword which must never be taken out of the scabbard.

And yet the gentleness of English civilization is mixed up with barbarities and anachronisms. Our criminal law is as out-of-date as the muskets in the Tower. Over against the Nazi Storm Trooper you have got to set that typically English figure, the hanging judge, some gouty old bully with his mind rooted in the nineteenth century, handing out savage sentences. In England people are still hanged by the neck and flogged with the cat o' nine tails. Both of these punishments are obscene as well as cruel, but there has never been any genuinely popular outcry against them. People accept them (and Dartmoor, and Borstal) almost as they accept the weather. They are part of 'the law', which is assumed to be unalterable.

Here one comes upon an all-important English trait: the respect for constitutionalism and legality, the belief in 'the law' as something above the State and above the individual, something which is cruel and stupid, of course, but at any rate *incorruptible*.

It is not that anyone imagines the law to be just. Everyone knows that there is one law for the rich and another for the poor. But no one accepts the implications of this, everyone takes it for granted that the law, such as it is, will be respected, and feels a sense of outrage when it is not. Remarks like 'They can't run me in; I haven't done anything wrong', or 'They can't do that; it's against the law', are part of the atmosphere of England. The professed enemies of society have this feeling as strongly as anyone else. One sees it in prison-books like Wilfred Macartney's *Walls Have Mouths* or Jim Phelan's *Jail Journey*, in the solemn idiocies that take place at the trials of conscientious objectors, in letters to the papers from eminent Marxist professors, pointing out that this or that is a 'miscarriage of British justice'. Everyone believes in his heart that the law can be, ought to be, and, on the whole, will be impartially administered. The totalitarian idea that there is no such thing as law, there is only power, has never taken root. Even the intelligentsia have only accepted it in theory.

An illusion can become a half-truth, a mask can alter the expression of a face. The familiar arguments to the effect that democracy is 'just the same as' or 'just as bad as' totalitarianism never take account of this fact. All such arguments boil down to saying that half a loaf is the same as no bread. In England such concepts as justice, liberty and objective truth are still believed in. They may be illusions, but they are very powerful illusions. The belief in them influences conduct, national life is different because of them. In proof of which, look about you. Where are the rubber truncheons, where is the castor oil? The sword is still in the scabbard, and while it stays there corruption cannot go beyond a certain point. The English electoral system, for instance, is an all but open fraud. In a dozen obvious ways it is gerrymandered in the interest of the moneyed class. But until some deep change has occurred in the public mind, it cannot become *completely* corrupt. You do not arrive at the polling booth to find men with revolvers telling you which way to vote, nor are the votes miscounted, nor is there any direct bribery. Even hypocrisy is a powerful safeguard. The hanging judge, that evil old man in scarlet robe and horsehair wig, whom nothing short of dynamite will ever teach what century he is living in, but who will at any rate interpret the law according to the books and will in no circumstances take a money bribe, is one of the symbolic figures of England. He is a symbol of the strange mixture of reality and illusion, democracy and privilege, humbug and decency, the subtle network of compromises, by which the nation keeps itself in its familiar shape.

III

I have spoken all the while of 'the nation', 'England', 'Britain', as though forty-five million souls could somehow be treated as a unit. But is not England notoriously two nations, the rich and the poor? Dare one pretend that there is anything in common between people with £100,000 a year and people with £1 a week? And even Welsh and Scottish readers are likely to have been offended because I have used the word 'England' oftener than 'Britain', as though the whole population dwelt in London and the Home Counties and neither north nor west possessed a culture of its own.

One gets a better view of this question if one considers the minor point first. It is quite true that the so-called races of Britain feel themselves to be very different from one another. A Scotsman, for instance, does not thank you if you call him an Englishman. You can see the hesitation we feel on this point by the fact that we call our islands by no less than six different names, England, Britain, Great Britain, the British Isles, the United Kingdom and, in very exalted moments, Albion. Even the differences between north and south England loom large in our own eyes. But somehow these differences fade away the moment that any two Britons are confronted by a European. It is very rare to meet a foreigner, other than an American, who can distinguish between English and Scots or even English and Irish. To a Frenchman, the Breton and the Auvergnat seem very different beings, and the accent of Marseilles is a stock joke in Paris. Yet we speak of 'France' and 'the French', recognizing France as an entity, a single civilization, which in fact it is. So also with ourselves. Looked at from the outside, even the cockney and the Yorkshireman have a strong family resemblance.

And even the distinction between rich and poor dwindles somewhat when one regards the nation from the outside. There is no question about the inequality of wealth in England. It is grosser than in any European country, and you have only to look down the nearest street to see it. Economically, England is certainly two nations, if not three or four. But at the same time the vast majority of the people *feel* themselves to be a single nation and are conscious of resembling one another more than they resemble foreigners. Patriotism is usually stronger than class-hatred, and always stronger than any kind of internationalism. Except for a brief moment in 1920 (the 'Hands off Russia' movement) the British working class have never thought or acted internationally. For two and a half years they watched their comrades in Spain slowly strangled, and never aided them by even a single strike.[2] But when their own country (the country of Lord Nuffield and Mr Montagu Norman) was in danger, their attitude was very different. At the moment when it seemed likely that England might be invaded, Anthony Eden appealed over the radio for Local Defence Voulunteers. He got a quarter of a million men in the first twenty-four hours, and another million in the subsequent month. One has only to compare these figures with, for instance, the number of conscientious objectors to see how vast is the strength of traditional loyalties compared with new ones.

In England patriotism takes different forms in different classes, but it runs like a connecting thread through nearly all of them. Only the Europeanized intelligentsia are really immune to it. As a positive emotion it is stronger in the middle class than in the upper class – the cheap public

2. It is true that they aided them to a certain extent with money. Still, the sums raised for the various aid-Spain funds would not equal five per cent of the turnover of the football pools during the same period. [Author's footnote.]

schools, for instance, are more given to patriotic demonstrations than the expensive ones – but the number of definitely treacherous rich men, the Laval-Quisling type, is probably very small. In the working class patriotism is profound, but it is unconscious. The working man's heart does not leap when he sees a Union Jack. But the famous 'insularity' and 'xenophobia' of the English is far stronger in the working class than in the bourgeoisie. In all countries the poor are more national than the rich, but the English working class are outstanding in their abhorrence of foreign habits. Even when they are obliged to live abroad for years they refuse either to accustom themselves to foreign food or to learn foreign languages. Nearly every Englishman of working-class origin considers it effeminate to pronounce a foreign word correctly. During the war of 1914–18 the English working class were in contact with foreigners to an extent that is rarely possible. The sole result was that they brought back a hatred of all Europeans, except the Germans, whose courage they admired. In four years on French soil they did not even acquire a liking for wine. The insularity of the English, their refusal to take foreigners seriously, is a folly that has to be paid for very heavily from time to time. But it plays its part in the English mystique, and the intellectuals who have tried to break it down have generally done more harm than good. At bottom it is the same quality in the English character that repels the tourist and keeps out the invader.

Here one comes back to two English characteristics that I pointed out, seemingly at random, at the beginning of the last chapter. One is the lack of artistic ability. This is perhaps another way of saying that the English are outside the European culture. For there is one art in which they have shown plenty of talent, namely literature. But this is also the only art that cannot cross frontiers. Literature, especially poetry, and lyric poetry most of all, is a kind of family joke, with little or no value outside its own language-group. Except for Shakespeare, the best English poets are barely known in Europe, even as names. The only poets who are widely read are Byron, who is admired for the wrong reasons, and Oscar Wilde, who is pitied as a victim of English hypocrisy. And linked up with this, though not very obviously, is the lack of philosophical faculty, the absence in nearly all Englishmen of any need for an ordered system of thought or even for the use of logic.

Up to a point, the sense of national unity is a substitute for a 'world-view'. Just because patriotism is all but universal and not even the rich are uninfluenced by it, there can be moments when the whole nation suddenly swings together and does the same thing, like a herd of cattle facing a wolf. There was such a moment, unmistakably, at the time of the disaster in France.

After eight months of vaguely wondering what the war was about, the people suddenly knew what they had got to do: first, to get the army away from Dunkirk, and secondly to prevent invasion. It was like the awakening of a giant. Quick! Danger! The Philistines be upon thee, Samson! And then the swift unanimous action – and then, alas, the prompt relapse into sleep. In a divided nation that would have been exactly the moment for a big peace movement to arise. But does this mean that the instinct of the English will always tell them to do the right thing? Not at all, merely that it will tell them to do the same thing. In the 1931 General Election, for instance, we all did the wrong thing in perfect unison. We were as single-minded as the Gadarene swine. But I honestly doubt whether we can say that we were shoved down the slope against our will.

It follows that British democracy is less of a fraud than it sometimes appears. A foreign observer sees only the huge inequality of wealth, the unfair electoral system, the governing-class control over the press, the radio and education, and concludes that democracy is simply a polite name for dictatorship. But this ignores the considerable agreement that does unfortunately exist between the leaders and the led. However much one may hate to admit it, it is almost certain that between 1931 and 1940 the National Government represented the will of the mass of the people. It tolerated slums, unemployment and a cowardly foreign policy. Yes, but so did public opinion. It was a stagnant period, and its natural leaders were mediocrities.

In spite of the campaigns of a few thousand left-wingers, it is fairly certain that the bulk of the English people were behind Chamberlain's foreign policy. More, it is fairly certain that the same struggle was going on in Chamberlain's mind as in the minds of ordinary people. His opponents professed to see in him a dark and wily schemer, plotting to sell England to Hitler, but it is far likelier that he was merely a stupid old man doing his best according to his very dim lights. It is difficult otherwise to explain the contradictions of his policy, his failure to grasp any of the courses that were open to him. Like the mass of the people, he did not want to pay the price either of peace or of war. And public opinion was behind him all the while, in policies that were completely incompatible with one another. It was behind him when he went to Munich, when he tried to come to an understanding with Russia, when he gave the guarantee to Poland, when he honoured it, and when he prosecuted the war half-heartedly. Only when the results of his policy became apparent did it turn against him; which is to say that it turned against its own lethargy of the past seven years. Thereupon the people picked a leader nearer to their mood, Churchill, who was at any rate able to grasp that wars are not won without fighting. Later, perhaps, they will pick another leader who can grasp that only Socialist nations can fight effectively.

Do I mean by all this that England is a genuine democracy? No, not even a reader of the *Daily Telegraph* could quite swallow that.

England is the most class-ridden country under the sun. It is a land of snobbery and privilege, ruled largely by the old and silly. But in any calculation about it one has got to take into account its emotional unity, the tendency of nearly all its inhabitants to feel alike and act together in moments of supreme crisis. It is the only great country in Europe that is not obliged to drive hundreds of thousands of its nationals into exile or the concentration camp. At this moment, after a year of war, newspapers and pamphlets abusing the Government, praising the enemy and clamouring for surrender are being sold on the streets, almost without interference. And this is less from a respect for freedom of speech than from a simple perception that these things don't matter. It is safe to let a paper like *Peace News* be sold, because it is certain that ninety-five per cent of the population will never want to read it. The nation is bound together by an invisible chain. At any normal time the ruling class will rob, mismanage, sabotage, lead us into the muck; but let popular opinion really make itself heard, let them get a tug from below that they cannot avoid feeling, and it is difficult for them not to respond. The left-wing writers who denounce the whole of the ruling class as 'pro-Fascist' are grossly over-simplifying. Even among the inner clique of politicians who brought us to our present pass, it is doubtful whether there were any *conscious* traitors. The corruption that happens in England is seldom of that kind. Nearly always it is more in the nature of self-deception, of the right hand not knowing what the left hand doeth. And being unconscious, it is limited. One sees this at its most obvious in the English press. Is the English press honest or dishonest? At normal times it is deeply dishonest. All the papers that matter live off their advertisements, and the advertisers exercise an indirect censorship over news. Yet I do not suppose there is one paper in England that can be straightforwardly bribed with hard cash. In the France of the Third Republic all but a very few of the newspapers could notoriously be bought over the counter like so many pounds of cheese. Public life in England has never been *openly* scandalous. It has not reached the pitch of disintegration at which humbug can be dropped.

England is not the jewelled isle of Shakespeare's much-quoted message, nor is it the inferno depicted by Dr Goebbels. More than either it resembles a family, a rather stuffy Victorian family, with not many black sheep in it but with all its cupboards bursting with skeletons. It has rich relations who have to be kow-towed to and poor relations who are horribly sat upon, and there is a deep conspiracy of silence about the source of the family income. It is a family in which the young are generally thwarted and most of the power is in the hands of irresponsible uncles and bedridden aunts. Still, it is a family. It has its private language and its common memories, and at the approach of an enemy it closes its ranks. A family with the wrong members in control – that, perhaps, is as near as one can come to describing England in a phrase.

IV

Probably the battle of Waterloo *was* won on the playing-fields of Eton, but the opening battles of all subsequent wars have been lost there. One of the dominant facts in English life during the past three quarters of a century has been the decay of ability in the ruling class.

In the years between 1920 and 1940 it was happening with the speed of a chemical reaction. Yet at the moment of writing it is still possible to speak of a ruling class. Like the knife which has had two new blades and three new handles, the upper fringe of English society is still almost what it was in the mid nineteenth century. After 1832 the old land-owning aristocracy steadily lost power, but instead of disappearing or becoming a fossil they simply intermarried with the merchants, manufacturers and financiers who had replaced them, and soon turned them into accurate copies of themselves. The wealthy ship-owner or cotton-miller set up for himself an alibi as a country gentleman, while his sons learned the right mannerisms at public schools which had been designed for just that purpose. England was ruled by an aristocracy constantly recruited from parvenus. And considering what energy the self-made men possessed, and considering that they were buying their way into a class which at any rate had a tradition of public service, one might have expected that able rulers could be produced in some such way.

And yet somehow the ruling class decayed, lost its ability, its daring, finally even its ruthlessness, until a time came when stuffed shirts like Eden or Halifax could stand out as men of exceptional talent. As for Baldwin, one could not even dignify him with the name of stuffed shirt. He was simply a hole in the air. The mishandling of England's domestic problems during the nineteen-twenties had been bad enough, but British foreign policy between 1931 and 1939 is one of the wonders of the world. Why? What had happened? What was it that at every decisive moment made every British statesman do the wrong thing with so unerring an instinct?

The underlying fact was that the whole position of the moneyed class had long ceased to be justifiable. There they sat, at the centre of a vast empire and a world-wide financial network, drawing interest and profits and spending them – on what? It was fair to say that life within the British Empire was in many ways better than life outside it. Still, the Empire was under-developed, India slept in the Middle Ages, the Dominions lay empty, with foreigners jealously barred out, and even England was full of slums and unemployment. Only half a million people, the people in the country houses, definitely benefited from the existing system. Moreover, the tendency of small businesses to merge together into large ones robbed more and more of the moneyed class of their function and turned them into mere *owners*, their work being done for them by salaried managers and technicians. For long past there had been in England an entirely functionless class, living on money that was invested they hardly knew where, the 'idle rich', the people whose photographs you can look at in the *Tatler* and the *Bystander*, always supposing that you want to. The existence of these people was by any standard unjustifiable. They were simply parasites, less useful to society than his fleas are to a dog.

By 1920 there were many people who were aware of all this. By 1930 millions were aware of it. But the British ruling class obviously could not admit to themselves that their usefulness was at an end. Had they done that they would have had to abdicate. For it was not possible for them to turn themselves into mere bandits, like the American millionaires, consciously clinging to unjust privileges and beating down opposition by bribery and tear-gas bombs. After all, they belonged to a class with a certain tradition, they had been to public schools where the duty of dying for your country, if necessary, is laid down as the first and greatest of the Commandments. They had to *feel* themselves true patriots, even while they plundered their countrymen. Clearly there was only one escape for them – into stupidity. They could keep society in its existing shape only by being *unable* to grasp that any improvement was possible. Difficult though this was, they achieved it, largely by fixing their eyes on the past and refusing to notice the changes that were going on round them.

There is much in England that this explains. It explains the decay of country life, due to the keeping-up of a sham feudalism which drives the more spirited workers off the land. It explains the immobility of the public schools, which have barely altered since the eighties of the last century. It explains the military incompetence which has again and again startled the world. Since the fifties every war in which England has engaged has started off with a series of disasters, after which the situation has been saved by people comparatively low in the social scale. The higher commanders, drawn from the aristocracy, could never prepare for modern war, because in order to do so they would have had to admit to themselves that the world was changing. They have always clung to obsolete methods and weapons, because they inevitably saw each war as a repetition of the last. Before the Boer War they prepared for the Zulu War, before the 1914 for the Boer War, and before the present war for 1914. Even at this moment hundreds of thousands of men in England are being trained with the bayonet, a weapon entirely useless except for opening tins. It is worth noticing that the navy and, latterly, the air force, have always been more efficient than the regular army. But the navy is only partially, and the air force hardly at all, within the ruling-class orbit.

It must be admitted that so long as things were peaceful the methods of the British ruling class served them well enough. Their own people manifestly tolerated them. However unjustly England might be organized, it was at any rate not torn by class warfare or haunted by secret police. The Empire was peaceful as no area of comparable size has ever been. Throughout its vast extent, nearly a quarter of the earth, there were fewer armed men than would be found necessary by a minor Balkan state. As people to live under, and looking at them merely from a liberal, *negative* standpoint, the British ruling class had their points. They were preferable to the truly modern men, the Nazis and Fascists. But it had long been obvious that they would be helpless against any serious attack from the outside.

They could not struggle against Nazism or Fascism, because they could not understand them. Neither could they have struggled against Communism, if Communism had been a serious force in western Europe. To understand Fascism they would have had to study the theory of Socialism, which would have forced them to realize that the economic system by which they lived was unjust, inefficient and out-of-date. But it was exactly this fact that they had trained themselves never to face. They dealt with Fascism as the cavalry generals of 1914 dealt with the machine-guns – by ignoring it. After years of aggression and massacres, they had grasped only one fact, that Hitler and Mussolini were hostile to Communism. Therefore, it was argued, they *must* be friendly to the British dividend-drawer. Hence the truly frightening spectacle of Conservative M.P.s wildly cheering the news that British ships, bringing food to the

Spanish Republican government, had been bombed by Italian aeroplanes. Even when they had begun to grasp that Fascism was dangerous, its essentially revolutionary nature, the huge military effort it was capable of making, the sort of tactics it would use, were quite beyond their comprehension. At the time of the Spanish Civil War, anyone with as much political knowledge as can be acquired from a sixpenny pamphlet on Socialism knew that, if Franco won, the result would be strategically disastrous for England; and yet generals and admirals who had given their lives to the study of war were unable to grasp this fact. This vein of political ignorance runs right through English official life, through Cabinet ministers, ambassadors, consuls, judges, magistrates, policemen. The policeman who arrests the 'red' does not understand the theories the 'red' is preaching; if he did his own position as bodyguard of the moneyed class might seem less pleasant to him. There is reason to think that even military espionage is hopelessly hampered by ignorance of the new economic doctrines and the ramifications of the underground parties.

The British ruling class were not altogether wrong in thinking that Fascism was on their side. It is a fact that any rich man, unless he is a Jew, has less to fear from Fascism than from either Communism or democratic Socialism. One ought never to forget this, for nearly the whole German and Italian propaganda is designed to cover it up. The natural instinct of men like Simon, Hoare, Chamberlain etc. was to come to an agreement with Hitler. But – and here the peculiar feature of English life that I have spoken of, the deep sense of national solidarity, comes in – they could only do so by breaking up the Empire and selling their own people into semi-slavery. A truly corrupt class would have done this without hesitation, as in France. But things had not gone that distance in England. Politicians who would make cringing speeches about 'the duty of loyalty to our conquerors' are hardly to be found in English public life. Tossed to and fro between their incomes and their principles, it was impossible that men like Chamberlain should do anything but make the worst of both worlds.

One thing that has always shown that the English ruling class are *morally* fairly sound, is that in time of war they are ready enough to get themselves killed. Several dukes, earls and what nots were killed in the recent campaign in Flanders. That could not happen if these people were the cynical scoundrels that they are sometimes declared to be. It is important not to misunderstand their motives, or one cannot predict their actions. What is to be expected of them is not treachery, or physical cowardice, but stupidity, unconscious sabotage, an infallible instinct for doing the wrong thing. They are not wicked, or not altogether wicked; they are merely unteachable. Only when their money and power are gone will the younger among them begin to grasp what century they are living in.

V

The stagnation of the Empire in the between-war years affected everyone in England, but it had an especially direct effect upon two important sub-sections of the middle class. One was the military and imperialist middle class, generally nicknamed the Blimps, and the other the left-wing intelligentsia. These two seemingly hostile types, symbolic opposites – the half-pay colonel with his bull neck and diminutive brain, like a dinosaur, the highbrow with his domed forehead and stalk-like neck – are mentally linked together and constantly interact upon one another; in any case they are born to a considerable extent into the same families.

Thirty years ago the Blimp class was already losing its vitality. The middle-class families celebrated by Kipling, the prolific lowbrow families whose sons officered the army and navy and swarmed over all the waste places of the earth from the Yukon to the Irrawaddy, were dwindling before 1914. The thing that had killed them was the telegraph. In a narrowing world, more and more governed from Whitehall, there was every year less room for individual initiative. Men like Clive, Nelson, Nicholson, Gordon would find no place for themselves in the modern British Empire. By 1920 nearly every inch of the colonial empire was in the grip of Whitehall. Well-meaning, over-civilized men, in dark suits and black felt hats, with neatly rolled umbrellas crooked over the left forearm, were imposing their constipated view of life on Malaya and Nigeria, Mombasa and Mandalay. The one-time empire builders were reduced to the status of clerks, buried deeper and deeper under mounds of paper and red tape. In the early twenties one could see, all over the Empire, the older officials, who had known more spacious days, writhing impotently under the changes that were happening. From that time onwards it has been next door to impossible to induce young men of spirit to take any part in imperial administration. And what was true of the official world was true also of the commercial. The great monopoly companies swallowed up hosts of petty traders. Instead of going out to trade adventurously in the Indies one went to an office stool in Bombay or Singapore. And life in Bombay or Singapore was actually duller and safer than life in London. Imperialist sentiment remained strong in the middle class, owing to family tradition, but the job of administering the Empire had ceased to appeal. Few able men went east of Suez if there was any way of avoiding it.

But the general weakening of imperialism, and to some extent of the whole British morale, that took place during the nineteen-thirties, was partly the work of the left-wing intelligentsia, itself a kind of growth that had sprouted from the stagnation of the Empire.

It should be noted that there is now no intelligentsia that is not in some sense 'left'. Perhaps the last right-wing intellectual was T. E. Lawrence. Since about 1930 everyone describable as an 'intellectual' has lived in a state of chronic discontent with the existing order. Necessarily so, because society as it was constituted had no room for him. In an Empire that was simply stagnant, neither being developed nor falling to pieces, and in an England ruled by people whose chief asset was their stupidity, to be 'clever' was to be suspect. If you had the kind of brain that could understand the poems of T. S. Eliot or the theories of Karl Marx, the higher-ups would see to it that you were kept out of any important job. The intellectuals could find a function for themselves only in the literary reviews and the left-wing political parties.

The mentality of the English left-wing intelligentsia can be studied in half a dozen weekly and monthly papers. The immediately striking thing about all these papers is their generally negative, querulous attitude, their complete lack at all times of any constructive suggestion. There is little in them except the irresponsible carping of people who have never been and never expect to be in a position of power. Another marked characteristic is the emotional shallowness of people who live in a world of ideas and have little contact with physical reality. Many intellectuals of the Left were flabbily pacifist up to 1935–9, and then promptly cooled off when the war started. It is broadly though not precisely true that the people who were most 'anti-Fascist' during the Spanish Civil War are most defeatist now. And underlying this is the really important fact about so many of the English intelligentsia – their severance from the common culture of the country.

In intention, at any rate, the English intelligentsia are Europeanized. They take their cookery from Paris and their opinions from Moscow. In the general patriotism of the country they form a sort of island of dissident thought. England is perhaps the only great country whose intellectuals are ashamed of their own nationality. In left-wing circles it is always felt that there is something slightly disgraceful in being an Englishman and that it is a duty to snigger at every English institution, from horse racing to suet puddings. It is a strange fact, but it is unquestionably true that almost any English intellectual would feel more ashamed of standing to attention during 'God save the King' than of stealing from a poor box. All through the critical years many left-wingers were chipping away at English morale, trying to spread an outlook that was sometimes squashily pacifist, sometimes violently pro-Russian, but always anti-British. It is questionable how much effect this had, but it certainly had some. If the English people suffered for several years a real weakening of morale, so that the Fascist nations judged that they were 'decadent' and that it was safe to plunge into war, the intellectual sabotage from the Left was partly responsible. Both the *New Statesman* and the *News Chronicle* cried out against the Munich settlement, but even they had done something to make it possible. Ten years of systematic Blimp-baiting affected even the Blimps themselves and made it harder than it had been before to get intelligent young men to enter the armed forces. Given the stagnation of the Empire the military middle class must have decayed in any case, but the spread of a shallow Leftism hastened the process.

It is clear that the special position of the English intellectuals during the past ten years, as purely *negative* creatures, mere anti-Blimps, was a by-product of ruling-class stupidity. Society could not use them, and they had not got it in them to see that devotion to one's country implies 'for better, for worse'. Both Blimps and highbrows took for granted, as though it were a law of nature, the divorce between patriotism and intelligence. If you were a patriot you read *Blackwood's Magazine* and publicly thanked God that you were 'not brainy'. If you were an intellectual you sniggered at the Union Jack and regarded physical courage as barbarous. It is obvious that this preposterous convention cannot continue. The Bloomsbury highbrow, with his mechanical snigger, is as out-of-date as the cavalry colonel. A modern nation cannot afford either of them. Patriotism and intelligence will have to come together again. It is the fact that we are fighting a war, and a very peculiar kind of war, that may make this possible.

VI

One of the most important developments in England during the past twenty years has been the upward and downward extension of the middle class. It has happened on such a scale as to make the old classification of society into capitalists, proletarians and petit bourgeois (small property-owners) almost obsolete.

England is a country in which property and financial power are concentrated in very few hands. Few people in modern England *own* anything at all, except clothes, furniture and possibly a house. The peasantry have long since disappeared, the independent shopkeeper is being destroyed, the small businessman is diminishing in numbers. But at the same time modern industry is so complicated that it cannot get along without great numbers of managers, salesmen, engineers, chemists and technicians of all kinds, drawing fairly large salaries. And these in turn call into being a professional class of doctors, lawyers, teachers, artists, etc. etc. The tendency of advanced capitalism has therefore been to enlarge the middle class and not to wipe it out as it once seemed likely to do.

But much more important than this is the spread of middle-class ideas and habits among the working class. The British working class are now better off in almost all ways than they were thirty years ago. This is partly due to the efforts of the trade unions, but partly to the mere advance of physical science. It is not always realized that within rather narrow limits the standard of life of a country can rise without a corresponding rise in real wages. Up to a point, civilization can lift itself up by its boot-tags. However unjustly society is organized, certain technical advances are bound to benefit the whole community, because certain kinds of goods are necessarily held in common. A millionaire cannot, for example, light the streets for himself while darkening them for other people. Nearly all citizens of civilized countries now enjoy the use of good roads, germ-free water, police protection, free libraries and probably free education of a kind. Public education in England has been meanly starved of money, but it has nevertheless improved, largely owing to the devoted efforts of the teachers, and the habit of reading has become enormously more widespread. To an increasing extent the rich and the poor read the same books, and they also see the same films and listen to the same radio programmes. And the differences in their way of life have been diminished by the mass-production of cheap clothes and improvements in housing. So far as outward appearance goes, the clothes of rich and poor, especially in the case of women, differ far less than they did thirty or even fifteen years ago. As to housing, England still has slums which are a blot on civilization, but much building has been done during the past ten years, largely by the local authorities. The modern council house, with its bathroom and electric light, is smaller than the stockbroker's villa, but it is recognizably the same kind of house, which the farm labourer's cottage is not. A person who has grown up in a council housing estate is likely to be – indeed, visibly *is* – more middle class in outlook than a person who has grown up in a slum.

The effect of all this is a general softening of manners. It is enhanced by the fact that modern industrial methods tend always to demand less muscular effort and therefore to leave people with more energy when their day's work is done. Many workers in the light industries are less truly manual labourers than is a doctor or a grocer. In tastes, habits, manners and outlook the working class and the middle class are drawing together. The unjust distinctions remain, but the real differences diminish. The old-style 'proletarian' – collarless, unshaven and with muscles warped by heavy labour – still exists, but he is constantly decreasing in numbers; he only predominates in the heavy-industry areas of the north of England.

After 1918 there began to appear something that had never existed in England before: people of indeterminate social class. In 1910 every human being in these islands could be 'placed' in an instant by his clothes, manners and accent. That is no longer the case. Above all, it is not the case in the new townships that have developed as a result of cheap motor cars and the southward shift of industry. The place to look for the germs of the future England is in light-industry areas and along the arterial roads. In Slough, Dagenham, Barnet, Letchworth, Hayes – everywhere, indeed, on the outskirts of great towns – the old pattern is gradually changing into something new. In those vast new wildernesses of glass and brick the sharp distinctions of the older kind of town, with its slums and mansions, or of the country, with its manor-houses and squalid cottages, no longer exist. There are wide gradations of income, but it is the same kind of life that is being lived at different levels, in labour-saving flats or council houses, along the concrete roads and in the naked democracy of the swimming-pools. It is a rather restless, cultureless life, centring round tinned food, *Picture Post*, the radio and the internal combustion engine. It is a civilization in which children grow up with an intimate knowledge of magnetoes and in complete ignorance of the Bible. To that civilization belong the people who are most at home in and most definitely *of* the modern world, the technicians and the higher-paid skilled workers, the airmen and their mechanics, the radio experts, film producers, popular journalists and industrial chemists. They are the indeterminate stratum at which the older class distinctions are beginning to break down.

This war, unless we are defeated, will wipe out most of the existing class privileges. There are every day fewer people who wish them to continue. Nor need we fear that as the pattern changes life in England will lose its peculiar flavour. The new red cities of Greater London are crude enough, but these things are only the rash that accompanies a change. In whatever shape England emerges from the war it will be deeply tinged with the characteristics that I have spoken of earlier. The intellectuals who hope to see it Russianized or Germanized will be disappointed. The gentleness, the hypocrisy, the thoughtlessness, the reverence for law and the hatred of uniforms will remain, along with the suet puddings and the misty skies. It needs some very great disaster, such as prolonged subjugation by a foreign enemy, to destroy a national culture. The Stock Exchange will be pulled down, the horse plough will give way to the tractor, the country houses will be turned into children's holiday camps, the Eton and Harrow match will be forgotten, but England will still be England, an everlasting animal stretching into the future and the past, and, like all living things, having the power to change out of recognition and yet remain the same.

PART II: SHOPKEEPERS AT WAR

I

I began this book to the tune of German bombs, and I begin this second chapter in the added racket of the barrage. The yellow gun-flashes are lighting the sky, the splinters are rattling on the housetops, and London Bridge is falling down, falling down, falling down. Anyone able to read a map knows that we are in deadly danger. I do not mean that we are beaten or need be beaten. Almost certainly the outcome depends on our own will. But at this moment we are in the soup, full fathom five, and we have been brought there by follies which we are still committing and which will drown us altogether if we do not mend our ways quickly.

What this war has demonstrated is that private capitalism – that is, an economic system in which land, factories, mines and transport are owned privately and operated solely for profit – *does not work.* It cannot deliver the goods. This fact had been known to millions of people for years past, but nothing ever came of it, because there was no real urge from below to alter the system, and those at the top had trained themselves to be impenetrably stupid on just this point. Argument and propaganda got one nowhere. The lords of property simply sat on their bottoms and proclaimed that all was for the best. Hitler's conquest of Europe, however, was a *physical* debunking of capitalism. War, for all its evil, is at any rate an unanswerable test of strength, like a try-your-grip machine. Great strength returns the penny, and there is no way of faking the result.

When the nautical screw was first invented, there was a controversy that lasted for years as to whether screw-steamers or paddle-steamers were better. The paddle-steamers, like all obsolete things, had their champions, who supported them by ingenious arguments. Finally, however, a distinguished admiral tied a screw-steamer and a paddle-steamer of equal horsepower stern to stern and set their engines running. That settled the question once and for all. And it was something similar that happened on the fields of Norway and of Flanders. Once and for all it was proved that a planned economy is stronger than a planless one. But it is necessary here to give some kind of definition to those much-abused words, Socialism and Fascism.

Socialism is usually defined as 'common ownership of the means of production'. Crudely: the State, representing the whole nation, owns everything, and everyone is a State employee. This does *not* mean that people are stripped of private possessions such as clothes and furniture, but it *does* mean that all productive goods, such as land, mines, ships and machinery, are the property of the State. The State is the sole large-scale producer. It is not certain that Socialism is in all ways superior to capitalism, but it is certain that, unlike capitalism, it can solve the problems of production and consumption. At normal times a capitalist economy can never consume all that it produces, so that there is always a wasted surplus (wheat burned in furnaces, herrings dumped back into the sea etc. etc.) and always unemployment. In time of war, on the other hand, it has difficulty in producing all that it needs, because nothing is produced unless someone sees his way to making a profit out of it.

In a Socialist economy these problems do not exist. The State simply calculates what goods will be needed and does its best to produce them. Production is only limited by the amount of labour and raw materials. Money, for internal purposes, ceases to be a mysterious all-powerful thing and becomes a sort of coupon or ration-ticket, issued in sufficient quantities to buy up such consumption goods as may be available at the moment.

However, it has become clear in the last few years that 'common ownership of the means of production' is not in itself a sufficient definition of Socialism. One must also add the following: approximate equality of incomes (it need be no more than approximate), political democracy, and abolition of all hereditary privilege, especially in education. These are simply the necessary safeguards against the reappearance of a class-system. Centralized ownership has very little meaning unless the mass of the people are living roughly upon an equal level, and have some kind of control over the government. 'The State' may come to mean no more than a self-elected political party, and oligarchy and privilege can return, based on power rather than on money.

But what then is Fascism?

Fascism, at any rate the German version, is a form of capitalism that borrows from Socialism just such features as will make it efficient for war purposes. Internally, Germany has a good deal in common with a Socialist state. Ownership has never been abolished, there are still capitalists and workers, and – this is the important point, and the real reason why rich men all over the world tend to sympathize with Fascism – generally speaking the same people are capitalists and the same people workers as before the Nazi revolution. But at the same time the State, which is simply the Nazi Party, is in control of everything. It controls investment, raw materials, rates of interest, working hours, wages. The factory owner still owns his factory, but he is for practical purposes reduced to the status of a manager. Everyone is in effect a State employee, though the salaries vary very greatly. The mere *efficiency* of such a system, the elimination of waste and obstruction, is obvious. In seven years it has built up the most powerful war machine the world has ever seen.

But the idea underlying Fascism is irreconcilably different from that which underlies Socialism. Socialism aims, ultimately, at a world-state of free and equal human beings. It takes the equality of human rights for granted. Nazism assumes just the opposite. The driving force behind the Nazi movement is the belief in human *inequality*, the superiority of Germans to all other races, the right of Germany to rule the world. Outside the German Reich it does not recognize any obligations. Eminent Nazi professors have 'proved' over and over again that only nordic man is fully human, have even mooted the idea that non-nordic peoples (such as ourselves) can interbreed with gorillas! Therefore, while a species of war-Socialism exists within the German state, its attitude towards conquered nations is frankly that of an exploiter. The function of the Czechs, Poles, French, etc. is simply to produce such goods as Germany may need, and get in return just as little as will keep them from open rebellion. If we are conquered, our job will probably be to manufacture weapons for Hitler's forthcoming wars with Russia and America. The Nazis aim, in effect, at setting up a kind of caste system, with four main castes corresponding rather closely to those of the Hindu religion. At the top comes the Nazi party, second come the mass of the German people, third come the conquered European populations. Fourth and last are to come the coloured peoples, the 'semi-apes' as Hitler calls them, who are to be reduced quite openly to slavery.

However horrible this system may seem to us, *it works*. It works because it is a planned system geared to a definite purpose, world-conquest, and not allowing any private interest, either of capitalist or worker, to stand in its way. British capitalism does not work, because it is a competitive system in which private profit is and must be the main objective. It is a system in which all the forces are pulling in opposite directions and the interests of the individual are as often as not totally opposed to those of the State.

All through the critical years British capitalism, with its immense industrial plant and its unrivalled supply of skilled labour, was unequal to the strain of preparing for war. To prepare for war on the modern scale you have got to divert the greater part of your national income to armaments, which means cutting down on consumption goods. A bombing plane, for instance, is equivalent in price to fifty small motor cars, or eight thousand pairs of silk stockings, or a million loaves of bread. Clearly you can't have *many* bombing planes without lowering the national standard of life. It is guns or butter, as Marshal Goering remarked. But in Chamberlain's England the transition could not be made. The rich would not face the necessary taxation, and while the rich are still visibly rich it is not possible to tax the poor very heavily either. Moreover, so long as *profit* was the main object the manufacturer had no incentive to change over from consumption goods to armaments. A businessman's first duty is to his shareholders. Perhaps England needs tanks, but perhaps it pays better to manufacture motor cars. To prevent war material from reaching the enemy is common sense, but to sell in the highest market is a business duty. Right at the end of August 1939 the British dealers were tumbling over one another in their eagerness to sell Germany tin, rubber, copper and shellac – and this in the clear, certain knowledge that war was going to break out in a week or two. It was about as sensible as selling somebody a razor to cut your throat with. But it was 'good business'.

And now look at the results. After 1934 it was known that Germany was rearming. After 1936 everyone with eyes in his head knew that war was coming. After Munich it was merely a question of how soon the war would begin. In September 1939 war broke out. *Eight months later* it was discovered that, so far as equipment went, the British army was barely beyond the standard of 1918. We saw our soldiers fighting their way desperately to the coast, with one aeroplane against three, with rifles against tanks, with bayonets against tommy-guns. There were not even enough revolvers to supply all the officers. After a year of war the regular army was still short of 300,000 tin hats. There had even, previously, been a shortage of uniforms – this in one of the greatest woollen-goods producing countries in the world!

What had happened was that the whole moneyed class, unwilling to face a change in their way of life, had shut their eyes to the nature of Fascism and modern war. And false optimism was fed to the general public by the gutter press, which lives on its advertisements and is therefore interested in keeping trade conditions normal. Year after year the Beaverbrook press assured us in huge headlines that THERE WILL BE NO WAR, and as late as the beginning of 1939 Lord Rothermere was describing Hitler as 'a great gentleman'. And while England in the moment of disaster proved to be short of every war material except ships, it is not recorded that there was any shortage of motor cars, fur coats, gramophones, lipstick, chocolates or silk stockings. And dare anyone pretend that the same tug-of-war between private profit and public necessity is not still continuing? England fights for her life, but business must fight for profits. You can hardly open a newspaper without seeing the two contradictory processes happening side by side. On the very same page you will find the Government urging you to save and the seller of some useless luxury urging you to spend. Lend to Defend, but Guinness is Good for You. Buy a Spitfire, but also buy Haig and Haig, Pond's Face Cream and Black Magic Chocolates.

But one thing gives hope – the visible swing in public opinion. If we can survive this war, the defeat in Flanders will turn out to have been one of the great turning-points in English history. In that spectacular disaster the working class, the middle class and even a section of the business community could see the utter rottenness of private capitalism. Before that the case against capitalism had never been *proved*. Russia, the only definitely Socialist country, was backward and far away. All criticism broke itself against the rat-trap faces of bankers and the brassy laughter of stockbrokers. Socialism? Ha! ha! ha! Where's the money to come from? Ha! ha! ha! The lords of property were firm in their seats, and they knew it. But after the French collapse there came something that could not be laughed away, something that neither cheque-books nor policemen were any use against – the bombing. Zweee – BOOM! What's that? Oh, only a bomb on the Stock Exchange. Zweee – BOOM! Another acre of somebody's valuable slum-property gone west. Hitler will at any rate go down in history as the man who made the City of London laugh on the wrong side of its face. For the first time in their lives the comfortable were uncomfortable, the professional optimists had to admit that there was something wrong. It was a great step forward. From that time onwards the ghastly job of trying to convince artificially stupefied people that a planned economy might be better than a free-for-all in which the worst man wins – that job will never be quite so ghastly again.

II

The difference between Socialism and capitalism is not primarily a difference of technique. One cannot simply change from one system to the other as one might install a piece of machinery in a factory, and then carry on as before, with the same people in positions of control. Obviously there is also needed a complete shift of power. New blood, new men, new ideas – in the true sense of the word, a revolution.

I have spoken earlier of the soundness and homogeneity of England, the patriotism that runs like a connecting thread through almost all classes. After Dunkirk anyone who had eyes in his head could see this. But it is absurd to pretend that the promise of that moment has been fulfilled. Almost certainly the mass of the people are now ready for the vast changes that are necessary; but those changes have not even begun to happen.

England is a family with the wrong members in control. Almost entirely we are governed by the rich, and by people who step into positions of command by right of birth. Few if any of these people are consciously treacherous, some of them are not even fools but as a class they are quite incapable of leading us to victory. They could not do it, even if their material interests did not constantly trip them up. As I pointed out earlier, they have been artificially stupefied. Quite apart from anything else, the rule of money sees to it that we shall be governed largely by the old – that is, by people utterly unable to grasp what age they are living in or what enemy they are fighting. Nothing was more desolating at the beginning of this war than the way in which the whole of the older generation conspired to pretend that it was the war of 1914–18 over again. All the old duds were back on the job, twenty years older, with the skull plainer in their faces. Ian Hay was cheering up the troops, Belloc was writing articles on strategy, Maurois doing broadcasts, Bairnsfather drawing cartoons. It was like a tea-party of ghosts. And that state of affairs has barely altered. The shock of disaster brought a few able men like Bevin to the front, but in general we are still commanded by people who managed to live through the years 1931–9 without even discovering that Hitler was dangerous. A generation of the unteachable is hanging upon us like a necklace of corpses.

As soon as one considers any problem of this war – and it does not matter whether it is the widest aspect of strategy or the tiniest detail of home organization – one sees that the necessary moves cannot be made while the social structure of England remains what it is. Inevitably, because of their position and upbringing, the ruling class are fighting for their own privileges, which cannot possibly be reconciled with the public interest. It is a mistake to imagine that war aims, strategy, propaganda and industrial organization exist in watertight compartments. All are interconnected. Every strategic plan, every tactical method, even every weapon will bear the stamp of the social system that produced it. The British ruling class are fighting against Hitler, whom they have always regarded and whom some of them still regard as their protector against Bolshevism. That does not mean that they will deliberately sell out; but it does mean that at every decisive moment they are likely to falter, pull their punches, do the wrong thing.

Until the Churchill Government called some sort of halt to the process, they have done the wrong thing with an unerring instinct ever since 1931. They helped Franco to overthrow the Spanish Government, although anyone not an imbecile could have told them that a Fascist Spain would be hostile to England. They fed Italy with war materials all through the winter of 1939–40, although it was obvious to the whole world that the Italians were going to attack us in the spring. For the sake of a few hundred thousand dividend-drawers they are turning India from an ally into an enemy. Moreover, so long as the moneyed classes remain in control, we cannot develop any but a *defensive* strategy. Every victory means a change in the *status quo*. How can we drive the Italians out of Abyssinia without rousing echoes among the coloured peoples of our own Empire? How can we even smash Hitler without the risk of bringing the German Socialists and Communists into power? The left-wingers who wail that 'this is a capitalist war' and that 'British Imperialism' is fighting for loot have got their heads screwed on backwards. The last thing the British moneyed class wish for is to acquire fresh territory. It would simply be an embarrassment. Their war aim (both unattainable and unmentionable) is simply to hang on to what they have got.

Internally, England is still the rich man's Paradise. All talk of 'equality of sacrifice' is nonsense. At the same time as factory-workers are asked to put up with longer hours, advertisements for 'Butler. One in family, eight in staff' are appearing in the press. The bombed-out populations of the East End go hungry and homeless while wealthier victims simply step into their cars and flee to comfortable country houses. The Home Guard swells to a million men in a few weeks, and is deliberately organized from above in such a way that only people with private incomes can hold positions of command. Even the rationing system is so arranged that it hits the poor all the time, while people with over £2,000 a year are practically unaffected by it. Everywhere privilege is squandering good will. In such circumstances even propaganda becomes almost impossible. As attempts to stir up patriotic feeling, the red posters issued by the Chamberlain Government at the beginning of the war broke all depth-records. Yet they could not have been much other than they were, for how could Chamberlain and his followers take the risk of rousing strong popular feeling *against Fascism*? Anyone who was genuinely hostile to Fascism must also be opposed to Chamberlain himself and to all the others who had helped Hitler into power. So also with external propaganda. In all Lord Halifax's speeches there is not one concrete proposal for which a single inhabitant of Europe would risk the top joint of his little finger. For what war aim can Halifax, or anyone like him, conceivably have, except to put the clock back to 1933?

It is only by revolution that the native genius of the English people can be set free. Revolution does not mean red flags and street fighting, it means a fundamental shift of power. Whether it happens with or without bloodshed is largely an accident of time and place. Nor does it mean the dictatorship of a single class. The people in England who grasp what changes are needed and are capable of carrying them through are not confined to any one class, though it is true that very few people with over £2,000 a year are among them. What is wanted is a conscious open revolt by ordinary people against inefficiency, class privilege and the rule of the old. It is not primarily a question of change of government. British governments do, broadly speaking, represent the will of the people, and if we alter our structure from below we shall get the government we need. Ambassadors, generals, officials and colonial adminstrators who are senile or pro-Fascist are more dangerous than Cabinet ministers whose follies have to be committed in public. Right through our national life we have got to fight against privilege, against the notion that a half-witted public-schoolboy is better for command than an intelligent mechanic. Although there are gifted and honest *individuals* among them, we have got to break the grip of the moneyed class as a whole. England has got to assume its real shape. The England that is only just beneath the surface, in the factories and the newspaper offices, in the aeroplanes and the submarines, has got to take charge of its own destiny.

In the short run, equality of sacrifice, 'war-Communism', is even more important than radical economic changes. It is very necessary that industry should be nationalized, but it is more urgently necessary that such monstrosities as butlers and 'private incomes' should disappear forthwith. Almost certainly the main reason why the Spanish Republic could keep up the fight for two and a half years against impossible odds was that there were no gross contrasts of wealth. The people suffered horribly, but they all suffered alike. When the private soldier had not a cigarette, the general had not one either. Given equality of sacrifice, the morale of a country like England would probably be unbreakable. But at present we have nothing to appeal to except traditional patriotism, which is deeper here than elsewhere, but is not necessarily bottomless. At some point or another you have got to deal with the man who says 'I should be no worse off under Hitler.' But what answer can you give him – that is, what answer that you can expect him to listen to – while common soldiers risk their lives for two and sixpence a day, and fat women ride about in Rolls-Royce cars, nursing pekineses?

It is quite likely that this war will last three years. It will mean cruel overwork, cold dull winters, uninteresting food, lack of amusements, prolonged bombing. It cannot but lower the general standard of living, because the essential act of war is to manufacture armaments instead of consumable goods. The working class will have to suffer terrible things. And they *will* suffer them, almost indefinitely, provided that they know what they are fighting for. They are not cowards, and they are not internationally minded. They can stand all that the Spanish workers stood, and more. But they will want some kind of proof that a better life is ahead for themselves and their children. The one sure earnest of that is that when they are taxed and overworked they shall see that the rich are being hit even harder. And if the rich squeal audibly, so much the better.

We can bring these things about, if we really want to. It is not true that public opinion has no power in England. It never makes itself heard without achieving something; it has been responsible for most of the changes for the better during the past six months. But we have moved with glacier-like slowness, and we have learned only from disasters. It took the fall of Paris to get rid of Chamberlain and the unnecessary suffering of scores of thousands of people in the East End to get rid or partially rid of Sir John Anderson. It is not worth losing a battle in order to bury a corpse. For we are fighting against swift evil intelligences, and time presses, and

> history to the defeated
> May say Alas! but cannot alter or pardon.

III

During the last six months there has been much talk of 'the Fifth Column'. From time to time obscure lunatics have been jailed for making speeches in favour of Hitler, and large numbers of German refugees have been interned, a thing which has almost certainly done us great harm in Europe. It is of course obvious that the idea of a large, organized army of Fifth Columnists suddenly appearing on the streets with weapons in their hands, as in Holland and Belgium, is ridiculous. Nevertheless a Fifth Column danger does exist. One can only consider it if one also considers in what way England might be defeated.

It does not seem probable that air bombing can settle a major war. England might well be invaded and conquered, but the invasion would be a dangerous gamble, and if it happened and failed it would probably leave us more united and less Blimp-ridden than before. Moreover, if England were overrun by foreign troops the English people would know that they had been beaten and would continue the struggle. It is doubtful whether they could be held down permanently, or whether Hitler wishes to keep an army of a million men stationed in these islands. A government of –, – and – (you can fill in the names) would suit him better. The English can probably not be bullied into surrender, but they might quite easily be bored, cajoled or cheated into it, provided that, as at Munich, they did not know that they were surrendering. It could happen most easily when the war seemed to be going well rather than badly. The threatening tone of so much of the German and Italian propaganda is a psychological mistake. It only gets home on intellectuals. With the general public the proper approach would be 'Let's call it a draw'. It is when a peace-offer along *those* lines is made that the pro-Fascists will raise their voices.

But who are the pro-Fascists? The idea of a Hitler victory appeals to the very rich, to the Communists, to Mosley's followers, to the pacifists, and to certain sections among the Catholics. Also, if things went badly enough on the Home Front, the whole of the poorer section of the working class might swing round to a position that was defeatist though not actively pro-Hitler.

In this motley list one can see the daring of German propaganda, its willingness to offer everything to everybody. But the various pro-Fascist forces are not consciously acting together, and they operate in different ways.

The Communists must certainly be regarded as pro-Hitler, and are bound to remain so unless Russian policy changes, but they have not very much influence. Mosley's Blackshirts, though now lying very low, are a more serious danger, because of the footing they probably possess in the armed forces. Still, even in its palmiest days Mosley's following can hardly have numbered 50,000. Pacifism is a psychological curiosity rather than a political movement. Some of the extremer pacifists, starting out with a complete renunciation of violence, have ended by warmly championing Hitler and even toying with antisemitism. This is interesting, but it is not important. 'Pure' pacifism, which is a by-product of naval power, can only appeal to people in very sheltered positions. Moreover, being negative and irresponsible, it does not inspire much devotion. Of the membership of the Peace Pledge Union, less than fifteen per cent even pay their annual subscriptions. None of these bodies of people, pacifists, Communists or Blackshirts, could bring a large-scale stop-the-war movement into being by their own efforts. But they might help to make things very much easier for a treacherous government negotiating surrender. Like the French Communists, they might become the half-conscious agents of millionaires.

The real danger is from above. One ought not to pay any attention to Hitler's recent line of talk about being the friend of the poor man, the enemy of plutocracy, etc. etc. Hitler's real self is in *Mein Kampf*, and in his actions. He has never persecuted the rich, except when they were Jews or when they tried actively to oppose him. He stands for a centralized economy which robs the capitalist of most of his power but leaves the structure of society much as before. The State controls industry, but there are still rich and poor, masters and men. Therefore, as against genuine Socialism, the moneyed class have always been on his side. This was crystal clear at the time of the Spanish Civil War, and clear again at the time when France surrendered. Hitler's puppet government are not working men, but a gang of bankers, gaga generals and corrupt right-wing politicians.

That kind of spectacular, *conscious* treachery is less likely to succeed in England, indeed is far less likely even to be tried. Nevertheless, to many payers of supertax this war is simply an insane family squabble which ought to be stopped at all costs. One need not doubt that a 'peace' movement is on foot somewhere in high places; probably a shadow Cabinet has already been formed. These people will get their chance not in the moment of defeat but in some stagnant period when boredom is reinforced by discontent. They will not talk about surrender, only about peace; and doubtless they will persuade themselves, and perhaps other people, that they are acting for the best. An army of unemployed led by millionaires quoting the Sermon on the Mount – that is our danger. But it cannot arise when we have once introduced a reasonable degree of social justice. The lady in the Rolls-Royce car is more damaging to morale than a fleet of Goering's bombing planes.

PART III: THE ENGLISH REVOLUTION

I

The English revolution started several years ago, and it began to gather momentum when the troops came back from Dunkirk. Like all else in England, it happens in a sleepy, unwilling way, but it is happening. The war has speeded it up, but it has also increased, and desparately, the necessity for speed.

Progress and reaction are ceasing to have anything to do with party labels. If one wishes to name a particular moment, one can say that the old distinction between Right and Left broke down when *Picture Post* was first published. What are the politics of *Picture Post*? Or of *Cavalcade*, or Priestley's broadcasts, or the leading articles in the *Evening Standard*? None of the old classifications will fit them. They merely point to the existence of multitudes of unlabelled people who have grasped within the last year or two that something is wrong. But since a classless, ownerless society is generally spoken of as 'Socialism', we can give that name to the society towards which we are now moving. The war and the revolution are inseparable. We cannot establish anything that a western nation would regard as Socialism without defeating Hitler; on the other hand we cannot defeat Hitler while we remain economically and socially in the nineteenth century. The past is fighting the future and we have two years, a year, possibly only a few months, to see to it that the future wins.

We cannot look to this or to any similar government to put through the necessary changes of its own accord. The initiative will have to come from below. That means that there will have to arise something that has never existed in England, a Socialist movement that actually has the mass of the people behind it. But one must start by recognizing why it is that English Socialism has failed.

In England there is only one Socialist party that has ever seriously mattered, the Labour Party. It has never been able to achieve any major change, because except in purely domestic matters it has never possessed a genuinely independent policy. It was and is primarily a party of the trade unions, devoted to raising wages and improving working conditions. This meant that all through the critical years it was directly interested in the prosperity of British capitalism. In particular it was interested in the maintenance of the British Empire, for the wealth of England was drawn largely from Asia and Africa. The standard of living of the trade-union workers, whom the Labour Party represented, depended indirectly on the sweating of Indian coolies. At the same time the Labour Party was a Socialist party, using Socialist phraseology, thinking in terms of an old-fashioned anti-imperialism and more or less pledged to make restitution to the coloured races. It had to stand for the 'independence' of India, just as it had to stand for disarmament and 'progress' generally. Nevertheless everyone was aware that this was nonsense. In the age of the tank and the bombing plane, backward agricultural countries like India and the African colonies can no more be independent than can a cat or a dog. Had any Labour government come into office with a clear majority and then proceeded to grant India anything that could truly be called independence, India would simply have been absorbed by Japan, or divided between Japan and Russia.

To a Labour government in power, three imperial policies would have been open. One was to continue administering the Empire exactly as before, which meant dropping all pretensions to Socialism. Another was to set the subject peoples 'free', which meant in practice handing them over to Japan, Italy and other predatory powers, and incidently causing a catastrophic drop in the British standard of living. The third was to develop a *positive* imperial policy, and aim at transforming the Empire into a federation of Socialist states, like a looser and freer version of the Union of Soviet Republics. But the Labour Party's history and background made this impossible. It was a party of the trade unions, hopelessly parochial in outlook, with little interest in imperial affairs and no contacts among the men who actually held the Empire together. It would have had to hand the administration of India and Africa and the whole job of imperial defence to men drawn from a different class and traditionally hostile to Socialism. Overshadowing everything was the doubt whether a Labour government which meant business could make itself obeyed. For all the size of its following, the Labour Party had no footing in the navy, little or none in the army or air force, none whatever in the Colonial Services, and not even a sure footing in the Home Civil Service. In England its position was strong but not unchallengeable, and outside England all the points were in the hands of its enemies. Once in power, the same dilemma would always have faced it: carry out your promises, and risk revolt, or continue with the same policy as the Conservatives, and stop talking about Socialism. The Labour leaders never found a solution, and from 1935 onwards it was very doubtful whether they had any wish to take office. They had degenerated into a Permanent Opposition.

Outside the Labour Party there existed several extremist parties, of whom the Communists were the strongest. The Communists had considerable influence in the Labour Party in the years 1920–26 and 1935–9. Their chief importance, and that of the whole left wing of the Labour movement, was the part they played in alienating the middle classes from Socialism.

The history of the past seven years has made it perfectly clear that Communism has no chance in western Europe. The appeal of Fascism is enormously greater. In one country after another the Communists have been rooted out by their more up-to-date enemies, the Nazis. In the English-speaking countries they never had a serious footing. The creed they were spreading could appeal only to a rather rare type of person, found chiefly in the middle-class intelligentsia, the type who has ceased to love his own country but still feels the need of patriotism, and therefore develops patriotic sentiments towards Russia. By 1940, after working for twenty years and spending a great deal of money, the British Communists had barely 20,000 members, actually a smaller number than they had started out with in 1920. The other Marxist parties were of even less importance. They had not the Russian money and prestige behind them, and even more than the Communists they were tied to the nineteenth-century doctrine of the class war. They continued year after year to preach this out-of-date gospel, and never drew any inference from the fact that it got them no followers.

Nor did any strong native Fascist movement grow up. Material conditions were not bad enough, and no leader who could be taken seriously was forthcoming. One would have had to look a long time to find a man more barren of ideas than Sir Oswald Mosley. He was as hollow as a jug. Even the elementary fact that Fascism must not offend national sentiment had escaped him. His entire movement was imitated slavishly from abroad, the uniform and the party programme from Italy and the salute from Germany, with the Jew-baiting tacked on as an afterthought, Mosley having actually started his movement with Jews among his most prominent followers. A man of the stamp of Bottomley or Lloyd George could perhaps have brought a real British Fascist movement into existence. But such leaders only appear when the psychological need for them exists.

After twenty years of stagnation and unemployment, the entire English Socialist movement was unable to produce a version of Socialism which the mass of the people could even find desirable. The Labour Party stood for a timid reformism, the Marxists were looking at the modern world through nineteenth-century spectacles. Both ignored agriculture and imperial problems, and both antagonized the middle classes. The suffocating stupidity of left-wing propaganda had frightened away whole classes of necessary people, factory managers, airmen, naval officers, farmers, white-collar workers, shopkeepers, policemen. All of these people had been taught to think of Socialism as something which menaced their livelihood, or as something seditious, alien, 'anti-British' as they would have called it. Only the intellectuals, the least useful section of the middle-class, gravitated towards the movement.

A Socialist Party which genuinely wished to achieve anything would have started by facing several facts which to this day are considered unmentionable in left-wing circles. It would have recognized that England is more united than most countries, that the British workers have a great deal to lose besides their chains, and that the differences in outlook and habits between class and class are rapidly diminishing. In general, it would have recognized that the old-fashioned 'proletarian revolution' is an impossibility. But all through the between-war years no Socialist programme that was both revolutionary and workable ever appeared; basically, no doubt, because no one genuinely wanted any major change to happen. The Labour leaders wanted to go on and on, drawing their salaries and periodically swapping jobs with the Conservatives. The Communists wanted to go on and on, suffering a comfortable martyrdom, meeting with endless defeats and afterwards putting the blame on other people. The left-wing intelligentsia wanted to go on and on, sniggering at the Blimps, sapping away at middle-class morale, but still keeping their favoured position as hangers-on of the dividend-drawers. Labour Party politics had become a variant of Conservatism, 'revolutionary' politics had become a game of make-believe.

Now, however, the circumstances have changed, the drowsy years have ended. Being a Socialist no longer means kicking theoretically against a system which in practice you are fairly well satisfied with. This time our predicament is real. It is 'the Philistines be upon thee, Samson'. We have got to make our words take physical shape, or perish. We know very well that with its present social structure England cannot survive, and we have got to make other people see that fact and act upon it. We cannot win the war without introducing Socialism, nor establish Socialism without winning the war. At such a time it is possible, as it was not in the peaceful years, to be both revolutionary and realistic. A Socialist movement which can swing the mass of the people behind it, drive the pro-Fascists out of positions of control, wipe out the grosser injustices and let the working class see that they have something to fight for, win over the middle classes instead of antagonizing them, produce a workable imperial policy instead of a mixture of humbug and Utopianism, bring patriotism and intelligence into partnership – for the first time, a movement of such a kind becomes possible.

II

The fact that we are at war has turned Socialism from a text-book word into a realizable policy.

The inefficiency of private capitalism has been proved all over Europe. Its injustice has been proved in the East End of London. Patriotism, against which the Socialists fought so long, has become a tremendous lever in their hands. People who at any other time would cling like glue to their miserable scraps of privilege, will surrender them fast enough when their country is in danger. War is the greatest of all agents of change. It speeds up all processes, wipes out minor distinctions, brings realities to the surface. Above all, war brings it home to the individual. That he is *not* altogether an individual. It is only because they are aware of this that men will die on the field of battle. At this moment it is not so much a question of surrendering leisure, comfort, economic liberty, social prestige. There are very few people in England who really want to see their country conquered by Germany. If it can be made clear that defeating Hitler means wiping out class privilege, the great mass of middling people, the £6 a week to £2,000 a year class, will probably be on our side. These people are quite indispensable, because they include most of the technical experts. Obviously the snobbishness and political ignorance of people like airmen and naval officers will be a very great difficulty. But without those airmen, destroyer commanders, etc. etc. we could not survive for a week. The only approach to them is through their patriotism. An intelligent Socialist movement will *use* their patriotism, instead of merely insulting it, as hitherto.

But do I mean that there will no opposition? Of course not. It would be childish to expect anything of the kind.

There will be a bitter political struggle, and there will be unconscious and half-conscious sabotage everywhere. At some point or other it may be necessary to use violence. It is easy to imagine a pro-Fascist rebellion breaking out in, for instance, India. We shall have to fight against bribery, ignorance and snobbery. The bankers and the larger businessmen, the landowners and dividend-drawers, the officials with their prehensile bottoms, will obstruct for all they are worth. Even the middle classes will writhe when their accustomed way of life is menaced. But just because the English sense of national unity has never disintegrated, because patriotism is finally stronger than class-hatred, the chances are that the will of the majority will prevail. It is no use imagining that one can make fundamental changes without causing a split in the nation; but the treacherous minority will be far smaller in time of war than it would be at any other time.

The swing of opinion is visibly happening, but it cannot be counted on to happen fast enough of its own accord. This war is a race between the consolidation of Hitler's empire and the growth of democratic consciousness. Everywhere in England you can see a ding-dong battle ranging to and fro – in Parliament and in the Government, in the factories and the armed forces, in the pubs and the air-raid shelters, in the newspapers and on the radio. Every day there are tiny defeats, tiny victories. Morrison for Home Secretary – a few yards forward. Priestley shoved off the air – a few yards back. It is a struggle between the groping and the unteachable, between the young and the old, between the living and the dead. But it is very necessary that the discontent which undoubtedly exists should take a purposeful and not merely obstructive form. It is time for *the people* to define their war aims. What is wanted is a simple, concrete programme of action, which can be given all possible publicity, and round which public opinion can group itself.

I suggest that the following six-point programme is the kind of thing we need. The first three points deal with England's internal policy, the other three with the Empire and the world:

1. Nationalization of land, mines, railways, banks and major industries.

2. Limitation of incomes, on such a scale that the highest tax-free income in Britain does not exceed the lowest by more than ten to one.

3. Reform of the educational system along democractic lines.

4. Immediate Dominion status for India, with power to secede when the war is over.

5. Formation of an Imperial General Council, in which the coloured peoples are to be represented.

6. Declaration of formal alliance with China, Abyssinia and all other victims of the Fascist powers.

The general tendency of this programme is unmistakable. It aims quite frankly at turning this war into a revolutionary war and England into a Socialist democracy. I have deliberately included in it nothing that the simplest person could not understand and see the reason for. In the form in which I have put it, it could be printed on the front page of the *Daily Mirror*. But for the purposes of this book a certain amount of amplification is needed.

1. *Nationalization*. One can 'nationalize' industry by the stroke of a pen, but the actual process is slow and complicated. What is needed is that the ownership of all major industry shall be formally vested in the State, representing the common people. Once that is done it becomes possible to eliminate the class of mere *owners* who live not by virtue of anything they produce but by the possession of title-deeds and share certificates. State-ownership implies, therefore, that nobody shall live without working, How sudden a change in the conduct of industry it implies is less certain. In a country like England we cannot rip down the whole structure and build again from the bottom, least of all in time of war. Inevitably the majority of industrial concerns will continue with much the same personnel as before, the one-time owners or managing directors carrying on with their jobs as State employees. There is reason to think that many of the smaller capitalists would actually welcome some such arrangement. The resistance will come from the big capitalists, the bankers, the landlords and the idle rich, roughly speaking the class with over £2,000 a year – and even if one counts in all their dependants there are not more than half a million of these people in England. Nationalization of agricultural land implies cutting out the landlord and the tithe drawer, but not necessarily interfering with the farmer. It is difficult to imagine any reorganization of English agriculture that would not retain most of the existing farms as units, at any rate at the beginning. The farmer, when he is competent, will continue as a salaried manager. He is virtually that already, with the added disadvantage of having to make a

profit and being permanently in debt to the bank. With certain kinds of petty trading, and even the small-scale ownership of land, the State will probably not interfere at all. It would be a great mistake to start by victimizing the smallholder class, for instance. These people are necessary, on the whole they are competent, and the amount of work they do depends on the feeling that they are 'their own masters'. But the State will certainly impose an upward limit to the ownership of land (probably fifteen acres at the very most), and will never permit any ownership of land in town areas.

From the moment that all productive goods have been declared the property of the State, the common people will feel, as they cannot feel now, that the State *is themselves*. They will be ready then to endure the sacrifices that are ahead of us, war or no war. And even if the face of England hardly seems to change, on the day that our main industries are formally nationalized the dominance of a single class will have been broken. From then onwards the emphasis will be shifted from ownership to management, from privilege to competence. It is quite possible that State-ownership will in itself bring about less social change than will be forced upon us by the common hardships of war. But it is the necessary first step without which any *real* reconstruction is impossible.

2. *Incomes*. Limitation of incomes implies the fixing of a minimum wage, which implies a managed internal currency based simply on the amount of consumption goods available. And this again implies a stricter rationing scheme than is now in operation. It is no use at this stage of the world's history to suggest that all human beings should have *exactly* equal incomes. It has been shown over and over again that without some kind of money reward there is no incentive to undertake certain jobs. On the other hand the money reward need not be very large. In practice it is impossible that earnings should be limited quite as rigidly as I have suggested. There will always be anomalies and evasions. But there is no reason why ten to one should not be the maximum normal variation. And within those limits some sense of equality is possible. A man with £3 a week and a man with £1,500 a year can feel themselves fellow creatures, which the Duke of Westminster and the sleepers on the Embankment benches cannot.

3. *Education*. In wartime, educational reform must necessarily be promise rather than performance. At the moment we are not in a position to raise the school-leaving age or increase the teaching staffs of the elementary schools. But there are certain immediate steps that we could take towards a democratic educational system. We could start by abolish-

ing the autonomy of the public schools and the older universities and flooding them with State-aided pupils chosen simply on grounds of ability. At present, public-school education is partly a training in class prejudice and partly a sort of tax that the middle classes pay to the upper class in return for the right to enter certain professions. It is true that that state of affairs is altering. The middle classes have begun to rebel against the expensiveness of education, and the war will bankrupt the majority of the public schools if it continues for another year or two. The evacuation is also producing certain minor changes. But there is a danger that some of the older schools, which will be able to weather the financial storm longest, will survive in some form or another as festering centres of snobbery. As for the 10,000 'private' schools that England possesses, the vast majority of them deserve nothing except suppression. They are simply commercial undertakings, and in many cases their educational level is actually lower than that of the elementary schools. They merely exist because of a widespread idea that there is something disgraceful in being educated by the public authorities. The State could quell this idea by declaring itself responsible for *all* education, even if at the start this were no more than a gesture. We need gestures as well as actions. It is all too obvious that our talk of 'defending democracy' is nonsense while it is a mere accident of birth that decides whether a gifted child shall or shall not get the education it deserves.

4. *India.* What we must offer India is not 'freedom', which, as I have said earlier, is impossible, but alliance, partnership – in a word, equality. But we must also tell the Indians that they are free to secede, if they want to. Without that there can be no equality of partnership, and our claim to be defending the coloured peoples against Fascism will never be believed. But it is a mistake to imagine that if the Indians were free to cut themselves adrift they would immediately do so. When a British government *offers* them unconditional independence, they will refuse it. For as soon as they have the power to secede the chief reasons for doing so will have disappeared.

A complete severance of the two countries would be a disaster for India no less than for England. Intelligent Indians know this. As things are at present, India not only cannot defend itself, it is hardly even capable of feeding itself. The whole administration of the country depends on a framework of experts (engineers, forest officers, railwaymen, soldiers, doctors) who are predominantly English and could not be replaced within five or ten years. Moreover, English is the chief lingua franca and nearly the whole of the Indian intelligentsia is deeply anglicized. Any transference to foreign rule – for if the British marched out of India the Japanese and other powers would immediately march in – would mean an immense dislocation. Neither the Japanese, the Russians, the Germans nor the Italians would be capable of administering India even at the low level of efficiency that is attained by the British. They do not possess the necessary supplies of technical experts or the knowledge of languages and local conditions, and they probably could not win the confidence of indispensable go-betweens such as the Eurasians. If India were simply 'liberated', i.e. deprived of British military protection, the first result would be a fresh foreign conquest, and the second a series of enormous famines which would kill millions of people within a few years.

What India needs is the power to work out its own constitution without British interference, but in some kind of partnership that ensures its military protection and technical advice. This is unthinkable until there is a Socialist government in England. For at least eighty years England has artificially prevented the development of India, partly from fear of trade competition if India industries were too highly develped, partly because backward peoples are more easily governed than civilized ones. It is a commonplace that the average Indian suffers far more from his own countrymen than from the British. The petty Indian capitalist exploits the town worker with the utmost ruthlessness, the peasant lives from birth to death in the grip of the money-lender. But all this is an indirect result of the British rule, which aims half-consciously at keeping India as backward as possible. The classes most loyal to Britain are the princes, the landowners and the business community – in general, the reactionary classes who are doing fairly well out of the *status quo*. The moment that England ceased to stand towards India in the relation of an exploiter, the balance of forces would be altered. No need then for the British to flatter the ridiculous Indian princes, with their gilded elephants and cardboard armies, to prevent the growth of the Indian trade unions, to play off Moslem against Hindu, to protect the worthless life of the money-lender, to receive the salaams of toadying minor officials, to prefer the half-barbarous Gurkha to the educated Bengali. Once check that stream of dividends that flows from the bodies of Indian coolies to the banking accounts of old ladies in Cheltenham, and the whole sahib–native nexus, with its haughty ignorance on one side and envy and servility on the other, can come to an end. Englishmen and Indians can work side by side for the development of India, and for the training of Indians in all the arts which, so far, they have been systematically prevented from learning. How many of the existing British personnel in India, commercial or official, would fall in with such an arrangement – which would mean ceasing once and for all to be 'sahibs' – is a different question. But, broadly speaking, more is to be hoped from the younger men and from those officials (civil engineers, forestry and agriculture experts, doctors, educationists) who have been scientifically educated. The higher officials, the provincial governors, commissioners, judges, etc. are hopeless; but they are also the most easily replaceable.

That, roughly, is what would be meant by Dominion status if it were offered to India by a Socialist government. It is an offer of partnership on equal terms until such time as the world has ceased to be ruled by bombing planes. But we must add to it the unconditional right to secede. It is the only way of proving that we mean what we say. And what applies to India applies, *mutatis mutandis*, to Burma, Malaya and most of our African possessions.

5 and 6 explain themselves. They are the necessary preliminary to any claim that we are fighting this war for the protection of peaceful peoples against Fascist aggression.

Is it impossibly hopeful to think that such a policy as this could get a following in England? A year ago, even six months ago, it would have been, but not now. Moreover – and this is the peculiar opportunity of this moment – it could be given the necessary publicity. There is now a considerable weekly press, with a circulation of millions, which would be ready to popularize – if not *exactly* the programme I have sketched above, at any rate *some* policy along those lines. There are even three or four daily papers which would be prepared to give it a sympathetic hearing. That is the distance we have travelled in the last six months.

But is such a policy realizable? That depends entirely on ourselves.

Some of the points I have suggested are of the kind that could be carried out immediately, others would take years or decades and even then would not be perfectly achieved. No political programme is ever carried out in its entirety. But what matters is that that or something like it should be our declared policy. It is always the *direction* that counts. It is of course quite hopeless to expect the present Government to pledge itself to any policy that implies turning this war into a revolutionary war. It is at best a government of compromise, with Churchill riding two horses like a circus acrobat. Before such measures as limitation of incomes become even thinkable, there will have to be a complete shift of power away from the old ruling class. If during this winter the war settles into another stagnant period, we ought in my opinion to agitate for a General Election, a thing which the Tory Party machine will make frantic efforts to prevent.

But even without an election we can get the government we want, provided that we want it urgently enough. A real shove from below will accomplish it. As to who will be in that government when it comes, I make no guess. I only know that the right men will be there when the people really want them, for it is movements that make leaders and not leaders movements.

Within a year, perhaps even within six months, if we are still unconquered, we shall see the rise of something that has never existed before, a specifically *English* Socialist movement. Hitherto there has been only the Labour Party, which was the creation of the working class but did not aim at any fundamental change, and Marxism, which was a German theory interpreted by Russians and unsuccessfully transplanted to England. There was nothing that really touched the heart of the English people. Throughout its entire history the English Socialist movement has never produced a song with a catchy tune – nothing like *La Marseillaise* or *La Cucuracha*, for instance. When a Socialist movement native to England appears, the Marxists, like all others with a vested interest in the past, will be its bitter enemies. Inevitably they will denounce it as 'Fascism'. Already it is customary among the more soft-boiled intellectuals of the Left to declare that if we fight against the Nazis we shall 'go Nazi' ourselves. They might almost equally well say that if we fight Negroes we shall turn black. To 'go Nazi' we should have to have the history of Germany behind us. Nations do not escape from their past merely by making a revolution. An English Socialist government will transform the nation from top to bottom, but it will still bear all over it the unmistakable marks of our own civilization, the peculiar civilization which I discussed earlier in this book.

It will not be doctrinaire, nor even logical. It will abolish the House of Lords, but quite probably will not abolish the Monarchy. It will leave anachronisms and loose ends everywhere, the judge in his ridiculous horsehair wig and the lion and the unicorn on the soldier's cap-buttons. It will not set up any explicit class dictatorship. It will group itself round the old Labour Party and its mass following will be in the trade unions, but it will draw into it most of the middle class and many of the younger sons of the bourgeoisie. Most of its directing brains will come from the new indeterminate class of skilled workers, technical experts, airmen, scientists, architects and journalists, the people who feel at home in the radio and ferro-concrete age. But it will never lose touch with the tradition of compromise and the belief in a law that is above the State. It will shoot traitors, but it will give them a solemn trial beforehand and occasionally it will acquit them. It will crush any open revolt promptly and cruelly, but it will interfere very little with the spoken and written word. Political parties with different names will still exist, revolutionary sects will still be publishing their newspapers and making as little impression as ever. It will disestablish the Church, but will not persecute religion. It will retain a vague reverence for the Christian moral code, and from time to time will refer to England as 'a Christian country'. The Catholic Church will war against it, but the Noncomformist sects and the bulk of the Anglican Church will be able to come to terms with it. It will show a power of assimilating the past which will shock foreign observers and sometimes make them doubt whether any revolution has happened.

But all the same it will have done the essential thing. It will have nationalized industry, scaled down incomes, set up a classless educational system. Its real nature will be apparent from the hatred which the surviving rich men of the world will feel for it. It will aim not at disintegrating the Empire but at turning it into a federation of Socialist states, freed not so much from the British flag as from the money-lender, the dividend-drawer and the wooden-headed British official. Its war strategy will be totally different from that of any property-ruled state, because it will not be afraid of the revolutionary after-effects when any existing régime is brought down. It will not have the smallest scruple about attacking hostile neutrals or stirring up native rebellion in enemy colonies. It will fight in such a way that even if it is beaten its memory will be dangerous to the victor, as the memory of the French Revolution was dangerous to Metternich's Europe. The dictators will fear it as they could not fear the existing British régime, even if its military strength were ten times what it is.

But at this moment, when the drowsy life of England has barely altered, and the offensive contrast of wealth and poverty still exists everywhere, even amid the bombs, why do I dare to say that all these things 'will' happen?

Because the time has come when one can predict the future in terms of an 'either – or'. Either we turn this war into a revolutionary war (I do not say that our policy will be *exactly* what I have indicated above – merely that it will be along those general lines) or we lose it, and much more besides. Quite soon it will be possible to say definitely that our feet are set upon one path or the other. But at any rate it is certain that with our present social structure we cannot win. Our real forces, physical, moral or intellectual, cannot be mobilized.

III

Patriotism has nothing to do with Conservatism. It is actually the opposite of Conservatism, since it is a devotion to something that is always changing and yet is felt to be mystically the same. It is the bridge between the future and the past. No real revolutionary has ever been an internationalist.

During the past twenty years the negative, *fainéant* outlook which has been fashionable among English left-wingers, the sniggering of the intellectuals at patriotism and physical courage, the persistent effort to chip away English morale and spread a hedonistic, what-do-I-get-out-of-it attitude to life, has done nothing but harm. It would have been harmful even if we had been living in the squashy League of Nations universe that these people imagined. In an age of fuehrers and bombing planes it was a disaster. However little we may like it, toughness is the price of survival. A nation trained to think hedonistically cannot survive amid peoples who work like slaves and breed like rabbits, and whose chief national industry is war. English Socialists of nearly all colours have wanted to make a stand against Fascism, but at the same time they have aimed at making their own countrymen unwarlike. They have failed, because in England traditional loyalties are stronger than new ones. But in spite of all the 'anti-Fascist' heroics of the left-wing press, what chance should we have stood when the real struggle with Fascism came, if the average Englishman had been the kind of creature that the *New Statesman*, the *Daily Worker* or even the *News Chronicle* wished to make him?

Up to 1935 virtually all English left-wingers were vaguely pacifist. After 1935 the more vocal of them flung themselves eagerly into the Popular Front movement, which was simply an evasion of the whole problem posed by Fascism. It set out to be 'anti-Fascist' in a purely negative way – 'against' Fascism without being 'for' any discoverable policy – and underneath it lay the flabby idea that when the time came the Russians would do our fighting for us. It is astonishing how this illusion fails to die. Every week sees its spate of letters to the press, pointing out that if we had a government with no Tories in it the Russians could hardly avoid coming round to our side. Or we are to publish high-sounding war aims (*vide* books like *Unser Kampf*, *A Hundred Million Allies – If We Choose*, etc.), whereupon the European populations will infallibly rise on our behalf. It is the same idea all the time – look abroad for your inspiration, get someone else to do your fighting for you. Underneath it lies the frightful inferiority complex of the English intellectual, the belief that the English are no longer a martial race, no longer capable of enduring.

In truth there is no reason to think that anyone will do our fighting for us yet awhile, except the Chinese, who have been doing it for three years already.[3] The Russians may be driven to fight on our side by the fact of a direct attack, but they have made it clear enough that they will not stand up to the German army if there is any way of avoiding it. In any case they are not likely to be attracted by the spectacle of a left-wing government in England. The present Russian régime must almost certainly be hostile to any revolution in the West. The subject peoples of Europe will rebel when Hitler begins to totter, but not earlier. Our potential allies are not the Europeans but on the one hand the Americans, who will need a year to mobilize their resources even if Big Business can be brought to heel, and on the other hand the coloured peoples, who cannot be even sentimentally on our side till our own revolution has started. For a long time, a year, two years, possibly three years, England has got to be the shock-absorber of the world. We have got to face bombing, overwork, influenza, boredom and treacherous peace offers. Manifestly it is a time to stiffen morale, not to weaken it. Instead of taking the mechanically anti-British attitude which is usual on the Left, it is better to consider what the world would really be like if the English-speaking culture perished. For it is childish to suppose that the other English-speaking countries, even the U.S.A., will be unaffected if Britain is conquered.

Lord Halifax, and all his tribe, believe that when the war is over things will be exactly as they were before. Back to the crazy pavement of Versailles, back to 'democracy', i.e. capitalism, back to dole queues and the Rolls-Royce cars, back to the grey top hats and the sponge-bag trousers, *in saecula saeculorum*. It is of course obvious that nothing of the kind is going to happen. A feeble imitation of it might just possibly happen in the case of a negotiated peace, but only for a short while. *Laissez-faire* capitalism is dead.[4] The choice lies between the kind of collective society that Hitler will set up and the kind that can arise if he is defeated.

If Hitler wins this war he will consolidate his rule over Europe, Africa and the Middle East, and if his armies have not been too greatly exhausted beforehand, he will wrench vast territories from Soviet Russia. He will

3. Written before the outbreak of the war in Greece. [Authors footnote.]

4. It is interesting to notice that Mr Kennedy, U.S.A. Ambassador in London, remarked on his return to New York in October 1940 that as a result of the war 'democracy is finished'. By 'democracy', of course, he meant private capitalism. [Author's footnote.]

set up a graded caste-society in which the German *Herrenvolk* ('master race' or 'aristocractic race') will rule over Slavs and other lesser peoples whose job it will be to produce low-priced agricultural products. He will reduce the coloured peoples once and for all to outright slavery. The real quarrel of the Fascist powers with British imperialism is that they know that it is disintegrating. Another twenty years along the present line of development, and India will be a peasant republic linked with England only by voluntary alliance. The 'semi-apes' of whom Hitler speaks with such loathing will be flying aeroplanes and manufacturing machine-guns. The Fascist dream of a slave empire will be at an end. On the other hand, if we are defeated we simply hand over our own victims to new masters who come fresh to the job and have not developed any scruples.

But more is involved than the fate of the coloured peoples. Two incompatible visions of life are fighting one another. 'Between democracy and totalitarianism,' says Mussolini, 'there can be no compromise.' The two creeds cannot even, for any length of time, live side by side. So long as democracy exists, even in its very imperfect English form, totalitarianism is in deadly danger. The whole English-speaking world is haunted by the idea of human equality, and though it would be simply a lie to say that either we or the Americans have ever acted up to our professions, still, the *idea* is there, and it is capable of one day becoming a reality. From the English-speaking culture, if it does not perish, a society of free and equal human beings will ultimately arise. But it is precisely the idea of human equality – the 'Jewish' or 'Judaeo-Christian' idea of equality – that Hitler came into the world to destroy. He has, heaven knows, said so often enough. The thought of a world in which black men would be as good as white men and Jews treated as human beings brings him the same horror and despair as the thought of endless slavery brings to us.

It is important to keep in mind how irreconcilable these two viewpoints are. Some time within the next year a pro-Hitler reaction within the left-wing intelligentsia is likely enough. There are premonitory signs of it already. Hitler's positive achievement appeals to the emptiness of these people, and, in the case of those with pacifist leanings, to their masochism. One knows in advance more or less what they will say. They will start by refusing to admit that Brtish capitalism is evolving into something different, or that the defeat of Hitler can mean any more than a victory for the British and American millionaires. And from that they will proceed to argue that, after all, democracy is 'just the same as' or 'just as bad as' totalitarianism. There is *not much* freedom of speech in England; therefore there is *no more* than exists in Germany. To be on the dole is a horrible experience; therefore it is *no worse* to be in the torture-chambers of the Gestapo. In general, two blacks make a white, half a loaf is the same as no bread.

But in reality, whatever may be true about democracy and totalitarianism, it is not true that they are the same. It would not be true, even if British democracy were incapable of evolving beyond its present stage. The whole conception of the militarized continental state, with its secret police, its censored literature and its conscript labour, is utterly different from that of the loose maritime democracy, with its slums and unemployment, its strikes and party politics. It is the difference between land power and sea power, between cruelty and inefficiency, between lying and self-deception, between the S.S. man and the rent-collector. And in choosing between them one chooses not so much on the strength of what they now are as of what they are capable of becoming. But in a sense it is irrelevant whether democracy, at its highest or at its lowest, is 'better' than totalitarianism. To decide that one would have to have access to absolute standards. The only question that matters is where one's real sympathies will lie when the pinch comes. The intellectuals who are so fond of balancing democracy against totalitarianism and 'proving' that one is as bad as the other are simply frivolous people who have never been shoved up against realities. They show the same shallow misunderstanding of Fascism now, when they are beginning to flirt with it, as a year or two ago, when they were squealing against it. The question is not, 'Can you make out a debating-society 'case' in favour of Hitler?' The question is, 'Do you genuinely accept that case? Are you willing to submit to Hitler's rule? Do you want to see England conquered, or don't you?' It would be better to be sure on that point before frivolously siding with the enemy. For there is no such thing as neutrality in war; in practice one must help one side or the other.

When the pinch comes, no one bred in the western tradition can accept the Fascist vision of life. It is important to realize that *now*, and to grasp what it entails. With all its sloth, hypocrisy and injustice, the English-speaking civilization is the only large obstacle in Hitler's path. It is a living contradiction of all the 'infallible' dogmas of Fascism. That is why all Fascist writers for years past have agreed that England's power must be destroyed. England must be 'exterminated', must be 'annihilated', must 'cease to exist'. Strategically it would be possible for this war to end with Hitler in secure possession of Europe, and with the British Empire intact and British seapower barely affected. But ideologically it is not possible; were Hitler to make an offer along those lines, it could only be treacherously, with a view to conquering England indirectly or renewing the attack at some more favourable moment. England cannot possibly be allowed to remain as a sort of funnel through which deadly ideas from beyond the Atlantic flow into the police states of Europe. And turning it round to our point of view, we see the vastness of the issue before us, the all-importance of preserving our democracy more or less as we have known it. But to *preserve* is always to *extend*. The choice before us is not so much between victory and defeat as between revolution and apathy. If the thing we are fighting for is altogether destroyed, it will have been destroyed partly by our own act.

It could happen that England could introduce the beginnings of Socialism, turn this war into a revolutionary war, and still be defeated. That is at any rate thinkable. But, terrible as it would be for anyone who is now adult, it would be far less deadly than the 'compromise peace' which a few rich men and their hired liars are hoping for. The final ruin of England could only be accomplished by an English government acting under orders from Berlin. But that cannot happen if England has awakened beforehand. For in that case the defeat would be unmistakable, the struggle would continue, the *idea* would survive. The difference between going down fighting, and surrendering without a fight, is by no means a question of 'honour' and schoolboy heroics. Hitler said once that to *accept* defeat destroys the soul of a nation. This sounds like a piece of claptrap, but it is strictly true. The defeat of 1870 did not lessen the world-influence of France. The Third Republic had more influence, intellectually, than the France of Napoleon III. But the sort of peace that Pétain, Laval and Co. have accepted can only be purchased by deliberately wiping out the national culture. The Vichy Government will enjoy a spurious independence only on condition that it destroys the distinctive marks of French culture: republicanism, secularism, respect for the intellect, absence of colour prejudice. We cannot be *utterly* defeated if we have made our revolution beforehand. We may see German troops marchng down Whitehall, but another process, ultimately deadly to the German power-dream, will have been started. The Spanish people were defeated, but the things they learned during those two and a half memorable years will one day come back upon the Spanish Fascists like a boomerang.

A piece of Shakespearean bombast was much quoted at the beginning of the war. Even Mr Chamberlain quoted it once, if my memory does not deceive me:

Come the four corners of the world in arms
And we shall shock them: naught shall make us rue
If England to herself do rest but true.

It is right enough, if you interpret it rightly. But England has got to be true to herself. She is not being true to herself while the refugees who have sought our shores are penned up in concentration camps, and company directors work out subtle schemes to dodge their Excess Profits Tax. It is goodbye to the *Tatler* and the *Bystander*, and farewell to the lady in the Rolls-Royce car. The heirs of Nelson and of Cromwell are not in the House of Lords. They are in the fields and the streets, in the factories and the armed forces, in the four-ale bar and the suburban back garden; and at present they are still kept under by a generation of ghosts. Compared with the task of bringing the real England to the surface, even the winning of the war, necessary though it is, is secondary. By revolution we become more ourselves, not less. There is no question of stopping short, striking a compromise, salvaging 'democracy', standing still. Nothing ever stands still. We must add to our heritage or lose it, we must grow greater or grow less, we must go forward or backward. I believe in England, and I believe that we shall go forward.

Part of *England Your England* with the title *The Ruling Class* appeared in *Horizon*, December 1940. *England Your England* was reprinted in *S.J.*; *E.Y.E.*; *O.R.* Also Parts I and II were reworked as a book, *The English People* (1947).

12. Wells, Hitler and the World State

In March or April, say the wiseacres, there is to be a stupendous knockout blow at Britain . . . What Hitler has to do it with, I cannot imagine. His ebbing and dispersed military resources are now probably not so very much greater than the Italians' before they were put to the test in Greece and Africa

The German air power has been largely spent. It is behind the times and its first-rate men are mostly dead or disheartened or worn out.

In 1914 the Hohenzollern army was the best in the world. Behind that screaming little defective in Berlin there is nothing of the sort . . . Yet our military 'experts' discuss the waiting phantom. In their imaginations it is perfect in its equipment and invincible in discipline. Sometimes it is to strike a decisive 'blow' through Spain and North Africa and on, or march through the Balkans, march from the Danube to Ankara, to Persia, to India, or 'crush Russia', or 'pour' over the Brenner into Italy. The weeks pass and the phantom does none of these things – for one excellent reason. It does not exist to that extent. Most of such inadequate guns and munitions as it possessed must have been taken away from it and fooled away in Hitler's silly feints to invade Britain. And its raw jerry-built discipline is wilting under the creeping realization that the Blitzkreig is spent, and the war is coming home to roost.

These quotations are not taken from the *Cavalry Quarterly* but from a series of newspaper articles by Mr H. G. Wells, written at the beginning of this year and now reprinted in a book entitled *Guide to the New World*. Since they were written, the German army has overrun the Balkans and reconquered Cyrenaica, it can march through Turkey or Spain at such time as may suit it, and it has undertaken the invasion of Russia. How that campaign will turn out I do not know, but it is worth noticing that the German general staff, whose opinion is probably worth something, would not have begun it if they had not felt fairly certain of finishing it within three months. So much for the idea that the German army is a bogey, its equipment inadequate, its morale breaking down, etc.etc.

What has Wells to set against the 'screaming little defective in Berlin'? The usual rigmarole about a World State, plus the Sankey Declaration, which is an attempted definition of fundamental human rights, of anti-totalitarian tendency. Except that he is now especially concerned with federal world control of air power, it is the same gospel as he has been preaching almost without interruption for the past forty years, always with an air of angry surprise at the human beings who can fail to grasp anything so obvious.

What is the use of saying that we need federal world control of the air? The whole question is how we are to get it. What is the use of pointing out that a World State is desirable? What matters is that not one of the five great military powers would think of submitting to such a thing. All sensible men for decades past have been substantially in agreement with what Mr Wells says; but the sensible men have no power and, in too many cases, no disposition to sacrifice themselves. Hitler is a criminal lunatic, and Hitler has an army of millions of men, aeroplanes in thousands, tanks in tens of thousands. For his sake a great nation has been willing to overwork itself for six years and then to fight for two years more, whereas for the common-sense, essentially hedonistic world-view which Mr Wells puts forward, hardly a human creature is willing to shed a pint of blood. Before you can even talk of world reconstruction, or even of peace, you have got to eliminate Hitler, which means bringing into being a dynamic not necessarily the same as that of the Nazis, but probably quite as unacceptable to 'enlightened' and hedonistic people. What has kept England on its feet during the past year? In part, no doubt, some vague idea about a better future, but chiefly the atavistic emotion of patriotism, the ingrained feeling of the English-speaking peoples that they are superior to foreigners. For the last twenty years the main object of English left-wing intellectuals has been to break this feeling down, and if they had succeeded, we might be watching the S.S. men patrolling the London streets at this moment. Similarly, why are the Russians fighting like tigers against the German invasion? In part, perhaps, for some half-remembered ideal of Utopian Socialism, but chiefly in defence of Holy Russia (the 'sacred soil of the Fatherland', etc. etc.), which Stalin has revived in an only slightly altered form. The energy that actually shapes the world springs from emotions – racial pride, leader-worship, religious belief, love of war – which liberal intellectuals mechanically write off as anachronisms, and which they have usually destroyed so completely in themselves as to have lost all power of action.

The people who say that Hitler is Antichrist, or alternatively, the Holy Ghost, are nearer an understanding of the truth than the intellectuals who for ten dreadful years have kept it up that he is merely a figure out of comic opera, not worth taking seriously. All that this idea really reflects is the sheltered conditions of English life. The Left Book Club was at bottom a product of Scotland Yard, just as the Peace Pledge Union is a product of the navy. One development of the last ten years has been the appearance of the 'political book', a sort of enlarged pamphlet combining history with political criticism, as an important literary form. But the best writers in this line – Trotsky, Rauschning, Rosenberg, Silone, Borkenau, Koestler and others – have none of them been Englishmen, and nearly all of them have been renegades from one or other extremist party, who have seen totalitarianism at close quarters and known the meaning of exile and persecution. Only in the English-speaking countries was it fashionable to believe, right up to the outbreak of war, that Hitler was an unimportant lunatic and the German tanks made of cardboard. Mr Wells, it will be seen from the quotations I have given above, believes something of the kind still. I do not suppose that either the bombs or the German campaign in Greece have altered his opinion. A lifelong habit of thought stands between him and an understanding of Hitler's power.

Mr Wells, like Dickens, belongs to the non-military middle class. The thunder of guns, the jingle of spurs, the catch in the throat when the old flag goes by, leave him manifestly cold. He has an invincible hatred of the fighting, hunting, swashbuckling side of life, symbolized in all his early books by a violent propaganda against horses. The principal villain of his *Outline of History* is the military adventurer, Napoleon. If one looks through nearly any book that he has written in the last forty years one finds the same idea constantly recurring: the supposed antithesis between the man of science who is working towards a planned World State and the reactionary who is trying to restore a disorderly past. In novels, Utopias, essays, films, pamphlets, the antithesis crops up, always more or less the same. On the one side science, order, progress, internationalism, aeroplanes, steel, concrete, hygiene: on the other side war, nationalism, religion, monarchy, peasants, Greek professors, poets, horses. History as he sees it is a series of victories won by the scientific man over the romantic man. Now, he is probably right in assuming that a 'reasonable', planned form of society, with scientists rather than witch-doctors in control, will prevail sooner or later, but that is a different matter from assuming that it is just round the corner. There survives somewhere or other an interesting controversy which took place between Wells and Churchill at the time of the Russian Revolution. Wells accuses Churchill of not really believing his own propaganda about the Bolsheviks being monsters dripping with blood etc., but of merely fearing that they were going to introduce an era of common sense and scientific control, in which flag-wavers like Churchill himself would have no place. Churchill's estimate of the Bolsheviks, however, was nearer the mark than Wells's. The early Bolsheviks may have been angels or demons, according as one chooses to regard them, but any any rate they were not sensible men. They were not introducing a Wellsian Utopia but a Rule of the Saints, which, like the English Rule of the Saints, was a military despotism enlivened by witchcraft trials. The same misconception reappears in an inverted form in Well's attitude to the Nazis. Hitler is all the war-lords and witch-doctors in history rolled into one. Therefore, argues Wells, he is an absurdity, a ghost from the past, a creature doomed to disappear almost immediately. But unfortunately the equation of science with common sense does not really hold good. The aeroplane, which was looked forward to as a civilizing influence but in practice has hardly been used except for dropping bombs, is the symbol of that fact. Modern Germany is far more scientific than England, and far more barbarous. Much of what Wells has imagined and worked for is physically there in Nazi Germany. The order, the planning, the State encouragement of science, the steel, the concrete, the aeroplanes, are all there, but all in the service of ideas appropriate to the Stone Age. Science is fighting on the side of superstition. But obviously it is impossible for Wells to accept this. It would contradict the world-view on which his own works are based. The war-lords and the witch-doctors *must* fail, the common-sense World State, as seen by a nineteenth-century liberal whose heart does not leap at the sound of bugles, *must* triumph. Treachery and defeatism apart, Hitler *cannot* be a danger. That he should finally win would be an impossible reversal of history, like a Jacobite restoration.

But is it not a sort of parricide for a person of my age (thirty-eight) to find fault with H. G. Wells? Thinking people who were born about the beginning of this century are in some sense Wells's own creation. How much influence any mere writer has, and especially a 'popular' writer whose work takes effect quickly, is questionable, but I doubt whether anyone who was writing books between 1900 and 1920, at any rate in the English language, influenced the young so much. The minds of all of us, and therefore the physical world, would be perceptibly different if Wells had never existed. Only, just the singleness of mind, the one-sided imagination that made him seem like an inspired prophet in the Edwardian age, make him a shallow, inadequate thinker now. When Wells was young, the antithesis between science and reaction was not false. Society was ruled by narrow-minded, profoundly incurious people, predatory businessmen, dull squires, bishops, politicians who could quote Horace but had never heard of algebra. Science was faintly disreputable and religious belief obligatory. Traditionalism, stupidity, snobbishness, patriotism, superstition and love of war seemed to be all on the same side; there was need of someone who could state the opposite point of view. Back in the nineteen-hundreds it was a wonderful experience for a boy to discover H. G. Wells. There you were, in a world of pedants, clergymen and golfers, with your future employers exhorting you to 'get on or get out', your parents systematically warping your sexual life, and your dull-witted schoolmasters sniggering over their Latin tags; and here was this wonderful man who could tell you about the inhabitants of the planets and the bottom of the sea, and who *knew* that the future was not going to be what respectable people imagined. A decade or so before aeroplanes were technically feasible Wells knew that within a little while men would be able to fly. He knew that because he himself *wanted* to be able to fly, and therefore felt sure that research in that direction would continue. On the other hand, even when I was a little boy, at a time when the Wright brothers had actually lifted their machine off the ground for fifty-nine seconds, the generally accepted opinion was that if God had meant us to fly He would have given us wings. Up to 1914 Wells was in the main a true prophet. In physical details his vision of the new world has been fulfilled to a surprising extent.

But because he belonged to the nineteenth century and to a non-military nation and class, he could not grasp the tremendous strength of the old world which was symbolized in his mind by fox-hunting Tories. He was, and still is, quite incapable of understanding that nationalism, religous bigotry and feudal loyalty are far more powerful forces than what he himself would describe as sanity. Creatures out of the Dark Ages have come marching into the present, and if they are ghosts they are at any rate ghosts which need a strong magic to lay them. The people who have shown the best understanding of Fascism are either those who have suffered under it or those who have a Fascist streak in themselves. A crude book like *The Iron Heel*, written nearly thirty years ago, is a truer prophecy of the future than either *Brave New World* or *The Shape of Things to Come.* If one had to choose among Wells's own contemporaries a writer who could stand towards him as a corrective, one might choose Kipling, who was not deaf to the evil voices of power and military 'glory'. Kipling would have understood the appeal of Hitler, or for that matter of Stalin, whatever his attitude towards them might be. Wells is too sane to understand the modern world. The succession of lower-middle-class novels which are his greatest achievement stopped short at the other war and never really began again, and since 1920 he has squandered his talents in slaying paper dragons. But how much it is, after all, to have any talents to squander.

Horizon, August 1941; *Cr.E.*; *D.D.*; *C.E.*

13. The Art of Donald McGill

Who does not know the 'comics' of the cheap stationers' windows, the penny or twopenny coloured postcards with their endless succession of fat women in tight bathing-dresses and their crude drawing and unbearable colours, chiefly hedge-sparrow's egg tint and Post Office red?

This question ought to be rhetorical, but it is a curious fact that many people seem to be unaware of the existence of these things, or else to have a vague notion that they are something to be found only at the seaside, like nigger minstrels or peppermint rock. Actually they are on sale everywhere – they can be bought at nearly any Woolworth's, for example – and they are evidently produced in enormous numbers, new series constantly appearing. They are not to be confused with the various other types of comic illustrated postcard, such as the sentimental ones dealing with puppies and kittens or the Wendyish, sub-pornographic ones which exploit the love-affairs of children. They are a genre of their own, specializing in very 'low' humour, the mother-in-law, baby's nappy, policemen's boots type of joke, and distinguishable from all the other kinds by having no artistic pretensions. Some half-dozen publishing houses issue them, though the people who draw them seem not to be numerous at any one time.

I have associated them especially with the name of Donald McGill because he is not only the most prolific and by far the best of contemporary postcard artists, but also the most representative, the most perfect in the tradition. Who Donald McGill is, I do not know. He is apparently a trade name, for at least one series of postcards is issued simply as 'The Donald McGill Comics', but he is also unquestionably a real person with a style of drawing which is recognizable at a glance. Anyone who examines his postcards in bulk will notice that many of them are not despicable even as drawings, but it would be mere dilettantism to pretend that they have any direct aesthetic value. A comic postcard is simply an illustration to a joke, invariably a 'low' joke, and it stands or falls by its ability to raise a laugh. Beyond that it has only 'ideological' interest. McGill is a clever draughtsman with a real caricaturist's touch in the drawing of faces, but the special value of his postcards is that they are so completely typical. They represent, as it were, the norm of the comic postcard. Without being in the least imitative, they are exactly what comic postcards have been any time these last forty years, and from them the meaning and purpose of the whole genre can be inferred.

Get hold of a dozen of these things, preferably McGill's – if you pick out from a pile the ones that seem to you funniest, you will probably find that most of them are McGill's – and spread them out on a table. What do you see?

Your first impression is of overwhelming vulgarity. This is quite apart from the ever-present obscenity, and apart also from the hideousness of the colours. They have an utter lowness of mental atmosphere which comes out not only in the nature of the jokes but, even more, in the grotesque, staring, blatant quality of the drawings. The designs, like those of a child, are full of heavy lines and empty spaces, and all the figures in them, every gesture and attitude, are deliberately ugly, the faces grinning and vacuous, the women monstrously parodied, with bottoms like Hottentots. Your second impression, however, is of indefinable familiarity. What do these things remind you of? What are they so like? In the first place, of course, they remind you of the barely different postcards which you probably gazed at in your childhood. But more than this, what you are really looking at is something as traditional as Greek tragedy, a sort of sub-world of smacked bottoms and scrawny mothers-in-law which is a part of western European consciousness. Not that the jokes, taken one by one, are necessarily stale. Not being debarred from smuttiness, comic postcards repeat themselves less often than the joke columns in reputable magazines, but their basic subject-matter, the *kind* of joke they are aiming at, never varies. A few are genuinely witty, in a Max Millerish style. Examples:

'I like seeing experienced girls home.'
'But I'm not experienced!'
'You're not home yet!'

'I've been struggling for years to get a fur coat. How did you get yours?'
'I left off struggling.'

Judge: 'You are prevaricating, sir. Did you or did you not sleep with this woman?'
Co-respondent: 'Not a wink, my lord!'

In general, however, they are not witty but humorous, and it must be said for McGill's postcards, in particular, that the drawing is often a good deal funnier than the joke beneath it. Obviously the outstanding characteristic of comic postcards is their obscenity, and I must discuss that more fully later. But I give here a rough analysis of their habitual subject-mattter, with such explanatory remarks as seem to be needed:

Sex. More than half, perhaps three quarters, of the jokes are sex jokes, ranging from the harmless to the all but unprintable. First favourite is probably the illegitimate baby. Typical captions: 'Could you exchange this lucky charm for a baby's feeding-bottle?' 'She didn't ask me to the christening, so I'm not going to the wedding.' Also newlyweds, old maids, nude statues and women in bathing-dresses. All of these are *ipso facto* funny, mere mention of them being enough to raise a laugh. The cuckoldry joke is very seldom exploited, and there are no references to homosexuality.

Conventions of the sex joke:

a. Marriage only benefits the woman. Every man is plotting seduction and every woman is plotting marriage. No woman ever remains unmarried voluntarily.
b. Sex-appeal vanishes at about the age of twenty-five. Well-preserved and good-looking people beyond their first youth are never represented. The amorous honeymooning couple reappear as the grim-visaged wife and hapless, mustachioed, red-nosed husband, no intermediate stage being allowed for.

Home life. Next to sex, the henpecked husband is the favourite joke. Typical caption: 'Did they get an X-ray of your wife's jaw at the hospital?' – 'No, they got a moving picture instead.'
Conventions:

a. There is no such thing as a happy marriage.
b. No man ever gets the better of a woman in argument.

Drunkenness. Both drunkenness and teetotalism are *ipso facto* funny.
Conventions:

a. All drunken men have optical illusions.
b. Drunkenness is something peculiar to middle-aged men. Drunken youths or women are never represented.

W.C. jokes. There is not a large number of these. Chamber-pots are *ipso facto* funny, and so are public lavatories. A typical postcard, captioned 'A Friend in Need', shows a man's hat blown off his head and disappearing down the steps of a ladies' lavatory.

Inter-working-class snobbery. Much in these postcards suggests that they are aimed at the better-off working class and poorer middle class. There are many jokes turning on malapropisms, illiteracy, dropped aitches and the rough manners of slum-dwellers. Countless postcards show draggled hags of the stage-charwoman type exchanging 'unladylike' abuse. Typical repartee: 'I wish you were a statue and I was a pigeon!' A certain number produced since the war treat evacuation from the anti-evacuee angle. There are the usual jokes about tramps, beggars and criminals, and the comic maidservant appears fairly frequently. Also the comic navvy, bargee, etc.; but there are no anti-trade-union jokes. Broadly speaking, everyone with much over or much under £5 a week is regarded as laughable. The 'swell' is almost as automatically a figure of fun as the slum-dweller!

Stock figures. Foreigners seldom or never appear. The chief locality joke is the Scotsman, who is almost inexhaustible. The lawyer is always a swindler, the clergyman always a nervous idiot who says the wrong thing. The 'knut' or 'masher' still appears, almost as in Edwardian days, in out-of-date-looking evening clothes and an opera hat, or even with spats and a knobby cane. Another survival is the Suffragette, one of the big jokes of the pre-1914 period and too valuable to be relinquished. She has reappeared, unchanged in physical appearance, as the Feminist lecturer or Temperance fanatic. A feature of the last few years is the complete absence of anti-Jew postcards. The 'Jew joke', always somewhat more ill-natured than the 'Scotch joke', disappeared abruptly soon after the rise of Hitler.

Politics. Any contemporary event, cult or activity which has comic possibilities (for example, 'free love', feminism, A.R.P., nudism) rapidly finds its way into the picture postcards, but their general atmosphere is extremely old-fashioned. The implied political outlook is a radicalism appropriate to about the year 1900. At normal times they are not only not patriotic, but go in for a mild guying of patriotism, with jokes about 'God save the King', the Union Jack, etc. The European situation only began to reflect itself in them at some time in 1939, and first did so through the comic aspects of A.R.P. Even at this date few postcards mention the war except in A.R.P. jokes (fat woman stuck in the mouth of Anderson shelter: wardens neglecting their duty while young woman undresses at window she had forgotten to black out, etc. etc.). A few express anti-Hitler sentiments of a not very vindictive kind. One, not McGill's, shows Hitler, with the usual hypertrophied backside, bending down to pick a flower. Caption: 'What would *you* do, chums?' This is about as high a flight of patriotism as any postcard is likely to attain. Unlike the twopenny weekly papers, comic postcards are not the product of any great monopoly company, and evidently they are not regarded as having any importance in forming public opinion. There is no sign in them of any attempt to induce an outlook acceptable to the ruling class.

Here one comes back to the outstanding, all-important feature of comic postcards – their obscenity. It is by this that everyone remembers them, and it is also central to their purpose, though not in a way that is immediately obvious.

A recurrent, almost dominant motif in comic postcards is the woman with the stuck-out behind. In perhaps half of them, or more than half, even when the point of the joke has nothing to do with sex, the same female figure appears, a plump 'voluptuous' figure with the dress clinging to it as tightly as another skin and with breasts or buttocks grossly over-emphasized, according to which way it is turned. There can be no doubt that these pictures lift the lid off a very widespread repression, natural enough in a country whose women when young tend to be slim to the point of skimpiness. But at the same time the McGill postcard – and this applies to all other postcards in this genre –is not intended as pornography but, a subtler thing, as a skit on pornography. The Hottentot figures of the women are caricatures of the Englishman's secret ideal, not portraits of it. When one examines McGill's postcards more closely, one notices that his brand of humour only has meaning in relation to a fairly strict moral code. Whereas in papers like *Esquire*, for instance, or *La Vie Parisienne*, the imaginary background of the jokes is always promiscuity, the utter breakdown of all standards, the background of the McGill postcard is marriage. The four leading jokes are nakedness, illegitimate babies, old maids and newly married couples, none of which would seem funny in a really dissolute or even 'sophisticated' society. The postcards dealing with honeymoon couples always have the enthusiastic indecency of those village weddings where it is still considered screamingly funny to sew bells to the bridal bed. In one, for example, a young bridegroom is shown getting out of bed the morning after his wedding night. 'The first morning in our own little home, darling!' he is saying; 'I'll go and get the milk and paper and bring you a cup of tea.' Inset is a picture of the front doorstep; on it are four newspapers and four bottles of milk. This is obscene, if you like, but it is not immoral. Its implication – and this is just the implication that *Esquire* or the *New Yorker* would avoid at all costs – is that marriage is something profoundly exciting and important, the biggest event in the average human being's life. So also with jokes about nagging wives and tyrannous mothers-in-law. They do at least imply a stable society in which marriage is indissoluble and family loyalty taken for granted. And bound up with this is something I noted earlier, the fact that there are no pictures, or hardly any, of good-looking people beyond their first youth. There is the 'spooning' couple and the middle- aged, cat-and-dog couple, but nothing in between. The liaison, the illicit but more or less decorous love-affair which used to be the stock joke of French comic papers, is not a postcard subject. And this reflects, on a comic level, the working-class outlook which takes it as a matter of course that youth and adventure – almost, indeed, individual life – end with marriage. One of the few authentic class-differences, as opposed to class-distinctions, still existing in England is that the working classes age very much earlier.

They do not live less long, provided that they survive their childhood, nor do they lose their physical activity earlier, but they do lose very early their youthful appearance. This fact is observable everywhere, but can be most easily verified by watching one of the higher age groups registering for military service; the middle- and upper-class members look, on average, ten years younger than the others. It is usual to attribute this to the harder lives that the working classes have to live, but it is doubtful whether any such difference now exists as would account for it. More probably the truth is that the working classes reach middle age earlier because they accept it earlier. For to look young after, say, thirty is largely a matter of wanting to do so. This generalization is less true of the better-paid workers, especially those who live in council houses and labour-saving flats, but it is true enough even of them to point to a difference of outlook. And in this, as usual, they are more traditional, more in accord with the Christian past than the well-to-do women who try to stay young at forty by means of physical jerks, cosmetics and avoidance of child-bearing. The impulse to cling to youth at all costs, to attempt to preserve your sexual attraction, to see even in middle age a future for yourself and not merely for your children, is a thing of recent growth and has only precariously established itself. It will probably disappear again when our standard of living drops and our birth-rate rises. 'Youth's a stuff will not endure' expresses the normal, traditional attitude. It is this ancient wisdom that McGill and his colleagues are reflecting, no doubt unconsciously, when they allow for no transition stage between the honeymoon couple and those glamourless figures, Mum and Dad.

I have said that at least half McGill's postcards are sex jokes, and a proportion, perhaps ten per cent, are far more obscene than anything else that is now printed in England. Newsagents are occasionally prosecuted for selling them, and there would be many more prosecutions if the broadest jokes were not invariably protected by double meanings. A single example will be enough to show how this is done. In one postcard, captioned 'They didn't believe her', a young woman is demonstrating, with her hands held apart, something about two feet long to a couple of open-mouthed acquaintances. Behind her on the wall is a stuffed fish in a glass case, and beside that is a photograph of a nearly naked athlete. Obviously it is not the fish that she is referring to, but this could never be proved. Now, it is doubtful whether there is any paper in England that would print a joke of this kind, and certainly there is no paper that does so habitually. There is an immense amount of pornography of a mild sort, countless illustrated papers cashing in on women's legs, but there is no popular literature specializing in the 'vulgar', farcical aspect of sex. On the other hand, jokes exactly like McGill's are the ordinary small change of the revue and music-hall stage, and are also to be heard on the radio, at moments when the censor happens to be nodding. In England the gap between what can be said and what can be printed is rather exceptionally wide. Remarks and gestures which hardly anyone objects to on the stage would raise a public outcry if any attempt were made to reproduce them on paper. (Compare Max Miller's[1] stage patter with his weekly column in the *Sunday Dispatch*.) The comic postcards are the only existing exception to this rule, the only medium in which really 'low' humour is considered to be printable. Only in postcards and on the variety stage can the stuck-out behind, dog and lamp-post, baby's nappy type of joke be freely exploited. Remembering that, one sees what function these postcards, in their humble way, are performing

What they are doing is to give expression to the Sancho Panza view of

1. Reviewing *Applesauce*, a variety show, in *Time and Tide*, 7 September 1940, Orwell wrote: 'Anyone wanting to see something really vulgar should visit the Holborn Empire, where you can get quite a good matinée seat for three shillings. Max Miller, of course, is the main attraction.

'Max Miller, who looks more like a Middlesex Street hawker than ever when he is wearing a tail coat and shiny top hat, is one of a long line of English comedians who have specialized in the Sancho Panza side of life, in real *lowness*. To do this probably needs more talent than to express nobility. Little Tich was a master at it. There was a music-hall farce which Little Tich used to act in, in which he was supposed to be factotum to a crook solicitor. The solicitor is giving him his instructions:

"Now, our client who's coming this morning is a widow with a good figure. Are you following me?'

'*Little Tich:* 'I'm ahead of you.'

'As it happens, I have seen this farce acted several times with other people in the same part, but I have never seen anyone who could approach the utter baseness that Little Tich could get into these simple words. There is a touch of the same quality in Max Miller. Quite apart from the laughs they give one, it is important that such comedians should exist. They express something which is valuable in our civilization and which might drop out of it in certain circumstances. To begin with, their genius is entirely masculine. A woman cannot be low without being disgusting, whereas a good male comedian can give the impression of something irredeemable and yet innocent, like a sparrow. Again, they are intensely national. They remind one how closely knit the civilization of England is, and how much it resembles a family, in spite of its out-of-date class distinctions. The startling obscenities which occur in *Applesauce* are only possible because they are expressed in '*doubles entendres* which imply a common background in the audience. Anyone who had not been brought up on the *Pink 'Un* would miss the point of them. So long as comedians like Max Miller are on the stage and the comic coloured postcards which express approximately the same view of life are in the stationers' windows, one knows that the popular culture of England is surviving . . .'

life, the attitude to life that Miss Rebecca West once summed up as 'extracting as much fun as possible from smacking behinds in basement kitchens'. The Don Quixote–Sancho Panza combination, which of course is simply the ancient dualism of body and soul in fiction form, recurs more frequently in the literature of the last four hundred years than can be explained by mere imitation. It comes up again and again, in endless variations, Bouvard and Pécuchet, Jeeves and Wooster, Bloom and Dedalus, Holmes and Watson (the Holmes–Watson variant is an exceptionally subtle one, because the usual physical characteristics of two partners have been transposed). Evidently it corresponds to something enduring in our civilization, not in the sense that either character is to be found in a 'pure' state in real life, but in the sense that the two principles, noble folly and base wisdom, exist side by side in nearly every human being. If you look into your own mind, which are you, Don Quixote or Sancho Panza? Almost certainly you are both. There is one part of you that wishes to be a hero or a saint, but another part of you is a little fat man who sees very clearly the advantages of staying alive with a whole skin. He is your unofficial self, the voice of the belly protesting against the soul. His tastes lie towards safety, soft beds, no work, pots of beer and women with 'voluptuous' figures. He it is who punctures your fine attitudes and urges you to look after Number One, to be unfaithful to your wife, to bilk your debts, and so on and so forth. Whether you allow yourself to be influenced by him is a different question. But it is simply a lie to say that he is not part of you, just as it is a lie to say that Don Quixote is not part of you either, though most of what is said and written consists of one lie or the other, usually the first

But though in varying forms he is one of the stock figures of literature, in real life, especially in the way society is ordered, his point of view never gets a fair hearing. There is a constant world-wide conspiracy to pretend that he is not there, or at least that he doesn't matter. Codes of law and morals, or religious systems, never have much room in them for a humorous view of life. Whatever is funny is subversive, every joke is ultimately a custard pie, and the reason why so large a proportion of jokes centre round obscenity is simply that all societies, as the price of survival, have to insist on a fairly high standard of sexual morality. A dirty joke is not, of course, a serious attack upon morality, but it is a sort of mental rebellion, a momentary wish that things were otherwise. So also with all other jokes, which always centre round cowardice, laziness, dishonesty or some other quality which society cannot afford to encourage. Society has always to demand a little more from human beings than it will get in practice. It has to demand faultless discipline and self-sacrifice, it must expect its subjects to work hard, pay their taxes, and be faithful to their wives, it must assume that men think it glorious to die on the battlefield and women want to wear themselves out with child-bearing. The whole of what one may call official literature is founded on such assumptions. I never read the proclamations of generals before battle, the speeches of fuehrers and prime ministers, the solidarity songs of public schools and left-wing political parties, national anthems, Temperance tracts, papal encyclicals and sermons against gambling and contraception, without seeming to hear in the background a chorus of raspberries from all the millions of common men to whom these high sentiments make no appeal. Nevertheless the high sentiments always win in the end, leaders who offer blood, toil, tears and sweat always get more out of their followers than those who offer safety and a good time. When it comes to the pinch, human beings are heroic. Women face childbed and the scrubbing brush, revolutionaries keep their mouths shut in the torture chamber, battleships go down with their guns still firing when their decks are awash. It is only that the other element in man, the lazy, cowardly, debt-bilking adulterer who is inside all of us, can never be suppressed altogether and needs a hearing occasionally.

The comic postcards are one expression of his point of view, a humble one, less important than the music halls, but still worthy of attention. In a society which is still basically Christian, they naturally concentrate on sex jokes; in a totalitarian society, if they had any freedom of expression at all, they would probably concentrate on laziness or cowardice, but at any rate on the unheroic in one form or another. It will not do to condemn them on the ground that they are vulgar and ugly. That is exactly what they are meant to be. Their whole meaning and virtue is in their unredeemed lowness, not only in the sense of obscenity, but lowness of outlook in every direction whatever. The slightest hint of 'higher' influences would ruin them utterly. They stand for the worm's-eye view of life, for the music-hall world where marriage is a dirty joke or a comic disaster, where the rent is always behind and the clothes are always up the spout, where the lawyer is always a crook and the Scotsman always a miser, where the newlyweds make fools of themselves on the hideous beds of seaside lodging houses and the drunken, red-nosed husbands roll home at four in the morning to meet the linen-nightgowned wives who wait for them behind the front door, poker in hand. Their existence, the fact that people want them, is symptomatically important. Like the music halls, they are a sort of saturnalia, a harmless rebellion against virtue.

They express only one tendency in the human mind, but a tendency which is always there and will find its own outlet, like water. On the whole, human beings want to be good, but not too good, and not quite all the time. For:

there is a just man that perisheth in his righteousness, and there is a wicked man that prolongeth his life in his wickedness. Be not righteous over much; neither make thyself over wise; why shouldest thou destroy thyself? Be not over much wicked, neither be thou foolish: why shouldest thou die before thy time?

In the past the mood of the comic postcard could enter into the central stream of literature, and jokes barely different from McGill's could casually be uttered between the murders in Shakespeare's tragedies. That is no longer possible, and a whole category of humour, integral to our literature till 1800 or thereabouts, has dwindled down to these ill-drawn postcards, leading a barely legal existence in cheap stationers' windows. The corner of the human heart that they speak for might easily manifest itself in worse forms, and I for one should be sorry to see them vanish.

Horizon, September 1941; *Cr.E.*, *D.D.*; *O.R.*; *C.E.*

14. Rudyard Kipling

It was a pity that Mr Eliot should be so much on the defensive in the long essay with which he prefaces this selection of Kipling's poetry,[1] but it was not to be avoided, because before one can even speak about Kipling one has to clear away a legend that has been created by two sets of people who have not read his works. Kipling is in the peculiar position of having been a by-word for fifty years. During five literary generations every enlightened person has despised him, and at the end of that time nine tenths of those enlightened persons are forgotten and Kipling is in some sense still there. Mr Eliot never satisfactorily explains this fact, because in answering the shallow and familiar charge that Kipling is a 'Fascist', he falls into the opposite error of defending him where he is not defensible. It is no use pretending that Kipling's view of life, as a whole, can be accepted or even forgiven by any civilized person. It is no use claiming,

1. *A Choice of Kipling's Verse* made by T.S. Eliot.

for instance, that when Kipling describes a British soldier beating a 'nigger' with a cleaning rod in order to get money out of him, he is acting merely as a reporter and does not necessarily approve what he describes. There is not the slightest sign anywhere in Kipling's work that he disapproves of that kind of conduct – on the contrary, there is a definite strain of sadism in him, over and above the brutality which a writer of that type has to have. Kipling *is* a jingo imperialist, he *is* morally insensitive and aesthetically disgusting. It is better to start by admitting that, and then to try to find out why it is that he survives while the refined people who have sniggered at him seem to wear so badly.

And yet the 'Fascist' charge has to be answered, because the first clue to any understanding of Kipling, morally or politically, is the fact that he was *not* a Fascist. He was further from being one than the most humane or the most 'progressive' person is able to be nowadays. An interesting instance of the way in which quotations are parroted to and fro without any attempt to look up their context or discover their meaning is the line from 'Recessional', 'Lesser breeds without the Law'. This line is always good for a snigger in pansy-left circles. It is assumed as a matter of course that the 'lesser breeds' are 'natives', and a mental picture is called up of some pukka sahib in a pith helmet kicking a coolie. In its context the sense of the line is almost the exact opposite of this. The phrase 'lesser breeds' refers almost certainly to the Germans, and especially the pan-German writers, who are 'without the Law' in the sense of being lawless, not in the sense of being powerless. The whole poem, conventionally thought of as an orgy of boasting, is a denunciation of power politics, British as well as German. Two stanzas are worth quoting (I am quoting this as politics, not as poetry):

If, drunk with sight of power, we loose
Wild tongues that have not Thee in awe,
Such boastings as the Gentiles use,
Or lesser breeds without the Law –
Lord God of hosts, be with us yet,
Lest we forget – lest we forget!

For heathen heart that puts her trust
In reeking tube and iron shard,
All valiant dust that builds on dust,
And guarding, calls not Thee to guard,
For frantic boast and foolish word –
Thy mercy on Thy People, Lord!

Much of Kipling's phraseology is taken from the Bible, and no doubt in the second stanza he had in mind the text from Psalm cxxvii: 'Except the Lord build the house, they labour in vain that build it; except the Lord keep the city, the watchman waketh but in vain.' It is not a text that makes much impression on the post-Hitler mind. No one, in our time, believes in any sanction greater than military power; no one believes that it is possible to overcome force except by greater force. There is no 'Law', there is only power. I am not saying that that is a true belief, merely that it is the belief which all modern men do actually hold. Those who pretend otherwise are either intellectual cowards, or power-worshippers under a thin disguise, or have simply not caught up with the age they are living in. Kipling's outlook is pre-Fascist. He still believes that pride comes before a fall and that the gods punish *hubris*. He does not foresee the tank, the bombing plane, the radio and the secret police, or their psychological results.

But in saying this, does not one unsay what I said about Kipling's jingoism and brutality? No, one is merely saying that the nineteenth-century imperialist outlook and the modern gangster outlook are two different things. Kipling belongs very definitely to the period 1885–1902. The Great War and its aftermath embittered him, but he shows little sign of having learned anything from any event later than the Boer War. He was the prophet of British imperalism in its expansionist phase (even more than his poems, his solitary novel, *The Light that Failed*, gives you the atmosphere of that time) and also the unofficial historian of the British army, the old mercenary army which began to change its shape in 1914. All his confidence, his bouncing vulgar vitality, sprang out of limitations which no Fascist or near-Fascist shares.

Kipling spent the later part of his life in sulking, and no doubt it was political disappointment rather than literary vanity that accounted for this. Somehow history had not gone according to plan. After the greatest victory she had ever known, Britain was a lesser world power than before, and Kipling was quite acute enough to see this. The virtue had gone out of the classes he idealized, the young were hedonistic or disaffected, the desire to paint the map red had evaporated. He could not understand what was happening, because he had never had any grasp of the economic forces underlying imperial expansion. It is notable that Kipling does not seem to realize, any more than the average soldier or colonial administrator, that an empire is primarily a money-making concern. Imperialism as he sees it is a sort of forcible evangelizing. You turn a Gatling gun on a mob of unarmed 'natives', and then you establish 'the Law', which includes roads, railways and a court-house. He could not foresee, therefore, that the same motives which brought the Empire into existence would end by destroying it. It was the same motive, for example, that caused the Malayan jungles to be cleared for rubber estates, and which now causes those estates to be handed over intact to the Japanese. The modern totalitarians know what they are doing, and the nineteenth-century English did not know what they were doing. Both attitudes have their advantages, but Kipling was never able to move forward from one into the other. His outlook, allowing for the fact that after all he was an artist, was that of the salaried bureaucrat who despises the 'box-wallah' and often lives a lifetime without realizing that the 'box-wallah' calls the tune.

But because he identifies himself with the official class, he does possess one thing which 'enlightened' people seldom or never possess, and that is a sense of responsibility. The middle-class Left hate him for this quite as much as for his cruelty and vulgarity. All left-wing parties in the highly industrialized countries are at bottom a sham, because they make it their business to fight against something which they do not really wish to destroy. They have international aims, and at the same time they struggle to keep up a standard of life with which those aims are incompatible. We all live by robbing Asiatic coolies, and those of us who are 'enlightened' all maintain that those coolies ought to be set free; but our standard of living, and hence our 'enlightenment', demands that the robbery shall continue. A humanitarian is always a hypocrite, and Kipling's understanding of this is perhaps the central secret of his power to create telling phrases. It would be difficult to hit off the one-eyed pacifism of the English in fewer words than in the phrase, 'making mock of uniforms that guard you while you sleep'. It is true that Kipling does not understand the economic aspect of the relationship between the highbrow and the Blimp. He does not see that the map is painted red chiefly in order that the coolie may be exploited. Instead of the coolie he sees the Indian Civil Servant; but even on that plane his grasp of function, of who protects whom, is very sound. He sees clearly that men can only be highly civilized while other men, inevitably less civilized, are there to guard and feed them

How far does Kipling really identify himself with the administrators, soldiers and engineers whose praises he sings? Not so completely as is sometimes assumed. He had travelled very widely while he was still a young man, he had grown up with a brilliant mind in mainly philistine surroundings, and some streak in him that may have been partly neurotic led him to prefer the active man to the sensitive man. The nineteenth-century Anglo-Indians, to name the least sympathetic of his idols, were at any rate people who did things. It may be that all that they did was evil, but they changed the face of the earth (it is instructive to look at a map of Asia and compare the railway system of India with that of the surrounding countries), whereas they could have achieved nothing, could not have maintained themselves in power for a single week, if the normal Anglo-Indian outlook had been that of, say, E. M. Forster. Tawdry and shallow though it is, Kipling's is the only literary picture that we possess of nineteenth-century Anglo-India, and he could only make it because he was just coarse enough to be able to exist and keep his mouth shut in clubs and regimental messes. But he did not greatly resemble the people he admired. I know from several private sources that many of the Anglo-Indians who were Kipling's contemporaries did not like or approve of him. They said, no doubt truly, that he knew nothing about India, and on the other hand, he was from their point of view too much of a highbrow. While in India he tended to mix with 'the wrong' people, and because of his dark complexion he was wrongly suspected of having a streak of Asiatic blood. Much in his development is traceable to his having been born in India and having left school early. With a slightly different background he might have been a good novelist or a superlative writer of music-hall songs. But how true is it that he was a vulgar flag-waver, a sort of publicity agent for Cecil Rhodes? It is true, but it is not true that he was a yes-man or a time-server. After his early days, if then, he never courted public opinion. Mr Eliot says that what is held against him is that he expressed unpopular views in a popular style. This narrows the issue by assuming that 'unpopular' means unpopular with the intelligentsia, but it is a fact that Kipling's 'message' was one that the big public did not want, and, indeed, has never accepted. The mass of the people, in the nineties as now, were anti-militarist, bored by the Empire, and only unconsciously patriotic. Kipling's official admirers are and were the 'service' middle class, the people who read *Blackwood's*. In the stupid early years of this century, the Blimps, having at last discovered someone who could be called a poet and who was on their side, set Kipling on a pedestal, and some of his more sententious poems, such as 'If', were given almost Biblical status. But it is doubtful whether the Blimps have ever read him with attention, any more than they have read the Bible. Much of what he says they could not possibly approve. Few people who have criticized England from the inside have said bitterer things about her than this gutter patriot. As a rule it is the British working class that he is attacking, but not always. That phrase about 'the flannelled fools at the wicket and the muddied oafs at the goal' sticks like an arrow to this day, and it is aimed at the Eton and Harrow match as well as the Cup-Tie Final. Some of the verses he wrote about the Boer War have a curiously modern ring, so far as their subject-matter goes. 'Stellenbosch', which must have been written about 1902, sums up what every intelligent infantry officer was saying in 1918, or is saying now, for that matter.

Kipling's romantic ideas about England and the Empire might not have mattered if he could have held them without having the class prejudices which at that time went with them. If one examines his best and more representative work, his soldier's poems, especially *Barrack-Room Ballads*, one notices that what more than anything else spoils them is an underlying air of patronage. Kipling idealizes the army officer, especially the junior officer, and that to an idiotic extent, but the private soldier, though lovable and romantic, has to be a comic. He is always made to speak in a sort of stylized cockney, not very broad but with all the aitches and final 'g's' carefully omitted. Very often the result is as embarrassing as the humorous recitation at a church social. And this accounts for the curious fact that one can often improve Kipling's poems, make them less facetious and less blatant, by simply going through them and transplanting them from cockney into standard speech. This is especially true of his refrains, which often have a truly lyrical quality. Two examples will do (one is about a funeral and the other about a wedding):

So it's knock out your pipes and follow me!
And it's finish up your swipes and follow me!
Oh, hark to the big drum calling.
Follow me – follow me home!

and again:

Cheer for the Sergeant's wedding –
Give them one cheer more!
Grey gun-horses in the lando,
And a rogue is married to a whore!

Here I have restored the aitches etc. Kipling ought to have known better. He ought to have seen that the two closing lines of the first of these stanzas are very beautiful lines, and that ought to have overridden his impulse to make fun of a working-man's accent. In the ancient ballads the lord and the peasant speak the same language. This is impossible to Kipling, who is looking down a distorting class perspective, and by a piece of poetic justice one of his best lines is spoiled – for 'follow me 'ome' is much uglier than 'follow me home'. But even where it makes no difference musically the facetiousness of his stage cockney dialect is irritating. However, he is more often quoted aloud than read on the printed page, and most people instinctively make the necessary alterations when they quote him.

Can one imagine any private soldier, in the nineties or now, reading *Barrack-Room Ballads* and feeling that here was a writer who spoke for him? It is very hard to do so. Any soldier capable of reading a book of verse would notice at once that Kipling is almost unconscious of the class war that goes on in an army as much as elsewhere. It is not only that he thinks the soldier comic, but that he thinks him patriotic, feudal, a ready admirer of his officers and proud to be a soldier of the Queen. Of course that is partly true, or battles could not be fought, but 'What have I done for thee, England, my England?' is essentially a middle-class query. Almost any working man would follow it up immediately with 'What has England done for me?' In so far as Kipling grasps this, he simply sets it down to 'the intense selfishness of the lower classes' (his own phrase). When he is writing not of British but of 'loyal' Indians he carries the 'Salaam, sahib' motif to sometimes disgusting lengths. Yet it remains true that he has far more interest in the common soldier, far more anxiety that he shall get a fair deal, than most of the 'liberals' of his day or our own. He sees that the soldier is neglected, meanly underpaid and hypocritically despised by the people whose incomes he safeguards. 'I came to realize', he says in his posthumous memoirs, 'the bare horrors of the private's life, and the unnecessary torments he endured.' He is accused of glorifying war, and perhaps he does so, but not in the usual manner, by pretending that war is a sort of football match. Like most people capable of writing battle poetry, Kipling had never been in battle, but his vision of war is realistic. He knows that bullets hurt, that under fire everyone is terrified, that the ordinary soldier never knows what the war is about or what is happening except in his own corner of the battlefield, and that British troops, like other troops, frequently run away:

> I 'eard the knives be'ind me, but I dursn't face my man,
> Nor I don't know where I went to, 'cause I didn't stop to see,
> Till I 'eard a beggar squealin' out for quarter as 'e ran,
> An' I thought I knew the voice an' – it was me!

Modernize the style of this, and it might have come out of one of the debunking war books of the nineteen-twenties. Or again

An' now the hugly bullets come peckin' through the dust
An' no one wants to face 'em, but every beggar must;
So, like a man in irons, which isn't glad to go,
They moves 'em off by companies uncommon stiff an' slow.

Compare this with:

'Forward the Light Brigade!'
Was there a man dismayed?
No! though the soldier knew
Someone had blundered.

If anything, Kipling overdoes the horrors, for the wars of his youth were hardly wars at all by our standards. Perhaps that is due to the neurotic strain in him, the hunger for cruelty. But at least he knows that men ordered to attack impossible objectives *are* dismayed, and also that fourpence a day is not a generous pension

How complete or truthful a picture has Kipling left us of the long-service, mercenary army of the late nineteenth century? One must say of this, as of what Kipling wrote about nineteenth-century Anglo-India, that it is not only the best but almost the only literary picture we have. He has put on record an immense amount of stuff that one could otherwise only gather from verbal tradition or from unreadable regimental histories. Perhaps this picture of army life seems fuller and more accurate than it is because any middle- class English person is likely to know enough to fill up the gaps. At any rate, reading the essay on Kipling that Mr Edmund Wilson has just published or is just about to publish,[2] I was struck by the number of things that are boringly familiar to us and seem to be barely intelligible to an American. But from the body of Kipling's early work there does seem to emerge a vivid and not seriously misleading picture of the old pre-machine-gun army – the sweltering barracks in Gibraltar or Lucknow, the red coats, the pipeclayed belts and the pillbox hats, the beer, the fights, the floggings, hangings and crucifixions, the bugle-calls, the smell of oats and horse-piss, the bellowing sergeants with foot-long moustaches, the bloody skirmishes, invariably mismanaged, the crowded troopships, the cholera-stricken camps, the 'native' concubines, the ultimate death in the workhouse. It is a crude, vulgar picture, in which a patriotic music-hall turn seems to have got mixed up with one of Zola's gorier passages, but from it future generations will be able to gather some idea of what a long-term volunteer army was like. On about the same

2. Published in a volume of collected essays, *The Wound and the Bow*. [Author's footnote 1945.]

level they will be able to learn something of British India in the days when motor cars and refrigerators were unheard of. It is an error to imagine that we might have had better books on these subjects if, for example, George Moore, or Gissing, or Thomas Hardy, had had Kipling's opportunities. That is the kind of accident that cannot happen. It was not possible that nineteenth-century England should produce a book like *War and Peace*, or like Tolstoy's minor stories of army life, such as *Sebastopol* or *The Cossacks*, not because the talent was necessarily lacking but because no one with sufficient sensitiveness to write such books would ever have made the appropriate contacts. Tolstoy lived in a great military empire in which it seemed natural for almost any young man of family to spend a few years in the army, whereas the British Empire was and still is demilitarized to a degree which continental observers find almost incredible. Civilized men do not readily move away from the centres of civilization, and in most languages there is a great dearth of what one might call colonial literature. It took a very improbable combination of circumstances to produce Kipling's gaudy tableau, in which Private Ortheris and Mrs Hauksbee pose against a background of palm trees to the sound of temple bells, and one necessary circumstance was that Kipling himself was only half civilized.

Kipling is the only English writer of our time who has added phrases to the language. The phrases and neologisms which we take over and use without remembering their origin do not always come from writers we admire. It is strange, for instance, to hear the Nazi broadcasters referring to the Russian soldiers as 'robots', thus unconsciously borrowing a word from a Czech democrat whom they would have killed if they could have laid hands on him. Here are half a dozen phrases coined by Kipling which one sees quoted in leaderettes in the gutter press or overhears in saloon bars from people who have barely heard his name. It will be seen that they all have a certain characteristic in common:

> East is East, and West is West.
> The white man's burden.
> What do they know of England who only England know?
> The female of the species is more deadly than the male.
> Somewhere East of Suez.
> Paying the Dane-geld.

There are various others, including some that have outlived their context by many years. The phrase 'killing Kruger with your mouth', for instance, was current till very recently. It is also possible that it was

Kipling who first let loose the use of the word 'Huns' for Germans; at any rate he began using it as soon as the guns opened fire in 1914. But what the phrases I have listed above have in common is that they are all of them phrases which one utters semi-derisively (as it might be 'For I'm to be Queen o' the May, mother, I'm to be Queen o' the May'), but which one is bound to make use of sooner or later. Nothing could exceed the contempt of the *New Statesman*, for instance, for Kipling, but how many times during the Munich period did the *New Statesman* find itself quoting that phrase about paying the Dane-geld?[3] The fact is that Kipling, apart from his snack-bar wisdom and his gift for packing much cheap picturesqueness into a few words ('Palm and Pine' – 'East of Suez' – 'The Road to Mandalay'), is generally talking about things that are of urgent interest. It does not matter, from this point of view, that thinking and decent people generally find themselves on the other side of the fence from him. 'White man's burden' instantly conjures up a real problem, even if one feels that it ought to be altered to 'black man's burden'. One may disagree to the middle of one's bones with the political attitude implied in 'The Islanders', but one cannot say that it is a frivolous attitude. Kipling deals in thoughts which are both vulgar and permanent. This raises the question of his special status as a poet, or verse-writer.

Mr Eliot describes Kipling's metrical work as 'verse' and not 'poetry', but adds that it is '*great* verse', and further qualifies this by saying that a writer can only be described as a 'great-verse-writer' if there is some of his work 'of which we cannot say whether it is verse or poetry'. Apparently Kipling was a versifier who occasionally wrote poems, in which case it was a pity that Mr Eliot did not specify these poems by name. The trouble is that whenever an aesthetic judgement on Kipling's work seems to be called for, Mr Eliot is too much on the defensive to be able to speak plainly. What he does not say, and what I think one ought to start by saying in any discussion of Kipling, is that most of Kipling's verse is so horribly vulgar that it gives one the same sensation as one gets from watching a third-rate music-hall performer recite 'The Pigtail of

3. On the first page of his recent book, *Adam and Eve*, Mr Middleton Murry quotes the well-known lines:

> ''There are nine and sixty ways
> Of constructing tribal lays,
> And every single one of them is right.'

He attributes these lines to Thackeray. This is probably what is known as a 'Freudian error'. A civilized person would prefer not to quote Kipling – i.e. would prefer not to feel that it was Kipling who had expressed his thought for him. [Author's footnote 1945.]

Wu Fang Fu' with the purple limelight on his face, *and yet* there is much of it that is capable of giving pleasure to people who know what poetry means. At his worst, and also his most vital, in poems like 'Gunga Din' or 'Danny Deever', Kipling is almost a shameful pleasure, like the taste of cheap sweets that some people secretly carry into middle life. But even with his best passages one has the same sense of being seduced by something spurious, and yet unquestionably seduced. Unless one is merely a snob and a liar it is impossible to say that no one who cares for poetry could not get any pleasure out of such lines as:

> For the wind is in the palm trees, and the temple bells they say,
> 'Come you back, you British soldier, come you back to Mandalay!'

and yet those lines are not poetry in the same sense as 'Felix Randal' or 'When icicles hang by the wall' are poetry. One can, perhaps, place Kipling more satisfactorily than by juggling with the words 'verse' and 'poetry', if one describes him simply as a good bad poet. He is as a poet what Harriet Beecher Stowe was as a novelist. And the mere existence of work of this kind, which is perceived by generation after generation to be vulgar and yet goes on being read, tells one something about the age we live in.

There is a great deal of good bad poetry in English, all of it, I should say, subsequent to 1790. Examples of good bad poems – I am deliberately choosing diverse ones – are 'The Bridge of Sighs', 'When all the World is Young,Lad', 'The Charge of the Light Brigade', Bret Harte's 'Dickens in Camp', 'The Burial of Sir John Moore', 'Jenny Kissed Me', 'Keith of Ravelston', 'Casabianca'. All of these reek of sentimentality, and yet – not these particular poems, perhaps, but poems of this kind, are capable of giving true pleasure to people who can see clearly what is wrong with them. One could fill a fair-sized anthology with good bad poems, if it were not for the significant fact that good bad poetry is usually too well known to be worth reprinting. It is no use pretending that in an age like our own, 'good' poetry can have any genuine popularity. It is, and must be, the cult of a very few people, the least tolerated of the arts. Perhaps that statement needs a certain amount of qualification. True poetry can sometimes be acceptable to the mass of the people when it disguises itself as something else. One can see an example of this in the folk-poetry that England still possesses, certain nursery rhymes and mnemonic rhymes, for instance, and the songs that soldiers make up, including the words that go to some of the bugle-calls. But in general ours is a civilization in which the very word 'poetry' evokes a hostile snigger or, at best, the sort of frozen disgust that most people feel when they hear the word 'God'. If you are good at playing the concertina you could probably go into the nearest public bar and get yourself an appreciative audience within five minutes. But what would be the attitude of that same audience if you suggested reading them Shakespeare's sonnets, for instance? Good bad poetry, however, can get across to the most unpromising audiences if the right atmosphere has been worked up before hand. Some months back Churchill produced a great effect by quoting Clough's 'Endeavour' in one of his broadcast speeches. I listened to this speech among people who could certainly not be accused of caring for poetry, and I am convinced that the lapse into verse impressed them and did not embarrass them. But not even Churchill could have got away with it if he had quoted anything much better than this

In so far as a writer of verse can be popular, Kipling has been and probably still is popular. In his own lifetime some of his poems travelled far beyond the bounds of the reading public, beyond the world of school prize-days, Boy Scout sing-songs, limp-leather editions, poker-work and calendars, and out in the yet vaster world of the music halls. Nevertheless, Mr Eliot thinks it worthwhile to edit him, thus confessing to a taste which others share but are not always honest enough to mention. The fact that such a thing as good bad poetry can exist is a sign of the emotional overlap between the intellectual and the ordinary man. The intellectual *is* different from the ordinary man, but only in certain sections of his personality, and even then not all the time. But what is the peculiarity of a good bad poem? A good bad poem is a graceful monument to the obvious. It records in memorable form – for verse is a mnemonic device, among other things – some emotion which very nearly every human being can share. The merit of a poem like 'When all the World is Young, Lad' is that, however sentimental it may be, its sentiment is 'true' sentiment in the sense that you are bound to find yourself thinking the thought it expresses sooner or later; and then, if you happen to know the poem, it will come back into your mind and seem better than it did before. Such poems are a kind of rhyming proverb, and it is a fact that definitely popular poetry is usually gnomic or sententious. One example from Kipling will do:

White hands cling to the bridle rein,
Slipping the spur from the booted heel;
Tenderest voices cry 'Turn again!'
Red lips tarnish the scabbarded steel:

Down to Gehenna or up to the Throne,
He travels the fastest who travels alone.

There is a vulgar thought vigorously expressed. It may not be true, but at any rate it is a thought that everyone thinks. Sooner or later you will have occasion to feel that he travels the fastest who travels alone, and there the thought is, ready made and, as it were, waiting for you. So the chances are that, having once heard this line, you will remember it.

One reason for Kipling's power as a good bad poet I have already suggested – his sense of responsibility, which made it possible for him to have a world-view, even though it happened to be a false one. Although he had no direct connexion with any political party, Kipling was a Conservative, a thing that does not exist nowadays. Those who now call themselves Conservatives are either Liberals, Fascists or the accomplices of Fascists. He identified himself with the ruling power and not with the opposition. In a gifted writer this seems to us strange and even disgusting, but it did have the advantage of giving Kipling a certain grip on reality. The ruling power is always faced with the question, 'In such and such circumstances, what would you *do*?', whereas the opposition is not obliged to take responsibility or make any real decisions. Where it is a permanent and pensioned opposition, as in England, the quality of its thought deteriorates accordingly. Moreover, anyone who starts out with a pessimistic, reactionary view of life tends to be justified by events, for Utopia never arrives and 'the gods of the copybook headings', as Kipling himself put it, always return. Kipling sold out to the British governing class, not financially but emotionally. This warped his political judgement, for the British ruling class were not what he imagined, and it led him into abysses of folly and snobbery, but he gained a corresponding advantage from having at least tried to imagine what action and responsibility are like. It is a great thing in his favour that he is not witty, not 'daring', has no wish to *épater les bourgeois*. He dealt largely in platitudes, and since we live in a world of platitudes, much of what he said sticks. Even his worst follies seem less shallow and less irritating than the 'enlightened' utterances of the same period, such as Wilde's epigrams or the collection of cracker-mottoes at the end of *Man and Superman*.

Horizon, February 1942; *Cr.E.*; *D.D.*; *O.R.*; *C.E.*

15. Looking Back on the Spanish War

I

First of all the physical memories, the sound, the smells and the surfaces of things

It is curious that more vividly than anything that came afterwards in the Spanish war I remember the week of so-called training that we received before being sent to the front – the huge cavalry barracks in Barcelona with its draughty stables and cobbled yards, the icy cold of the pump where one washed, the filthy meals made tolerable by pannikins of wine, the trousered militia-women chopping firewood, and the roll-call in the early mornings where my prosaic English name made a sort of comic interlude among the resounding Spanish ones, Manuel Gonzalez, Pedro Aguilar, Ramon Fenellosa, Roque Ballaster, Jaime Domenech, Sebastian Viltron, Ramon Nuvo Bosch. I name those particular men because I remember the faces of all of them. Except for two who were mere riff-raff and have doubtless become good Falangists by this time, it is probable that all of them are dead. Two of them I know to be dead. The eldest would have been about twenty-five, the youngest sixteen.

One of the essential experiences of war is never being able to escape from disgusting smells of human origin. Latrines are an overworked subject in war literature, and I would not mention them if it were not that the latrine in our barracks did its necessary bit towards puncturing my own illusions about the Spanish Civil War. The Latin type of latrine, at which you have to squat, is bad enough at its best, but these were made of some kind of polished stone so slippery that it was all you could do to keep on your feet. In addition they were always blocked. Now I have plenty of other disgusting things in my memory, but I believe it was these latrines that first brought home to me the thought, so often to recur; 'Here we are, soldiers of a revolutionary army, defending democracy against Fascism, fighting a war which is *about* something, and the detail of our lives is just as sordid and degrading as it could be in prison, let alone in a bourgeois army.' Many other things reinforced this impression later; for instance, the boredom and animal hunger of trench life, the squalid intrigues over scraps of food, the mean, nagging quarrels which people exhausted by lack of sleep indulge in.

The essential horror of army life (whoever has been a soldier will know what I mean by the essential horror of army life) is barely affected by the nature of the war you happen to be fighting in. Discipline, for instance, is ultimately the same in all armies. Orders have to be obeyed and enforced by punishment if necessary, the relationship of officer and man has to be the relationship of superior and inferior. The picture of war set forth in books like *All Quiet on the Western Front* is substantially true. Bullets, hurt, corpses stink, men under fire are often so frightened that they wet their trousers. It is true that the social background from which an army springs will colour its training, tactics and general efficiency, and also that the consciousness of being in the right can bolster up morale, though this affects the civilian population more than the troops. (People forget that a soldier anywhere near the front line is usually too hungry, or frightened, or cold, or, above all, too tired to bother about the political origins of the war.) But the laws of nature are not suspended for a 'red' army any more than for a 'white' one. A louse is a louse and a bomb is a bomb, even though the cause you are fighting for happens to be just.

Why is it worth while to point out anything so obvious? Because the bulk of the British and American intelligentsia were manifestly unaware of it then, and are now. Our memories are short nowadays, but look back a bit, dig out the files of *New Masses* or the *Daily Worker,* and just have a look at the romantic warmongering muck that our left-wingers were spilling at that time. All the stale old phrases! And the unimaginative callousness of it! The sang-froid with which London faced the bombing of Madrid! Here I am not bothering about the counter-propagandists of the Right, the Lunns, Garvins *et hoc genus*; they go without saying. But here were the very people who for twenty years had hooted and jeered at the 'glory' of war, at atrocity stories, at patriotism, even at physical courage, coming out with stuff that with the alteration of a few names would have fitted into the *Daily Mail* of 1918. If there was one thing that the British intelligentsia were committed to, it was the debunking version of war, the theory that war is all corpses and latrines and never leads to any good result. Well, the same people who in 1933 sniggered pityingly if you said that in certain circumstances you would fight for your country, in 1937 were denouncing you as a Trotsky-Fascist if you suggested that the stories in *New Masses* about freshly wounded men clamouring to get back into the fighting might be exaggerated. And the Left intelligentsia made their swing-over from 'War is hell' to 'War is glorious' not only with no sense of incongruity but almost without any intervening stage. Later the bulk of them were to make other transitions equally violent. There must be a quite large number of people, a sort of central core of the intelligentsia, who approved the 'King and Country' declaration in 1935, shouted for a 'firm line' against Germany in 1937, supported the People's Convention in 1940, and are demanding a Second Front now.

As far as the mass of the people go, the extraordinary swings of opinion which occur nowadays, the emotions which can be turned on and off like a tap, are the result of newspaper and radio hypnosis. In the intelligentsia I should say they result rather from money and mere physical safety. At a given moment they may be 'pro-war' or 'anti-war', but in either case they have no realistic picture of war in their minds. When they enthused over the Spanish war they knew, of course, that people were being killed and that to be killed is unpleasant, but they did feel that for a soldier in the Spanish Republican army the experience of war was somehow not degrading. Somehow the latrines stank less, discipline was less irksome. You have only to glance at the *New Statesman* to see that they believed that; exactly similar blah is being written about the Red Army at this moment. We have become too civilized to grasp the obvious. For the truth is very simple. To survive you often have to fight, and to fight you have to dirty yourself. War is evil, and it is often the lesser evil. Those who take the sword perish by the sword, and those who don't take the sword perish by smelly diseases. The fact that such a platitude is worth writing down shows what the years of *rentier* capitalism have done to us.

II

In connexion with what I have just said, a footnote on atrocities.

I have little direct evidence about the atrocities in the Spanish Civil War. I know that some were committed by the Republicans, and far more (they are still continuing) by the Fascists. But what impressed me then, and has impressed me ever since, is that atrocities are believed in or disbelieved in solely on grounds of political predilection. Everyone believes in the atrocities of the enemy and disbelieves in those of his own side, without ever bothering to examine the evidence. Recently I drew up a table of atrocities during the period between 1918 and the present; there was never a year when atrocities were not occurring somewhere or other, and there was hardly a single case when the Left and Right believed in the same stories simultaneously. And stranger yet, at any moment the situation can suddenly reverse itself and yesterday's proved-to-the-hilt atrocity story can become a ridiculous lie, merely because the political landscape has changed.

In the present war we are in the curious situation that our 'atrocity campaign' was done largely before the war started, and done mostly by the Left, the people who normally pride themselves on their incredulity. In the same period the Right, the atrocity-mongers of 1914–18, were gazing at Nazi Germany and flatly refusing to see any evil in it. Then as soon as war broke out it was the pro-Nazis of yesterday who were repeating horror stories, while the anti-Nazis suddenly found themselves doubting whether the Gestapo really existed. Nor was this solely the result of the Russo-German Pact. It was partly because before the war the Left had wrongly believed that Britain and Germany would never fight and were therefore able to be anti-German and anti-British simultaneously; partly also because official war propaganda, with its disgusting hypocrisy and self-righteousness, always tends to make thinking people sympathize with the enemy. Part of the price we paid for the systematic lying of 1914–18 was the exaggerated pro-German reaction which followed. During the years 1918–33 you were hooted at in left-wing circles if you suggested that Germany bore even a fraction of responsibility for the war. In all the denunciations of Versailles I listened to during those years I don't think I ever once heard the question, 'What would have happened if Germany had won?' even mentioned, let alone discussed. So also with atrocities. The truth, it is felt, becomes untruth when your enemy utters it. Recently I noticed that the very people who swallowed any and every horror story about the Japanese in Nanking in 1937 refused to believe exactly the same stories about Hong Kong in 1942. There was even a tendency to feel that the Nanking atrocities had become, as it were retrospectively untrue because the British Government now drew attention to them.

But unfortunately the truth about atrocities is far worse than that they are lied about and made into propaganda. The truth is that they happen. The fact often adduced as a reason for scepticism – that the same horror stories come up in war after war – merely makes it rather more likely that these stories are true. Evidently they are widespread fantasies, and war provides an opportunity of putting them into practice. Also, although it has ceased to be fashionable to say so, there is little question that what one may roughly call the 'whites' commit far more and worse atrocities than the 'reds'. There is not the slightest doubt, for instance, about the behaviour of the Japanese in China. Nor is there much doubt about the long tale of Fascist outrages during the last ten years in Europe. The volume of testimony is enormous, and a respectable proportion of it comes from the German press and radio. These things really happened, that is the thing to keep one's eye on. They happened even though Lord

Halifax said they happened. The raping and butchering in Chinese cities, the tortures in the cellars of the Gestapo, the elderly Jewish professors flung into cesspools, the machine-gunning of refugees along the Spanish roads – they all happened, and they did not happen any the less because the *Daily Telegraph* has suddenly found out about them when it is five years too late

III

Two memories, the first not proving anything in particular, the second, I think, giving one a certain insight into the atmosphere of a revolutionary period.

Early one morning another man and I had gone out to snipe at the Fascists in the trenches outside Huesca. Their line and ours here lay three hundred yards apart, at which range our aged rifles would not shoot accurately, but by sneaking out to a spot about a hundred yards from the Fascist trench you might, if you were lucky, get a shot at someone through a gap in the parapet. Unfortunately the ground between was a flat beet-field with no cover except a few ditches, and it was necessary to go out while it was still dark and return soon after dawn, before the light became too good. This time no Fascists appeared, and we stayed too long and were caught by the dawn. We were in a ditch, but behind us were two hundred yards of flat ground with hardly enough cover for a rabbit. We were still trying to nerve ourselves to make a dash for it when there was an uproar and a blowing of whistles in the Fascist trench. Some of our aeroplanes were coming over. At this moment a man, presumably carrying a message to an officer, jumped out of the trench and ran along the top of the parapet in full view. He was half-dressed and was holding up his trousers with both hands as he ran. I refrained from shooting at him. It is true that I am a poor shot and unlikely to hit a running man at a hundred yards, and also that I was thinking chiefly about getting back to our trench while the Fascists had their attention fixed on the aeroplanes. Still, I did not shoot partly because of that detail about the trousers. I had come here to shoot at 'Fascists'; but a man who is holding up his trousers isn't a 'Fascist', he is visibly a fellow creature, similar to yourself, and you don't feel like shooting at him

What does this incident demonstrate? Nothing very much, because it is the kind of thing that happens all the time in all wars. The other is different. I don't suppose that in telling it I can make it moving to you who read it, but I ask you to believe that it is moving to me, as an incident characteristic of the moral atmosphere of a particular moment in time

One of the recruits who joined us while I was at the barracks was a wild-looking boy from the back streets of Barcelona. He was ragged and barefooted. He was also extremely dark (Arab blood, I dare say), and made gestures you do not usually see a European make; one in particular – the arm outstretched, the palm vertical – was a gesture characteristic of Indians. One day a bundle of cigars, which you could still buy dirt cheap at that time, was stolen out of my bunk. Rather foolishly I reported this to the officer, and one of the scallywags I have already mentioned promptly came forward and said quite untruly that twenty-five pesetas had been stolen from his bunk. For some reason the officer instantly decided that the brown-faced boy must be the thief. They were very hard on stealing in the militia, and in theory people could be shot for it. The wretched boy allowed himself to be led off to the guardroom to be searched. What most struck me was that he barely attempted to protest his innocence. In the fatalism of his attitude you could see the desperate poverty in which he had been bred. The officer ordered him to take his clothes off. With a humility which was horrible to me he stripped himself naked, and his clothes were searched. Of course neither the cigars nor the money were there; in fact he had not stolen them. What was most painful of all was that he seemed no less ashamed after his innocence had been established. That night I took him to the pictures and give him brandy and chocolate. But that too was horrible – I mean the attempt to wipe out an injury with money. For a few minutes I had half believed him to be a thief, and that could not be wiped out.

Well, a few weeks later at the front I had trouble with one of the men in my section. By this time I was a 'cabo', or corporal, in command of twelve men. It was static warfare, horribly cold, and the chief job was getting sentries to stay awake and at their posts. One day a man suddenly refused to go to a certain post, which he said quite truly was exposed to enemy fire. He was a feeble creature, and I seized hold of him and began to drag him towards his post. This roused the feelings of the others against me, for Spaniards, I think, resent being touched more than we do. Instantly I was surrounded by a ring of shouting men: 'Fascist! Fascist! Let that man go! This isn't a bourgeois army. Fascist!' etc.etc. As best I could in my bad Spanish I shouted back that orders had got to be obeyed, and the row developed into one of those enormous arguments by means of which discipline is gradually hammered out in revolutionary armies. Some said I was right, others said I was wrong. But the point is that the one who took my side the most warmly of all was the brown-faced boy. As soon as he saw what was happening he sprang into the ring and began passionately defending me. With his strange, wild, Indian gesture he kept exclaiming, 'He's the best corporal we've got!' (*¡No hay cabo como el!)* Later on he applied for leave to exchange into my section.

Why is this incident touching to me? Because in any normal circumstances it would have been impossible for good feelings ever to be re-established between this boy and myself. The implied accusation of theft would not have been made any better, probably somewhat worse, by my efforts to make amends. One of the effects of safe and civilized life is an immense oversensitiveness which makes all the primary emotions seem somewhat disgusting. Generosity is as painful as meanness, gratitude as hateful as ingratitude. But in Spain in 1936 we were not living in a normal time. It was a time when generous feelings and gestures were easier than they ordinarily are. I could relate a dozen similar incidents, not really communicable but bound up in my own mind with the special atmosphere of the time, the shabby clothes and the gay-coloured revolutionary posters, the universal use of the word 'comrade', the anti-Fascist ballads printed on flimsy paper and sold for a penny, the phrases like 'international proletarian solidarity', pathetically repeated by ignorant men who believed them to mean something. Could you feel friendly towards somebody, and stick up for him in a quarrel, after you had been ignominiously searched in his presence for property you were supposed to have stolen from him? No, you couldn't; but you might if you had both been through some emotionally widening experience. That is one of the by-products of revolution, though in this case it was only the beginnings of a revolution, and obviously foredoomed to failure.

IV

The struggle for power between the Spanish Republican parties is an unhappy, far-off thing which I have no wish to revive at this date. I only mention it in order to say: believe nothing, or next to nothing, of what you read about internal affairs on the Government side. It is all, from whatever source, party propaganda – that is to say, lies. The broad truth about the war is simple enough. The Spanish bourgeoisie saw their chance of crushing the labour movement, and took it, aided by the Nazis and by the forces of reaction all over the world. It is doubtful whether more than that will ever be established.

I remember saying once to Arthur Koestler, 'History stopped in 1936,' at which he nodded in immediate understanding. We were both thinking of totalitarianism in general, but more particuarly of the Spanish Civil War. Early in life I had noticed that no event is ever correctly reported in a newspaper, but in Spain, for the first time, I saw newspaper reports which did not bear any relation to the facts, not even the relationship which is implied in an ordinary lie. I saw great battles reported where there had been no fighting, and complete silence where hundreds of men had been killed. I saw troops who had fought bravely denounced as cowards and traitors, and others who had never seen a shot fired hailed as the heroes of imaginary victories, and I saw newspapers in London retailing these lies and eager intellectuals building emotional superstructures over events that had never happened. I saw, in fact, history being written not in terms of what happened but of what ought to have happened according to various 'party lines'. Yet in a way, horrible as all this was, it was unimportant. It concerned secondary issues – namely, the struggle for power between the Comintern and the Spanish left-wing parties, and the efforts of the Russian Government to prevent revolution in Spain. But the broad picture of the war which the Spanish Government presented to the world was not untruthful. The main issues were what it said they were. But as for the Fascists and their backers, how could they come even as near to the truth as that? How could they possibly mention their real aims? Their version of the war was pure fantasy, and in the circumstances it could not have been otherwise.

The only propaganda line open to the Nazis and Fascists was to represent themselves as Christian patriots saving Spain from a Russian dictatorship. This involved pretending that life in Government Spain was just one long massacre (*vide* the *Catholic Herald* or the *Daily Mail* – but these were child's play compared with the continental Fascist press), and it involved immensely exaggerating the scale of Russian intervention. Out of the huge pyramid of lies which the Catholic and reactionary press all over the world built up, let me take just one point – the presence in Spain of a Russian army. Devout Franco partisans all believed in this; estimates of its strength went as high as half a million. Now, there was no Russian army in Spain. There may have been a handful of airmen and other technicians, a few hundred at the most, but an army there was not. Some thousands of foreigners who fought in Spain, not to mention millions of Spaniards, were witnesses of this. Well, their testimony made no impression at all upon the Franco propagandists, not one of whom had set foot in Government Spain. Simultaneously these people refused utterly to admit the fact of German or Italian intervention, at the same time as the German and Italian press were openly boasting about the exploits of their 'legionaries'. I have chosen to mention only one point, but in fact the whole of Fascist propaganda about the war was on this level.

This kind of thing is frightening to me, because it often gives me the feeling that the very concept of objective truth is fading out of the world. After all, the chances are that those lies, or at any rate similar lies, will pass into history. How will the history of the Spanish war be written? If Franco remains in power his nominees will write the history books, and (to stick to my chosen point) that Russian army which never existed will become historical fact, and schoolchildren will learn about it generations hence. But suppose Fascism is finally defeated and some kind of democratic government restored in Spain in the fairly near future; even then, how is the history of the war to be written? What kind of records will Franco have left behind him? Suppose even that the records kept on the Government side are recoverable – even so, how is a true history of the war to be written? For, as I have pointed out already, the Government also dealt extensively in lies. From the anti-Fascist angle one could write a broadly truthful history of the war, but it would be a partisan history, unreliable on every minor point. Yet, after all, *some* kind of history will be written, and after those who actually remember the war are dead, it will be universally accepted. So for all practical purposes the lie will have become truth.

I know it is the fashion to say that most of recorded history is lies anyway. I am willing to believe that history is for the most part inaccurate and biased, but what is peculiar to our own age is the abandonment of the idea that history *could* be truthfully written. In the past people deliberately lied, or they unconsciously coloured what they wrote, or they struggled after the truth, well knowing that they must make many mistakes; but in each case they believed that 'the facts' existed and were more or less discoverable. And in practice there was always a considerable body of fact which would have been agreed to by almost everyone. If you look up the history of the last war in, for instance, the *Encyclopaedia Britannica,* you will find that a respectable amount of the material is drawn from German sources. A British and a German historian would disagree deeply on many things, even on fundamentals, but there would still be that body of, as it were, neutral fact on which neither would seriously challenge the other. It is just this common basis of agreement, with its implication that human beings are all one species of animal, that totalitarianism destroys. Nazi theory indeed specifically denies that such a thing as 'the truth' exists.

There is, for instance, no such thing as 'science'. There is only 'German science', 'Jewish science' etc. The implied objective of this line of thought is a nightmare world in which the Leader, or some ruling clique, controls not only the future but *the past*. If the Leader says of such and such an event, 'It never happened' – well, it never happened. If he says that two and two are five – well, two and two are five. This prospect frightens me much more than bombs – and after our experiences of the last few years that is not a frivolous statement.

But is it perhaps childish or morbid to terrify oneself with visions of a totalitarian future? Before writing off the totalitarian world as a nightmare that can't come true, just remember that in 1925 the world of today would have seemed a nightmare that couldn't come true. Against that shifting phantasmagoric world in which black may be white tomorrow and yesterday's weather can be changed by decree, there are in reality only two safeguards. One is that however much you deny the truth, the truth goes on existing, as it were, behind your back, and you consequently can't violate it in ways that impair military efficiency. The other is that so long as some parts of the earth remain unconquered, the liberal tradition can be kept alive. Let Fascism, or possibly even a combination of several Fascisms, conquer the whole world, and those two conditions no longer exist. We in England underrate the danger of this kind of thing, because our traditions and our past security have given us a sentimental belief that it all comes right in the end and the thing you most fear never really happens. Nourished for hundreds of years on a literature in which Right invariably triumphs in the last chapter, we believe half-instinctively that evil always defeats itself in the long run. Pacifism, for instance, is founded largely on this belief. Don't resist evil, and it will somehow destroy itself. But why should it? What evidence is there that it does? And what instance is there of a modern industrialized state collapsing unless conquered from the outside by military force?

Consider for instance the re-institution of slavery. Who could have imagined twenty years ago that slavery would return to Europe? Well, slavery has been restored under our noses. The forced-labour camps all over Europe and North Africa where Poles, Russians, Jews and political prisoners of every race toil at road-making or swamp-draining for their bare rations, are simple chattel slavery. The most one can say is that the buying and selling of slaves by individuals is not yet permitted. In other ways – the breaking-up of families, for instance – the conditions are probably worse than they were on the American cotton plantations. There is no reason for thinking that this state of affairs will change while any totalitarian domination endures. We don't grasp its full implications, because in our mystical way we feel that a régime founded on slavery *must* collapse. But it is worth comparing the duration of the slave empires of antiquity with that of any modern state. Civilizations founded on slavery have lasted for such periods as four thousand years.

When I think of antiquity, the detail that frightens me is that those hundreds of millions of slaves on whose backs civilization rested generation after generation have left behind them no record whatever. We do not even know their names. In the whole of Greek and Roman history, how many slaves' names are known to you? I can think of two, or possibly three. One is Spartacus and the other is Epictetus. Also, in the Roman room at the British Museum there is a glass jar with the maker's name inscribed on the bottom, '*Felix fecit*'. I have a vivid mental picture of poor Felix (a Gaul with red hair and a metal collar round his neck), but in fact he may not have been a slave; so there are only two slaves whose names I definitely know, and probably few people can remember more. The rest have gone down into utter silence.

V

The backbone of the resistance against Franco was the Spanish working class, especially the urban trade-union members. In the long run – it is important to remember that it is only in the long run – the working class remains the most reliable enemy of Fascism, simply because the working class stands to gain most by a decent reconstruction of society. Unlike other classes or categories, it can't be permanently bribed.

To say this is not to idealize the working class. In the long struggle that has followed the Russian Revolution it is the manual workers who have been defeated, and it is impossible not to feel that it was their own fault. Time after time, in country after country, the organized working-class movements have been crushed by open, illegal violence, and their comrades abroad, linked to them in theoretical solidarity, have simply looked on and done nothing; and underneath this, secret cause of many betrayals, has lain the fact that between white and coloured workers there is not even lip-service to solidarity. Who can believe in the class-conscious international proletariat after the events of the past ten years? To the British working class the massacre of their comrades in Vienna, Berlin, Madrid, or wherever it might be, seemed less interesting and less important than yesterday's football match. Yet this does not alter the fact that the working class will go on struggling against Fascism after the others have caved in. One feature of the Nazi conquest of France was the astonishing defections among the intelligentsia, including some of the left-wing political intelligentsia. The intelligentsia are the people who squeal loudest against Fascism, and yet a respectable proportion of them collapse into defeatism when the pinch comes. They are far-sighted enough to see the odds against them, and moreover they can be bribed – for it is evident that the Nazis think it worth while to bribe intellectuals. With the working class it is the other way about. Too ignorant to see through the trick that is being played on them, they easily swallow the promises of Fascism, yet sooner or later they always take up the struggle again. They must do so, because in their own bodies they always discover that the promises of Fascism cannot be fulfilled. To win over the working class permanently, the Fascists would have to raise the general standard of living, which they are unable and probably unwilling to do. The struggle of the working class is like the growth of a plant. The plant is blind and stupid, but it knows enough to keep pushing upwards towards the light, and it will do this in the face of endless discouragements. What are the workers struggling for? Simply for the decent life which they are more and more aware is now technically possible. Their consciousness of this aim ebbs and flows. In Spain, for a while, people were acting consciously, moving towards a goal which they wanted to reach and believed they could reach. It accounted for the curiously buoyant feeling that life in Government Spain had during the early months of the war. The common people knew in their bones that the Republic was their friend and Franco was their enemy. They knew that they were in the right, because they were fighting for something which the world owed them and was able to give them

One has to remember this to see the Spanish war in its true perspective. When one thinks of the cruelty, squalor, and futility of war – and in this particular case of the intrigues, the persecutions, the lies and the misunderstandings – there is always the temptation to say: 'One side is as bad as the other. I am neutral.' In practice, however, one cannot be neutral, and there is hardly such a thing as a war in which it makes no difference who wins. Nearly always one side stands more or less for progress, the other side more or less for reaction. The hatred which the Spanish Republic excited in millionaires, dukes, cardinals, play-boys, Blimps and what-not would in itself be enough to show one how the land lay. In essence it was a class war. If it had been won, the cause of the common people everywhere would have been strengthened. It was lost, and the dividend-drawers all over the world rubbed their hands. That was the real issue; all else was froth on its surface.

VI

The outcome of the Spanish war was settled in London, Paris, Rome, Berlin – at any rate not in Spain. After the summer of 1937 those with eyes in their heads realized that the Government could not win the war unless there was some profound change in the international set-up, and in deciding to fight on Negrin and the others may have been partly influenced by the expectation that the world war which actually broke out in 1939 was coming in 1938. The much-publicized disunity on the Government side was not a main cause of defeat. The Government militias were hurriedly raised, ill-armed and unimaginative in their military outlook, but they would have been the same if complete political agreement had existed from the start. At the outbreak of war the average Spanish factory-worker did not even know how to fire a rifle (there had never been universal conscription in Spain), and the traditional pacifism of the Left was a great handicap. The thousands of foreigners who served in Spain made good infantry, but there were very few experts of any kind among them. The Trotskyist thesis that the war could have been won if the revolution had not been sabotaged was probably false. To nationalize factories, demolish churches, and issue revolutionary manifestos would not have made the armies more efficient. The Fascists won because they were the stronger; they had modern arms and the others hadn't. No political strategy could offset that.

The most baffling thing in the Spanish war was the behaviour of the great powers. The war was actually won for Franco by the Germans and Italians, whose motives were obvious enough. The motives of France and Britain are less easy to understand. In 1936 it was clear to everyone that if Britain would only help the Spanish Government, even to the extent of a few million pounds' worth of arms, Franco would collapse and German strategy would be severely dislocated. By that time one did not need to be a clairvoyant to foresee that war between Britain and Germany was coming; one could even foretell within a year or two when it would come. Yet in the most mean, cowardly, hypocritical way the British ruling class did all they could to hand Spain over to Franco and the Nazis. Why? Because they were pro-Fascist, was the obvious answer. Undoubtedly they were, and yet when it came to the final showdown they chose to stand up to Germany. It is still very uncertain what plan they acted on in backing Franco, and they may have had no clear plan at all. Whether the British ruling class are wicked or merely stupid is one of the most difficult questions of our time, and at certain moments a very important question. As to the Russians, their motives in the Spanish war are completely inscrutable. Did they, as the pinks believed, intervene in Spain in order to defend democracy and thwart the Nazis? Then why did they intervene on such a niggardly scale and finally leave Spain in the lurch? Or did they, as the Catholics maintained, intervene in order to foster revolution in Spain? They why did they do all in their power to crush the Spanish revolutionary movements, defend private property and hand power to the middle class as against the working class? Or did they, as the Trotskyists suggested, intervene simply in order to *prevent* a Spanish revolution? Then why not have backed Franco? Indeed, their actions are most easily explained if one assumes that they were acting on several contradictory motives. I believe that in the future we shall come to feel that Stalin's foreign policy, instead of being so diabolically clever as it is claimed to be, has been merely opportunistic and stupid. But at any rate, the Spanish Civil War demonstrated that the Nazis knew what they were doing and their opponents did not. The war was fought at a low technical level and its major strategy was very simple. That side which had arms would win. The Nazis and the Italians gave arms to their Spanish Fascist friends, and the western democracies and the Russians didn't give arms to those who should have been their friends. So the Spanish Republic perished, having 'gained what no republic missed'.

Whether it was right, as all left-wingers in other countries undoubtedly did, to encourage the Spaniards to go on fighting when they could not win is a question hard to answer. I myself think it was right, because I believe that it is better even from the point of view of survival to fight and be conquered than to surrender without fighting. The effects on the grand strategy of the struggle against Fascism cannot be assessed yet. The ragged, weaponless armies of the Republic held out for two and a half years, which was undoubtedly longer than their enemies expected. But whether that dislocated the Fascist timetable, or whether, on the other hand, it merely postponed the major war and gave the Nazis extra time to get their war machine into trim, is still uncertain

VII

I never think of the Spanish war without two memories coming into my mind. One is of the hospital ward at Lerida and the rather sad voices of the wounded militiamen singing some song with a refrain that ended:

'Una resolucion,
Luchar hast' al fin!'

Well, they fought to the end all right. For the last eighteen months of the war the Republican armies must have been fighting almost without cigarettes, and with precious little food. Even when I left Spain in the middle of 1937, meat and bread were scarce, tobacco a rarity, coffee and sugar almost unobtainable

The other memory is of the Italian militiaman who shook my hand in the guardroom, the day I joined the militia. I wrote about this man at the beginning of my book on the Spanish war,[1] and do not want to repeat what I said there. When I remember – oh, how vividly! – his shabby uniform and fierce, pathetic, innocent face, the complex side-issues of the war seem to fade away and I see clearly that there was at any rate no doubt as to who was in the right. In spite of power politics and journalistic lying, the central issue of the war was the attempt of people like this to win the decent life which they knew to be their birthright. It is difficult to think of this particular man's probable end without several kinds of bitterness. Since I met him in the Lenin Barracks he was probably a Trotskyist or an Anarchist, and in the peculiar conditions of our time, when people of that sort are not killed by the Gestapo they are usually killed by the G.P.U. But that does not affect the long-term issues. This man's face, which I saw only for a minute or two, remains with me as a sort of visual reminder of what the war was really about. He symbolizes for me the flower of the European working class, harried by the police of all countries, the people who fill the mass graves of the Spanish battlefields and are now, to the tune of several millions, rotting in forced-labour camps.

When one thinks of all the people who support or have supported Fascism, one stands amazed at their diversity. What a crew! Think of a programme which at any rate for a while could bring Hitler, Pétain, Montagu Norman, Pavelitch, William Randolph Hearst, Streicher, Buchman, Ezra Pound, Juan March, Cocteau, Thyssen, Father Coughlin, the Mufti of Jerusalem, Arnold Lunn, Antonescu, Spengler, Beverly

1. *Homage to Catalonia.*

Nichols, Lady Houston, and Marinetti all into the same boat! But the clue is really very simple. They are all people with something to lose, or people who long for a hierarchical society and dread the prospect of a world of free and equal human beings. Behind all the ballyhoo that is talked about 'godless' Russia and the 'materialism' of the working class lies the simple intention of those with money or privileges to cling to them. Ditto, though it contains a partial truth, with all the talk about the worthlessness of social reconstruction not accompanied by a 'change of heart'. The pious ones, from the Pope to the yogis of California, are great on the 'changes of heart', much more reassuring from their point of view than a change in the economic system. Pétain attributes the fall of France to the common people's 'love of pleasure'. One sees this in its right perspective if one stops to wonder how much pleasure the ordinary French peasant's or working-man's life would contain compared with Pétain's own. The damned impertinence of these politicians, priests, literary men, and what not who lecture the working-class Socialist for his 'materialism'! All that the working man demands is what these others would consider the indispensable minimum without which human life cannot be lived at all. Enough to eat, freedom from the haunting terror of unemployment, the knowledge that your children will get a fair chance, a bath once a day, clean linen reasonably often, a roof that doesn't leak, and short enough working hours to leave you with a little energy when the day is done. Not one of those who preach against 'materialism' would consider life liveable without these things. And how easily that minimum could be attained if we chose to set our minds to it for only twenty years! To raise the standard of living of the whole world to that of Britain would not be a greater undertaking than the war we are now fighting. I don't claim, and I don't know who does, that that would solve anything in itself. It is merely that privation and brute labour have to be abolished before the real problems of humanity can be tackled. The major problem of our time is the decay of the belief in personal immortality, and it cannot be dealt with while the average human being is either drudging like an ox or shivering in fear of the secret police. How right the working classes are in their 'materialism'! How right they are to realize that the belly comes before the soul, not in the scale of values but in point of time! Understand that, and the long horror that we are enduring becomes at least intelligible. All the considerations that are likely to make one falter – the siren voices of a Pétain or of a Gandhi, the inescapable fact that in order to fight one has to degrade oneself, the equivocal moral position of Britain, with its democratic phrases and its coolie empire, the sinister development of Soviet Russia, the squalid farce of left-wing politics – all this fades away and one sees only the struggle of the gradually awakening common people against the lords of property and their hired liars and bumsuckers. The question is very simple. Shall people like that Italian soldier be allowed to live the decent, fully human life which is now technically achievable, or shan't they? Shall the common man be pushed back into the mud, or shall he not? I myself believe, perhaps on insufficient grounds, that the common man will win his fight sooner or later, but I want it to be sooner and not later – some time within the next hundred years, say, and not some time within the next ten thousand years. That was the real issue of the Spanish war, and of the present war, and perhaps of other wars yet to come

I never saw the Italian militiaman again, nor did I ever learn his name. It can be taken as quite certain that he is dead. Nearly two years later, when the war was visibly lost, I wrote these verses in his memory:

The Italian soldier shook my hand
Beside the guard-room table;
The strong hand and the subtle hand
Whose palms are only able

To meet within the sounds of guns,
But oh! what peace I knew then
In gazing on his battered face
Purer than any woman's!

For the flyblown words that make me spew
Still in his ears were holy,
And he was born knowing that I had learned
Out of books and slowly.

The treacherous guns had told their tale
And we both had bought it,
But my gold brick was made of gold –
Oh! who ever would have thought it?

Good luck go with you, Italian soldier!
But luck is not for the brave;
What would the world give back to you?
Always less than you gave.

Between the shadow and the ghost,
Between the white and the red,

Between the bullet and the lie,
Where would hide your head?

For where is Manuel Gonzalez,
And where is Pedro Aguilar,
And where is Ramon Fenellosa?
The earthworms know where they are.

Your name and your deeds were forgotten
Before your bones were dry,
And the lie that slew you is buried
Under a deeper lie;

But the thing that I saw in your face
No power can disinherit:
No bomb that ever burst
Shatters the crystal spirit.

Written [Autumn 1942]; Sections I, II, III, and vii printed in *New Road* [June?] 1943; full version in *S.J.*; *E.Y.E.*; *C.E.*

16. W.B. Yeats

One thing that Marxist criticism has not succeeded in doing is to trace the connexion between 'tendency' and literary style. The subject-matter and imagery of a book can be explained in sociological terms, but its texture seemingly cannot. Yet some such connexion there must be. One knows, for instance, that a Socialist would not write like Chesterton or a Tory imperialist like Bernard Shaw, though *how* one knows it is not easy to say. In the case of Yeats, there must be some kind of connexion between his wayward, even tortured style of writing and his rather sinister vision of life. Mr Menon[1] is chiefly concerned with the esoteric philosophy underlying Yeats's work, but the quotations which are scattered all through his interesting book serve to remind one how artificial Yeats's manner of writing was. As a rule, this artificiality is accepted as Irishism, or Yeats is even credited with simplicity because he uses short words, but

1. *The Development of William Butler Yeats* by V. K. Narayana Menon.

in fact one seldom comes on six consecutive lines of his verse in which there is not an archaism or an affected turn of speech. To take the nearest example:

> Grant me an old man's Frenzy,
> My self must I remake
> Till I am Timon and Lear
> Or that William Blake
> Who beat upon the wall
> Till Truth obeyed his call.

The unnecessary 'that' imports a feeling of affectation, and the same tendency is present in all but Yeats's best passages. One is seldom long away from a suspicion of 'quaintness', something that links up not only with the nineties, the Ivory Tower and 'calf covers of pissed-on green', but also with Rackham's drawings, Liberty art-fabrics and the *Peter Pan* never-never land, of which, after all, 'The Happy Townland' is merely a more appetizing example. This does not matter, because, on the whole, Yeats gets away with it, and if his straining after effect is often irritating, it can also produce phrases ('the chill, footless years', 'the mackerel-crowded seas') which suddenly overwhelm one like a girl's face seen across a room. He is an exception to the rule that poets do not use poetical language:

> How many centuries spent
> The sedentary soul
> In toils of measurement
> Beyond eagle or mole,
> Beyond hearing or seeing,
> Or Archimedes' guess,
> To raise into being
> That loveliness?

Here he does not flinch from a squashy vulgar word like 'loveliness', and after all it does not seriously spoil this wonderful passage. But the same tendencies, together with a sort of raggedness which is no doubt intentional, weaken his epigrams and polemical poems. For instance (I am quoting from memory) the epigram against the critics who damned *The Playboy of the Western World*:

> Once when midnight smote the air
> Eunuchs ran through Hell and met
> On every crowded street to stare
> Upon great Juan riding by;

Even like these to rail and sweat,
Staring upon his sinewy thigh.

The power which Yeats has within himself gives him the analogy ready made and produces the tremendous scorn of the last line, but even in this short poem there are six or seven unnecessary words. It would probably have been deadlier if it had been neater.

Mr Menon's book is incidentally a short biography of Yeats, but he is above all interested in Yeats's philosophical 'system', which in his opinion supplies the subject-matter of more of Yeats's poems than is generally recognized. This system is set forth fragmentarily in various places, and at full length in *A Vision*, a privately printed book which I have never read but which Mr Menon quotes from extensively. Yeats gave conflicting accounts of its origin, and Mr Menon hints pretty broadly that the 'documents' on which it was ostensibly founded were imaginary. Yeats's philosophical system, says Mr Menon, 'was at the back of his intellectual life almost from the beginning. His poetry is full of it. Without it his later poetry becomes almost completely unintelligible.' As soon as we begin to read about the so-called system we are in the middle of a hocus-pocus of Great Wheels, gyres, cycles of the moon, reincarnation, disembodied spirits, astrology and what not. Yeats hedges as to the literalness with which he believed in all this, but he certainly dabbled in spiritualism and astrology, and in earlier life had made experiments in alchemy. Although almost buried under explanations, very difficult to understand, about the phases of the moon, the central idea of his philosophical system seems to be our old friend, the cyclical universe,in which everything happens over and over again. One has not, perhaps, the right to laugh at Yeats for his mystical beliefs – for I believe it could be shown that *some* degree of belief in magic is almost universal – but neither ought one to write such things off as mere unimportant eccentricities. It is Mr Menon's perception of this that gives his book its deepest interest. 'In the first flush of admiration and enthusiasm', he says, 'most people dismissed the fantastical philosophy as the price we have to pay for a great and curious intellect. One did not quite realize where he was heading. And those who did, like Pound and perhaps Eliot, approved the stand that he finally took. The first reaction to this did not come, as one might have expected, from the politically minded young English poets. They were puzzled because a less rigid or artificial system than that of *A Vision* might not have produced the great poetry of Yeats's last days.' It might not, and yet

Yeats's philosophy has some very sinister implications, as Mr Menon points out.

Translated into political terms, Yeats's tendency is Fascist. Throughout most of his life, and long before Fascism was ever heard of, he had had the outlook of those who reach Fascism by the aristocratic route. He is a great hater of democracy, of the modern world, science, machinery, the concept of progress – above all, of the idea of human equality. Much of the imagery of his work is feudal, and it is clear that he was not altogether free from ordinary snobbishness. Later these tendencies took clearer shape and led him to 'the exultant acceptance of authoritarianism as the only solution. Even violence and tyranny are not necessarily evil because the people, knowing not evil and good, would become perfectly acquiescent to tyranny . . . Everything must come from the top. Nothing can come from the masses.' Not much interested in politics, and no doubt disgusted by his brief incursions into public life, Yeats nevertheless makes political pronouncements. He is too big a man to share the illusions of Liberalism, and as early as 1920 he foretells in a justly famous passage ('The Second Coming') the kind of world that we have actually moved into. But he appears to welcome the coming age, which is to be 'hierarchical, masculine, harsh, surgical', and is influenced both by Ezra Pound and by various Italian Fascist writers. He describes the new civilization which he hopes and believes will arrive: 'an aristocratic civilization in its most completed form, every detail of life hierarchical, every great man's door crowded at dawn by petitioners, great wealth everywhere in a few men's hands, all dependent upon a few, up to the Emperor himself, who is a God dependent on a greater God, and everywhere, in Court, in the family, an inequality made law.' The innocence of this statement is as interesting as its snobbishness. To begin with, in a single phrase, 'great wealth in a few men's hands', Yeats lays bare the central reality of Fascism, which the whole of its propaganda is designed to cover up. The merely political Fascist claims always to be fighting for justice: Yeats, the poet, sees at a glance that Fascism means injustice, and acclaims it for that very reason. But at the same time he fails to see that the new authoritarian civilization, if it arrives, will not be aristocratic, or what he means by aristocratic. It will not be ruled by noblemen with Van Dyck faces, but by anonymous millionaires, shiny-bottomed bureaucrats and murdering gangsters. Others who have made the same mistake have afterwards changed their views and one ought not to assume that Yeats, if he had lived longer, would necessarily have followed his friend Pound, even in sympathy. But the tendency of the passage I have quoted above is obvious, and its complete throwing overboard of whatever good the past two thousand years have achieved is a disquieting symptom.

How do Yeats's political ideas link up with his leaning towards occultism? It is not clear at first glance why hatred of democracy and a tendency to believe in crystal-gazing should go together. Mr Menon only discusses this rather shortly, but it is possible to make two guesses. To begin with, the theory that civilization moves in recurring cycles is one way out for people who hate the concept of human equality. It it is true that 'all this', or something like it, 'has happened before', then science and the modern world are debunked at one stroke and progress becomes for ever impossible. It does not much matter if the lower orders are getting above themselves, for, after all, we shall soon be returning to an age of tyranny. Yeats is by no means alone in this outlook. If the universe is moving round on a wheel, the future must be foreseeable, perhaps even in some detail. It is merely a question of discovering the laws of its motion, as the early astronomers discovered the solar year. Believe that, and it becomes difficult not to believe in astrology or some similar system. A year before the war, examining a copy of *Gringoire*, the French Fascist weekly, much read by army officers, I found in it no less than thirty-eight advertisements of clairvoyants. Secondly, the very concept of occultism carries with it the idea that knowledge must be a secret thing, limited to a small circle of initiates. But the same idea is integral to Fascism. Those who dread the prospect of universal suffrage, popular education, freedom of thought, emancipation of women, will start off with a predilection towards secret cults. There is another link between Fascism and magic in the profound hostility of both to the Christian ethical code.

No doubt Yeats wavered in his beliefs and held at different times many different opinions, some enlightened, some not. Mr Menon repeats for him Eliot's claim that he had the longest period of development of any poet who has ever lived. But there is one thing that seems constant, at least in all of his work that I can remember, and that is his hatred of modern western civilization and desire to return to the Bronze Age, or perhaps to the Middle Ages. Like all such thinkers, he tends to write in praise of ignorance. The Fool in his remarkable play, *The Hour-Glass*, is a Chestertonian figure, 'God's fool', the 'natural born innocent', who is always wiser than the wise man. The philosopher in the play dies on the knowledge that all his lifetime of thought has been wasted (I am quoting from memory again):

The stream of the world has changed its course,
And with the stream my thoughts have run
Into some cloudly, thunderous spring
That is its mountain-source;
Ay, to a frenzy of the mind,
That all that we have done's undone
Our speculation but as the wind.[2]

Beautiful words, but by implication profoundly obscurantist and reactionary; for if it is really true that a village idiot, as such, is wiser than a philosopher, then it would be better if the alphabet had never been invented. Of course, all praise of the past is partly sentimental, because we do not live in the past. The poor do not praise poverty. Before you can despise the machine, the machine must set you free from brute labour. But that is not to say that Yeats's yearning for a more primitive and more hierarchical age was not sincere. How much of all this is traceable to mere snobbishness, product of Yeats's own position as an impoverished offshoot of the aristocracy, is a different question. And the connexion between his obscurantist opinions and his tendency towards 'quaintness' of language remains to be worked out; Mr Menon hardly touches upon it.

This is a very short book, and I would greatly like to see Mr Menon go ahead and write another book on Yeats, starting where this one leaves off. 'If the greatest poet of our times is exultantly ringing in an era of Fascism, it seems a somewhat disturbing symptom,' he says on the last page, and leaves it at that. It is a disturbing symptom, because it is not an isolated one. By and large the best writers of our time have been reactionary in tendency, and though Fascism does not offer any real return to the past, those who yearn for the past will accept Fascism sooner than its probable alternatives. But there are other lines of approach, as we have seen during the past two or three years. The relationship between Fascism and the literary intelligentsia badly needs investigating, and Yeats might well be the starting-point. He is best studied by someone like Mr Menon, who can approach a poet primarily as a poet, but who also knows that a writer's political and religious beliefs are not excrescences to be laughed away, but something that will leave their mark even on the smallest detail of his work.

Horizon, January 1943; *Cr.E.*; *D.D.*; *C.E.*

2. The last three lines actually read:

"Aye, to some frenzy of the mind
For all that we have done's undone
Our speculation but as the wind.'

17. Poetry and the Microphone

About a year ago I and a number of others were engaged in broadcasting literary programmes to India, and among other things we broadcast a good deal of verse by contemporary and near-contemporary English writers – for example, Eliot, Herbert Read, Auden, Spender, Dylan Thomas, Henry Treece, Alex Comfort, Robert Bridges, Edmund Blunden, D. H. Lawrence. Whenever it was possible we had poems broadcast by the people who wrote them. Just why these particular programmes (a small and remote outflanking movement in the radio war) were instituted there is no need to explain here, but I should add that the fact that we were broadcasting to an Indian audience dictated our technique to some extent. The essential point was that our literary broadcasts were aimed at the Indian university students, a small and hostile audience, unapproachable by anything that could be described as British propaganda. It was known in advance that we could not hope for more than a few thousand listeners at the most, and this gave us an excuse to be more 'highbrow' than is generally possible on the air.

If you are broadcasting poetry to people who know your language but don't share your cultural background, a certain amount of comment and explanation is unavoidable, and the formula we usually followed was to broadcast what purported to be a monthly literary magazine. The editorial staff were supposedly sitting in their office, discussing what to put into the next number. Somebody suggested one poem, someone else suggested another, there was a short discussion and then came the poem itself, read in a different voice, preferably the author's own. This poem naturally called up another, and so the programme continued, usually with at least half a minute of discussion between any two items. For a half-hour programme, six voices seemed to be the best number. A programme of this sort was necessarily somewhat shapeless, but it could be given a certain appearance of unity by making it revolve round a single central theme. For example, one number of our imaginary magazine was devoted to the subject of war. It included two poems by Edmund Blunden, Auden's 'September 1941', extracts from a long poem by G. S. Fraser ('A Letter to Anne Ridler'), Byron's 'Isles of Greece' and an extract from T. E. Lawrence's *Revolt in the Desert.* These half-dozen items, with the arguments that preceded and followed them, covered reasonably well the possible attitudes towards war. The poems and the prose extract took about twenty minutes to broadcast, the arguments about eight minutes.

This formula may seem slightly ridiculous and also rather patronizing, but its advantage is that the element of mere instruction, the textbook motif, which is quite unavoidable if one is going to broadcast serious and sometimes 'difficult' verse, becomes a lot less forbidding when it appears as an informal discussion. The various speakers can ostensibly say to one another what they are in reality saying to the audience. Also, by such an approach you at least give a poem a context, which is just what poetry lacks from the average man's point of view. But of course there are other methods. One which we frequently used was to set a poem in music. It is announced that in a few minutes' time such and such a poem will be broadcast; then the music plays for perhaps a minute, then fades out into the poem, which follows without any title or announcement, then the music is faded in again and plays up for another minute or two – the whole thing taking perhaps five minutes. It is necessary to choose appropriate music, but needless to say, the real purpose of the music is to insulate the poem from the rest of the programme. By this method you can have, say, a Shakespeare sonnet within three minutes of a news bulletin without, at any rate to my ear, any gross incongruity.

These programmes that I have been speaking of were of no great value in themselves, but I have mentioned them because of the ideas they aroused in myself and some others about the possibilities of the radio as a means of popularizing poetry. I was early struck by the fact that the broadcasting of a poem by the person who wrote it does not merely produce an effect upon the audience, if any, but also on the poet himself. One must remember that extremely little in the way of broadcasting poetry has been done in England, and that many people who write verse have never even considered the idea of reading it aloud. By being set down at a microphone, especially if this happens at all regularly, the poet is brought into a new relationship with his work, not otherwise attainable in our time and country. It is a commonplace that in modern times – the last two hundred years, say – poetry has come to have less and less connexion either with music or with the spoken word. It needs print in order to exist at all, and it is no more expected that a poet, as such, will know how to sing or even to declaim than it is expected that an architect will know how to plaster a ceiling. Lyrical and rhetorical poetry have almost ceased to be written, and a hostility towards poetry on the part of the common man has come to be taken for granted in any country where everyone can read. And where such a breach exists it is always inclined to widen, because the concept of poetry as primarily something printed, and something intelligible only to a minority, encourages obscurity and 'cleverness'. How many people do not feel quasi-instinctively that there must be something wrong with any poem whose meaning can be taken in at a single glance? It seems unlikely that these tendencies will be checked unless it again becomes normal to read verse aloud, and it is difficult to see how this can be brought about except by using the radio as a medium. But the special advantage of the radio, its power to select the right audience, and to do away with stage-fright and embarrassment, ought here to be noticed.

In broadcasting your audience is conjectural, but it is an audience of *one*. Millions may be listening, but each is listening alone, or as a member of a small group, and each has (or ought to have) the feeling that you are speaking to him individually. More than this, it is reasonable to assume that your audience is sympathetic, or at least interested, for anyone who is bored can promptly switch you off by turning a knob. But though presumably sympathetic, the audience *has no power over you*. It is just here that a broadcast differs from a speech or a lecture. On the platform, as anyone used to public speaking knows, it is almost impossible not to take your tone from the audience. It is always obvious within a few minutes what they will respond to and what they will not, and in practice you are almost compelled to speak for the benefit of what you estimate as the stupidest person present, and also to ingratiate yourself by means of the ballyhoo known as 'personality'. If you don't do so, the result is always an atmosphere of frigid embarrassment. That grisly thing, a 'poetry reading', is what it is because there will always be some among the audience who are bored or all but frankly hostile and who can't remove themselves by the simple act of turning a knob. And it is at bottom the same difficulty – the fact that a theatre audience is not a selected one – that makes it impossible to get a decent performance of Shakespeare in England. On the air these conditions do not exist. The poet *feels* that he is addressing people to whom poetry means something, and it is a fact that poets who are used to broadcasting can read into the microphone with a virtuosity they would not equal if they had a visible audience in front of them. The element of make-believe that enters here does not greatly matter. The point is that in the only way now possible the poet has been brought into a situation in which reading verse aloud seems a natural unembarrassing thing, a normal exchange between man and man: also he has been led to think of his work as *sound* rather than as a pattern on paper. By that much the reconciliation between poetry and the common man is nearer. It already exists at the poet's end of the aether-waves, whatever may be happening at the other end

However, what is happening at the other end cannot be disregarded. It will be seen that I have been speaking as though the whole subject of poetry were embarrassing, almost indecent, as though popularizing poetry were essentially a strategic manoeuvre, like getting a dose of medicine down a child's throat or establishing tolerance for a persecuted sect. But unfortunately that or something like it is the case. There can be no doubt that in our civilization poetry is by far the most discredited of the arts, the only art, indeed, in which the average man refuses to discern *any* value. Arnold Bennett was hardly exaggerating when he said that in the English-speaking countries the word 'poetry' would disperse a crowd quicker than a fire-hose. And as I have pointed out, a breach of this kind tends to widen simply because of its existence, the common man becoming more and more anti-poetry, the poet more and more arrogant and unintelligible, until the divorce between poetry and popular culture is accepted as a sort of law of nature, although in fact it belongs only to our own time and to a comparatively small area of the earth. We live in an age in which the average human being in the highly civilized countries is aesthetically inferior to the lowest savage. This state of affairs is generally looked upon as being incurable by any *conscious* act, and on the other hand is expected to right itself of its own accord as soon as society takes a comelier shape. With slight variations the Marxist, the Anarchist and the religious believer will all tell you this, and in broad terms it is undoubtedly true. The ugliness amid which we live has spiritual and economic causes and is not to be explained by the mere going-astray of tradition at some point or other. But it does not follow that no improvement is possible within our present framework, nor that an aesthetic improvement is not a necessary part of the general redemption of society. It is worth stopping to wonder, therefore, whether it would not be possible even now to rescue poetry from its special position as the most hated of the arts and win for it at least the same degree of toleration as exists for music. But one has to start by asking, in what way and to what extent is poetry unpopular?

On the face of it, the unpopularity of poetry is as complete as it could be. But on second thoughts, this has to be qualified in a rather peculiar way. To begin with, there is still an appreciable amount of folk poetry (nursery rhymes etc.) which is universally known and quoted and forms part of the background of everyone's mind. There is also a handful of ancient songs and ballads which have never gone out of favour. In addition there is the popularity, or at least the toleration, of 'good bad' poetry, generally of a patriotic or sentimental kind. This might seem beside the point if it were not that 'good bad' poetry has all the characteristics which, ostensibly, make the average man dislike true poetry. It is in verse, it rhymes, it deals in lofty sentiments and unusual language – all this to a very marked degree, for it is almost axiomatic that bad poetry is more 'poetical' than good poetry. Yet if not actively liked it is at least tolerated. For example, just before writing this I have been listening to a couple of B.B.C. comedians doing their usual turn before the 9 o'clock news. In the last three minutes one of the two comedians suddenly announces that he 'wants to be serious for a moment' and proceeds to recite a piece of patriotic balderdash entitled 'A Fine Old English Gentleman', in praise of His Majesty the King. Now, what is the reaction of the audience to this sudden lapse into the worst sort of rhyming heroics? It cannot be very violently negative, or there would be a sufficient volume of indignant letters to stop the B.B.C. doing this kind of thing. One must conclude that though the big public is hostile to *poetry*, it is not strongly hostile to *verse*. After all, if rhyme and metre were disliked for their own sakes, neither songs nor dirty limericks could be popular. Poetry is disliked because it is associated with unintelligibility, intellectual pretentiousness and a general feeling of Sunday-on-a-weekday. Its name creates in advance the same sort of bad impression as the word 'God', or a parson's dog-collar. To a certain extent, popularizing poetry is a question of breaking down an acquired inhibition. It is a question of getting people to listen instead of uttering a mechanical raspberry. If true poetry could be introduced to the big public in such a way as to make it seem *normal*, as that piece of rubbish I have just listened to presumably seemed normal, then part of the prejudice against it might be overcome

It is difficult to believe that poetry can ever be popularized again without some deliberate effort at the education of public taste, involving strategy and perhaps even subterfuge. T. S. Eliot once suggested that poetry, particularly dramatic poetry, might be brought back into the consciousness of ordinary people through the medium of the music hall; he might have added the pantomime, whose vast possibilities do not seem ever to have been completely explored. 'Sweeney Agonistes' was perhaps written with some such idea in mind, and it would in fact be conceivable as a music-hall turn, or at least as a scene in a revue. I have suggested the radio as a more hopeful medium, and I have pointed out its technical advantages, particularly from the point of view of the poet. The reason why such a suggestion sounds hopeless at first hearing is that few people are able to imagine the radio being used for the dissemination of anything except tripe. People listen to the stuff that does actually dribble from the loudspeakers of the world, and conclude that it is for that and nothing else that the wireless exists. Indeed the very word 'wireless' calls up a picture either of roaring dictators or of genteel throaty voices announcing that three of our aircraft have failed to return. Poetry on the air sounds like the Muses in striped trousers. Nevertheless one ought not to confuse the capabilities of an instrument with the use it is actually put to. Broadcasting is what it is, not because there is something inherently vulgar, silly and dishonest about the whole apparatus of microphone and transmitter, but because all the broadcasting that now happens all over the world is under the control of governments or great monopoly companies which are actively interested in maintaining the *status quo* and therefore in preventing the common man from becoming too intelligent. Something of the same kind has happened to the cinema, which, like the radio, made its appearance during the monopoly stage of capitalism and is fantastically expensive to operate. In all the arts the tendency is similar. More and more the channels of production are under control of bureaucrats, whose aim is to destroy the artist or at least to castrate him. This would be a bleak outlook if it were not that the totalitarianization which is now going on, and must undoubtedly continue to go on, in every country of the world, is mitigated by another process which it was not easy to foresee even as short a time as five years ago.

This is, that the huge bureaucratic machines of which we are all part are beginning to work creakily because of their mere size and their constant growth. The tendency of the modern state is to wipe out the freedom of the intellect, and yet at the same time every state, especially under the pressure of war, finds itself more and more in need of an intelligentsia to do its publicity for it. The modern state needs, for example, pamphlet-writers, poster artists, illustrators, broadcasters, lecturers, film producers, actors, song composers, even painters and sculptors, not to mention psychologists, sociologists, bio-chemists, mathematicians and what-not. The British Government started the present war with the more or less openly declared intention of keeping the literary intelligentsia out of it; yet after three years of war almost every writer, however undesirable his political history or opinions, has been sucked into the various Ministries or the B.B.C. and even those who enter the armed forces tend to find themselves after a while in Public Relations or some other essentially literary job. The Government has absorbed these people, unwillingly enough, because it found itself unable to get on without them. The ideal, from the official point of view, would have been to put all publicity into the hands of 'safe' people like A. P. Herbert or Ian Hay: but since not enough of these were available, the existing intelligentsia had to be utilized, and the tone and even to some extent the content of official propaganda have been modified accordingly. No one acquainted with the Government pamphlets, A.B.C.A.[1] lectures, documentary films and broadcasts to occupied countries which have been issued during the past two years imagines that our rulers would sponsor this kind of thing if they could help it. Only, the bigger the machine of government becomes, the more loose ends and forgotten corners there are in it. This is perhaps a small consolation, but it is not a despicable one. It means that in countries where there is already a strong liberal tradition, bureaucratic tyranny can perhaps never be complete. The striped-trousered ones will rule, but so long as they are forced to maintain an intelligentsia, the intelligentsia will have a certain amount of autonomy. If the Government needs, for example, documentary films, it must employ people specially interested in the technique of the film, and it must allow them the necesary minimum of freedom; consequently, films that are all wrong from the bureaucratic point of view will always have a tendency to appear. So also with painting, photography, script-writing, reportage, lecturing and all the other arts and half-arts of which a complex modern state has need.

The application of this to the radio is obvious. At present the loudspeaker is the enemy of the creative writer, but this may not necessarily remain true when the volume and scope of broadcasting increase. As things are, although the B.B.C. does keep up a feeble show of interest in contemporary literature, it is harder to capture five minutes on the air in which to broadcast a poem than twelve hours in which to disseminate lying propaganda, tinned music, stale jokes, faked 'discussions' or what-have-you. But that state of affairs may alter in the way I have indicated, and when that time comes serious experiment in the broadcasting of verse, with complete disregard for the various hostile influences which prevent any such thing at present, would become possible. I don't claim it as certain that such an experiment would have very great results. The radio was bureaucratized so early in its career that the relationship between broadcasting and literature has never been thought out. It is not certain that the microphone is the instrument by which poetry could be brought back to the common people and it is not even certain that poetry would gain by being more of a spoken and less

1. The Army Bureau of Current Affairs.

of a written thing. But I do urge that these possibilities exist, and that those who care for literature might turn their minds more often to this much-despised medium, whose powers for good have perhaps been obscured by the voices of Professor Joad and Doctor Goebbels.

Written [Autumn 1943]; *New Saxon Pamphlet* [No. 3, March 1945]; *S.J.*; *E.Y.E.*; *C.E.*

18. In Defence of English Cooking

We have heard a good deal of talk in recent years about the desirability of attracting foreign tourists to this country. It is well known that England's two worst faults, from a foreign visitor's point of view, are the gloom of our Sundays and the difficulty of buying a drink.

Both of these are due to fanatical minorities who will need a lot of quelling, including extensive legislation. But there is one point on which public opinion could bring about a rapid change for the better: I mean cooking.

It is commonly said, even by the English themselves, that English cooking is the worst in the world. It is supposed to be not merely incompetent, but also imitative, and I even read quite recently, in a book by a French writer, the remark: 'The best English cooking is, of course, simply French cooking.'

Now that is simply not true. As anyone who has lived long abroad will know, there is a whole host of delicacies which it is quite impossible to obtain outside the English-speaking countries. No doubt the list could be added to, but here are some of the things that I myself have sought for in foreign countries and failed to find.

First of all, kippers, Yorkshire pudding, Devonshire cream, muffins and crumpets. Then a list of puddings, that would be interminable if I gave it in full: I will pick out for special mention Christmas pudding, treacle tart and apple dumplings. Then an almost equally long list of cakes: for instance, dark plum cake (such as you used to get at Buzzard's before the war), short-bread and saffron buns. Also innumerable kinds of biscuit, which exist, of course, elsewhere, but are generally admitted to be better and crisper in England.

Then there are the various ways of cooking potatoes that are peculiar to our own country. Where else do you see potatoes roasted under the joint, which is far and away the best way of cooking them? Or the delicious potato cakes that you get in the north of England? And it is far better to cook new potatoes in the English way – that is, boiled with mint and then served with a little melted butter or margarine – than to fry them as is done in most countries.

Then there are the various sauces peculiar to England. For instance, bread sauce, horse-radish sauce, mint sauce and apple sauce; not to mention redcurrant jelly, which is excellent with mutton as well as with hare, and various kinds of sweet pickle, which we seem to have in greater profusion than most countries.

What else? Outside these islands I have never seen a haggis, except one that came out of a tin, nor Dublin prawns, nor Oxford marmalade, nor several other kinds of jam (marrow jam and bramble jelly, for instance), nor sausages of quite the same kind as ours.

Then there are the English cheeses. There are not many of them but I fancy that Stilton is the best cheese of its type in the world, with Wensleydale not far behind. English apples are also outstandingly good, particularly the Cox's Orange Pippin.

And finally, I would like to put in a word for English bread. All the bread is good, from the enormous Jewish loaves flavoured with caraway seeds to the Russian rye bread which is the colour of black treacle. Still, if there is anything quite as good as the soft part of the crust from an English cottage loaf (how soon shall we be seeing cottage loaves again?) I do not know of it.

No doubt some of the things I have named above could be obtained in continental Europe, just as it is possible in London to obtain vodka or bird's nest soup. But they are all native to our shores, and over huge areas they are literally unheard of.

South of, say, Brussels, I do not imagine that you would succeed in getting hold of a suet pudding. In French there is not even a word that exactly translates 'suet'. The French, also, never use mint in cookery and do not use black currants except as a basis of a drink.

It will be seen that we have no cause to be ashamed of our cookery, so far as originality goes or so far as the ingredients go. And yet it must be admitted that there is a serious snag from the foreign visitor's point of view. This is, that you practically don't find good English cooking outside a private house. If you want, say, a good, rich slice of Yorkshire pudding you are more likely to get it in the poorest English home than in a restaurant, which is where the visitor necessarily eats most of his meals.

It is a fact that restaurants which are distinctively English and which also sell good food are very hard to find. Pubs, as a rule, sell no food at all, other than potato crips and tasteless sandwiches. The expensive restaurants and hotels almost all imitate French cookery and write their menus in French, while if you want a good cheap meal you gravitate naturally towards a Greek, Italian or Chinese restaurant. We are not likely to succeed in attracting tourists while England is thought of as a country of bad food and unintelligible by-laws. At present one cannot do much about it, but sooner or later rationing will come to an end, and then will be the moment for our national cookery to revive. It is not a law of nature that every restaurant in England should be either foreign or bad, and the first step towards an improvement will be a less long-suffering attitude in the British public itself.

Evening Standard, 15 December 1945

19. Benefit of Clergy: Some Notes on Salvador Dali

Autobiography is only to be trusted when it reveals something disgraceful. A man who gives a good account of himself is probably lying, since any life when viewed from the inside is simply a series of defeats. However, even the most flagrantly dishonest book (Frank Harris's autobiographical writings are an example) can without intending it give a true picture of its author. Dali's recently published *Life*[1] comes under this heading. Some of the incidents in it are flatly incredible, others have been rearranged and romanticized, and not merely the humiliation but the persistent *ordinariness* of everyday life has been cut out. Dali is even by his own diagnosis narcissistic, and his autobiography is simply a strip-tease act conducted in pink limelight. But as a record of fantasy, of the perversion of instinct that has been made possible by the machine age, it has great value.

Here, then, are some of the episodes in Dali's life, from his earliest years onward. Which of them are true and which are imaginary hardly matters: the point is that this is the kind of thing that Dali would have *liked* to do.

1. *The Secret Life of Salvador Dali*, Dial Press, New York.

When he is six years old there is some excitement over the appearance of Halley's comet:

> Suddenly one of my father's office clerks appeared in the drawing-room doorway and announced that the comet could be seen from the terrace . . . While crossing the hall I caught sight of my little three-year-old sister crawling unobtrusively through a door-way. I stopped, hesitated a second, then gave her a terrible kick in the head as though it had been a ball, and continued running, carried away with a 'delirious joy' induced by this savage act. But my father, who was behind me, caught me and led me down into his office, where I remained as a punishment till dinner-time.

A year earlier than this Dali had 'suddenly, as most of my ideas occur' flung another little boy off a suspension bridge. Several other incidents of the same kind are recorded, including (*this was when he was twenty-nine years old*) knocking down and trampling on a girl 'until they had to tear her, bleeding, out of my reach'.

When he is about five he gets hold of a wounded bat which he puts into a tin pail. Next morning he finds that the bat is almost dead and is covered with ants which are devouring it. He puts it in his mouth, ants and all, and bites it almost in half.

When he is adolescent a girl falls desperately in love with him. He kisses and caresses her so as to excite her as much as possible, but refuses to go further. He resolves to keep this up for five years (he calls it his 'five year plan'), enjoying her humiliation and the sense of power it gives him. He frequently tells her that at the end of five years he will desert her, and when the time comes he does so.

Till well into adult life he keeps up the practice of masturbation, and likes to do this, apparently, in front of a looking-glass. For ordinary purposes he is impotent, it appears, till the age of thirty or so. When he first meets his future wife, Gala, he is greatly tempted to push her off a precipice. He is aware that there is something that she wants him to do to her, and after their first kiss the confession is made:

> I threw back Gala's head, pulling it by the hair, and trembling with complete hysteria, I commanded:
>
> 'Now tell me what you want me to do with you! But tell me slowly, looking me in the eye, with the crudest, the most ferociously erotic words that can make both of us feel the greatest shame!'
>
> . . . Then Gala, transforming the last glimmer of her expression of pleasure into the hard light of her own tyranny, answered:
>
> 'I want you to kill me'!

He is somewhat disappointed by this demand, since it is merely what he wanted to do already. He contemplates throwing her off the bell-tower of the cathedral of Toledo, but refrains from doing so.

During the Spanish Civil War he astutely avoids taking sides, and makes a trip to Italy. He feels himself more and more drawn towards the aristocracy, frequents smart *salons*, finds himself wealthy patrons, and is photographed with the plump Vicomte de Noailles, whom he describes as his 'Maecenas'. When the European war approaches he has one preoccupation only: how to find a place which has good cookery and from which he can make a quick bolt if danger comes too near. He fixes on Bordeaux, and duly flees to Spain during the Battle of France. He stays in Spain long enough to pick up a few anti-red atrocity stories, then makes for America. They story ends in a blaze of respectability. Dali, at thirty-seven, has become a devoted husband, is cured of his aberrations, or some of them, and is completely reconciled to the Catholic Church. He is also, one gathers, making a good deal of money.

However, he has by no means ceased to take pride in the pictures of his Surrealist period, with titles like 'The Great Masturbator', 'Sodomy of a Skull with a Grand Piano', etc. There are reproductions of these all the way through the book. Many of Dali's drawings are simply representational and have a characteristic to be noted later. But from his Surrealist paintings and photographs the two things that stand out are sexual perversity and necrophilia. Sexual objects and symbols – some of them well known, like our old friend the high-heeled slipper, others, like the crutch and the cup of warm milk, patented by Dali himself – recur over and over again, and there is a fairly well-marked excretory motif as well. Of his painting, *'Le Jeu Lugubre'*, he says, 'the drawers bespattered with excrement were painted with such minute and realistic complacency that the whole little Surrealist group was anguished by the question: Is he coprophagic or not?' Dali adds firmly that he is *not*, and that he regards this aberration as 'repulsive', but it seems to be only at that point that his interest in excrement stops. Even when he recounts the experience of watching a woman urinate standing up, he has to add the detail that she missses her aim and dirties her shoes. It is not given to any one person to have all the vices, and Dali also boasts that he is not homosexual, but otherwise he seems to have as good an outfit of perversions as anyone could wish for.

However, his most notable characteristic is his necrophilia. He himself freely admits to this, and claims to have been cured of it. Dead faces, skulls, corpses of animals occur fairly frequently in his pictures, and the ants which devoured the dying bat make countless reappearances. One photograph shows an exhumed corpse, far gone in decomposition. Another shows the dead donkeys putrefying on top of grand pianos which formed part of the Surrealist film, *Le Chien Andalou*. Dali still looks back on these donkeys with great enthusiasm.

> I 'made up' the putrefaction of the donkeys with great pots of sticky glue which I poured over them. Also I emptied their eye-sockets and made them larger by hacking them out with scissors. In the same way I furiously cut their mouths open to make the rows of their teeth show to better advantage, and I added several jaws to each mouth, so that it would appear that although the donkeys were already rotting they were vomiting up a little more of their own death, above those other rows of teeth formed by the keys of the black pianos.

And finally there is the picture – apparently some kind of faked photograph – of 'Mannequin rotting in a taxi-cab'. Over the already somewhat bloated face and breast of an apparently dead girl, huge snails are crawling. In the caption below the picture Dali notes that these are Burgundy snails – that is, the edible kind.

Of course, in this long book of 400 quarto pages there is more than I have indicated, but I do not think that I have given an unfair account of its moral atmosphere and mental scenery. It is a book that stinks. If it were possible for a book to give a physical stink off its pages, this one would – a thought that might please Dali, who before wooing his future wife for the first time rubbed himself all over with an ointment made of goat's dung boiled up in fish glue. But against this has to be set the fact that Dali is a draughtsman of very exceptional gifts. He is also, to judge by the minuteness and the sureness of his drawings, a very hard worker. He is an exhibitionist and a careerist, but he is not a fraud. He has fifty times more talent than most of the people who would denounce his morals and jeer at his paintings. And these two sets of facts, taken together, raise a question which for lack of any basis of agreement seldom gets a real discussion.

The point is that you have here a direct, unmistakable assault on sanity and decency; and even – since some of Dali's pictures would tend to poison the imagination like a pornographic postcard – on life itself. What Dali has done and what he has imagined is debatable, but in his outlook, his character, the bedrock decency of a human being does not exist. He is as antisocial as a flea. Clearly, such people are undesirable, and a society in which they can flourish has something wrong with it.

Now, if you showed this book, with its illustrations, to Lord Elton, to

Mr Alfred Noyes, to *The Times* leader-writers who exult over the 'eclipse of the highbrow' – in fact, to any 'sensible' art-hating English person – it is easy to imagine what kind of response you would get. They would flatly refuse to see any merit in Dali whatever. Such people are not only unable to admit that what is morally degraded can be aesthetically right, but their real demand of every artist is that he shall pat them on the back and tell them that thought is unnecessary. And they can be especially dangerous at a time like the present, when the Ministry of Information and the British Council put power into their hands. For their impulse is not only to crush every new talent as it appears, but to castrate the past as well. Witness the renewed highbrow-baiting that is now going on in this country and America, with its outcry not only against Joyce, Proust and Lawrence, but even against T.S. Eliot.

But if you talk to the kind of person who *can* see Dali's merits, the response that you get is not as a rule very much better. If you say that Dali, though a brilliant draughtsman, is a dirty little scoundrel, you are looked upon as a savage. If you say that you don't like rotting corpses, and that people who do like rotting corpses are mentally diseased, it is assumed that you lack the aesthetic sense. Since 'Mannequin rotting in a taxi-cab' is a good composition (as it undoubtedly is), it cannot be a disgusting, degrading picture; whereas Noyes, Elton, etc., would tell you that because it is disgusting it cannot be a good composition. And between these two fallacies there is no middle position; or, rather, there is a middle position, but we seldom hear much about it. On the one side *Kulturbolschewismus*: on the other (though the phrase itself is out of fashion) 'Art for Art's sake'. Obscenity is a very difficult question to discuss honestly. People are too frightened either of seeming to be shocked or of seeming not to be shocked, to be able to define the relationship between art and morals.

It will be seen that what the defenders of Dali are claiming is a kind of *benefit of clergy*. The artist is to be exempt from the moral laws that are binding on ordinary people. Just pronounce the magic word 'art', and everything is OK. Rotting corpses with snails crawling over them are OK; kicking little girls on the head is OK; even a film like *L'Age d'Or* is OK.[2] It is also OK that Dali should batten on France for years and then

2. Dali mentions *L'Age d'Or* and adds that its first public showing was broken up by hooligans, but he does not say in detail what it was about. According to Henry Miller's account of it, it showed among other things some fairly detailed shots of a woman defecating. [Author's footnote.]

scuttle off like a rat as soon as France is in danger. So long as you can paint well enough to pass the test, all shall be forgiven you.

One can see how false this is if one extends it to cover the ordinary crime. In an age like our own, when the artist is an altogether exceptional person, he must be allowed a certain amount of irresponsibility, just as a pregnant woman is. Still, no one would say that a pregnant woman should be allowed to commit murder, nor would anyone make such a claim for the artist, however gifted. If Shakespeare returned to the earth tomorrow, and if it were found that his favourite recreation was raping little girls in railway carriages, we should not tell him to go ahead with it on the ground that he might write another *King Lear*. And, after all, the worse crimes are not always the punishable ones. By encouraging necrophilic reveries one probably does quite as much harm as by, say, picking pockets at the races. One ought to be able to hold in one's head simultaneously the two facts that Dali is a good draughtsman and a disgusting human being. The one does not invalidate or, in a sense, affect the other. The first thing that we demand of a wall is that it shall stand up. If it stands up, it is a good wall, and the question of what purpose it serves is separable from that. And yet even the best wall in the world deserves to be pulled down if it surrounds a concentration camp. In the same way it should be possible to say, 'This is a good book or a good picture, and it ought to be burned by the public hangman.' Unless one can say that, at least in imagination, one is shirking the implications of the fact that an artist is also a citizen and a human being.

Not, of course, that Dali's autobiography, or his pictures, ought to be suppressed. Short of the dirty postcards that used to be sold in Mediterranean seaport towns, it is doubtful policy to suppress anything, and Dali's fantasies probably cast useful light on the decay of capitalist civilization. But what he clearly needs is diagnosis. The question is not so much *what* he is, as *why* he is like that. It ought not to be in doubt that he is a diseased intelligence, probably not much altered by his alleged conversion, since genuine penitents, or people who have returned to sanity, do not flaunt their past vices in that complacent way. He is a symptom of the world's illness. The important thing is not to denounce him as a cad who ought to be horse-whipped or to defend him as a genius who ought not to be questioned, but to find out *why* he exhibits that particular set of aberrations.

The answer is probably discoverable in his pictures, and those I myself am not competent to examine. But I can point to one clue which perhaps takes one part of the distance. This is the old-fashioned, over-ornate,

Edwardian style of drawing to which Dali tends to revert when he is not being Surrealist. Some of Dali's drawings are reminiscent of Dürer, one (p. 113) seems to show the influence of Beardsley, another (p. 269) seems to borrow something from Blake. But the most persistent strain is the Edwardian one. When I opened the book for the first time and looked at its innumerable marginal illustrations, I was haunted by a resemblance which I could not immediately pin down. I fetched up at the ornamental candlestick at the beginning of Part I (p. 7). What did this remind me of? Finally I tracked it down. It reminded me of a large, vulgar, expensively got-up edition of Anatole France (in translation) which must have been published about 1914. That had ornamental chapter headings and tailpieces after this style. Dali's candlestick displays at one end a curly fish-like creature that looks curiously familiar (it seems to be based on the conventional dolphin), and at the other is the burning candle. This candle, which recurs in one picture after another, is a very old friend. You will find it, with the same picturesque gouts of wax arranged on its sides, in those phony electric lights done up as candlesticks which are popular in sham-Tudor country hotels. This candle, and the design beneath it, convey at once an intense feeling of sentimentality. As though to counteract this, Dali has spattered a quill-ful of ink all over the page, but without avail. The same impression keeps popping up on page after page. The design at the bottom of page 62, for instance, would nearly go into *Peter Pan*. The figure on page 224, in spite of having her cranium elongated into an immense sausage-like shape, is the witch of the fairy-tale books. The horse on page 234 and the unicorn on page 218 might be illustrations to James Branch Cabell. The rather pansified drawings of youths on pages 97, 100 and elsewhere convey the same impression. Picturesqueness keeps breaking in. Take away the skulls, ants, lobsters, telephones and other paraphernalia, and every now and again you are back in the world of Barrie, Rackham, Dunsany and *Where the Rainbow Ends*.

Curiously enough, some of the naughty-naughty touches in Dali's autobiography tie up with the same period. When I read the passage I quoted at the beginning, about the kicking of the little sister's head. I was aware of another phantom resemblance. What was it? Of course! *Ruthless Rhymes for Heartless Homes* by Harry Graham. Such rhymes were very popular round about 1912, and one that ran

> Poor little Willy is crying so sore,
> A sad little boy is he,

For he's broken his little sister's neck
And he'll have no jam for tea.

might almost have been founded on Dali's anecdote. Dali, of course, is aware of his Edwardian leanings, and makes capital out of them, more or less in a spirit of pastiche. He professes an especial affection for the year 1900, and claims that every ornamental object of 1900 is full of mystery, poetry, eroticism, madness, perversity, etc. Pastiche, however, usually implies a real affection for the thing parodied. It seems to be, if not the rule, at any rate distinctly common for an intellectual bent to be accompanied by a non-rational, even childish urge in the same direction. A sculptor, for instance, is interested in planes and curves, but he is also a person who enjoys the physical act of mucking about with clay or stone. An engineer is a person who enjoys the feel of tools, the noise of dynamos and the smell of oil. A psychiatrist usually has a leaning towards some sexual aberration himself. Darwin became a biologist partly because he was a country gentleman and fond of animals. It may be, therefore, that Dali's seemingly perverse cult of Edwardian things (for example, his 'discovery' of the 1900 subway-entrances) is merely the symptom of a much deeper, less conscious affection. The innumerable, beautifully executed copies of text-book illustrations, solemnly labelled *le rossignol*, *une montre* and so on, which he scatters all over his margins, may be meant partly as a joke. The little boy in knickerbockers playing with a diabolo on page 103 is a perfect period piece. But perhaps these things are also there because Dali can't help drawing that kind of thing, because it is to that period and that style of drawing that he really belongs.

If so, his aberrations are partly explicable. Perhaps they are a way of assuring himself that he is not commonplace. The two qualities that Dali unquestionably possesses are a gift for drawing and an atrocious egoism. 'At seven,' he says in the first paragraph of his book, 'I wanted to be Napoleon. And my ambition has been growing steadily ever since.' This is worded in a deliberately startling way, but no doubt it is substantially true. Such feelings are common enough. 'I knew I was a genius,' somebody once said to me, 'long before I knew what I was going to be a genius *about*.' And suppose that you have nothing in you except your egoism and a dexterity that goes no higher than the elbow; suppose that your real gift is for a detailed, academic, representational style of drawing, your real *métier* to be an illustrator of scientific textbooks. How then do you become Napoleon?

There is always one escape: *into wickedness*. Always do the thing that will shock and wound people. At five, throw a little boy off a bridge, strike an old doctor across the face with a whip and break his spectacles – or, at any rate, dream about doing such things. Twenty years later, gouge the eyes out of dead donkeys with a pair of scissors. Along those lines you can always feel yourself original. And after all, it pays! It is much less dangerous than crime. Making all allowance for the probable suppressions in Dali's autobiography, it is clear that he has not had to suffer for his eccentricities as he would have done in an earlier age. He grew up in the corrupt world of the nineteen-twenties, when sophistication was immensely widespread and every European capital swarmed with aristocrats and *rentiers* who had given up sport and politics and taken to patronizing the arts. If you threw dead donkeys at people, they threw money back. A phobia for grasshoppers – which a few decades back would merely have provoked a snigger – was now an interesting 'complex' which could be profitably exploited. And when that particular world collapsed before the German army, America was waiting. You could even top it all up with religious conversion, moving at one hop and without a shadow of repentance from the fashionable *salons* of Paris to Abraham's bosom.

That, perhaps, is the essential outline of Dali's history. But why his aberrations should be the particular ones they were, and why it should be so easy to 'sell' such horrors as rotting corpses to a sophisticated public – those are questions for the psychologist and the sociological critic. Marxist criticism has a short way with such phenomena as Surrealism. They are 'bourgeois decadence' (much play is made with the phrases 'corpse poisons' and 'decaying *rentier* class'), and that is that. But though this probably states a fact, it does not establish a connexion. One would still like to know *why* Dali's leaning was towards necrophilia (and not, say, homosexuality), and *why* the *rentiers* and the aristocrats should buy his pictures instead of hunting and making love like their grandfathers. Mere moral disapproval does not get one any further. But neither ought one to pretend, in the name of 'detachment', that such pictures as 'Mannequin rotting in a taxi-cab' are morally neutral. They are diseased and disgusting, and any investigation ought to start out from that fact.

[Written [June] 1944. 'Benefit of Clergy' made a sort of phantom appearance in the *Saturday Book* for 1944. The book was in print when its publishers, Messrs Hutchinson, decided that this essay must be suppressed on grounds of obscenity. It was accordingly cut out of each copy, though for technical reasons it was impossible to remove its title from the table of contents.' Author's note to *Cr.E.*; *D.D.*; *C.E.*]

20. Raffles and Miss Blandish

Nearly half a century after his first appearance, Raffles, 'the amateur cracksman', is still one of the best-known characters in English fiction. Very few people would need telling that he played cricket for England, had bachelor chambers in Albany and burgled the Mayfair houses which he also entered as a guest. Just for that reason he and his exploits make a suitable background against which to examine a more modern crime story such as *No Orchids for Miss Blandish*. Any such choice is necessarily arbitrary – I might equally well have chosen *Arsène Lupin*, for instance – but at any rate *No Orchids* and the Raffles books[1] have the common quality of being crime stories which play the limelight on the criminal rather than the policeman. For sociological purposes they can be compared. *No Orchids* is the 1939 version of glamorized crime, *Raffles* the 1900 version. What I am concerned with here is the immense difference in moral atmosphere between the two books, and the change in the popular attitude that this probably implies.

At this date, the charm of *Raffles* is partly in the period atmosphere and partly in the technical excellence of the stories. Hornung was a very conscientious and on his level a very able writer. Anyone who cares for sheer efficiency must admire his work. However, the truly dramatic thing about Raffles, the thing that makes him a sort of byword even to this day (only a few weeks ago, in a burglary case, a magistrate referred to the prisoner as 'a Raffles in real life'), is the fact that he is a *gentleman*. Raffles is presented to us – that this is rubbed home in countless scraps of dialogue and casual remarks – not as an honest man who has gone astray, but as a public-school man who has gone astray. His remorse, when he feels any, is almost purely social; he has disgraced 'the old school', he has lost his right to enter 'decent society', he has forfeited his amateur status and become a cad. Neither Raffles nor Bunny appear to feel at all strongly that stealing is wrong in itself, though Raffles does once justify himself by the casual remark that 'the distribution of property is all wrong anyway'. They think of themselves not as sinners but as renegades, or

1. *Raffles*, *A Thief in the Night* and *Mr Justice Raffles* by E. W. Hornung. The third of these is definitely a failure, and only the first has the true Raffles atmosphere. Hornung wrote a number of crime stories, usually with a tendency to take the side of the criminal. A successful book in rather the same vein as *Raffles* is *Stingaree*. [Author's footnote.]

simply as outcasts. And the moral code of most of us is still so close to Raffles's own that we do feel his situation to be an especially ironical one. A West End club man who is really a burglar! That is almost a story in itself, is it not? But how if it were a plumber or a greengrocer who was really a burglar? Would there be anything inherently dramatic in that? No – although the theme of the 'double life', of respectability covering crime, is still there. Even Charles Peace in his clergyman's dog-collar seems somewhat less of a hypocrite than Raffles in his I Zingari blazer.

Raffles, of course, is good at all games, but it is peculiarly fitting that his chosen game should be cricket. This allows not only of endless analogies between his cunning as a slow bowler and his cunning as a burglar, but also helps to define the exact nature of his crime. Cricket is not in reality a very popular game in England – it is nowhere near so popular as football, for instance – but it gives expression to a well-marked trait in the English character, the tendency to value 'form' or 'style' more highly than success. In the eyes of any true cricket-lover it is possible for an innings of ten runs to be 'better' (i.e. more elegant) than an innings of a hundred runs: cricket is also one of the very few games in which the amateur can excel the professional. It is a game full of forlorn hopes and sudden dramatic changes of fortune, and its rules are so ill-defined that their interpretation is partly an ethical business. When Larwood, for instance, practised body-line bowling in Australia he was not actually breaking any rule: he was merely doing something that was 'not cricket'. Since cricket takes up a lot of time and is rather an expensive game to play, it is predominantly an upper-class game, but for the whole nation it is bound up with such concepts as 'good form', 'playing the game', etc., and it has declined in popularity just as the tradition of 'don't hit a man when he's down' has declined. It is not a twentieth-century game, and nearly all modern-minded people dislike it. The Nazis, for instance, were at pains to discourage cricket, which had gained a certain footing in Germany before and after the last war. In making Raffles a cricketer as well as a burglar, Hornung was not merely providing him with a plausible disguise; he was also drawing the sharpest moral contrast that he was able to imagine.

Raffles, no less than *Great Expectations* or *Le Rouge et le Noir,* is a story of snobbery, and it gains a great deal from the precariousness of Raffles's social position. A cruder writer would have made the 'gentleman burglar' a member of the peerage, or at least a baronet. Raffles, however, is of upper-middle-class origin and is only accepted by the aristocracy because of his personal charm. 'We were in Society but not of it,' he says to

Bunny towards the end of the book; and 'I was asked about for my cricket.' Both he and Bunny accept the values of 'society' unquestioningly, and would settle down in it for good if only they could get away with a big enough haul. The ruin that constantly threatens them is all the blacker because they only doubtfully 'belong'. A duke who has served a prison sentence is still a duke, whereas a mere man about town, if once disgraced, ceases to be 'about town' for evermore. The closing chapters of the book, when Raffles has been exposed and is living under an assumed name, have a 'twilight of the gods' feeling, a mental atmosphere rather similar to that of Kipling's poem, 'Gentleman Rankers':

> Yes, a trooper of the forces –
> Who has run his own six horses! etc.

Raffles now belongs irrevocably to the 'cohorts of the damned'. He can still commit successful burglaries, but there is no way back into Paradise, which means Piccadilly and the M.C.C.[2] According to the public-school code there is only one means of rehabilitation: death in battle. Raffles dies fighting against the Boers (a practised reader would foresee this from the start), and in the eyes of both Bunny and his creator this cancels his crimes.

Both Raffles and Bunny, of course, are devoid of religious belief, and they have no real ethical code, merely certain rules of behaviour which they observe semi-instinctively. But it is just here that the deep moral difference between *Raffles* and *No Orchids* becomes apparent. Raffles and Bunny, after all, are gentlemen, and such standards as they do have are not to be violated. Certain things are 'not done', and the idea of doing them hardly arises. Raffles will not, for example, abuse hospitality. He will commit a burglary in a house where he is staying as a guest, but the victim must be a fellow guest and not the host. He will not commit murder,[3] and he avoids violence wherever possible and prefers to carry out his robberies unarmed. He regards friendship as sacred, and is chivalrous though not moral in his relations with women. He will take extra risks in the name of 'sportsmanship', and sometimes even for aesthetic reasons. And above all, he is intensely patriotic. He celebrates the Diamond Jubilee ('For sixty years, Bunny, we've been ruled over by absolutely the finest sovereign the world has ever seen') by dispatching to

2. Marylebone Cricket Club.

3. Actually Raffles does kill one man and is more or less consciously responsible for the death of two others. But all three of them are foreigners and have behaved in a very reprehensible manner. He also, on one occasion, contemplates murdering a blackmailer. It is however, a fairly well-established convention in crime stories that murdering a blackmailer 'doesn't count'. [Author's footnote, 1945.]

the Queen through the post, an antique gold cup which he has stolen from the British Museum. He steals, from partly political motives, a pearl which the German Emperor is sending to one of the enemies of Britain, and when the Boer War begins to go badly his one thought is to find his way into the fighting line. At the front he unmasks a spy at the cost of revealing his own identity, and then dies gloriously by a Boer bullet. In this combination of crime and patriotism he resembles his near-contemporary Arsène Lupin, who also scores off the German Emperor and wipes out his very dirty past by enlisting in the Foreign Legion.

It is important to note that by modern standards Raffles's crimes are very petty ones. Four hundred pounds' worth of jewellery seems to him an excellent haul. And though the stories are convincing in their physical detail, they contain very little sensationalism – very few corpses, hardly any blood, no sex crimes, no sadism, no perversions of any kind. It seems to be the case that the crime story, at any rate on its higher levels, has greatly increased in blood-thirstiness during the past twenty years. Some of the early detective stories do not even contain a murder. The Sherlock Holmes stories, for instance, are not all murders, and some of them do not even deal with an indictable crime. So also with the John Thorndyke stories, while of the Max Carrados stories only a minority are murders. Since 1918, however, a detective story not containing a murder has been a great rarity, and the most disgusting details of dismemberment and exhumation are commonly exploited. Some of the Peter Wimsey stories, for instance, display an extremely morbid interest in corpses. The Raffles stories, written from the angle of the criminal, are much less antisocial than many modern stories written from the angle of the detective. The main impression that they leave behind is of boyishness. They belong to a time when people had standards, though they happened to be foolish standards. Their key-phrase is 'not done'. The line that they draw between good and evil is as senseless as a Polynesian taboo, but at least, like the taboo, it has the advantage that everyone accepts it.

So much for *Raffles*. Now for a header into the cesspool. *No Orchids for Miss Blandish*, by James Hadley Chase, was published in 1939, but seems to have enjoyed its greatest popularity in 1940, during the Battle of Britain and the blitz. In its main outlines its story is this:

Miss Blandish, the daughter of a millionaire, is kidnapped by some gangsters who are almost immediately surprised and killed off by a larger and better organized gang. They hold her to ransom and extract half a million dollars from her father. Their original plan had been to kill her as soon as the ransom-money was received, but a chance keeps her alive. One of the gang is a young man named Slim, whose sole pleasure in life consists in driving knives into other people's bellies. In childhood he had graduated by cutting up living animals with a pair of rusty scissors. Slim is sexually impotent, but takes a kind of fancy to Miss Blandish. Slim's mother, who is the real brains of the gang, sees in this the chance of curing Slim's impotence, and decides to keep Miss Blandish in custody till Slim shall have succeeded in raping her. After many efforts and much persuasion, including the flogging of Miss Blandish with a length of rubber hosepipe, the rape is achieved. Meanwhile Miss Blandish's father has hired a private detective, and by means of bribery and torture the detective and the police manage to round up and exterminate the whole gang. Slim escapes with Miss Blandish and is killed after a final rape, and the detective prepares to restore Miss Blandish to her family. By this time, however, she has developed such a taste for Slim's caresses[4] that she feels unable to live without him, and she jumps out of the window of a sky-scraper.

Several other points need noticing before one can grasp the full implications of this book. To begin with, its central story bears a very marked resemblance to William Faulkner's novel *Sanctuary*. Secondly, it is not, as one might expect, the product of an illiterate hack, but a brilliant piece of writing, with hardly a wasted word or a jarring note anywhere. Thirdly, the whole book, *recit* as well as dialogue, is written in the American language; the author, an Englishman who has (I believe) never been in the United States, seems to have made a complete mental transference to the American underworld. Fourthly, the book sold, according to its publishers, no less than half a million copies.

I have already outlined the plot, but the subject-matter is much more sordid and brutal than this suggests. The book contains eight full-dress murders, an unassessable number of casual killings and woundings, an exhumation (with a careful reminder of the stench), the flogging of Miss Blandish, the torture of another woman with red-hot cigarette-ends, a strip-tease act, a third-degree scene of unheard-of cruelty and much else of the same kind. It assumes great sexual sophistication in its readers (there is a scene for instance, in which a gangster, presumably of masochistic tendency, has an orgasm in the moment of being knifed), and it takes for granted the most complete corruption and self-seeking as the norm of human behaviour. The detective, for instance, is almost as great a rogue as the gangsters, and actuated by nearly the same motives.

4. Another reading of the final episode is possible. It may mean merely that Miss Blandish is pregnant. But the interpretation I have given above seems more in keeping with the general brutality of the book. [Author's footnote, 1945.]

Like them, he is in pursuit of 'five hundred grand'. It is necessary to the machinery of the story that Mr Blandish should be anxious to get his daughter back, but apart from this, such things as affection, friendship, good nature or even ordinary politeness simply do not enter. Nor, to any great extent, does normal sexuality. Ultimately only one motive is at work throughout the whole story: the pursuit of power.

It should be noticed that the book is not in the ordinary sense pornography. Unlike most books that deal in sexual sadism, it lays the emphasis on the cruelty and not on the pleasure. Slim, the ravisher of Miss Blandish, has 'wet, slobbering lips': this is disgusting, and it is meant to be disgusting. But the scenes describing cruelty to women are comparatively perfunctory. The real highspots of the book are cruelties committed by men upon other men: above all, the third-degreeing of the gangster, Eddie Schultz, who is lashed into a chair and flogged on the windpipe with truncheons, his arms broken by fresh blows as he breaks loose. In another of Mr Chase's books, *He won't Need It Now*, the hero, who is intended to be a sympathetic and perhaps even noble character, is described as stamping on somebody's face, and then, having crushed the man's mouth in, grinding his heel round and round in it. Even when physical incidents of this kind are not occurring, the mental atmosphere of these books is always the same. Their whole theme is the struggle for power and the triumph of the strong over the weak. The big gangsters wipe out the little ones as mercilessly as a pike gobbling up the little fish in a pond; the police kill off the criminals as cruelly as the angler kills the pike. If ultimately one sides with the police against the gangsters, it is merely because they are better organized and more powerful, because, in fact, the law is a bigger racket than crime. Might is right: *vae victis*.

As I have mentioned already, *No Orchids* enjoyed its greatest vogue in 1940, though it was successfully running as a play till some time later. It was, in fact, one of the things that helped to console people for the boredom of being bombed. Early in the war the *New Yorker* had a picture of a little man approaching a news-stall littered with papers with such headlines as 'Great Tank Battles in Northern France', 'Big Naval Battle in the North Sea', 'Huge Air Battles over the Channel', etc., etc. The little man is saying '*Action Stories*, please'. That little man stood for all the drugged millions to whom the world of the gangsters and the prize-ring is more 'real', more 'tough', than such things as wars, revolutions, earthquakes, famines and pestilences. From the point of view of a reader of *Action Stories*, a description of the London blitz, or of the struggles of the European underground parties, would be 'sissy stuff'. On the other hand, some puny gun-battle in Chicago, resulting in perhaps half a dozen deaths, would seem genuinely 'tough'. This habit of mind is now extremely widespread. A soldier sprawls in a muddy trench, with the machine-gun bullets crackling a foot or two overhead, and whiles away his intolerable boredom by reading an American gangster story. And what is it that makes that story so exciting? Precisely the fact that people are shooting at each other with machine-guns! Neither the soldier nor anyone else sees anything curious in this. It is taken for granted that an imaginary bullet is more thrilling than a real one.

The obvious explanation is that in real life one is usually a passive victim, whereas in the adventure story one can think of oneself as being at the centre of events. But there is more to it than that. Here it is necessary to refer again to the curious fact of *No Orchids* being written – with technical errors, perhaps, but certainly with considerable skill – in the American language.

There exists in America an enormous literature of more or less the same stamp as *No Orchids*. Quite apart from books, there is the huge array of 'pulp magazines', graded so as to cater for different kinds of fantasy, but nearly all having much the same mental atmosphere. A few of them go in for straight pornography, but the great majority are quite plainly aimed at sadists and masochists. Sold at threepence a copy under the title of Yank Mags,[5] these things used to enjoy considerable popularity in England, but when the supply dried up owing to the war, no satisfactory substitute was forthcoming. English imitations of the 'pulp magazine' do now exist, but they are poor things compared with the original. English crook films, again, never approach the American crook film in brutality. And yet the career of Mr Chase shows how deep the American influence has already gone. Not only is he himself living a continuous fantasy-life in the Chicago underworld, but he can count on hundreds of thousands of readers who know what is meant by a 'clipshop' or the 'hotsquat', do not have to do mental arithmetic when confronted by 'fifty grand', and understand at sight a sentence like 'Johnnie was a rummy and only two jumps ahead of the nut-factory.' Evidently there are great numbers of English people who are partly Americanized in language and, one ought to add, in moral outlook. For there was no popular protest against *No Orchids*. In the end it was withdrawn, but only retrospectively, when a later work, *Miss Callaghan Comes to Grief*, brought Mr Chase's

5. They are said to have been imported into this country as ballast, which accounted for their low price and crumpled appearance. Since the war the ships have been ballasted with something more useful, probably gravel. [Author's footnote.]

books to the attention of the authorities. Judging by casual conversations at the time, ordinary readers got a mild thrill out of the obscenities of *No Orchids*, but saw nothing undesirable in the book as a whole. Many people, incidentally, were under the impression that it was an American book reissued in England.

The thing that the ordinary reader *ought* to have objected to – almost certainly would have objected to, a few decades earlier – was the equivocal attitude towards crime. It is implied throughout *No Orchids* that being a criminal is only reprehensible in the sense that it does not pay. Being a policeman pays better, but there is no moral difference, since the police use essentially criminal methods. In a book like *He Won't Need It Now* the distinction between crime and crime prevention practically disappears. This is a new departure for English sensational fiction, in which till recently there has always been a sharp distinction between right and wrong and a general agreement that virtue must triumph in the last chapter. English books glorifying crime (modern crime, that is – pirates and highwaymen are different) are very rare. Even a book like *Raffles*, as I have pointed out, is governed by powerful taboos, and it is clearly understood that Raffles's crimes must be expiated sooner or later. In America, both in life and fiction, the tendency to tolerate crime, even to admire the criminal so long as he is successful, is very much more marked. It is, indeed, ultimately this attitude that has made it possible for crime to flourish upon so huge a scale. Books have been written about Al Capone that are hardly different in tone from the books written about Henry Ford, Stalin, Lord Northcliffe and all the rest of the 'log cabin to White House' brigade. And switching back eighty years, one finds Mark Twain adopting much the same attitude towards the disgusting bandit Slade, hero of twenty-eight murders, and towards the Western desperadoes generally. They were successful, they 'made good', therefore he admired them.

In a book like *No Orchids* one is not, as in the old-style crime story, simply escaping from dull reality into an imaginary world of action. One's escape is essentially into cruelty and sexual perversion. *No Orchids* is aimed at the power instinct, which *Raffles* or the Sherlock Holmes stories are not. At the same time the English attitude towards crime is not so superior to the American as I may have seemed to imply. It too is mixed up with power worship, and has become more noticeably so in the last twenty years. A writer who is worth examining is Edgar Wallace, especially in such typical books as *The Orator* and the Mr J. G. Reeder stories. Wallace was one of the first crime-story writers to break away from the old tradition of the private detective and make his central figure a Scotland Yard official. Sherlock Holmes is an amateur, solving his problems without the help and even, in the earlier stories, against the opposition of the police. Moreover, like Lupin, he is essentially an intellectual, even a scientist. He reasons logically from observed fact, and his intellectuality is constantly contrasted with the routine methods of the police. Wallace objected strongly to this slur, as he considered it, on Scotland Yard, and in several newspaper articles he went out of his way to denounce Holmes by name. His own ideal was the detective inspector who catches criminals not because he is intellectually brilliant but because he is part of an all-powerful organization. Hence the curious fact that in Wallace's most characteristic stories the 'clue' and the 'deduction' play no part. The criminal is always defeated either by an incredible coincidence, or because in some unexplained manner the police know all about the crime beforehand. The tone of the stories makes it quite clear that Wallace's admiration for the police is pure bully-worship. A Scotland Yard detective is the most powerful kind of being that he can imagine, while the criminal figures in his mind as an outlaw against whom anything is permissible, like the condemned slaves in the Roman arena. His policemen behave much more brutally than British policemen do in real life – they hit people without provocation, fire revolvers past their ears to terrify them and so on – and some of the stories exhibit a fearful intellectual sadism. (For instance, Wallace likes to arrange things so that the villain is hanged on the same day as the heroine is married.) But it is sadism after the English fashion: that is to say, it is unconscious, there is not overtly any sex in it, and it keeps within the bounds of the law. The British public tolerates a harsh criminal law and gets a kick out of monstrously unfair murder trials: but still that is better, on any count, than tolerating or admiring crime. If one must worship a bully, it is better that he should be a policeman than a gangster. Wallace is still governed to some extent by the concepts of 'not done'. In *No Orchids* anything is 'done' so long as it leads on to power. All the barriers are down, all the motives are out in the open. Chase is a worse symptom than Wallace, to the extent that all-in wrestling is worse than boxing, or Fascism is worse than capitalist democracy.

In borrowing from William Faulkner's *Sanctuary*, Chase only took the plot; the mental atmosphere of the two books is not similar. Chase really derives from other sources, and this particular bit of borrowing is only symbolic. What it symbolizes is the vulgarization of ideas which is constantly happening, and which probably happens faster in an age of print. Chase has been described as 'Faulkner for the masses', but it would be more accurate to describe him as Carlyle for the masses. He is a popular writer – there are many such in America, but they are still rarities in England – who has caught up with what it is now fashionable to call 'realism', meaning the doctrine that might is right. The growth of 'realism' has been the great feature of the intellectual history of our own age. Why this should be so is a complicated question. The interconnexion between sadism, masochism, success worship, power worship, nationalism and totalitarianism is a huge subject whose edges have barely been scratched, and even to mention it is considered somewhat indelicate. To take merely the first example that comes to mind, I believe no one has ever pointed out the sadistic element in Bernard Shaw's work, still less suggested that this probably has some connexion with Shaw's admiration for dictators. Fascism is often loosely equated with sadism, but nearly always by people who see nothing wrong in the most slavish worship of Stalin. The truth is, of course, that the countless English intellectuals who kiss the arse of Stalin are not different from the minority who give their allegiance to Hitler or Mussolini, nor from the efficiency experts who preached 'punch', 'drive', 'personality' and 'learn to be a Tiger man' in the nineteen-twenties, nor from the older generation of intellectuals, Carlyle, Creasy and the rest of them, who bowed down before German militarism. All of them are worshipping power and successful cruelty. It is important to notice that the cult of power tends to be mixed up with a love of cruelty and wickedness *for their own sakes.* A tyrant is all the more admired if he happens to be a blood-stained crook as well, and 'the end justifies the means' often becomes, in effect, 'the means justify themselves provided they are dirty enough'. This idea colours the outlook of all sympathizers with totalitarianism, and accounts, for instance, for the positive delight with which many English intellectuals greeted the Nazi–Soviet Pact. It was a step only doubtfully useful to the U.S.S.R., but it was entirely unmoral, and for that reason to be admired; the explanations of it, which were numerous and self-contradictory, could come afterwards.

Until recently the characteristic adventure stories of the English-speaking peoples have been stories in which the hero fights *against odds.* This is true all the way from Robin Hood to Popeye the Sailor. Perhaps the basic myth of the western world is Jack the Giant-Killer, but to be brought up to date this should be renamed Jack the Dwarf-Killer, and there already exists a considerable literature which teaches, either overtly or implicitly, that one should side with the big man against the little man.

Most of what is now written about foreign policy is simply an embroidery on this theme, and for several decades such phrases as 'Play the game', 'Don't hit a man when he's down' and 'It's not cricket' have never failed to draw a snigger from anyone of intellectual pretensions. What is comparatively new is to find the accepted pattern according to which (a) right is right and wrong is wrong, whoever wins, and (b) weakness must be respected, disappearing from popular literature as well. When I first read D. H. Lawrence's novels, at the age of about twenty, I was puzzled by the fact that there did not seem to be any classification of the characters into 'good' and 'bad'. Lawrence seemed to sympathize with all of them about equally, and this was so unusual as to give me the feeling of having lost my bearings. Today no one would think of looking for heroes and villains in a serious novel, but in lowbrow fiction one still expects to find a sharp distinction between right and wrong and between legality and illegality. The common people, on the whole, are still living in the world of absolute good and evil from which the intellectuals have long since escaped. But the popularity of *No Orchids* and the American books and magazines to which it is akin shows how rapidly the doctrine of 'realism' is gaining ground.

Several people, after reading *No Orchids*, have remarked to me, 'It's pure Fascism'. This is a correct description, although the book has not the smallest connexion with politics and very little with social or economic problems. It has merely the same relation to Fascism as, say, Trollope's novels have to nineteenth-century capitalism. It is a day-dream appropriate to a totalitarian age. In his imagined world of gangsters Chase is presenting, as it were, a distilled version of the modern political scene, in which such things as mass bombing of civilians, the use of hostages, torture to obtain confessions, secret prisons, execution without trial, floggings with rubber truncheons, drownings in cesspools, systematic falsification of records and statistics, treachery, bribery and quislingism are normal and morally neutral, even admirable when they are done in a large and bold way. The average man is not directly interested in politics and, when he reads, he wants the current struggles of the world to be translated into a simple story about individuals. He can take an interest in Slim and Fenner as he could not in the G.P.U. and the Gestapo. People worship power in the form in which they are able to understand it. A twelve-year-old boy worships Jack Dempsey. An adolescent in a Glasgow slum worships Al Capone. An aspiring pupil at a business college worships Lord Nuffield. A *New Statesman* reader worships Stalin. There is a difference in intellectual maturity, but none in moral outlook. Thirty years ago the heroes of popular fiction had nothing in common with Mr Chase's gangsters and detectives, and the idols of the English liberal intelligentsia were also comparatively sympathetic figures. Between Holmes and Fenner on the one hand, and between Abraham Lincoln and Stalin on the other, there is a similar gulf.

One ought not to infer too much from the success of Mr Chase's books. It is possible that it is an isolated phenomenon, brought about by the mingled boredom and brutality of war. But if such books should definitely acclimatize themselves in England, instead of being merely a half-understood import from America, there would be good grounds for dismay. In choosing *Raffles* as a background for *No Orchids* I deliberately chose a book which by the standards of its time was morally equivocal. Raffles, as I have pointed out, has no real moral code, no religion, certainly no social consciousness. All he has is a set of reflexes – the nervous system, as it were, of a gentleman. Give him a sharp tap on this reflex or that (they are called 'sport', 'pal', 'woman', 'king and country' and so forth), and you get a predictable reaction. In Mr Chase's books there are no gentlemen and no taboos. Emancipation is complete. Freud and Machiavelli have reached the outer suburbs. Comparing the schoolboy atmosphere of the one book with the cruelty and corruption of the other, one is driven to feel that snobbishness, like hypocrisy, is a check upon behaviour whose value from a social point of view has been underrated.

Horizon, October 1944; *Politics*, November 1944; *Cr.E.*; *D.D.*; *C.E.*

21. Arthur Koestler

One striking fact about English literature during the present century is the extent to which it has been dominated by foreigners – for example, Conrad, Henry James, Shaw, Joyce, Yeats, Pound and Eliot. Still, if you chose to make this a matter of national prestige and examine our achievement in the various branches of literature, you would find that England made a fairly good showing until you came to what may be roughly described as political writing, or pamphleteering. I mean by this the special class of literature that has arisen out of the European political struggle since the rise of Fascism. Under this heading novels, autobiographies, books of 'reportage', sociological treatises and plain pamphlets can all be lumped together, all of them having a common origin and to a great extent the same emotional atmosphere.

Some out of the outstanding figures in this school of writers are Silone, Malraux, Salvemini, Borkenau, Victor Serge and Koestler himself. Some of these are imaginative writers, some not, but they are all alike in that they are trying to write contemporary history, but *unofficial* history, the kind that is ignored in the text-books and lied about in the newspapers. Also they are all alike in being continental Europeans. It may be an exaggeration, but it cannot be a very great one, to say that whenever a book dealing with totalitarianism appears in this country, and still seems worth reading six months after publication, it is a book translated from some foreign language. English writers, over the past dozen years, have poured forth an enormous spate of political literature, but they have produced almost nothing of aesthetic value, and very little of historical value either. The Left Book Club, for instance, has been running ever since 1936. How many of its chosen volumes can you even remember the names of? Nazi Germany, Soviet Russia, Spain, Abyssinia, Austria, Czechoslovakia – all that these and kindred subjects have produced, in England, are slick books of reportage, dishonest pamphlets in which propaganda is swallowed whole and then spewed up again, half digested, and a very few reliable guide books and text-books. There has been nothing resembling, for instance, *Fontamara* or *Darkness at Noon*, because there is almost no English writer to whom it has happened to see totalitarianism from the inside. In Europe, during the past decade and more, things have been happening to middle-class people which in England do not even happen to the working class. Most of the European writers I mentioned above, and scores of others like them, have been obliged to break the law in order to engage in politics at all; some of them have thrown bombs and fought in street battles, many have been in prison or the concentration camp, or fled across frontiers with false names and forged passports. One cannot imagine, say, Professor Laski indulging in activities of that kind. England is lacking, therefore, in what one might call concentration-camp literature. The special world created by secret-police forces, censorship of opinion, torture, and frame-up trials is, of course, known about and to some extent disapproved of, but it has made very little emotional impact. One result of this is that there exists in England almost no literature of disillusionment about the Soviet Union. There is the attitude of ignorant disapproval, and there is the attitude of uncritical admiration, but very little in between. Opinion on the Moscow sabotage trials, for instance, was divided, but divided chiefly on the question of whether the accused were guilty. Few people were able to see that, whether justified or not, the trials were an unspeakable horror. And English disapproval of the Nazi outrages has also been an unreal thing, turned on and off like a tap according to political expediency. To understand such things one has to be able to imagine oneself as the victim, and for an Englishman to write *Darkness at Noon* would be as unlikely an accident as for a slave-trader to write *Uncle Tom's Cabin.*

Koestler's published work really centres about the Moscow trials. His main theme is the decadence of revolutions owing to the corrupting effects of power, but the special nature of the Stalin dictatorship has driven him back into a position not far removed from pessimistic Conservatism. I do not know how many books he has written in all. He is a Hungarian whose earlier books were written in German, and five books have been published in England: *Spanish Testament*, *The Gladiators*, *Darkness at Noon*, *Scum of the Earth*, and *Arrival and Departure.* The subject-matter of all of them is similar, and none of them ever escapes for more than a few pages from the atmosphere of nightmare. Of the five books, the action of three takes place entirely or almost entirely in prison.

In the opening months of the Spanish Civil War Koestler was the *News Chronicle's* correspondent in Spain, and early in 1937 he was taken prisoner when the Fascists captured Malaga. He was nearly shot out of hand, then spent some months imprisoned in a fortress, listening every night to the roar of rifle fire as batch after batch of Republicans was executed, and being most of the time in acute danger of execution himself. This was not a chance adventure which 'might have happened to anybody', but was in accordance with Koestler's life-style. A politically indifferent person would not have been in Spain at that date, a more cautious observer would have got out of Malaga before the Fascists arrived, and a British or American newspaper man would have been treated with more consideration. The book that Koestler wrote about this, *Spanish Testament,* has remarkable passages, but apart from the scrappiness that is usual in a book of reportage, it is definitely false in places. In the prison scenes Koestler successfully establishes the nightmare atmosphere which is, so to speak, his patent, but the rest of the book is too much coloured by the Popular Front orthodoxy of the time. One or two passages even look as though they had been doctored for the purposes of the Left Book Club. At that time Koestler still was, or recently had been, a member of the Communist Party, and the complex politics of the civil war made it impossible for any Communist to write honestly about the internal struggle on the Government side. The sin of nearly all left-wingers from 1933 onward is that they have wanted to be anti-Fascist without being anti-totalitarian. In 1937 Koestler already knew this, but did not feel free to say so. He came much nearer to saying it – indeed, he did say it, though he put on a mask to do so– in his next book, *The Gladiators*, which was published about a year before the war and for some reason attracted very little attention.

The Gladiators is in some ways an unsatisfactory book. It is about Spartacus, the Thracian gladiator who raised a slaves' rebellion in Italy round about 65 B.C., and any book on such a subject is handicapped by challenging comparison with *Salammbô*. In our own age it would not be possible to write a book like *Salammbô*, even if one had the talent. The great thing about *Salammbô*, even more important than its physical detail, is its utter mercilessness. Flaubert could think himself into the stony cruelty of antiquity, because in the mid-nineteenth century one still had peace of mind. One had time to travel in the past. Nowadays the present and the future are too terrifying to be escaped from, and if one bothers with history it is in order to find modern meanings there. Koestler makes Spartacus into an allegorical figure, a primitive version of the proletarian dictator. Whereas Flaubert has been able, by a prolonged effort of the imagination, to make his mercenaries truly pre-Christian, Spartacus is a modern man dressed up. But this might not matter if Koestler were fully aware of what his allegory means. Revolutions always go wrong – that is the main theme. It is on the question of *why* they go wrong that he falters, and his uncertainty enters into the story and makes the central figures enigmatic and unreal.

For several years the rebellious slaves are uniformly successful. Their numbers swell to a hundred thousand, they overrun great areas of Southern Italy, they defeat one punitive expedition after another, they ally themselves with the pirates who at that time were the masters of the Mediterranean, and finally they set to work to build a city of their own, to be named the City of the Sun. In this city human beings are to be free and equal, and above all, they are to be happy: no slavery, no hunger, no injustice, no floggings, no executions. It is the dream of a just society which seems to haunt the human imagination ineradicably and in all ages, whether it is called the Kingdom of Heaven or the classless society, or whether it is thought of as a Golden Age which once existed in the past and from which we have degenerated. Needless to say, the slaves fail to achieve it. No sooner have they formed themselves into a community than their way of life turns out to be as unjust, laborious and fear-ridden as any other. Even the cross, symbol of slavery, has to be revived for the punishment of malefactors. The turning-point comes when Spartacus finds himself obliged to crucify twenty of his oldest and most faithful followers. After that the City of the Sun is doomed, the slaves split up and are defeated in detail, the last fifteen thousand of them being captured and crucified in one batch.

The serious weakness of this story is that the motives of Spartacus himself are never made clear. The Roman lawyer Fulvius, who joins the rebellion and acts as its chronicler, sets forth the familiar dilemma of ends and means. You can achieve nothing unless you are willing to use force and cunning, but in using them you pervert your original aims. Spartacus, however, is not represented as power hungry, nor, on the other hand, as a visionary. He is driven onwards by some obscure force which he does not understand, and he is frequently in two minds as to whether it would not be better to throw up the whole adventure and flee to Alexandria while the going is good. The slaves' republic is in any case wrecked rather by hedonism than by the struggle for power. The slaves are discontented with their liberty because they still have to work, and the final break-up happens because the more turbulent and less civilized slaves, chiefly Gauls and Germans, continue to behave like bandits after the republic has been established. This may be a true account of events – naturally we know very little about the slave rebellions of antiquity – but by allowing the Sun City to be destroyed because Crixus the Gaul cannot be prevented from looting and raping, Koestler has faltered between allegory and history. If Spartacus is the prototype of the modern revolutionary – and obviously he is intended as that – he should have gone astray because of the impossibility of combining power with righteousness. As it is, he is an almost passive figure, acted upon rather than acting, and at times not convincing. The story partly fails because the central problem of revolution has been avoided or, at least, has not been solved.

It is again avoided in a subtler way in the next book, Koestler's masterpiece, *Darkness at Noon*. Here, however, the story is not spoiled, because it deals with individuals and its interest is psychological. It is an episode picked out from a background that does not have to be questioned. *Darkness at Noon* describes the imprisonment and death of an Old Bolshevik, Rubashov, who first denies and ultimately confesses to crimes which he is well aware he has not committed. The grown-upness, the lack of surprise or denunciation, the pity and irony with which the story is told, show the advantage, when one is handling a theme of this kind, of being a European. The book reaches the stature of tragedy, whereas an English or American writer could at most have made it into a polemical tract. Koestler has digested his material and can treat it on the aesthetic level. At the same time his handling of it has a political implication, not important in this case but likely to be damaging in later books.

Naturally the whole book centres round one question: Why did Rubashov confess? He is not guilty – that is, not guilty of anything except the essential crime of disliking the Stalin régime. The concrete acts of treason in which he is supposed to have engaged are all imaginary. He has not even been tortured, or not very severely. He is worn down by solitude, toothache, lack of tobacco, bright lights glaring in his eyes, and continuous questioning, but these in themselves would not be enough to overcome a hardened revolutionary. The Nazis have previously done worse to him without breaking his spirit. The confessions obtained in the Russian state trials are capable of three explanations.

1. That the accused were guilty.

2. That they were tortured, and perhaps blackmailed by threats to relatives and friends.

3. That they were actuated by despair, mental bankruptcy and the habit of loyalty to the Party.

For Koestler's purpose in *Darkness at Noon* 1 is ruled out, and though this is not the place to discuss Russian purges, I must add that what little verifiable evidence there is suggests that the trials of the Bolsheviks were frame-ups. If one assumes that the accused were not guilty – at any rate, not guilty of the particular things they confessed to – then 2 is the common-sense explanation. Koestler, however, plumps for 3, which is also accepted by the Trotskyist Boris Souvarine, in his pamphlet *Cauchemar en U.R.S.S.* Rubashov ultimately confesses because he cannot find in his own mind any reason for not doing so. Justice and objective truth have long ceased to have any meaning for him. For decades he has been simply the creature of the Party, and what the Party now demands is that he shall confess to non-existent crimes. In the end, though he had to be bullied and weakened first, he is somewhat proud of his decision to confess. He feels superior to the poor Czarist officer who inhabits the next cell and who talks to Rubashov by tapping on the wall. The Czarist officer is shocked when he learns that Rubashov intends to capitulate. As he sees it from his 'bourgeois' angle, everyone ought to stick to his guns, even a Bolshevik. Honour, he says, consists in doing what you think right. 'Honour is to be useful without fuss,' Rubashov taps back; and he reflects with a certain satisfaction that he is tapping with his pince-nez while the other, the relic of the past, is tapping with a monocle. Like Bukharin, Rubashov is 'looking out upon black darkness'. What is there, what code, what loyalty, what notion of good and evil, for the sake of which he can defy the Party and endure further torment? He is not only alone, he is also hollow. He has himself committed worse crimes than the one that is now being perpetrated against him. For example, as a secret envoy of the Party in Nazi Germany, he has got rid of disobedient followers by betraying them to the Gestapo. Curiously enough, if he has any inner strength to draw upon, it is the memories of his boyhood when he was the son of a landowner. The last thing he remembers, when he is shot from behind, is the leaves of poplar trees on his father's estate. Rubashov belongs to the older generation of Bolsheviks that was largely wiped out in the purges. He is aware of art and literature, and of the world outside Russia. He contrasts sharply with Gletkin, the young G.P.U. man who conducts his interrogation, and who is the typical 'good party man', completely without scruples or curiosity, a thinking gramophone. Rubashov, unlike Gletkin, does not have the Revolution as his starting-point. His mind was not a blank sheet when the Party got hold of it. His superiority to the other is finally traceable to his bourgeois origin.

One cannot, I think, argue that *Darkness at Noon* is simply a story dealing with the adventures of an imaginary individual. Clearly it is a political book, founded on history and offering an interpretation of disputed events. Rubashov might be called Trotsky, Bukharin Rakovsky or some other relatively civilized figure among the Old Bolsheviks. If one writes about the Moscow trials one must answer the question, 'Why did the accused confess?' and which answer one makes is a political decision. Koestler answers, in effect, 'Because these people had been rotted by the Revolution which they served', and in doing so he comes near to claiming that revolutions are of their nature bad. If one assumes that the accused in the Moscow trials were made to confess by means of some kind of terrorism, one is only saying that one particular set of revolutionary leaders has gone astray. Individuals, and not the situation, are to blame. The implication of Koestler's book, however, is that Rubashov in power would be no better than Gletkin: or rather, only better in that his outlook is still partly pre-revolutionary. Revolution, Koestler seems to say, is a corrupting process. Really enter into the Revolution and you must end up as either Rubashov or Gletkin. It is not merely that 'power corrupts': so also do the ways of attaining power. Therefore, all efforts to regenerate society *by violent means* lead to the cellars of the O.G.P.U., Lenin leads to Stalin, and would have come to resemble Stalin if he had happened to survive.

Of course, Koestler does not say this explicitly, and perhaps is not altogether conscious of it. He is writing about darkness, but it is darkness at what ought to be noon. Part of the time he feels that things might have turned out differently. The notion that so-and-so has 'betrayed', that things have only gone wrong because of individual wickedness, is ever present in left-wing thought. Later, in *Arrival and Departure*, Koestler swings over much further towards the anti-revolutionary position, but in between these two books there is another, *Scum of the Earth*, which is straight autobiography and has only an indirect bearing upon the problems raised by *Darkness at Noon*. True to his life-style, Koestler was caught in France by the outbreak of war and, as a foreigner and a known anti-Fascist, was promptly arrested and interned by the Daladier Government. He spent the first nine months of war mostly in a prison camp, then, during the collapse of France, escaped and travelled by devious routes to England, where he was once again thrown into prison as an enemy alien. This time he was soon released, however. The book is a valuable piece of reportage, and together with a few other scraps of honest writing that happened to be produced at the time of the débâcle, it is a reminder of the depths that bourgeois democracy can descend to. At this moment, with France newly liberated and the witch-hunt after collaborators in full swing, we are apt to forget that in 1940 various observers on the spot considered that about forty per cent of the French population was either actively pro-German or completely apathetic. Truthful war books are never acceptable to non-combatants, and Koestler's book did not have a very good reception. Nobody came well out of it – neither the bourgeois politicians, whose idea of conducting an anti-Fascist war was to jail every left-winger they could lay their hands on, nor the French Communists, who were effectively pro-Nazi and did their best to sabotage the French war effort, nor the common people, who were just as likely to follow mountebanks like Doriot as responsible leaders. Koestler records some fantastic conversations with fellow victims in the concentration camp, and adds that till then, like most middle-class Socialists and Communists, he had never made contact with real proletarians, only with the educated minority. He draws the pessimistic conclusion: 'Without education of the masses, no social progress; without social progress, no education of the masses.' In *Scum of the Earth* Koestler ceases to idealize the common people. He has abandoned Stalinism, but he is not a Trotskyist either. This is the book's real link with *Arrival and Departure*, in which what is normally called a revolutionary outlook is dropped, perhaps for good.

Arrival and Departure is not a satisfactory book. The pretence that it is a novel is very thin; in effect it is a tract purporting to show that revolutionary creeds are rationalizations of neurotic impulses. With all too neat a symmetry, the book begins and ends with the same action – a leap into a foreign country. A young ex-Communist who has made his escape from Hungary jumps ashore in Portugal, where he hopes to enter the service of Britain, at that time the only power fighting against Germany. His enthusiasm is somewhat cooled by the fact that the British Consulate is uninterested in him and almost ignores him for a period of several months, during which his money runs out and other astuter refugees escape to America. He is successively tempted by the World in the form of a Nazi propagandist, the Flesh in the form of a French girl, and – after a nervous breakdown – the Devil in the form of a psychoanalyst. The psychoanalyst drags out of him the fact that his revolutionary enthusiasm is not founded on any real belief in historical necessity, but on a morbid guilt complex arising from an attempt in early childhood to blind his baby brother. By the time that he gets an opportunity of serving the Allies he has lost all reason for wanting to do so, and he is on the point of leaving for America when his irrational impulses seize hold of him again. In practice he cannot abandon the struggle. When the book ends, he is floating down in a parachute over the dark landscape of his native country, where he will be employed as a secret agent of Britain.

As a political statement (and the book is not much more), this is insufficient. Of course it is true in many cases, and it may be true in all cases, that revolutionary activity is the result of personal maladjustment. Those who struggle against society are, on the whole, those who have reason to dislike it, and normal healthy people are no more attracted by violence and illegality than they are by war. The young Nazi in *Arrival and Departure* makes the penetrating remark that one can see what is wrong with the left-wing movement by the ugliness of its women. But after all, this does not invalidate the Socialist case. Actions have results, irrespective of their motives. Marx's ultimate motives may well have been envy and spite, but this does not prove that his conclusions were false. In making the hero of *Arrival and Departure* take his final decision from a mere instinct not to shirk action and danger, Koestler is making him suffer a sudden loss of intelligence. With such a history as he has behind him, he would be able to see that certain things have to be done, whether our reasons for doing them are 'good' or 'bad'. History has to move in a certain direction, even if it has to be pushed that way by neurotics. In *Arrival and Departure* Peter's idols are overthrown one after the other. The

Russian Revolution has degenerated, Britain, symbolized by the aged consul with gouty fingers, is no better, the international class-conscious proletariat is a myth. But the conclusion (since, after all, Koestler and his hero 'support' the war) ought to be that getting rid of Hitler is still a worthwhile objective, a necessary bit of scavenging in which motives are almost irrelevant.

To take a rational political decision one must have a picture of the future. At present Koestler seems to have none, or rather to have two which cancel out. As an ultimate objective he believes in the Earthly Paradise, the Sun State which the gladiators set out to establish, and which has haunted the imagination of Socialists, Anarchists and religious heretics for hundreds of years. But his intelligence tells him that the Earthly Paradise is receding into the far distance and that what is actually ahead of us is bloodshed, tyranny and privation. Recently he described himself as 'short-term pessimist'. Every kind of horror is blowing up over the horizon, but somehow it will all come right in the end. This outlook is probably gaining ground among thinking people: it results from the very great difficulty, once one has abandoned orthodox religious belief, of accepting life on earth as inherently miserable, and on the other hand, from the realization that to make life liveable is a much bigger problem that it recently seemed. Since about 1930 the world has given no reason for optimism whatever. Nothing is in sight except a welter of lies, hatred, cruelty and ignorance, and beyond our present troubles loom vaster ones which are only now entering into the European consciousness. It is quite possible that man's major problems will *never* be solved. But it is also unthinkable! Who is there who dares to look at the world of today and say to himself, 'It will always be like this: even in a million years it cannot get appreciably better?' So you get the quasi-mystical belief that for the present there is no remedy, all political action is useless, but that somewhere in space and time human life will cease to be the miserable brutish thing it now is.

The only easy way out is that of the religious believer, who regards this life merely as a preparation for the next. But few thinking people now believe in life after death, and the number of those who do is probably diminishing. The Christian churches would probably not survive on their own merits if their economic basis were destroyed. The real problem is how to restore the religious attitude while accepting death as final. Men can only be happy when they do not assume that the object of life is happiness. It is most unlikely, however, that Koestler would accept this.

There is a well-marked hedonistic strain in his writings, and his failure to find a political position after breaking with Stalinism is a result of this.

The Russian Revolution, the central event in Koestler's life, started out with high hopes. We forget these things now, but a quarter of a century ago it was confidently expected that the Russian Revolution would lead to Utopia. Obviously this has not happened. Koestler is too acute not to see this, and too sensitive not to remember the original objective. Moreover, from his European angle he can see such things as purges and mass deportations for what they are; he is not, like Shaw or Laski, looking at them through the wrong end of the telescope. Therefore he draws the conclusion: This is what revolutions lead to. There is nothing for it except to be a 'Short-term' pessimist', i.e. to keep out of politics, make a sort of oasis within which you and your friends can remain sane, and hope that somehow things will be better in a hundred years. At the basis of this lies his hedonism, which leads him to think of the Earthly Paradise as desirable. Perhaps, however, whether desirable or not, it isn't possible. Perhaps some degree of suffering is ineradicable from human life, perhaps the choice before man is always a choice of evils, perhaps even the aim of Socialism is not to make the world perfect but to make it better. All revolutions are failures, but they are not all the same failure. It is his unwillingness to admit this that has led Koestler's mind temporarily into a blind alley and that makes *Arrival and Departure* seem shallow compared with the earlier books.

Written [September] 1944; *Cr.E.*; *D.D.*; *Focus 2 1946*; *C.E.*

22. Antisemitism in Britain

There are about 400,000 known Jews in Britain, and in addition some thousands or, at most, scores of thousands of Jewish refugees who have entered the country from 1934 onwards. The Jewish population is almost entirely concentrated in half a dozen big towns and is mostly employed in the food, clothing and furniture trades. A few of the big monopolies, such as the I.C.I., one or two leading newspapers and at least one big chain of department stores are Jewish-owned or partly Jewish-owned, but it would be very far from the truth to say that British business life is dominated by Jews. The Jews seem, on the contrary, to have failed to keep up with the modern tendency towards big amalgamations and to have remained fixed in those trades which are necessarily carried out on a small scale and by old-fashioned methods.

I start off with these background facts, which are already known to any well-informed person, in order to emphasize that there is no real Jewish 'problem' in England. The Jews are not numerous or powerful enough, and it is only in what are loosely called 'intellectual circles' that they have any noticeable influence. Yet it is generally admitted that antisemitism is on the increase, that it has been greatly exacerbated by the war, and that humane and enlightened people are not immune to it. It does not take violent forms (English people are almost invariably gentle and law-abiding), but it is ill-natured enough, and in favourable circumstances it could have political results. Here are some samples of antisemitic remarks that have been made to me during the past year or two:

Middle-aged office employee: 'I generally come to work by bus. It takes longer, but I don't care about using the Underground from Golders Green nowadays. There's too many of the Chosen Race travelling on that line.'

Tobacconist (woman): 'No, I've got no matches for you. I should try the lady down the street. *She's* always got matches. One of the Chosen Race, you see.'

Young intellectual, Communist or near-Communist: 'No, I do *not* like Jews. I've never made any secret of that. I can't stick them. Mind you, I'm not antisemitic, of course.'

Middle-class woman: 'Well, no one could call me antisemitic, but I do think the way these Jews behave is too absolutely stinking. The way they push their way to the head of queues, and so on. They're so abominably selfish. I think they're responsible for a lot of what happens to them.'

Milk roundsman: 'A Jew don't do no work, not the same as what an Englishman does. 'E's too clever. We work with this 'ere' (flexes his biceps). 'They work with that there' (taps his forehead).

Chartered accountant, intelligent, left-wing in an undirected way: 'These bloody Yids are all pro-German. They'd change sides tomorrow if the Nazis got here. I see a lot of them in my business. They admire Hitler at the bottom of their hearts. They'll always suck up to anyone who kicks them.'

Intelligent woman, on being offered a book dealing with antisemitism and German atrocities: 'Don't show it to me, *please* don't show it to me. It'll only make me hate the Jews more than ever.'

I could fill pages with similar remarks, but these will do to go on with. Two facts emerge from them. One – which is very important and which I must return to in a moment – is that above a certain intellectual level people are ashamed of being antisemitic and are careful to draw a distinction between 'antisemitism' and 'disliking Jews'. The other is that antisemitism is an irrational thing. The Jews are accused of specific offences (for instance, bad behaviour in food queues) which the person speaking feels strongly about, but it is obvious that these accusations merely rationalize some deep-rooted prejudice. To attempt to counter them with facts and statistics is useless, and may sometimes be worse than useless. As the last of the above-quoted remarks shows, people can remain antisemitic, or at lease anti-Jewish, while being fully aware that their outlook is indefensible. If you dislike somebody, you dislike him and there is an end of it: your feelings are not made any better by a recital of his virtues.

It so happens that the war has encouraged the growth of antisemitism and even, in the eyes of many ordinary people, given some justification for it. To begin with, the Jews are one people of whom it can be said with complete certainty that they will benefit by an Allied victory. Consequently the theory that 'this is a Jewish war' has a certain plausibility, all the more so because the Jewish war effort seldom gets its fair share of recognition. The British Empire is a huge heterogeneous organization held together largely by mutual consent, and it is often necessary to flatter the less reliable elements at the expense of the more loyal ones. To publicize the exploits of Jewish soldiers, or even to admit the existence of a considerable Jewish army in the Middle East, rouses hostility in South Africa, the Arab countries and elsewhere: it is easier to ignore the whole subject and allow the man in the street to go on thinking that Jews are exceptionally clever at dodging military service. Then again, Jews are to be found in exactly those trades which are bound to incur unpopularity with the civilian public in war-time. Jews are mostly concerned with selling food, clothes, furniture and tobacco – exactly the commodities of which there is a chronic shortage, with consequent overcharging, black-marketing and favouritism. And again, the common charge that Jews behave in an exceptionally cowardly way during air raids was given a certain amount of colour by the big raids of 1940. As it happened, the Jewish quarter of Whitechapel was one of the first areas to be heavily blitzed, with the natural result that swarms of Jewish refugees distributed themselves all over London. If one judged merely from these war-time phenomena, it would be easy to imagine that antisemitism is a quasi-rational thing, founded on mistaken premises. And naturally the antisemite thinks of himself as a reasonable being. Whenever I have touched on this subject in a newspaper article, I have always had a considerable 'come-back', and invariably some of the letters are from well-balanced, middling people – doctors for example – with no apparent economic grievance. These people always say (as Hitler says in *Mein Kampf*) that they started out with no anti-Jewish prejudice but were driven into their present position by mere observation of the facts. Yet one of the marks of antisemitism is an ability to believe stories that could not possibly be true. One could see a good example of this in the strange accident that occurred in London in 1942, when a crowd, frightened by a bomb-burst nearby, fled into the mouth of an Underground station, with the result that something over a hundred people were crushed to death. The very same day it was repeated all over London that 'the Jews were responsible'. Clearly, if people will believe this kind of thing, one will not get much further by arguing with them. The only useful approach is to discover *why* they can swallow absurdities on one particular subject while remaining sane on others.

But now let me come back to that point I mentioned earlier – that there is widespread awareness of the prevalence of antisemitic feeling, and unwillingness to admit sharing it. Among educated people, antisemitism is held to be an unforgivable sin and in a quite different category from other kinds of racial prejudice. People will go to remarkable lengths to demonstrate that they are *not* antisemitic. Thus, in 1943 an intercession service on behalf of the Polish Jews was held in a synagogue in St John's Wood. The local authorities declared themselves anxious to participate in it, and the service was attended by the mayor of the borough in his robes and chain, by representatives of all the churches, and by detachments of R.A.F., Home Guards, nurses, Boy Scouts and what-not. On the surface it was a touching demonstration of solidarity with the suffering Jews. But it was essentially a *conscious* effort to behave decently by people whose subjective feelings must in many cases have been very different. That quarter of London is partly Jewish, antisemitism is rife there, and, as I well knew, some of the men sitting round me in the synagogue were tinged by it. Indeed, the commander of my own platoon of Home Guards, who had been especially keen beforehand that we should 'make a good show' at the intercession service, was an ex-member of Mosley's

Blackshirts. While this division of feeling exists, tolerance of mass violence against Jews, or, what is more important, antisemitic legislation, are not possible in England. It is not at present possible, indeed, that antisemitism should *become respectable.* But this is less of an advantage than it might appear.

One effect of the persecutions in Germany has been to prevent antisemitism from being seriously studied. In England a brief inadequate survey was made by Mass Observation a year or two ago, but if there has been any other investigation of the subject, then its findings have been kept strictly secret. At the same time there has been conscious suppression, by all thoughtful people, of anything likely to wound Jewish susceptibilities. After 1934 the 'Jew joke' disappeared as though by magic from postcards, periodicals and the music-hall stage, and to put an unsympathetic Jewish character into a novel or short story came to be regarded as antisemitism. On the Palestine issue, too, it was *de rigueur* among enlightened people to accept the Jewish case as proved and avoid examining the claims of the Arabs – a decision which might be correct on its own merits, but which was adopted primarily because the Jews were in trouble and it was felt that one must not criticize them. Thanks to Hitler, therefore, you had a situation in which the press was in effect censored in favour of the Jews while in private antisemitism was on the up-grade, even, to some extent, among sensitive and intelligent people. This was particularly noticeable in 1940 at the time of the internment of the refugees. Naturally, every thinking person felt that it was his duty to protest against the wholesale locking-up of unfortunate foreigners who for the most part were only in England because they were opponents of Hitler. Privately, however, one heard very different sentiments expressed. A minority of the refugees behaved in an exceedingly tactless way, and the feeling against them necessarily had an antisemetic undercurrent, since they were largely Jews. A very eminent figure in the Labour Party – I won't name him, but he is one of the most respected people in England – said to me quite violently: 'We never asked these people to come to this country. If they choose to come here, let them take the consequences.' Yet this man would as a matter of course have associated himself with any kind of petition or manifesto against the internment of aliens. This feeling that antisemitism is something sinful and disgraceful, something that a civilized person does not suffer from, is unfavourable to a scientific approach, and indeed many people will admit that they are frightened of probing too deeply into the subject. They are frightened, that is to say, of discovering not only that antisemitism is spreading, but that they themselves are infected by it.

To see this in perspective one must look back a few decades, to the days when Hitler was an out-of-work house-painter whom nobody had heard of. One would then find that though antisemitism is sufficiently in evidence now, it is probably *less* prevalent in England than it was thirty years ago. It is true that antisemitism as a fully thought-out racial or religious doctrine has never flourished in England. There has never been much feeling against intermarriage, or against Jews taking a prominent part in public life. Nevertheless, thirty years ago it was accepted more or less as a law of nature that a Jew was a figure of fun and – though superior in intelligence – slightly deficient in 'character'. In theory a Jew suffered from no legal disabilities, but in effect he was debarred from certain professions. He would probably not have been accepted as an officer in the navy, for instance, nor in what is called a 'smart' regiment in the army. A Jewish boy at a public school almost invariably had a bad time. He could, of course, live down his Jewishness if he was exceptionally charming or athletic, but it was an initial disability comparable to a stammer or a birthmark. Wealthy Jews tended to disguise themselves under aristocratic English or Scottish names, and to the average person it seemed quite natural that they should do this, just as it seems natural for a criminal to change his identity if possible. About twenty years ago, in Rangoon, I was getting into a taxi with a friend when a small ragged boy of a fair complexion rushed up to us and began a complicated story about having arrived from Colombo on a ship and wanting money to get back. His manner and appearance were difficult to 'place', and I said to him:

'You speak very good English. What nationality are you?'

He answered eagerly in his chi-chi accent: 'I am a *Joo*, sir!'

And I remember turning to my companion and saying, only partly in joke, 'He admits it openly.' All the Jews I had known till then were people who were ashamed of being Jews, or at any rate preferred not to talk about their ancestry, and if forced to do so tended to use the word 'Hebrew'.

The working-class attitude was no better. The Jew who grew up in Whitechapel took it for granted that he would be assaulted, or at least hooted at, if he ventured into one of the Christian slums nearby, and the 'Jew joke' of the music halls and the comic papers was almost consistently ill-natured.[1] There was also literary Jew-baiting, which in the hands of Belloc, Chesterton and their followers reached an almost continental level of scurrility. Non-Catholic writers were sometimes guilty of the same thing in a milder form. There has been a perceptible antisemitic strain in English literature from Chaucer onwards, and without even getting up from this table to consult a book I can think of passages which *if written now* would be stigmatized as antisemitism, in the works of Shakespeare, Smollett, Thackeray, Bernard Shaw, H. G. Wells, T. S. Eliot, Aldous Huxley and various others. Offhand, the only English writers I can think of who, before the days of Hitler, made a definite effort to stick up for Jews are Dickens and Charles Reade. And however little the average intellectual may have agreed with the opinions of Belloc and Chesterton, he did not acutely disapprove of them. Chesterton's endless tirades against Jews, which he thrust into stories and essays upon the flimsiest pretexts, never got him into trouble – indeed Chesterton was one of the most generally respected figures in English literary life. Anyone who wrote in that strain *now* would bring down a storm of abuse upon himself, or more probably would find it impossible to get his writings published.

If, as I suggest, prejudice against Jews has always been pretty widespread in England, there is no reason to think that Hitler has genuinely diminished it. He has merely caused a sharp division between the politically conscious person who realizes that this is not a time to throw stones at the Jews, and the unconscious person whose native antisemitism is increased by the nervous strain of the war. One can assume, therefore, that many people who would perish rather than admit to antisemitic feelings are secretly prone to them. I have already indicated that I believe antisemitism to be essentially a neurosis, but of course it has its rationalizations, which are sincerely believed in and are partly true. The rationalization put forward by the common man is that the Jew is an exploiter. The partial justification for this is that the Jew, in England, is generally a small businessman – that is to say a person whose depredations are more obvious and intelligible than those of, say, a bank or an insurance

1. It is interesting to compare the 'Jew joke' with that other stand-by of the music halls, the 'Scotch joke', which superficially it resembles. Occasionally a story is told (e.g. the Jew and the Scotsman who went into a pub together and both died of thirst) which puts both races on an equality, but in general the Jew is credited *merely* with cunning and avarice while the Scotsman is credited with physical hardihood as well. This is seen, for example, in the story of the Jew and the Scotsman who go together to a meeting which has been advertised as free. Unexpectedly there is a collection, and to avoid this the Jew faints and the Scotsman carries him out. Here the Scotsman performs the athletic feat of carrying the other. It would seem vaguely wrong if it were the other way about. [Author's footnote.]

company. Higher up the intellectual scale, antisemitism is rationalized by saying that the Jew is a person who spreads disaffection and weakens national morale. Again there is some superficial justification for this. During the past twenty-five years the activities of what are called 'intellectuals' have been largely mischievous. I do not think it an exaggeration to say that if the 'intellectuals' had done their work a little more thoroughly, Britain would have surrendered in 1940. But the disaffected intelligentsia inevitably included a large number of Jews. With some plausibility it can be said that the Jews are the enemies of our native culture and our national morale. Carefully examined, the claim is seen to be nonsense, but there are always a few prominent individuals who can be cited to support it. During the past few years there has been what amounts to a counter-attack against the rather shallow Leftism which was fashionable in the previous decade and which was exemplified by such organizations as the Left Book Club. This counter-attack (see for instance such books as Arnold Lunn's *The Good Gorilla* or Evelyn Waugh's *Put Out More Flags*) has an antisemitic strain, and it would probably be more marked if the subject were not so obviously dangerous. It so happens that for some decades past Britain has had no nationalist intelligentsia worth bothering about. But British nationalism, i.e. nationalism of an intellectual kind, may revive, and probably will revive if Britain comes out of the present war greatly weakened. The young intellectuals of 1950 may be as naïvely patriotic as those of 1914. In that case the kind of antisemitism which flourished among the anti-Dreyfusards in France, and which Chesterton and Belloc tried to import into this country, might get a foothold.

I have no hard-and-fast theory about the origins of antisemitism. The two current explanations, that it is due to economic causes, or on the other hand, that it is a legacy from the Middle Ages, seem to me unsatisfactory, though I admit that if one combines them they can be made to cover the facts. All I would say with confidence is that antisemitism is part of the larger problem of nationalism, which has not yet been seriously examined, and that the Jew is evidently a scapegoat, though *for what* he is a scapegoat we do not yet know. In this essay I have relied almost entirely on my own limited experience, and perhaps every one of my conclusions would be negatived by other observers. The fact is that there are almost no data on this subject. But for what they are worth I will summarize my opinions. Boiled down, they amount to this:

There is more antisemitism in England than we care to admit, and the war has accentuated it, but it is not certain that it is on the increase if one thinks in terms of decades rather than years.

It does not at present lead to open persecution, but it has the effect of making people callous to the sufferings of Jews in other countries.

It is at bottom quite irrational and will not yield to argument.

The persecutions in Germany have caused much concealment of antisemitic feeling and thus obscured the whole picture.

The subject needs serious investigation.

Only the last point is worth expanding. To study any subject scientifically one needs a detached attitude, which is obviously harder when one's own interests or emotions are involved. Plenty of people who are quite capable of being objective about sea urchins, say, or the square root of 2, become schizophrenic if they have to think about the sources of their own income. What vitiates nearly all that is written about antisemitism is the assumption in the writer's mind that *he himself* is immune to it. 'Since I know that antisemitism is irrational,' he argues, 'it follows that I do not share it.' He thus fails to start his investigation in the one place where he could get hold of some reliable evidence – that is, in his own mind.

It seems to me a safe assumption that the disease loosely called nationalism is now almost universal. Antisemitism is only one manifestation of nationalism, and not everyone will have the disease in that particular form. A Jew, for example, would not be antisemitic: but then many Zionist Jews seem to me to be merely antisemites turned upside-down, just as many Indians and Negroes display the normal colour prejudices in an inverted form. The point is that something, some psychological vitamin, is lacking in modern civilization, and as a result we are all more or less subject to this lunacy of believing that whole races or nations are mysteriously good or mysteriously evil. I defy any modern intellectual to look closely and honestly into his own mind without coming upon nationalistic loyalties and hatreds of one kind or another. It is the fact that he can feel the emotional tug of such things, and yet see them dispassionately for what they are, that gives him his status as an intellectual. It will be seen, therefore that the starting point for any investigation of antisemitism should not be 'Why does this obviously irrational belief appeal to other people?' but 'Why does antisemitism appeal to *me*? What is there about it that I feel to be true?' If one asks this question one at least discovers one's own rationalizations, and it may be possible to find out what lies beneath them. Antisemitism should be investigated – and I will not say by antisemites, but at any rate by people who know that they are not immune to that kind of emotion. When

Hitler has disappeared a real inquiry into this subject will be possible, and it would probably be best to start not by debunking antisemitism, but by marshalling all the justifications for it that can be found, in one's own mind or anybody else's. In that way one might get some clues that would lead to its psychological roots. But that antisemitism will be definitively *cured*, without curing the larger disease of nationalism, I do not believe.

Written [early February 1945]; *Contemporary Jewish Record*, April 1945; *S.J.*; *E.Y.E.*; *C.E.*

23. In Defence of P. G. Wodehouse

When the Germans made their rapid advance through Belgium in the early summer of 1940, they captured, among other things, Mr P. G. Wodehouse, who had been living throughout the early part of the war in his villa at Le Touquet, and seems not to have realized until the last moment that he was in any danger. As he was led away into captivity, he is said to have remarked, 'Perhaps after this I shall write a serious book.' He was placed for the time being under house arrest, and from his subsequent statements it appears that he was treated in a fairly friendly way, German officers in the neighbourhood frequently 'dropping in for a bath or a party'.

Over a year later, on 25 June 1941, the news came that Wodehouse had been released from internment and was living at the Adlon Hotel in Berlin. On the following day the public was astonished to learn that he had agreed to do some broadcasts of a 'non-political' nature over the German radio. The full texts of these broadcasts are not easy to obtain at this date, but Wodehouse seems to have done five of them between 26 June and 2 July, when the Germans took him off the air again. The first broadcast, on 26 June, was not made on the Nazi radio but took the form an interview with Harry Flannery, the representative of the Columbia Broadcasting System, which still had its correspondents in Berlin. Wodehouse also published in the *Saturday Evening Post* an article which he had written while still in the internment camp.

The article and the broadcasts dealt mainly with Wodehouse's experiences in internment, but they did include a very few comments on the war. The following are fair samples:

I never was interested in politics. I'm quite unable to work up any kind of belligerent feeling. Just as I'm about to feel belligerent about some country I meet a decent sort of chap. We go out together and lose any fighting thoughts or feelings

A short time ago they had a look at us on parade and got the right idea; at least they sent us to the local lunatic asylum. And I have been there forty-two weeks. There is a good deal to be said for internment. It keeps you out of the saloon and helps you to keep up with your reading. The chief trouble is that it means you are away from home for a long time. When I join my wife I had better take along a letter of introduction to be on the safe side.

In the days before the war I had always been modestly proud of being an Englishman, but now that I have been some months resident in this bin or repository of Englishmen I am not so sure . . . The only concession I want from Germany is that she gives me a loaf of bread, tells the gentlemen with muskets at the main gate to look the other way, and leaves the rest to me. In return I am prepared to hand over India, an autographed set of my books, and to reveal the secret process of cooking sliced potatoes on a radiator. This offer holds good till Wednesday week.

The first extract quoted above caused great offence. Wodehouse was also censured for using (in the interview with Flannery) the phrase 'whether Britain wins the war or not', and he did not make things better by describing in another broadcast the filthy habits of some Belgian prisoners among whom he was interned. The Germans recorded this broadcast and repeated it a number of times. They seem to have supervised his talks very lightly, and they allowed him not only to be funny about the discomforts of internment but to remark that 'the internees at Trost camp all fervently believe that Britain will eventually win'. The general upshot of the talks, however, was that he had not been ill treated and bore no malice.

These broadcasts caused an immediate uproar in England. There were questions in Parliament, angry editorial comments in the press, and a stream of letters from fellow authors, nearly all of them disapproving, though one or two suggested that it would be better to suspend judgement, and several pleaded that Wodehouse probably did not realize what he was doing. On 15 July, the Home Service of the B.B.C. carried an extremely violent Postscript by 'Cassandra' of the *Daily Mirror*, accusing Wodehouse of 'selling his country'. This postscript made free use of such expressions as 'quisling' and 'worshipping the Fuehrer'. The main charge was that Wodehouse had agreed to do German propaganda as a way of buying himself out of the internment camp.

'Cassandra's' Postscript caused a certain amount of protest, but on the whole it seems to have intensified popular feeling against Wodehouse. One result of it was that numerous lending libraries withdrew Wodehouse's books from circulation. Here is a typical news item:

Within twenty-four hours of listening to the broadcast of Cassandra, the *Daily Mirror* columnist, Portadown (North Ireland) Urban District Council banned P. G. Wodehouse's books from their public library. Mr Edward McCann said that Cassandra's broadcast had clinched the matter. Wodehouse was funny no longer. (*Daily Mirror*.)

In addition the B.B.C. banned Wodehouse's lyrics from the air and was still doing so a couple of years later. As late as December 1944 there were demands in Parliament that Wodehouse should be put on trial as a traitor.

There is an old saying that if you throw enough mud some of it will stick, and the mud has stuck to Wodehouse in a rather peculiar way. An impression has been left behind that Wodehouse's talks (not that anyone remembers what he said in them) showed him up not merely as a traitor but as an ideological sympathizer with Fascism. Even at the time several letters to the press claimed that 'Fascist tendencies' could be detected in his books, and the charge has been repeated since. I shall try to analyse the mental atmosphere of those books in a moment, but it is important to realize that the events of 1941 do not convict Wodehouse of anything worse than stupidity. The really interesting question is how and why he could be so stupid. When Flannery met Wodehouse (released, but still under guard) at the Adlon Hotel in June 1941, he saw at once that he was dealing with a political innocent, and when preparing him for their broadcast interview he had to warn him against making some exceedingly unfortunate remarks, one of which was by implication slightly anti-Russian. As it was, the phrase 'whether England wins or not' did get through. Soon after the interview Wodehouse told him that he was also going to broadcast on the Nazi radio, apparently not realizing that this action had any special significance. Flannery comments:[1]

By this time the Wodehouse plot was evident. It was one of the best Nazi publicity stunts of the war, the first with a human angle . . . Plack (Goebbels's assistant) had gone to the camp near Gleiwitz to see Wodehouse, found that the author was completely without political sense, and had an idea. He suggested to Wodehouse that in return for being released from the prison camp he write a series of broadcasts about his experiences; there would be no censorship and he would put them on the air himself. In making that proposal Plack showed that he

1. *Assignment to Berlin* by Harry W. Flannery. [Author's footnote.]

knew his man. He knew that Wodehouse made fun of the English in all his stories and that he seldom wrote in any other way, that he was still living in the period about which he wrote and had no conception of Nazism and all it meant. Wodehouse was his own Bertie Wooster.

The striking of an actual bargain between Wodehouse and Plack seems to be merely Flannery's own interpretation. The arrangement may have been of a much less definite kind, and to judge from the broadcasts themselves, Wodehouse's main idea in making them was to keep in touch with his public and – the comedian's ruling passion – to get a laugh. Obviously they are not the utterances of a quisling of the type of Ezra Pound or John Amery,[2] nor, probably, of a person capable of understanding the nature of quislingism. Flannery seems to have warned Wodehouse that it would be unwise to broadcast, but not very forcibly. He adds that Wodehouse (though in one broadcast he refers to himself as an Englishman) seemed to regard himself as an American citizen. He had contemplated naturalization, but had never filled in the necessary papers. He even used, to Flannery, the phrase, 'We're not at war with Germany.'

I have before me a bibliography of P. G. Wodehouse's works. It names round about fifty books, but is certainly incomplete. It is as well to be honest, and I ought to start by admitting that there are many books by Wodehouse – perhaps a quarter or a third of the total – which I have not read. It is not, indeed, easy to read the whole output of a popular writer who is normally published in cheap editions. But I have followed his work fairly closely since 1911, when I was eight years old, and am well acquainted with its peculiar mental atmosphere – an atmosphere which has not, of course, remained completely unchanged, but shows little alteration since about 1925. In the passage from Flannery's book which I quoted above there are two remarks which would immediately strike any attentive reader of Wodehouse. One is to the effect that Wodehouse 'was still living in the period about which he wrote', and the other that the Nazi Propaganda Ministry made use of him because he 'made fun of the English'. The second statement is based on a misconception to which I will return presently. But Flannery's other comment is quite true and contains in it part of the clue to Wodehouse's behaviour.

2. John Amery(1912–45), right-wing politician and son of Leo Amery, who was a Conservative and patriotic M.P. and Secretary for India 1940–45. John Amery was an ardent admirer of Hitler, and had broadcast from Germany during the war urging British subjects in captivity to fight for Germany against England and Russia, and also made public speeches throughout occupied Europe on behalf of the German régime. He was executed for treason by the British in December 1945

A thing that people often forget about P.G. Wodehouse's novels is how long ago the better-known of them were written. We think of him as in some sense typifying the silliness of the nineteen-twenties and nineteen-thirties, but in fact the scenes and characters by which he is best remembered had all made their appearance before 1925. Psmith first appeared in 1909, having been foreshadowed by other characters in early school stories. Blandings Castle, with Baxter and the Earl of Emsworth both in residence, was introduced in 1915. The Jeeves–Wooster cycle began in 1919, both Jeeves and Wooster having made brief appearances earlier. Ukridge appeared in 1924. When one looks through the list of Wodehouse's books from 1902 onwards, one can observe three fairly well-marked periods. The first is the school-story period. It includes such books as *The Gold Bat*, *The Pothunters*, etc., and has its high-spot in *Mike* (1909). *Psmith in the City*, published in the following year, belongs in this category, though it is not directly concerned with school life. The next is the American period. Wodehouse seems to have lived in the United States from about 1913 to 1920, and for a while showed signs of becoming Americanized in idiom and outlook. Some of the stories in *The Man with Two Left Feet* (1917) appear to have been influenced by O.Henry, and other books written about this time contain Americanisms (e.g. 'highball' for 'whisky and soda') which an Englishman would not normally use *in propria persona*. Nevertheless, almost all the books of this period – *Psmith, Journalist*; *The Little Nugget*; *The Indiscretions of Archie*; *Piccadilly Jim* and various others – depend for their effect on the *contrast* between English and American manners. English characters appear in an American setting, or vice versa: there is a certain number of purely English stories, but hardly any purely American ones. The third period might fitly be called the country-house period. By the early nineteen-twenties Wodehouse must have been making a very large income, and the social status of his characters moved upwards accordingly, though the Ukridge stories form a partial exception. The typical setting is now a country mansion, a luxurious bachelor flat or an expensive golf club. The school-boy athleticism of the earlier books fades out, cricket and football giving way to golf, and the element of farce and burlesque becomes more marked. No doubt many of the later books, such as *Summer Lightning*, are light comedy rather than pure farce, but the occasional attempts at moral earnestness which can be found in *Psmith, Journalist*; *The Little Nugget*; *The Coming of Bill*; *The Man with Two Left Feet* and some of the school stories, no longer appear. Mike Jackson has turned into Bertie Wooster. That, however, is not a very startling metamorphosis, and one of the most noticeable things about Wodehouse is his *lack* of development. Books like *The Gold Bat* and *Tales of St Austin's*, written in the opening years of this century, already have the familiar atmosphere. How much of a formula the writing of his later books had become one can see from the fact that he continued to write stories of English life although throughout the sixteen years before his internment he was living at Hollywood and Le Touquet.

Mike, which is now a difficult book to obtain in an unabridged form, must be one of the best 'light' school stories in English. But though its incidents are largely farcical, it is by no means a satire on the public-school system, and *The Gold Bat*, *The Pothunters*, etc., are even less so. Wodehouse was educated at Dulwich, and then worked in a bank and graduated into novel writing by way of very cheap journalism. It is clear that for many years he remained 'fixated' on his old school and loathed the unromantic job and the lower-middle-class surroundings in which he found himself. In the early stories the 'glamour' of public-school life (house matches, fagging, teas round the study fire, etc.), is laid on fairly thick, and the 'play the game' code of morals is accepted with not many reservations. Wrykyn, Wodehouse's imaginary public school, is a school of a more fashionable type than Dulwich, and one gets the impression that between *The Gold Bat* (1904) and *Mike* (1908) Wrykyn itself has become more expensive and moved farther from London. Psychologically the most revealing book of Wodehouse's early period is *Psmith in the City*. Mike Jackson's father has suddenly lost his money, and Mike, like Wodehouse himself, is thrust at the age of about eighteen into an ill-paid subordinate job in a bank. Psmith is similarly employed, though not from financial necessity. Both this book and *Psmith, Journalist* (1915) are unusual in that they display a certain amount of political consciousness. Psmith at this stage chooses to call himself a Socialist – in his mind, and no doubt in Wodehouse's, this means no more than ignoring class distinctions – and on one occasion the two boys attend an open-air meeting on Clapham Common and go home to tea with an elderly Socialist orator, whose shabby-genteel home is described with some accuracy. But the most striking feature of the book is Mike's inability to wean himself from the atmosphere of school. He enters upon his job without any pretence of enthusiasm, and his main desire is not, as one might expect, to find a more interesting and useful job, but simply to be playing cricket. When he has to find himself lodgings he chooses to settle at Dulwich, because there he will be near a school and will be able to hear the agreeable sound of the ball striking against the bat. The climax of the book comes when Mike gets the chance to play in a county match and simply walks out of his job in order to do so. The point is that Wodehouse here sympathizes with Mike: indeed he identified himself with him, for it is clear enough that Mike bears the same relation to Wodehouse as Julien Sorel to Stendhal. But he created many other heroes essentially similar. Through the books of this and the next period there passes a whole series of young men to whom playing games and 'keeping fit' are a sufficient life-work. Wodehouse is almost incapable of imagining a desirable job. The great thing is to have money of your own, or, failing that, to find a sinecure. The hero of *Something Fresh* (1915) escapes from low-class journalism by becoming physical-training instructor to a dyspeptic millionaire: this is regarded as a step up, morally as well as financially.

In the books of the third period there is no narcissism and no serious interludes, but the implied moral and social background has changed much less than might appear at first sight. If one compares Bertie Wooster with Mike, or even with the rugger-playing prefects of the earliest school stories, one sees that the only real difference between them is that Bertie is richer and lazier. His ideals would be almost the same as theirs, but he fails to live up to them. Archie Moffam, in *The Indiscretions of Archie* (1921), is a type intermediate between Bertie and the earlier heroes: he is an ass, but he is also honest, kind-hearted, athletic and courageous. From first to last Wodehouse takes the public-school code of behaviour for granted, with the difference that in his later, more sophisticated period he prefers to show his characters violating it or living up to it against their will:

'Bertie! You wouldn't let down a pal?'
'Yes, I would.'
'But we were at school together, Bertie.'
'I don't care.'
'The old school, Bertie, the old school!'
'Oh, well – dash it!'

Bertie, a sluggish Don Quixote, has no wish to tilt at windmills, but he would hardly think of refusing to do so when honour calls. Most of the people whom Wodehouse intends as sympathetic characters are parasites, and some of them are plain imbeciles, but very few of them could be described as immoral. Even Ukridge is a visionary rather than a plain crook. The most immoral, or rather un-moral, of Wodehouse's characters is Jeeves, who acts as a foil to Bertie Wooster's comparative high-mindedness and perhaps symbolizes the widespread English belief that intelligence and unscrupulousness are much the same thing. How closely Wodehouse sticks to conventional morality can be seen from the fact that nowhere in his books is there anything in the nature of a sex joke. This is an enormous sacrifice for a farcical writer to make. Not only are there no dirty jokes, but there are hardly any compromising situations: the horns-on-the-forehead motif is almost completely avoided. Most of the full-length books, of course, contain a 'love interest', but it is always at the light-comedy level: the love affair, with its complications and its idyllic scenes, goes on and on, but as the saying goes, 'nothing happens'. It is significant that Wodehouse, by nature a writer of farces, was able to collaborate more than once with Ian Hay, a serio-comic writer and an exponent (*vide Pip*, etc.) of the 'clean-living Englishman' tradition at its silliest.

In *Something Fresh* Wodehouse had discovered the comic possibilities of the English aristocracy, and a succession of ridiculous but, save in a very few instances, not actually contemptible barons, earls and what-not followed accordingly. This had the rather curious effect of causing Wodehouse to be regarded, outside England, as a penetrating satirist of English society. Hence Flannery's statement that Wodehouse 'made fun of the English', which is the impression he would probably make on a German or even an American reader. Some time after the broadcasts from Berlin I was discussing them with a young Indian Nationalist who defended Wodehouse warmly. He took it for granted that Wodehouse *had* gone over to the enemy, which from his own point of view was the right thing to do. But what interested me was to find that he regarded Wodehouse as an anti-British writer who had done useful work by showing up the British aristocracy in their true colours. This is a mistake that it would be very difficult for an English person to make, and is a good instance of the way in which books, especially humorous books, lose their finer nuances when they reach a foreign audience. For it is clear enough that Wodehouse is not anti-British, and not anti-upper-class either. On the contrary, a harmless old-fashioned snobbishness is perceptible all through his work. Just as an intelligent Catholic is able to see that the blasphemies of Baudelaire or James Joyce are not seriously damaging to the Catholic faith, so an English reader can see that in creating such characters as Hildebrand Spencer Poyns de Burgh John Hanneyside Coombe-Crombie, 12th Earl of Dreever, Wodehouse is not really attacking the social hierarchy. Indeed, no one who genuinely despised titles would write of them so much. Wodehouse's attitude towards the

English social system is the same as his attitude towards the public-school moral code – a mild facetiousness covering an unthinking acceptance. The Earl of Emsworth is funny because an earl ought to have more dignity, and Bertie Wooster's helpless dependence on Jeeves is funny partly because the servant ought not to be superior to the master. An American reader can mistake these two, and others like them, for hostile caricatures because he is inclined to be anglophobe already and they correspond to his preconceived ideas about a decadent aristocracy. Bertie Wooster, with his spats and his cane, is the traditional stage Englishman. But, as any English reader would see, Wodehouse intends him as a sympathetic figure, and Wodehouse's real sin has been to present the English upper classes as much nicer people than they are. All through his books certain problems are consistently avoided. Almost without exception his moneyed young men are unassuming, good mixers, not avaricious: their tone is set for them by Psmith, who retains his own upper-class exterior but bridges the social gap by addressing everyone as 'Comrade'.

But there is another important point about Bertie Wooster: his out-of-dateness. Conceived in 1917 or thereabouts, Bertie really belongs to an epoch earlier than that. He is the 'knut' of the pre-1914 period, celebrated in such songs as 'Gilbert the Filbert' or 'Reckless Reggie of the Regent's Palace'. The kind of life that Wodehouse writes about by preference, the life of the 'clubman' or 'man about town', the elegant young man who lounges all the morning in Piccadilly with a cane under his arm and a carnation in his button-hole, barely survived into the nineteen-twenties. It is significant that Wodehouse could publish in 1936 a book entitled *Young Men in Spats*. For who was wearing spats at that date? They had gone out of fashion quite ten years earlier. But the traditional 'knut', the 'Piccadilly Johnny', *ought* to wear spats, just as the pantomime Chinese ought to wear a pigtail. A humorous writer is not obliged to keep up to date, and having struck one or two good veins, Wodehouse continued to exploit them with a regularity that was no doubt all the easier because he did not set foot in England during the sixteen years that preceded his internment. His picture of English society had been formed before 1914, and it was a naïve, traditional and, at bottom, admiring picture. Nor did he ever become genuinely Americanized. As I have pointed out, spontaneous Americanisms do occur in the books of the middle period, but Wodehouse remained English enough to find American slang an amusing and slightly shocking novelty. He loves to thrust a slang phrase or a crude fact in among Wardour Street English ('With a hollow groan Ukridge borrowed five shillings from me and went out into the night'), and expressions like 'a piece of cheese' or 'bust him on the noggin' lend themselves to this purpose. But the trick had been developed before he made any American contacts, and his use of garbled quotations is a common device of English writers running back to Fielding. As Mr John Hayward has pointed out,[3] Wodehouse owes a good deal to his knowledge of English literature and especially of Shakespeare. His books are aimed, not, obviously, at a high-brow audience, but at an audience educated along traditional lines. When, for instance, he describes somebody as heaving 'the kind of sigh that Prometheus might have heaved when the vulture dropped in for its lunch', he is assuming that his readers will know something of Greek mythology. In his early days the writers he admired were probably Barry Pain, Jerome K. Jerome, W. W. Jacobs, Kipling and F. Anstey, and he has remained closer to them than to the quick-moving American comic writers such as Ring Lardner or Damon Runyon. In his radio interview with Flannery, Wodehouse wondered whether 'the kind of people and the kind of England I write about will live after the war', not realizing that they were ghosts already. 'He was still living in the period about which he wrote', says Flannery, meaning, probably, the nineteen-twenties. But the period was really the Edwardian age, and Bertie Wooster, if he ever existed, was killed round about 1915.

If my analysis of Wodehouse's mentality is accepted, the idea that in 1941 he consciously aided the Nazi propaganda machine becomes untenable and even ridiculous. He *may* have been induced to broadcast by the promise of an earlier release (he was due for release a few months later, on reaching his sixtieth birthday) but he cannot have realized that what he did would be damaging to British interests. As I have tried to show, his moral outlook has remained that of a public-school boy, and according to the public-school code, treachery in time of war is the most unforgivable of all the sins. But how could he fail to grasp that what he did would be a big propaganda score for the Germans and would bring down a torrent of disapproval on his own head? To answer this one must take two things into consideration. First, Wodehouse's complete lack – so far as one can judge from his printed works – of political awareness. It is nonsense to talk of 'Fascist tendencies' in his books. There are no post-1918 tendencies at all. Throughout his work there is a certain uneasy awareness of the problem of class distinctions, and scattered through it at various dates there are ignorant though not unfriendly references to

3. 'P. G. Wodehouse' by John Hayward. (*The Saturday Book*, 1942.) I believe this is the only full-length critical essay on Wodehouse. [Author's footnote.]

Socialism. In *The Heart of a Goof* (1926) there is a rather silly story about a Russian novelist, which seems to have been inspired by the factional struggle then raging in the U.S.S.R. But the references in it to the Soviet system are entirely frivolous and, considering the date, not markedly hostile. That is about the extent of Wodehouse's political consciousness, so far as it is discoverable from his writings. Nowhere, so far as I know, does he so much as use the word 'Fascism' or 'Nazism'. In left-wing circles, indeed in 'enlightened' circles of any kind, to broadcast on the Nazi radio, to have any truck with Nazis whatever, would have seemed just as shocking an action before the war as during it. But that is a habit of mind that had been developed during nearly a decade of ideological struggle against Fascism. The bulk of the British people, one ought to remember, remained anaesthetic to that struggle until late into 1940. Abyssinia, Spain, China, Austria, Czechoslovakia – the long series of crimes and aggressions had simply slid past their consciousness or were dimly noted as quarrels occurring among foreigners and 'not our business'. One can gauge the general ignorance from the fact that the ordinary Englishman thought of 'Fascism' as an exclusively Italian thing and was bewildered when the same word was applied to Germany. And there is nothing in Wodehouse's writings to suggest that he was better informed, or more interested in politics, than the general run of his readers.

The other thing one must remember is that Wodehouse happened to be taken prisoner at just the moment when the war reached its desperate phase. We forget these things now, but until that time feelings about the war had been noticeably tepid. There was hardly any fighting, the Chamberlain Government was unpopular, eminent publicists were hinting that we should make compromise peace as quickly as possible, trade-union and Labour-Party branches all over the country were passing anti-war resolutions. Afterwards, of course, things changed. The army was with difficulty extricated from Dunkirk, France collapsed, Britain was alone, the bombs rained on London, Goebbels announced that Britain was to be 'reduced to degradation and poverty'. By the middle of 1941 the British people knew what they were up against and feelings against the enemy were far fiercer than before. But Wodehouse had spent the intervening year in internment, and his captors seem to have treated him reasonably well. He had missed the turning-point of the war, and in 1941 he was still reacting in terms of 1939. He was not alone in this. On several occasions about this time the Germans brought captured British soldiers to the microphone, and some of them made remarks at least as tactless as Wodehouse's. They attracted no attention, however. And even an outright quisling like John Amery was afterwards to arouse much less indignation than Wodehouse had done.

But why? Why should a few rather silly but harmless remarks by an elderly novelist have provoked such an outcry? One has to look for the probable answer amid the dirty requirements of propaganda warfare.

There is one point about the Wodehouse broadcasts that is almost certainly significant – the date. Wodehouse was released two or three days before the invasion of the U.S.S.R., and at a time when the higher ranks of the Nazi party must have known that the invasion was imminent. It was vitally necessary to keep America out of the war as long as possible, and in fact, about this time, the German attitude towards the U.S.A. did become more conciliatory than it had been before. The Germans could hardly hope to defeat Russia, Britain and the U.S.A. in combination, but if they could polish off Russia quickly – and presumably they expected to do so – the Americans might never intervene. The release of Wodehouse was only a minor move, but it was not a bad sop to throw to the American isolationists. He was well known in the United States, and he was – or so the Germans calculated – popular with the anglophobe public as a caricaturist who made fun of the silly-ass Englishman with his spats and monocle. At the microphone he could be trusted to damage British prestige in one way or another, while his release would demonstrate that the Germans were good fellows and knew how to treat their enemies chivalrously. That presumably was the calculation, though the fact that Wodehouse was only broadcasting for about a week suggests that he did not come up to expectations.

But on the British side similar though opposite calculations were at work. For the two years following Dunkirk, British morale depended largely upon the feeling that this was not only a war for democracy but a war which the common people had to win by their own efforts. The upper classes were discredited by their appeasement policy and by the disasters of 1940, and a social-levelling process appeared to be taking place. Patriotism and left-wing sentiments were associated in the popular mind, and numerous able journalists were at work to tie the association tighter. Priestley's 1940 broadcasts and 'Cassandra's' articles in the *Daily Mirror* were good examples of the demagogic propaganda flourishing at that time. In this atmosphere, Wodehouse made an ideal whipping-boy. For it was generally felt that the rich were treacherous, and Wodehouse – as 'Cassandra' vigorously pointed out in his broadcast – was a rich man. But he was the kind of rich man who could be attacked with impunity and without risking any damage to the structure of society. To denounce Wodehouse was not like denouncing, say, Beaverbrook. A mere novelist, however large his earnings may happen to be, is not *of* the possessing class. Even if his income touches £50,000 a year he has only the outward semblance of a millionaire. He is a lucky outsider who has fluked into a fortune – usually a very temporary fortune – like the winner of the Calcutta Derby Sweep. Consequently, Wodehouse's indiscretion gave a good propaganda opening. It was a chance to 'expose' a wealthy parasite without drawing attention to any of the parasites who really mattered.

In the desperate circumstances of the time, it was excusable to be angry at what Wodehouse did, but to go on denouncing him three or four years later – and more, to let an impression remain that he acted with conscious treachery – is not excusable. Few things in this war have been more morally disgusting than the present hunt after traitors and quislings. At best it is largely the punishment of the guilty by the guilty. In France, all kinds of petty rats – police officials, penny-a-lining journalists, women who have slept with German soldiers – are hunted down while almost without exception the big rats escape. In England the fiercest tirades against quislings are uttered by Conservatives who were practising appeasement in 1938 and Communists who were advocating it in 1940. I have striven to show how the wretched Wodehouse – just because success and expatriation had allowed him to remain mentally in the Edwardian age – became the *corpus vile* in a propaganda experiment, and I suggest that it is now time to regard the incident as closed. If Ezra Pound is caught and shot by the American authorities, it will have the effect of establishing his reputation as a poet for hundreds of years; and even in the case of Wodehouse, if we drive him to retire to the United States and renounce his British citizenship we shall end by being horribly ashamed of ourselves. Meanwhile, if we really want to punish the people who weakened national morale at critical moments, there are other culprits who are nearer home and better worth chasing

Written [February] 1945; *Windmill*, No.2 [July] 1945; *Cr.E.*; *D.D.*; *O.R.*; *C.E.*

24. Notes on Nationalism

Somewhere or other Byron makes use of the French word *longueur*, and remarks in passing that though in England we happen not to have the *word*, we have the *thing* in considerable profusion. In the same way, there is a habit of mind which is now so widespread that it affects our thinking on nearly every subject, but which has not yet been given a name. As the nearest existing equivalent I have chosen the word 'nationalism', but it will be seen in a moment that I am not using it in quite the ordinary sense, if only because the emotion I am speaking about does not always attach itself to what is called a nation – that is, a single race or a geographical area. It can attach itself to a church or a class, or it may work in a merely negative sense, *against* something or other and without the need for any positive object of loyalty.

By 'nationalism' I mean first of all the habit of assuming that human beings can be classified like insects and that whole blocks of millions or tens of millions of people can be confidently labelled 'good' or 'bad'.[1] But secondly – and this is much more important – I mean the habit of identifying oneself with a single nation or other unit, placing it beyond good and evil and recognizing no other duty than that of advancing its interests. Nationalism is not to be confused with patriotism. Both words are normally used in so vague a way that any definition is liable to be challenged, but one must draw a distinction between them, since two different and even opposing ideas are involved. By 'patriotism' I mean devotion to a particular place and a particular way of life, which one believes to be the best in the world but has no wish to force upon other people. Patriotism is of its nature defensive, both militarily and culturally. Nationalism, on the other hand, is inseparable from the desire for power. The abiding purpose of every nationalist is to

1. Nations, and even vaguer entities such as the Catholic Church or the proletariat, are commonly thought of as individuals and often referred to as 'she'. Patently absurd remarks such as 'Germany is naturally treacherous' are to be found in any newspaper one opens, and reckless generalizations about national character ('The Spaniard is a natural aristocrat' or 'Every Englishman is a hypocrite') are uttered by almost everyone. Intermittently these generalizations are seen to be unfounded, but the habit of making them persists, and people of professedly international outlook, e.g. Tolstoy or Bernard Shaw, are often guilty of them. [Author's footnote.]

secure more power and more prestige, *not* for himself but for the nation or other unit in which he has chosen to sink his own individuality.

So long as it is applied merely to the more notorious and identifiable nationalist movements in Germany, Japan and other countries, all this is obvious enough. Confronted with a phenomenon like Nazism, which we can observe from the outside, nearly all of us would say much the same things about it. But here I must repeat what I said above, that I am only using the word 'nationalism' for lack of a better. Nationalism, in the extended sense in which I am using the word, includes such movements and tendencies as Communism, political Catholicism, Zionism, Antisemitism, Trotskyism and Pacifism. It does not necessarily mean loyalty to a government or a country, still less to *one's own* country, and it is not even strictly necessary that the units in which it deals should actually exist. To name a few obvious examples, Jewry, Islam, Christendom, the Proletariat and the White Race are all of them the objects of passionate nationalistic feeling: but their existence can be seriously questioned, and there is no definition of any one of them that would be universally accepted.

It is also worth emphasizing once again that nationalist feeling can be purely negative. There are, for example, Trotskyists who have become simply the enemies of the U.S.S.R. without developing a corresponding loyalty to any other unit. When one grasps the implications of this, the nature of what I mean by nationalism becomes a good deal clearer. A nationalist is one who thinks solely, or mainly, in terms of competitive prestige. He may be a positive or a negative nationalist – that is, he may use his mental energy either in boosting or in denigrating – but at any rate his thoughts always turn on victories, defeats, triumphs, and humiliations. He sees history, especially contemporary history, as the endless rise and decline of great power units, and every event that happens seems to him a demonstration that his own side is on the up-grade and some hated rival on the down-grade. But finally, it is important not to confuse nationalism with mere worship of success. The nationalist does not go on the principle of simply ganging up with the strongest side. On the contrary, having picked his side, he persuades himself that it *is* the strongest, and is able to stick to his belief even when the facts are overwhelmingly against him. Nationalism is power hunger tempered by self-deception. Every nationalist is capable of the most flagrant dishonesty, but he is also – since he is conscious of serving something bigger than himself – unshakeably certain of being in the right.

Now that I have given this lengthy definition, I think it will be admitted that the habit of mind I am talking about is widespread among the

English intelligentsia, and more widespread there than among the mass of the people. For those who feel deeply about contemporary politics, certain topics have become so infected by considerations of prestige that a genuinely rational approach to them is almost impossible. Out of the hundreds of examples that one might choose, take this question: Which of the three great allies, the U.S.S.R., Britain and the U.S.A., has contributed most to the defeat of Germany? In theory it should be possible to give a reasoned and perhaps even a conclusive answer to this question. In practice, however, the necessary calculations cannot be made, because anyone likely to bother his head about such a question would inevitably see it in terms of competitive prestige. He would therefore *start* by deciding in favour of Russia, Britain or America as the case might be, and only *after* this would begin searching for arguments that seemed to support his case. And there are whole strings of kindred questions to which you can only get an honest answer from someone who is indifferent to the whole subject involved, and whose opinion on it is probably worthless in any case. Hence, partly, the remarkable failure in our time of political and military prediction. It is curious to reflect that out of all the 'experts' of all the schools, there was not a single one who was able to foresee so likely an event as the Russo-German Pact of 1939.[2] And when the news of the Pact broke, the most wildly divergent explanations of it were given, and predictions were made which were falsified almost immediately, being based in nearly every case not on a study of probabilities but on a desire to make the U.S.S.R. seem good or bad, strong or weak. Political or military commentators, like astrologers, can survive almost any mistake, because their more devoted followers do not look to them for an appraisal of the facts but for the stimulation of nationalistic loyalties.[3] And aesthetic judgements, especially literary

2. A few writers of conservative tendency, such as Peter Drucker, foretold an agreement between Germany and Russia, but they expected an actual alliance or amalgamation which would be permanent. No Marxist or other left-wing writer, of whatever colour, came anywhere near foretelling the Pact. [Author's footnote.]

3. The military commentators of the popular press can mostly be classified as pro-Russian or anti-Russian, pro-Blimp or anti-Blimp. Such errors as believing the Maginot Line impregnable, or predicting that Russia would conquer Germany in three months, have failed to shake their reputation, because they were always saying what their own particular audience wanted to hear. The two military critics most favoured by the intelligentsia are Captain Liddell Hart and Major-General Fuller, the first of whom teaches that the defence is stronger than the attack, and the second that the attack is stronger than the defence. This contradiction has not prevented both of them from being accepted as authorities by the same public. The secret reason for their vogue in left-wing circles is that both of them are at odds with the War Office. [Author's footnote.]

judgements, are often corrupted in the same way as political ones. It would be difficult for an Indian nationalist to enjoy reading Kipling or for a Conservative to see merit in Mayakovsky, and there is always a temptation to claim that any book whose tendency one disagrees with must be a bad book from a *literary* point of view. People of strongly nationalistic outlook often perform this sleight of hand without being conscious of dishonesty.

In England, if one simply considers the number of people involved, it is probable that the dominant form of nationalism is old-fashioned British jingoism. It is certain that this is still widespread, and much more so than observers would have believed a dozen years ago. However, in this essay I am concerned chiefly with the reactions of the intelligentsia, among whom jingoism and even patriotism of the old kind are almost dead, thought they now seem to be reviving among a minority. Among the intelligentsia, it hardly needs saying that the dominant form of nationalism is Communism – using this word in a very loose sense, to include not merely Communist Party members but 'fellow-travellers' and russophiles generally. A Communist, for my purpose here, is one who looks upon the U.S.S.R. as his Fatherland and feels it his duty to justify Russian policy and advance Russian interests at all costs. Obviously such people abound in England today, and their direct and indirect influence is very great. But many other forms of nationalism also flourish, and it is by noticing the points of resemblance between different and even seemingly opposed currents of thought that one can best get the matter into perspective.

Ten or twenty years ago, the form of nationalism most closely corresponding to Communism today was political Catholicism. Its most outstanding exponent – though he was perhaps an extreme case rather than a typical one – was G. K. Chesterton. Chesterton was a writer of considerable talent who chose to suppress both his sensibilities and his intellectual honesty in the cause of Roman Catholic propaganda. During the last twenty years or so of his life, his entire output was in reality an endless repetition of the same thing, under its laboured cleverness as simple and boring as 'Great is Diana of the Ephesians'. Every book that he wrote, every paragraph, every sentence, every incident in every story, every scrap of dialogue, had to demonstrate beyond possibility of mistake the superiority of the Catholic over the Protestant or the pagan. But Chesterton was not content to think of this superiority as merely intellectual or spiritual: it had to be translated into terms of national prestige and military power, which entailed an ignorant idealization of the Latin countries, especially France. Chesterton had not lived long in France, and his picture of it – as a land of Catholic peasants incessantly singing the *Marseillaise* over glasses of red wine – had about as much relation to reality as *Chu Chin Chow* has to everyday life in Baghdad. And with this went not only an enormous over-estimation of French military power (both before and after 1914–18 he maintained that France, by itself, was stronger than Germany), but a silly and vulgar glorification of the actual process of war. Chesterton's battle poems, such as 'Lepanto' or 'The Ballad of Saint Barbara', make 'The Charge of the Light Brigade' read like a pacifist tract: they are perhaps the most tawdry bits of bombast to be found in our language. The interesting thing is that had the romantic rubbish which he habitually wrote about France and the French army been written by somebody else about Britian and the British army, he would have been the first to jeer. In home politics he was a Little Englander, a true hater of jingoism and imperialism, and according to his lights a true friend of democracy. Yet when he looked outwards into the international field, he could foresake his principles without even noticing that he was doing so. Thus, his almost mystical belief in the virtues of democracy did not prevent him from admiring Mussolini. Mussolini had destroyed the representative government and the freedom of the press for which Chesterton had struggled so hard at home, but Mussolini was an Italian and had made Italy strong, and that settled the matter. Nor did Chesterton ever find a word to say against imperialism and the conquest of coloured races when they were practised by Italians or Frenchmen. His hold on reality, his literary taste, and even to some extent his moral sense, were dislocated as soon as his nationalistic loyalties were involved.

Obviously there are considerable resemblances between political Catholicism, as exemplified by Chesterton, and Communism. So there are between either of these and, for instance, Scottish nationalism, Zionism, Antisemitism, or Trotskyism. It would be an over-simplification to say that all forms of nationalism are the same, even in their mental atmosphere, but there are certain rules that hold good in all cases. The following are the principal characteristics of nationalist thought:

Obsession. As nearly as possible, no nationalist ever thinks, talks, or writes about anything except the superiority of his own power unit. It is difficult if not impossible for any nationalist to conceal his allegiance. The smallest slur upon his own unit, or any implied praise of a rival organization, fills him with uneasiness which he can only relieve by making some sharp retort. If the chosen unit is an actual country, such as Ireland or India, he will generally claim superiority for it not only in military power and political virtue, but in art, literature, sport, the structure of the language, the physical beauty of the inhabitants, and perhaps even in climate, scenery and cooking. He will show great sensitiveness about such things as the correct display of flags, relative size of headlines and the order in which different countries are named.[4] Nomenclature plays a very important part in nationalist thought. Countries which have won their independence or gone through a nationalist revolution usually change their names, and any country or other unit round which strong feelings revolve is likely to have several names, each of them carrying a different implication. The two sides in the Spanish Civil War had between them nine or ten names expressing different degrees of love and hatred. Some of these names (e.g. 'Patriots' for Franco-supporters, or 'Loyalists' for Government-supporters) were frankly question-begging, and there was no single one of them which the two rival factions could have agreed to use. All nationalists consider it a duty to spread their own language to the detriment of rival languages, and among English-speakers this struggle reappears in subtler form as a struggle between dialects. Anglophobe Americans will refuse to use a slang phrase if they know it to be of British origin, and the conflict between Latinizers and Germanizers often has nationalist motives behind it. Scottish nationalists insist on the superiority of Lowland Scots, and Socialists whose nationalism takes the form of class hatred tirade against the B.B.C. accent and even the broad A. One could multiply instances. Nationalist thought often gives the impression of being tinged by belief in sympathetic magic – a belief which probably comes out in the widespread custom of burning political enemies in effigy, or using pictures of them as targets in shooting galleries.

Instability. The intensity with which they are held does not prevent nationalist loyalties from being transferable. To begin with, as I have pointed out already, they can be and often are fastened upon some foreign country. One quite commonly finds that great national leaders, or the founders of nationalist movements, do not even belong to the country they have glorified. Sometimes they are outright foreigners, or more often they come from peripheral areas where nationality is doubtful. Examples are Stalin, Hitler, Napoleon, de Valera, Disraeli, Poincaré, Beaverbrook. The Pan-German movement was in part the creation of an

4. Certain Americans have expressed dissatisfaction because 'Anglo-American' is the normal form of combination of these two words. It has been proposed to substitute 'Americo-British'. [Author's footnote.]

Englishman, Houston Chamberlain. For the past fifty or a hundred years, transferred nationalism has been a common phenomenon among literary intellectuals. With Lafcadio Hearne the transference was to Japan, with Carlyle and many others of his time to Germany, and in our own age it is usually to Russia. But the peculiarly interesting fact is that *re*-transference is also possible. A country or other unit which has been worshipped for years may suddenly become detestable, and some other object of affection may take its place with almost no interval. In the first version of H. G. Wells's *Outline of History*, and others of his writings about that time, one finds the United States praised almost as extravagantly as Russia is praised by Communists today: yet within a few years this uncritical admiration had turned into hostility. The bigoted Communist who changes in a space of weeks, or even of days, into an equally bigoted Trotskyist is a common spectacle. In continental Europe Fascist movements were largely recruited from among Communists, and the opposite process may well happen within the new few years. What remains constant in the nationalist is his own state of mind: the object of his feelings is changeable, and may be imaginary.

But for an intellectual, transference has an important function which I have already mentioned shortly in connexion with Chesterton. It makes it possible for him to be much *more* nationalistic – more vulgar, more silly, more malignant, more dishonest – than he could ever be on behalf of his native country, or any unit of which he had real knowledge. When one sees the slavish or boastful rubbish that is written about Stalin, the Red army, etc. by fairly intelligent and sensitive people, one realizes that this is only possible because some kind of dislocation has taken place. In societies such as ours, it is unusual for anyone describable as an intellectual to feel a very deep attachment to his own country. Public opinion – that is, the section of public opinion of which he as an intellectual is aware – will not allow him to do so. Most of the people surrounding him are sceptical and disaffected, and he may adopt the same attitude from imitativeness or sheer cowardice: in that case he will have abandoned the form of nationalism that lies nearest to hand without getting any closer to a genuinely internationalist outlook. He still feels the need for a Fatherland, and it is natural to look for one somewhere abroad. Having found it, he can wallow unrestrainedly in exactly those emotions from which he believes that he has emancipated himself. God, the King, the Empire, the Union Jack – all the overthrown idols can reappear under different names, and because they are not recognized for what they are they can be worshipped with a good conscience. Transferred nationalism, like the use of scapegoats, is a way of attaining salvation without altering one's conduct.

Indifference to Reality. All nationalists have the power of not seeing resemblances between similar sets of facts. A British Tory will defend self-determination in Europe and oppose it in India with no feeling of inconsistency. Actions are held to be good or bad, not on their own merits but according to who does them, and there is almost no kind of outrage – torture, the use of hostages, forced labour, mass deportations, imprisonment without trial, forgery, assassination, the bombing of civilians – which does not change its moral colour when it is committed by 'our' side. The Liberal *News Chronicle* published, as an example of shocking barbarity, photographs of Russians hanged by the Germans, and then a year or two later published with warm approval almost exactly similar photographs of Germans hanged by the Russians.[5] It is the same with historical events. History is thought of largely in nationalist terms, and such things as the Inquisition, the tortures of the Star Chamber, the exploits of the English buccaneers (Sir Francis Drake, for instance, who was given to sinking Spanish prisoners alive), the Reign of Terror, the heroes of the Mutiny blowing hundreds of Indians from guns, or Cromwell's soldiers slashing Irishwomen's faces with razors, become morally neutral or even meritorious when it is felt that they were done in the 'right' cause. If one looks back over the past quarter of a century, one finds that there was hardly a single year when atrocity stories were not being reported from some part of the world: and yet in not one single case were these atrocities – in Spain, Russia, China, Hungary, Mexico, Amritsar, Smyrna – believed in and disapproved of by the English intelligentsia as a whole. Whether such deeds were reprehensible, or even whether they happened, was always decided according to political predilection.

The nationalist not only does not disapprove of atrocities committed by his own side, but he has a remarkable capacity for not even hearing about them. For quite six years the English admirers of Hitler contrived not to learn of the existence of Dachau and Buchenwald. And those who are loudest in denouncing the German concentration camps are often

5. The *News Chronicle* advised its readers to visit the news film at which the entire execution could be witnessed, with close-ups. The *Star* published with seeming approval photographs of nearly naked female collaborationists being baited by the Paris mob. These photographs had a marked resemblance to the Nazi photographs of Jews being baited by the Berlin mob. [Author's footnote.]

quite unaware, or only very dimly aware, that there are also concentration camps in Russia. Huge events like the Ukraine famine of 1933, involving the deaths of millions of people, have actually escaped the attention of the majority of English russophiles. Many English people have heard almost nothing about the extermination of German and Polish Jews during the present war. Their own antisemitism has caused this vast crime to bounce off their consciousness. In nationalist thought there are facts which are both true and untrue, known and unknown. A known fact may be so unbearable that it is habitually pushed aside and not allowed to enter into logical processes, or on the other hand it may enter into every calculation and yet never be admitted as a fact, even in one's own mind.

Every nationalist is haunted by the belief that the past can be altered. He spends part of his time in a fantasy world in which things happen as they should – in which, for example, the Spanish Armada was a success or the Russian Revolution was crushed in 1918 – and he will transfer fragments of this world to the history books whenever possible. Much of the propagandist writing of our time amounts to plain forgery. Material facts are suppressed, dates altered, quotations removed from their context and doctored so as to change their meaning. Events which, it is felt, ought not to have happened are left unmentioned and ultimately denied.[6] In 1927 Chiang Kai-Shek boiled hundreds of Communists alive, and yet within ten years he had become one of the heroes of the Left. The re-alignment of world politics had brought him into the anti-Fascist camp, and so it was felt that the boiling of the Communists 'didn't count', or perhaps had not happened. The primary aim of propaganda is, of course, to influence contemporary opinion, but those who rewrite history do probably believe with part of their minds that they are actually thrusting facts into the past. When one considers the elaborate forgeries that have been committed in order to show that Trotsky did not play a valuable part in the Russian Civil War, it is difficult to feel that the people responsible are merely lying. More probably they feel that their own version *was* what happened in the sight of God, and that one is justified in rearranging the records accordingly.

Indifference to objective truth is encouraged by the sealing-off of one part of the world from another, which makes it harder and harder to discover what is actually happening. There can often be a genuine doubt

6. An example is the Russo-German Pact, which is being effaced as quickly as possible from public memory. A Russian corresondent informs me that mention of the Pact is already being omitted from Russian year-books which table recent political events. [Author's footnote.]

about the most enormous events. For example, it is impossible to calculate within millions, perhaps even tens of millions, the number of deaths caused by the present war. The calamities that are constantly being reported – battles, massacres, famines, revolutions – tend to inspire in the average person a feeling of unreality. One has no way of verifying the facts, one is not even fully certain that they have happened, and one is always presented with totally different interpretations from different sources. What were the rights and wrongs of the Warsaw rising of August 1944? Is it true about the German gas ovens in Poland? Who was really to blame for the Bengal famine? Probably the truth is discoverable, but the facts will be so dishonestly set forth in almost any newspaper that the ordinary reader can be forgiven either for swallowing lies or for failing to form an opinion. The general uncertainty as to what is really happening makes it easier to cling to lunatic beliefs. Since nothing is ever quite proved or disproved, the most unmistakable fact can be impudently denied. Moreover, although endlessly brooding on power, victory, defeat, revenge, the nationalist is often somewhat uninterested in what happens in the real world. What he wants is to *feel* that his own unit is getting the better of some other unit, and he can more easily do this by scoring off an adversary than by examining the facts to see whether they support him. All nationalist controversy is at the debating-society level. It is always entirely inconclusive, since each contestant invariably believes himself to have won the victory. Some nationalists are not far from schizophrenia, living quite happily amid dreams of power and conquest which have no connexion with the physical world.

I have examined as best I can the mental habits which are common to all forms of nationalism. The next thing is to classify those forms, but obviously this cannot be done comprehensively. Nationalism is an enormous subject. The world is tormented by innumerable delusions and hatreds which cut across one another in an extremely complex way, and some of the most sinister of them have not yet even impinged on the European consciousness. In this essay I am concerned with nationalism as it occurs among the English intelligentsia. In them, much more often than in ordinary English people, it is unmixed with patriotism and can therefore be studied pure. Below are listed the varieties of nationalism now flourishing among English intellectuals, with such comments as seem to be needed. It is convenient to use three headings, Positive, Transferred and Negative, though some varieties will fit into more than one category:

Positive Nationalism

1. *Neo-Toryism.* Exemplified by such people as Lord Elton, A. P. Herbert, G. M. Young, Professor Pickthorn, by the literature of the Tory Reform Committee, and by such magazines as the *New English Review* and the *Nineteenth Century and After.* The real motive force of neo-Toryism, giving it its nationalistic character and differentiating it from ordinary Conservatism, is the desire not to recognize that British power and influence have declined. Even those who are realistic enough to see that Britain's military position is not what it was, tend to claim that 'English ideas' (usually left undefined) must dominate the world. All neo-Tories are anti-Russian, but sometimes the main emphasis is anti-American. The significant thing is that this school of thought seem to be gaining ground among youngish intellectual, sometimes ex-Communists, who have passed through the usual process of disillusionment and become disillusioned with that. The anglophobe who suddenly becomes violently pro-British is a fairly common figure. Writers who illustrate this tendency are F. A. Voigt, Malcolm Muggeridge, Evelyn Waugh, Hugh Kingsmill, and a psychologically similar development can be observed in T. S. Eliot, Wyndham Lewis and various of their followers.

2. *Celtic Nationalism.* Welsh, Irish, and Scottish nationalism have points of difference but are alike in their anti-English orientation. Members of all three movements have opposed the war while continuing to describe themselves as pro-Russian, and the lunatic fringe has even contrived to be simultaneously pro-Russian and pro-Nazi. But Celtic nationalism is not the same thing as anglophobia. Its motive force is a belief in the past and future greatness of the Celtic peoples, and it has a strong tinge of racialism. The Celt is supposed to be spiritually superior to the Saxon – simpler, more creative, less vulgar, less snobbish, etc. – but the usual power hunger is there under the surface. One sympton of it is the delusion that Eire, Scotland or even Wales could preserve its independence unaided and owes nothing to British protection. Among writers, good examples of this school of thought are Hugh MacDiarmid and Sean O'Casey. No modern Irish writer, even of the stature of Yeats or Joyce, is completely free from traces of nationalism.

3. *Zionism.* This has the usual characteristics of a nationalist movement, but the American variant of it seems to be more violent and malignant than the British. I classify it under Direct and not Transferred nationalism

because it flourishes almost exclusively among the Jews themselves. In England, for several rather incongruous reasons, the intelligentsia are mostly pro-Jew on the Palestine issue, but they do not feel strongly about it. All English people of goodwill are also pro-Jew in the sense of disapproving of Nazi persecution. But any actual nationalistic loyalty, or belief in the innate superiority of Jews, is hardly to be found among Gentiles.

Transferred Nationalism

1. *Communism*

2. *Political Catholicism*

3. *Colour Feeling.* The old-style contemptuous attitude towards 'natives' has been much weakened in England, and various pseudo-scientific theories emphasizing the superiority of the white race have been abandoned.[7] Among the intelligentsia, colour feeling only occurs in the transposed form, that is, as a belief in the innate superiority of the coloured races. This is now increasingly common among English intellectuals, probably resulting more often from masochism and sexual frustration than from contact with the Oriental and Negro nationalist movements. Even among those who do not feel strongly on the colour question, snobbery and imitation have a powerful influence. Almost any English intellectual would be scandalized by the claim that the white races are superior to the coloured, whereas the opposite claim would seem to him unexceptionable even if he disagreed with it. Nationalistic attachment to the coloured races is usually mixed up with the belief that their sex lives are superior, and there is a large underground mythology about the sexual prowess of Negroes.

4. *Class Feeling.* Among upper-class and middle-class intellectuals, only

7. A good example is the sunstroke superstition. Until recently it was believed that the white races were much more liable to sunstroke than the coloured, and that a white man could not safely walk about in tropical sunshine without a pith helmet. There was no evidence whatever for this theory, but it served the purpose of accentuating the difference between 'natives' and Europeans. During the present war the theory has been quietly dropped and whole armies manoeuvre in the tropics without pith helmets. So long as the sunstroke superstition survived, English doctors in India appear to have believed in it as firmly as laymen. [Author's footnote.]

in the transposed form – i.e. as a belief in the superiority of the proletariat. Here again, inside the intelligentsia, the pressure of public opinion is overwhelming. Nationalistic loyalty towards the proletariat, and most vicious theoretical hatred of the bourgeoisie, can and often do co-exist with ordinary snobbishness in everyday life.

5. *Pacifism.* The majority of pacifists either belong to obscure religious sects or are simply humanitarians who object to taking life and prefer not to follow their thoughts beyond that point. But there is a minority of intellectual pacifists whose real though unadmitted motive appears to be hatred of western democracy and admiration for totalitarianism. Pacifist propaganda usually boils down to saying that one side is as bad as the other, but if one looks closely at the writings of the younger intellectual pacifists, one finds that they do not by any means express impartial disapproval but are directed almost entirely against Britain and the United States. Moreoever they do not as a rule condemn violence as such, but only violence used in defence of the western countries. The Russians, unlike the British, are not blamed for defending themselves by warlike means, and indeed all pacifist propaganda of this type avoids mention of Russia or China. It is not claimed, again, that the Indians should abjure violence in their struggle against the British. Pacifist literature abounds with equivocal remarks which, if they mean anything, appear to mean that statesmen of the type of Hitler are preferable to those of the type of Churchill, and that violence is perhaps excusable if it is violent enough. After the fall of France, the French pacifists, faced by a real choice which their English colleagues have not had to make, mostly went over to the Nazis, and in England there appears to have been some small overlap of membership between the Peace Pledge Union and the Blackshirts. Pacifist writers have written in praise of Carlyle, one of the intellectual fathers of Fascism. All in all it is difficult not to feel that pacifism, as it appears among a section of the intelligentsia, is secretly inspired by an admiration for power and successful cruelty. The mistake was made of pinning this emotion to Hitler, but it could easily be retransferred.

Negative Nationalism

1. *Anglophobia.* Within the intelligentsia, a derisive and mildly hostile attitude towards Britain is more or less compulsory, but it is an unfaked emotion in many cases. During the war it was manifested in the defeatism

of the intelligentsia, which persisted long after it had become clear that the Axis powers could not win. Many people were undisguisedly pleased when Singapore fell or when the British were driven out of Greece, and there was a remarkable unwillingness to believe in good news, e.g. el Alamein, or the number of German planes shot down in the Battle of Britain. English left-wing intellectuals did not, of course, actually want the Germans or Japanese to win the war, but many of them could not help getting a certain kick out of seeing their own country humiliated, and wanted to feel that the final victory would be due to Russia, or perhaps America, and not to Britain. In foreign politics many intellectuals follow the principle that any faction backed by Britain must be in the wrong. As a result, 'enlightened' opinion is quite largely a mirror-image of Conservative policy. Anglophobia is always liable to reversal, hence that fairly common spectacle, the pacifist of one war who is a bellicist in the next.

2. *Antisemitism.* There is little evidence about this at present, because the Nazi persecutions have made it necessary for any thinking person to side with the Jews against their oppressors. Anyone educated enough to have heard the word 'antisemitism' claims as a matter of course to be free of it, and anti-Jewish remarks are carefully eliminated from all classes of literature. Actually, antisemitism appears to be widespread, even among intellectuals, and the general conspiracy of silence probably helps to exacerbate it. People of Left opinions are not immune to it, and their attitude is sometimes affected by the fact that Trotskyists and Anarchists tend to be Jews. But antisemitism comes more naturally to people of Conservative tendency, who suspect the Jews of weakening national morale and diluting the national culture. Neo-Tories and political Catholics are always liable to succumb to antisemitism, at least intermittently.

3. *Trotskyism.* The word is used so loosely as to include Anarchists, democratic Socialists and even Liberals. I use it here to mean a doctrinaire Marxist whose main motive is hostility to the Stalin régime. Trotskyism can be better studied in obscure pamphlets or in papers like the *Socialist Appeal* than in the works of Trotsky himself, who was by no means a man of one idea. Although in some places, for instance in the United States, Trotskyism is able to attract a fairly large number of adherents and develop into an organized movement with a petty fuehrer of its own, its inspiration is essentially negative. The Trotskyist is *against* Stalin just as

the Communist is *for* him, and, like the majority of Communists, he wants not so much to alter the external world as to feel that the battle for prestige is going in his own favour. In each case there is the same obsessive fixation on a single subject, the same inability to form a genuinely rational opinion based on probabilities. The fact that Trotskyists are everywhere a persecuted minority, and that the accusation usually made against them, i.e. of collaborating with the Fascists, is absolutely false, creates an impression that Trotskyism is intellectually and morally superior to communism; but it is doubtful whether there is much difference. The most typical Trotskyists, in any case, are ex-Communists, and no one arrives at Trotskyism except via one of the left-wing movements. No Communist, unless tethered to his party by years of habit, is secure against a sudden lapse into Trotskyism. The opposite process does not seem to happen equally often, though there is no clear reason why it should not.

In the classification I have attempted above, it will seem that I have often exaggerated, oversimplified, made unwarranted assumptions and have left out of account the existence of ordinarily decent motives. This was inevitable, because in this essay I am trying to isolate and identify tendencies which exist in all our minds and pervert our thinking, without necessarily occurring in a pure state or operating continuously. It is important at this point to correct the over-simplified picture which I have been obliged to make. To begin with, one has no right to assume that *everyone*, or even every intellectual, is infected by nationalism. Secondly, nationalism can be intermittent and limited. An intelligent man may half-succumb to a belief which attracts him but which he knows to be absurd, and he may keep it out of his mind for long periods, only reverting to it in moments of anger or sentimentality, or when he is certain that no important issue is involved. Thirdly, a nationalistic creed may be adopted in good faith from non-nationalist motives. Fourthly, several kinds of nationalism, even kinds that cancel out, can coexist in the same person.

All the way through I have said 'the nationalist does this' or 'the nationalist does that', using for purposes of illustration the extreme, barely sane type of nationalist who has no neutral areas in his mind and no interest in anything except the struggle for power. Actually such people are fairly common, but they are not worth powder and shot. In real life Lord Elton, D. N. Pritt, Lady Houston, Ezra Pound, Lord Vansittart, Father Coughlin and all the rest of their dreary tribe have to be fought against, but their intellectual deficiencies hardly need pointing out. Monomania is not interesting, and the fact that no nationalist of the more bigoted kind can write a book which still seems worth reading after a lapse of years has a certain deodorizing effect. But when one has admitted that nationalism has not triumphed everywhere, that there are still people whose judgements are not at the mercy of their desires, the fact does remain that the pressing problems – India, Poland, Palestine, the Spanish Civil War, the Moscow trials, the American Negroes, the Russo-German Pact or what have you – cannot be, or at least never are, discussed upon a reasonable level. The Eltons and Pritts and Coughlins, each of them simply an enormous mouth bellowing the same lie over and over again, are obviously extreme cases, but we deceive ourselves if we do not realize that we can all resemble them in unguarded moments. Let a certain note be struck, let this or that corn be trodden on – and it may be a corn whose very existence has been unsuspected hitherto – and the most fair-minded and sweet-tempered person may suddenly be transformed into a vicious partisan, anxious only to 'score' over his adversary and indifferent as to how many lies he tells or how many logical errors he commits in doing so. When Lloyd George, who was an opponent of the Boer War, announced in the House of Commons that the British communiqués, if one added them together, claimed the killing of more Boers than the whole Boer nation contained, it is recorded that Arthur Balfour rose to his feet and shouted 'Cad!' Very few people are proof against lapses of this type. The Negro snubbed by a white woman, the Englishman who hears England ignorantly criticized by an American, the Catholic apologist reminded of the Spanish Armada, will all react in much the same way. One prod to the nerve of nationalism, and the intellectual decencies can vanish, the past can be altered, and the plainest facts can be denied.

If one harbours anywhere in one's mind a nationalistic loyalty or hatred, certain facts, although in a sense known to be true, are inadmissible. Here are just a few examples. I list below five types of nationalist, and against each I append a fact which it is impossible for that type of nationalist to accept, even in his secret thoughts:

British Tory. Britain will come out of this war with reduced power and prestige.

Communist. If she had not been aided by Britain and America, Russia would have been defeated by Germany.

Irish Nationalist. Eire can only remain independent because of British protection.

Trotskyist. The Stalin régime is accepted by the Russian masses.

Pacifist. Those who 'abjure' violence can only do so because others are committing violence on their behalf.

All of these facts are grossly obvious if one's emotions do not happen to be involved: but to the kind of person named in each case they are also *intolerable*, and so they have to be denied, and false theories constructed upon their denial. I come back to the astonishing failure of military prediction in the present war. It is, I think, true to say that the intelligentsia have been more wrong about the progress of the war than the common people, and that they were more swayed by partisan feelings. The average intellectual of the Left believed, for instance, that the war was lost in 1940, that the Germans were bound to overrun Egypt in 1942, that the Japanese would never be driven out of the lands they had conquered, and that the Anglo-American bombing offensive was making no impression on Germany. He could believe these things because his hatred of the British ruling class forbade him to admit that British plans could succeed. There is no limit to the follies that can be swallowed if one is under the influence of feelings of this kind. I have heard it confidently stated, for instance, that the American troops had been brought to Europe not to fight the Germans but to crush an English revolution. One has to belong to the intelligentsia to believe things like that: no ordinary man could be such a fool. When Hitler invaded Russia, the officials of the M.O.I. issued 'as background' a warning that Russia might be expected to collapse in six weeks. On the other hand the Communists regarded every phase of the war as a Russian victory, even when the Russians were driven back almost to the Caspian Sea and had lost several million prisoners. There is no need to multiply instances. The point is that as soon as fear, hatred, jealousy and power worship are involved, the sense of reality becomes unhinged. And, as I have pointed out already, the sense of right and wrong becomes unhinged also. There is no crime, absolutely none, that cannot be condoned when 'our' side commits it. Even if one does not deny that the crime has happened, even if one knows that it is exactly the same crime as one has condemned in some other case, even if one admits in an intellectual sense that it is unjustified – still one cannot *feel* that it is wrong. Loyalty is involved, and so pity ceases to function.

The reason for the rise and spread of nationalism is far too big a question to be raised here. It is enough to say that, in the forms in which it appears among English intellectuals, it is a distorted reflection of the frightful battles actually happening in the external world, and that its worst follies have been made possible by the break-down of patriotism and religious belief. If one follows up this train of thought, one is in danger of being led into a species of Conservatism, or into political quietism. It can be plausibly argued, for instance – it is even probably true – that patriotism is an inoculation against nationalism, that monarchy is a guard against dictatorship, and that organized religion is a guard against superstition. Or again it can be argued that *no* unbiased outlook is possible, that *all* creeds and causes involve the same lies, follies and barbarities; and this is often advanced as a reason for keeping out of politics altogether. I do not accept this argument, if only because in the modern world no one describable as an intellectual *can* keep out of politics in the sense of not caring about them. I think one must engage in politics – using the word in a wide sense – and that one must have preferences: that is, one must recognize that some causes are objectively better than others, even if they are advanced by equally bad means. As for the nationalistic loves and hatreds that I have spoken of, they are part of the make-up of most of us, whether we like it or not. Whether it is possible to get rid of them I do not know, but I do believe that it is possible to struggle against them, and that this is essentially a *moral* effort. It is a question first of all of discovering what one really is, what one's own feelings really are, and then of making allowance for the inevitable bias. If you hate and fear Russia, if you are jealous of the wealth and power of America, if you despise Jews, if you have a sentiment of inferiority towards the British ruling class, you cannot get rid of those feelings simply by taking thought. But you can at least recognize that you have them, and prevent them from contaminating your mental processes. The emotional urges which are inescapable, and are perhaps even necessary to political action, should be able to exist side by side with an acceptance of reality. But this, I repeat, needs a *moral* effort, and contemporary English literature, so far as it is alive at all to the major issues of our time, shows how few of us are prepared to make it.

Written [May 1945]; *Polemic*, [No 1, October 1945]; *S.J.*; *E.Y.E.*; *C.E.*

25. Good Bad Books

Not long ago a publisher commissioned me to write an introduction for a reprint of a novel by Leonard Merrick. This publishing house, it appears, is going to reissue a long series of minor and partly-forgotten novels of the twentieth century. It is a valuable service in these bookless days, and I rather envy the person whose job it will be to scout round the threepenny boxes, hunting down copies of his boyhood favourites.

A type of book which we hardly seem to produce in these days, but which flowered with great richness in the late nineteenth and early twentieth centuries, is what Chesterton called the 'good bad book': that is, the kind of book that has no literary pretensions but which remains readable when more serious productions have perished. Obviously outstanding books in this line are *Raffles* and the Sherlock Holmes stories, which have kept their place when innumerable 'problem novels', 'human documents' and 'terrible indictments' of this or that have fallen into deserved oblivion. (Who has worn better, Conan Doyle or Meredith?) Almost in the same class as these I put R. Austin Freeman's earlier stories – 'The Singing Bone', 'The Eye of Osiris' and others – Ernest Bramah's *Max Carrados*, and, dropping the standard a bit, Guy Boothby's Tibetan thriller, *Dr Nikola*, a sort of schoolboyversion of Huc's *Travels in Tartary* which would probably make a real visit to Central Asia seem a dismal anticlimax.

But apart from thrillers, there were the minor humorous writers of the period. For example, Pett Ridge – but I admit his full-length books no longer seem readable – E. Nesbit (*The Treasure Seekers*), George Birmingham, who was good so long as he kept off politics, the pornographic Binstead ('Pitcher' of the *Pink 'Un*), and, if American books can be included, Booth Tarkington's Penrod stories. A cut above most of these was Barry Pain. Some of Pain's humorous writings are, I suppose, still in print, but to anyone who comes across it I recommend what must now be a very rare book – *The Octave of Claudius*, a brilliant exercise in the macabre. Somewhat later in time there was Peter Blundell, who wrote in the W. W. Jacobs vein about Far Eastern seaport towns, and who seems to be rather unaccountably forgotten, in spite of having been praised in print by H. G. Wells.

However, all the books I have been speaking of are frankly 'escape' literature. They form pleasant patches in one's memory, quiet corners where the mind can browse at odd moments, but they hardly pretend to have anything to do with real life. There is another kind of good bad book which is more seriously intended, and which tells us, I think, something about the nature of the novel and the reasons for its present decadence. During the last fifty years there has been a whole series of writers – some of them are still writing – whom it is quite impossible to call 'good' by any strictly literary standard, but who are natural novelists and who seem to attain sincerity partly because they are not inhibited by good taste. In this class I put Leonard Merrick himself, W. L. George, J. D. Beresford, Ernest Raymond, May Sinclair, and – at a lower level than the others but still essentially similar – A. S. M. Hutchinson.

Most of these have been prolific writers, and their output has naturally varied in quality. I am thinking in each case of one or two outstanding books: for example, Merrick's *Cynthia*, J. D. Beresford's *A Candidate for Truth*, W. L. George's *Caliban*, May Sinclair's *The Combined Maze* and Ernest Raymond's *We, the Accused*. In each of these books the author has been able to identify himself with his imagined characters, to feel with them and invite sympathy on their behalf, with a kind of abandonment that cleverer people would find it difficult to achieve. They bring out the fact that intellectual refinement can be a disadvantage to a story-teller, as it would be to a music-hall comedian.

Take, for example, Ernest Raymond's *We, the Accused* – a peculiarly sordid and convincing murder story, probably based on the Crippen case. I think it gains a great deal from the fact that the author only partly grasps the pathetic vulgarity of the people he is writing about, and therefore does not despise them. Perhaps it even – like Theordore Dreiser's *An American Tragedy* – gains something from the clumsy long-winded manner in which it is written; detail is piled on detail, with almost no attempt at selection, and in the process an effect of terrible, grinding cruelty is slowly built up. So also with *A Candidate for Truth*. Here there is not the same clumsiness, but there is the same ability to take seriously the problems of commonplace people. So also with *Cynthia* and at any rate the earlier part of *Caliban*. The greater part of what W. L. George wrote was shoddy rubbish, but in this particular book, based on the career of Northcliffe, he achieved some memorable and truthful pictures of lower-middle-class London life. Parts of this book are probably autobiographical, and one of the advantages of good bad writers is their lack of shame in writing autobiography. Exhibitionism and self-pity are the bane of the novelist, and yet if he is too frightened of them his creative gift may suffer.

The existence of good bad literature – the fact that one can be amused or excited or even moved by a book that one's intellect simply refuses to take seriously – is a reminder that art is not the same thing as cerebration. I imagine that by any test that could be devised, Carlyle would be found to be a more intelligent man than Trollope. Yet Trollope has remained readable and Carlyle has not: with all his cleverness he had not even the wit to write in plain straightforward English. In novelists, almost as much as in poets, the connexion between intelligence and creative power is hard to establish. A good novelist may be a prodigy of self-discipline like Flaubert, or he may be an intellectual sprawl like Dickens. Enough talent to set up dozens of ordinary writers has been poured into Wyndham Lewis's so-called novels, such as *Tarr* or *Snooty Baronet*. Yet it would be a very heavy labour to read one of these books right through. Some indefinable quality, a sort of literary vitamin, which exists even in a book like *If Winter Comes*, is absent from them.

Perhaps the supreme example of the 'good bad' book is *Uncle Tom's Cabin*. It is an unintentionally ludicrous book, full of preposterous melodramatic incidents; it is also deeply moving and essentially true; it is hard to say which quality outweighs the other. But *Uncle Tom's Cabin*, after all, is trying to be serious and to deal with the real world. How about the frankly escapist writers, the purveyors of thrills and 'light' humour? How about *Sherlock Holmes*, *Vice Versa*, *Dracula*, *Helen's Babies* or *King Solomon's Mines*? All of these are definitely absurd books, books which one is more inclined to laugh *at* than *with*, and which were hardly taken seriously even by their authors; yet they have survived, and will probably continue to do so. All one can say is that, while civilization remains such that one needs distraction from time to time, 'light' literature has its appointed place; also that there is such a thing as sheer skill, or native grace, which may have more survival value than erudition or intellectual power. There are music-hall songs which are better poems than three quarters of the stuff that gets into the anthologies:

> Come where the booze is cheaper,
> Come where the pots hold more,
> Come where the boss is a bit of a sport,
> Come to the pub next door!

Or again:

> Two lovely black eyes –
> Oh, what a surprise!
> Only for calling another man wrong,
> Two lovely black eyes!

I would far rather have written either of these than, say, 'The Blessed Damozel' or 'Love in the Valley'. And by the same token I would back *Uncle Tom's Cabin* to outlive the complete works of Virginia Woolf or George Moore, though I know of no strictly literary test which would show where the superiority lies.

Tribune, 2 November 1945; *S.E.*

26. The Sporting Spirit

Now that the brief visit of the Dynamo football team[1] has come to an end, it is possible to say publicly what many thinking people were saying privately before the Dynamos ever arrived. That is, that sport is an unfailing cause of ill-will, and that if such a visit as this had any effect at all on Anglo-Soviet relations, it could only be to make them slightly worse than before.

Even the newspapers have been unable to conceal the fact that at least two of the four matches played led to much bad feeling. At the Arsenal match, I am told by someone who was there, a British and a Russian player came to blows and the crowd booed the referee. The Glasgow match, someone else informs me, was simply a free-for-all from the start. And then there was the controversy, typical of our nationalistic age, about the composition of the Arsenal team. Was it really an all-England team, as claimed by the Russians, or merely a league team, as claimed by the British? And did the Dynamos end their tour abruptly in order to avoid playing an all-England team? As usual, everyone answers these questions according to his political predilections. Not quite everyone, however. I noted with interest, as an instance of the vicious passions that football provokes, that the sporting correspondent of the russophile *News Chronicle* took the anti-Russian line and maintained that Arsenal was *not* an all-

1. The Moscow Dynamos, a Russian football team, toured Britain in the autumn of 1945 playing against leading British clubs.

England team. No doubt the controversy will continue to echo for years in the footnotes of history books. Meanwhile the result of the Dynamos' tour, in so far as it has had any result, will have been to create fresh animosity on both sides.

And how could it be otherwise? I am always amazed when I hear people saying that sport creates goodwill between the nations, and that if only the common peoples of the world could meet one another at football or cricket, they would have no inclination to meet on the battlefield. Even if one didn't know from concrete examples (the 1936 Olympic Games, for instance) that international sporting contests lead to orgies of hatred, one could deduce it from general principles.

Nearly all the sports practised nowadays are competitive. You play to win, and the game has little meaning unless you do your utmost to win. On the village green, where you pick up sides and no feeling of local patriotism is involved, it is possible to play simply for the fun and exercise: but as soon as the question of prestige arises, as soon as you feel that you and some larger unit will be disgraced if you lose, the most savage combative instincts are aroused. Anyone who has played even in a school football match knows this. At the international level sport is frankly mimic warfare. But the significant thing is not the behaviour of the players but the attitude of the spectators: and, behind the spectators, of the nations who work themselves into furies over these absurd contests, and seriously believe – at any rate for short periods – that running, jumping and kicking a ball are tests of national virtue.

Even a leisurely game like cricket, demanding grace rather than strength, can cause much ill-will, as we saw in the controversy over body-line bowling and over the rough tactics of the Australian team that visited England in 1921. Football, a game in which everyone gets hurt and every nation has its own style of play which seems unfair to foreigners, is far worse. Worst of all is boxing. One of the most horrible sights in the world is a fight between white and coloured boxers before a mixed audience. But a boxing audience is always disgusting, and the behaviour of the women, in particular, is such that the army, I believe, does not allow them to attend its contests. At any rate, two or three years ago, when Home Guards and regular troops were holding a boxing tournament, I was placed on guard at the door of the hall, with orders to keep the women out.

In England, the obsession with sport is bad enough, but even fiercer passions are aroused in young countries where games playing and nationalism are both recent developments. In countries like India or

Burma, it is necessary at football matches to have strong cordons of police to keep the crowd from invading the field. In Burma, I have seen the supporters of one side break through the police and disable the goalkeeper of the opposing side at a critical moment. The first big football match that was played in Spain about fifteen years ago led to an uncontrollable riot. As soon as strong feelings of rivalry are aroused, the notion of playing the game according to the rules always vanishes. People want to see one side on top and the other side humiliated, and they forget that victory gained through cheating or through the intervention of the crowd is meaningless. Even when the spectators don't intervene physically they try to influence the game by cheering their own side and 'rattling' opposing players with boos and insults. Serious sport has nothing to do with fair play. It is bound up with hatred, jealousy, boastfulness, disregard of all rules and sadistic pleasure in witnessing violence: in other words it is war minus the shooting.

Instead of blah-blahing about the clean, healthy rivalry of the football field and the great part played by the Olympic Games in bringing the nations together, it is more useful to inquire how and why this modern cult of sport arose. Most of the games we now play are of ancient origin, but sport does not seem to have been taken very seriously between Roman times and the nineteenth century. Even in the English public schools the games cult did not start till the later part of the last century. Dr Arnold, generally regarded as the founder of the modern public school, looked on games as simply a waste of time. Then, chiefly in England and the United States, games were built up into a heavily-financed activity, capable of attracting vast crowds and rousing savage passions, and the infection spread from country to country. It is the most violently combative sports, football and boxing, that have spread the widest. There cannot be much doubt that the whole thing is bound up with the rise of nationalism – that is, with the lunatic modern habit of identifying oneself with large power units and seeing everything in terms of competitive prestige. Also, organized games are more likely to flourish in urban communities where the average human being lives a sedentary or at least a confined life, and does not get much opportunity for creative labour. In a rustic community a boy or young man works off a good deal of his surplus energy by walking, swimming, snowballing, climbing trees, riding horses, and by various sports involving cruelty to animals, such as fishing, cock-fighting and ferreting for rats. In a big town one must indulge in group activities if one wants an outlet for one's physical strength or for one's sadistic impulses. Games are taken seriously in London and New York, and they were taken seriously in Rome and Byzantium: in the Middle Ages they were played, and probably played with much physical brutality, but they were not mixed up with politics nor a cause of group hatreds.

If you wanted to add to the vast fund of ill-will existing in the world at this moment, you could hardly do it better than by a series of football matches between Jews and Arabs, Germans and Czechs, Indians and British, Russians and Poles, and Italians and Jugoslavs, each match to be watched by a mixed audience of 100,000 spectators. I do not, of course, suggest that sport is one of the main causes of international rivalry; big-scale sport is itself, I think, merely another effect of the causes that have produced nationalism. Still, you do make things worse by sending forth a team of eleven men, labelled as national champions, to do battle against some rival team, and allowing it to be felt on all sides that whichever nation is defeated will 'lose face'.

I hope, therefore, that we shan't follow up the visit of the Dynamos by sending a British team to the U.S.S.R. If we must do so, then let us send a second-rate team which is sure to be beaten and cannot be claimed to represent Britain as a whole. There are quite enough real causes of trouble already, and we need not add to them by encouraging young men to kick each other on the shins amid the roars of infuriated spectators.

Tribune, 14 December 1945; *S.E.*

27. Nonsense Poetry

In many languages, it is said, there is no nonsense poetry, and there is not a great deal of it even in English. The bulk of it is in nursery rhymes and scraps of folk poetry, some of which may not have been strictly nonsensical at the start, but have become so because their original application has been forgotten. For example, the rhyme about Margery Daw:

See-saw, Margery Daw,
Dobbin shall have a new master.
He shall have but a penny day
Because he can't go any faster.

Or the other version that I learned in Oxfordshire as a little boy:

> See-saw, Margery Daw,
> Sold her bed and lay upon straw.
> Wasn't she a silly slut
> To sell her bed and lie upon dirt?

It may be that there was once a real person called Margery Daw, and perhaps there was even a Dobbin who somehow came into the story. When Shakespeare makes Edgar in *King Lear* quote 'Pillicock sat on Pillicock hill', and similar fragments, he is uttering nonsense, but no doubt these fragments come from forgotten ballads in which they once had a meaning. The typical scrap of folk poetry which one quotes almost unconsciously is not exactly nonsense but a sort of musical comment on some recurring event, such as 'One a penny, two a penny, Hot-Cross buns', or 'Polly, put the kettle on, we'll all have tea'. Some of these seemingly frivolous rhymes actually express a deeply pessimistic view of life, the churchyard wisdom of the peasant. For instance:

> Solomon Grundy,
> Born on Monday,
> Christened on Tuesday,
> Married on Wednesday,
> Took ill on Thursday,
> Worse on Friday,
> Died on Saturday,
> Buried on Sunday,
> And that was the end of Solomon Grundy.

which is a gloomy story, but remarkably similar to yours or mine.

Until Surrealism made a deliberate raid on the unconscious, poetry that aimed at being nonsense, apart from the meaningless refrains of songs, does not seem to have been common. This gives a special position to Edward Lear, whose nonsense rhymes have just been edited by Mr R. L. Megroz,[2] who was also responsible for the Penguin edition a year or two before the war. Lear was one of the first writers to deal in pure fantasy, with imaginary countries and made-up words, without any satirical purposes. His poems are not all of them equally nonsensical; some of them get their effect by a perversion of logic, but they are all alike in that their underlying feeling is sad and not bitter. They express a kind of amiable lunacy, a natural sympathy with whatever is weak and absurd. Lear could fairly be called the originator of the limerick, though

2. *The Lear Omnibus* edited by R. L. Megroz.

verses in almost the same metrical form are to be found in earlier writers, and what is sometimes considered a weakness in his limericks – that is, the fact that the rhyme is the same in the first and last lines – is part of their charm. The very slight change increases the impression of ineffectuality, which might be spoiled if there were some striking surprise. For example:

There was a young lady of Portugal
Whose ideas were excessively nautical;
She climbed up a tree
To examine the sea,
But declared she would never leave Portugal.

It is significant that almost no limericks since Lear's have been both printable and funny enough to seem worth quoting. But he is really seen at his best in certain longer poems, such as 'The Owl and the Pussy-Cat' or the 'The Courtship of the Yonghy-Bonghy-Bò:

On the Coast of Coromandel,
Where the early pumpkins blow,
In the middle of the woods
Lived the Yonghy-Bonghy-Bò.
Two old chairs, and half a candle –
One old jug without a handle –
These were all his worldly goods:
In the middle of the woods,
These were all the wordly goods
Of the Yonghy-Bonghy-Bò
Of the Yonghy-Bonghy-Bò.

Later there appears a lady with some white Dorking hens, and an inconclusive love affair follows. Mr Megroz thinks, plausibly enough, that this may refer to some incident in Lear's own life. He never married, and it is easy to guess that there was something seriously wrong in his sex life. A psychiatrist could no doubt find all kinds of significance in his drawings and in the recurrence of certain made-up words such as 'runcible'. His health was bad, and as he was the youngest of twenty-one children in a poor family, he must have known anxiety and hardship in very early life. It is clear that he was unhappy and by nature solitary, in spite of having good friends.

Aldous Huxley, in praising Lear's fantasies as a sort of assertion of freedom, has pointed out that the 'They' of the limericks represent common sense, legality and the duller virtues generally. 'They' are the realists, the practical men, the sober citizens in bowler hats who are always anxious to stop you doing anything worth doing. For instance:

There was an Old Man of Whitehaven,
Who danced a quadrille with a raven;
But they said, 'It's absurd
To encourage this bird!'
So they smashed that Old Man of Whitehaven.

To smash somebody just for dancing a quadrille with a raven is exactly the kind of thing that 'They' would do. Herbert Read has also praised Lear, and is inclined to prefer his verse to that of Lewis Carroll, as being purer fantasy. For myself, I must say that I find Lear funniest when he is least arbitrary and when a touch of burlesque or perverted logic makes its appearance. When he gives his fancy free play, as in his imaginary names, or in things like 'Three Receipts for Domestic Cookery', he can be silly and tiresome. 'The Pobble Who Has No Toes' is haunted by the ghost of logic, and I think it is the element of sense in it that makes it funny. The Pobble, it may be remembered, went fishing in the Bristol Channel:

And all the Sailors and Admirals cried,
When they saw him nearing the further side –
'He has gone to fish, for his Aunt Jobiska's
Runcible Cat with crimson whiskers!'

The thing that is funny here is the burlesque touch, the Admirals. What is arbitary – the word 'runcible', and the cat's crimson whiskers – is merely rather embarrassing. While the Pobble was in the water some unidentified creatures came and ate his toes off, and when he got home his aunt remarked:

'It's a fact the whole world knows,
That Pobbles are happier without their toes,'

which once again is funny because it has a meaning, and one might even say a political significance. For the whole theory of authoritarian governments is summed up in the statement that Pobbles were happier without their toes. So also with the well-known limerick:

There was an Old Person of Basing,
Whose presence of mind was amazing;
He purchased a steed,
Which he rode at full speed,
And escaped from the people of Basing.

It is not quite arbitrary. The funniness is in the gentle implied criticism of the people of Basing, who once again are 'They', the respectable ones, the right-thinking, art-hating majority.

The writer closest to Lear among his contemporaries was Lewis Carroll, who, however, was less essentially fantastic – and, in my opinion, funnier. Since then, as Mr Megroz points out in his Introduction, Lear's influence has been considerable, but it is hard to believe that it has been altogether good. The silly whimsiness of present-day children's books could perhaps be partly traced back to him. At any rate, the idea of deliberately setting out to write nonsense, though it came off in Lear's case, is a doubtful one. Probably the best nonsense poetry is produced gradually and accidentally, by communities rather than by individuals. As a comic draughtsman, on the other hand, Lear's influence must have been beneficial. James Thurber, for instance, must surely owe something to Lear, directly or indirectly.

Tribune, 21 December 1945; *S.E.*

28. The Prevention of Literature

About a year ago I attended a meeting of the PEN Club, the occasion being the tercentenary of Milton's *Areopagitica* – a pamphlet, it may be remembered, in defence of freedom of the press. Milton's famous phrase about the sin of 'killing' a book was printed on the leaflets, advertising the meeting, which had been circulated beforehand.

There were four speakers on the platform. One of them delivered a speech which did deal with the freedom of the press, but only in relation to India; another said, hesitantly, and in very general terms, that liberty was a good thing; a third delivered an attack on the laws relating to obscenity in literature. The fourth devoted most of his speech to a defence of the Russian purges. Of the speeches from the body of the hall, some reverted to the question of obscenity and the laws that deal with it, others were simply eulogies of Soviet Russia. Moral liberty – the liberty to discuss sex questions frankly in print – seemed to be generally approved, but political liberty was not mentioned. Out of this concourse of several hundred people, perhaps half of whom were directly connected with the writing trade, there was not a single one who could point out that freedom of the press, if it means anything at all, means the freedom to criticize and oppose. Significantly, no speaker quoted from the pamphlet which was ostensibly being commemorated. Nor was there any mention of the various books that have been 'killed' in this country and the United States during the war. In its net effect the meeting was a demonstration in favour of censorship.[1]

There was nothing particularly surprising in this. In our age, the idea of intellectual liberty is under attack from two directions. On the one side are its theoretical enemies, the apologists of totalitarianism, and on the other its immediate, practical enemies, monopoly and bureaucracy. Any writer or journalist who wants to retain his integrity finds himself thwarted by the general drift of society rather than by active persecution. The sort of things that are working against him are the concentration of the press in the hands of a few rich men, the grip of monopoly on radio and the films, the unwillingness of the public to spend money on books, making it necessary for nearly every writer to earn part of his living by hack work, the encroachment of official bodies like the M.O.I.[2] and the British Council, which help the writer to keep alive but also waste his time and dictate his opinions, and the continuous war atmosphere of the past ten years, whose distorting effects no one has been able to escape. Everything in our age conspires to turn the writer, and every other kind of artist as well, into a minor official, working on themes handed to him from above and never telling what seems to him the whole of the truth. But in struggling against his fate he gets no help from his own side: that is, there is no large body of opinion which will assure him that he is in the right. In the past, at any rate throughout the Protestant centuries, the idea of rebellion and the idea of intellectual integrity were mixed up. A heretic – political, moral, religious, or aesthetic – was one who refused to outrage his own conscience. His outlook was summed up in the words of the Revivalist hymn:

1. It is fair to say that the PEN Club celebrations, which lasted a week or more, did not always stick at quite the same level. I happened to strike a bad day. But an examination of the speeches (printed under the title *Freedom of Expression*) shows that almost nobody in our own day is able to speak out as roundly in favour of intellectual liberty as Milton could do three hundred years ago – and this in spite of the fact that Milton was writing in a period of civil war. [Author's footnote.]

2. Ministry of Information

Dare to be a Daniel,
Dare to stand alone;
Dare to have a purpose firm,
Dare to make it known.

To bring this hymn up to date one would have to add a 'Don't' at the beginning of each line. For it is the peculiarity of our age that the rebels against the existing order, at any rate the most numerous and characteristic of them, are also rebelling against the idea of individual integrity. 'Daring to stand alone' is ideologically criminal as well as practically dangerous. The independence of the writer and the artist is eaten away by vague economic forces, and at the same time it is undermined by those who should be its defenders. It is with the second process that I am concerned here.

Freedom of thought and of the press are usually attacked by arguments which are not worth bothering about. Anyone who has experience of lecturing and debating knows them off backwards. Here I am not trying to deal with the familiar claim that freedom is an illusion, or with the claim that there is more freedom in totalitarian countries than in democratic ones, but with the much more tenable and dangerous proposition that freedom is undesirable and that intellectual honesty is a form of antisocial selfishness. Although other aspects of the question are usually in the foreground the controversy over freedom of speech and of the press is at the bottom a controversy over the desirability, or otherwise, of telling lies. What is really at issue is the right to report contemporary events truthfully, or as truthfully as is consistent with the ignorance, bias and self-deception from which every observer necessarily suffers. In saying this I may seem to be saying that straightforward 'reportage' is the only branch of literature that matters: but I will try to show later that at every literary level, and probably in every one of the arts, the same issue arises in more or less subtilized forms. Meanwhile, it is necessary to strip away the irrelevancies in which this controversy is usually wrapped up.

The enemies of intellectual liberty always try to present their case as a plea for discipline versus individualism. The issue truth-versus-untruth is as far as possible kept in the background. Although the point of emphasis may vary, the writer who refuses to sell his opinions is always branded as a mere egoist. He is accused, that is , either of wanting to shut himself up in an ivory tower, or of making an exhibitionist display of his own personality, or of resisting the inevitable current of history in an attempt to cling to unjustified privileges. The Catholic and the Communist are alike in assuming that an opponent cannot be both honest and intelligent.

Each of them tacitly claims that 'the truth' has already been revealed, and that the heretic, if he is not simply a fool, is secretly aware of 'the truth' and merely resists it out of selfish motives. In Communist literature the attack on intellectual liberty is usually masked by oratory about 'petty-bourgeois individualism', 'the illusions of nineteenth-century liberalism', etc., and backed up by words of abuse such as 'romantic' and 'sentimental', which, since they do not have any agreed meaning, are difficult to answer. In this way the controversy is manoeuvred away from its real issue. One can accept, and most enlightened people would accept, the Communist thesis that pure freedom will only exist in a classless society, and that one is more nearly free when one is working to bring such a society about. But slipped in with this is the quite unfounded claim that the Communist Party is itself aiming at the establishment of the classless society, and that in the U.S.S.R. this aim is actually on the way to being realized. If the first claim is allowed to entail the second, there is almost no assault on common sense and common decency that cannot be justified. But meanwhile, the real point has been dodged. Freedom of the intellect means the freedom to report what one has seen, heard, and felt, and not to be obliged to fabricate imaginary facts and feelings. The familiar tirades against 'escapism', 'individualism', 'romanticism' and so forth, are merely a forensic device, the aim of which is to make the perversion of history seem respectable

Fifteen years ago, when one defended the freedom of the intellect, one had to defend it against Conservatives, against Catholics, and to some extent – for they were not of great importance in England – against Fascists. Today one has to defend it against Communists and 'fellow-travellers'. One ought not to exaggerate the direct influence of the small English Communist Party, but there can be no question about the poisonous effect of the Russian *mythos* on English intellectual life. Because of it, known facts are suppressed and distorted to such an extent as to make it doubtful whether a true history of our times can ever be written. Let me give just one instance out of the hundreds that could be cited. When Germany collapsed, it was found that very large numbers of Soviet Russians – mostly, no doubt, from non-political motives – had changed sides and were fighting for the Germans. Also, a small but not negligible proportion of the Russian prisoners and Displaced Persons refused to go back to the U.S.S.R., and some of them, at least, were repatriated against their will. These facts, known to many journalists on the spot, went almost unmentioned in the British press, while at the same time russophile publicists in England continued to justify the purges and deportations of

1936–8 by claiming that the U.S.S.R., 'had no quislings'. The fog of lies and misinformation that surrounds such subjects as the Ukraine famine, the Spanish Civil War, Russian policy in Poland, and so forth, is not due entirely to conscious dishonesty, but any writer or journalist who is fully sympathetic to the U.S.S.R. – sympathetic, that is, in the way the Russians themselves would want him to be – does have to acquiesce in deliberate falsification on important issues. I have before me what must be a very rare pamphlet, written by Maxim Litvinov in 1918 and outlining the recent events in the Russian Revolution. It makes no mention of Stalin, but gives high praise to Trotsky, and also to Zinoviev, Kamenev and others. What could be the attitude of even the most intellectually scrupulous Communist towards such a pamphlet? At best, the obscurantist attitude of saying that it is an undesirable document and better suppressed. And if for some reason it were decided to issue a garbled version of the pamphlet, denigrating Trotsky and inserting references to Stalin, no Communist who remained faithful to his Party could protest. Forgeries almost as gross as this have been committed in recent years. But the significant thing is not that they happen, but that even when they are known about they provoke no reaction from the left-wing intelligentsia as a whole. The argument that to tell the truth would be 'inopportune' or would 'play into the hands of' somebody or other is felt to be unanswerable, and few people are bothered by the prospect of the lies which they condone getting out of the newspapers and into the history books.

The organized lying practised by totalitarian states is not, as is sometimes claimed, a temporary expedient of the same nature as military deception. It is something integral to totalitarianism, something that would still continue even if concentration camps and secret police forces had ceased to be necessary. Among intelligent Communists there is an underground legend to the effect that although the Russian Government is obliged now to deal in lying propaganda, frame-up trials, and so forth, it is secretly recording the true facts and will publish them at some future time. We can, I believe, be quite certain that this is not the case, because the mentality implied by such an action is that of a liberal historian who believes that the past cannot be altered and that a correct knowledge of history is valuable as a matter of course. From the totalitarian point of view history is something to be created rather than learned. A totalitarian state is in effect a theocracy, and its ruling caste, in order to keep its position, has to be thought of as infallible. But since, in practice, no one is infallible, it is frequently necessary to rearrange past events in order to show that this or that mistake was not made, or that this or that imaginary triumph actually happened. Then, again, every major change in policy demands a corresponding change of doctrine and a revaluation of prominent historical figures. This kind of thing happens everywhere, but is clearly likelier to lead to outright falsification in societies where only one opinion is permissible at any given moment. Totalitarianism demands, in fact, the continuous alteration of the past, and in the long run probably demands a disbelief in the very existence of objective truth. The friends of totalitarianism in this country tend to argue that since absolute truth is not attainable, a big lie is no worse than a little lie. It is pointed out that all historical records are biassed and inaccurate, or, on the other hand, that modern physics has proved that what seems to us the real world is an illusion, so that to believe in the evidence of one's senses is simply vulgar philistinism. A totalitarian society which succeeded in perpetuating itself would probably set us a schizophrenic system of thought, in which the laws of common sense held good in everyday life and in certain exact sciences, but could be disregarded by the politician, the historian, and the sociologist. Already there are countless people who would think it scandalous to falsify a scientific text-book, but would see nothing wrong in falsifying an historical fact. It is at the point where literature and politics cross that totalitarianism exerts is greatest pressure on the intellectual. The exact sciences are not, at this date, menaced to anything like the same extent. This partly accounts for the fact that in all countries it is easier for the scientists than for the writers to line up behind their respective governments.

To keep the matter in perspective, let me repeat what I said at the beginning of this essay; that in England the immediate enemies of truthfulness, and hence of freedom of thought, are the press lords, the film magnates, and the bureaucrats, but that on a long view the weakening of the desire for liberty among the intellectuals themselves is the most serious symptom of all. It may seem that all this time I have been talking about the effects of censorship, not on literature as a whole, but merely on one department of political journalism. Granted that Soviet Russia constitutes a sort of forbidden area in the British press, granted that issues like Poland, the Spanish Civil War, the Russo-German Pact, and so forth, are debarred from serious discussion, and that if you possess information that conflicts with the prevailing orthodoxy you are expected to distort it or to keep quiet about it – granted all this, why should literature in the wider sense be affected? Is every writer a politician, and is every book necessarily a work of straightforward 'reportage'? Even under the tightest dictatorship, cannot the individual writer remain free inside his own mind and distil or disguise his unorthodox ideas in such a way that the authorities will be too stupid to recognize them? And in any case, if the writer himself is in agreement with the prevailing orthodoxy, why should it have a cramping effect on him? Is not literature, or any of the arts, likeliest to flourish in societies in which there are no major conflicts of opinion and no sharp distinction between the artist and his audience? Does one have to assume that every writer is a rebel, or even that a writer as such is an exceptional person?

Whenever one attempts to defend intellectual liberty against the claims of totalitarianism, one meets with these arguments in one form or another. They are based on a complete misunderstanding of what literature is, and how – one should perhaps rather say why – it comes into being. They assume that a writer is either a mere entertainer or else a venal hack who can switch from one line of propaganda to another as easily as an organ-grinder changing tunes. But after all, how is it that books ever come to be written? Above a quite low level, literature is an attempt to influence the viewpoint of one's contemporaries by recording experience. And so far as freedom of expression is concerned, there is not much difference between a mere journalist and the most 'unpolitical' imaginative writer. The journalist is unfree, and is conscious of unfreedom, when he is forced to write lies or suppress what seems to him important news: the imaginative writer is unfree when he has to falsify his subjective feelings, which from his point of view are facts. He may distort and caricature reality in order to make his meaning clearer, but he cannot misrepresent the scenery of his own mind: he cannot say with any conviction that he likes what he dislikes, or believes what he disbelieves. If he is forced to do so, the only result is that his creative faculties dry up. Nor can he solve the problem by keeping away from controversial topics. There is no such thing as genuinely non-political literature, and least of all in an age like our own, when fears, hatreds, and loyalties of a directly political kind are near to the surface of everyone's consciousness. Even a single taboo can have an all-round crippling effect upon the mind, because there is always the danger that any thought which is freely followed up may lead to the forbidden thought. It follows that the atmosphere of totalitarianism is deadly to any kind of prose writer, though a poet, at any rate a lyric poet, might possible find it breathable. And in any totalitarian society that survives for more than a couple of generations, it is probable that prose literature, of the kind that has existed during the past four hundred years, must actually come to an end.

Literature has sometimes flourished under despotic régimes, but, as has often been pointed out, the despotisms of the past were not totalitarian. Their repressive apparatus was always inefficient, their ruling classes were usually either corrupt or apathetic or half-liberal in outlook, and the prevailing religious doctrines usually worked against perfectionism and the notion of human infallibility. Even so it is broadly true that prose literature has reached its highest levels in periods of democracy and free speculation. What is new in totalitarianism is that its doctrines are not only unchallengeable but also unstable. They have to be accepted on pain of damnation, but on the other hand they are always liable to be altered at a moment's notice. Consider, for example, the various attitudes, completely imcompatible with one another, which an English Communist or 'fellow-traveller' has had to adopt towards the war between Britain and Germany. For years before September 1939 he was expected to be in a continuous stew about 'the horrors of Nazism' and to twist everything he wrote into a denunciation of Hitler: after September 1939, for twenty months, he had to believe that Germany was more sinned against than sinning, and the word 'Nazi', at least so far as print went, had to drop right out of his vocabulary. Immediately after hearing the 8 o'clock news bulletin on the morning of 22 June 1941, he had to start believing once again that Nazism was the most hideous evil the world had ever seen. Now, it is easy for a politician to make such changes: for a writer the case is somewhat different. If he is to switch his allegiance at exactly the right moment, he must either tell lies about his subjective feelings, or else suppress them altogether. In either case he has destroyed his dynamo. Not only will ideas refuse to come to him but the very words he uses will seem to stiffen under his touch. Political writing in our time consists almost entirely of prefabricated phrases bolted together like the pieces of a child's Meccano set. It is the unavoidable result of self-censorship. To write in plain, vigorous language one has to think fearlessly, and if one thinks fearlessly one cannot be politically orthodox. It might be otherwise in an 'age of faith', when the prevailing orthodoxy has been long established and is not taken too seriously. In that case it would be possible, or might be possible, for large areas of one's mind to remain unaffected by what one officially believed. Even so, it is worth noticing that prose literature almost disappeared during the only age of faith that Europe has ever enjoyed. Throughout the whole of the Middle Ages there was almost no imaginative prose literature and very little in the way of historical writing: and the intellectual leaders of society expressed their most serious thoughts in a dead language which barely altered during a thousand years.

Totalitarianism, however, does not so much promise an age of faith as an age of schizophrenia. A society becomes totalitarian when its structure becomes flagrantly artificial: that is, when its ruling class has lost its function but succeeds in clinging to power by force or fraud. Such a society, no matter how long it persists, can never afford to become either tolerant or intellectually stable. It can never permit either the truthful recording of facts, or the emotional sincerity, that literary creation demands. But to be corrupted by totalitarianism one does not have to live in a totalitarian country. The mere prevalence of certain ideas can spread a kind of poison that makes one subject after another impossible for literary purposes. Wherever there is an enforced orthodoxy – or even two orthodoxies, as often happens – good writing stops. This was well illustrated by the Spanish Civil War. To many English intellectuals the war was a deeply moving experience, but not an experience about which they could write sincerely. There were only two things that you were allowed to say, and both of them were palpable lies: as a result, the war produced acres of print but almost nothing worth reading

It is not certain whether the effects of totalitarianism upon verse need be so deadly as its effects on prose. There is a whole series of converging reasons why it is somewhat easier for a poet than for a prose writer to feel at home in an authoritarian society. To begin with, bureaucrats and other 'practical' men usually despise the poet too deeply to be much interested in what he is saying. Secondly, what the poet is saying – that is, what his poem 'means' if translated into prose – is relatively unimportant even to himself. The thought contained in a poem is always simple, and is no more the primary purpose of the poem than the anecdote is the primary purpose of a picture. A poem is an arrangement of sounds and associations, as a painting is an arrangement of brush-marks. For short snatches, indeed, as in the refrain of a song, poetry can even dispense with meaning altogether. It is therefore fairly easy for a poet to keep away from dangerous subjects and avoid uttering heresies: and even when he does utter them, they may escape notice. But above all, good verse, unlike good prose, is not necessarily an individual product. Certain kinds of poems, such as ballads, or, on the other hand, very artifical verse forms, can be composed co-operatively by groups of people. Whether the ancient English and Scottish ballads were originally produced by individuals, or by the people at large, is disputed, but at any rate they are non-individual in the sense that they constantly change in passing from mouth to mouth. Even in print no two versions of a ballad are ever quite the same. Many primitive peoples compose verse communally. Someone begins to improvise, probably accompanying himself on a musical instrument, somebody else chips in with a line or a rhyme when the first singer breaks down, and so the process continues until there exists a whole song or ballad which has no identifiable author.

In prose, this kind of intimate collaboration is quite impossible. Serious prose, in any case, has to be composed in solitude, whereas the excitement of being part of a group is actually an aid to certain kinds of versification. Verse – and perhaps good verse of its kind, though it would not be the highest kind – might survive under even the most inquisitorial régime. Even in a society where liberty and individuality had been extinguished, there would still be need either for patriotic songs and heroic ballads celebrating vitories, or for elaborate exercises in flattery: and these are the kinds of poem that can be written to order, or composed communally, without necessarily lacking artistic value. Prose is a different matter, since the prose writer cannot narrow the range of his thoughts without killing his inventiveness. But the history of totalitarian societies, or of groups of people who have adopted the totalitarian outlook, suggests that loss of liberty is inimical to all forms of literature. German literature almost disappeared during the Hitler régime, and the case was not much better in Italy. Russian literature, so far as one can judge by translations, has deteriorated markedly since the early days of the Revolution, though some of the verse appears to be better than the prose. Few if any Russian novels that it is possible to take seriously have been translated for about fifteen years. In western Europe and America large sections of the literary intelligentsia have either passed through the Communist Party or been warmly sympathetic to it, but this whole leftward movement has produced extraordinarily few books worth reading. Orthodox Catholicism, again, seems to have a crushing effect upon certain literary forms, especially the novel. During a period of three hundred years, how many people have been at once good novelists and good Catholics? The fact is that certain themes cannot be celebrated in words, and tyranny is one of them. No one ever wrote a good book in praise of the Inquisition. Poetry might survive, in a totalitarian age, and certain arts or half-arts, such as architecture, might even find tyranny beneficial, but the prose writer would have no choice between silence and death. Prose literature as we know it is the product of rationalism, of the Protestant centuries, of the autonomous individual. And the destruction of intellectual liberty cripples the journalist, the sociological writer, the historian, the novelist, the critic and the poet, in that order. In the future it is possible that a new kind of literature, not involving individual feeling or truthful observation, may arise, but no such thing is at present imaginable. It seems much likelier that if the liberal culture that we have lived in since the Renaissance actually comes to an end, the literary art will perish with it.

Of course, print will continue to be used, and it is interesting to speculate what kinds of reading matter would survive in a rigidly totalitarian society. Newspapers will presumably continue until television technique reaches a higher level, but apart from newspapers it is doubtful even now whether the great mass of people in the industrialized countries feel the need for any kind of literature. They are unwilling, at any rate, to spend anywhere near as much on reading matter as they spend on several other recreations. Probably novels and stories will be completely superseded by film and radio productions. Or perhaps some kind of low-grade sensational fiction will survive, produced by a sort of conveyor-belt process that reduces human initiative to the minimum.

It would probably not be beyond human ingenuity to write books by machinery. But a sort of mechanizing process can already be seen at work in the film and radio, in publicity and propaganda, and in the lower reaches of journalism. The Disney films, for instance, are produced by what is essentially a factory process, the work being done partly mechanically and partly by teams of artists who have to subordinate their individual style. Radio features are commonly written by tired hacks to whom the subject and the manner of treatment are dictated beforehand: even so, what they write is merely a kind of raw material to be chopped into shape by producers and censors. So also with the innumerable books and pamphlets commissioned by government departments. Even more machine-like is the production of short stories, serials and poems for the very cheap magazines. Papers such as the *Writer* abound with advertisements of Literary Schools, all of them offering you ready-made plots at a few shillings a time. Some, together with the plot, supply the opening and closing sentences of each chapter. Others furnish you with a sort of algebraical formula by the use of which you can construct your plots for yourself. Other offer packs of cards marked with characters and situations, which have only to be shuffled and dealt in order to produce ingenious stories automatically. It is probably in some such way that the literature of a totalitarian society would be produced, if literature were still felt to be necessary. Imagination – even consciousness, so far as possible – would be eliminated from the process of writing. Books would be planned in their broad lines by bureaucrats, and would pass through so many hands that when finished they would be no more an individual product than a Ford car at the end of the assembly line. It goes without saying that anything so produced would be rubbish; but anything that was not rubbish would endanger the structure of the State. As for the surviving literature of the past, it would have to be suppressed or at least elaborately rewritten.

Meanwhile totalitarianism has not fully triumphed everywhere. Our own society is still, broadly speaking, liberal. To exercise your right of free speech you have to fight against economic pressure and against strong sections of public opinion, but not, as yet, against a secret police force. You can say or print almost anything so long as you are willing to do it in a hole-and-corner way. But what is sinister, as I said at the beginning of this essay, is that the conscious enemies of liberty are those to whom liberty ought to mean most. The big public do not care about the matter one way or the other. They are not in favour of persecuting the heretic, and they will not exert themselves to defend him. They are at once too sane and too stupid to acquire the totalitarian outlook. The direct, conscious attack on intellectual decency comes from the intellectuals themselves.

It is possible that the russophile intelligentsia, if they had not succumbed to that particular myth, would have succumbed to another of much the same kind. But at any rate the Russian myth is there, and the corruption it causes stinks. When one sees highly educated men looking on indifferently at oppression and persecution, one wonders which to despise more, their cynicism or their shortsightedness. Many scientists, for example, are the uncritical admirers of the U.S.S.R. They appear to think that the destruction of liberty is of no importance so long as their own line of work is for the moment unaffected. The U.S.S.R. is a large, rapidly developing country which has acute need of scientific workers and, consequently, treats them generously. Provided that they steer clear of dangerous subjects such as psychology, scientists are privileged persons. Writers, on the other hand, are viciously persecuted. It is true that literary prostitutes like Ilya Ehrenburg or Alexei Tolstoy are paid huge sums of money, but the only thing which is of any value to the writer as such – his freedom of expression – is taken away from him. Some, at least, of the English scientists who speak so enthusiastically of the opportunities enjoyed by scientists in Russia are capable of understanding this. But their reflection appears to be: 'Writers are persecuted in Russia. So what? I am not a writer.' They do not see that any attack on intellectual liberty, and on the concept of objective truth, threatens in the long run every department of thought.

For the moment the totalitarian state tolerates the scientist because it needs him. Even in Nazi Germany, scientists, other than Jews, were relatively well treated, and the German scientific community, as a whole, offered no resistance to Hitler. At this stage of history, even the most autocratic ruler is forced to take account of physical reality, partly because of the lingering-on of liberal habits of thought, partly because of the need to prepare for war. So long as physical reality cannot be altogether ignored, so long as two and two have to make four when you are, for example, drawing the blue-print of an aeroplane, the scientist has his function, and can even be allowed a measure of liberty. His awakening will come later, when the totalitarian state is firmly established. Meanwhile, if he wants to safeguard the integrity of science, it is his job to develop some kind of solidarity with his literary colleagues and not regard it as a matter of indifference when writers are silenced or driven to suicide, and newspapers systematically falsified.

But however it may be with the physical sciences, or with music, painting, and architecture, it is – as I have tried to show – certain that literature is doomed if liberty of thought perishes. Not only is it doomed in any country which retains a totalitarian structure; but any writer who adopts the totalitarian outlook, who finds excuses for persecution and the falsification of reality, thereby destroys himself as a writer. There is no way out of this. No tirades against 'individualism' and 'the ivory tower', no pious platitudes to the effect that 'true individuality is only attained through identification with the community', can get over the fact that a bought mind is a spoiled mind. Unless spontaneity enters at some point or another, literary creation is impossible, and language itself becomes ossified. At some time in the future, if the human mind becomes something totally different from what it now is, we may learn to separate literary creation from intellectual honesty. At present we know only that the imagination, like certain wild animals, will not breed in captivity. Any writer or journalist who denies that fact – and nearly all the current praise of the Soviet Union contains or implies such a denial – is, in effect, demanding his own destruction.

Polemic, No. 2, January 1946; *S.E.*; *O.R.*; *C.E.*

29. Books v. Cigarettes

A couple of years ago a friend of mine, a newspaper editor, was fire-watching with some factory workers. They fell to talking about his newspaper, which most of them read and approved of, but when he asked them what they thought of the literary section, the answer he got was: 'You don't suppose we read that stuff, do you? Why, half the time you're talking about books that cost twelve and sixpence! Chaps like us couldn't spend twelve and sixpence on a book.' These, he said, were men who thought nothing of spending several pounds on a day trip to Blackpool.

This idea that the buying, or even the reading , of books is an expensive hobby and beyond the reach of the average person is so widespread that it deserves some detailed examination. Exactly what reading costs, reckoned in terms of pence per hour, is difficult to estimate, but I have made a start by inventorying my own books and adding up their total price. After allowing for various other expenses, I can make a fairly good guess at my expenditure over the last fifteen years.

The books that I have counted and priced are the ones I have here, in my flat. I have about an equal number stored in another place, so that I shall double the final figure in order to arrive at the complete amount. I have counted oddments such as proof copies, defaced volumes, cheap paper-covered editions, pamphlets, or magazines, unless bound up into book form. Nor have I counted the kind of junky books – old school text-books and so forth – that accumulate in the bottoms of cupboards. I have counted only those books which I have acquired voluntarily, or else would have acquired voluntarily, and which I intend to keep. In this category I find that I have 442 books, acquired in the following ways:

Bought (mostly second-hand)	251
Given to me or bought with book tokens	33
Review copies and complimentary copies	143
Borrowed and not returned	10
Temporarily on loan	5
TOTAL	442

Now as to the method of pricing. Those books that I have bought I have listed at their full price, as closely as I can determine it. I have also listed at their full price the books that have been given to me, and those that I have temporarily borrowed, or borrowed and kept. This is because book-giving, book-borrowing and book-stealing more or less even out. I possess books that do not strictly speaking belong to me, but many other people also have books of mine: so that the books I have not paid for can be taken as balancing others which I have paid for but no longer possess. On the other hand I have listed the review and complimentary copies at half-price. That is about what I would have paid for them second-hand, and they are mostly books that I would only have bought second-hand, if at all. For the prices I have sometimes had to rely on guesswork, but my figures will not be far out. The costs were as follows:

	£	s.	d.
Bought	36	9	0
Gifts	10	10	0
Review copies, etc.	25	11	9
	£	s.	d.
Borrowed and not returned	4	16	9
On Loan	3	10	0
Shelves	2	0	0
TOTAL	82	17	6

Adding the other batch of books that I have elsewhere, it seems that I possess altogether nearly 900 books, at a cost of £165 15s. This is the accumulation of about fifteen years – actually more, since some of these books date from my childhood: but call it fifteen years. This works out at £11 1s. a year, but there are other charges that must be added in order to estimate my full reading expenses. The biggest will be for newspapers and periodicals, and for this I think £8 a year would be a reasonable figure. Eight pounds a year covers the cost of two daily papers, one evening paper, two Sunday papers, one weekly review and one or two monthly magazines. This brings the figure up to £19. 1s., but to arrive at the grand total one has to make a guess. Obviously one often spends money on books without afterwards having anything to show for it. There are library subscriptions, and there are also the books, chiefly Penguins and other cheap editions, which one buys and then loses or throws away. However, on the basis of my other figures, it looks as though £6 a year would be quite enough to add for expenditure of this kind. So my total reading expenses over the past fifteen years have been in the neighbourhood of £25 a year.

Twenty-five pounds a year sounds quite a lot until you begin to measure it against other kinds of expenditure. It is nearly 9s. 9d. a week, and at present 9s. 9d. is the equivalent of about 83 cigarettes (Players): even before the war it would have bought you less than 200 cigarettes. With prices as they now are, I am spending far more on tobacco than I do on books. I smoke six ounces a week, at half a crown an ounce, making nearly £40 a year. Even before the war when the same tobacco cost 8d. an ounce, I was spending over £10 a year on it: and if I also averaged a pint of beer a day, at 6d., these two items together will have cost me close on £20 a year. This was probably not much above the national average. In 1938 the people of this country spent nearly £10 per head per annum on alcohol and tobacco: however, 20 per cent of the population were children under fifteen and another 40 per cent were women, so that the average smoker and drinker must have been spending much more than £10. In 1944, the annual expenditure per head on these items was no less than £23. Allow for the women and children as before, and £40 is a reasonable individual figure. Forty pounds a year would just about pay for a packet of Woodbines every day and half a pint of mild six days a week – not a magnificent allowance. Of course, all prices are now inflated, including the price of books: still, it looks as though the cost of reading, even if you buy books instead of borrowing them and take in a fairly large number of periodicals, does not amount to more than the combined cost of smoking and drinking.

It is difficult to establish any relationship between the price of books and the value one gets out of them. 'Books' includes novels, poetry, text-books, works of reference, sociological treatises and much else, and length and price do not correspond to one another, especially if one habitually buys books second-hand. You may spend ten shillings on a poem of 500 lines, and you may spend sixpence on a dictionary which you consult at odd moments over a period of twenty years. There are books that one reads over and over again, books that become part of the furniture of one's mind and alter one's whole attitude to life, books that one dips into but never reads through, books that one reads at a single sitting and forgets a week later: and the cost in terms of money, may be the same in each case. But if one regards reading simply as a recreation, like going to the pictures, then it is possible to make a rough estimate of what it costs. If you read nothing but novels and 'light' literature, and bought every book that you read, you would be spending – allowing eight shillings as the price of a book, and four hours as the time spent in reading it – two shillings an hour. This is about what it costs to sit in one of the more expensive seats in the cinema. If you concentrated on more serious books, and still bought everything that you read, your expenses would be about the same. The books would cost more but they would take longer to read. In either case you would still possess the books after you had read them, and they would be saleable at about a third of their purchase price. If you bought only second-hand books, your reading expenses would, of course, be much less: perhaps sixpence an hour would be a fair estimate. And on the other hand if you don't buy books, but merely borrow them from the lending library, reading costs you round about a halfpenny an hour: if you borrow them from the public library, it costs you next door to nothing.

I have said enough to show that reading is one of the cheaper recreations: after listening to the radio probably *the* cheapest. Meanwhile, what is the actual amount that the British public spends on books? I cannot discover any figures, though no doubt they exist. But I do know that before the war this country was publishing annually about 15,000 books, which included reprints and school books. If as many as 10,000 copies of each book were sold – and even allowing for the school books, this is probably a high estimate – the average person was only buying, directly or indirectly, about three books a year. These three books taken together might cost £1, or probably less.

These figures are guesswork, and I should be interested if someone would correct them for me. But if my estimate is anywhere near right, it is not a proud record for a country which is nearly 100 per cent literate and where the ordinary man spends more on cigarettes than an Indian peasant has for his whole livelihood. And if our book consumption remains as low as it has been, at least let us admit that it is because reading is a less exciting pastime than going to the dogs, the pictures or the pub, and not because books, whether bought or borrowed, are too expensive

Tribune, 8 February 1946; *S.E.*

30. Decline of the English Murder

It is Sunday afternoon, preferably before the war. The wife is already asleep in the armchair, and the children have been sent out for a nice long walk. You put your feet up on the sofa, settle your spectacles on your nose, and open the *News of the World*. Roast beef and Yorkshire, or roast pork and apple sauce, followed up by suet pudding and driven home, as it were, by a cup of mahogany-brown tea, have put you in just the right mood. Your pipe is drawing sweetly, the sofa cushions are soft underneath you, the fire is well alight, the air is warm and stagnant. In these blissful circumstances, what is it that you want to read about?

Naturally, about a murder. But what kind of murder? If one examines the murders which have given the greatest amount of pleasure to the British public, the murders whose story is known in its general outline to almost everyone and which have been made into novels and rehashed over and over again by the Sunday papers, one finds a fairly strong family resemblance running through the greater number of them. Our great period in murder, our Elizabethan period, so to speak, seems to have been between roughly 1850 and 1925, and the murderers whose reputation has stood the test of time are the following: Dr Palmer of Rugeley, Jack the Ripper, Neill Cream, Mrs Maybrick, Dr Crippen, Seddon, Joseph Smith, Armstrong, and Bywaters and Thompson. In addition, in 1919 or thereabouts, there was another very celebrated case which fits into the general pattern but which I had better not mention by name, because the accused man was acquitted.

Of the above-mentioned nine cases, at least four have had successful novels based on them, one has been made into a popular melodrama, and the amount of literature surrounding them, in the form of newspaper write-ups, criminological treatises and reminiscences by lawyers and police officers, would make a considerable library. It is difficult to believe that any recent English crime will be remembered so long and so intimately, and not only because the violence of external events has made murder seem unimportant, but because the prevalent type of crime seems to be changing. The principal *cause célèbre* of the war years was the so-called Cleft Chin Murder, which has now been written up in a popular booklet;[1] the verbatim account of the trial was published some time last

1. *The Cleft Chin Murder* by R. Alwyn Raymond.

year by Messrs Jarrolds with an introduction by Mr. Bechhofer-Roberts. Before returning to this pitiful and sordid case, which is only interesting from a sociological and perhaps a legal point of view, let me try to define what it is that the readers of Sunday papers mean when they say fretfully that 'you never seem to get a good murder nowadays'.

In considering the nine murders I named above, one can start by excluding the Jack the Ripper case, which is in a class by itself. Of the other eight, six were poisoning cases, and eight of the ten criminals belonged to the middle class. In one way or another, sex was a powerful motive in all but two cases, and in at least four cases respectability – the desire to gain a secure position in life, or not to forfeit one's social position by some scandal such as a divorce – was one of the main reasons for committing murder. In more than half the cases, the object was to get hold of a certain known sum of money such as a legacy or an insurance policy, but the amount involved was nearly always small. In most of the cases the crime only came to light slowly, as the result of careful investigation which started off with the suspicions of neighbours or relatives; and in nearly every case there was some dramatic coincidence, in which the finger of Providence could be clearly seen, or one of those episodes that no novelist would dare to make up, such as Crippen's flight across the Atlantic with his mistress dressed as a boy, or Joseph Smith playing 'Nearer, my God, to Thee' on the harmonium while one of his wives was drowning in the next room. The background of all these crimes, except Neill Cream's, was essentially domestic; of twelve victims, seven were either wife or husband of the murderer.

With all this in mind one can construct what would be, from a *News of the World* reader's point of view, the 'perfect' murder. The murderer should be a little man of the professional class – a dentist or a solicitor, say – living an intensely respectable life somewhere in the suburbs, and preferably in a semi-detached house, which will allow the neighbours to hear suspicious sounds through the wall. He should be either chairman of the local Conservative Party branch, or a leading Nonconformist and strong Temperance advocate. He should go astray through cherishing a guilty passion for his secretary or the wife of a rival professional man, and should only bring himself to the point of murder after long and terrible wrestles with his conscience. Having decided on murder, he should plan it all with the utmost cunning, and only slip up over some tiny, unforeseeable detail. The means chosen should, of course, be poison. In the last analysis he should commit murder because this seems to him less disgraceful, and less damaging to his career, than being detected in adultery. With this kind of background, a crime can have dramatic and even tragic qualities which make it memorable and excite pity for both victim and murderer. Most of the crimes mentioned above have a touch of this atmosphere, and in three cases, including the one I referred to but did not name, the story approximates to the one I have outlined.

Now compare the Cleft Chin Murder. There is no depth of feeling in it. It was almost chance that the two people concerned committed that particular murder, and it was only by good luck that they did not commit several others. The background was not domesticity, but the anonymous life of the dance halls and the false values of the American film. The two culprits were an eighteen-year-old ex-waitress named Elizabeth Jones, and an American army deserter, posing as an officer, named Karl Hulten. They were only together for six days, and it seems doubtful whether, until they were arrested, they even learned one another's true names. They met casually in a teashop, and that night went out for a ride in a stolen army truck. Jones described herself as a strip-tease artist, which was not strictly true (she had given one unsuccessful performance in this line), and declared that she wanted to do something dangerous, 'like being a gun-moll'. Hulten described himself as a big-time Chicago gangster, which was also untrue. They met a girl bicycling along the road, and to show how tough he was Hulten ran over her with his truck, after which the pair robbed her of the few shillings that were on her. On another occasion they knocked out a girl to whom they had offered a lift, took her coat and handbag and threw her into a river. Finally, in the most wanton way, they murdered a taxi-driver who happened to have £8 in his pocket. Soon afterwards they parted. Hulten was caught because he had foolishly kept the dead man's car, and Jones made spontaneous confessions to the police. In court each prisoner incriminated the other. In between crimes, both of them seem to have behaved with the utmost callousness: they spent the dead taxi-driver's £8 at the dog races.

Judging from her letters, the girl's case has a certain amount of psychological interest, but this murder probably captured the headlines because it provided distraction amid the doodle-bugs and the anxieties of the Battle of France. Jones and Hulten committed their murder to the tune of V1,[2] and were convicted to the tune of V2.[3] There was also considerable excitement because – as has become usual in England – the man was sentenced to death and the girl to imprisonment.

2. The V1, an unmanned aircraft developed by the Germans and used by them to bomb London from June 1944: they were nicknamed 'doodlebugs' by the Londoners.

3. The V2, a rocket bomb used by the Germans on London from September 1944.

According to Mr Raymond, the reprieving of Jones caused widespread indignation and streams of telegrams to the Home Secretary: in her native town, 'She should hang' was chalked on the walls beside pictures of a figure dangling from a gallows. Considering that only ten women have been hanged in Britain in this century, and that the practice has gone out largely because of popular feeling against it, it is difficult not to feel that this clamour to hang an eighteen-year-old girl was due partly to the brutalizing effects of war. Indeed, the whole meaningless story, with its atmosphere of dance-halls, movie palaces, cheap perfume, false names and stolen cars, belongs essentially to a war period.

Perhaps it is significant that the most talked-of English murder of recent years should have been committed by an American and an English girl who had become partly americanized. But it is difficult to believe that this case will be so long remembered as the old domestic poisoning dramas, product of a stable society where the all-prevailing hypocrisy did at least ensure that crimes as serious as murder should have strong emotions behind them

Tribune, 15 February 1946; *S.E.*; *O.R.*

31. Politics and the English Language

Most people who bother with the matter at all would admit that the English language is in a bad way, but it is generally assumed that we cannot by conscious action do anything about it. Our civilization is decadent, and our language – so the arguments runs – must inevitably share in the general collapse. It follows that any struggle against the abuse of language is a sentimental archaism, like preferring candles to electric light or hansom cabs to aeroplanes. Underneath this lies the half-conscious belief that language is a natural growth and not an instrument which we shape for our own purposes.

Now, it is clear that the decline of a language must ultimately have political and economic causes: it is not due simply to the bad influences of this or that individual writer. But an effect can become a cause, reinforcing the original cause and producing the same effect in an intensified form, and so on indefinitely. A man may take to drink because he feels himself to be a failure, and then fail all the more completely because he drinks. It is rather the same thing that is happening to the English language. It becomes ugly and inaccurate because our thoughts are foolish, but the slovenliness of our language makes it easier for us to have foolish thoughts. The point is that the process is reversible. Modern English, especially written English, is full of bad habits which spread by imitation and which can be avoided if one is willing to take the necessary trouble. If one gets rid of these habits one can think more clearly, and to think clearly is a necessary first step towards political regeneration: so that the fight against bad English is not frivolous and is not the exclusive concern of professional writers. I will come back to this presently, and I hope that by that time the meaning of what I have said here will have become clearer. Meanwhile, here are five specimens of the English language as it is now habitually written.

These five passages have not been picked out because they are especially bad – I could have quoted far worse if I had chosen – but because they illustrate various of the mental vices from which we now suffer. They are a little below the average, but are fairly representative samples. I number them so I can refer back to them when necessary:

1. I am not, indeed, sure whether it is not true to say that the Milton who once seemed not unlike a seventeenth-century Shelley had not become, out of an experience ever more bitter in each year, more alien (*sic*) to the founder of that Jesuit sect which nothing could induce him to tolerate.

Professor Harold Laski (Essay in *Freedom of Expression*)

2. Above all, we cannot play ducks and drakes with a native battery of idioms which prescribes such egregious collocations of vocables as the Basic *put up with* for *tolerate* or *put at a loss* for *bewilder*.

Professor Lancelot Hogben (*Interglossa*).

3. On the one side we have the free personality: by definition it is not neurotic, for it has neither conflict nor dream. Its desires, such as they are, are transparent, for they are just what institutional approval keeps in the forefront of consciousness; another institutional pattern would alter their number and intensity; there is little in them that is natural, irreducible, or culturally dangerous. But *on the other side*, the social bond itself is nothing but the mutual reflection of these self-secure integrities. Recall the definition of love. Is not this the very picture of a small academic? Where is there a place in this hall of mirrors for either personality or fraternity?

Essay on psychology in *Politics* (New York).

4. All the 'best people' from the gentlemen's clubs, and all the frantic Fascist captains, united in common hatred of Socialism and bestial horror of the rising

tide of the mass revolutionary movement, have turned to acts of provocation, to foul incendiarism, to medieval legends of poisoned wells, to legalize their own destruction to proletarian organizations, and rouse the agitated petty-bourgeoisie to chauvinistic fervour on behalf of the fight against the revolutionary way out of the crisis.

Communist pamphlet.

5. If a new spirit *is* to be infused into this old country, there is one thorny and contentious reform which must be tackled, and that is the humanization and galvanization of the B.B.C. Timidity here will bespeak canker and atrophy of the soul. The heart of Britain may be sound and of strong beat, for instance, but the British lion's roar at present is like that of Bottom in Shakespeare's *Midsummer Night's Dream* – as gentle as any sucking dove. A virile new Britain cannot continue indefinitely to be traduced in the eyes, or rather ears, of the world by the effete languors of Langham Place, brazenly masquerading as 'standard English'. When the Voice of Britain is heard at nine o'clock, better far and infinitely less ludicrous to hear aitches honestly dropped than the present priggish, inflated, inhibited, school-ma'amish arch braying of blameless, bashful mewing maidens!

Letter in *Tribune*.

Each of these passages has faults of its own, but, quite apart from avoidable ugliness, two qualities are common to all of them. The first is staleness of imagery: the other is lack of precision. The writer either has a meaning and cannot express it, or he inadvertently says something else, or he is almost indifferent as to whether his words mean anything or not. This mixture of vagueness and sheer incompetence is the most marked characteristic of modern English prose, and especially of any kind of political writing. As soon as certain topics are raised, the concrete melts into the abstract and no one seems able to think of turns of speech that are not hackneyed: prose consists less and less of *words* chosen for the sake of their meaning, and more of *phrases* tacked together like the sections of a prefabricated hen-house. I list below, with notes and examples, various of the tricks by means of which the work of prose construction is habitually dodged:

Dying metaphors. A newly invented metaphor assists thought by evoking a visual image, while on the other hand a metaphor which is technically 'dead' (e.g. *iron resolution*) has in effect reverted to being an ordinary word and can generally be used without loss of vividness. But in between these two classes there is a huge dump of worn-out metaphors which have lost all evocative power and are merely used because they save people the trouble of inventing phrases for themselves. Examples are: *Ring the changes on, take up the cudgels for, toe the line, ride roughshod over, stand shoulder to shoulder with, play into the hands of, no axe to grind, grist to the mill, fishing in troubled waters, rift within the lute, on the order of the day, Achilles' heel, swan song, hotbed.* Many of these are used without knowledge of their meaning (what is a 'rift', for instance?), and incompatible metaphors are frequently mixed, a sure sign that the writer is not interested in what he is saying. Some metaphors now current have been twisted out of their original meaning without those who use them even being aware of the fact. For example, *toe the line* is sometimes written *tow the line*. Another example is *the hammer and the anvil*, now always used with the implication that the anvil gets the worst of it. In real life it is always the anvil that breaks the hammer, never the other way about: a writer who stopped to think what he was saying would be aware of this, and would avoid perverting the original phrase.

Operators, or *verbal false limbs*. These save the trouble of picking out appropriate verbs and nouns, and at the same time pad each sentence with extra syllables which give it an appearance of symmetry. Characteristic phrases are: *render inoperative, militate against, prove unacceptable, make contact with, be subject to, give rise to, give grounds for, have the effect of, play a leading part (role) in, make itself felt, take effect, exhibit a tendency to, serve the purpose of*, etc.etc. The keynote is the elimination of simple verbs. Instead of being a single word, such as *break, stop, spoil, mend, kill*, a verb becomes a *phrase*, made up of a noun or adjective tacked on to some general-purposes verb such as *prove, serve, form, play, render*. In addition, the passive voice is wherever possible used in preference to the active, and noun constructions are used instead of gerunds (*by examination of* instead of *by examining*). The range of verbs is further cut down by means of the *-ize* and *de-* formations, and banal statements are given an appearance of profundity by means of the *not un-* formation. Simple conjunctions and prepositions are replaced by such phrases as *with respect to, having regard to, the fact that, by dint of, in view of, in the interests of, on the hypothesis that*; and the ends of sentences are saved from anticlimax by such resounding commonplaces as *greatly to be desired, cannot be left out of account, a development to be expected in the near future, deserving of serious consideration, brought to a satisfactory conclusion*, and so on and so forth.

Pretentious diction. Words like *phenomenon, element, individual* (as noun), *objective, categorical, effective, virtual, basic, primary, promote, constitute, exhibit, exploit, utilize, eliminate, liquidate*, are used to dress up simple statements and give an air of scientific impartiality to biassed judgements. Adjectives like *epoch-making, epic, historic, unforgettable, triumphant, age-old, inevitable, inexorable, veritable*, are used to dignify the sordid processes of international politics, while writing that aims at glorifying war usually takes on an archaic colour, its characteristic words being: *realm, throne, chariot, mailed fist, trident, sword, shield, buckler, banner, jackboot, clarion*. Foreign words and expressions such as *cul de sac, ancien régime, deus ex machina, mutatis mutandis, status quo, Gleichschaltung, Weltanschauung*, are used to give an air of culture and elegance. Except for the useful abbreviations *i.e., e.g.*, and *etc.*, there is no real need for any of the hundreds of foreign phrases now current in English. Bad writers, and especially scientific, political and sociological writers, are nearly always haunted by the notion that Latin or Greek words are grander than Saxon ones, and unnecessary words like *expedite, ameliorate, predict, extraneous, deracinated, clandestine, sub-aqueous* and hundreds of others constantly gain ground from their Anglo-Saxon opposite numbers.[1] The jargon peculiar to Marxist writing (*hyena, hangman, cannibal, petty bourgeois, these gentry, lackey, flunkey, mad dog, White Guard*, etc) consists largely of words and phrases translated from Russian, German or French; but the normal way of coining a new word is to use a Latin or Greek root with the appropriate affix and, where necessary, the *-ize* formation. It is often easier to make up words of this kind (*deregionalize, impermissible, extramarital, non-fragmentatory* and so forth) than to think up the English words that will cover one's meaning. The result, in general, is an increase in slovenliness and vagueness.

Meaningless words. In certain kinds of writing, particularly in art criticism and literary criticism, it is normal to come across long passages which are almost completely lacking in meaning.[2] Words like *romantic, plastic, values, human, dead, sentimental, natural, vitality*, as used in art criticism,

1. An interesting illustration of this is the way in which the English flower names which were in use till very recently are being ousted by Greek ones, *snapdragon* becoming *antirrhinum*, *forget-me-not* becoming *myosotis*, etc. It is hard to see any practical reason for this change of fashion: it is probably due to an instinctive turning-away from the more homely word and a vague feeling that the Greek word is scientific. [Author's footnote.]

2. Example: 'Comfort's catholicity of perception and image, strangely Whitmanesque in range, almost the exact opposite in aesthetic compulsion, continues to evoke that trembling atmospheric accumulative hinting at a cruel, an inexorably serene timelessness. . . Wrey Gardiner scores by aiming at simple bullseyes with precision. Only they are not so simple, and through this contented sadness runs more than the surface bitter-sweet of resignation.' (*Poetry Quarterly*.) [Author's footnote.]

are strictly meaningless, in the sense that they not only do not point to any discoverable object, but are hardly even expected to do so by the reader. When one critic writes, 'The outstanding features of Mr X's work is its living quality', while another writes, 'The immediately striking thing about Mr X's work is its peculiar deadness', the reader accepts this as a simple difference of opinion. If words like *black* and *white* were involved, instead of the jargon words *dead* and *living*, he would see at once that language was being used in an improper way. Many political words are similarly abused. The word *Fascism* has now no meaning except in so far as it signifies 'something not desirable'. The words *democracy, socialism, freedom, patriotic, realistic, justice*, have each of them several different meanings which cannot be reconciled with one another. In the case of a word like *democracy*, not only is there no agreed definition, but the attempt to make one is resisted from all sides. It is almost universally felt that when we call a country democratic we are praising it: consequently the defenders of every kind of régime claim that it is a democracy, and fear that they might have to stop using the word if it were tied down to any one meaning. Words of this kind are often used in a consciously dishonest way. That is, the person who uses them has his own private definition, but allows his hearer to think he means something quite different. Statements like *Marshal Pétain was a true patriot, The Soviet press is the freest in the world, The Catholic Church is opposed to persecution*, are almost always made with intent to deceive. Other words used in variable meanings, in most cases more or less dishonestly, are: *class, totalitarian, science, progressive, reactionary, bourgeois, equality*.

Now that I have made this catalogue of swindles and perversions, let me give another example of the kind of writing that they lead to. This time it must of its nature be an imaginary one. I am going to translate a passage of good English into modern English of the worst sort. Here is a well-known verse from *Ecclesiastes*:

> I returned, and saw under the sun, that the race is not to the swift, nor the battle to the strong, neither yet bread to the wise, nor yet riches to men of understanding, nor yet favour to men of skill; but time and chance happeneth to them all.

Here it is in modern English:

> Objective consideration of contemporary phenomena compels the conclusion that success or failure in competitive activities exhibits no tendency to be commensurate with innate capacity, but that a considerable element of the unpredictable must invariably be taken into account.

This is a parody, but not a very gross one. Exhibit 3, above, for instance, contains several patches of the same kind of English. It will be seen that I have not made a full translation. The beginning and ending of the sentence follow the original meaning fairly closely, but in the middle the concrete illustrations – race, battle, bread – dissolve into the vague phrase 'success or failure in competitive activities'. This had to be so, because no modern writer of the kind I am discussing – no one capable of using phrases like 'objective consideration of contemporary phenomena' – would ever tabulate his thoughts in that precise and detailed way. The whole tendency of modern prose is away from concreteness. Now analyse these two sentences a little more closely. The first contains 49 words but only 60 syllables, and all its words are those of everyday life. The second contains 38 words of 90 syllables: 18 of its words are from Latin roots, and one from Greek. The first sentence contains six vivid images, and only one phrase ('time and chance') that could be called vague. The second contains not a single fresh, arresting phrase, and in spite of its 90 syllables it gives only a shortened version of the meaning contained in the first. Yet without a doubt it is the second kind of sentence that is gaining ground in modern English. I do not want to exaggerate. This kind of writing is not yet universal, and outcrops of simplicity will occur here and there in the worst-written page. Still if you or I were told to write a few lines on the uncertainty of human fortunes, we should probably come much nearer to my imaginary sentence than to the one from *Ecclesiastes*.

As I have tried to show, modern writing at its worst does not consist in picking out words for the sake of their meaning and inventing images in order to make the meaning clearer. It consists in gumming together long strips of words which have already been set in order by someone else, and making the results presentable by sheer humbug. The attraction of this way of writing is that it is easy. It is easier – even quicker, once you have the habit – to say *In my opinion it is a not unjustifiable assumption that* than to say *I think*. If you use ready-made phrases, you not only don't have to hunt about for words; you also don't have to bother with the rhythms of your sentences, since these phrases are generally so arranged as to be more or less euphonious. When you are composing in a hurry – when you are dictating to a stenographer, for instance, or making a public speech – it is natural to fall into a pretentious, latinized style. Tags like *a consideration which we should do well to bear in mind* or *a conclusion to which all of us would readily assent* will save many a sentence from coming down with a bump. By using stale metaphors, similes and idioms, you save much mental effort, at the cost of leaving your meaning vague, not

* euphonious – agreeable in sound

only for your reader but for yourself. This is the significance of mixed metaphors. The sole aim of a metaphor is to call up a visual image. When these images clash – as in *The Fascist octopus has sung its swan song, the jackboot is thrown into the melting-pot* – it can be taken as certain that the writer is not seeing a mental image of the objects he is naming; in other words he is not really thinking. Look again at the examples I gave at the beginning of this essay. Professor Laski (1) uses five negatives in 53 words. One of these is superfluous, making nonsense of the whole passage, and in addition there is the slip *alien* for akin, making further nonsense, and several avoidable pieces of clumsiness which increase the general vagueness. Professor Hogben (2) plays ducks and drakes with a battery which is able to write prescriptions, and, while disapproving of the everyday phrase *put up with*, is unwilling to look *egregious* up in the dictionary and see what it means. (3), if one takes an uncharitable attitude towards it, is simply meaningless: probably one could work out its intended meaning by reading the whole of the article in which it occurs. In (4) the writer knows more or less what he wants to say, but an accumulation of stale phrases chokes him like tea-leaves blocking a sink. In (5) words and meaning have almost parted company. People who write in this manner usually have a general emotional meaning – they dislike one thing and want to express solidarity with another – but they are not interested in the detail of what they are saying. A scrupulous writer, in every sentence that he writes, will ask himself at least four questions, thus: What am I trying to say? What words will express it? What image or idiom will make it clearer? Is this image fresh enough to have an effect? And he will probably ask himself two more: Could I put it more shortly? Have I said anything that is avoidably ugly? But you are not obliged to go to all this trouble. You can shirk it by simply throwing your mind open and letting the ready-made phrases come crowding in. They will construct your sentences for you – even think your thoughts for you, to a certain extent – and at need they will perform the important service of partially concealing your meaning even from yourself. It is at this point that the special connexion between politics and the debasement of language becomes clear.

In our time it is broadly true that political writing is bad writing. Where it is not true, it will generally be found that the writer is some kind of rebel, expressing his private opinions, and not a 'party line'. Orthodoxy, of whatever colour, seems to demand a lifeless, imitative style. The political dialects to be found in pamphlets, leading articles, manifestos, White Papers and the speeches of Under-Secretaries do, of course, vary from party to party, but they are all alike in that one almost never finds in them a fresh, vivid, home-made turn of speech. When one watches some tired hack on the platform mechanically repeating the familiar phrases – *bestial atrocities, iron heel, blood-stained tyranny, free peoples of the world, stand shoulder to shoulder* – one often has a curious feeling that one is not watching a live human being but some kind of dummy: a feeling which suddenly becomes stronger at moments when the light catches the speaker's spectacles and turns them into blank discs which seem to have no eyes behind them. And this is not altogether fanciful. A speaker who uses that kind of phraseology has gone some distance towards turning himself into a machine. The appropriate noises are coming out of his larynx, but his brain is not involved as it would be if he were choosing his words for himself. If the speech he is making is one that he is accustomed to make over and over again, he may be almost unconscious of what he is saying, as one is when one utters the responses in church. And this reduced state of consciousness, if not indispensable, is at any rate favourable to political conformity.

In our time, political speech and writing are largely the defence of the indefensible. Things like the continuance of British rule in India, the Russian purges and deportations, the dropping of the atom bombs on Japan, can indeed be defended, but only by arguments which are too brutal for most people to face, and which do not square with the professed aims of political parties. Thus political language has to consist largely of euphemism, question-begging and sheer cloudy vagueness. Defenceless villages are bombarded from the air, the inhabitants driven out into the countryside, the cattle machine-gunned, the huts set on fire with incendiary bullets: this is called *pacification*. Millions of peasants are robbed of their farms and sent trudging along the roads with no more than they can carry: this is called *transfer of population* or *rectification of frontiers*. People are imprisoned for years without trial, or shot in the back of the neck or sent to die of scurvy in Arctic lumber camps: this is called *elimination of unreliable elements*. Such phraseology is needed if one wants to name things without calling up mental pictures of them. Consider for instance some comfortable English professor defending Russian totalitarianism. He cannot say outright, 'I believe in killing off your opponents when you can get good results by doing so'. Probably, therefore, he will say something like this:

> While freely conceding that the Soviet régime exhibits certain features which the humanitarian may be inclined to deplore, we must, I think, agree that a certain curtailment of the right to political opposition is an unavoidable concom-

itant of transitional periods, and that the rigours which the Russian people have been called upon to undergo have been amply justified in the sphere of concrete achievement.

The inflated style is itself a kind of euphemism. A mass of Latin words falls upon the facts like soft snow, blurring the outlines and covering up all the details. The great enemy of clear language is insincerity. When there is a gap between one's real and one's declared aims, one turns as it were instinctively to long words and exhausted idioms, like a cuttlefish squirting out ink. In our age there is no such thing as 'keeping out of politics'. All issues are political issues, and politics itself is a mass of lies, evasions, folly, hatred and schizophrenia. When the general atmosphere is bad, language must suffer. I should expect to find – this is a guess which I have not sufficient knowledge to verify – that the German, Russian and Italian languages have all deteriorated in the last ten or fifteen years, as a result of dictatorship.

But if thought corrupts language, language can also corrupt thought. A bad usage can spread by tradition and imitation, even among people who should and do know better. The debased language that I have been discussing is in some ways very convenient. Phrases like *a not unjustifiable assumption, leaves much to be desired, would serve no good purpose, a consideration which we should do well to bear in mind*, are a continuous temptation, a packet of aspirins always at one's elbow. Look back through this essay, and for certain you will find that I have again and again committed the very faults I am protesting against. By this morning's post I have received a pamphlet dealing with conditions in Germany. The author tells me that he 'felt impelled' to write it. I open it at random, and here is almost the first sentence that I see: '(The Allies) have an opportunity not only of achieving a radical transformation of Germany's social and political structure in such a way as to avoid a nationalistic reaction in Germany itself, but at the same time of laying the foundations of a co-operative and unified Europe.' You see, he 'feels impelled' to write – feels, presumably, that he has something new to say – and yet his words, like cavalry horses answering the bugle, group themselves automatically into the familiar dreary pattern. This invasion of one's mind by ready-made phrases (*lay the foundations, achieve a radical transformation*) can only be prevented if one is constantly on guard against them, and every such phrase anaesthetizes a portion of one's brain.

I said earlier that the decadence of our language is probably curable. Those who deny this would argue, if they produced an argument at all, that language merely reflects existing social conditions, and that we cannot influence its development by any direct tinkering with words and constructions. So far as the general tone or spirit of a language goes, this may be true, but it is not true in detail. Silly words and expressions have often disappeared, not through any evolutionary process but owing to the conscious action of a minority. Two recent examples were *explore every avenue* and *leave no stone unturned*, which were killed by the jeers of a few journalists. There is a long list of fly-blown metaphors which could similarly be got rid of if enough people would interest themselves in the job; and it should also be possible to laugh the *not un-* formation out of existence,[3] to reduce the amount of Latin and Greek in the average sentence, to drive out foreign phrases and strayed scientific words, and, in general, to make pretentiousness unfashionable. But all these are minor points. The defence of the English language implies more than this, and perhaps it is best to start by saying what it does *not* imply.

To begin with, it has nothing to do with archaism, with the salvaging of obsolete words and turns of speech, or with the setting-up of a 'standard English' which must never be departed from. On the contrary, it is especially concerned with the scrapping of every word or idiom which has outworn its usefulness. It has nothing to do with correct grammar and syntax, which are of no importance so long as one makes one's meaning clear or with the avoidance of Americanisms, or with having what is called a 'good prose style'. On the other hand it is not concerned with fake simplicity and the attempt to make written English colloquial. Nor does it even imply in every case preferring the Saxon word to the Latin one, though it does imply using the fewest and shortest words that will cover one's meaning. What is above all needed is to let the meaning choose the word, and not the other way about. In prose, the worst thing you can do with words is to surrender them. When you think of a concrete object, you think wordlessly, and then, if you want to describe the thing you have been visualizing, you probably hunt about till you find the exact words that seem to fit it. When you think of something abstract you are more inclined to use words from the start, and unless you make a conscious effort to prevent it, the existing dialect will come rushing in and do the job for you, at the expense of blurring or even changing your meaning. Probably it is better to put off using words as long as possible and get one's meanings as clear as one can through pictures or sensations. Afterwards one can choose – not simply

3. One can cure onself of the *not un-* formation by memorizing this sentence: *A not unblack dog was chasing a not unsmall rabbit across a not ungreen field.* [Author's footnote.]

accept – the phrases that will best cover the meaning, and then switch round and decide what impression one's words are likely to make on another person. This last effort of the mind cuts out all stale or mixed images, all prefabricated phrases, needless repetitions, and humbug and vagueness generally. But one can often be in doubt about the effect of a word or a phrase, and one needs rules that one can rely on when instinct fails. I think the following rules will cover most cases:

i. Never use a metaphor, simile or other figure of speech which you are used to seeing in print.

ii. Never use a long word where a short one will do.

iii. If it is possible to cut a word out, always cut it out.

iv. Never use the passive where you can use the active.

v. Never use a foreign phrase, a scientific word or a jargon word if you can think of an everyday English equivalent.

vi. Break any of these rules sooner than say anything outright barbarous. *

These rules sound elementary, and so they are, but they demand a deep change of attitude in anyone who has grown used to writing in the style now fashionable. One could keep all of them and still write bad English, but one could not write the kind of stuff that I quoted in those five specimens at the beginning of this article.

I have not here been considering the literary use of language, but merely language as an instrument for expressing and not for concealing or preventing thought. Stuart Chase and others have come near to claiming that all abstract words are meaningless, and have used this as a pretext for advocating a kind of political quietism. Since you don't know what Fascism is, how can you struggle against Fascism? One need not swallow such absurdities as this, but one ought to recognize that the present political chaos is connected with the decay of language, and that one can probably bring about some improvement by starting at the verbal end. If you simplify your English, you are freed from the worst follies of orthodoxy. You cannot speak any of the necessary dialects, and when you make a stupid remark its stupidity will be obvious, even to yourself. Political language – and with variations this is true of all political parties, from Conservatives to Anarchists – is designed to make lies sound truthful and murder respectable, and to give an appearance of solidity to pure wind. One cannot change this all in a moment, but one can at least change one's own habits, and from time to time one can even, if one jeers loudly enough, send some worn-out and useless phrase – some *jackboot*,

* barbarous - below standard of correctness

Achilles' heel, hotbed, melting pot, acid test, veritable inferno or other lump of verbal refuse – into the dustbin where it belongs.

Horizon, April 1946; *Modern British Writing* ed. Denys Val Baker, 1947; *S.E.*; *O.R.*; *C.E.*

32. Some Thoughts on the Common Toad

Before the swallow, before the daffodil, and not much later than the snowdrop, the common toad salutes the coming of spring after his own fashion, which is to emerge from a hole in the ground, where he has lain buried since the previous autumn, and crawl as rapidly as possible towards the nearest suitable patch of water. Something – some kind of shudder in the earth, or perhaps merely a rise of a few degrees in the temperature – has told him that it is time to wake up: though a few toads appear to sleep the clock round and miss out a year from time to time – at any rate, I have more than once dug them up, alive and apparently well, in the middle of summer.

At this period, after his long fast, the toad has a very spiritual look, like a strict Anglo-Catholic towards the end of Lent. His movements are languid but purposeful, his body is shrunken, and by contrast his eyes look abnormally large. This allows one to notice, what one might not at another time, that a toad has about the most beautiful eye of any living creature. It is like gold, or more exactly it is like the golden-coloured semi-precious stone which one sometimes sees in signet-rings, and which I think is called a chrysoberyl.

For a few days after getting into the water the toad concentrates on building up his strength by eating small insects. Presently he has swollen to his normal size again, and then he goes through a phase of intense sexiness. All he knows, at least if he is a male toad, is that he wants to get his arms round something, and if you offer him a stick, or even your finger, he will cling to it with surprising strength and take a long time to discover that it is not a female toad. Frequently one comes upon shapeless masses of ten or twenty toads rolling over and over in the water, one clinging to another without distinction of sex. By degrees, however, they sort themselves out into couples, with the male duly sitting on the female's back. You can now distinguish males from females, because the male is smaller, darker and sits on top, with his arms tightly clasped round the female's neck. After a day or two the spawn is laid in long strings which wind themselves in and out of the reeds and soon become invisible. A few more weeks, and the water is alive with masses of tiny tadpoles which rapidly grow larger, sprout hind-legs, then forelegs, then shed their tails: and finally, about the middle of the summer, the new generation of toads, smaller than one's thumb-nail but perfect in every particular, crawl out of the water to begin the game anew.

I mention the spawning of the toads because it is one of the phenomena of spring which most deeply appeal to me, and because the toad, unlike the skylark and the primrose, has never had much of a boost from poets. But I am aware that many people do not like reptiles or amphibians, and I am not suggesting that in order to enjoy the spring you have to take an interest in toads. There are also the crocus, the missel-thrush, the cuckoo, the blackthorn, etc. The point is that the pleasures of spring are available to everybody, and cost nothing. Even in the most sordid street the coming of spring will register itself by some sign or other, if it is only a brighter blue between the chimney pots or the vivid green of an elder sprouting on a blitzed site. Indeed it is remarkable how Nature goes on existing unofficially, as it were, in the very heart of London. I have seen a kestrel flying over the Deptford gasworks, and I have heard a first-rate performance by a blackbird in the Euston Road. There must be some hundreds of thousands, if not millions, of birds living inside the four-mile radius, and it is rather a pleasing thought that none of them pays a halfpenny of rent.

As for spring, not even the narrow and gloomy streets round the Bank of England are quite able to exclude it. It comes seeping in everywhere, like one of those new poison gases which pass through all filters. The spring is commonly referred to as 'a miracle', and during the past five or six years this worn-out figure of speech has taken on a new lease of life. After the sort of winters we have had to endure recently, the spring does seem miraculous, because it has become gradually harder and harder to believe that it is actually going to happen. Every February since 1940 I have found myself thinking that this time winter is going to be permanent. But Persephone, like the toads, always rises from the dead at about the same moment. Suddenly, towards the end of March, the miracle happens and the decaying slum in which I live is transfigured. Down in the square the sooty privets have turned bright green, the leaves are thickening on the chestnut trees, the daffodils are out, the wallflowers are budding, the policeman's tunic looks positively a pleasant shade of blue, the fishmonger greets his customers with a smile, and even the sparrows are quite a different colour, having felt the balminess of the air and nerved themselves to take a bath, their first since last September.

Is it wicked to take a pleasure in spring and other seasonal changes? To put it more precisely, is it politically reprehensible, while we are all groaning, or at any rate ought to be groaning, under the shackles of the capitalist system, to point out that life is frequently more worth living because of a blackbird's song, a yellow elm tree in October, or some other natural phenomenon which does not cost money and does not have what the editors of left-wing newspapers call a class angle? There is no doubt that many people think so. I know by experience that a favourable reference to 'Nature' in one of my articles is liable to bring me abusive letters, and though the key-word in these letters is usually 'sentimental', two ideas seem to be mixed up in them. One is that any pleasure in the actual process of life encourages a sort of political quietism. People, so the thought runs, ought to be discontented, and it is our job to multiply our wants and not simply to increase our enjoyment of the things we have already. The other idea is that this is the age of machines and that to dislike the machine, or even to want to limit its domination, is backward-looking, reactionary and slightly ridiculous. This is often backed up by the statement that a love of Nature is a foible of urbanized people who have no notion what Nature is really like. Those who really have to deal with the soil, so it is argued, do not love the soil, and do not take the faintest interest in birds or flowers, except from a strictly utilitarian point of view. To love the country one must live in the town, merely taking an occasional week-end ramble at the warmer times of year.

This last idea is demonstrably false. Medieval literature, for instance, including the popular ballads, is full of an almost Georgian enthusiasm for Nature, and the art of agricultural peoples such as the Chinese and Japanese centres always round trees, birds, flowers, rivers, mountains. The other idea seems to me to be wrong in a subtler way. Certainly we ought to be discontented, we ought not simply to find out ways of making the best of a bad job, and yet if we kill all pleasure in the actual process of life, what sort of future are we preparing for ourselves? If a man cannot enjoy the return of spring, why should he be happy in a labour-saving Utopia? What will he do with the leisure that the machine will give him? I have always suspected that if our economic and political problems are ever really solved, life will become simpler instead of more complex, and that the sort of pleasure one gets from finding the first primrose will loom larger than the sort of pleasure one gets from eating an ice to the tune of a Wurlitzer. I think that by retaining one's childhood love of such things as trees, fishes, butterflies and – to return to my first instance – toads, one makes a peaceful and decent future a little more probable, and that by preaching the doctrine that nothing is to be admired except steel and concrete, one merely makes it a little surer that human beings will have no outlet for their surplus energy except in hatred and leader worship.

At any rate, spring is here, even in London N.1, and they can't stop you enjoying it. This is a satisfying reflection. How many a time have I stood watching the toads mating, or a pair of hares having a boxing match in the young corn, and thought of all the important persons who would stop me enjoying this if they could. But luckily they can't. So long as you are not actually ill, hungry, frightened or immured in a prison or a holiday camp, spring is still spring. The atom bombs are piling up in the factories, the police are prowling through the cities, the lies are streaming from the loudspeakers, but the earth is still going round the sun, and neither the dictators nor the bureaucrats, deeply as they disapprove of the process, are able to prevent it.

Tribune, 12 April 1946; *New Republic*, 20 May 1946; *S.E.*; *O.R.*

33. A Good Word for the Vicar of Bray

Some years ago a friend took me to the little Berkshire church of which the celebrated Vicar of Bray was once the incumbent. (Actually it is a few miles from Bray, but perhaps at that time the two livings were one.) In the churchyard there stands a magnificent yew tree which, according to a notice at its foot, was planted by no less a person than the Vicar of Bray himself. And it struck me at the time as curious that such a man should have left such a relic behind him.

The Vicar of Bray, though he was well equipped to be a leader-writer on *The Times*, could hardly be described as an admirable character. Yet, after this lapse of time, all that is left of him is a comic song and a beautiful tree which has rested the eyes of generation after generation and must surely have outweighed any bad effects which he produced by his political quislingism.

Thibaw, the last King of Burma, was also far from being a good man. He was a drunkard, he had five hundred wives – he seems to have kept them chiefly for show, however – and when he came to the throne his first act was to decapitate seventy or eighty of his brothers. Yet he did posterity a good turn by planting the dusty streets of Mandalay with tamarind trees which cast a pleasant shade until the Japanese incendiary bombs burned them down in 1942.

The poet, James Shirley, seems to have generalized too freely when he said that 'Only the actions of the just Smell sweet and blossom in their dust'. Sometimes the actions of the unjust make quite a good showing after the appropriate lapse of time. When I saw the Vicar of Bray's yew tree it reminded me of something, and afterwards I got hold of a book of selections from the writings of John Aubrey and reread a pastoral poem which must have been written some time in the first half of the seventeenth century, and which was inspired by a certain Mrs Overall.

Mrs Overall was the wife of a Dean and was extensively unfaithful to him. According to Aubrey she 'could scarcely denie any one', and she had 'the loveliest Eies that were ever seen, but wondrous wanton'. The poem (the 'shepherd swaine' seems to have been somebody called Sir John Selby) starts off:

Downe lay the Shepherd Swaine
So sober and demure
Wishing for his wench againe
So bonny and so pure
With his head on hillock lowe
And his arms akimboe
And all was for the loss of his
Hye nonny nonny noe . . .

Sweet she was, as kind a love
As ever fetter'd Swaine;
Never such a daynty one
Shall man enjoy again;
Sett a thousand on a rowe
I forbid that any showe
Ever the like of her
Hye nonny nonny noe.

As the poem proceeds through another six verses, the refrain 'Hye nonny nonny noe' takes on an unmistakably obscene meaning, but it ends with the exquisite stanza:

But gone she is the prettiest lasse
That ever trod on plaine.
What ever hath betide of her
Blame not the Shepherd Swaine.
For why? She was her owne Foe,
And gave herself the overthrowe
By being so franke of her
Hye nonny nonny noe.

Mrs Overall was no more an exemplary character than the Vicar of Bray, though a more attractive one. Yet in the end all that remains of her is a poem which still gives pleasure to many people, though for some reason it never gets into the anthologies. The suffering which she presumably caused, and the misery and futility in which her own life must have ended, have been transformed into a sort of lingering fragrance like the smell of tobacco plants on a summer evening.

But to come back to trees. The planting of a tree, especially one of the long-living hardwood trees, is a gift to which you can make to posterity at almost no cost and with almost no trouble, and if the tree takes root it will far outlive the visible effect of any of your other actions, good or evil. A year or two ago I wrote a few paragraphs in *Tribune* about some sixpenny rambler roses from Woolworth's which I had planted before the war. This brought me an indignant letter from a reader who said that roses are bourgeois, but I still think that my sixpence was better spent than if it had gone on cigarettes or even on one of the excellent Fabian Research Pamphlets.

Recently I spent a day at the cottage where I used to live, and noted with a pleased surprise – to be exact, it was a feeling of having done good unconsciously – the progress of the things I had planted nearly ten years ago. I think it is worth recording what some of them cost, just to show what you can do with a few shillings if you invest them in something that grows.

First of all there were the two ramblers from Woolworth's, and three polyantha roses, all at sixpence each. Then there were two bush roses which were part of a job lot from a nursery garden. This job lot consisted of six fruit trees, three rose bushes and two gooseberry bushes, all for ten shillings. One of the fruit trees and one of the rose bushes died, but the rest are all flourishing. The sum total is five fruit trees, seven roses and two gooseberry bushes, all for twelve and sixpence. These plants have not entailed much work, and have had nothing spent on them beyond the original amount. They never even received any manure, except what I occasionally collected in a bucket when one of the farm horses happened to have halted outside the gate.

Between them, in nine years, those seven rose bushes will have given what would add up to a hundred or a hundred and fifty months of bloom. The fruit trees, which were mere saplings when I put them in, are now just about getting in their stride. Last week one of them, a plum, was a mass of blossom, and the apples looked as if they were going to do fairly well. What had originally been the weakling of the family, a Cox's Orange Pippin – it would hardly have been included in the job lot if it had been a good plant – had grown into a sturdy tree with plenty of fruit spurs on it. I maintain that it was a public-spirited action to plant that Cox, for these trees do not fruit quickly and I did not expect to stay there long. I never had an apple of it myself, but it looks as if someone else will have quite a lot. By their fruits ye shall know them, and the Cox's Orange Pippin is a good fruit to be known by. Yet I did not plant it with the conscious intention of doing anybody a good turn. I just saw the job lot going cheap and stuck the things into the ground without much preparation.

A thing which I regret, and which I will try to remedy some time, is that I have never in my life planted a walnut. Nobody does plant them nowadays – when you see a walnut it is almost invariably an old tree. If you plant a walnut you are planting it for your grandchildren, and who cares a damn for his grandchildren? Nor does anybody plant a quince, a mulberry or a medlar. But these are garden trees which you can only be expected to plant if you have a patch of ground of your own. On the other hand, in any hedge or in any piece of waste ground you happen to be walking through, you can do something to remedy the appalling massacre of trees, especially oaks, ashes, elms and beeches, which has happened during the war years.

Even an apple tree is liable to live for about a hundred years, so that the Cox I planted in 1936 may still be bearing fruit well into the twenty-first century. An oak or a beech may live for hundreds of years and be a pleasure to thousands or tens of thousands of people before it is finally sawn up into timber. I am not suggesting that one can discharge all one's obligations towards society by means of a private re-afforestation scheme. Still, it might not be a bad idea, every time you commit an antisocial act, to make a note of it in your diary, and then, at the appropriate season, push an acorn into the ground.

And, if even one in twenty of them came to maturity, you might do quite a lot of harm in your lifetime, and still, like the Vicar of Bray, end up as a public benefactor after all.

Tribune, 26 April 1946; *S.E.*; *O.R.*

34. Confessions of a Book Reviewer

In a cold but stuffy bed-sitting room littered with cigarette ends and half-empty cups of tea, a man in a moth-eaten dressing-gown sits at a rickety table, trying to find room for his typewriter among the piles of dusty papers that surround it. He cannot throw the papers away because the wastepaper basket is already overflowing, and besides, somewhere among the unanswered letters and unpaid bills it is possible that there is a cheque for two guineas which he is nearly certain he forgot to pay into the bank. There are also letters with addresses which ought to be entered in his address book. He has lost his address book, and the thought of looking for it, or indeed of looking for anything, afflicts him with acute suicidal impulses.

He is a man of thirty-five, but looks fifty. He is bald, has varicose veins and wears spectacles, or would wear them if his only pair were not chronically lost. If things are normal with him he will be suffering from malnutrition, but if he has recently had a lucky streak he will be suffering from a hangover. At present it is half past eleven in the morning, and according to his schedule he should have started work two hours ago; but even if he had made any serious effort to start he would have been frustrated by almost continuous ringing of the telephone bell, the yells of the baby, the rattle of an electic drill out in the street, and the heavy boots of his creditors clumping up and down the stairs. The most recent interruption was the arrival of the second post, which brought him two circulars and an income-tax demand printed in red.

Needless to say this person is a writer. He might be a poet, a novelist, or a writer of film scripts or radio features, for all literary people are very much alike, but let us say that he is a book reviewer. Half hidden among the pile of papers is a bulky parcel containing five volumes which his editor has sent with a note suggesting that they 'ought to go well together'. They arrived four days ago, but for forty-eight hours the reviewer was prevented by moral paralysis from opening the parcel. Yesterday in a resolute moment he ripped the string off it and found the five volumes to be *Palestine at the Cross Roads*, *Scientific Dairy Farming*, *A Short History of European Democracy* (this one is 680 pages and weighs four pounds), *Tribal Customs in Portuguese East Africa*, and a novel, *It's Nicer*

Lying Down, probably included by mistake. His review – 800 words, say – has got to be 'in' by midday tomorrow.

Three of these books deal with subjects of which he is so ignorant that he will have to read at least fifty pages if he is to avoid making some howler which will betray him not merely to the author (who of course knows all about the habits of book reviewers), but even to the general reader. By four in the afternoon he will have taken the books out of their wrapping papers but will still be suffering from a nervous inability to open them. The prospects of having to read them, and even the smell of the paper, affects him like the prospect of eating cold ground-rice pudding flavoured with castor oil. And yet curiously enough his copy will get to the office in time. Somehow it always does get there in time. At about nine p.m. his mind will grow relatively clear , and until the small hours he will sit in a room which grows colder and colder, while the cigarette smoke grows thicker and thicker, skipping expertly through one book after another and laying each down with a final comment, 'God, what tripe!' In the morning, blear-eyed, surly and unshaven, he will gaze for an hour or two at a blank sheet of paper until the menacing finger of the clock frightens him into action. Then suddenly he will snap into it. All the stale old phrases – ' a book that no one should miss', 'something memorable on every page', 'of special value are the chapters dealing with, etc. etc.' – will jump into their places like iron filings obeying the magnet, and the review will end up at exactly the right length and with just about three minutes to go. Meanwhile another wad of ill-assorted, unappetizing books will have arrived by post. So it goes on. And yet with what high hopes this downtrodden, nerve-racked creature started his career, only a few years ago.

Do I seem to exaggerate? I ask any regular reviewer – anyone who reviews, say, a minimum of a hundred books a year – whether he can deny in honesty that his habits and character are such as I have described. Every writer, in any case, is rather that kind of person, but the prolonged, indiscriminate reviewing of books is a quite exceptionally thankless, irritating and exhausting job. It not only involves praising trash – though it does involve that, as I will show in a moment – but constantly *inventing* reactions towards books about which one has no spontaneous feelings whatever. The reviewer, jaded though he may be, is professionally interested in books, and out of the thousands that appear annually, there are probably fifty or a hundred that he would enjoy writing about. If he is a top-notcher in his profession he may get hold of ten or twenty of them: more probably he gets hold of two or three. The rest of his work however conscientious he may be in praising or damning, is in essence humbug. He is pouring his immortal spirit down the drain, half a pint at a time.

The great majority of reviews give an inadequate or misleading account of the book that is dealt with. Since the war publishers have been less able than before to twist the tails of literary editors and evoke a paean of praise for every book that they produce, but on the other hand the standard of reviewing has gone down owing to lack of space and other inconveniences. Seeing the results, people sometimes suggest that the solution lies in getting book reviewing out of the hands of hacks. Books on specialized subjects ought to be dealt with by experts, and on the other hand a good deal of reviewing, especially of novels, might well be done by amateurs. Nearly every book is capable of arousing passionate feeling, if it is only a passionate dislike, in some or other reader, whose ideas about it would surely be worth more than those of a bored professional. But, unfortunately, as every editor knows, that kind of thing is very difficult to organize. In practice the editor always finds himself reverting to his team of hacks – his 'regulars', as he calls them.

None of this is remediable so long as it is taken for granted that every book deserves to be reviewed. It is almost impossible to mention books in bulk without grossly overpraising the great majority of them. Until one has some kind of professional relationship with books one does not discover how bad the majority of them are. In much more than nine cases out of ten the only objectively truthful criticism would be 'This book is worthless', while the truth about the reviewer's own reaction would probably be 'This book does not interest me in any way, and I would not write about it unless I were paid to'. But the public will not pay to read that kind of thing. Why should they? They want some kind of guide to the books they are asked to read, and they want some kind of evaluation. But as soon as values are mentioned, standards collapse. For if one says – and nearly every reviewer says this kind of thing at least once a week – that *King Lear* is a good play and *The Four Just Men* is a good thriller, what meaning is there in the word 'good'?

The best practice, it has always seemed to me, would be simply to ignore the great majority of books and to give very long reviews – 1,000 words is a bare minimum – to the few that seem to matter. Short notes of a line or two on forthcoming books can be useful, but the usual middle-length review of about 600 words is bound to be worthless even if the reviewer genuinely wants to write it. Normally he doesn't want to write it, and the week-in, week-out production of snippets soon reduces him to the crushed figure in a dressing gown whom I described at the beginning of this article. However, everyone in this world has someone else whom he can look down on, and I must say, from experience of both trades, that the book reviewer is better off than the film critic, who cannot even do his work at home, but has to attend trade shows at eleven in the morning and, with one or two notable exceptions, is expected to sell his honour for a glass of inferior sherry.

Tribune, 3 May 1946; *New Republic*, 5 August 1946; *S.E.*

Politics vs Literature: An Examination of *Gulliver's Travels*

In *Gulliver's Travels* humanity is attacked, or criticized, from at least three different angles, and the implied character of Gulliver himself necessarily changes somewhat in the process. In Part I he is the typical eighteenth-century voyager, bold, practical and unromantic, his homely outlook skilfully impressed on the reader by the biographical details at the beginning, by his age (he is a man of forty, with two children, when his adventures start), and by the inventory of the things in his pockets, especially his spectacles, which make several appearances. In Part II he has in general the same character, but at moments when the story demands it he has a tendency to develop into an imbecile who is capable of boasting of 'our noble Country, the Mistress of Arts and Arms, the Scourge of France' etc., etc., and at the same time of betraying every available scandalous fact about the country which he professes to love. In Part III he is much as he was in Part I, though, as he is consorting chiefly with the courtiers and men of learning, one has the impression that he has risen in the social scale. In Part IV he conceives a horror of the human race which is not apparent, or only intermittently apparent, in the earlier books, and changes into a sort of unreligious anchorite whose one desire is to live in some desolate spot where he can devote himself to meditating on the goodness of the Houyhnhnms. However, these inconsistencies are forced upon Swift by the fact that Gulliver is there chiefly to provide a contrast. It is necessary, for instance, that he should appear sensible in Part I and at least intermittently silly in Part II, because in both books the essential manoeuvre is the same, i.e. to make the human being look ridiculous by imagining him as a creature six inches high. Whenever Gulliver is not acting as a stooge there is a sort of continuity in his character, which comes out especially in his resourcefulness and his observation of physical detail. He is much the same kind of person, with the same prose style, when he bears off the warships of Blefuscu, when he rips open the belly of the monstrous rat, and when he sails away upon the ocean in his frail coracle made from the skins of Yahoos. Moreover, it is difficult not to feel that in his shrewder moments Gulliver is simply Swift himself, and there is at least one incident in which Swift seems to be venting his private grievance against contemporary society. It will be remembered that when the Emperor of Lilliput's palace catches fire, Gulliver puts it out by urinating on it. Instead of being congratulated on his presence of mind, he finds that he has committed a capital offence by making water in the precincts of the palace, and

I was privately assured, that the Empress, conceiving the greatest Abhorrence of what I had done, removed to the most distant Side of the Court, firmly resolved that those buildings should never be repaired for her Use; and, in the Presence of her chief Confidents, could not forbear vowing Revenge.

According to Professor G.M. Trevelyan (*England under Queen Anne*), part of the reason for Swift's failure to get preferment was that the Queen was scandalized by *A Tale of a Tub* – a pamphlet in which Swift probably felt he had done a great service to the English Crown, since it scarifies the Dissenters and still more the Catholics while leaving the Established Church alone. In any case no one would deny that *Gulliver's Travels* is a rancorous as well as a pessimistic book, and that especially in Parts I and III it often descends into political partisanship of a narrow kind. Pettiness and magnanimity, republicanism and authoritarianism, love of reason and lack of curiousity, are all mixed up in it. The hatred of the human body with which Swift is especially associated is only dominant in Part IV, but somehow this new preoccupation does not come as a surprise. One feels that all these adventures, and all these changes of mood, could have happened to the same person, and the inter-connexion between Swift's political loyalties and his ultimate despair is one of the most interesting features of the book.

Politically, Swift was one of those people who are driven into a sort of perverse Toryism by the follies of the progressive part of the moment. Part I of *Gulliver's Travels*, ostensibly a satire on human greatness, can be seen, if one looks a little deeper, to be simply an attack on England, on the dominant Whig Party, and on the war with France, which – however bad the motives of the Allies may have been – did save Europe from being tyrannized over by a single reactionary power. Swift was not a Jacobite nor strictly speaking a Tory, and his declared aim in the war was merely a moderate peace treaty and not the outright defeat of England. Nevertheless there is a tinge of quislingism in his attitude, which comes out in the ending of Part I and slightly interferes with the allegory. When Gulliver flees from Lilliput (England) to Blefuscu (France) the assumption that a human being six inches high is inherently contemptible seems to be dropped. Whereas the people of Lilliput have behaved towards Gulliver with the utmost treachery and meanness, those of Blefuscu behave generously and straightforwardly, and indeed this section of the book ends on a different note from the all-round disillusionment of the earliest chapters. Evidently Swift's animus is, in the first place, against *England*. It is 'your Natives' (i.e. Gulliver's fellow countrymen) whom the King of Brobdingnag considers to be 'the most pernicious Race of little odious Vermin that Nature ever suffered to crawl upon the surface of the Earth', and the long passage at the end, denouncing colonization and foreign conquest, is plainly aimed at England, although the contrary is elaborately stated. The Dutch, England's allies and target of one of Swift's most famous pamphlets, are also more or less wantonly attacked in Part III. There is even what sounds like a personal note in the passage in which Gulliver records his satisfaction that the various countries he has discovered cannot be made colonies of the British Crown:

> The *Houyhnhnms*, indeed, appear not to be so well prepared for War, a Science to which they are perfect Strangers, and especially against missive Weapons. However, supposing myself to be a Minister of State, I could never give my advice for invading them. . . Imagine twenty thousand of them breaking into the midst of an *European* army, confounding the Ranks, overturning the Carriages, battering the Warriors' Faces into Mummy, by terrible Yerks from their hinder Hoofs . . .

Considering that Swift does not waste words, that phrase, 'battering the warriors' faces into mummy', probably indicates a secret wish to see the invincible armies of the Duke of Marlborough treated in a like manner. There are similar touches elsewhere. Even the country mentioned in Part III, where 'the Bulk of the People consist, in a Manner, wholly of Discoverers, Witnesses, Informers, Accusers, Prosecutors, Evidences, Swearers, together with their several subservient and subaltern Instruments, all under the Colours, the Conduct, and Pay of Ministers of State', is called Langdon, which is within one letter of being an anagram of England. (As the early editions of the book contain misprints, it may perhaps have been intended as a complete anagram.) Swift's *physical* repulsion from humanity is certainly real enough, but one has the feeling that his debunking of human grandeur, his diatribes against lords, politicians, court favourites, etc. have mainly a local application and spring from the fact that he belonged to the unsuccessful party. He denounces injustice and oppression, but he gives no evidence of liking democracy. In spite of his enormously greater powers, his implied position is very similar to that of the innumerable silly-clever Conservatives of our own day – people like Sir Alan Herbert, Professor G. M. Young, Lord Elton, the Tory Reform Committee or the long line of Catholic apologists from W. H. Mallock onwards: people who specialize in cracking neat jokes at the expense of whatever is 'modern' and 'progressive', and whose opinions are often all the more extreme because they know that they cannot influence the actual drift of events. After all, such a pamphlet as *An Argument to prove that the Abolishing of Christianity* etc. is very like 'Timothy Shy' having a bit of clean fun with the Brains Trust, or Father Ronald Knox exposing the errors of Bertrand Russell. And the ease with which Swift has been forgiven – and forgiven sometimes, by devout believers – for the blasphemies of *A Tale of a Tub* demonstrates clearly enough the feebleness of religious sentiments as compared with political ones.

However, the reactionary cast of Swift's mind does not show itself chiefly in his political affiliations. The important thing is his attitude towards science, and, more broadly, towards intellectual curiosity. The famous Academy of Lagado, described in Part III of *Gulliver's Travels*, is no doubt a justified satire on most of the so-called scientists of Swift's own day. Significantly, the people at work in it are described as 'Projectors', that is, people not engaged in disinterested research but merely on the look-out for gadgets which will save labour and bring in money. But there is no sign – indeed, all through the book there are many signs to the contrary – that 'pure' science would have struck Swift as a worth-while activity. The more serious kind of scientist has already had a kick in the pants in Part II, when the 'Scholars' patronized by the King of Brobdingnag try to account for Gulliver's small stature:

After much Debate, they concluded unanimously that I was only *Relplum Scalcath*, which is interpreted literally, *Lusus Naturae*; a Determination exactly agreeable to the modern philosophy of *Europe*, whose Professors, disdaining the old Evasion of *occult Causes*, whereby the followers of *Aristotle* endeavoured in vain to disguise their Ignorance, have invented this wonderful Solution of all Difficulties, to the unspeakable Advancement of human Knowledge.

If this stood by itself one might assume that Swift is merely the enemy of *sham* science. In a number of places, however, he goes out of his way to proclaim the uselessness of all learning or speculation not directed towards some practical end:

The Learning of (the Brobdingnagians) is very defective, consisting only in Morality, History, Poetry, and Mathematics, wherein they must be allowed to excel. But, the last of these is wholly applied to what may be useful in Life, to the Improvement of Agriculture, and all mechanical Arts; so that among us it would be little esteemed. And as to Ideas, Entities, Abstractions, and Transcendentals, I could never drive the least Conception into their Heads.

The Houyhnhnms, Swift's ideal beings, are backward even in a mechanical sense. They are unacquainted with metals, have never heard of boats, do not, properly speaking, practise agriculture (we are told that the oats which they live upon 'grow naturally') and appear not to have invented wheels.[1] They have no alphabet, and evidently have not much curiosity about the physical world. They do not believe that any inhabited country exists beside their own, and though they understand the motions of the sun and moon, and the nature of eclipses, 'this is the utmost Progress of their *Astronomy*'. By contrast, the philosophers of the flying island of Laputa are so continuously absorbed in mathematical speculations that before speaking to them one has to attract their attention by flapping them on the ear with a bladder. They have catalogued ten thousand fixed stars, have settled the periods of ninety-three comets, and have discovered, in advance of the astronomers of Europe, that Mars has two moons – all of which information Swift evidently regards as ridiculous, useless and uninteresting. As one might expect, he believes that the scientist's place, if he has a place, is in the laboratory, and that scientific knowledge has no bearing on political matters:

What I . . . thought altogether unaccountable, was the strong Disposition I observed in them towards News and Politics, perpetually enquiring into Public Affairs, giving their judgements in Matters of State, and passionately disputing every Inch of a Party Opinion. I have, indeed, observed the same Disposition

1. Houyhnhnms too old to walk are described as being carried in 'sledges' or in 'a kind of vehicle, drawn like a sledge'. Presumably these had no wheels. [Author's footnote.]

among most of the Mathematicians I have known in *Europe*, though I could never discover the least Analogy between the two Sciences; unless those People suppose, that, because the smallest Circle hath as many Degrees as the largest, therefore the Regulation and Management of the World require no more Abilities, than the Handling and turning of a Globe.

Is there not something familiar in that phrase 'I could never discover the least analogy between the two sciences'? It has precisely the note of the popular Catholic apologists who profess to be astonished when a scientist utters an opinion on such questions as the existence of God or the immortality of the soul. The scientist, we are told, is an expert only in one restricted field: why should his opinions be of value in any other? The implication is that theology is just as much an exact science as, for instance, chemistry, and that the priest is also an expert whose conclusions on certain subjects must be accepted. Swift in effect makes the same claim for the politician, but he goes one better in that he will not allow the scientist – either the 'pure' scientist or the *ad hoc* investigator – to be a useful person in his own line. Even if he had not written Part III of *Gulliver's Travels*, one could infer from the rest of the book that, like Tolstoy and like Blake, he hates the very idea of studying the processes of Nature. The 'Reason' which he so admires in the Houyhnhnms does not primarily mean the power of drawing logical inferences from observed facts. Although he never defines it, it appears in most contexts to mean either common sense – i.e. acceptance of the obvious and contempt for quibbles and abstractions – or absence of passion and superstition. In general he assumes that we know all that we need to know already, and merely use our knowledge incorrectly. Medicine, for instance, is a useless science, because if we lived in a more natural way, there would be no diseases. Swift, however, is not a simple-lifer or an admirer of the Noble Savage. He is in favour of civilization and the arts of civilization. Not only does he see the value of good manners, good conservation, and even learning of a literary and historical kind, he also sees that agriculture, navigation and architecture need to be studied and could with advantage be improved. But his implied aim is a static, incurious civilization – the world of his own day, a little cleaner, a little saner, with no radical change and no poking into the unknowable. More than one would expect in anyone so free from accepted fallacies, he reveres the past, especially classical antiquity, and believes that modern man has degenerated sharply during the past hundred years.[2] In the island of sorcerers, where the spirits of the dead can be called up at will:

> I desired that the Senate of *Rome* might appear before me in one large Chamber, and a modern Representative in Counterview, in another. The first seemed to be an Assembly of Heroes and Demy-Gods, the other a Knot of Pedlars, Pick-Pockets, Highwaymen, and Bullies.

Although Swift uses this section of Part III to attack the truthfulness of recorded history, his critical spirit deserts him as soon as he is dealing with Greeks and Romans. He remarks, of course, upon the corruption of imperial Rome, but he has an almost unreasoning admiration for some of the leading figures of the ancient world:

> I was struck with profound Veneration at the Sight of *Brutus*, and could easily discover the most consummate Virtue, the greatest Intrepidity and Firmness of Mind, the truest Love of his Country, and general Benevolence for mankind, in every Lineament of his Countenance. . . I had the Honour to have much Conversation with *Brutus*, and was told, that his Ancester *Junius*, *Socrates*, *Epaminondas*, *Cato* the younger, *Sir Thomas More*, and himself, were perpetually together: a *Sextumvirate*, to which all the Ages of the World cannot add a seventh.

It will be noticed that of these six people only one is a Christian. This is an important point. If one adds together Swift's pessimism, his reverence for the past, his incuriosity and his horror of the human body, one arrives at an attitude common among religious reactionaries – that is, people who defend an unjust order of society by claiming that this world cannot be substantially improved and only the 'next world' matters. However, Swift shows no sign of having any religious beliefs, at least in an ordinary sense of the words. He does not appear to believe seriously in life after death, and his idea of goodness is bound up with republicanism, love of liberty, courage, 'benevolence' (meaning in effect public spirit), 'reason' and other pagan qualities. This reminds one that there is another strain in Swift, not quite congruous with his disbelief in progress and his general hatred of humanity.

To begin with, he has moments when he is 'constructive' and even 'advanced'. To be occasionally inconsistent is almost a mark of vitality in Utopia books, and Swift sometimes inserts a word of praise into a passage that ought to be purely satirical. Thus, his ideas about the education of

2. The physical decadence which Swift claims to have observed may have been a reality at that date. He attributes it to syphilis, which was a new disease in Europe and may have been more virulent than it is now. Distilled liquors, also, were a novelty in the seventeenth century and must have led at first to a great increase in drunkenness. [Author's footnote.]

the young are fathered on to the Lilliputians, who have much the same views on this subject as the Houyhnhnms. The Lilliputians also have various social and legal institutions (for instance, there are old age pensions, and people are rewarded for keeping the law as well as punished for breaking it) which Swift would have liked to see prevailing in his own country. In the middle of this passage Swift remembers his satirical intention and adds, 'In relating these and the following Laws, I would only be understood to mean the original Institutions, and not the most scandalous Corruptions into which these people are fallen by the degenerate Nature of Man': but as Lilliput is supposed to represent England, and the laws he is speaking of have never had their parallel in England, it is clear that the impulse to make constructive suggestions has been too much for him. But Swift's greatest contribution to political thought, in the narrower sense of the words, is his attack, especially in Part III, on what would now be called totalitarianism. He has an extraordinarily clear prevision of the spy-haunted 'police-State', with its endless heresy-hunts and treason trials, all really designed to neutralize popular discontent by changing it into war hysteria. And one must remember that Swift is here inferring the whole from a quite small part, for the feeble governments of his own day did not give him illustrations ready-made. For example, there is the professor at the School of Political Projectors who 'shewed me a large Paper of Instructions for discovering Plots and Conspiracies', and who claimed that one can find people's secret thoughts by examining their excrement:

> Because Men are never so serious, thoughtful, and intent, as when they are at Stool, which he found by frequent Experiment: for in such Conjectures, when he used merely as a Trial to consider what was the best Way of murdering the King, his Ordure would have a Tincture of Green; but quite different when he thought only of raising an Insurrection, or burning the Metropolis.

The professor and his theory are said to have been suggested to Swift by the – from our point of view – not particularly astonishing or disgusting fact that in a recent State Trial some letters found in somebody's privy had been put in evidence. Later in the same chapter we seem to be positively in the middle of the Russian purges:

> In the Kingdom of Tribnia, by the Natives called Langdon . . . the Bulk of the People consist, in a Manner, wholly of Discoverers, Witnesses, Informers, Accusers, Prosecutors, Evidences, Swearers. . . It is first agreed, and settled among them, what suspected Persons shall be accused of a Plot: Then, 'effectual Care is taken to secure all their Letters and Papers, and put the Owners in Chains.

These papers are delivered to a Sett of Artists, very dexterous in finding out the mysterious Meanings of Words, Syllables, and Letters. . . Where this Method fails, they have two others more effectual, which the Learned among them call *Acrostics* and *Anagrams*. *First*, they can decypher all initial Letters into political Meanings: Thus, N shall signify a Plot, B a Regiment of Horse, L a Fleet at Sea: Or, *Secondly*, by transposing the Letters of the Alphabet in any suspected Paper, they can lay open the deepest Designs of a discontented Party. So, for Example, if I should say in a Letter to a Friend, *Our Brother Tom has just got the Piles*, a skilful Decypherer would discover that the same Letters, which compose that Sentence, may be analysed in the following Words: *Resist – a Plot is brought Home – The Tour*.[3] And this is the anagrammatic Method.

Other professors at the same school invent simplified languages, write books by machinery, educate their pupils by inscribing the lessons on a wafer and causing them to swallow it, or propose to abolish individuality altogether by cutting off part of the brain of one man and grafting it on to the head of another. There is something queerly familiar in the atmosphere of these chapters, because, mixed up with much fooling, there is a perception that one of the aims of totalitarianism is not merely to make sure that people will think the right thoughts, but actually to make them *less conscious*. Then, again, Swift's account of the Leader who is usually to be found ruling over a tribe of Yahoos, and of the 'favourite' who acts first as a dirty-worker and later as a scapegoat, fits remarkably well into the pattern of our own times. But are we to infer from all this that Swift was first and foremost an enemy of tyranny and a champion of the free intelligence? No: his views, so far as one can discern them, are not markedly liberal. No doubt he hates lords, kings, bishops, generals, ladies of fashion, orders, titles and flummery generally, but he does not seem to think better of the common people than of their rulers, or to be in favour of increased social equality, or to be enthusiastic about representative institutions. The Houyhnhnms are organized upon a sort of caste system which is racial in character, the horses which do the menial work being of different colours from their masters and not interbreeding with them. The educational system which Swift admires in the Lilliputians takes hereditary class distinctions for granted, and the children of the poorest class do not go to school, because 'their Business being only to till and cultivate the Earth . . . therefore their Education is of little Consequence to the Public'. Nor does he seem to have been strongly in favour of freedom of speech and the press, in spite of the toleration which his own writings enjoyed. The King of Brobdingnag is

3. Tower. [Author's footnote.]

astonished at the multiplicity of religious and political sects in England, and considers that those who hold 'opinions prejudicial to the public' (in the context this seems to mean simply heretical opinions), though they need not be obliged to change them, ought to be obliged to conceal them: for 'as it was Tyranny in any Government to require the first, so it was Weakness not to enforce the second'. There is a subtler indication of Swift's own attitude in the manner in which Gulliver leaves the land of the Houyhnhnms. Intermittently, at least, Swift was a kind of anarchist, and Part IV of *Gulliver's Travels* is a picture of an anarchistic society, not governed by law in the ordinary sense, but by the dictates of 'Reason', which are voluntarily accepted by everyone. The General Assembly of the Houyhnhnms 'exhorts' Gulliver's master to get rid of him, and his neighbours put pressure on him to make him comply. Two reasons are given. One is that the presence of this unusual Yahoo may unsettle the rest of the tribe, and the other is that a friendly relationship between a Houyhnhnm and a Yahoo is 'not agreeable to Reason or Nature, or a Thing ever heard of before among them'. Gulliver's master is somewhat unwilling to obey, but the 'exhortation' (a Houyhnhnm, we are told, is never *compelled* to do anything, he is merely 'exhorted' or 'advised') cannot be disregarded. This illustrates very well the totalitarian tendency which is implicit in the anarchist or pacifist vision of society. In a society in which there is no law, and in theory no compulsion, the only arbiter of behaviour is public opinion. But public opinion, because of the tremendous urge to conformity in gregarious animals, is less tolerant than any system of law. When human beings are governed by 'thou shalt not', the individual can practise a certain amount of eccentricity: when they are supposedly governed by 'love' or 'reason', he is under continuous pressure to make him behave and think in exactly the same way as everyone else. The Houyhnhnms, we are told, were unanimous on almost all subjects. The only question they ever *discussed* was how to deal with the Yahoos. Otherwise there was no room for disagreement among them, because the truth is always either self-evident, or else it is undiscoverable and unimportant. They had apparently no word for 'opinion' in their language, and in their conversations there was no 'difference of sentiments'. They had reached, in fact, the highest stage of totalitarian organization, the stage when conformity has become so general that there is no need for a police force. Swift approves of this kind of thing because among his many gifts neither curiosity nor good nature was included. Disagreement would always seem to him sheer perversity. 'Reason', among the Houyhnhnms, he says, 'is not a Point Problematical, as with us, where men can argue with Plausibility on both Sides of a Question; but strikes you with immediate Conviction; as it must needs do, where it is not mingled, obscured, or discoloured by Passion and Interest'. In other words, we know everything already, so why should dissident opinions be tolerated? The totalitarian society of the Houyhnhnms, where there can be no freedom and no development, follows naturally from this.

We are right to think of Swift as a rebel and iconoclast, but except in certain secondary matters, such as his insistence that women should receive the same education as men, he cannot be labelled 'left'. He is a Tory anarchist, despising authority while disbelieving in liberty, and preserving the aristocratic outlook while seeing clearly that the existing aristocracy is degenerate and contemptible. When Swift utters one of his characteristic diatribes against the rich and powerful, one must probably, as I said earlier, write off something for the fact that he himself belonged to the less successful party, and was personally disappointed. The 'outs', for obvious reasons, are always more radical than the 'ins'.[4] But the most essential thing in Swift is his inability to believe that life – ordinary life on the solid earth, and not some rationalized, deodorized version of it – could be made worth living. Of course, no honest person claims that happiness is *now* a normal condition among adult human beings; but perhaps it *could* be made normal, and it is upon this question that all serious political controversy really turns. Swift has much in common – more, I believe, than has been noticed – with Tolstoy, another disbeliever in the possiblity of happiness. In both men you have the same anarchistic outlook covering an authoritarian cast of mind; in both a similar hostility to science, the same impatience with opponents, the same inability to see the importance of any question not interesting to themselves; and in both cases a sort of horror of the actual process of life, though in Tolstoy's case it was arrived at later and in a different way. The sexual unhappiness of the two men was not of the same kind, but there was this in common,

4. At the end of the book, as typical specimens of human folly and viciousness, Swift names 'a Lawyer, a Pickpocket, a Colonel, a Fool, a Lord, a Gamester, a Politician, a Whore-master, a Physician, an Evidence, a Suborner, an Attorney, a Traitor, or the like'. One sees here the irresponsible violence of the powerless. The list lumps together those who break the conventional code, and those who keep it. For instance, if you automatically condemn a colonel, as such, on what grounds do you condemn a traitor? Or again, if you want to suppress pickpockets, you must have laws, which means that you must have lawyers. But the whole closing passage, in which the hatred is so authentic, and the reason given for it so inadequate, is somehow unconvincing. One has the feeling that personal animosity is at work. [Author's footnote.]

that in both of them a sincere loathing was mixed up with a morbid fascination. Tolstoy was a reformed rake who ended by preaching complete celibacy, while continuing to practise the opposite into extreme old age. Swift was presumably impotent, and had an exaggerated horror of human dung: he also thought about it incessantly, as is evident throughout his works. Such people are not likely to enjoy even the small amount of happiness that falls to most human beings, and, from obvious motives, are not likely to admit that earthly life is capable of much improvement. Their incuriosity, and hence their intolerance, spring from the same root.

Swift's disgust, rancour and pessimism would make sense against the background of a 'next world' to which this one is the prelude. As he does not appear to believe seriously in any such thing, it becomes necessary to construct a paradise supposedly existing on the surface of the earth, but something quite different from anything we know, with all that he disapproves of – lies, folly, change, enthusiasm, pleasure, love and dirt – eliminated from it. As his ideal being he chooses the horse, an animal whose excrement is not offensive. The Houyhnhnms are dreary beasts – this is so generally admitted that the point is not worth labouring. Swift's genius can make them credible, but there can have been very few readers in whom they have excited any feeling beyond dislike. And this is not from wounded vanity at seeing animals preferred to men; for, of the two, the Houyhnhnms are much liker to human beings than are the Yahoos, and Gulliver's horror of the Yahoos, together with his recognition that they are the same kind of creature as himself, contains a logical absurdity. This horror comes upon him at his very first sight of them. 'I never beheld' he says, 'in all my Travels, so disagreeable an Animal, nor one against which I naturally conceived so strong an Antipathy.' But in comparison with what are the Yahoos disgusting? Not with the Houyhnhnms, because at this time Gulliver has not seen a Houyhnhnm. It can only be in comparison with himself, i.e. with a human being. Later, however, we are told that the Yahoos *are* human beings, and human society becomes insupportable to Gulliver because all men are Yahoos. In that case why did he not conceive his disgust of humanity earlier? In effect we are told that the Yahoos are fantastically different from men, and yet are the same. Swift has overreached himself in his fury, and is shouting at his fellow creatures: 'You are filthier than you are!' However, it is impossible to feel much sympathy with the Yahoos, and it is not because they oppress the Yahoos that the Houyhnhnms are unattractive. They are unattractive because the 'Reason' by which they are governed is really a desire for death. They are exempt from love, friendship, curiosity, fear, sorrow and – except in their feelings towards the Yahoos, who occupy rather the same place in their community as the Jews in Nazi Germany – anger and hatred. 'They have no Fondness for their Colts or Foles, but the Care they take, in educating them, proceeds entirely from the Dictates of *Reason*.' They lay store by 'Friendship' and 'Benevolence', but 'these are not confined to particular Objects, but universal to the whole Race'. They also value conversation, but in their conversations there are no differences of opinion, and 'nothing passed but what was useful, expressed in the fewest and most significant Words'. They practise strict birth control, each couple producing two offspring and thereafter abstaining from sexual intercourse. Their marriages are arranged for them by their elders, on eugenic principles, and their language contains no word for 'love', in the sexual sense. When somebody dies they carry on exactly as before, without feeling any grief. It will be seen that their aim is to be as like a corpse as is possible while retaining physical life. One or two of their characteristics, it is true, do not seem to be strictly 'reasonable' in their own usage of the word. Thus, they place a great value not only on physical hardihood but on athleticism, and they are devoted to poetry. But these exceptions may be less arbitrary than they seem. Swift probably emphasizes the physical strength of the Houyhnhnms in order to make clear that they could never be conquered by the hated human race, while a taste for poetry may figure among their qualities because poetry appeared to Swift as the antithesis of science, from his point of view the most useless of all pursuits. In Part III he names 'Imagination, Fancy, and Invention' as desirable faculties in which the Laputan mathematicians (in spite of their love of music) were wholly lacking. One must remember that although Swift was an admirable writer of comic verse, the kind of poetry he thought valuable would probably be didactic poetry. The poetry of the Houyhnhnms, he says,

> must be allowed to excel (that of) all other Mortals; wherein the Justness of their Similes, and the Minuteness, as well as exactness, of their Descriptions, are, indeed, inimitable. Their Verses abound very much in both of these; and usually contain either some exalted Notions of Friendship and Benevolence, or the Praises of those who were Victors in Races, and other bodily Exercises.

Alas, not even the genius of Swift was equal to producing a specimen by which we could judge the poetry of the Houyhnhnms. But it sounds as though it were chilly stuff (in heroic couplets, presumably), and not seriously in conflict with the principles of 'Reason'.

Happiness is notoriously difficult to describe, and pictures of a just and well-ordered society are seldom either attractive or convincing. Most creators of 'favourable' Utopias, however, are concerned to show what life could be like if it were lived more fully. Swift advocates a simple refusal of life, justifying this by the claim that 'Reason' consists in thwarting your instincts. The Houyhnhnms, creatures without a history, continue for generation after generation to live prudently, maintaining their population at exactly the same level, avoiding all passion, suffering from no diseases, meeting death indifferently, training up their young in the same principles – and all for what? In order that the same process may continue indefinitely. The notions that life here and now is worth living, or that it could be made worth living, or that it must be sacrificed for some future good, are all absent. The dreary world of the Houyhnhnms was about as good a Utopia as Swift could construct, granting that he neither believed in a 'next world' nor could get any pleasure out of certain normal activities. But it is not really set up as something desirable in itself, but as the justification for another attack on humanity. The aim, as usual, is to humiliate Man by reminding him that he is weak and ridiculous, and above all that he stinks; and the ultimate motive, probably, is a kind of envy, the envy of the ghost for the living, of the man who knows he cannot be happy for the others who – so he fears – may be a little happier than himself. The political expression of such an outlook must be either reactionary or nihilistic, because the person who holds it will want to prevent society from developing in some direction in which his pessimism may be cheated. One can do this either by blowing everything to pieces, or by averting social change. Swift ultimately blew everything to pieces in the only way that was feasible before the atomic bomb – that is, he went mad – but, as I have tried to show, his political aims were on the whole reactionary ones.

From what I have written it may have seemed that I am *against* Swift, and that my object is to refute him and even to belittle him. In a political and moral sense I am against him so far as I understand him. Yet curiously enough he is one of the writers I admire with least reserve, and *Gulliver's Travels*, in particular is a book which it seems impossible for me to grow tired of. I read it first when I was eight – one day short of eight, to be exact, for I stole and furtively read the copy which was to be given me next day on my eighth birthday – and I have certainly not read it less than half a dozen times since. Its fascination seems inexhaustible. If I had to make a list of six books which were to be preserved when all others were destroyed, I would certainly put *Gulliver's Travels* among them. This raises the question: what is the relationship between agreement with a writer's opinions, and enjoyment of his work?

If one is capable of intellectual detachment, one can *perceive* merit in a writer whom one deeply disagrees with, but *enjoyment* is a different matter. Supposing that there is such a thing as good or bad art, then the goodness or badness must reside in the work of art itself – not independently of the observer, indeed, but independently of the mood of the observer. In one sense, therefore, it cannot be true that a poem is good on Monday and bad on Tuesday. But if one judges the poem by the appreciation it arouses, then it can certainly be true, because appreciation, or enjoyment, is a subjective condition which cannot be commanded. For a great deal of his waking life, even the most cultivated person has no aesthetic feelings whatever, and the power to have aesthetic feelings is very easily destroyed. When you are frightened, or hungry, or are suffering from toothache or seasickness, *King Lear* is no better from your point of view than *Peter Pan*. You may know in an intellectual sense that it is better, but that is simply a fact which you remember; you will not *feel* the merit of *King Lear* until you are normal again. And aesthetic judgement can be upset just as disastrously – more disastrously, because the cause is less readily recognized – by political or moral disagreement. If a book angers, wounds or alarms you, then you will not enjoy it, whatever its merits may be. If it seems to you a really pernicious book, likely to influence other people in some undesirable way, then you will probably construct an aesthetic theory to show that it *has* no merits. Current literary criticism consists quite largely of this kind of dodging to and fro between two sets of standards. And yet the opposite process can also happen: enjoyment can overwhelm disapproval, even though one clearly recognizes that one is enjoying something inimical. Swift, whose world-view is so peculiarly unacceptable, but who is nevertheless an extremely popular writer, is a good instance of this. Why is it that we don't mind being called Yahoos, although firmly convinced that we are *not* Yahoos?

It is not enough to make the usual answer that of course Swift was wrong, in fact he was insane, but he was 'a good writer'. It is true that the literary quality of a book is to some small extent separable from its subject-matter. Some people have a native gift for using words, as some people have a naturally 'good eye' at games. It is largely a question of timing and of instinctively knowing how much emphasis to use. As an example near at hand, look back at the passage I quoted earlier, starting 'In the Kingdom of Tribnia, by the Natives called Langdon'. It derives much of its force from the final sentence: 'And this is the anagrammatic Method.' Strictly speaking this sentence is unnecessary, for we have already seen the anagram deciphered, but the mock-solemn repetition, in which one seems to hear Swift's own voice uttering the words, drives home the idiocy of the activities described, like the final tap to a nail. But not all the power and simplicity of Swift's prose, nor the imaginative effort that has been able to make not one but a whole series of impossible words more credible than the majority of history books – none of this would enable us to enjoy Swift if his world-view were truly wounding or shocking. Millions of people, in many countries, must have enjoyed *Gulliver's Travels* while more or less seeing its anti-human implications: and even the child who accepts Parts I and II as a simple story gets a sense of absurdity from thinking of human beings six inches high. The explanation must be that Swift's world-view is felt to be *not* altogether false – or it would probably be more accurate to say, not false all the time. Swift is a diseased writer. He remains permanently in a depressed mood which in most people is only intermittent, rather as though someone suffering from jaundice or the after-effects of influenza should have the energy to write books. But we all know that mood, and something in us responds to the expression of it. Take, for instance, one of his most characteristic works, 'The Lady's Dressing Room': one might add the kindred poem, 'Upon a Beautiful Young Nymph Going to Bed'. Which is truer, the viewpoint expressed in these poems, or the viewpoint implied in Blake's phrase, 'The naked female human form divine'? No doubt Blake is nearer the truth, and yet who can fail to feel a sort of pleasure in seeing that fraud, feminine delicacy, exploded for once? Swift falsifies his picture of the whole world by refusing to see anything in human life except dirt, folly and wickedness, but the part which he abstracts from the whole does exist, and it is something which we all know about while shrinking from mentioning it. Part of our minds – in any normal person it is the dominant part – believes that man is a noble animal and life is worth living: but there is also a sort of inner self which at least intermittently stands aghast at the horror of existence. In the queerest way, pleasure and disgust are linked together. The human body is beautiful: it is also repulsive and ridiculous, a fact which can be verified at any swimming pool. The sexual organs are objects of desire and also of loathing, so much so that in many languages, if not in all languages, their names are used as words of abuse. Meat is delicious, but a butcher's shop makes one feel sick: and indeed all our food springs ultimately from dung and dead bodies, the two things which of all others seem to us the most horrible. A child, when it is past the infantile stage but still looking at the world with fresh eyes, is moved by horror almost as often as by wonder – horror of snot and spittle, of the dogs' excrement on the pavement, the dying toad full of maggots, the sweaty smell of grown-ups, the hideousness of old men, with their bald heads and bulbous noses. In his endless harping on disease, dirt and deformity, Swift is not actually inventing anything, he is merely leaving something out. Human behaviour, too, especially in politics, is as he describes it, although it contains other more important factors which he refuses to admit. So far as we can see, both horror and pain are necessary to the continuance of life on this planet, and it is therefore open to pessimists like Swift to say: 'If horror and pain must always be with us, how can life be significantly improved?' His attitude is in effect the Christian attitude, minus the bribe of a 'next world' – which, however, probably has less hold upon the minds of believers than the conviction that this world is a vale of tears and the grave is a place of rest. It is, I am certain, a wrong attitude, and one which could have harmful effects upon behaviour; but something in us responds to it, as it responds to the gloomy words of the burial service and the sweetish smell of corpses in a country church.

It is often argued, at least by people who admit the importance of subject-matter, that a book cannot be 'good' if it expresses a palpably false view of life. We are told that in our own age, for instance, any book that has genuine literary merit will also be more or less 'progressive' in tendency. This ignores the fact that throughout history a similar struggle between the progress and reaction has been raging, and that the best books of any one age have always been written from several different viewpoints, some of them palpably more false than others. In so far as the writer is a propagandist, the most one can ask of him is that he shall genuinely believe in what he is saying, and that it shall not be something blazingly silly. Today, for example, one can imagine a good book being written by a Catholic, a Communist, a Fascist, a Pacifist, an Anarchist, perhaps by an old-style Liberal or an ordinary Conservative: one cannot imagine a good book being written by a spiritualist, a Buchmanite or a member of the Ku Klux Klan. The views that a writer holds must be compatible with sanity, in the medical sense, and with the power of continuous thought: beyond that what we ask of him is talent, which is probably another name for conviction. Swift did not possess ordinary wisdom, but he did possess a terrible intensity of vision, capable of picking out a single hidden truth and then magnifying it and distorting it. The durability of *Gulliver's Travels* goes to show that if the force of belief is behind it, a world-view which only just passes the test of sanity is sufficient to produce a great work of art.

Polemic, No. 5, September–October 1946; *S.E.*; *O.R.*; *C.E.*

36. How the Poor Die

In the year 1929 I spent several weeks in the Hôpital X, in the fifteenth *arrondissement* of Paris. The clerks put me through the usual third-degree at the reception desk, and indeed I was kept answering questions for some twenty minutes before they would let me in. If you have ever had to fill up forms in a Latin country you will know the kind of questions I mean. For some days past I have been unequal to translating Réaumur into Fahrenheit, but I know that my temperature was round about 103, and by the end of the interview I had some difficulty in standing on my feet. At my back a resigned little knot of patients, carrying bundles done up in coloured handkerchiefs, waiting their turn to be questioned.

After the questioning came the bath – a compulsory routine for all newcomers, apparently, just as in prison or the workhouse. My clothes were taken away from me, and after I had sat shivering for some minutes in five inches of warm water I was given a linen nightshirt and a short blue flannel dressing-gown – no slippers, they had none big enough for me, they said – and led out into the open air. This was a night in February and I was suffering from pneumonia. The ward we were going to was 200 yards away and it seemed that to get to it you had to cross the hospital grounds. Someone stumbled in front of me with a lantern. The gravel path was frosty underfoot, and the wind whipped the nightshirt round my bare calves. When we got into the ward I was aware of a strange feeling of familiarity whose origin I did not succeed in pinning down till later in the night. It was a long, rather low, ill-lit room, full of murmuring voices and with three rows of beds surprisingly close together. There was a foul smell, faecal and yet sweetish. As I lay down I saw on a bed nearly opposite me a small, round-shouldered, sandy-haired man sitting half naked while a doctor and a student performed some strange operation on him. First the doctor produced from his black bag a dozen small glasses like wine glasses, then the student burned a match inside each glass to exhaust the air, then the glass was popped on to the man's back or chest and the vacuum drew up a huge yellow blister. Only after some moments did I realize what they were doing to him. It was something called cupping, a treatment which you can read about in old medical text-books but which till then I had vaguely thought of as one of those things they do to horses.

The cold air outside had probably lowered my temperature, and I watched this barbarous remedy with detachment and even a certain amount of amusement. The next moment, however, the doctor and the student came across to my bed, hoisted me upright and without a word began applying the same set of glasses, which had not been sterilized in any way. A few feeble protests that I uttered got no more response than if I had been an animal. I was very much impressed by the impersonal way in which the two men started on me. I had never been in the public ward of a hospital before, and it was my first experience of doctors who handle you without speaking to you, or, in a human sense, taking any notice of you. They only put on six glasses in my case, but after doing so they scarified the blisters and applied the glasses again. Each glass now drew out about a dessert-spoonful of dark-coloured blood. As I lay down again, humiliated, disgusted and frightened by the thing that had been done to me, I reflected that now at least they would leave me alone. But no, not a bit of it. There was another treatment coming, the mustard poultice, seemingly a matter of routine like the hot bath. Two slatternly nurses had already got the poultice ready, and they lashed it round my chest as tight as a strait jacket while some men who were wandering about the ward in shirt and trousers began to collected round my bed with half-sympathetic grins. I learned later that watching a patient have a mustard poultice was a favourite pastime in the ward. These things are normally applied for a quarter of an hour and certainly they are funny enough if you don't happen to be the person inside. For the first five minutes the pain is severe, but you believe you can bear it. During the second five minutes this belief evaporates, but the poultice is buckled at the back and you can't get it off. This is the period the onlookers most enjoy. During the last five minutes, I noted a sort of numbness supervenes. After the poultice had been removed a waterproof pillow packed with ice was thrust beneath my head and I was left alone. I did not sleep and to the best of my knowledge this was the only night of my life – I mean the only night spent in bed – in which I have not slept at all, not even a minute.

During my first hour in the Hôpital X, I had had a whole series of different and contradictory treatments, but this was misleading, for in general you got very little treatment at all, either good or bad, unless you were ill in some interesting and instructive way. At five in the morning the nurses came round, woke the patients and took their temperatures, but did not wash them. If you were well enough you washed yourself, otherwise you depended on the kindness of some walking patient. It was generally patients, too, who carried the bed-bottles and the grim bed-pan, nicknamed *la casserole*. At eight breakfast arrived, called army fashion *la soupe*. It was soup, too, a thin vegetable soup with slimy hunks of bread floating about in it. Later in the day the tall, solemn, black-bearded doctor made his rounds, with an *interne* and a troop of students following at his heels, but there were about sixty of us in the ward and it was evident that he had other wards to attend to as well. There were many beds past which he walked day after day, sometimes followed by imploring cries. On the other hand if you had some disease with which the students wanted to familiarize themselves you got plenty of attention of a kind. I myself, with an exceptionally fine specimen of a bronchial rattle, sometimes had as many as a dozen students queueing up to listen to my chest. It was a queer feeling – queer, I mean, because of their intense interest in learning their job, together with a seeming lack of any perception that the patients were human beings. It is strange to relate, but sometimes as some young student stepped forward to take his turn at manipulating you he would be actually tremulous with excitement, like a boy who has at last got his hands on some expensive piece of machinery. And then ear after ear – ears of young men, of girls, of Negroes – pressed against your back, relays of fingers solemnly but clumsily tapping, and not from any one of them did you get a word of conversation or a look direct in your face. As a non-paying patient, in the uniform nightshirt, you were primarily *a specimen*, a thing I did not resent but could never quite get used to.

After some days I grew well enough to sit up and study the surrounding patients. The stuffy room, with its narrow beds so close together that you could easily touch your neighbour's hand, had every sort of disease in it except, I suppose, acutely infectious cases. My right-hand neighbour was a little red-haired cobbler with one leg shorter than the other, who used to announce the death of any other patient (this happened a number of times, and my neighbour was always the first to hear of it) by whistling to me, exclaiming '*Numéro 43*!' (or whatever it was) and flinging his arms above his head. This man had not much wrong with him, but in most of the other beds within my angle of vision some squalid tragedy or some plain horror was being enacted. In the bed that was foot to foot with mine there lay, until he died (I didn't see him die – they moved him to another bed), a little weazened man who was suffering from I do not know what disease, but something that made his whole body so intensely sensitive that any movement from side to side, sometimes even the weight of the bed-clothes, would make him shout out with pain. His worst suffering was when he urinated, which he did with the greatest difficulty. A nurse would bring him the bed-bottle and then for a long time stand beside his bed, whistling, as grooms are said to do with horses, until at last with an agonized shriek of '*Je pisse*!' he would get started. In the bed next to him the sandy-haired man whom I had seen being cupped used to cough up blood-streaked mucus at all hours. My left-hand neighbour was a tall, flaccid-looking young man who used periodically to have a tube inserted into his back and astonishing quantities of frothy liquid drawn off from some part of his body. In the bed beyond that a veteran of the war of 1870 was dying, a handsome old man with a white imperial, round whose bed, at all hours when visiting was allowed, four elderly female relatives dressed all in black sat exactly like crows, obviously scheming for some pitiful legacy. In the bed opposite me in the further row was an old bald-headed man with drooping moustaches and greatly swollen face and body, who was suffering from some disease that made him urinate almost incessantly. A huge glass receptable stood always beside his bed. One day his wife and daughter came to visit him. At the sight of them the old man's bloated face lit up with a smile of surprising sweetness, and as his daughter, a pretty girl of about twenty, approached the bed I saw that his hand was slowly working its way from under the bed-clothes. I seemed to see in advance the gesture that was coming – the girl kneeling beside the bed, the old man's hand laid on her head in his dying blessing. But no, he merely handed her the bed-bottle, which she promptly took from him and emptied into the receptacle.

About a dozen beds away from me was *numéro 57* – I think that was his number – a cirrhosis of the liver case. Everyone in the ward knew him by sight because he was sometimes the subject of a medical lecture. On two afternoons a week the tall, grave doctor would lecture in the ward to a party of students, and on more than one occasion old *numéro 57* was wheeled on a sort of trolley into the middle of the ward, where the doctor would roll back his nightshirt, dilate with his fingers a huge flabby protuberance on the man's belly – the diseased liver, I suppose – and explain solemnly that this was a disease attributable to alcoholism, commoner in the wine-drinking countries. As usual he neither spoke to his patient nor gave him a smile, a nod or any kind of recognition. While he talked, very grave and upright, he would hold the wasted body beneath his two hands, sometimes giving it a gentle roll to and fro, in just the attitude of a woman handling a rolling-pin. Not that *numéro 57* minded this kind of thing. Obviously he was an old hospital inmate, a regular exhibit at lectures, his liver long since marked down for a bottle in some pathological museum. Utterly uninterested in what was said about him, he would lie with his colourless eyes gazing at nothing, while the doctor showed him off like a piece of antique china. He was a man of about sixty, astonishingly shrunken. His face, pale as vellum, had shrunken away till it seemed no bigger than a doll's.

One morning my cobbler neighbour woke me by plucking at my pillow before the nurses arrived. '*Numéro 57*!' – he flung his arms above his head. There was a light in the ward, enough to see by. I could see old *numéro 57* lying crumpled up on his side, his face sticking out over the side of the bed, and towards me. He had died some time during the night, nobody knew when. When the nurses came they received the news of his death indifferently and went about their work. After a long time, an hour or more, two other nurses marched in abreast like soldiers, with a great clumping of sabots, and knotted the corpse up in the sheets, but it was not removed till some time later. Meanwhile, in the better light, I had time for a good look at *numéro 57*. Indeed I lay on my side to look at him. Curiously enough he was the first dead European I had seen. I had seen dead men before, but always Asiatics and usually people who had died violent deaths. *Numéro 57*'s eyes were still open, his mouth also open, his small face contorted into an expression of agony. What most impressed me however was the whiteness of his face. It had been pale before, but now it was little darker than the sheets. As I gazed at the tiny, screwed-up face it struck me that this disgusting piece of refuse, waiting to be carted away and dumped on a slab in the dissecting room, was an example of 'natural' death, one of the things you pray for in the Litany. There you are, then, I thought, that's what is waiting for you, twenty, thirty, forty years hence: that is how the lucky ones die, the ones who live to be old. One wants to live, of course, indeed one only stays alive by virtue of the fear of death, but I think now, as I thought then, that it's better to die violently and not too old. People talk about the horrors of war, but what weapon has a man invented that even approaches in cruelty some of the commoner diseases? 'Natural' death, almost by definition, means something slow, smelly and painful. Even at that, it makes a difference if you can achieve it in your own home and not in a public institution. This poor old wretch who had just flickered out like a candle-end was not even important enough to have anyone watching by his deathbed. He was merely a number, then a 'subject' for the students' scalpels. And the sordid publicity of dying in such a place! In the Hôpital X the beds were very close together and there were no screens. Fancy, for instance, dying like the little man whose bed was for a while foot to foot with mine, the one who cried out when the bed-clothes touched him! I dare say *Je pisse!* were his last recorded words. Perhaps the dying don't bother about such things – that at least would be the standard answer: nevertheless dying people are often more or less normal in their minds till within a day or so of the end.

In the public wards of a hospital you see horrors that you don't seem to meet with among people who manage to die in their own homes, as though certain diseases only attacked people at the lower income levels. But it is a fact that you would not in any English hospitals see some of the things I saw in the Hôpital X. This business of people just dying like animals, for instance, with nobody standing by, nobody interested, the death not even noticed till the morning – this happened more than once. You certainly would not see that in England, and still less would you see a corpse left exposed to the view of the other patients. I remember that once in a cottage hospital in England a man died while we were at tea, and though there were only six of us in the ward the nurses managed things so adroitly that the man was dead and his body removed without our even hearing about it till tea was over. A thing we perhaps underrate in England is the advantage we enjoy in having large numbers of well-trained and rigidly-disciplined nurses. No doubt English nurses are dumb enough, they may tell fortunes with tea-leaves, wear Union Jack badges and keep photographs of the Queen on their mantelpieces, but at least they don't let you lie unwashed and constipated on an unmade bed, out of sheer laziness. The nurses at the Hôpital X still had a tinge of Mrs Gamp about them, and later, in the military hospitals of Republican Spain, I was to see nurses almost too ignorant to take a temperature. You wouldn't, either, see in England such dirt as existed in the Hôpital X. Later on, when I was well enough to wash myself in the bathroom, I found that there was kept there a huge packing-case into which the scraps of food and dirty dressings from the ward were flung, and the wainscottings were infested by crickets.

When I had got back my clothes and grown strong on my legs I fled from the Hôpital X, before my time was up and without waiting for a medical discharge. It was not the only hospital I have fled from, but its gloom and bareness, its sickly smell and, above all, something in its mental atmosphere stand out in my memory as exceptional. I had been taken there because it was the hospital belonging to my *arrondissement*, and I did not learn till after I was in it that it bore a bad reputation. A year or two later the celebrated swindler, Madame Hanaud, who was ill while on remand, was taken to the Hôpital X, and after a few days of it she managed to elude her guards, took a taxi and drove back to the prison, explaining that she was more comfortable there. I have no doubt that the Hôpital X was quite untypical of French hospitals even at that date. But the patients, nearly all of them working men, were surprisingly resigned. Some of them seemed to find the conditions almost comfortable, for at least two were destitute malingerers who found this a good way of getting through the winter. The nurses connived because the malingerers made themselves useful by doing odd jobs. But the attitude of the majority was: of course this is a lousy place, but what else do you expect? It did not seem strange to them that you should be woken at five and then wait three hours before starting the day on watery soup, or that people should die with no one at their bedside, or even that your chance of getting medical attention should depend on catching the doctor's eye as he went past. According to their traditions that was what hospitals were like. If you are seriously ill, and if you are too poor to be treated in your own home, then you must go into hospital, and once there you must put up with harshness and discomfort, just as you would in the army. But on top of this I was interested to find a lingering belief in the old stories that have now almost faded from memory in England – stories, for instance, about doctors cutting you open out of sheer curiosity or thinking it funny to start operating before you were properly 'under'. There were dark tales about a little operating room said to be situated just beyond the bathroom. Dreadful screams were said to issue from this room. I saw nothing to confirm these stories and no doubt they were all nonense, though I did see two students kill a sixteen-year-old boy, or nearly kill him (he appeared to be dying when I left the hospital, but he may have recovered later) by mischievous experiment which they probably could not have tried on a paying patient. Well within living memory it used to be believed in London that in some of the big hospitals patients were killed off to get dissection subjects. I didn't hear this tale repeated at the Hôpital X, but I should think some of the men there would have found it credible. For it was a hospital in which not the methods, perhaps, but something of the atmosphere of the nineteenth century had managed to survive, and therein lay its peculiar interest.

During the past fifty years or so there has been a great change in the relationship between doctor and patient. If you look at almost any literature before the later part of the nineteenth century, you find that a hospital is popularly regarded as much the same thing as a prison, and an old-fashioned, dungeon-like prison at that. A hospital is a place of filth, torture and death, a sort of antechamber to the tomb. No one who was not more or less destitute would have thought of going into such a place for treatment. And especially in the early part of the last century, when medical science had grown bolder than before without being any more successful, the whole business of doctoring was looked on with horror and dread by ordinary people. Surgery, in particular, was believed to be no more than a peculiarly gruesome form of sadism, and dissection, possible only with the aid of body-snatchers, was even confused with necromancy. From the nineteenth century you could collect a large horror-literature connected with doctors and hospitals. Think of poor old George III, in his dotage, shrieking for mercy as he sees his surgeons approaching to 'bleed him till he faints'! Think of the conversations of Bob Sawyer and Benjamin Allen, which no doubt are hardly parodies, or the field hospitals in *La Débâcle* and *War and Peace*, or that shocking description of an amputation in Melville's *Whitejacket*! Even the names given to doctors in nineteenth-century English fiction, Slasher, Carver, Sawyer, Fillgrave and so on, and the generic nickname 'sawbones', are about as grim as they are comic. The anti-surgery tradition is perhaps best expressed in Tennyson's poem, 'The Children's Hospital', which is essentially a pre-chloroform document though it seems to have been written as late as 1880. Moreover, the outlook which Tennyson records in this poem had a lot to be said for it. When you consider what an operation without anaesthetics must have been like, what it notoriously *was* like, it is difficult not to suspect the motives of people who would undertake such things. For these bloody horrors which the students so eagerly looked forward to ('A magnificent sight if Slasher does it!') were admittedly more or less useless: the patient who did not die of shock usually died of gangrene, a result which was taken for granted. Even now doctors can be found whose motives are questionable. Anyone who has had much illness, or who has listened to medical students talking, will know what I mean. But anaesthetics were a turning-point, and disinfectants were another. Nowhere in the world, probably, would you now see the kind of scene described by Axel Munthe in *The Story of San Michele*, when the sinister surgeon in top-hat and frock-coat, his starched shirtfront spattered with blood and pus, carves up patient after patient with the same knife and flings the severed limbs into a pile beside the table. Moreover, national health insurance has partly done away with the idea that a working-class patient is a pauper who deserves little consideration. Well into this century it was usual for 'free' patients at the big hospitals to have their teeth extracted with no anaesthetic. They don't pay, so why should they have anaesthetic – that was the attitude. That too has changed.

And yet every institution will always bear upon it some lingering memory of its past. A barrack-room is still haunted by the ghost of Kipling, and it is difficult to enter a workhouse without being reminded of *Oliver Twist*. Hospitals began as a kind of casual ward for lepers and the like to die in, and they continued as places where medical students learned their art on the bodies of the poor. You can still catch a faint suggestion of their history in their characteristically gloomy architecture. I would be far from complaining about the treatment I have received in any English hospital, but I do know that it is a sound instinct that warns people to keep out of hospitals if possible, and especially out of the public wards. Whatever the legal position may be, it is unquestionable that you have far less control over your own treatment, far less certainty that frivolous experiments will not be tried on you, when it is a case of 'accept the discipline or get out'. And it is a great thing to die in your own bed, though it is better still to die in your boots. However great the kindness and the efficiency, in every hospital death there will be some cruel, squalid detail, something perhaps too small to be told but leaving terribly painful memories behind, arising out of the haste, the crowding, the impersonality of a place where every day people are dying among strangers.

The dread of hospitals probably still survives among the very poor and in all of us it has only recently disappeared. It is a dark patch not far beneath the surface of our minds. I have said earlier that, when I entered the ward at the Hôpital X, I was conscious of a strange feeling of familiarity. What the scene reminded me of, of course, was the reeking, pain-filled hospitals of the nineteenth century, which I had never seen but of which I had a traditional knowledge. And something, perhaps the black-clad doctor with his frowsy black bag, or perhaps only the sickly smell, played the queer trick of unearthing from my memory that poem of Tennyson's, 'The Children's Hospital', which I had not thought of for twenty years. It happened that as a child I had had it read aloud to me by a sick-nurse whose own working life might have stretched back to the time when Tennyson wrote the poem. The horrors and sufferings of the old-style hospitals were a vivid memory to her. We had shuddered over the poem together, and then seemingly I had forgotten it. Even its name would probably have recalled nothing to me. But the first glimpse of the ill-lit, murmurous room, with the beds so close together, suddenly roused the train of thought to which it belonged, and in the night that followed I found myself remembering the whole story and atmosphere of the poem, with many of its lines complete.

Now, [N.S.], No. 6 [November 1946]; *S.E.*, *O.R.*, *C.E.*

37. Riding Down from Bangor

The reappearance of *Helen's Babies*,[1] in its day one of the most popular books in the world – within the British Empire alone it was pirated by twenty different publishing firms, the author receiving a total profit of £40 from a sale of some hundreds of thousand or millions of copies – will ring a bell in any literate person over thirty-five. Not that the present edition is an altogether satisfactory one. It is a cheap little book with rather unsuitable illustrations, various American dialect words appear to have been cut out of it, and the sequel, *Other People's Children*, which was often bound up with it in earlier editions, is missing. Still, it is pleasant to see *Helen's Babies* in print again. It had become almost a rarity in recent years, and it is one of the best of the little library of American books on which people born at about the turn of the century were brought up.

The books one reads in childhood, and perhaps most of all the bad and good bad books, create in one's mind a sort of false map of the world, a series of fabulous countries into which one can retreat at odd moments throughout the rest of life, and which in some cases can even survive a visit to the real countries which they are supposed to represent. The pampas, the Amazon, the coral islands of the Pacific, Russia, land of birchtree and samovar, Transylvania with its boyars and vampires, the China of Guy Boothby, the Paris of du Maurier – one could continue the list for a long time. But one other imaginary country that I acquired early in life was called America. If I pause on the word 'America', and, deliberately putting aside the existing reality, call up my childhood vision of it, I see two pictures – composite pictures, of course, from which I am omitting a good deal of the detail.

1. *Helen's Babies* by John Habberton, first published in 1876.

One is of a boy sitting in a whitewashed stone schoolroom. He wears braces and has patches on his shirt, and if it is summer he is barefooted. In the corner of the school room there is a bucket of drinking water with a dipper. The boy lives in a farm-house, also of stone and also whitewashed, which has a mortgage on it. He aspires to be President, and is expected to keep the woodpile full. Somewhere in the background of the picture but completely dominating it, is a huge black Bible. The other picture is of a tall, angular man, with a shapeless hat pulled down over his eyes, leaning against a wooden paling and whittling at a stick. His lower jaw moves slowly but ceaselessly. At very long intervals he emits some piece of wisdom such as 'A woman is the orneriest critter there is,'ceptin' a mule', or 'When you don't know a thing to do, don't do a thing', but more often it is a jet of tobacco juice that issues from the gap in his front teeth. Between them those two pictures summed up my earliest impression of America. And of the two, the first – which, I suppose, represented New England, the other representing the South – had the stronger hold upon me.

The books from which these pictures were derived included, of course, books which it is still possible to take seriously, such as *Tom Sawyer* and *Uncle Tom's Cabin*, but the most richly American flavour was to be found in minor works which are now almost forgotten. I wonder, for instance, if anyone still reads *Rebecca of Sunnybrook Farm*, which remained a popular favourite long enough to be filmed with Mary Pickford in the leading part. Or how about the 'Katy' books by Susan Coolidge (*What Katy Did at School*, etc.), which, although girls' books and therefore 'soppy', had the fascination of foreignness? Louisa M. Alcott's *Little Women* and *Good Wives* are, I suppose, still flickeringly in print, and certainly they still have their devotees. As a child I loved both of them, though I was less pleased by the third of the trilogy, *Little Men*. That model school where the worst punishment was to have to whack the schoolmaster, on 'this hurts me more than it hurts you' principles, was rather difficult to swallow.

Helen's Babies belonged in much the same world as *Little Women*, and must have been published round about the same date. Then there were Artemus Ward, Bret Harte, and various songs, hymns and ballads, besides poems dealing with the Civil War, such as 'Barbara Fritchie'("Shoot if you must this old grey head, But spare your country's flag,'she said') and 'Little Gifford of Tennessee'. There were other books so obscure that it hardly seems worth mentioning them, and magazine stories of which I remember nothing except that the old homestead always seemed to have a mortgage on it. There was also *Beautiful Joe*, the American reply to *Black Beauty*, of which you might just possibly pick up a copy in a sixpenny box. All the books I have mentioned were written well before 1900, but something of the special American flavour lingered on into this century in, for instance, the Buster Brown coloured supplements, and even in Booth Tarkington's 'Penrod' stories, which will have been written round about 1910. Perhaps there was even a tinge of it in Ernest Thompson Seton's animal books (*Wild Animals I have Known*, etc.), which have now fallen from favour but which drew tears from the pre-1914 child as surely as *Misunderstood* had done from the children of a generation earlier.

Somewhat later my picture of nineteenth-century America was given greater precision by a song which is still fairly well known and which can be found (I think) in the *Scottish Students' Song Book*. As usual in these bookless days I cannot get hold of a copy, and I must quote fragments from memory. It begins:

> Riding down from Bangor
> On an Eastern train,
> Bronzed with weeks of hunting
> In the woods of Maine –
> Quite extensive whiskers,
> Beard, moustache as well –
> Sat a student fellow,
> Tall and slim and swell.

Presently an aged couple and a 'village maiden', described as 'beautiful, petite', get into the carriage. Quantities of cinders are flying about, and before long the student fellow gets one in his eye: the village maiden extracts it for him, to the scandal of the aged couple. Soon after this the train shoots into a long tunnel, 'black as Egypt's night'. When it emerges into the daylight again the maiden is covered with blushes, and the cause of her confusion is revealed when

> There suddenly appeared
> A tiny little ear-ring
> In that horrid student's beard!

I do not know the date of the song, but the primitiveness of the train (no lights in the carriage, and a cinder in one's eye a normal accident) suggests that it belongs well back in the nineteenth century.

What connects this song with books like *Helen's Babies* is first of all a sort of sweet innocence – the climax, the thing you are supposed to be slightly shocked at, is an episode with which any modern piece of naughty-naughty would *start* – and, secondly, a faint vulgarity of language mixed up with a certain cultural pretentiousness. *Helen's Babies* is intended as a humorous, even a farcical book, but it is haunted all the way through by words like 'tasteful' and 'ladylike', and it is funny chiefly because its tiny disasters happen against a background of conscious gentility. 'Handsome, intelligent, composed, tastefully dressed, without a suspicion of the flirt or the languid woman of fashion about her, she awakened to the utmost my every admiring sentiment' – thus is the heroine described, figuring elsewhere as 'erect, fresh, neat, composed, bright-eyed, fair-faced, smiling and observant'. One gets beautiful glimpses of a now-vanished world in such remarks as: 'I believe you arranged the floral decorations at St Zephaniah's Fair last winter, Mr Burton? 'Twas the most tasteful display of the season.' But in spite of the occasional use of ''twas' and other archaisms – 'parlour' for sitting-room, 'chamber' for bedroom, 'real' as an adverb, and so forth – the book does not 'date' very markedly, and many of its admirers imagine it to have been written round about 1900. Actually it was written in 1875, a fact which one might infer from internal evidence, since the hero, aged twenty-eight, is a veteran of the Civil War.

The book is very short and the story is a simple one. A young bachelor is prevailed on by his sister to look after her house and her two sons, aged five and three, while she and her husband go on a fortnight's holiday. The children drive him almost mad by an endless succession of such acts as falling into ponds, swallowing poison, throwing keys down wells, cutting themselves with razors, and the like, but also facilitate his engagement to 'a charming girl, whom, for about a year, I had been adoring from afar'. These events take place in an outer suburb of New York, in a society which now seems astonishingly sedate, formal, domesticated and, according to current conceptions, un-American. Every action is governed by etiquette. To pass a carriage full of ladies when your hat is crooked is an ordeal; to recognize an acquaintance in church is ill-bred; to become engaged after a ten days' courtship is a severe social lapse. We are accustomed to thinking of American society as more crude, adventurous and, in a cultural sense, democratic than our own, and from writers like Mark Twain, Whitman and Bret Harte, not to mention the cowboy and Red Indian stories of the weekly papers, one draws a picture of a wild anarchic world peopled by eccentrics and desperadoes who have no traditions and no attachment to one place. That aspect of nineteenth-century America did of course exist, but in the more populous eastern States a society similar to Jane Austen's seems to have survived longer than it did in England. And it is hard not to feel that it was a better kind of society than that which arose from the sudden industrialization of the later part of the century. The people in *Helen's Babies* or *Little Women* may be mildly ridiculous, but they are uncorrupted. They have something that is perhaps best described as integrity, or good morale, founded partly on an unthinking piety. It is a matter of course that everyone attends church on Sunday morning and says grace before meals and prayers at bedtime: to amuse the children one tells them Bible stories, and if they ask for a song it is probably 'Glory, glory Hallelujah'. Perhaps it is also a sign of spiritual health in the light literature of this period that death is mentioned freely. 'Baby Phil', the brother of Budge and Toddie, has died shortly before *Helen's Babies* opens, and there are various tear-jerking references to his 'tiny coffin'. A modern writer attempting a story of this kind would have kept coffins out of it.

English children are still americanized by way of the films, but it would no longer be generally claimed that American books are the best ones for children. Who, without misgivings, would bring up a child on the coloured 'comics' in which sinister professors manufacture atomic bombs in the underground laboratories while Superman whizzes through the clouds, the machine-gun bullets bouncing of his chest like peas, and plantinum blondes are raped, or very nearly, by steel robots and fifty-foot dinosaurs? It is a far cry from Superman to the Bible and the woodpile. The earlier children's books, or books readable by children, had not only innocence but a sort of native gaiety, a buoyant, carefree feeling, which was the product, presumably, of the unheard-of freedom and security which nineteenth-century America enjoyed. That is the connecting link between books so seemingly far apart as *Little Women* and *Life on the Mississippi*. The society described in the one is subdued, bookish and home-loving, while the other tells of a crazy world of bandits, gold mines, duels, drunkenness and gambling halls: but in both one can detect an underlying confidence in the future, a sense of freedom and opportunity.

Nineteenth-century America was a rich, empty country which lay outside the main stream of world events, and in which the twin nightmares that beset nearly every modern man, the nightmare of unemployment and the nightmare of State interference, had hardly come into being. There were social distinctions, more marked than those of today, and there was poverty (in *Little Women*, it will be remembered, the family is at one time so hard up that one of the girls sells her hair to the barber), but there was not, as there is now, an all-prevailing sense of helplessness. There was room for everybody, and if you worked hard you could be certain of a living – could even be certain of growing rich: this was generally believed, and for the greater part of the population it was even broadly true. In other words, the civilization of nineteenth-century America was capitalist civilization at its best. Soon after the Civil War the inevitable deterioration started. But for some decades, at least, life in America was much better fun than life in Europe – there was more happening, more colour, more variety, more opportunity – and the books and songs of that period had a sort of bloom, a childlike quality. Hence, I think, the popularity of *Helen's Babies* and other 'light' literature, which made it normal for the English child of thirty or forty years ago to grow up with a theoretical knowledge of racoons, woodchucks, chipmunks, gophers, hickory trees, water-melons and other unfamiliar fragments of the American scene.

Tribune, 22 November 1946; *S.E.*

38. Lear, Tolstoy and the Fool

Tolstoy's pamphlets are the least-known part of his work, and his attack on Shakespeare [1] is not even an easy document to get hold of, at any rate in an English translation. Perhaps, therefore, it will be useful if I give a summary of the pamphlet before trying to discuss it.

Tolstoy begins by saying that throughout life Shakespeare has aroused in him 'an irresistible repulsion and tedium'. Conscious that the opinion of the civilized world is against him, he has made one attempt after another on Shakespeare's works, reading and rereading them in Russian, English and German; but 'I invariably underwent the same feelings: repulsion, weariness and bewilderment'. Now, at the age of seventy-five, he has once again reread the entire works of Shakespeare, including the historical plays, and

1. *Shakespeare and the Drama.* Written about 1903 as an introduction to another pamphlet, *Shakespeare and the Working Classes,* by Ernest Crosby. [Author's footnote.]

I have felt with even greater force, the same feelings – this time, however, not of bewilderment, but of firm, indubitable conviction that the unquestionable glory of a great genius which Shakespeare enjoys, and which compels writers of our time to imitate him and readers and spectators to discover in him non-existent merits – thereby distorting their aesthetic and ethical understanding – is a great evil, and is every untruth.

Shakespeare, Tolstoy adds, is not merely no genius, but is not even 'an average author', and in order to demonstrate this fact he will examine *King Lear*, which, as he is able to show by quotations from Hazlitt, Brandes and others, has been extravagantly praised and can be taken as an example of Shakespeare's best work.

Tolstoy then makes a sort of exposition of the plot of *King Lear*, finding it at every step to be stupid, verbose, unnatural, unintelligible, bombastic, vulgar, tedious and full of incredible events, 'wild ravings', 'mirthless jokes', anachronisms, irrelevancies, obscenities, worn-out stage conventions and other faults both moral and aesthetic. *Lear* is, in any case, a plagiarism of an earlier, and much better play, *King Leir*, by an unknown author, which Shakespeare stole and then ruined. It is worth quoting a specimen paragraph to illustrate the manner in which Tolstoy goes to work. Act III, Scene 2 (in which Lear, Kent and the Fool are together in the storm) is summarized thus:

> Lear walks about the heath and says the words which are meant to express his despair: he desired that the winds should blow so hard that they (the winds) should crack their cheeks and that the rain should flood everything, that lightning should singe his white head, and the thunder flatten the world and destroy all germs 'that make ungrateful man'! The fool keeps uttering still more senseless words. Enter Kent: Lear says that for some reason during this storm all criminals shall be found out and convicted. Kent, still unrecognized by Lear, endeavours to persuade him to take refuge in a hovel. At this point the fool utters a prophecy in no wise related to the situation and they all depart.

Tolstoy's final verdict on *Lear* is that no unhypnotized observer, if such an observer existed, could read it to the end with any feeling except 'aversion and weariness'. And exactly the same is true of 'all the other extolled dramas of Shakespeare, not to mention the senseless dramatized tales, *Pericles*, *Twelfth Night*, *The Tempest*, *Cymbeline*, *Troilus and Cressida*'.

Having dealt with *Lear* Tolstoy draws up a more general indictment against Shakespeare. He finds that Shakespeare has a certain technical skill which is partly traceable to his having been an actor, but otherwise no merits whatever. He has no power of delineating character or of making words and actions spring naturally out of situations, his language is uniformly exaggerated and ridiculous, he constantly thrusts his own random thoughts into the mouth of any character who happens to be handy, he displays a 'complete absence of aesthetic feeling', and his words 'have nothing whatever in common with art and poetry'. 'Shakespeare might have been whatever you like', Tolstoy concludes, 'but he was not an artist.' Moreover, his opinions are not original or interesting, and his tendency is 'of the lowest and most immoral'. Curiously enough, Tolstoy does not base this last judgement on Shakespeare's own utterances, but on the statements of two critics, Gervinus and Brandes. According to Gervinus (or at any rate Tolstoy's reading of Gervinus), 'Shakespeare taught. . .that one *may be too good*', while according to Brandes, 'Shakespeare's fundamental principle . . . is that *the end justifies the means*.' Tolstoy adds on his own account that Shakespeare was a jingo patriot of the worst type, but apart from this he considers that Gervinus and Brandes have given a true and adequate description of Shakespeare's view on life.

Tolstoy then recapitulates in a few paragraphs the theory of art which he had expressed at greater length elsewhere. Put still more shortly, it amounts to a demand for dignity of subject-matter, sincerity, and good craftsmanship. A great work of art must deal with some subject which is 'important to the life of mankind', it must express something which the author genuinely feels, and it must use such technical methods as will produce the desired effect. As Shakespeare is debased in outlook, slipshod in execution and incapable of being sincere even for a moment, he obviously stands condemned.

But here there arises a difficult question. If Shakespeare is all Tolstoy has shown him to be, how did he ever come to be so generally admired? Evidently the answer can only lie in a sort of mass hypnosis, or 'epidemic suggestion'. The whole civilized world has somehow been deluded into thinking Shakespeare a good writer, and even the plainest demonstration to the contrary makes no impression, because one is not dealing with a reasoned opinion but with something akin to religious faith. Throughout history, says Tolstoy, there has been an endless series of these 'epidemic suggestions' – for example, the Crusades, the search for the Philopher's Stone, the craze for tulip growing which once swept over Holland, and so on and so forth. As a contemporary instance he cites, rather significantly, the Dreyfus Case, over which the whole world grew violently excited for no sufficient reason. There are also sudden short-lived crazes for new political and philosophical theories, or for this or that writer, artist or scientist – for example, Darwin, who (in 1903) is 'beginning to be forgotten'. And in some cases a quite worthless popular idol may remain in favour for centuries, for 'it also happens that such crazes, having arisen in consequence of special reasons accidentally favouring their establishment, correspond in such a degree to the views of life spread in society, and especially in literary circles, that they are maintained for a long time'. Shakespeare's plays have continued to be admired over a long period because 'they corresponded to the irreligious and immoral frame of mind of the upper classes of his time and ours'.

As to the manner in which Shakespeare's fame *started*, Tolstoy explains it as having been 'got up' by German professors towards the end of the eighteenth century. His reputation 'originated in Germany, and thence was transferred to England'. The Germans chose to elevate Shakespeare because, at a time when there was no German drama worth speaking about and French classical literature was beginning to seem frigid and artificial, they were captivated by Shakespeare's 'clever development of scenes' and also found in him a good expression of their own attitude towards life. Goethe pronounced Shakespeare a great poet, whereupon all the other critics flocked after him like a troop of parrots, and the general infatuation has lasted ever since. The result has been a further debasement of the drama – Tolstoy is careful to include his own plays when condemning the contemporary stage – and a further corruption of the prevailing moral outlook. It follows that 'the false glorification of Shakespeare' is an important evil which Tolstoy feels it his duty to combat.

This, then, is the substance of Tolstoy's pamphlet. One's first feeling is that in describing Shakespeare as a bad writer he is saying something demonstrably untrue. But this is not the case. In reality there is no kind of evidence or argument by which one can show that Shakespeare, or any other writer, is 'good'. Nor is there any way of definitely proving that – for instance – Warwick Deeping is 'bad'. Ultimately there is no test of literary merit except survival, which is itself merely an index to majority opinion. Artistic theories such as Tolstoy's are quite worthless, because they not only start out with arbitrary assumptions, but depend on vague terms ('sincere', 'important' and so forth) which can be interpreted in any way one chooses. Properly speaking one cannot *answer* Tolstoy's attack. The interesting question is: why did he make it? But it should be noticed in passing that he uses many weak or dishonest arguments. Some of these are worth pointing out, not because they invalidate his main charge but because they are, so to speak, evidence of malice.

To begin with, his examination of *King Lear* is not 'impartial', as he twice claims. On the contrary, it is a prolonged exercise in misrepresentation. It is obvious that when you are summarizing *King Lear* for the benefit of someone who has not read it, you are not really being impartial if you introduce an important speech (Lear's speech when Cordelia is dead in his arms) in this manner: 'Again begin Lear's awful ravings, at which one feels ashamed, as at unsuccessful jokes.' And in a long series of instances Tolstoy slightly alters or colours the passages he is criticizing, always in such a way as to make the plot appear a little more complicated and improbable, or the language a little more exaggerated. For example, we are told that Lear 'has no necessity or motive for his abdication', although his reason for abdicating (that he is old and wishes to retire from the cares of state) has been clearly indicated in the first scene. It will be seen that even in the passage which I quoted earlier, Tolstoy has wilfully misunderstood one phrase and slightly changed the meaning of another, making nonsense of a remark which is reasonable enough in its context. None of these misreadings is very gross in itself, but their cumulative effect is to exaggerate the psychological incoherence of the play. Again, Tolstoy is not able to explain why Shakespeare's plays were still in print, and still on the stage, two hundred years after his death (*before* the 'epidemic suggestion' started, that is); and his whole account of Shakespeare's rise to fame is guesswork punctuated by outright mis-statements. And again, various of his accusations contradict one another: for example, Shakespeare is a mere entertainer and 'not in earnest', but on the other hand he is constantly putting his own thoughts into the mouths of his characters. On the whole it is difficult to feel that Tolstoy's criticisms are uttered in good faith. In any case it is impossible that he should fully have believed in his main thesis – believed, that is to say, that for a century or more the entire civilized world had been taken in by a huge and palpable lie which he alone was able to see through. Certainly his dislike of Shakespeare is real enough, but the reasons for it may be different, or partly different, from what he avows; and therein lies the interest of his pamphlet.

At this point one is obliged to start guessing. However, there is one possible clue, or at least there is a question which may point the way to a clue. It is: why did Tolstoy, with thirty or more plays to choose from, pick out *King Lear* as his especial target? True, *Lear* is so well known and has been so much praised that it could justly be taken as representative of Shakespeare's best work: still, for the purpose of hostile analysis Tolstoy would probably choose the play he disliked most. Is it not possible that he bore an especial enmity towards this particular play because he was aware, consciously or unconsciously, of the resemblance between Lear's story and his own? But it is better to approach this clue from the opposite direction – that is, by examining *Lear* itself, and the qualities in it that Tolstoy fails to mention.

One of the first things an English reader would notice in Tolstoy's pamphlet is that it hardly deals with Shakespeare as a poet. Shakespeare is treated as a dramatist, and in so far as his popularity is not spurious, it is held to be due to tricks of stagecraft which give good opportunities to clever actors. Now, so far as the English-speaking countries go, this is not true. Several of the plays which are most valued by lovers of Shakespeare (for instance, *Timon of Athens*) are seldom or never acted, while some of the most actable, such as *A Midsummer Night's Dream*, are the least admired. Those who care most for Shakespeare value him in the first place for his use of language, the 'verbal-music' which even Bernard Shaw, another hostile critic, admits to be 'irrestible'. Tolstoy ignores this, and does not seem to realize that a poem may have a special value for those who speak the language in which it was written. However, even if one puts oneself in Tolstoy's place and tries to think of Shakespeare as a foreign poet it is still clear that there is something that Tolstoy has left out. Poetry, it seems, is *not* solely a matter of sound and association, and valueless outside its own language-group: otherwise, how is it that some poems, including poems written in dead languages, succeed in crossing frontiers? Clearly a lyric like 'Tomorrow is Saint Valentine's Day' could not be satisfactorily translated, but in Shakespeare's major work there is something describable as poetry that can be separated from the words. Tolstoy is right in saying that *Lear* is not a very good play, as a play. It is too drawn-out and has too many characters and sub-plots. One wicked daughter would have been quite enough, and Edgar is a superfluous character: indeed it would probably be a better play if Gloucester and both his sons were eliminated. Nevertheless, something, a kind of pattern, or perhaps only an atmosphere, survives the complications and the *longueurs*. *Lear* can be imagined as a puppet show, a mime, a ballet, a series of pictures. Part of its poetry, perhaps the most essential part, is inherent in the story and is dependent neither on any particular set of words, nor on flesh-and-blood presentation.

Shut your eyes and think of *King Lear*, if possible without calling to mind any of the dialogue. What do you see? Here at any rate is what I see: a majestic old man in a long black robe, with flowing white hair and beard, a figure out of Blake's drawings (but also, curiously enough, rather like Tolstoy), wandering through a storm and cursing the heavens, in company with a Fool and a lunatic. Presently the scene shifts, and the old man, still cursing, still understanding nothing, is holding a dead girl in his arms while the Fool dangles on a gallows somewhere in the background. This is the bare skeleton of the play, and even here Tolstoy wants to cut out most of what is essential. He objects to the storm, as being unnecessary, to the Fool, who in his eyes is simply a tedious nuisance and an excuse for making bad jokes, and to the death of Cordelia, which, as he sees it, robs the play of its moral. According to Tolstoy, the earlier play, *King Leir*, which Shakespeare adapted,

> terminates more naturally and more in accordance with the moral demands of the spectator than does Shakespeare's: namely, by the King of the Gauls conquering the husbands of the elder sisters, and by Cordelia, instead of being killed, restoring Leir to his former position.

In other words the tragedy ought to have been a comedy, or perhaps a melodrama. It is doubtful whether the sense of tragedy is compatible with belief in God: at any rate, it is not compatible with disbelief in human dignity and with the kind of 'moral demand' which feels cheated when virtue fails to triumph. A tragic situation exists precisely when virtue does *not* triumph but when it is still felt that man is nobler than the forces which destroy him. It is perhaps more significant that Tolstoy sees no justification for the presence of the Fool. The Fool is integral to the play. He acts not only as a sort of chorus, making the central situation clearer by commenting on it more intelligently than the other characters, but as a foil to Lear's frenzies. His jokes, riddles and scraps of rhyme, and his endless digs at Lear's high-minded folly, ranging from mere derision to a sort of melancholy poetry ('All thy other titles thou hast given away; that thou wast born with'), are like a trickle of sanity running through the play, a reminder that somewhere or other, in spite of the injustices, cruelties, intrigues, deceptions and misunderstandings that are being enacted here, life is going on much as usual. In Tolstoy's impatience with the Fool one gets a glimpse of his deeper quarrel with Shakespeare. He objects, with some justification, to the raggedness of Shakespeare's plays, the irrelevancies, the incredible plots, the exaggerated language: but what at bottom he probably most dislikes is a sort of exuberance, a tendency to take – not so much a pleasure, as simply an interest in the actual process of life. It is a mistake to write Tolstoy off as a moralist attacking an artist. He never said that art, as such, is wicked or meaningless, nor did he even say that technical virtuosity is unimportant. But his main aim, in his later years, was to narrow the range of human consciousness. One's interests, one's points of attachment to the physical world and the day-to-day struggle, must be as few and not as many as possible. Literature must consist of parables, stripped of detail and almost independent of language. The parables – this is where Tolstoy differs from the average vulgar puritan – must themselves be works of art, but pleasure and curiosity must be excluded from them. Science, also, must be divorced from curiosity. The business of science, he says, is not to discover what happens, but to teach men how they ought to live. So also with history and politics. Many problems (for example, the Dreyfus Case) are simply not worth solving, and he is willing to leave them as loose ends. Indeed his whole theory of 'crazes' or 'epidemic suggestions', in which he lumps together such things as the Crusades and the Dutch passion of tulip growing, shows a willingness to regard many human activities as mere ant-like rushings to and fro, inexplicable and uninteresting. Clearly he could have no patience with a chaotic, detailed, discursive writer like Shakespeare. His reaction is that of an irritable old man who is being pestered by a noisy child. 'Why do you keep jumping up and down like that? Why can't you sit still like I do?' In a way the old man is in the right, but the trouble is that the child has a feeling in its limbs which the old man has lost. And if the old man knows of the existence of this feeling, the effect is merely to increase his irritation: he would make children senile, if he could. Tolstoy does not know, perhaps, just *what* he misses in Shakespeare, but he is aware that he misses something, and he is determined that others shall be deprived of it as well. By nature he was imperious as well as egotistical. Well after he was grown up he would still occasionally strike his servant in moments of anger, and somewhat later, according to his English biographer, Derrick Leon, he felt 'a frequent desire upon the slenderest provocation to slap the faces of those with whom he disagreed'. One does not necessarily get rid of that kind of temperament by undergoing religious conversion, and indeed it is obvious that the illusion of having been reborn may allow one's native vices to flourish more freely than ever, though perhaps in subtler forms. Tolstoy was capably of abjuring physical violence and of seeing what this implies, but he was not capable of tolerance or humility, and even if one knew nothing of his other writings, one could deduce his tendency towards spiritual bullying from this single pamphlet.

However, Tolstoy is not simply trying to rob others of a pleasure he does not share. He is doing that, but his quarrel with Shakespeare goes further. It is the quarrel between the religious and the humanist attitudes towards life. Here one comes back to the central theme of *King Lear*, which Tolstoy does not mention, although he sets forth the plot in some detail.

Lear is one of the minority of Shakespeare's plays that are unmistakably *about* something. As Tolstoy justly complains, much rubbish has been written about Shakespeare as a philosopher, as a psychologist, as a 'great moral teacher', and what-not. Shakespeare was not a systematic thinker, his most serious thoughts are uttered irrelevantly or indirectly, and we do not know to what extent he wrote with a 'purpose' or even how much of the work attributed to him was actually written by him. In the Sonnets he never even refers to the plays as part of his achievement, though he does make what seems to be a half-ashamed allusion to his career as an actor. It is perfectly possible that he looked on at least half of his plays as mere pot-boilers and hardly bothered about purpose or probability so long as he could patch up something, usually from stolen material, which would more or less hang together on the stage. However, that is not the whole story. To begin with, as Tolstoy himself points out, Shakespeare has a habit of thrusting uncalled-for general reflections into the mouths of his characters. This is a serious fault in a dramatist but it does not fit in with Tolstoy's picture of Shakespeare as a vulgar hack who has no opinions of his own and merely wishes to produce the greatest effect with the least trouble. And more than this, about a dozen of his plays, written for the most part later than 1600, do unquestionably have a meaning and even a moral. They revolve round a central subject which in some cases can be reduced to a single word. For example, *Macbeth* is about ambition, *Othello* is about jealousy, and *Timon of Athens* is about money. The subject of *Lear* is renunciation, and it is only by being wilfully blind that one can fail to understand what Shakespeare is saying.

Lear renounces his throne but expects everyone to continue treating him as a king. He does not see that if he surrenders power, other people will take advantage of his weakness: also that those who flatter him the most grossly, i.e. Regan and Goneril, are exactly the ones who will turn against him. The moment he finds that he can no longer make people obey him as he did before, he falls into a rage which Tolstoy describes as 'strange and unnatural', but which in fact is perfectly in character. In his madness and despair, he passes through two moods which again are natural enough in his circumstances, though in one of them it is probable that he is being used partly as a mouthpiece for Shakespeare's own opinions. One is the mood of disgust in which Lear repents, as it were, for having been a king, and grasps for the first time the rottenness of formal justice and vulgar morality. The other is a mood of impotent fury in which he wreaks imaginary revenges upon those who have wronged him. 'To have a thousand with red burning spits Come hissing in upon 'em!', and:

> It were a delicate stratagem to shoe
> A troop of horse with felt: I'll put't in proof;
> And when I have stol'n upon these sons-in-law,
> Then kill, kill, kill, kill, kill!

Only at the end does he realize, as a sane man, that power, revenge and victory are not worth while:

> No, no, no, no! Come, let's away to prison . . .
> . . . . and we'll wear out,
> In a wall'd prison, packs and sects of great ones
> That ebb and flow by the moon.

But by the time he makes this discovery it is too late, for his death and Cordelia's are already decided on. That is the story, and, allowing for some clumsiness in the telling, it is a very good story.

But is it not also curiously similar to the history of Tolstoy himself? There is a general resemblance which one can hardly avoid seeing, because the most impressive event in Tolstoy's life, as in Lear's, was a huge and gratuitous act of renunciation. In his old age he renounced his estate, his title and his copyrights, and made an attempt – a sincere attempt, though it was not successful – to escape from his privileged position and live the life of a peasant. But the deeper resemblance lies in the fact that Tolstoy, like Lear, acted on mistaken motives and failed to get the results he had hoped for. According to Tolstoy, the aim of every human being is happiness, and happiness can only be attained by doing the will of God. But doing the will of God means casting off all earthly pleasures and ambitions, and living only for others. Ultimately, therefore, Tolstoy renounced the world under the expectation that this would make him happier. But if there is one thing certain about his later years, it is that he was *not* happy. On the contrary, he was driven almost to the edge of madness by the behaviour of the people about him, who persecuted him precisely *because* of his renunciation. Like Lear, Tolstoy was not humble and not a good judge of character. He was inclined at moments to revert to the attitudes of an aristocrat, in spite of his peasant's blouse, and he even had two children whom he believed in and who ultimately turned against him – though, of course, in a less sensational manner than Regan and Goneril. His exaggerated revulsion from sexuality was also distinctly similar to Lear's. Tolstoy's remark that marriage is 'slavery, satiety, repulsion' and means putting up with the proximity of 'ugliness, dirtiness, smell, sores', is matched by Lear's well-known outburst:

> But to the girdle do the gods inherit,
> Beneath is all the fiends;
> There's hell, there's darkness, there's sulphurous pit,
> Burning, scalding, stench, consumption, etc. etc.

And though Tolstoy could not foresee it when he wrote his essay on Shakespeare, even the ending of his life – the sudden unplanned flight across country, accompanied only by a faithful daughter, the death in a cottage in a strange village – seems to have in it a sort of phantom reminiscence of *Lear*.

Of course, one cannot assume that Tolstoy was aware of this resemblance, or would have admitted it if it had been pointed out to him. But his attitude towards the play must have been influenced by its theme. Renouncing power, giving away your lands, was a subject on which he had reason to feel deeply. Probably, therefore, he would be more angered and disturbed by the moral that Shakespeare draws than he would be in the case of some other play – *Macbeth*, for example – which did not touch so closely on his own life. But what exactly *is* the moral of *Lear*? Evidently there are two morals, one explicit, the other implied in the story.

Shakespeare starts by assuming that to make yourself powerless is to invite an attack. This does not mean that *everyone* will turn against you (Kent and the Fool stand by Lear from first to last), but in all probability *someone* will. If you throw away your weapons, some less scrupulous person will pick them up. If you turn the other cheek, you will get a harder blow on it than you got on the first one. This does not always happen, but it is to be expected, and you ought not to complain if it does happen. The second blow is, so to speak, part of the act of turning the other cheek. First of all, therefore, there is the vulgar, common-sense moral drawn by the Fool: 'Don't relinquish power, don't give away your lands.' But there is also another moral. Shakespeare never utters it in so many words, and it does not very much matter whether he was fully aware of it. It is contained in the story, which, after all, he made up, or altered to suit his purposes. It is: 'Give away your lands if you want to, but don't expect to gain happiness by doing so. Probably you won't gain happiness. If you live for others, you must live *for others*, and not as a roundabout way of getting an advantage for yourself.'

Obviously neither of these conclusions could have been pleasing to Tolstoy. The first of them expresses the ordinary, belly-to-earth selfishness from which he was genuinely trying to escape. The other conflicts with his desire to eat his cake and have it – that is, to destroy his own egoism and by so doing to gain eternal life. Of course, *Lear* is not a sermon in favour of altruism. It merely points out the results of practising self-denial for selfish reasons. Shakespeare had a considerable streak of worldliness in him, and if he had been forced to take sides in his own play, his sympathies would probably have lain with the Fool. But at least he could see the whole issue and treat it at the level of tragedy. Vice is punished, but virtue is not rewarded. The morality of Shakespeare's later tragedies is not religious in the ordinary sense, and certainly is not Christian. Only two of them, *Hamlet* and *Othello*, are supposedly occurring inside the Christian era, and even in those, apart from the antics of the ghost in *Hamlet*, there is no indication of a 'next world' where everything is to be put right. All of these tragedies start out with the humanist assumption that life, although full of sorrow, is worth living, and that Man is a noble animal – a belief which Tolstoy in his old age did not share.

Tolstoy was not a saint, but he tried very hard to make himself a saint, and the standards he applied to literature were other-worldly ones. It is important to realize that the difference between a saint and an ordinary human being is a difference of kind and not degree. That is, the one is not to be regarded as an imperfect form of the other. The saint, at any rate Tolstoy's kind of saint, is not trying to work an improvement in earthly life: he is trying to bring it to an end and put something different in its place. One obvious expression of this is the claim that celibacy is 'higher' than marriage. If only, Tolstoy says in effect, we would stop breeding, fighting, struggling and enjoying, if we could get rid not only of our sins but of everything else that binds us to the surface of the earth – including love, in the ordinary sense of caring more for one human being than another – then the whole painful process would be over and the Kingdom of Heaven would arrive. But a normal human being does not want the Kingdom of Heaven: he wants life on earth to continue. This is not solely because he is 'weak', 'sinful' and anxious for a 'good time'. Most people get a fair amount of fun out of their lives, but on balance life is suffering, and only the very young or the very foolish imagine otherwise. Ultimately it is the Christian attitude which is self-interested and hedonistic, since the aim is always to get away from the painful struggle of earthly life and find eternal peace in some kind of Heaven or Nirvana. The humanist attitude is that the struggle must continue and that death is the price of life. 'Men must endure Their going hence, even as their coming hither: Ripeness is all' – which is an un-Christian sentiment. Often there is a seeming truce between the humanist and the religious believer, but in fact their attitudes cannot be reconciled: one must choose between this world and the next. And the enormous majority of human beings, if they understood the issue, would choose this world. They do make that choice when they continue working, breeding and dying instead of crippling their faculties in the hope of obtaining a new lease of existence elsewhere.

We do not know a great deal about Shakespeare's religious beliefs, and from the evidence of his writings it would be difficult to prove that he had any. But at any rate he was not a saint or a would-be saint: he was a human being, and in some ways not a very good one. It is clear, for instance, that he liked to stand well with the rich and powerful, and was capable of flattering them in the most servile way. He is also noticeably cautious, not to say cowardly, in his manner of uttering unpopular opinions. Almost never does he put a subversive or sceptical remark into the mouth of a character likely to be identified with himself. Throughout his plays the acute social critics, the people who are not taken in by accepted fallacies, are buffoons, villains, lunatics or persons who are shamming insanity or are in a state of violent hysteria. *Lear* is a play in which this tendency is particularly well marked. It contains a great deal of veiled social criticism – a point Tolstoy misses – but it is all uttered either by the Fool, by Edgar when he is pretending to be mad, or by Lear during his bouts of madness. In his sane moments Lear hardly ever makes an intelligent remark. And yet the very fact that Shakespeare had to use these subterfuges shows how widely his thoughts ranged. He could not restrain himself from commenting on almost everything, although he put on a series of masks in order to do so. If one has once read Shakespeare with attention, it is not easy to go a day without quoting him, because there are not many subjects of major importance that he does not discuss or at least mention somewhere or other, in his unsystematic but illuminating way. Even the irrelevancies that litter every one of his plays – the puns and riddles, the lists of names, the scraps of reportage like the conversation of the carriers in *Henry IV*, the bawdy jokes, the rescued fragments of forgotten ballads – are merely the products of excessive vitality. Shakespeare was not a philosopher or a scientist, but he did have curiosity: he loved the surface of the earth and the process of life – which, it should be repeated, is *not* the same thing as wanting to have a good time and stay alive as long as possible. Of course, it is not because of the quality of his thought that Shakespeare has survived, and he might not even be remembered as a dramatist if he had not also been a poet. His main hold on us is through language. How deeply Shakespeare himself was fascinated by the music of words can probably be inferred from the speeches of Pistol. What Pistol says is largely meaningless, but if one considers his lines singly they are magnificent rhetorical verse. Evidently, pieces of resounding nonsense ('Let floods o'erswell, and fiends for food howl on', etc.) were constantly appearing in Shakespeare's mind of their own accord, and a half-lunatic character had to be invented to use them up. Tolstoy's native tongue was not English, and one cannot blame him for being unmoved by Shakespeare's verse, nor even, perhaps, for refusing to believe that Shakespeare's skill with words was something out of the ordinary. But he would also have rejected the whole notion of valuing poetry for its texture – valuing it, that is to say, as a kind of music. If it could somehow have been proved to him that his whole explanation of Shakespeare's rise to fame is mistaken, that inside the English speaking world, at any rate, Shakespeare's popularity is genuine, that his mere skill in placing one syllable beside another has given acute pleasure to generation after generation of English-speaking people – all this would not have been counted as a merit to Shakespeare, but rather the contrary. It would simply have been one more proof of the irreligious, earthbound nature of Shakespeare and his admirers. Tolstoy would have said that poetry is to be judged by its meaning, and that seductive sounds merely cause false meanings to go unnoticed. At every level it is the same issue – this world against the next: and certainly the music is something that belongs to this world.

A sort of doubt has always hung round the character of Tolstoy, as round the character of Gandhi. He was not a vulgar hypocrite, as some people declared him to be, and he would probably have imposed even greater sacrifices on himself than he did, if he had not been interfered with at every step by the people surrounding him, especially his wife. But on the other hand it is dangerous to take such men as Tolstoy at their disciples' valuation. There is always the possibility – the probability, indeed – that they have done no more than exchange one form of egoism for another. Tolstoy renounced wealth, fame and privilege; he abjured violence in all its forms and was ready to suffer for doing so; but it is not so easy to believe that he abjured the principle of coercion, or at least the *desire* to coerce others. There are families in which the father will say to his child, 'You'll get a thick ear if you do that again,' while the mother, her eyes brimming over with tears, will take the child in her arms and murmur lovingly, 'Now, darling, *is* it kind to Mummy to do that?' And who would maintain that the second method is less tyrannous than the first? The distinction that really matters is not between violence and non-violence, but between having and not having the appetite for power. There are people who are convinced of the wickedness both of armies and of police forces, but who are nevertheless much more intolerant and inquisitorial in outlook than the normal person who believes that it is necessary to use your violence in certain circumstances. They will not say to somebody else, 'Do this, that and the other or you will go to prison,' but they will, if they can, get inside his brain and dictate his thoughts for him in the minutest particulars. Creeds like pacifism and anarchism, which seem on the surface to imply a complete renunciation of power, rather encourage this habit of mind. For if you have embraced a creed which appears to be free from the ordinary dirtiness of politics – a creed from which you yourself cannot expect to draw any material advantage – surely that proves that you are in the right? And the more you are in the right, the more natural that everyone else should be bullied into thinking likewise.

If we are to believe what he says in his pamphlet, Tolstoy had never been able to see any merit in Shakespeare, and was always astonished to find that his fellow writers, Turgenev, Fet and others, thought differently. We may be sure that in his unregenerate days Tolstoy's conclusion would have been: 'You like Shakespeare – I don't. Let's leave it at that.' Later, when his perception that it takes all sorts to make a world had deserted him, he came to think of Shakespeare's writings as something dangerous to himself. The more pleasure people took in Shakespeare, the less they would listen to Tolstoy. Therefore nobody must be *allowed* to enjoy Shakespeare, just as nobody must be allowed to drink alcohol or smoke tobacco. True, Tolstoy would not prevent them by force. He is not demanding that the police shall impound every copy of Shakespeare's works. But he will do dirt on Shakespeare, if he can. He will try to get inside the mind of every lover of Shakespeare and kill his enjoyment by every trick he can think of, including – as I have shown in my summary of his pamphlet – arguments which are self-contradictory or even doubtfully honest.

But finally the most striking thing is how little difference it all makes. As I said earlier, one cannot *answer* Tolstoy's pamphlet, at least on its main counts. There is no argument by which one can defend a poem. It defends itself by surviving, or it is indefensible. And if this test is valid, I think the verdict in Shakespeare's case must be 'not guilty'. Like every other writer, Shakespeare will be forgotten sooner or later, but it is unlikely that a heavier indictment will ever be brought against him. Tolstoy was perhaps the most admired literary man of his age, and he was certainly not its least able pamphleteer. He turned all his powers of denunciation against Shakespeare, like all the guns of a battleship roaring simultaneously. And with what result? Forty years later, Shakespeare is still there, completely unaffected, and of the attempt to demolish him nothing remains except the yellowing pages of a pamphlet which hardly anyone has read, and which would be forgotten altogether if Tolstoy had not also been the author of *War and Peace* and *Anna Karenina.*

Polemic, No. 7, March 1947; *S.E.*; *O.R.*; *C.E.*

39. Such, Such Were the Joys[1]

I

Soon after I arrived at St Cyprian's (not immediately, but after a week or two, just when I seemed to be settling into the routine of school life) I began wetting my bed. I was now aged eight, so that this was a reversion to a habit which I must have grown out of at least fours years earlier.

Nowadays, I believe, bed-wetting in such circumstances is taken for granted. It is a normal reaction in children who have been removed from their homes to a strange place. In those days, however, it was looked on as a disgusting crime which the child committed on purpose and for which the proper cure was a beating. For my part I did not need to be told it was a crime. Night after night I prayed, with a fervour never previously attained in my prayers. 'Please God, do not let me wet my bed! Oh, please God, do not let me wet my bed!', but it made remarkably little difference. Some nights the thing happened, others not. There was no volition about it, no consciousness. You did not properly speaking *do* the deed: you merely woke up in the morning and found that the sheets were wringing wet.

After the second or third offence I was warned that I should be beaten next time, but I received the warning in a curiously roundabout way. One afternoon, as we were filing out from tea, Mrs W—, the Headmaster's wife, was sitting at the head of one of the tables, chatting with a lady of whom I knew nothing, except that she was on an afternoon's visit to the school. She was an intimidating, masculine-looking person wearing a riding-habit, or something that I took to be a riding-habit. I was just

1. In the version of this piece already published in the United States, St Cyprian's was called 'Crossgates'. Other old boys writing of the school followed Cyril Connolly and called it 'St Wulfric's', the name it was first given in *Enemies of Promise*. The text printed here is of Orwell's original typescript, but the names of his school fellows and the assistant masters have been changed.

leaving the room when Mrs W— called me back, as though to introduce me to the visitor.

Mrs W— was nicknamed Flip, and I shall call her by that name, for I seldom think of her by any other. (Officially, however, she was addressed as Mum, probably a corruption of the 'Ma'am' used by public schoolboys to their housemasters' wives.) She was a stocky square-built woman with hard red cheeks, a flat top to her head, prominent brows and deep-set, suspicious eyes. Although a great deal of the time she was full of false heartiness, jollying one along with mannish slang ('*Buck* up, old chap!' and so forth), and even using one's Christian name, her eyes never lost their anxious, accusing look. It was very difficult to look her in the face without feeling guilty, even at moments when one was not guilty of anything in particular.

'Here is a little boy,' said Flip, indicating me to the strange lady, 'who wets his bed every night. Do you know what I am going to do if you wet your bed again?' she added, turning to me. 'I am going to get the Sixth Form to beat you.'

The strange lady put on an air of being inexpressibly shocked, and exclaimed 'I-should-*think*-so!' And here there occurred one of those wild, almost lunatic misunderstandings which are part of the daily experience of childhood. The Sixth Form were a group of older boys who were selected as having 'character' and were empowered to beat smaller boys. I had not yet learned of their existence, and I mis-heard the phrase 'the Sixth Form' as 'Mrs Form'. I took it as referring to the strange lady – I thought, that is, that her name was Mrs Form. It was an improbable name, but a child has no judgement in such matters. I imagined, therefore, that it was *she* who was to be deputed to beat me. It did not strike me as strange that this job should be turned over to a casual visitor in no way connected with the school. I merely assumed that 'Mrs Form' was a stern disciplinarian who enjoyed beating people (somehow her appearance seemed to bear this out) and I had an immediate terrifying vision of her arriving for the occasion in full riding kit and armed with a hunting-whip. To this day I can feel myself almost swooning with shame as I stood, a very small, round-faced boy in short corduroy knickers, before the two women. I could not speak. I felt that I should die if 'Mrs Form' were to beat me. But my dominant feeling was not fear or even resentment: it was simply shame because one more person, and that a woman, had been told of my disgusting offence.

A little later, I forget how, I learned that it was not after all 'Mrs Form' who would do the beating. I cannot remember whether it was that very night that I wetted my bed again, but at any rate I did wet it again quite soon. Oh, the despair, the feeling of cruel injustice, after all my prayers and resolutions, at once again waking between the clammy sheets! There was no chance of hiding what I had done. The grim statuesque matron, Margaret by name, arrived in the dormitory specially to inspect my bed. She pulled back the clothes, then drew herself up, and the dreaded words seemed to come rolling out of her like a peal of thunder:

'REPORT YOURSELF to the Headmaster after breakfast!'

I put REPORT YOURSELF in capitals because that was how it appeared in my mind. I do not know how many times I heard that phrase during my early years at St Cyprian's. It was only very rarely that it did not mean a beating. The words always had a portentous sound in my ears, like muffled drums or the words of the death sentence.

When I arrived to report myself, Flip was doing something or other at the long shiny table in the ante-room to the study. Her uneasy eyes searched me as I went past. In the study the Headmaster, nicknamed Sambo, was waiting. Sambo was a round-shouldered, curiously oafish-looking man, not large but shambling in gait, with a chubby face which was like that of an overgrown baby, and which was capable of good humour. He knew, of course, why I had been sent to him, and had already taken a bone-handled riding-crop out of the cupboard, but it was part of the punishment of reporting yourself that you had to proclaim your offence with your own lips. When I had said my say, he read me a short but pompous lecture, then seized me by the scruff of the neck, twisted me over and began beating me with the riding-crop. He had a habit of continuing his lecture while he flogged you, and I remember the words 'you dir-ty lit-tle boy' keeping time with the blows. The beating did not hurt (perhaps. as it was the first time, he was not hitting me very hard), and I walked out feeling very much better. The fact that the beating had not hurt was a sort of victory and partially wiped out the shame of the bed-wetting. I was even incautious enough to wear a grin on my face. Some small boys were hanging about in the passage outside the door of the ante-room.

'D'you get the cane?'

'It didn't hurt,' I said proudly.

Flip had heard everything. Instantly her voice came screaming after me:

'Come here! Come here this instant! What was that you said?

'I said it didn't hurt,' I faltered out.

'How dare you say a thing like that? Do you think that is the proper thing to say? Go in and REPORT YOURSELF AGAIN!'

This time Sambo laid on in real earnest. He continued for a length of time that frightened and astonished me – about five minutes, it seemed – ending up by breaking the riding-crop. The bone handle went flying across the room.

'Look what you've made me do!' he said furiously, holding up the broken crop.

I had fallen into a chair, weakly snivelling. I remember that this was the only time throughout my boyhood when a beating actually reduced me to tears, and curiously enough I was not even now crying because of the pain. The second beating had not hurt very much either. Fright and shame seemed to have anaesthetized me. I was crying partly because I felt that this was expected of me, partly from genuine repentance, but partly also because of a deeper grief which is peculiar to childhood and not easy to convey: a sense of desolate loneliness and helplessness, of being locked up not only in a hostile world but in a world of good and evil where the rules were such that it was actually not possible for me to keep them.

I knew that the bed-wetting was (a) wicked and (b) outside my control. The second fact I was personally aware of, and the first I did not question. It was possible, therefore, to commit a sin without knowing that you committed it, without wanting to commit it, and without being able to avoid it. Sin was not necessarily something that you did: it might be something that happened to you. I do not want to claim that this idea flashed into my mind as a complete novelty at this very moment, under the blows of Sambo's cane: I must have had glimpses of it even before I left home, for my early childhood had not been altogether happy. But at any rate this was the great, abiding lesson of my boyhood: that I was in a world where it was *not possible* for me to be good. And the double beating was a turning-point, for it brought home to me for the first time the harshness of the environment into which I had been flung. Life was more terrible, and I was more wicked, than I had imagined. At any rate, as I sat snivelling on the edge of a chair in Sambo's study, with not even the self-possession to stand up while he stormed at me, I had a conviction of sin and folly and weakness, such as I do not remember to have felt before.

In general, one's memories of any period must necessarily weaken as one moves away from it. One is constantly learning new facts, and old ones have to drop out to make way for them. At twenty I could have written the history of my school-days with an accuracy which would be quite impossible now. But it can also happen that one's memories grow sharper after a long lapse of time, because one is looking at the past with fresh eyes and can isolate and, as it were, notice facts which previously existed undifferentiated among a mass of others. Here are two things which in a sense I remembered, but which did not strike me as strange or interesting until quite recently. One is that the second beating seemed to me a just and reasonable punishment. To get one beating, and then to get another and far fiercer one on top of it, for being so unwise as to show that the first had not hurt – that was quite natural. The gods are jealous, and when you have good fortune you should conceal it. The other is that I accepted the broken riding-crop as my own crime. I can still recall my feeling as I saw the handle lying on the carpet – the feeling of having done an ill-bred clumsy thing, and ruined an expensive object. *I* had broken it: so Sambo told me, and so I believed. This acceptance of guilt lay unnoticed in my memory for twenty or thirty years.

So much for the episode of bed-wetting. But there is one more thing to be remarked. This is that I did not wet my bed again – at least, I did wet it once again, and received another beating, after which the trouble stopped. So perhaps this barbarous remedy does work, though at a heavy price, I have no doubt.

II

St Cyprian's was an expensive and snobbish school which was in process of becoming more snobbish, and, I imagine, more expensive. The public school with which it had special connexions was Harrow, but during my time an increasing proportion of the boys went on to Eton. Most of them were the children of rich parents, but on the whole they were the un-aristocratic rich, the sort of people who live in huge shrubberied houses in Bournemouth or Richmond, and who have cars and butlers but not country estates. There were a few exotics among them – some South American boys, sons of Argentine beef barons, one or two Russians, and even a Siamese prince, or someone who was described as a prince.

Sambo had two great ambitions. One was to attract titled boys to the school, and the other was to train up pupils to win scholarships at public schools, above all at Eton. He did, towards the end of my time, succeed in getting hold of two boys with real English titles. One of them, I remember, was a wretched drivelling little creature, almost an albino, peering upwards out of weak eyes, with a long nose at the end of which a dewdrop always seemed to be trembling. Sambo always gave these boys their titles when mentioning them to a third person, and for the first few days he actually addressed them to their faces as 'Lord So-and-so'. Needless to say he found ways of drawing attention to them when any visitor was being shown round the school. Once, I remember, the little fair-haired boy had a choking fit at dinner, and a stream of snot ran out of his nose on to his plate in a way horrible to see. Any lesser person would have been called a dirty little beast and ordered out of the room instantly: but Sambo and Flip laughed it off in a 'boys will be boys' spirit.

All the very rich boys were more or less undisguisedly favoured. The school still had a faint suggestion of the Victorian 'private academy' with its 'parlour boarders', and when I later read about that kind of school in Thackeray I immediately saw the resemblance. The rich boys had milk and biscuits in the middle of the morning, they were given riding lessons once or twice a week, Flip mothered them and called them by their Christian names, and above all they were never caned. Apart from the South Americans, whose parents were safely distant, I doubt whether Sambo ever caned any boy whose father's income was much above £2,000 a year. But he was sometimes willing to sacrifice financial profit to scholastic prestige. Occasionally, by special arrangement, he would take at greatly reduced fees some boy who seemed likely to win scholarships and thus bring credit on the school. It was on these terms that I was at St Cyprian's myself: otherwise my parents could not have afforded to send me to so expensive a school.

I did not at first understand that I was being taken at reduced fees; it was only when I was about eleven that Flip and Sambo began throwing the fact in my teeth. For my first two or three years I went through the ordinary educational mill: then, soon after I had started Greek (one started Latin at eight, Greek at ten), I moved into the scholarship class, which was taught, so far as classics went, largely by Sambo himself. Over a period of two or three years the scholarship boys were crammed with learning as cynically as a goose is crammed for Christmas. And with what learning! This business of making a gifted boy's career depend on a competitive examination, taken when he is only twelve or thirteen, is an evil thing at best, but there do appear to be preparatory schools which send scholars to Eton, Winchester, etc. without teaching them to see everything in terms of marks. At St Cyprian's the whole process was frankly a preparation for a sort of confidence trick. Your job was to learn exactly those things that would give an examiner the impression that you knew more than you did know, and as far as possible to avoid burdening your brain with anything else. Subjects which lacked examination-value, such as geography, were almost completely neglected, mathematics was also neglected if you were a 'classical', science was not taught in any form – indeed it was so despised that even an interest in natural history was discouraged – and even the books you were encouraged to read in your spare time were chosen with one eye on the 'English paper'. Latin and Greek, the main scholarship subjects, were what counted, but even these were deliberately taught in a flashy, unsound way. We never, for example, read right through even a single book of a Greek or Latin author: we merely read short passages which were picked out because they were the kind of thing likely to be set as an 'unseen translation'. During the last year or so before we went up for our scholarships, most of our time was spent in simply working our way through the scholarship papers of previous years. Sambo had sheaves of these in his possession, from every one of the major public schools. But the greatest outrage of all was the teaching of history.

There was in those days a piece of nonsense called the Harrow History Prize, an annual competition for which many preparatory schools entered. It was a tradition for St Cyprian's to win it every year, as well we might, for we had mugged up every paper that had been set since the competition started, and the supply of possible questions was not inexhaustible. They were the kind of stupid question that is answered by rapping out a name or a quotation. Who plundered the Begams? Who was beheaded in an open boat? Who caught the Whigs bathing and ran away with their clothes? Almost all our historical teaching was on this level. History was a series of unrelated, unintelligible but – in some way that was never explained to us – important facts with resounding phrases tied to them. Disraeli brought peace with honour. Clive was astonished at his moderation. Pitt called in the New World to redress the balance of the Old. And the dates, and the mnemonic devices! (Did you know, for example, that the initial letters of 'A black Negress was my aunt: there's her house behind the barn' are also the initial letters of the battles in the Wars of the Roses?) Flip, who 'took' the higher forms in history, revelled in this kind of thing. I recall positive orgies of dates, with the keener boys leaping up and down in their places in their eagerness to shout out the right answers, and at the same time not feeling the faintest interest in the meaning of the mysterious events they were naming.

'1587?'

'Massacre of St Bartholomew!'

'1707?'

'Death of Aurangzeeb!'

'1713?'

'Treaty of Utrecht!'

'1773?'

'Boston Tea Party!'

'1520?'

'Oo, Mum, please, Mum –'

'Please, Mum, please, Mum! Let me tell him, Mum!'

'Well! 1520?'

'Field of the Cloth of Gold!'

And so on.

But history and such secondary subjects were not bad fun. It was in 'classics' that the real strain came. Looking back, I realize that I then worked harder than I have ever done since, and yet at the time it never seemed possible to make quite the effort that was demanded of one. We would sit round the long shiny table, made of some very pale-coloured hard wood, with Sambo goading, threatening, exhorting, sometimes joking, very occasionally praising, but always prodding, prodding away at one's mind to keep it up to the right pitch of concentration, as one might keep a sleepy person awake by sticking pins in him.

'Go on, you little slacker! Go on, you idle, worthless little boy! The whole trouble with you is that you're bone and horn idle. You eat too much, that's why. You wolf down enormous meals, and then when you come here you're half asleep. Go on, now, put your back into it. You're not *thinking*. Your brain doesn't sweat.'

He would tap away at one's skull with his silver pencil, which, in my memory, seems to have been about the size of a banana, and which certainly was heavy enough to raise a bump: or he would pull the short hairs round one's ears, or, occasionally, reach out under the table and kick one's shin. One some days nothing seemed to go right, and then it would be: 'All right, then, I know what you want. You've been asking for it the whole morning. Come along, you useless little slacker. Come into the study.' And then whack, whack, whack, whack, and back one would come, red-wealed and smarting – in later years Sambo had abandoned his riding-crop in favour of a thin rattan cane which hurt very much more – to settle down to work again. This did not happen very often, but I do remember, more than once, being led out of the room in the middle of a Latin sentence, receiving a beating and then going straight ahead with the same sentence, just like that. It is a mistake to think such methods do not work. They work very well for their special purpose. Indeed, I doubt whether classical education ever has been or can be successfully carried on without corporal punishment. The boys themselves believed in its efficacy. There was a boy named Beacham, with no brains to speak of, but evidently in acute need of a scholarship. Sambo was flogging him towards the goal as one might do with a foundered horse. He went up for a scholarship at Uppingham, came back with a consciousness of having done badly, and a day or two later received a severe beating for idleness. 'I wish I'd had that caning before I went up for the exam,' he said sadly – a remark which I felt to be contemptible, but which I perfectly well understood.

The boys of the scholarship class were not all treated alike. If a boy were the son of rich parents to whom the saving of fees was not all-important, Sambo would goad him along in a comparatively fatherly way, with jokes and digs in the ribs and perhaps an occasional tap with the pencil, but no hair-pulling and no caning. It was the poor but 'clever' boys who suffered. Our brains were a gold-mine in which he had sunk money, and the dividends must be squeezed out of us. Long before I had grasped the nature of my financial relationship with Sambo, I had been made to understand that I was not on the same footing as most of the other boys. In effect there were three castes in the school. There was the minority with an aristocratic or millionaire background, there were the children of the ordinary suburban rich, who made up the bulk of the school, and there were a few underlings like myself, the sons of clergymen, Indian civil servants, struggling widows and the like. These poorer ones were discouraged from going in for 'extras' such as shooting and carpentry, and were humiliated over clothes and petty possessions. I never, for instance, succeeded in getting a cricket bat of my own, because 'Your parents wouldn't be able to afford it'. This phrase pursued me throughout my schooldays. At St Cyprian's we were not allowed to keep the money we brought back with us, but had to 'give it in' on the first day of term, and then from time to time were allowed to spend it under supervision. I and similarly-placed boys were always choked off from buying expensive toys like model aeroplanes, even if the necessary money stood to our credit. Flip, in particular, seemed to aim consciously at inculcating a humble outlook in the poorer boys. 'Do you think that's the sort of thing a boy like you should buy?' I remember her saying to somebody – and she said this in front of the whole school: 'You know you're not going to grow up with money, don't you? Your people aren't rich. You must learn to be sensible. Don't get above yourself!' There was also the weekly pocket-money, which we took out in sweets, dispensed by Flip from a large table. The millionaires had sixpence a week, but the normal sum was threepence. I and one or two others were only allowed twopence. My parents had not given instructions to this effect, and the saving of a penny a week could not conceivably have made any difference to them: it was a mark of status. Worse yet was the detail of the birthday cakes. It was usual for each boy, on his birthday, to have a large iced cake with candles, which was shared out at tea between the whole school. It was provided as a matter of routine and went on his parents' bill. I never had such a cake, though my parents would have paid for it readily enough. Year after year, never daring to ask, I would miserably hope that this year a cake would appear. Once or twice I even rashly pretended to my companions that this time I *was* going to have a cake. Then came tea-time, and no cake, which did not make me more popular.

Very early it was impressed upon me that I had no chance of a decent future unless I won a scholarship at a public school. Either I won my scholarship, or I must leave school at fourteen and become, in Sambo's favourite phrase 'a little office boy at forty pounds a year'. In my circumstances it was natural that I should believe this. Indeed, it was universally taken for granted at St Cyprian's that unless you went to a 'good' public school (and only about fifteen schools came under this heading) you were ruined for life. It is not easy to convey to a grown-up person the sense of strain, of nerving oneself for some terrible, all-deciding combat, as the date of the examination crept nearer – eleven years old, twelve years old, then thirteen, the fatal year itself! Over a period of about two years, I do not think there was ever a day when 'the exam', as I called it, was quite out of my waking thoughts. In my prayers it figured invariably: and whenever I got the bigger portion of a wishbone, or picked up a horseshoe, or bowed seven times to the new moon, or succeeded in passing through a wishing-gate without touching the sides, then the wish I earned by doing so went on 'the exam' as a matter of course. And yet curiously enough I was also tormented by an almost irresistible impulse *not* to work. There were days when my heart sickened at the labours ahead of me, and I stood stupid as an animal before the most elementary difficulties. In the holidays, also, I could not work. Some of the scholarship boys received extra tuition from a certain Mr Batchelor, a likeable, very hairy man who wore shaggy suits and lived in a typical bachelor's 'den' – book-lined walls, overwhelming stench of tobacco – somewhere in the town. During the holidays Mr Batchelor used to send us extracts from Latin authors to translate, and we were supposed to send back a wad of work once a week. Somehow I could not do it. The empty paper and the black Latin dictionary lying on the table, the consciousness of a plain duty shirked, poisoned my leisure, but somehow I could not start, and by the end of the holidays I would only have sent Mr Batchelor fifty or a hundred lines. Undoubtedly part of the reason was that Sambo and his cane were far away. But in term-time, also, I would go through periods of idleness and stupidity when I would sink deeper and deeper into disgrace and even achieve a sort of feeble, snivelling defiance, fully conscious of my guilt and yet unable or unwilling – I could not be sure which – to do any better. Then Sambo or Flip would send for me, and this time it would not even be a caning.

Flip would search me with her baleful eyes. (What colour were those eyes, I wonder? I remember them as green, but actually no human being has green eyes. Perhaps they were hazel.) She would start off in her peculiar, wheedling, bullying style, which never failed to get right through one's guard and score a hit on one's better nature.

'I don't think it's awfully decent of you to behave like this, is it? Do you think it's quite playing the game by your mother and father to go on idling your time away, week after week, month after month? Do you *want* to throw all your chances away? You know your people aren't rich, don't you? You know they can't afford the same things as other boys' parents. How are they to send you to a public school if you don't win a scholarship? I know how proud your mother is of you. Do you *want* to let her down?'

'I don't think he wants to go to a public school any longer,' Sambo would say, addressing himself to Flip with a pretence that I was not there. 'I think he's given up that idea. He wants to be a little office boy at forty pounds a year.'

The horrible sensation of tears – a swelling in the breast, a tickling behind the nose – would already have assailed me. Flip would bring out her ace of trumps:

'And do you think it's quite fair to *us*, the way you're behaving? After all we've done for you? You *do* know what we've done for you, don't you?' Her eyes would pierce deep into me, and though she never said it straight out, I did know. 'We've had you here all these years – we even had you here for a week in the holidays so that Mr Batchelor could coach you. We don't *want* to have to send you away, you know, but we can't keep a boy here just to eat up our food, term after term. *I* don't think it's very straight, the way you're behaving. Do you?'

I never had any answer except a miserable 'No, Mum', or 'Yes, Mum', as the case might be. Evidently it was *not* straight, the way I was behaving. And at some point or other the unwanted tear would always force its way out of the corner of my eye, roll down my nose and splash.

Flip never said in plain words that I was a non-paying pupil, no doubt because vague phrases like 'all we've done for you' had a deeper emotional appeal. Sambo, who did not aspire to be loved by his pupils, put it more brutally, though, as was usual with him in pompous language. 'You are living on my bounty' was his favourite phrase in this context. At least once I listened to these words between blows of the cane. I must say that these scenes were not frequent, and except on one occasion they did not take place in the presence of other boys. In public I was reminded that I was poor and that my parents 'wouldn't be able to afford' this or that, but I was not actually reminded of my dependent position. It was a final unanswerable argument, to be brought forth like an instrument of torture when my work became exceptionally bad.

To grasp the effect of this kind of thing on a child of ten or twelve, one has to remember that the child has little sense of proportion or probability. A child may be a mass of egoism and rebelliousness, but it has no accumulated experience to give it confidence in its own judgements. On the whole it will accept what it is told, and it will believe in the most fantastic way in the knowledge and powers of the adults surrounding it. Here is an example.

I have said that at St Cyprian's we were not allowed to keep our own money. However, it was possible to hold back a shilling or two, and sometimes I used furtively to buy sweets which I kept hidden in the loose ivy on the playing-field wall. One day when I had been sent on an errand I went into a sweet-shop a mile or more from the school and bought some chocolates. As I came out of the shop I saw on the opposite pavement a small sharp-faced man who seemed to be staring very hard at my school cap. Instantly a horrible fear went through me. There could be no doubt as to who the man was. He was a spy placed there by Sambo! I turned away unconcernedly, and then, as though my legs were doing it of their own accord, broke into a clumsy run. But when I got round the next corner I forced myself to walk again, for to run was a sign of guilt, and obviously there would be other spies posted here and there about the town. All that day and the next I waited for the summons to the study, and was surprised when it did not come. It did not seem to me strange that the headmaster of a private school should dispose of any army of informers, and I did not even imagine that he would have to pay them. I assumed that any adult, inside the school or outside, would collaborate voluntarily in preventing us from breaking the rules. Sambo was all-powerful; it was natural that his agents should be everywhere. When this episode happened I do not think I can have been less than twelve years old.

I hated Sambo and Flip, with a sort of shamefaced, remorseful hatred, but it did not occur to me to doubt their judgement. When they told me that I must either win a public-school scholarship or become an office boy at fourteen, I believed that those were the unavoidable alternatives before me. And above all, I believed Sambo and Flip when they told me they were my benefactors. I see now, of course, that from Sambo's point of view I was a good speculation. He sank money in me, and he looked to get it back in the form of prestige. If I had 'gone off', as promising boys sometimes do, I imagine that he would have got rid of me swiftly. As it was I won him two scholarships when the time came, and no doubt he made full use of them in his prospectuses. But it is difficult for a child to realize that a school is primarily a commercial venture. A child believes that the school exists to educate and that the school-master disciplines him either for his own good, or from a love of bullying. Flip and Sambo had chosen to befriend me, and their friendship included canings, reproaches and humiliations, which were good for me and saved me from an office stool. That was their version, and I believed in it. It was therefore clear that I owed them a vast debt of gratitude. But I was *not* grateful, as I very well knew. On the contrary, I hated both of them. I could not control my subjective feelings, and I could not conceal them from myself. But it is wicked, is it not, to hate your benefactors? So I was taught, and so I believed. A child accepts the codes of behaviour that are presented to it, even when it breaks them. From the age of eight, or even earlier, the consciousness of sin was never far away from me. If I contrived to seem callous and defiant, it was only a thin cover over a mass of shame and dismay. All through my boyhood I had a profound conviction that I was no good, that I was wasting my time, wrecking my talents, behaving with monstrous folly and wickedness and ingratitude – and all this, it seemed, was inescapable, because I lived among laws which were absolute, like the law of gravity, but which it was not possible for me to keep.

III

No one can look back on his schooldays and say with truth that they were altogether unhappy.

I have good memories of St Cyprian's, among a horde of bad ones. Sometimes on summer afternoons there were wonderful expeditions across the Downs to a village called Birling Gap, or to Beachy Head, where one bathed dangerously among the chalk boulders and came home covered with cuts. And there were still more wonderful mid-summer evenings when, as a special treat, we were not driven off to bed as usual but allowed to wander about the grounds in the long twilight, ending up with a plunge into the swimming bath at about nine o'clock. There was the joy of waking early on summer mornings and getting in an hour's undisturbed reading (Ian Hay, Thackeray, Kipling and H. G. Wells were the favourite authors of my boyhood) in the sunlit, sleeping dormitory. There was also cricket, which I was no good at but with which I conducted a sort of hopeless love affair up to the age of about eighteen. And there was the pleasure of keeping caterpillars – the silky green and purple puss-moth, the ghostly green poplar-hawk, the privet-hawk. large as one's third finger, specimens of which could be illicitly purchased for sixpence at a shop in the town – and, when one could escape long enough from the master who was 'taking the walk', there was the excitement of dredging the dew-ponds on the Downs for enormous newts with orange-coloured bellies. This business of being out for a walk, coming across something of fascinating interest and then being dragged away from it by a yell from the master, like a dog jerked onwards by the leash, is an important feature of school life, and helps to build up the conviction, so strong in many children, that the things you most want to do are always unattainable.

Very occasionally, perhaps once during each summer, it was possible to escape altogether from the barrack-like atmosphere of school, when Brown, the second master, was permitted to take one or two boys for an afternoon of butterfly hunting on a common a few miles away. Brown was a man with white hair and a red face like a strawberry, who was good at natural history, making models and plaster casts, operating magic lanterns, and things of that kind. He and Mr Batchelor were the only adults in any way connected with the school whom I did not either dislike or fear. Once he took me into his room and showed me in confidence a plated, pearl-handled revolver – his 'six-shooter', he called it – which he kept in a box under his bed, and oh, the joy of those occasional expeditions! The ride of two or three miles on a lonely little branch line, the afternoon of charging to and fro with large green nets, the beauty of the enormous dragonflies which hovered over the tops of the grasses, the sinister killing-bottle with its sickly smell, and then tea in the parlour of a pub with large slices of pale-coloured cake! The essence of it was in the railway journey, which seemed to put magic distances between yourself and school.

Flip, characteristically, disapproved of these expeditions, though not actually forbidding them. 'And have you been catching *little butterflies?*' she would say with a vicious sneer when one got back, making her voice as babyish as possible. From her point of view, natural history ('bug-hunting' she would probably have called it) was a babyish pursuit which a boy should be laughed out of as early as possible. Moreover it was somehow faintly plebeian, it was traditionally associated with boys who wore spectacles and were no good at games, it did not help you to pass exams, and above all it smelt of science and therefore seemed to menace classical education. It needed a considerable moral effort to accept Brown's invitation. How I dreaded that sneer of *little butterflies*! Brown, however, who had been at the school since its early days, had built up a certain independence for himself: he seemed to handle Sambo, and ignored Flip a good deal. If it ever happened that both of them were away, Brown acted as deputy headmaster, and on those occasions instead of reading the appointed lesson for the day at morning chapel, he would read us stories from the Apocrypha.

Most of the good memories of my childhood, and up to the age of about twenty, are in some way connected with animals. So far as St Cyprian's goes, it also seems, when I look back, that all my good memories are of summer. In winter your nose ran continually, your fingers were too numb to button your shirt (this was an especial misery on Sundays, when we wore Eton collars), there was the daily nightmare of football – the cold, the mud, the hideous greasy ball that came whizzing at one's face, the gouging knees and trampling boots of the bigger boys. Part of the trouble was that in winter, after about the age of ten, I was seldom in good health, at any rate during term-time. I had defective bronchial tubes and a lesion in one lung which was not discovered till many years later. Hence I not only had a chronic cough, but running was a torment to me. In those days however, 'wheeziness', or 'chestiness', as it was called, was either diagnosed as imagination or was looked on as essentially a moral disorder, caused by overeating. 'You wheeze like a concertina,' Sambo would say disapprovingly as he stood behind my chair; 'You're perpetually stuffing yourself with food, that's why.' My cough was referred to as a 'stomach cough', which made it sound both disgusting and reprehensible. The cure for it was hard running, which, if you kept it up long enough, ultimately 'cleared your chest'.

It is curious, the degree – I will not say of actual hardship, but of squalor and neglect – that was taken for granted in upper-class schools of that period. Almost as in the days of Thackeray, it seemed natural that a little boy of eight or ten should be a miserable, snotty-nosed creature, his face almost permanently dirty, his hands chapped, his nails bitten, his handkerchief a sodden horror, his bottom frequently blue with bruises. It was partly the prospect of actual physical discomfort that made the thought of going back to school lie in one's breast like a lump of lead during the last few days of the holidays. A characteristic memory of St Cyprian's is the astonishing hardness of one's bed on the first night of term. Since this was an expensive school, I took a social step upwards by attending it, and yet the standard of comfort was in every way far lower than in my own home, or indeed, than it would have been in a prosperous working-class home. One only had a hot bath once a week, for instance. The food was not only bad, it was also insufficient. Never before or since have I seen butter or jam scraped on bread so thinly. I do not think I can be imagining the fact that we were underfed, when I remember the lengths we would go in order to steal food. On a number of occasions I remember creeping down at two or three o'clock in the morning through what seemed like miles of pitch-dark stairways and passages – barefooted, stopping to listen after each step, paralysed with about equal fear of Sambo, ghosts and burglars – to steal stale bread from the pantry. The assistant masters had their meals with us, but they had somewhat better food, and if one got half a chance it was usual to steal left-over scraps of bacon rind or fried potato when their plates were removed.

As usual, I did not see the sound commercial reason for this underfeeding. On the whole I accepted Sambo's view that a boy's appetite is a sort of morbid growth which should be kept in check as much as possible. A maxim often repeated to us at St Cyprian's was that it is healthy to get up from a meal feeling as hungry as when you sat down. Only a generation earlier than this it had been common for school dinners to start off with a slab of unsweetened suet pudding, which, it was frankly said, 'broke the boys' appetites'. But the underfeeding was probably less flagrant at preparatory schools, where a boy was wholly dependent on the official diet, than at public schools, where he was allowed – indeed, expected – to buy extra food for himself. At some schools, he would literally not have had enough to eat unless he had bought regular supplies of eggs, sausages, sardines, etc.; and his parents had to allow him money for this purpose. At Eton, for instance, at any rate in College, a boy was as given no solid meal after midday dinner. For his afternoon tea he was given only tea and bread and butter, and at eight o'clock he was given a miserable supper of soup or fried fish, or more often bread and cheese, with water to drink. Sambo went down to see his eldest son at Eton and came back in snobbish ecstacies over the luxury in which the boys lived. 'They give them fried fish for supper!' he exclaimed, beaming all over his chubby face. 'There's no school like it in the world.' Fried fish! The habitual supper of the poorest of the working class! At very cheap boarding schools it was no doubt worse. A very early memory of mine is of seeing the boarders at a grammar school – the sons, probably, of farmers and shopkeepers – being fed on boiled lights.

Whoever writes about his childhood must beware of exaggeration and self-pity. I do not claim that I was a martyr or that St Cyprian's was a sort of Dotheboys Hall. But I should be falsifying my own memories if I did not record that they are largely memories of disgust. The overcrowded, underfed, underwashed life that we led *was* disgusting, as I recall it. If I shut my eyes and say 'school', it is of course the physical surroundings that first come back to me: the flat playing-field with its cricket pavilion and the little shed by the rifle range, the draughty dormitories, the dusty splintery passages, the square of asphalt in front of the gymnasium, the raw-looking pinewood chapel at the back. And at almost every point some filthy detail obtrudes itself. For example, there were the pewter bowls out of which we had our porridge. They had overhanging rims, and under the rims there were accumulations of sour porridge, which could be flaked off in long strips. The porridge itself, too, contained more lumps, hairs and unexplained black things than one would have thought possible, unless someone were putting them there on purpose. It was never safe to start on that porridge without investigating it first. And there was the slimy water of the plunge bath – it was twelve or fifteen feet long, the whole school was supposed to go into it every morning, and I doubt whether the water was changed at all frequently – and the always-damp towels with their cheesy smell: and, on occasional visits in the winter, the murky seawater of the local Baths, which came straight in from the beach and on which I once saw floating a human turd. And the sweaty smell of the changing-room with its greasy basins, and, giving on this, the row of filthy, dilapidated lavatories, which had no fastenings of any kind on the doors, so that whenever you were sitting there someone was sure to come crashing in. It is not easy for me to think of my schooldays without seeming to breathe in a whiff of something cold and evil-smelling – a sort of compound of sweaty stockings, dirty towels, faecal smells blowing along corridors, forks with old food between the prongs, neck-of-mutton stew, and the banging doors of the lavatories and the echoing chamber-pots in the dormitories.

It is true that I am by nature not gregarious, and the W.C. and dirty handkerchief side of life is necessarily more obtrusive when great numbers of human beings are crushed together in a small space. It is just as bad in an army, and worse, no doubt, in a prison. Besides, boyhood is the age of disgust. After one has learned to differentiate, and before one has become hardened – between seven and eighteen, say – one seems always to be walking the tight-rope over a cesspool. Yet I do not think I exaggerate the squalor of school life, when I remember how health and cleanliness were neglected, in spite of the hoo-ha about fresh air and cold water and keeping in hard training. It was common to remain constipated for days together. Indeed, one was hardly encouraged to keep one's bowels open, since the only aperients tolerated were castor oil or another almost equally horrible drink called liquorice powder. One was supposed to go into the plunge bath every morning, but some boys shirked it for days on end, simply making themselves scarce when the bell sounded, or else slipping along the edge of the bath among the crowd, and then wetting their hair with a little dirty water off the floor. A little boy of eight or nine will not necessarily keep himself clean unless there is someone to see that he does it. There was a new boy named Hazel, a pretty, mother's darling of a boy, who came a little while before I left. The first thing I noticed about him was the beautiful pearly whiteness of his teeth. By the end of that term his teeth were an extraordinary shade of green. During all that time, apparently, no one had taken sufficient interest in him to see that he brushed them.

But of course the differences between home and school were more than physical. That bump on the hard mattress, on the first night of term, used to give me a feeling of abrupt awakening, a feeling of: 'This is reality, this is what you are up against.' Your home might be far from perfect, but at least it was a place ruled by love rather than by fear, where you did not have to be perpetually on your guard against the people surrounding you. At eight years old you were suddenly taken out of this warm nest and flung into a world of force and fraud and secrecy, like a gold-fish into a tank full of pike. Against no matter what degree of bullying you had no redress. You could only have defended yourself by sneaking, which, except in a few rigidly defined circumstances, was the unforgivable sin. To write home and ask your parents to take you away would have been even less thinkable, since to do so would have been to admit yourself unhappy and unpopular, which a boy will never do. Boys are Erewhonians: they think that misfortune is disgraceful and must be concealed at all costs. It might perhaps have been considered permissible to complain to your parents about bad food, or an unjustified caning, or some other ill-treatment inflicted by masters and not by boys. The fact that Sambo never beat the richer boys suggests that such complaints were made occasionally. But in my own peculiar circumstances I could never have asked my parents to intervene on my behalf. Even before I understood about the reduced fees, I grasped that they were in some way under an obligation to Sambo, and therefore could not protect me against him. I have mentioned already that throughout my time at St. Cyprian's I never had a cricket bat of my own. I had been told this was because 'your parents couldn't afford it'. One day in the holidays, by some casual remark, it came out that they had provided ten shillings to buy me one: yet no cricket bat appeared. I did not protest to my parents, let alone raise the subject with Sambo. How could I? I was dependent on him, and the ten shillings was merely a fragment of what I owed him. I realize now, of course, that it is immensely unlikely that Sambo had simply stuck to the money. No doubt the matter had slipped his memory. But the point is that I assumed that he had stuck to it, and that he had a right to do so if he chose.

How difficult it is for a child to have any real independence of attitude could be seen in our behaviour towards Flip. I think it would be true to say that every boy in the school hated and feared her. Yet we all fawned on her in the most abject way, and the top layer of our feelings towards her was a sort of guilt-stricken loyalty. Flip, although the discipline of the school depended more on her than on Sambo, hardly pretended to dispense strict justice. She was frankly capricious. An act which might get you a caning one day might next day be laughed off as a boyish prank, or even commended because it 'showed you had guts'. There were days when everyone cowered before those deep-set, accusing eyes, and there were days when she was like a flirtatious queen surrounded by courtier-lovers, laughing and joking, scattering largesse, or the promise of largesse ('And if you win the Harrow History Prize I'll give you a new case for your camera!'), and occasionally even packing three or four favoured boys into her Ford car and carrying them off to a teashop in town, where they were allowed to buy coffee and cakes. Flip was inextricably mixed up in my mind with Queen Elizabeth, whose relations with Leicester and Essex and Raleigh were intelligible to me from a very early age. A word we all constantly used in speaking of Flip was 'favour'. I'm in good favour,' we would say, or 'I'm in bad favour.' Except for the handful of wealthy or titled boys, no one was permanently in good favour, but on the other hand even the outcasts had patches of it from time to time.

Thus, although my memories of Flip are mostly hostile, I also remember considerable periods when I basked under her smiles, when she called me 'old chap' and used my Christian name, and allowed me to frequent her private library, where I first made acquaintance with *Vanity Fair*. The high-water mark of good favour was to be invited to serve at table on Sunday nights when Flip and Sambo had guests to dinner. In clearing away, of course, one had a chance to finish off the scraps, but one also got a servile pleasure from standing behind the seated guests and darting deferentially forward when something was wanted. Whenever one had the chance to suck up, one did suck up, and at the first smile one's hatred turned into a sort of cringing love. I was always tremendously proud when I succeeded in making Flip laugh. I have even, at her command, written *vers d'occasion*, comic verses to celebrate memorable events in the life of the school.

I am anxious to make it clear that I was not a rebel, except by force of circumstances. I accepted the codes that I found in being. Once, towards the end of my time, I even sneaked to Brown about a suspected case of homosexuality. I did not know very well what homosexuality was, but I knew that it happened and was bad, and that this was one of the contexts in which it was proper to sneak. Brown told me I was 'a good fellow', which made me feel horribly ashamed. Before Flip one seemed as helpless as a snake before the snake-charmer. She had a hardly-varying vocabulary of praise and abuse, a whole series of set phrases, each of which promptly called forth the appropriate response. There was '*Buck* up, old chap!', which inspired one to paroxysms of energy; there was 'Don't *be* such a fool!' (or, 'It's path*et*ic, isn't it?') which made one feel a born idiot; and there was 'It isn't very straight of you, is it?', which always brought one to the brink of tears. And yet all the while, at the middle of one's heart, there seemed to stand an incorruptible inner self who knew that whatever one did – whether one laughed or snivelled or went into frenzies of gratitude for small favours – one's only true feeling was hatred.

IV

I had learned early in my career that one can do wrong against one's will, and before long I also learned that one can do wrong without ever discovering what one has done or why it was wrong. There were sins that were too subtle to be explained, and there were others that were too terrible to be clearly mentioned. For example, there was sex, which was always smouldering just under the surface and which suddenly blew up into a tremendous row when I was about twelve.

At some preparatory schools homosexuality is not a problem but I think that St Cyprian's may have acquired a 'bad tone' thanks to the presence of the South American boys, who would perhaps mature a year or two earlier than an English boy. At that age I was not interested, so I do not actually know what went on, but I imagine it was group masturbation. At any rate, one day the storm suddenly burst over our heads. There were summonses, interrogations, confessions, floggings, repentances, solemn lectures of which one understood nothing except that some irredeemable sin known as 'swinishness' or 'beastliness' had been committed. One of the ringleaders, a boy named Horne, was flogged, according to eye-witnesses, for a quarter of an hour continuously before being expelled. His yells rang through the house. But we were all implicated, more or less, or felt ourselves to be implicated. Guilt seemed to hang in the air like a pall of smoke. A solemn, black-haired imbecile of an assistant master, who was later to be a Member of Parliament, took the older boys to a secluded room and delivered a talk on the Temple of the Body.

'Don't you realize what a wonderful thing your body is?' he said gravely. 'You talk of your motor-car engines, your Rolls-Royces and Daimlers and so on. Don't you understand that no engine ever made is fit to be compared with your body? And then you go and wreck it, ruin it – for life!'

He turned his cavernous black eyes on me and added quite sadly:

'And you, whom I'd always believed to be quite a decent person after your fashion – you, I hear, are one of the very worst.'

A feeling of doom descended upon me. So I was guilty too. I too had done the dreadful thing, whatever it was, that wrecked you for life, body and soul, and ended in suicide or the lunatic asylum. Till then I had hoped that I was innocent, and the conviction of sin which now took possession of me was perhaps all the stronger because I did not know what I had done. I was not among those who were interrogated and flogged, and it was not until the row was well over that I even learned about the trivial accident that had connected my name with it. Even then I understood nothing. It was not till about two years later that I fully grasped what that lecture on the Temple of the Body had referred to.

At this time I was in an almost sexless state, which is normal, or at any rate common, in boys of that age; I was therefore in the position of simultaneously knowing and not knowing what used to be called the

Facts of Life. At five or six, like many children, I had passed through a phase of sexuality. My friends were the plumber's children up the road, and we used sometimes to play games of a vaguely erotic kind. One was called 'playing at doctors', and I remember getting a faint but definitely pleasant thrill from holding a toy trumpet, which was supposed to be a stethoscope, against a little girl's belly. About the same time I fell deeply in love, a far more worshipping kind of love than I have ever felt for anyone since, with a girl named Elsie at the convent school which I attended. She seemed to me grown up, so I suppose she must have been fifteen. After that, as often happens, all sexual feelings seemed to go out of me for many years. At twelve I knew more than I had known as a young child, but I understood less, because I no longer knew the essential fact that there is something pleasant in sexual activity. Between roughly seven and fourteen, the whole subject seemed to me uninteresting and, when for some reason I was forced to think of it, disgusting. My knowledge of the so-called Facts of Life was derived from animals, and was therefore distorted, and in any case was only intermittent. I knew that animals copulated and that human beings had bodies resembling those of animals: but that human beings also copulated I only knew as it were, reluctantly, when something, a phrase in the Bible, perhaps, compelled me to remember it. Not having desire, I had no curiosity, and was willing to leave many questions unanswered. Thus, I knew in principle how the baby gets into the woman, but I did not know how it gets out again, because I had never followed the subject up. I knew all the dirty words, and in my bad moments I would repeat them to myself, but I did not know what the worst of them meant, nor want to know. They were abstractly wicked, a sort of verbal charm. While I remained in this state, it was easy for me to remain ignorant of any sexual misdeeds that went on about me, and to be hardly wiser even when the row broke. At most, through the veiled and terrible warnings of Flip, Sambo and all the rest of them, I grasped that the crime of which we were all guilty was somehow connected with the sexual organs. I had noticed, without feeling much interest, that one's penis sometimes stands up of its own accord (this starts happening to a boy long before he has any conscious sexual desires), and I was inclined to believe, or half-believe, that *that* must be the crime. At any rate, it was something to do with the penis – so much I understood. Many other boys, I have no doubt, were equally in the dark.

After the talk on the Temple of the Body (days later, it seems in retrospect: the row seemed to continue for days), a dozen of us were seated at a long shiny table which Sambo used for the scholarship class, under Flip's lowering eye. A long desolate wail rang out from a room somewhere above. A very small boy named Ronalds, aged no more than about ten, who was implicated in some way, was being flogged, or was recovering from a flogging. At the sound, Flip's eyes searched our faces, and settled upon me.

'*You see*,' she said.

I will not swear that she said 'You see what you have done,' but that was the sense of it. We were all bowed down with shame. It was *our* fault. Somehow or other we had led poor Ronalds astray: *we* were responsible for his agony and his ruin. Then Flip turned upon another boy named Heath. It is thirty years ago, and I cannot remember for certain whether she merely quoted a verse from the Bible, or whether she actually brought out the Bible and made Heath read it; but at any rate the text indicated was: 'Whoso shall offend one of these little ones that believe in me, it were better for him that a millstone were hanged about his neck, and that he were drowned in the depth of the sea.'

That, too, was terrible. Ronalds was one of these little ones, we had offended him; it were better that a millstone were hanged about our necks and that we were drowned in the depth of the sea.

'Have you thought about that, Heath – have you thought what it means?' Flip said. And Heath broke down into snivelling tears.

Another boy, Beacham, whom I have mentioned already, was similarly overwhelmed with shame by the accusation that he 'had black rings round his eyes'.

'Have you looked in the glass lately, Beacham?' said Flip. 'Aren't you ashamed to go about with a face like that? Do you think everyone doesn't know what it means when a boy has black rings round his eyes?'

Once again the load of guilt and fear seemed to settle down upon me. Had *I* got black rings round my eyes? A couple of years later I realized that these were supposed to be a symptom by which masturbators could be detected. But already, without knowing this, I accepted black rings as a sure sign of depravity, *some* kind of depravity. And many times, even before I grasped the supposed meaning, I have gazed anxiously into the glass, looking for the first hint of that dreaded stigma, the confession which the secret sinner writes upon his own face.

These terrors wore off, or became merely intermittent, without affecting what one might call my official beliefs. It was still true about the madhouse and the suicide's grave, but it was no longer acutely frightening. Some months later it happened that I once again saw Horne, the ringleader who had been flogged and expelled. Horne was one of the outcasts, the son of poor middle-class parents, which was no doubt part of the reason why Sambo had handled him so roughly. The term after his expulsion he went on to Eastbourne College, the small local public school, which was hideously despised at St Cyprian's and looked on as 'not really' a public school at all. Only a very few boys from St Cyprian's went there, and Sambo always spoke of them with a sort of contemptuous pity. You had no chance if you went to a school like that: at the best your destiny would be a clerkship. I thought of Horne as a person who at thirteen had already forfeited all hope of any decent future. Physically, morally and socially he was finished. Moreover I assumed that his parents had only sent him to Eastbourne College because after his disgrace no 'good' school would have him.

During the following term, when we were out for a walk, we passed Horne in the street. He looked completely normal. He was a strongly-built, rather good-looking boy with black hair. I immediately noticed that he looked better than when I had last seen him – his complexion, previously rather pale, was pinker – and that he did not seem embarrassed at meeting us. Apparently he was not ashamed either of having been expelled, or of being at Eastbourne College. If one could gather anything from the way he looked at us as we filed past, it was that he was glad to have escaped from St Cyprian's. But the encounter made very little impression on me. I drew no inference from the fact that Horne, ruined in body and soul, appeared to be happy and in good health. I still believed in the sexual mythology that had been taught me by Sambo and Flip. The mysterious, terrible dangers were still there. Any morning the black rings might appear round your eyes and you would know that you too were among the lost ones. Only it no longer seemed to matter very much. These contradictions can exist easily in the mind of a child, because of its own vitality. It accepts – how can it do otherwise? – the nonsense that its elders tell it, but its youthful body, and the sweetness of the physical world, tell it another story. It was the same with Hell, which up to the age of about fourteen I officially believed in. Almost certainly Hell existed, and there were occasions when a vivid sermon could scare you into fits. But somehow it never lasted. The fire that waited for you was real fire, it would hurt in the same way as when you burnt your finger, and *for ever*, but most of the time you could contemplate it without bothering.

V

The various codes which were presented to you at St Cyprian's – religious, moral, social and intellectual – contradicted one another if you worked out their implications. The essential conflict was between the tradition of the nineteenth-century asceticism and the actually existing luxury and snobbery of the pre-1914 age. On the one side were low-church Bible Christianity, sex puritanism, insistence on hard work, respect for academic distinction, disapproval of self-indulgence: on the other, contempt for 'braininess', and worship of games, contempt for foreigners and the working class, an almost neurotic dread of poverty, and, above all, the assumption not only that money and privilege are the things that matter, but that it is better to inherit them than to have to work for them. Broadly, you were bidden to be at once a Christian and a social success, which is impossible. At the time I did not perceive that the various ideals which were set before us cancelled out. I merely saw that they were all, or nearly all, unattainable, so far as I was concerned, since they all depended not only on what you did but on what you *were*.

Very early, at the age of ten or eleven, I reached the conclusion – no one told me this, but on the other hand I did not simply make it up out of my own head: somehow it was in the air I breathed – that you were no good unless you had £100,000. I had perhaps fixed on this particular sum as a result of reading Thackeray. The interest on £100,000 would be £4,000 a year (I was in favour of a safe 4 per cent), and this seemed to me the minimum income that you must possess if you were to belong to the real top crust, the people in the country houses. But it was clear that I could never find my way into that paradise, to which you did not really belong unless you were born into it. You could only *make* money, if at all, by a mysterious operation called 'going into the City', and when you came out of the City, having won your £100,000, you were fat and old. But the truly enviable thing about the top-notchers was that they were rich while young. For people like me, the ambitious middle class, the examination-passers, only a bleak, laborious kind of success was possible. You clambered upwards on a ladder of scholarships into the Civil Service or the Indian Civil Service, or possibly you became a barrister. And if at any point you 'slacked' or 'went off' and missed one of the rungs of the ladder, you became 'a little office boy at forty pounds a year'. But even if you climbed to the highest niche that was open to you, you could still only be an underling, a hanger-on of the people who really counted.

Even if I had not learned this from Sambo and Flip, I would have learned it from other boys,. Looking back, it is astonishing how intimately, intelligently snobbish we all were, how knowledgeable about names and addresses, how swift to detect small differences in accents and manners and the cut of clothes. There were some boys who seemed to drip money from their pores even in the bleak misery of the middle of a winter term. At the beginning and end of the term, especially, there was naïvely snobbish chatter about Switzerland, and Scotland with its ghillies and grouse moors, and 'my uncle's yacht', and 'our place in the country', and 'my pony' and 'my pater's touring car'. There never was, I suppose, in the history of the world a time when the sheer vulgar fatness of wealth, without any kind of aristocratic elegance to redeem it, was so obtrusive as in those years before 1914. It was the age when crazy millionaires in curly top-hats and lavender waistcoats gave champagne parties in rococo house-boats on the Thames, the age of diabolo and hobble skirts, the age of the 'knut' in his grey bowler and cut-away coat, the age of *The Merry Widow*, Saki's novels, *Peter Pan* and *Where the Rainbow Ends*, the age when people talked about chocs and cigs and ripping and topping and heavenly, when they went for divvy week-ends at Brighton and had scrumptious teas at the Troc. From the whole decade before 1914 there seems to breathe forth a smell of the more vulgar, un-grown-up kind of luxury, a smell of brilliantine and *crème-de-menthe* and soft centred chocolates – an atmosphere, as it were, of eating everlasting strawberry ices on green lawns to the tune of the Eton Boating Song. The extraordinary thing was the way in which everyone took it for granted that this oozing, bulging wealth of the English upper and upper-middle classes would last for ever, and was part of the order of things. After 1918 it was never quite the same again. Snobbishness and expensive habits came back, certainly, but they were self-conscious and on the defensive. Before the war the worship of money was entirely unreflecting and untroubled by any pang of conscience. The goodness of money was as unmistakable as the goodness of health or beauty, and a glittering car, a title or a horde of servants was mixed up in people's minds with the idea of actual moral virtue.

At St Cyprian's, in term-time, the general bareness of life enforced a certain democracy, but any mention of the holidays, and the consequent competitive swanking about cars and butlers and country houses, promptly called class distinctions into being. The school was pervaded by a curious cult of Scotland, which brought out the fundamental contradiction in our standard of values. Flip claimed Scottish ancestry, and she favoured the Scottish boys, encouraging them to wear kilts in their ancestral tartan instead of the school uniform, and even christened her youngest child by a Gaelic name. Ostensibly we were supposed to admire the Scots because they were 'grim' and 'dour' ('stern' was perhaps the key word), and irresistible on the field of battle. In the big schoolroom there was a steel engraving of the charge of the Scots Greys at Waterloo, all looking as though they enjoyed every moment of it. Our picture of Scotland was made up of burns, braes, kilts, sporrans, claymores, bagpipes and the like, all somehow mixed up with the invigorating effects of porridge, Protestantism and a cold climate. But underlying this was something quite different. The real reason for the cult of Scotland was that only very rich people could spend their summers there. And the pretended belief in Scottish superiority was a cover for the bad conscience of the occupying English, who had pushed the Highland peasantry off their farms to make way for the deer forests, and then compensated them by turning them into servants. Flip's face always beamed with innocent snobbishness when she spoke of Scotland. Occasionally she even attempted a trace of Scottish accent. Scotland was a private paradise which a few initiates could talk about and make outsiders feel small.

'You going to Scotland this hols?'

'Rather! We go every year.'

'My pater's got three miles of river.'

'My pater's giving me a new gun for the twelfth. There's jolly good black game where we go. Get out, Smith! What are you listening for? You've never been to Scotland. I bet you don't know what a blackcock looks like.'

Following on this, imitations of the cry of a blackcock, of the roaring of a stag, of the accent of 'our ghillies', etc. etc.

And the questionings that new boys of doubtful social origin were sometimes put through – questions quite surprising in their mean-minded particularity, when one reflects that the inquisitors were only twelve or thirteen!

'How much a year has your pater got? What part of London do you live in? Is that Knightsbridge or Kensington? How many bathrooms has your house got? How many servants do your people keep? Have you got a butler? Well, then, have you got a cook? Where do you get your clothes made? How many shows did you go to in the hols? How much money did you bring back with you?' etc. etc.

I have seen a little new boy, hardly older than eight, desperately lying his way through such a catechism:

'Have your people got a car?'

'Yes.'

'What sort of car?'

'Daimler.'

'How many horse-power?'

(Pause, and leap in the dark.)'Fifteen.'

'What kind of lights?'

The little boy is bewildered.

'What kind of lights? Electric or acetylene?'

(A longer pause, and another leap in the dark.) 'Acetylene.'

'Coo! He says his pater's car's got acetylene lamps. They went out years ago. It must be as old as the hills.'

'Rot! He's making it up. He hasn't got a car. He's just a navvy. Your pater's a navvy.'

And so on.

By the social standards that prevailed about me, I was no good, and could not be any good. But all the different kinds of virtue seemed to be mysteriously interconnected and to belong to much the same people. It was not only money that mattered: there were also strength, beauty, charm, athleticism and something called 'guts' or 'character', which in reality meant the power to impose your will on others. I did not possess any of these qualities. At games for instance, I was hopeless. I was a fairly good swimmer and not altogether contemptible at cricket, but these had no prestige value, because boys only attach importance to a game if it requires strength and courage. What counted was football, at which I was a funk. I loathed the game, and since I could see no pleasure or usefulness in it, it was very difficult for me to show courage at it. Football, it seemed to me, is not really played for the pleasure of kicking a ball about, but is a species of fighting. The lovers of football are large, boisterous, nobbly boys who are good at knocking down and trampling on slightly smaller boys. That was the pattern of school life – a continuous triumph of the strong over the weak. Virtue consisted in winning: it consisted in being bigger, stronger, handsomer, richer, more popular, more elegant, more unscrupulous than other people – in dominating them, bullying them, making them suffer pain, making them look foolish, getting the better of them in every way. Life was hierarchical and whatever happened was right. There were the strong, who deserved to win and always did win, and there were the weak, who deserved to lose and always did lose, everlastingly.

I did not question the prevailing standards, because so far as I could see there were no others. How could the rich, the strong, the elegant, the fashionable, the powerful, be in the wrong? It was their world, and the rules they made for it must be the right ones. And yet from a very early age I was aware of the impossibility of any *subjective* conformity. Always at the centre of my heart the inner self seemed to be awake, pointing out the difference between the moral obligation and the psychological *fact*. It was the same in all matters, worldly or otherwordly. Take religion, for instance. You were supposed to love God, and I did not question this. Till the age of about fourteen I believed in God, and believed that the accounts given of him were true. But I was well aware that I did not love him. On the contrary, I hated him, just as I hated Jesus and the Hebrew patriarchs. If I had sympathetic feelings towards any character in the Old Testament, it was towards such people as Cain, Jezebel, Haman, Agag, Sisera: in the New Testament my friends, if any, were Ananias, Caiaphas, Judas and Pontius Pilate. But the whole business of religion seemed to be strewn with psychological impossibilities. The Prayer Book told you, for example, to love God and fear him: but how could you love someone whom you feared? With your private affections it was the same. What you *ought* to feel was usually clear enough but the appropriate emotion could not be commanded. Obviously it was my duty to feel grateful towards Flip and Sambo; but I was not grateful. It was equally clear that one ought to love one's father, but I knew very well that I merely disliked my own father, whom I had barely seen before I was eight and who appeared to me simply as a gruff-voiced elderly man forever saying 'Don't'. It was not that one did not want to possess the right qualities or feel the correct emotions, but that one could not. The good and the possible never seemed to coincide.

There was a line of verse that I came across not actually while I was at St Cyprian's, but a year or two later, and which seemed to strike a sort of leaden echo in my heart. It was: 'The armies of unalterable law'. I understood to perfection what it meant to be Lucifer, defeated and justly defeated, with no possibility of revenge. The schoolmasters with their canes, the millionaires with their Scottish castles, the athletes with their curly hair – these were the armies of unalterable law. It was not easy, at that date, to realize that in fact it *was* alterable. And according to that law I was damned. I had no money, I was weak, I was ugly, I was unpopular, I had a chronic cough, I was cowardly, I smelt. This picture, I should add, was not altogether fanciful. I was an unattractive boy, St Cyprian's soon made me so, even if I had not been so before. But a child's belief in its own shortcomings is not much influenced by facts. I believed, for example, that I 'smelt', but this was based simply on general probability. It was notorious that disagreeable people smelt, and therefore presumably I did so too. Again, until after I had left school for good I continued to believe that I was preternaturally ugly. It was what my schoolfellows had told me, and I had no other authority to refer to. The conviction that it was *not possible* for me to be a success went deep enough to influence my actions till far into adult life. Until I was about thirty I always planned my life on the assumption not only that any major undertaking was bound to fail, but that I could only expect to live a few years longer.

But this sense of guilt and inevitable failure was balanced by something else: that is, the instinct to survive. Even a creature that is weak, ugly, cowardly, smelly and in no way justifiable still wants to stay alive and be happy after its own fashion. I could not invert the existing scale of values, or turn myself into a success, but I could accept my failure and make the best of it. I could resign myself to being what I was, and then endeavour to survive on those terms.

To survive, or at least to preserve any kind of independence, was essentially criminal, since it meant breaking rules which you yourself recognized. There was a boy named Johnny Hale who for some months oppressed me horribly. He was a big, powerful, coarsely handsome boy with a very red face and curly black hair, who was forever twisting somebody's arm, wringing somebody's ear, flogging somebody with a riding-crop (he was a member of the Sixth Form), or performing prodigies of activity on the football field. Flip loved him (hence the fact he was habitually called by his Christian name) and Sambo commended him as a boy who 'had character' and 'could keep order'. He was followed about by a group of toadies who nicknamed him Strong Man.

One day, when we were taking off our overcoats in the changing-room, Hale picked on me for some reason. I 'answered him back', whereupon he gripped my wrist, twisted it round and bent my forearm back upon itself in a hideously painful way. I remember his handsome, jeering red face bearing down upon mine. He was, I think, older than I, besides being enormously stronger. As he let go of me a terrible, wicked resolve formed itself in my heart. I would get back on him by hitting him when he did not expect it. It was a strategic moment, for the master who had been 'taking' the walk would be coming back almost immediately, and then there could be no fight. I let perhaps a minute go by, walked up to Hale with the most harmless air I could assume, and then, getting the weight of my body behind it, smashed my fist into his face. He was flung backwards by the blow, and some blood ran out of his mouth. His always sanguine face turned almost black with rage. Then he turned away to rinse his mouth at the washbasins.

'*All right*!' he said to me between his teeth as the master led us way.

For days after this he followed me about, challenging me to fight. Although terrified out of my wits, I steadily refused to fight. I said that the blow in the face had served him right and there was an end of it. Curiously enough he did not simply fall upon me there and then, which public opinion would probably have supported him in doing. So gradually the matter tailed off, and there was no fight.

Now, I had behaved wrongly, by my own code no less than his. To hit him unawares was wrong. But to refuse afterwards to fight knowing that if we fought he would beat me – that was far worse: it was cowardly. If I had refused because I disapproved of fighting, or because I genuinely felt the matter to be closed, it would have been all right; but I had refused merely because I was afraid. Even my revenge was made empty by that fact. I had struck the blow in a moment of mindless violence, deliberately not looking far ahead and merely determined to get my own back for once and damn the consequences. I had had time to realize that what I did was wrong, but it was the kind of crime from which you could get some satisfaction. Now all was nullified. There had been a sort of courage in the first act, but my subsequent cowardice had wiped it out.

The fact I hardly noticed was that though Hale formally challenged me to fight, he did not actually attack me. Indeed, after receiving that one blow he never oppressed me again. It was perhaps twenty years before I saw the significance of this. At the time I could not see beyond the moral dilemma that is presented to the weak in a world governed by the strong: Break the rules, or perish. I did not see that in that case the weak have the right to make a different set of rules for themselves; because, even if such an idea had occurred to me, there was no one in my environment who could have confirmed me in it. I lived in a world of boys, gregarious animals, questioning nothing, accepting the law of the stronger and avenging their own humiliations by passing them down to someone smaller. My situation was that of countless other boys, and if potentially I was more of a rebel than most, it was only because, by boyish standards, I was a poorer specimen. But I never did rebel intellectually, only emotionally. I had nothing to help me except my dumb selfishness, my inability – not, indeed, to despise myself, but to *dislike* myself – my instinct to survive.

It was about a year after I hit Johnny Hale in the face that I left St Cyprian's for ever. It was the end of a winter term. With a sense of coming out from darkness into sunlight I put on my Old Boy's tie as we dressed for the journey. I well remember the feeling of that brand-new silk tie round my neck, a feeling of emancipation, as though the tie had been at once a badge of manhood and an amulet against Flip's voice and Sambo's cane. I was escaping from bondage. It was not that I expected, or even intended, to be any more successful at a public school than I had been at St Cyprian's. But still, I was escaping. I knew that at a public-school there would be more privacy, more neglect, more chance to be idle and self-indulgent and degenerate. For years I had been resolved – unconsciously at first, but consciously later on – that when once my scholarship was won I would 'slack off' and cram no longer. This resolve, by the way, was so fully carried out that between the ages of thirteen and twenty-two or three I hardly ever did a stroke of avoidable work.

Flip shook hands to say good-bye. She even gave me my Christian name for the occasion. But there was a sort of patronage, almost a sneer, in her face and in her voice. The tone in which she said good-bye was nearly the one in which she had been used to say *little butterflies*. I had won two scholarships, but I was a failure, because success was measured not by what you did but by what you *were*. I was 'not a good type of boy' and could bring no credit on the school. I did not possess character or courage or health or strength or money, or even good manners, the power to look like a gentlemen.

'Good-bye,' Flip's parting smile seemed to say; 'it's not worth quarrelling now. You haven't made much of a success of your time at St Cyprian's, have you? And I don't suppose you'll get on awfully well at public school either. We made a mistake, really, in wasting our time and money on you. This kind of education hasn't much to offer to a boy with your background and your outlook. Oh, don't think we don't understand you! We know all about those ideas you have at the back of your head, we know you disbelieve in everything we've taught you, and we know you aren't in the least grateful for all we've done for you. But there's no use in bringing it all up now. We aren't responsible for you any longer, and we shan't be seeing you again. Let's just admit that you're one of our failures and part without ill-feeling. And so, good-bye.'

That at least was what I read into her face. And yet how happy I was, that winter morning, as the train bore me away with the gleaming new silk tie (dark green, pale blue and black, if I remember rightly) round my neck! The world was opening before me, just a little, like a grey sky which exhibits a narrow crack of blue. A public school would be better fun than St Cyprian's, but at bottom equally alien. In a world where the prime necessities were money, titled relatives, athleticism, tailor-made clothes, neatly-brushed hair, a charming smile, I was no good. All I had gained was a breathing-space. A little quietude, a little self-indulgence, a little respite from cramming – and then ruin. What kind of ruin I did not know: perhaps the colonies or an office-stool, perhaps prison or an early death. But first a year or two in which one could 'slack off' and get the benefit of one's sins, like Doctor Faustus. I believed firmly in my evil destiny, and yet I was acutely happy. It is the advantage of being thirteen that you can not only live in the moment, but do so with full consciousness, foreseeing the future and yet not caring about it. Next term I was going to Wellington. I had also won a scholarship at Eton, but it was uncertain whether there would be a vacancy, and I was going to Wellington first. At Eton you had a room to yourself – a room which might even have a fire in it. At Wellington you had your own cubicle, and could make yourself cocoa in the evenings. The privacy of it, the grown-upness! And there would be libraries to hang about in, and summer afternoons when you could shirk games and mooch about the countryside alone, with no master driving you along. Meanwhile there were the holidays. There was the .22 rifle that I had bought the previous holidays (the Crackshot, it was called, costing twenty-two and sixpence), and Christmas was coming next week. There were also the pleasures of overeating. I thought of some particularly voluptuous cream buns which could be bought for twopence each at a shop in our town. (This was 1916, and food-rationing had not yet started.) Even the detail that my journey-money had been slightly miscalculated, leaving about a shilling over – enough for an unforeseen cup of coffee and a cake or two somewhere on the way – was enough to fill me with bliss. There was time for a bit of happiness before the future closed in upon me. But I did know that the future was dark. Failure, failure, failure – failure behind me, failure ahead of me – that was by far the deepest conviction that I carried away.

VI

All this was thirty years ago and more. The question is: Does a child at school go through the same kind of experiences nowadays.

The only honest answer, I believe, is that we do not with certainty know. Of course it is obvious that the present-day *attitude* towards education is enormously more humane and sensible than that of the past. The snobbishness that was an integral part of my own education would be almost unthinkable today, because the society that nourished it is dead. I recall a conversation that must have taken place about a year before I left St Cyprian's. A Russian boy, large and fair-haired, a year older than myself, was questioning me.

'How much a year has your father got?'

I told him what I thought it was, adding a few hundreds to make it sound better. The Russian boy, neat in his habits, produced a pencil and a small note-book and made a calculation.

'My father has over two hundred times as much money as yours,' he announced with a sort of amused contempt.

That was in 1915. What happened to that money a couple of years later, I wonder? And still more I wonder, do conversations of that kind happen at preparatory schools now?

Clearly there has been a vast change of outlook, a general growth of 'enlightment', even among ordinary, unthinking middle-class people. Religious belief, for instance, has largely vanished, dragging other kinds of nonsense after it. I imagine that very few people nowadays would tell a child that if it masturbates it will end in the lunatic asylum. Beating, too, has become discredited, and has even been abandoned at many schools. Nor is the underfeeding of children looked on as a normal, almost meritorious act. No one now would openly set out to give his pupils as little food as they could do with, or tell them that it is healthy to get up from a meal as hungry as you sat down. The whole status of children has improved, partly because they have grown relatively less numerous. And the diffusion of even a little psychological knowledge has made it harder for parents and schoolteachers to indulge their aberrations in the name of discipline. Here is a case, not known to me personally, but known to someone I can vouch for, and happening within my own lifetime. A small girl, daughter of a clergyman, continued wetting her bed at an age when she should have grown out of it. In order to punish her for this dreadful deed, her father took her to a large garden party and there introduced her to the whole company as a little girl who wetted her bed: and to underline her wickedness he had previously painted her face black. I do not suggest that Flip and Sambo would actually have done a thing like this, but I doubt whether it would have much surprised them. After all, things do change. And yet – !

The question is not whether boys are still buckled into Eton collars on Sunday, or told that babies are dug up under gooseberry bushes. That kind of thing is at an end, admittedly. The real question is whether it is still normal for a schoolchild to live for years amid irrational terrors and lunatic misunderstandings. And here one is up against the very great difficulty of knowing what a child really feels and thinks. A child which appears reasonably happy may actually be suffering horrors which it cannot or will not reveal. It lives in a sort of alien under-water world which we can only penetrate by memory or divination. Our chief clue is the fact that we were once children ourselves, and many people appear to forget the atmosphere of their own childhood almost entirely. Think for instance of the unnecessary torments that people will inflict by sending a child back to school with clothes of the wrong pattern, and refusing to see that this matters! Over things of this kind a child will sometimes utter a protest, but a great deal of the time its attitude is one of simple concealment. Not to expose your true feelings to an adult seems to be instinctive from the age of seven or eight onwards. Even the affection that one feels for a child, the desire to protect and cherish it, is a cause of misunderstanding. One can love a child, perhaps, more deeply than one can love another adult, but it is rash to assume that the child feels any love in return. Looking back on my own childhood, after the infant years were over, I do not believe that I ever felt love for any mature person, except my mother, and even her I did not trust, in the sense that shyness made me conceal most of my real feelings from her. Love, the spontaneous, unqualified emotion of love, was something I could only feel for people who were young. Towards people who were old – and remember that 'old' to a child means over thirty, or even over twenty-five – I could feel reverence, respect, admiration or compunction, but I seemed cut off from them by a veil of fear and shyness mixed up with physical distaste. People are too ready to forget the child's *physical* shrinking from the adult. The enormous size of grown-ups, their ungainly, rigid bodies, their coarse, wrinkled skins, their great relaxed eyelids, their yellow teeth, and the whiffs of musty clothes and beer and sweat and tobacco that disengage from them at every movement! Part of the reason for the ugliness of adults, in a child's eyes, is that the child is usually looking upwards, and few faces are at their best when seen from below. Besides, being fresh and unmarked itself, the child has impossibly high standards in the matter of skin and teeth and complexion. But the greatest barrier of all is the child's misconception about age. A child can hardly envisage life beyond thirty, and in judging people's ages it will make fantastic mistakes. It will think that a person of twenty-five is forty, that a person of forty is sixty-five, and so on. Thus, when I fell in love with Elsie I took her to be grown-up. I met her again, when I was thirteen and she, I think, must have been twenty-three; she now seemed to me a middle-aged woman, somewhat past her best. And the child thinks of growing old as an almost obscene calamity, which for some mysterious reason will never happen to itself. All who have passed the age of thirty are joyless grotesques, endlessly fussing about things of no importance and staying alive without, so far as the child can see, having anything to live for. Only child life is real life. The schoolmaster who imagines that he is loved and trusted by his boys is in fact mimicked and laughed at behind his back. An adult who does not seem dangerous nearly always seems ridiculous.

I base these generalizations on what I can recall of my own childhood outlook. Treacherous though memory is, it seems to me the chief means we have of discovering how a child's mind works. Only by resurrecting our own memories can we realize how incredibly distorted is the child's vision of the world. Consider this, for example. How would St Cyprian's appear to me now, if I could go back, at my present age, and see it as it was in 1915? What should I think of Sambo and Flip, those terrible, all-powerful monsters? I should see them as a couple of silly, shallow, ineffectual people, eagerly clambering up a social ladder which any thinking person could see to be on the point of collapse. I would no more be frightened of them than I would be frightened of a dormouse. Moreover, in those days they seemed to me fantastically old, whereas – though of this I am not certain – I imagine they must have been somewhat younger than I am now. And how would Johnny Hale appear, with his blacksmith's arms and his red, jeering face? Merely a scruffy little boy, barely distinguishable from hundreds of other scruffy little boys. The two sets of facts can lie side by side in my mind, because those happen to be my own memories. But it would be very difficult for me to see with the eyes of any other child, except by an effort of the imagination which might lead me completely astray. The child and the adult live in different worlds. If that is so, we cannot be certain that school, at any rate boarding school, is not still for many children as dreadful an experience as it used to be. Take away God, Latin, the cane, class distinctions and sexual taboos, and the fear, the hatred, the snobbery and the misunderstanding might still all be there. It will have been seen that my own main trouble was an utter lack of any sense of proportion or probability. This led me to accept outrages and believe absurdities, and to suffer torments over things which were in fact of no importance. It is not enough to say that I was 'silly' and 'ought to have known better'. Look back into your own childhood and think of the nonsense you used to believe and the trivialities which could make you suffer. Of course my own case had its individual variations, but essentially it was that of countless other boys. The weakness of the child is that it starts with a blank sheet. It neither understands nor questions the society in which it lives, and because of its credulity other people can work upon it, infecting it with the sense of inferiority and the dread of offending against mysterious, terrible laws.

It may be that everything that happened to me at St Cyprian's could happen in the most 'enlightened' school, though perhaps in subtler forms. Of one thing, however, I do feel fairly sure, and that is that boarding schools are worse than day schools. A child has a better chance with the sanctuary of its home near at hand. And I think the characteristic faults of the English upper and middle classes may be partly due to the practice, general until recently, of sending children away from home as young as nine, eight or even seven.

I have never been back to St Cyprian's. Reunions, old boys' dinners and such-like leave me something more than cold, even when my memories are friendly. I have never even been down to Eton, where I was relatively happy, though I did once pass through it in 1933 and noted with interest that nothing seemed to have changed, except that the shops now sold radios. As for St Cyprian's, for years I loathed its very name so deeply that I could not view it with enough detachment to see the significance of the things that happened to me there. In a way, it is only within the last decade that I have really thought over my schooldays, vividly though their memory has always haunted me. Nowadays, I believe, it would make very little impression on me to see the place again, if it still exists. (I remember hearing a rumour some years ago that it had been burnt down.) If I had to pass through Eastbourne I would not make a detour to avoid the school: and if I happened to pass the school itself I might even stop for a moment by the low brick wall, with the steep bank running down from it, and look across the flat playing field at the ugly building with the square of asphalt in front of it. And if I went inside and smelt again the inky, dusty smell of the big schoolroom, the rosiny smell of the chapel, the stagnant smell of the swimming bath and the cold reek of the lavatories, I think I should only feel what one invariably feels in revisiting any scene of childhood: How small everything has grown, and how terrible is the deterioration in myself! But it is a fact that for many years I could hardly have borne to look at it again. Except upon dire necessity I would not have set foot in Eastbourne. I even conceived a prejudice against Sussex, as the county that contained St Cyprian's, and as an adult I have only once been in Sussex, on a short visit. Now, however, the place is out of my system for good. Its magic works no longer, and I have not even enough animosity left to make me hope that Flip and Sambo are dead or that the story of the school being burnt down was true.

Written by May 1947; *Partisan Review*, September–October 1952; *S.J.*; *O.R.*

40. Writers and Leviathan

The position of the writer in an age of State control is a subject that has already been fairly largely discussed, although most of the evidence that might be relevant is not yet available. In this place I do not want to express an opinion either for or against State patronage of arts, but merely to point out that *what kind* of State rules over us must depend partly on the prevailing intellectual atmosphere: meaning, in this context, partly on the attitude of writers and artists themselves, and on their willingness or otherwise to keep the spirit of liberalism alive. If we find ourselves in ten years' time cringing before somebody like Zhdanov, it will probably be because that is what we have deserved. Obviously there are strong tendencies towards totalitarianism at work within the English literary intelligentsia already. But here I am not concerned with any organized and conscious movement such as Communism, but merely with the effect, on people of goodwill, of political thinking and the need to take sides politically.

This is a political age. War, Fascism, concentration camps, rubber truncheons, atomic bombs, etc. are what we daily think about, and therefore to a great extent what we write about, even when we do not name them openly. We cannot help this. When you are on a sinking ship, your thoughts will be about sinking ships. But not only is our subject-matter narrowed, but our whole attitude towards literature is coloured by loyalties which we at least intermittently realize to be non-literary. I often have the feeling that even at the best of times literary criticism is fraudulent, since in the absence of any accepted standards whatever – any *external* reference which can give meaning to the statement that such and such a book is 'good' or 'bad' – every literary judgement consists in trumping up a set of rules to justify an instinctive preference. One's real reaction to a book, when one has a reaction at all, is usually, 'I like this book' or 'I don't like it', and what follows is a rationalization. But 'I like this book' is not, I think, a non-literary reaction; the non-literary reaction is 'This book is on my side, and therefore I must discover merits in it.' Of course, when one praises a book for political reasons one may be emotionally sincere, in the sense that one does feel strong approval of it, but also it often happens that party solidarity demands a plain lie. Anyone used to reviewing books for political periodicals is well aware of this. In general, if you are writing for a paper that you are in agreement with, you sin by commission, and if for a paper of the opposite stamp, by omission. At any rate, innumerable controversial books – books for or against Soviet Russia, for or against Zionism, for or against the Catholic Church, etc. – are judged before they are read, and in effect before they are written. One knows in advance what reception they will get in what papers. And yet, with a dishonesty that sometimes is not even quarter-conscious, the pretence is kept up that genuinely literary standards are being applied.

Of course, the invasion of literature by politics was bound to happen. It must have happened, even if the special problem of totalitarianism had never arisen, because we have developed a sort of compunction which our grandfathers did not have, an awareness of the enormous injustice and misery of the world, and a guilt-stricken feeling that one ought to be doing something about it, which makes a purely aesthetic attitude towards life impossible. No one, now, could devote himself to literature as single-mindedly as Joyce or Henry James. But unfortunately, to accept political responsibility now means yielding oneself over to orthodoxies and 'party lines', with all the timidity and dishonesty that that implies. As against the Victorian writers, we have the disadvantage of living among clear-cut political ideologies and of usually knowing at a glance what thoughts are heretical. A modern literary intellectual lives and writes in constant dread – not, indeed, of public opinion in the wider sense, but of public opinion within his own group. As a rule, luckily, there is more than one group, but also at any given moment there is a dominant orthodoxy, to offend against which needs a thick skin and sometimes means cutting one's income in half for years on end. Obviously, for about fifteen years past, the dominant orthodoxy, especially among the young, has been 'left'. The key words are 'progressive', 'democratic' and 'revolutionary', while the labels which you must at all costs avoid having gummed upon you are 'bourgeois', 'reactionary' and 'Fascist'. Almost everyone nowadays, even the majority of Catholics and Conservatives, is 'progressive', or at least wishes to be thought so. No one, so far as I know, ever describes himself as a 'bourgeois', just as no one literate enough to have heard the word ever admits to being guilty of antisemitism. We are all of us good democrats, anti-Fascist, anti-imperialist, contemptuous of class distinctions, impervious to colour prejudice, and so on and so forth. Nor is there much doubt that the present-day 'left' orthodoxy is better than the rather snobbish, pietistic Conservative orthodoxy which prevailed twenty years ago, when the *Criterion* and (on a lower level) the *London Mercury* were the dominant literary magazines. For at least its implied objective is a viable form of society which large numbers of people actually want. But it also has its own falsities which, because they cannot be admitted, make it impossible for certain questions to be seriously discussed.

The whole left-wing ideology, scientific and Utopian, was evolved by people who had no immediate prospect of attaining power. It was, therefore, an extremist ideology, utterly contemptuous of kings, governments, laws, prisons, police forces, armies, flags, frontiers, patriotism, religion, conventional morality, and, in fact, the whole existing scheme of things. Until well within living memory the forces of the Left in all countries were fighting against a tyranny which appeared to be invincible, and it was easy to assume that if only *that* particular tyranny – capitalism – could be overthrown, Socialism would follow. Moreover, the Left had inherited from Liberalism certain distinctly questionable beliefs, such as the belief that the truth will prevail and persecution defeats itself, or that man is naturally good and is only corrupted by his environment. This perfectionist ideology has persisted in nearly all of us, and it is in the name of it that we protest when (for instance) a Labour government votes huge incomes to the King's daughters or shows hesitation about nationalizing steel. But we have also accumulated in our minds a whole series of unadmitted contradictions, as a result of successive bumps against reality.

The first big bump was the Russian Revolution. For somewhat complex reasons, nearly the whole of the English Left has been driven to accept the Russian régime as 'Socialist', while silently recognizing that its spirit and practice are quite alien to anything that is meant by 'Socialism' in this country. Hence there has arisen a sort of schizophrenic manner of thinking, in which words like 'democracy' can bear two irreconcilable meanings, and such things as concentration camps and mass deportations can be right and wrong simultaneously. The next blow to the left-wing ideology was the rise of Fascism, which shook the pacifism and internationalism of the Left without bringing about a definite restatement of doctrine. The experience of German occupation taught the European peoples something that the colonial peoples knew already, namely, that class antagonisms are not all-important and that there is such a thing as national interest. After Hitler it was difficult to maintain seriously that 'the enemy is in your own country' and that national independence is of no value. But though we all know this and act upon it when necessary, we still feel that to say it aloud would be a kind of treachery. And finally, the greatest difficulty of all, there is the fact that the Left is now in power and is obliged to take responsibility and make genuine decisions.

Left governments almost invariably disappoint their supporters because, even when the prosperity which they have promised is achievable, there is always need of an uncomfortable transition period about which little has been said beforehand. At this moment we see our own Government, in its desperate economic straits, fighting in effect against its own past propaganda. The crisis that we are now in is not a sudden unexpected calamity, like an earthquake, and it was not caused by the war, but merely hastened by it. Decades ago it could be foreseen that something of this kind was going to happen. Ever since the nineteenth century our national income, dependent partly on interest from foreign investments, and on assured markets and cheap raw materials in colonial countries, had been extremely precarious. It was certain that, sooner or later, something would go wrong and we should be forced to make our exports balance our imports: and when that happened the British standard of living, including the working-class standard, was bound to fall, at least temporarily. Yet the left-wing parties, even when they were vociferously anti-imperialist, never made these facts clear. On occasion they were ready to admit that the British workers had benefited, to some extent, by the looting of Asia and Africa, but they always allowed it to appear that we could give up our loot and yet in some way contrive to remain prosperous. Quite largely, indeed, the workers were won over to Socialism by being told that they were exploited, whereas the brute truth was that, in world terms, they were exploiters. Now, to all appearances, the point has been reached when the working-class living-standard *cannot* be maintained, let alone raised. Even if we squeeze the rich out of existence, the mass of the people must either consume less or produce more. Or am I exaggerating the mess we are in? I may be, and I should be glad to find myself mistaken. But the point I wish to make is that this question, among people who are faithful to the Left ideology, cannot be genuinely discussed. The lowering of wages and raising of working hours are felt to be inherently anti-Socialist measures, and must therefore be dismissed in advance, whatever the economic situation may be. To suggest that they may be unavoidable is merely to risk being plastered with those labels that we are all terrified of. It is far safer to evade the issue and pretend that we can put everything right by redistributing the existing income.

To accept an orthodoxy is always to inherit unresolved contradictions. Take for instance the fact that all sensitive people are revolted by industrialism and its products, and yet are aware that the conquest of poverty and the emancipation of the working class demand not less industrialization, but more and more. Or take the fact that certain jobs are absolutely necessary and yet are never done except under some kind of coercion. Or take the fact that it is impossible to have a positive foreign policy without having powerful armed forces. One could multiply examples. In every such case there is a conclusion which is perfectly plain but which can only be drawn if one is privately disloyal to the official ideology. The normal response is to push the question, unanswered, into a corner of one's mind, and then continue repeating contradictory catchwords. One does not have to search far through the reviews and magazines to discover the effects of this kind of thinking.

I am not, of course, suggesting that mental dishonesty is peculiar to Socialists and left-wingers generally, or is commonest among them. It is merely that acceptance of *any* political discipline seems to be incompatible with literary integrity. This applies equally to movements like Pacifism and Personalism, which claim to be outside the ordinary political struggle. Indeed, the mere sound of words ending in -ism seems to bring with it the smell of propaganda. Group loyalties are necessary, and yet they are poisonous to literature, so long as literature is the product of individuals. As soon as they are allowed to have any influence, even a negative one, on creative writing, the result is not only falsification, but often the actual drying-up of the inventive faculties.

Well, then what? Do we have to conclude that it is the duty of every writer to 'keep out of politics'? Certainly not! In any case, as I have already said, no thinking person can or does genuinely keep out of politics, in an age like the present one. I only suggest that we should draw up a sharper distinction than we do at present between our political and our literary loyalties, and should recognize that a willingness to *do* certain distasteful but necessary things does not carry with it any obligation to swallow the beliefs that usually go with them. When a writer engages in politics he should do so as a citizen, as a human being, but not *as a writer.* I do not think that he has the right, merely on the score of his sensibilities, to shirk the ordinary dirty work of politics. Just as much as anyone else, he should be prepared to deliver lectures in draughty halls, to chalk pavements, to canvass voters, to distribute leaflets, even to fight in civil wars if it seems necessary. But whatever else he does in the service of his party, he should never write for it. He should make it clear that his writing is a thing apart. And he should be able to act co-operatively while, if he chooses, completely rejecting the official ideology. He should never turn back from a train of thought because it may lead to a heresy, and he should not mind very much if his unorthodoxy is smelt out, as it probably will be. Perhaps it is even a bad sign in a writer if he is not suspected of reactionary tendencies today, just as it was a bad sign if he was not suspected of Communist sympathies twenty years ago.

But does all this mean that a writer should not only refuse to be dictated to by political bosses, but also that he should refrain from writing *about* politics? Once again, certainly not! There is no reason why he should not write in the most crudely political way, if he wishes to. Only he should do so as an individual, an outsider, at the most an unwelcome guerrilla on the flank of a regular army. This attitude is quite compatible with ordinary political usefulness. It is reasonable, for example, to be willing to fight in a war because one thinks the war ought to be won, and at the same time to refuse to write war propaganda. Sometimes, if a writer is honest, his writings and his political activities may actually contradict one another. There are occasions when that is plainly undesirable: but then the remedy is not to falsify one's impulses, but to remain silent.

To suggest that a creative writer, in a time of conflict, must split his life into two compartments, may seem defeatist or frivolous: yet in practice I do not see what else he can do. To lock yourself up in an ivory tower is impossible and undesirable. To yield subjectively, not merely to a party machine, but even to a group ideology, is to destroy yourself as a writer. We feel this dilemma to be a painful one, because we see the need of engaging in politics while also seeing what a dirty, degrading business it is. And most of us still have a lingering belief that every choice, even every political choice, is between good and evil, and that if a thing is necessary it is also right. We should, I think, get rid of this belief, which belongs to the nursery. In politics one can never do more than decide which of two evils is the lesser, and there are some situations from which one can only escape by acting like a devil or a lunatic. War, for example, may be necessary, but it is certainly not right or sane. Even a General Election is not exactly a pleasant or edifying spectacle. If you have to take part in such things – and I think you do have to, unless you are armoured by old age or stupidity or hypocrisy – then you also have to keep part of yourself inviolate. For most people the problem does not arise in the same form, because their lives are split already. They are truly alive only in their leisure hours, and there is no emotional connexion between their work and their political activities. Nor are they generally asked, in the name of political loyalty, to debase themselves as workers. The artist, and especially the writer, is asked just that – in fact, it is the only thing the politicians ever ask of him. If he refuses, that does not mean that he is condemned to inactivity. One half of him, which in a sense is the whole of him, can act as resolutely, even as violently if need be, as anyone else. But his writings, in so far as they have any value, will always be the product of the saner self that stands aside, records the things that are done and admits their necessity, but refuses to be deceived as to their true nature.

Written [March] 1948; *Politics and Letters*, Summer 1948; *New Leader* (New York), 19 June 1948; *S.J.*; *E.Y.E.*; *C.E.*

41. Reflections on Gandhi

Saints should always be judged guilty until they are proved innocent, but the tests that have to be applied to them are not, of course, the same in all cases. In Gandhi's case the questions one feels inclined to ask are: to what extent was Gandhi moved by vanity – by the consciousness of himself as a humble, naked old man, sitting on a praying-mat and shaking empires by sheer spiritual power – and to what extend did he compromise his own principles by entering into politics, which of their nature are inseparable from coercion and fraud? To give a definite answer one would have to study Gandhi's acts and writings in immense detail, for his whole life was a sort of pilgrimage in which every act was significant. But this partial autobiography, which ends in the nineteen-twenties, is strong evidence in his favour, all the more because it covers what he would have called the unregenerate part of his life and reminds one that inside the saint, or near-saint, there was a very shrewd, able person who could, if he had chosen, have been a brilliant success as a lawyer, an administrator or perhaps even a businessman.

At about the time when the autobiography[1] first appeared I remember reading its opening chapters in the ill-printed pages of some Indian newspaper. They made a good impression on me, which Gandhi himself, at that time, did not. The things that one associated with him – homespun cloth, 'soul forces' and vegetarianism – were unappealing, and his

1. *The Story of my Experiments with Truth* by M. K. Gandhi, translated from the Gujarati by Mahadev Desai.

medievalist programme was obviously not viable in a backward, starving, overpopulated country. It was also apparent that the British were making use of him, or thought they were making use of him. Strictly speaking, as a Nationalist, he was an enemy, but since in every crisis he would exert himself to prevent violence – which, from the British point of view, meant preventing any effective action whatever – he could be regarded as 'our man'. In private this was sometimes cynically admitted. The attitude of the Indian millionaires was similar. Gandhi called upon them to repent, and naturally they preferred him to the Socialists and Communists who, given the chance, would actually have taken their money away. How reliable such calculations are in the long run is doubtful; as Gandhi himself says 'in the end deceivers deceive only themselves'; but at any rate the gentleness with which he was nearly always handled was due partly to the feeling that he was useful. The British Conservatives only became really angry with him when, as in 1942, he was in effect turning his non-violence against a different conqueror.

But I could see even then that the British officials who spoke of him with a mixture of amusement and disapproval also genuinely liked and admired him, after a fashion. Nobody ever suggested that he was corrupt, or ambitious in any vulgar way, or that anything he did was actuated by fear or malice. In judging a man like Gandhi one seems instinctively to apply high standards, so that some of his virtues have passed almost unnoticed. For instance, it is clear even from the autobiography that his natural physical courage was quite outstanding: the manner of his death was a later illustration of this, for a public man who attached any value to his own skin would have been more adequately guarded. Again, he seems to have been quite free from that maniacal suspiciousness which, as E.M. Forster rightly says in *A Passage to India*, is the besetting Indian vice, as hypocrisy is the British vice. Although no doubt he was shrewd enough in detecting dishonesty, he seems wherever possible to have believed that other people were acting in good faith and had a better nature through which they could be approached. And though he came of a poor middle-class family, started life rather unfavourably, and was probably of unimpressive physical appearance, he was not afflicted by envy or by the feeling of inferiority. Colour feeling, when he first met it in its worst form in South Africa, seems rather to have astonished him. Even when he was fighting what was in effect a colour war he did not think of people in terms of race or status. The governor of a province, a cotton millionaire, a half-starved Dravidian coolie, a British private soldier, were all equally human beings, to be approached in much the same way. It is noticeable that even in the worst possible circumstances, as in South Africa, when he was making himself unpopular as the champion of the Indian community, he did not lack European friends.

Written in short lengths for newspaper serialization, the autobiography is not a literary masterpiece, but is the more impressive because of the commonplaceness of much of its material. It is well to be reminded that Gandhi started out with the normal ambitions of a young Indian student and only adopted his extremist opinions by degrees and, in some cases, rather unwillingly. There was a time, it is interesting to learn, when he wore a top-hat, took dancing lessons, studied French and Latin, went up the Eiffel Tower, and even tried to learn the violin – all this with the idea of assimilating European civilization as thoroughly as possible. He was not one of those saints who are marked out by their phenomenal piety from childhood onwards, nor one of the other kind who forsake the world after sensational debaucheries. He makes full confession of the misdeeds of his youth, but in fact there is not much to confess. As a frontispiece to the book, there is a photograph of Gandhi's possessions at the time of his death. The whole outfit could be purchased for about £5, and Gandhi's sins, at least his fleshly sins, would make the same sort of appearance if placed all in one heap. A few cigarettes, a few mouthfuls of meat, a few annas pilfered in childhood from the maidservant, two visits to a brothel (on each occasion he got away without 'doing anything'), one narrowly escaped lapse with his landlady in Plymouth, one outburst of temper – that is about the whole collection. Almost from childhood onwards he had a deep earnestness, an attitude ethical rather than religious, but, until he was about thirty, no very definite sense of direction. His first entry into anything describable as public life was made by way of vegetarianism. Underneath his less ordinary qualities one feels all the time the solid middle-class businessmen who were his ancestors. One feels that even after he had abandoned personal ambition he must have been a resourceful, energetic lawyer and a hard headed political organizer, careful in keeping down expenses, an adroit handler of committees and an indefatigable chaser of subscriptions. His character was an extraordinarily mixed one, but there was almost nothing in it that you can put your finger on and call bad, and I believe that even Gandhi's worst enemies would admit that he was an interesting and unusual man who enriched the world simply by being alive. Whether he was also a lovable man, and whether his teachings can have much value for those who do not accept the religious beliefs on which they are founded, I have never felt fully certain.

Of late years it has been the fashion to talk about Gandhi as though he were not only sympathetic to the western left-wing movement, but were even integrally part of it. Anarchists and pacifists, in particular, have claimed him for their own, noticing only that he was opposed to centralism and State violence and ignoring the other-wordly, anti-humanist tendency of his doctrines. But one should, I think, realize that Gandhi's teachings cannot be squared with the belief that Man is the measure of all things, and that our job is to make life worth living on this earth, which is the only earth we have. They make sense only on the assumption that God exists and that the world of solid objects is an illusion to be escaped from. It is worth considering the disciplines which Gandhi imposed on himself and which – though he might not insist on every one of his followers observing every detail – he considered indispensable if one wanted to serve either God or humanity. First of all, no meat eating, and if possible no animal food in any form. (Gandhi himself, for the sake of his health, had to compromise on milk, but seems to have felt this to be a backsliding.) No alcohol or tobacco, and no spices or condiments, even of a vegetable kind, since food should be taken not for its own sake, but solely in order to preserve one's strength. Secondly, if possible, no sexual intercourse. If sexual intercourse must happen, then it should be for the sole purpose of begetting children and presumably at long intervals. Gandhi himself, in his middle thirties, took the vow of *bramahcharya*, which means not only complete chastity but the elimination of sexual desire. This condition, it seems, is difficult to attain without a special diet and frequent fasting. One of the dangers of milk drinking is that it is apt to arouse sexual desire. And finally – this is the cardinal point – for the seeker after goodness there must be no close friendships and no exclusive loves whatever.

Close friendships, Gandhi says, are dangerous, because 'friends react on one another' and through loyalty to a friend one can be led into wrong-doing. This is unquestionably true. Moreover, if one is to love God, or to love humanity as a whole, one cannot give one's preference to any individual person. This again is true, and it marks the point at which the humanistic and the religious attitudes cease to be reconcilable. To an ordinary human being, love means nothing if it does not mean loving some people more than others. The autobiography leaves it uncertain whether Gandhi behaved in an inconsiderate way to his wife and children, but at any rate it makes clear that on three occasions he was willing to let his wife or a child die rather than administer the animal food prescribed by the doctor. It is true that the threatened death never actually occurred, and also that Gandhi – with, one gathers, a good deal of moral pressure in the opposite direction –always gave the patient the choice of staying alive at the price of committing a sin: still, if the decision had been solely his own, he would have forbidden the animal food, whatever the risks might be. There must, he says, be some limit to what we will do in order to remain alive, and the limit is well on this side of chicken broth. This attitude is perhaps a noble one, but in the sense which – I think – most people would give to the word, it is inhuman. The essence of being human is that one does not seek perfection, that one *is* sometimes willing to commit sins for the sake of loyalty, that one does not push asceticism to the point where it makes friendly intercourse impossible, and that one is prepared in the end to be defeated and broken up by life, which is the inevitable price of fastening one's love upon other human individuals. No doubt alcohol, tobacco and so forth are things that a saint must avoid, but sainthood is also a thing that human beings must avoid. There is an obvious retort to this, but one should be wary about making it. In this yogi-ridden age, it is too readily assumed that 'non-attachment' is not only better than a full acceptance of earthly life, but that the ordinary man only rejects it because it is too difficult: in other words, that the average human being is a failed saint. It is doubtful whether this is true. Many people genuinely do not wish to be saints, and it is probable that some who achieve or aspire to sainthood have never felt much temptation to be human beings. If one could follow it to its psychological roots, one would, I believe, find that the main motive for 'non-attachment' is a desire to escape from the pain of living, and above all from love, which, sexual or non-sexual, is hard work. But it is not necessary here to argue whether the other-wordly or the humanistic ideal is 'higher'. The point is that they are incompatible. One must choose between God and Man, and all 'radicals' and 'progressives', from the mildest Liberal to the most extreme Anarchist, have in effect chosen Man.

However, Gandhi's pacifism can be separated to some extent from his other teachings. Its motive was religious, but he claimed also for it that it was a definite technique, a method, capable of producing desired political results. Gandhi's attitude was not that of most western pacifists. *Satyagraha*, first evolved in South Africa, was a sort of non-violent warfare, a way of defeating the enemy without hurting him and without feeling or arousing hatred. It entailed such things as civil disobedience, strikes, lying down in front of railway trains, enduring police charges without running away and without hitting back, and the like. Gandhi objected to 'passive resistance' as a translation of *Satyargraha*: in Gujarati, it seems, the word means 'firmness in the truth'. In his early days Gandhi served as a stretcher-bearer on the British side in the Boer War, and he was prepared to do the same again in the war of 1914–18. Even after he had completely abjured violence he was honest enough to see that in war it is usually necessary to take sides. He did not – indeed, since his whole political life centred round a struggle for national independence, he could not – take the sterile and dishonest line of pretending that in every war both sides are exactly the same and it makes no difference who wins. Nor did he, like most western pacifists, specialize in avoiding awkward questions. In relation to the late war, one question that every pacifist had a clear obligation to answer was: 'What about the Jews? Are you prepared to see them exterminated? If not, how do you propose to save them without resorting to war?' I must say that I have never heard, from any western pacifist, an honest answer to this question, though I have heard plenty of evasions, usually of the 'you're another' type. But it so happens that Gandhi was asked a somewhat similar question in 1938 and that his answer is on record in Mr Louis Fischer's *Gandhi and Stalin*. According to Mr Fischer Gandhi's view was that the German Jews ought to commit collective suicide, which 'would have aroused the world and the people of Germany to Hitler's violence'. After the war he justified himself: the Jews had been killed anyway, and might as well have died significantly. One has the impression that this attitude staggered even so warm an admirer as Mr Fischer, but Gandhi was merely being honest. If you are not prepared to take life, you must often be prepared for lives to be lost in some other way. When, in 1942, he urged non-violent resistance against a Japanese invasion, he was ready to admit that it might cost several million deaths.

At the same time there is reason to think that Gandhi, who after all was born in 1869, did not understand the nature of totalitarianism and saw everything in terms of his own struggle against the British Government. The important point here is not so much that the British treated him forbearingly as that he was always able to command publicity. As can be seen from the phrase quoted above, he believed in 'arousing the world', which is only possible if the world gets a chance to hear what you are doing. It is difficult to see how Gandhi's methods could be applied in a country where opponents of the régime disappear in the middle of the night and are never heard of again. Without a free press and the right of assembly, it is impossible not merely to appeal to outside opinion, but to bring a mass movement into being, or even to make your intentions known to your adversary. Is there a Gandhi in Russia at this moment?

And if there is, what is he accomplishing? The Russian masses could only practise civil disobedience if the same idea happened to occur to all of them simultaneously, and even then, to judge by the history of the Ukraine famine, it would make no difference. But let it be granted that non-violent resistance can be effective against one's own government, or against an occupying power: even so, how does one put it into practice internationally? Gandhi's various conflicting statements on the late war seems to show that he felt the difficulty of this. Applied to foreign politics, pacifism either stops being pacifist or becomes appeasement. Moreover the assumption, which served Gandhi so well in dealing with individuals, that all human beings are more or less approachable and will respond to a generous gesture, needs to be seriously questioned. It is not necessarily true, for example, when you are dealing with lunatics. Then the question becomes: Who is sane? Was Hitler sane? And is it not possible for one whole culture to be insane by the standards of another? And, so far as one can gauge the feelings of whole nations, is there any apparent connexion between a generous deed and a friendly response? Is gratitude a factor in international politics?

These and kindred questions need discussion, and need it urgently, in the few years left to us before somebody presses the button and the rockets begin to fly. It seems doubtful whether civilization can stand another major war, and it is at least thinkable that the way out lies through non-violence. It is Gandhi's virtue that he would have been ready to give honest consideration to the kind of question that I have raised above; and indeed, he probably did discuss most of these questions somewhere or other in his innumerable newspaper articles. One feels of him that there was much that he did not understand, but not that there was anything that he was frightened of saying or thinking. I have never been able to feel much liking for Gandhi, but I do not feel sure that as a political thinker he was wrong in the main, nor do I believe that his life was a failure. It is curious that when he was assassinated, many of his warmest admirers exclaimed sorrowfully that he had lived just long enough to see his life work in ruins, because India was engaged in a civil war which had always been foreseen as one of the by-products of the transfer of power. But it was not in trying to smooth down Hindu–Moslem rivalry that Gandhi had spent his life. His main political objective, the peaceful ending of British rule, had after all been attained. As usual, the relevant facts cut across one another. On the one hand, the British did get out of India without fighting, an event which very few observers indeed would have predicted until about a year before it happened. On the other hand, this was done by a Labour Government, and it is certain that a Conservative Government, especially a government headed by Churchill, would have acted differently. But if, by 1945, there had grown up in Britain a large body of opinion sympathetic to Indian independence, how far was this due to Gandhi's personal influence? And if, as may happen, India and Britain finally settle down into a decent and friendly relationship, will this be partly because Gandhi, by keeping up his struggle obstinately and without hatred, disinfected the political air? That one even thinks of asking such questions indicates his stature. One may feel, as I do, a sort of aesthetic distaste for Gandhi, one may reject the claims of sainthood made on his behalf (he never made any such claim himself, by the way), one may also reject sainthood as an ideal and therefore feel that Gandhi's basic aims were anti-human and reactionary: but regarded simply as a politician, and compared with the other leading political figures of our time, how clean a smell he has managed to leave behind!

Partisan Review, January 1949; *S.E.*; *O.R.*; *C.E.*

READ MORE IN PENGUIN

BY THE SAME AUTHOR

A Clergyman's Daughter

Intimidated by her father, the Rector of Knype Hill, Dorothy performs her submissive roles of dutiful daughter and bullied housekeeper, passing her days in church activities, penance and housework, her thoughts circumscribed by the task in hand. But suddenly her routine shatters and Dorothy finds herself down and out in London. She is wearing silk stockings, has money in her pocket and cannot remember her name . . .

Coming Up For Air

Fat and forty-five, George Bowling is Orwell's *homme moyen sensuel.* George sells insurance, lives in a semi-detached house and imagines himself completely a 'part of the modern world'. But, also fearing the modern world, the world of 1939, he attempts to escape to the past world of his childhood – to the peacefulness of civilization 'before the radio, before aeroplanes, before Hitler'. 'The author's ironic humour is fresher than ever. This is an Orwell not to miss – *Observer*

Keep the Aspidistra Flying

Gordon Comstock, poet *manqué*, gives up a 'good' job in an advertising agency to become a part-time bookshop assistant, thereby gaining the time to write. Despite some modest success, he embarks on a long, deliberate slide into penury which results in a solitary, squalid existence. With characteristic irony and perception, Orwell traces the disaffection with society and the desire to renounce contemporary values which he himself had experienced. 'A completely harrowing and stark account of poverty . . . written in clear and violent language' – Cyril Connolly

BY THE SAME AUTHOR

Burmese Days

Set in the days of Empire, with the British ruling in Burma, *Burmese Days* describes both the indigenous corruption and the Imperial bigotry of a time when 'after all, natives were natives – interesting, no doubt, but finally only a "subject" people, an inferior people with black faces'. 'I recommend it to anyone who enjoys a spate of efficient indignation, graphic description, excellent narrative, excitement, and irony tempered with vitriol' – Cyril Connolly

Animal Farm

'It is the history of a revolution that went wrong – and of the excellent excuses that were forthcoming at every step for the perversion of the original doctrine,' wrote Orwell for the first edition of *Animal Farm* in 1945. His simple and tragic fable, telling of what happens when the animals drive out Mr Jones and attempt to run their farm themselves, has since become one of the most famous novels in the English language.

Nineteen Eighty-Four

Newspeak, Doublethink, Big Brother, the Thought Police – George Orwell's world-famous novel coined new and potent words of warning for us all. Alive with Swiftian wit and passion, it is one of the most brilliant satires on totalitarianism and the power-hungry ever written. 'It is a volley against the authoritarian in every personality, a polemic against every orthodoxy, an anarchistic blast against every unquestioning conformist . . . a great novel and a great tract' – Ben Pimlott

BY THE SAME AUTHOR

In Penguin Twentieth-Century Classics – the authoritative texts of Orwell's three classics of political reportage:

The Road to Wigan Pier

Commissioned by the Left Book Club, Orwell set out to write the urban equivalent of Cobbett's *Rural Rides* and describe the great industrial wastelands of Yorkshire and Lancashire. The polemical portrait of the unemployed and dispossessed that resulted from his first-hand observation of the devastating effects of poverty, apathy, despair, malnutrition and overcrowding remains indelibly burned into our collective conscience.

Homage to Catalonia

'The Spanish war and other events in 1936–7 turned the scale and thereafter I knew where I stood. Every line of serious work that I have written since 1936 has been written, directly or indirectly, *against* totalitarianism and *for* democractic Socialism, as I understand it'. In this famous account of his experience as a militaman in the Spanish Civil War, Orwell brings to bear the full force of his humanity, passion and clarity, describing with bitter intensity the bright hopes and cynical betrayals of that chaotic episode. 'Home to Catalonia is that phoenix, a book which is at the same time a work of first-class literature and a political document of the greatest importance' – Geoffrey Gorer

also published:

Down and Out in Paris and London
Decline of the English Murder and Other Essays
Inside the Whale and Other Essays
The Lion and the Unicorn Socialism and the English Genius

and the celebrated biography by Bernard Crick:

George Orwell: A Life